The Bloomsbury Companion to Plato

Bloomsbury Companions

The *Bloomsbury Companions* series is a major series of single volume companions to key research fields in the humanities aimed at postgraduate students, scholars and libraries. Each companion offers a comprehensive reference resource giving an overview of key topics, research areas, new directions and a manageable guide to beginning or developing research in the field. A distinctive feature of the series is that each companion provides practical guidance on advanced study and research in the field, including research methods and subject-specific resources.

Titles currently available in the series:

Aesthetics, edited by Anna Christina Ribeiro
Analytic Philosophy, edited by Barry Dainton and Howard Robinson
Aristotle, edited by Claudia Baracchi
Continental Philosophy, edited by John Mullarkey and Beth Lord
Epistemology, edited by Andrew Cullison
Ethics, edited by Christian Miller
Existentialism, edited by Jack Reynolds, Felicity Joseph and Ashley Woodward
Hegel, edited by Allegra de Laurentiis and Jeffrey Edwards
Heidegger, edited by Francois Raffoul and Eric Sean Nelson
Hobbes, edited by S.A. Lloyd
Hume, edited by Alan Bailey and Dan O'Brien
Kant, edited by Gary Banham, Dennis Schulting and Nigel Hems
Leibniz, edited by Brendan Look
Locke, edited by S.-J. Savonious-Wroth, Paul Schuurman and Jonathan Walmsley
Metaphysics, edited by Neil A. Manson and Robert W. Barnard
Philosophy of Language, edited by Manuel García-Carpintero and Max Kölbel
Philosophy of Mind, edited by James Garvey
Philosophy of Science, edited by Steven French and Juha Saatsi
Political Philosophy, edited by Andrew Fiala
Pragmatism, edited by Sami Pihlström
Socrates, edited by John Bussanich and Nicholas D. Smith
Spinoza, edited by Wiep van Bunge

THE BLOOMSBURY COMPANION TO PLATO

EDITED BY

Gerald A. Press

Associate Editors: Francisco Gonzalez, Debra Nails and Harold Tarrant

Bloomsbury Companions

Bloomsbury Academic
An imprint of Bloomsbury Publishing Plc

B L O O M S B U R Y
LONDON · OXFORD · NEW YORK · NEW DELHI · SYDNEY

Bloomsbury Academic
An imprint of Bloomsbury Publishing Plc

50 Bedford Square	1385 Broadway
London	New York
WC1B 3DP	NY 10018
UK	USA

www.bloomsbury.com

BLOOMSBURY and the Diana logo are trademarks of Bloomsbury Publishing Plc

First published in paperback 2015

First published as *The Continuum Companion to Plato* 2012

British Library Cataloguing-in-Publication Data
A catalogue record for this book is available from the British Library.

ISBN: PB: 978-1-4742-5091-7
ePub: 978-1-4742-5092-4
ePDF: 978-1-4742-5093-1

Library of Congress Cataloging-in-Publication Data
A catalogue record for this book is available from the Library of Congress.

Typeset by Newgen Knowledge Works (P) Ltd., Chennai, India
Printed and bound in Great Britain

CONTENTS

CONTENTS

CONTENTS

ACKNOWLEDGEMENTS

The editor would like to thank the publisher for supporting this project, as well as several members of the staff who assisted in it over the years: Evander Lomke, Sarah Campbell and Tom Crick. I especially appreciate the ongoing help and advice Merilyn Holme has provided over several years.

I am grateful to the President, Provost and Dean of Hunter College for a sabbatical in 2009–10 that gave me the extra time I required for organizing, managing and writing the project. I want to thank the Research Foundation of the City University of New York for a PSC-CUNY Research Grant that enabled me to hire an Editorial Assistant to edit contributions as they were received. My thanks goes to Elvira Basevich, the Editorial Assistant, for her dedicated and painstaking work in editing individual contributions and compiling the Bibliography. Thanks also to Gregory Smulewicz-Zucker for compiling and editing the List of Contributors and John Storm for editorial advice on several of the articles and the Introduction.

I would like to thank each of the contributors for their work on this project and their willingness to adapt their articles to the overall plan and needs of the volume and to say in fewer words than they often wished what might have been said in more. Special thanks to Sarah Hutton and Samuel Scolnicov for advice at moments of special need.

Most of all, I want to thank the Associate Editors of this volume, Francisco Gonzalez, Debra Nails and Harold Tarrant, for their collaborative hard work over the 3 years of working on the project in defining the contents, selecting the contributors, editing the submissions and providing specific advice and suggestions in instances too numerous to count. They have been examples throughout of the intellectual moderation, courage, wisdom and justice that make the scholarly life happiest and best.

LIST OF ABBREVIATIONS

In this work, after the first mention of a Platonic dialogue or other Platonic work, the following abbreviations are used:

Alcibiades (Alc. I, 2)
Amatores (Amat.)
Apology (Ap.)
Axiochus (Ax.)
Charmides (Chrm.)
Clitophon (Clit.)
Cratylus (Cra.)
Critias (Criti.)
Crito (Cri.)
Definitions (Def.)
Demodocus (Demod.)
Epigrams (Epigr.)
Epinomis (Epin.)
Epistles (Ep. I, 2, *etc.)*
Eryxias (Erx.)
Euthydemus (Euthd.)
Euthyphro (Euthphr.)
Gorgias (Grg.)
Halcyon (Hal.)
Hipparchus (Hipparch.)
Hippias Major (Hp. Ma.)
Hippias Minor (Hp. Mi.)

Ion
Laches (La.)
Laws/Leges (Lg.)
Lysis (Ly.)
Menexenus (Mx.)
Meno (Men.)
Minos (Min.)
On Justice (Just.)
On Virtue (Virt.)
Parmenides (Prm.)
Phaedo (Phd.)
Phaedrus (Phdr.)
Philebus (Phlb.)
Protagoras (Prt.)
Republic (R.)
Sisyphus (Sis.)
Sophist (Sph.)
Statesman/Politicus (Plt.)
Symposium (Smp.)
Theaetetus (Tht.)
Theages (Thg.)
Timaeus (Ti.)

OTHER ANCIENT AUTHORS

'DK' Diels-Kranz, Hermann Diels and Walther Kranz. *Die Fragmente der Vorsokratiker*.

This is a standard source for fragments of the pre-Socratic philosophers. 'A' numbers refer to testimonies about the philosopher; 'B' numbers refer to fragments of their actual words.

D. L. Diogenes Laertius. *Lives and Opinions of Eminent Philosophers*.

This is a third-century CE doxography that is an important source of the views of ancient philosophers.

OTHER ABBREVIATIONS

Antid.	(*Antidosis*)	no.	(number)
b.	(born)	nos.	(numbers)
bk	(book)	n.s.	(new series)
bks	(books)	n.d.	(no date of publication)
c.	(circa)	*Od.*	(Homer, *Odyssey*)
cf.	(confer, compare)	*passim*	(often)
ch.	(chapter)	pt	(part)
chs	(chapters)	q.v.	(*quod vide*, see the article entitled)
d.	(died)		
ed.	(editor/edited by)	repr.	(reprint/ed)
edn	(edition)	rev.	(revised)
eds	(editors)	sc.	(scilicet)
f.	(fragment)	*Theog.*	(*Theogony*)
ff.	(fragments)	trans.	(translated by, translator/s)
fl.	(floruit)	vol.	(volume)
Il.	(Homer, *Iliad*)	vols	(volumes)

LIST OF CONTRIBUTORS

Hayden W. Ausland
Professor of Classics
University of Montana
Missoula, MT
USA

Dirk Baltzly
Associate Professor of Philosophy
Monash University
Victoria
Australia

Frederick Beiser
Professor of Philosophy
Syracuse University
Syracuse, NY
USA

Elizabeth Belfiore
Professor of Philosophy, Emerita
University of Minnesota
Minneapolis, MN
USA

Eugenio Benitez
Associate Professor of Philosophy
The University of Sydney
Australia

Hugh H. Benson
Professor of Philosophy
University of Oklahoma
Norman, OK
USA

Robbert van den Berg
Lecturer
Leiden University
The Netherlands

David Blank
Professor of Classics
University of California
Los Angeles, CA
USA

Ruby Blondell
Professor of Classics
University of Washington
Seattle, WA
USA

Thomas C. Brickhouse
Professor of Philosophy
Lynchburg College
Lynchburg, VA
USA

Luc Brisson
Director of Research
Centre Jean Pépin
CNRS, Paris
France

Stuart Brown
Professor Emeritus
The Open University
Milton Keynes, Buckinghamshire
UK

Margaret Cameron
Assistant Professor of Philosophy
University of Victoria
Canada

Timothy Chappell
Professor of Philosophy
The Open University
UK

Antonio Chu
Associate Professor of Philosophy
Metropolitan State College of Denver
Denver, CO
USA

Catherine Collobert
Associate Professor of Philosophy and
Classics
University of Ottawa
Canada

John Dillon
Emeritus Fellow
Trinity College, Dublin
Ireland

Monique Dixsaut
Emeritus Professor
Panthéon-Sorbonne University, Paris
France

Jacques Antoine Duvoisin
St. John's College
Santa Fe, NM
USA

Rafael Ferber
Professor of Philosophy
University of Lucerne
Switzerland

Richard Foley
Assistant Professor of Classical Studies
University of Missouri
Columbia, MO
USA

Dorothea Frede
Mills Adjunct Professor of Philosophy
University of California
Berkeley, CA
USA

Francesco Fronterotta
Associate Professor in History of Ancient
Philosophy
University of Salento, Lecce
Italy

Alessandra Fussi
Associate Professor of Philosophy
University of Pisa
Italy

Francisco Gonzalez
Professor of Philosophy
University of Ottawa
Canada

Jill Gordon
Professor of Philosophy
Colby College
Waterville, ME
USA

LIST OF CONTRIBUTORS

Herbert Granger
Professor of Philosophy
Wayne State University
Detroit, MI
USA

Stephen Halliwell
Professor of Greek
University of St. Andrews
Fife, Scotland
UK

Verity Harte
Professor of Philosophy and Classics
Yale University
New Haven, CT
USA

Angela Hobbs
Associate Professor of Philosophy
University of Warwick
UK

Carl A. Huffman
Professor of Classical Studies, of Greek
Language and Literature
DePauw University
Greencastle, IN
USA

Sarah Hutton
Professor of English
Aberystwyth University
Wales
UK

Christopher Janaway
Professor of Philosophy
University of Southampton
UK

Thomas Johansen
Reader in Ancient Philosophy
Brasenose College, Oxford University
UK

Mark Joyal
Professor of Classics
University of Manitoba
Canada

Rachana Kamtekar
Associate Professor of Philosophy
University of Arizona
Tucson, AZ
USA

George Karamanolis
Lecturer in Ancient Philosophy
University of Crete
Greece

J. B. Kennedy
Centre for the History of Science, Technology
and Medicine
Manchester University
Manchester
UK

David Konstan
Professor Emeritus of Classics and
Comparative Literature
Brown University
Providence, RI
USA

Taneli Kukkonen
Professor of History
University of Jyväskylä
Finland

Melissa Lane
Professor of Politics
Princeton University
Princeton, NJ
USA

Oliver Leaman
Professor of Philosophy
University of Kentucky
Lexington, KY
USA

Gabriel Richardson Lear
Professor of Philosophy
University of Chicago
Chicago, IL
USA

Mi-Kyoung Lee
Associate Professor of Philosophy
University of Colorado
Boulder, CO
USA

Fiona Leigh
Department of Philosophy
University College, London
UK

J. H. Lesher
Professor of Philosophy
University of North Carolina
Chapel Hill, NC
USA

Susan B. Levin
Associate Professor of Philosophy
Smith College
Northampton, MA
USA

V. Bradley Lewis
Associate Professor of Philosophy
The Catholic University of America
Washington, DC
USA

A. A. Long
Professor of Classics and of Literature
University of California
Berkeley, CA
USA

Menahem Luz
Senior Lecturer in Philosophy and History
University of Haifa
Israel

Michail Maiatsky
National Research University
Moscow
Russia

Richard Marback
Associate Professor of English
Wayne State University
Detroit, MI
USA

Marina McCoy
Associate Professor of Philosophy
Boston College
Boston, MA
USA

Mark McPherran
Professor of Philosophy
Simon Fraser University
Vancouver
Canada

Fred D. Miller, Jr.
Professor of Philosophy
Bowling Green State University
Bowling Green, OH
USA

David Mirhady
Associate Professor of Classics
Simon Fraser University
Vancouver
Canada

Christopher Moore
Lecturer in Philosophy
The University of Texas
Austin, TX
USA

Kathryn A. Morgan
Professor of Classics
University of California
Los Angeles, CA
USA

LIST OF CONTRIBUTORS

Debra Nails
Professor of Philosophy
Michigan State University
East Lansing, MI
USA

Andrea Nightingale
Professor of Classics and Comparative
Literature
Stanford University
Stanford, CA
USA

Noburu Notomi
Professor of Philosophy
Keio University
Japan

Nickolas Pappas
Professor of Philosophy
City College of New York and the CUNY
Graduate Center
New York, NY
USA

Richard D. Parry
Emeritus Professor of
Philosophy
Agnes Scott College
Decatur, GA
USA

Richard Patterson
Professor of Philosophy
Emory University
Atlanta, GA
USA

E. E. Pender
Senior Lecturer, Department of Classics
University of Leeds, Leeds
UK

Sandra Peterson
Professor of Philosophy
University of Minnesota
Minneapolis, MN
USA

Ronald Polansky
Professor of Philosophy
Duquesne University
Pittsburgh, PA
USA

Jean-François Pradeau
Professor of Philosophy
University of Lyon
France

Gerald A. Press
Professor of Philosophy
Hunter College and C.U.N.Y. Graduate
Center
New York, NY
USA

William Prior
Professor of Philosophy
Santa Clara University
Santa Clara, CA
USA

Naomi Reshotko
Professor of Philosophy
University of Denver
Denver, CO
USA

Gretchen Reydams-Schils
Professor of Philosophy
University of Notre Dame
Notre Dame, IN
USA

T. M. Robinson
Emeritus Professor of Philosophy and Classics
University of Toronto
Canada

David Roochnik
Professor of Philosophy
Boston University
Boston, MA
USA

David T. Runia
Master of Queen's College
Queen's College, University of Melbourne
Australia

Daniel C. Russell
Professor of Philosophy
Wichita State University
Wichita, KS
USA

Kenneth Sayre
Professor of Philosophy
University of Notre Dame
Notre Dame, IN
USA

D. C. Schindler
Associate Professor of Philosophy
Villanova University
Villanova, PA
USA

Samuel Scolnicov
Emeritus Professor of Philosophy
The Hebrew University of Jerusalem
Israel

Allan Silverman
Professor of Philosophy
Ohio State University
Columbus, OH
USA

Nicholas D. Smith
Professor of Humanities
Lewis & Clark College
Portland, OR
USA

Richard Stalley
Emeritus Professor of Ancient Philosophy
University of Glasgow
UK

Thomas Alexander Szlezák
Ordinarius for Greek Philology and Director
of Plato Archives
Eberhard Karls University, Tubingen
Germany

Harold Tarrant
Professor of Classics
University of Newcastle
Australia

Holger Thesleff
Emeritus Professor of Greek
University of Helsinki
Finland

Christine J. Thomas
Associate Professor of Philosophy
Dartmouth College
Dartmouth, NH
USA

Andrea Tschemplik
Associate Professor of Philosophy and
Religion
American University
Washington, DC
USA

Joanne B. Waugh
Associate Professor of Philosophy
University of South Florida
Tampa, FL
USA

LIST OF CONTRIBUTORS

Silke-Maria Weineck
Associate Professor of Germanic Languages
and Literature
University of Michigan
Ann Arbor, MI
USA

Roslyn Weiss
Professor of Philosophy
Lehigh University
Bethlehem, PA
USA

A. Gabrièle Wersinger
Professor of Philosophy
University of Rheims
France

James Wilberding
Lecturer in History
University of Newcastle
Newcastle upon Tyne
UK

Charles M. Young
Professor of Philosophy
Claremont Graduate University
Claremont, CA
USA

Catherine Zuckert
Professor of Political Science
University of Notre Dame
Notre Dame, IN
USA

INTRODUCTION

People usually think of Plato as a philosopher. That is correct, as far as it goes; but it can be argued that Plato was not merely *a* philosopher. He actually created and gave the initial definition to the specific intellectual practise and way of life that has been called philosophy ever since, even though his own philosophic work was far less narrow than what has been common under the label philosophy in the last century. He is also the most influential of all the ancient philosophers, and perhaps of all philosophers. The other major ancient philosopher usually mentioned in this regard, Aristotle, was a member of Plato's school, the Academy, for 20 years and can be seen as a kind of Platonist. Besides the sustained influence that these two have exerted on the subsequent history of Western philosophy, there was a third major ancient philosopher, Plotinus. Although Plotinus considered himself only to have explained more clearly what Plato said obscurely, he is today thought to have founded a rather different line of thought, now called Neoplatonism. Neoplatonism turns out to have been a very powerful influence from late antiquity to the nineteenth century even though this was unrecognized until one hundred and 50 years ago. In a way, then, all of the most influential ancient philosophy is Platonic.

Plato was not only a philosopher, however; and his importance and influence extend far beyond the specific field of philosophy. By common consent, he was the greatest writer of the ancient Greek language, even including classical Greek oratory, poetry, drama and history; he was also a superb tragic and comic dramatist, a fine poet, a composer of brilliant speeches, a ferocious social critic and reformer, a political, musical, educational and medical theorist, a mathematician, mythmaker, cosmologist and even, perhaps, a city planner. Due to this extraordinary richness in his writings, Plato's influence can be found in many fields other than philosophy. He is a truly 'interdisciplinary' figure. In recent years, discussions of Plato are to be found in professional books and journals on aesthetics, anthropology, archaeology, art history, classical philology, city planning, drama, education, geography, Greek, history, law, literature, mathematics, medicine, music, penology, philosophy, politics, psychology, religious studies, rhetoric and sociology. Besides their extraordinarily complex and persistent influence on philosophers from his own day to the present, Plato's dialogues have inspired poetry, dramatic performances, movies, sculptures, paintings and musical compositions. A computer program is named after Plato.

1

Mathematical discussions of Platonic numbers and Platonic solids still occur. Scholars have written about Platonism in Music and the Platonics are a Rumanian rock band.

Plato is unique among the most prolific ancient authors in that every single text mentioned by an ancient source as having been written by him has survived somehow into the present, something not true, for example, about the tragedies of Aeschylus and Sophocles or the dialogues and treatises of Aristotle. Yet we have less certain factual knowledge about him than about many others and disputes continue about the authenticity of Letters attributed to him and about political involvements on his part described in some of those Letters. Similarly, there are more and more fundamental disagreements about Plato than about any other philosopher. It is notorious that Plato scholars dispute not only about the proper interpretations of his works but also about the proper principles on which interpretations are to be based. Even so, his dialogues retain an apparently endless capacity to inspire interest and motivate discussion.

In the scholarly world of the last 100 to 150 years, the study of Plato has developed important divisions and conceptual antinomies. Since the Renaissance, and especially since the late eighteenth and early nineteenth centuries, a distinctly modern interest in historical accuracy has increasingly supplanted the more ancient interest in Plato because of the impersonal and eternal truths to be found in his writings. Pursuing the question 'What did Plato really think?' has motivated the continuing clarification of the differences between Plato and the various Platonisms of the later tradition and has generated a number of influential interpretive commitments.

Interpreters who turn to the dialogues to discover Plato's true doctrines, however,

quickly encounter difficulties. Different and even mutually exclusive views of the same matter – for example, the composition of the soul or the characteristics of the best human society – seem to be put forward in different dialogues. How could it be that Plato really thinks that the soul is simple and has no parts (*Phaedo*) and that it has three parts (*Phaedrus*, *Republic*)? How could Plato hold that the best city would be governed by philosophers selected for their intellectual qualities and rigorously educated (*Republic*) and that it would be ruled by elected magistrates and a citizen assembly (*Laws*)? And what true Platonic views are we to extract from the many dialogues that end by explicitly stating that the participants have not discovered the correct answer to the question under discussion and that they must therefore begin again?

One of the most widespread modern ideas about Plato to grow out of the pursuit of his true views was 'developmentalism', the belief that apparent doctrinal inconsistencies among the dialogues can be explained as products of Plato's intellectual development from a youthful and uncritical follower of Socrates to a much more systematic and dogmatic thinker in his middle and later years. Based on either or both thematic considerations and statistical analysis of certain details of the dialogues' style, it was believed that one could clearly distinguish groups of 'early', 'middle' and 'late' dialogues and correspondingly different phases in Plato's philosophic development. This developmental view was very widely accepted for much of the twentieth century, but opposed by a smaller group of interpreters, notably Paul Shorey and Harold Cherniss, who held that Plato's true views had an underlying unity throughout.

As far reaching as the division between a developmentalist and a 'unitarian' interpretation, as the latter is sometimes called, and reflecting the increased specialization and disciplinary separation in educational curricula, another division grew between the Plato whose written texts are taught in departments of Greek or of classics and the Plato whose theories and arguments are taught in departments of philosophy. This disciplinary division reflected and, at the same time, encouraged the belief that literature was something separate and distinct from philosophy, so that, in the study of Plato one could separate the literary and dramatic aspects of the dialogues for study by philologists and assign the study of theories, arguments and ideas to philosophers. The literary and dramatic aspects could be thought of as the form in which content was presented that was independent of that form.

Finally, among philosophers, two further divisions developed in the mid-twentieth century. The first was between those who sought to recover the truth from Plato's dialogues by emphasizing minute logical analysis of arguments extracted from their dialogical contexts and those who thought the truth lay in a broader confrontation with fundamental assumptions. The latter were sometimes referred to as 'continental' because they tended to be from continental Europe while the former tended to be from England and the English speaking countries. They are sometimes referred to as 'analytical' both for their methods of logical analysis and assessment and for selecting only overtly 'logical' parts of dialogues for study.

A second division was created by those who, following the lead of Gregory Vlastos, thought that study of a subset of Plato's 'early' dialogues could be used as sources for the discovery of the true philosophy of Socrates, rather than the philosophy of Plato, although debates existed from the beginning about the historicity of Plato's Socrates in separation from the rather different Socrates that is found in the contemporaneous writings of Xenophon and Aristophanes.

In Plato scholarship of the last 25 to 30 years, however, four major developments have undermined and resolved these divisions. First, through the work of Holger Thesleff, Debra Nails and others, it has come to be widely recognized that despite the general developmental consensus, there was never, in fact, agreement about exactly which dialogues went into the three groups. More significantly, it was shown that neither thematic nor stylistic evidence unambiguously supports the division of Plato's dialogues into three groups. Evidence of revision and school accumulation has provided further evidence that assuming the dialogues to have been written in the way modern books are, at one time and by the author alone, is misleading. This has led to the demise of the developmental consensus that existed 50 years ago and a considerable weakening of the developmental-unitarian opposition. They also serve to undermine the project of finding an historically significant Socratic philosophy in Plato's 'early' dialogues, and, in fact, those who pursue 'Socratic philosophy' now do so without making historical claims.

Second, interpreters in many disciplines have increasingly recognized that Plato made extensive use of a large variety of literary and dramatic elements. The dialogues are rich in images and metaphors, puns, jokes and other forms of humour like multiple kinds of irony. Plato has borrowed story lines from mythology and literature, language from poetry and rhetoric and characters and settings from history, but has transformed them so as to create connections and resonances between the literary elements on the one hand and central philosophic themes and ideas on the other. Evidence of reworking and revising his own material suggests that this was deliberate on Plato's part. The tendency of current work is to recognize, therefore, that form and content cannot be detached from each other without misrepresenting the complex wholes that Plato worked so hard to produce. Similarly, Platonic doctrines should not simply be read off of the dramatic, dialectical conversations of which most dialogues consist, nor should arguments be extracted for analysis and assessment in separation from their dialogical settings, specific characters, settings, topics and overall conversations. The more inter-disciplinary and holistic approach in recent scholarship has generated a growing appre-ciation of the philosophic importance of dra-matic and literary characteristics and has led to identification of a variety of structures in the dialogues – pedagogical, pedimental and musical – other than the logical structure of arguments and conclusions, and to recogni-tion that Plato's dialogues are philosophical texts of an essentially different kind from the expository writings of most philosophers in the Western canon.

In line with this, third, interpreters have come to appreciate the character of Socrates in the dialogues as something other than the two-dimensional mouthpiece for Platonic doctrines he was long thought to be. On the contrary, his character is forever inquiring, viewing all conclusions as open to recon-sideration and revision. This resonates with what happens in nearly all of the dialogues: they end by explicitly denying that the par-ticipants have come to know the answer to the question they have been discussing. These facts are consistent with Plato's choice to write no treatises, but only dialogues in which he himself never speaks and suggest that Plato's philosophizing might be, unlike much of the subsequent Western tradition, nondogmatic, open-ended and nonauthoritarian.

Fourth, reflection on facts and reports about the writings and views of Plato's stu-dents in the ancient world by John Dillon, Harold Tarrant and others has led to a clearer understanding of the evolution of Platonic thinking, the ways in which the ancients understood the dialogues and the Platonic thought in them. Thus, we have come to a clearer recognition of the similarities and differences between the Old Academy in the first generation after Plato's death and the later, ancient New Academy, Middle Platonism and Neoplatonism. This, in turn, has enabled us to see more clearly the sources of beliefs about Plato's thought that are, to some extent, still influential today and to see that they are not simply part of Plato's own thought as expressed in the dialogues (more detailed treatments of interpretive develop-ments will be found in Chapter 5).

We are in a period of significant change in the orientation and content of thinking about Plato. The trend is towards more holistic, con-textual and interdisciplinary approaches. Due to this, the time is ripe not only for a new guide book to Plato, but for a new *kind* of guide or companion. This volume is unlike existing ones in several important ways. Rather than limit-ing the topics included to philosophy, in our choice of contents we have also gathered arti-cles on characters, education, language, myth, poetry, rhetoric, textual history and a variety of special features of the dialogues as written texts. Contributors include not only philoso-phers, but specialists in Classics, Comparative Literature, English, Greek, History and Political Science; and they are professors in Australia, Canada, England, Finland, France, Germany, Greece, Ireland, Israel, Italy, Japan, the Netherlands, Russia, Scotland, Switzerland, the United States and Wales.

Rather than a small number – perhaps 10 to 20 – of long articles on a proportionally limited array of subjects, we have gathered a rather large number – more than 140 – on a very large array of subjects. And rather than articles that share a single methodology or interpretive approach, we have been pluralistic, seeking to include many different approaches. In fact, our aim was to have all of the current approaches represented in order to give as complete a picture as possible of the current state of knowledge and research about Plato. Pluralism in interpretation is not only a fact, however, it is, importantly, how error and vacuity are avoided (Heath 2002).

In sum, the aim was for the greatest possible breadth of coverage so that the volume would be encyclopaedic in what it offers readers. It should be useful to undergraduates and graduate students as well as interested general readers, and even professionals who may need a quick orientation on an aspect of Plato's work, thought or later influence. Articles are designed to offer a concise, lucid 'starting point' or introduction to their topics and to indicate the main problems that have been debated and the main lines of these debates. But beyond providing basic knowledge of a topic, it is hoped that the extent of the topics treated and the diversity of specializations and scholarly orientations represented will help keep readers' preconceptions open to revision, so that we, like Plato's Socrates, may be reflective and critical, constantly evaluating and reevaluating our own assumptions.

The volume is divided into five chapters. Chapter 1, Plato's Life – Historical and Intellectual Context, begins with Plato's biography and then includes a number of individuals, groups, cultural practises and movements that elucidate the intellectual context in which Plato lived and wrote. Chapter 2 is introduced by a general discussion of the entire body of Platonic writings and the manuscript tradition. After this, in alphabetical order are individual articles on each dialogue, as well as one each on the dubious and spurious ones and on the Letters. Chapter 3 includes articles on a variety of specific features of the dialogues as texts, such as their use of drama, humour and irony and a variety of structures that recent interpreters have identified as ways of understanding Plato's thought as expressed in the dialogues. Chapter 4, the longest, deals with a wide variety of themes and topics explicitly treated in the dialogues. Chapter 5 concerns the Later Reception, Interpretation and Influence of Plato and the Dialogues. It begins with the history of the Academy in antiquity, and continues through later ancient Platonisms, the medieval, renaissance, modern and contemporary interpretive approaches.

TECHNICAL TOOLS AND CONVENTIONS

The volume makes use of several technical tools and conventions of which the reader should be aware. Translations of Plato, unless otherwise indicated, are taken from those in Cooper, J.M. (ed.) (1997), *Plato: Complete Works*. Indianapolis: Hackett Publishing Co. Since its appearance, this has been the standard English collection of translations.

Important Greek terms are transliterated into the Roman alphabet and set in italics, for example, *akrasia* (lacking control of oneself) and *paideia* (education). We use macrons to distinguish the Greek eta (*ê*) from epsilon (*e*), for example, *epistêmê* (knowledge), *merê* (parts), *genê* (kinds) and *eidê* (forms). We also use macrons to distinguish the Greek omega (*ô*) from omicron (*o*), for example, *erôs* (love) and *logos* (account). The Greek letter upsilon is sometimes transliterated as *y* (as in *psychê*) and sometimes *u* (as in *muthos*). Although this is inconsistent, it accurately reflects the absence of a scholarly consensus on the question.

Although the words Form and Idea are often used interchangeably, in discussions of Plato we use 'form' only and do not capitalize.

Multiple forms of crossreferencing are used in this volume. Besides the Table of Contents that lists each article by title in each section, there is an Index of Names and an Index of Topics at the back of the volume. The most frequent form of crossreference is the abbreviation, q.v., used within articles to refer interested readers to a related article by title. Thus, the sentence 'The dialogues offer many more candidate methods (q.v.) for discovering reality amid appearances' refers the reader to the article on Method, which can be found either through the Table of Contents or through the Index. The titles of the dialogues and the names Plato and Socrates are not crossreferenced because they are used so often.

BIBLIOGRAPHY

Each article is intended to give the reader a clear, concise introduction to the subject or topic indicated in its title. To inform the reader where to learn more about the topic and specific aspects of it, secondary sources are indicated through references within the article in an abbreviated form: author's last name and year of publication and, perhaps specific page numbers. Thus 'Heath 2002' cited above will be found to refer uniquely to 'Heath, M. (2002), *Interpreting Classical*

Texts. London.' Similarly, 'Gerson 2003:79–88' uniquely refers to Lloyd P. Gerson, *Knowing Persons* published in Oxford and to pages 79–88 in that volume. Full information about all citations is given in the Bibliography, pp. 309–47. Other examples are given below:

Reference in the text	Full citation
Derrida 1972a.	Derrida, J. (1972a), 'Plato's pharmacy,' in B. Johnson (Trans.), *Disseminations*. Chicago (repr. of 'La pharmacie de Platon,' *Quel Tel*, pp. 32–3).
Ferber 2002:189	Ferber, R. (2002), 'The Absolute Good and the Human Goods,' in G. Reale and S. Scolnicov (eds), *New Images of Plato: Dialogues on the Idea of the Good.* Sankt Augustin, pp. 187–96.
Kraut 2008:pt4	Kraut, R. (2008), 'Plato,' *The Stanford Encyclopedia of Philosophy*, E.N. Zalta (ed.), http://plato.stanford.edu/archives/fall2008/entries/plato/>, accessed 1 June 2008.
Rowe 1989:177	Rowe, C. (1989), 'The Unity of the Phaedrus: A Reply to Heath,' *Oxford Studies in Ancient Philosophy*. 7, 175–88.

The understanding of Plato – or any other author – is a collaborative, dialectical and historical process. The hope of the editors is that the present volume will be a part of that process. It is collaborative in that contributors offer together their views of topics on the study of which they have spent a great deal of time and energy. It is dialectical both because the reasoned views of contributors disagree on various points and because we try to make clear to the reader the reasons for our sometimes differing views. It is historical insofar as we offer more than a dozen articles on the historical contexts in which Plato wrote and more than 20 articles on the history and varieties of reception and interpretation of Plato. Views of the right answers as well as identification of the important questions are always – as a matter of fact – under discussion. This is the nature of the world of knowledge. Collaboration in pursuit of truth happens both through cooperation and through disagreement. Rational criticism and disagreement, as Plato's Socrates might agree, are intellectual, social and ethical goods.

Gerald A. Press

1

PLATO'S LIFE – HISTORICAL AND INTELLECTUAL CONTEXT

PLATO'S LIFE

Holger Thesleff

Little is certain, but some facts and hypotheses can be sifted from a great variety of sources and traditions about Plato. Modern accounts include Davies (1971), Friedländer (1958), Guthrie (1975), Nails (2002), Ryle (1966) and Thesleff (1982:20–39), on which the following is based.

We know that Plato died in 347 BCE; his year of birth was 426 or later. Both parents belonged to the old Athenian aristocracy. His father died early, and his mother remarried to her uncle who also died, perhaps before Plato was 13. Plato, his sister and brothers grew up with his mother's family in Athens. This 'clan', impoverished in the Peloponnesian War like many other landowners, was dominated by Critias, a gifted sophist and dramatist, later leader of the Thirty, who sought peace with Sparta to stop the Periclean democracy-based Athenian imperialism.

When Plato had reached his early teens, life in Athens was marked by prolonged war, poverty, political cynicism and ideological confusion. Yet, cultural life flourished in the city. As a sensitive young man with literary and intellectual preferences, Plato could seek compensation for the depressive circumstances in poetry and drama, rhetoric and philosophy (qq.v.), private discussions and homoerotic play in gymnasia.

Some detect lines of escapism in Plato's attitudes. In spite of his professed early interest in Athenian politics, there is little evidence that he appeared in public or took physical risks, although it is reported that he served in the army three times (D. L. 3.8). Problems of ethics were in the foreground of his thinking from his early years. His political sympathies passed from the Thirty to the moderate democrats (who then contributed to the death of Socrates), ending in deep disillusionment with human society (see *Ep.* 7 324b–6b).

The impact of Socrates and his circle was of fundamental importance to Plato. Socrates was a moral model for him and gave the dialectical frame to his thinking (q.v. Dialectic, Elenchus). But Plato's early commitment to speculative theory is due to influence from various pre-Socratics (q.v.) and mathematicians. After the death of Socrates, Plato seems to have spent some time with the Socratic Euclides in Megara. The theory of the utopian state may have taken shape before 392 when *Republic* bks 2–5 was perhaps parodied in Aristophanes' *Ecclesiazusae* (Thesleff 1997). Plato's mathematical orientation was stimulated by his brilliant young friend Theaetetus. His *Apology* did not settle the anti-Socratic sentiments. In the 390s he seems also to have presented entertaining and provocative sketches of Socratic discussions to groups of friends (q.v. Public), but the preserved written dialogues are almost certainly written at a later date.

The date and circumstances of Plato's first voyage to the West are controversial, but there can be little doubt about the following general lines. Plato left Athens about 386 BCE, possibly frustrated by lack of intellectual response in Athens. In Tarentum in southern Italy he met Archytas, a local political leader who knew Pythagorean traditions better than Socrates' friends did (q.v. Pythagoreans; *Phaedo*); he was later in communication with Plato's circle. Probably from Locri, famous for its ancient laws, Plato went over to Sicily. At the court of Syracuse he met the ruler's twenty-year old relative, Dion, who became his lifelong intimate friend and whose role in Plato's political experiments should not be underestimated. After Plato's return home (after dramatic events variously described in the sources), Anniceris the Cyrenaic purchased a piece of land in the Akadêmeia park that became Plato's school (D. L. 3.1; q.v. Academy).

From the mid-380s onwards, Plato spent his time quietly in the Academy outside the city walls. He had perhaps started to teach his own philosophy in partial contrast to other Socratics, the sophists and Isocrates (q.v.). Some of his written works now reached a larger public. He gathered around him a small group of intellectual friends who were prepared to

search into the basics of the good, of being, and of knowledge (q.v. Epistemology), and to themselves become part of a new philosophical elite. This latter ambition was supported by Dion in particular who had some hopes for a 'philosophers' rule' in Syracuse. Most of Plato's prominent students (D. L. 3.46) were in fact non-Athenians.

Plato was averse to practical politics, preferring spirited philosophical elenchus and a private 'being together' (*sunousia*). The Athenians tended to mistrust esoteric clubs, so it is understandable that Plato acquired the stigma of haughty arrogance to outsiders (Xenophon, *Ap*. 1). Plato's alleged Pythagorean models were already exaggerated in antiquity. Contrary to the Pythagoreans, Plato made no point of secrecy or mystic initiation, despite some play in *Symposium* (q.v. Esoterism; Love), and that he accepted women 'officially' in the school in Athens may be doubted, though Diogenes lists two by name (D. L. 3.46).

The apparently unexpected death of Dionysius I (367 BCE) meant a sudden new turn. Dion immediately invited Plato to assist him in organizing a philosopher-led state in Sicily. The new ruler, Dionysius II, did not meet the expectations of Dion and Plato (whatever they were), and court intrigues soon forced Dion into exile; but Plato was persuaded to stay until the following spring. The explanations given in *Ep*. 7 reflect Plato's own loyalty to Dion, his uncertainty and his idealism when confronted with life's practicalities.

Back in Athens, where the Academy kept contacts with Syracuse, Plato was engaged in new challenges from younger friends, including Aristotle, and his third voyage to Sicily in 361 signalled the end of his Sicilian adventure. Dionysius had been reported to 'have time' for Platonic philosophy now, but Plato soon discovered that he was bluffing. Dion's enemies saw their chance. Only with the help of Archytas did Plato escape an imminent death. Dion later managed to seize power in Syracuse, in spite of Plato's warning, and was murdered as a 'tyrant'.

By Greek standards, Plato was now an old man. His younger friends had taken over many Academic activities. The dialogues from Plato's later years reflect a wide variety of new philosophic stimuli and polemics.

During Plato's last years the scene in Athens was dominated by the Macedonian question. Athenian nationalism did not appeal to the internationally oriented Academy. The old master preferred to stay far from the glowing political debates. But by his friends, including Aristotle, Plato was venerated as an architect of philosophy and a benign and wise moral leader. After his death in 347 he was the subject of some kind of hero cult in the Academy. We have copies of a bust by Silanion which, though posthumous, is not particularly idealized.

The third-century BCE biographer, Diogenes Laertius, cites some 43 sources indiscriminately, including Alcimus, Alexander, Alexandrides, Alexis, Amphis, Anaxilaïdes, Anaxilas, Antigonus, Antileon, Antisthenes, Apollodorus, Archytas, Aristippus, Aristophanes (grammarian), Aristoxenus, Athenodorus, Chamaeleon, Clearchus, Cratinus, Dicaearchus, Euphorion, Eupolis, Favorinus, Heraclides, Hermippus, Idomeneus, Mnesistratus, Molon, Myroninus, Neanthes, Onetor, Pamphila, Panaetius, Polemo, Praxiphanes, Sabinus, Satyrus, Speusippus, Theopompus, Thrasylus, Timon, Timotheus and Xenophon. Apollodorus and Favorinus and Philodemus and Olympiodorus are also important to the biographical tradition, and Plato's controversial *Ep.* 7 is crucial.

ARISTOPHANES AND INTELLECTUALS

Harold Tarrant

The plays of Aristophanes and his rivals offer something of a comic mirror of the intellectual world in which Plato's Socrates is situated. Plato's boyhood had coincided with a period of intellectual ferment at Athens. Pericles had associated with intellectuals such as the cosmologist Anaxagoras and the music-theorist Damon (*Alcibiades* 118c), and another prominent Athenian, Archelaus, had studied with Anaxagoras and developed cosmological ideas of his own. Particularly rich individuals like Callias, son of Hipponicus, host character in the *Protagoras*, were also liable to play host to visiting itinerant intellectuals, including those we know as 'sophists'. However, there was probably little immediate impact on ordinary Athenians until, as Thucydides reports when discussing the effects of the plague at Athens (2.53), war forced people to rethink their attitudes to the gods and to morality. His work shows an Athens little interested in discussing traditional moral values as opposed to civic expediency and personal hedonism.

The comic playwright Aristophanes, whose creative life began in 427 BCE and extended into the 380s, like his fellow comic poets, presented various intellectuals on stage, most obviously in *Clouds*, produced in 423 BCE. The very fact that the new ideas had become suitable material for comedy suggests that ordinary citizens were certainly aware of them and perhaps concerned about their implications. The leading intellectual here is none other than Socrates himself, but, in spite of several details that seem to capture Socrates' idiosyncrasies rather well, his portrait is so different from anything found in Plato that many suppose him to be simply a convenient figure on whom to father virtually all of the new ideas regardless of who had first propounded them. Insofar as this 'Socrates' figure runs an intellectual school or *phrontistêrion*, the play is an exercise of the imagination. Yet, that granted, one should note that Plato's Socrates expresses some interest in virtually all new ideas, in spite of his professed lack of expertise in any. Some, however, read more into Aristophanes' portrait of Socrates, and Vander Waerdt (1994b) notes that the playwright seems to have a good understanding of many contemporary theories that could have influenced Socrates, especially those of Diogenes of Apollonia.

At 314–426 the emphasis falls on cosmology and a consequent naturalistic explanation of the usual manifestations of divine power. Socrates' 'gods' are the Clouds, who are employed in the explanation of rain and thunderstorms in preference to Zeus. Yet, Socrates also comes across as a priestly character (compare *Birds* 1553–64) who is both aloof and aloft (212–25), and conducts private ceremonies while invoking deities (254–66). This combination of pre-Socratic-style cosmology and priestly attitudes and functions can now be matched in the Derveni Papyrus, particularly since the reconstruction and publication of the first fragmentary columns in 1997. The author, who discusses rituals designed to avert hostile spirits (presumably on death), and then subjects a poem of 'Orpheus' about Zeus to a consistently allegorical reading, quotes Heraclitus and is influenced by the ideas of Anaxagoras and his immediate followers. The date of this work could in theory be anywhere between 430 and 350 BCE, but an early date would have made it more topical. It is noteworthy that air in the papyrus is the physical manifestation of intelligence (meaning Zeus, and some other divinities

identified with him), and that airy stuffs, including Air, the Gulf (between heaven and earth), Clouds, Respiration and perhaps Mist (Derveni Papyrus 424, 627, 814), are the intelligences that Socrates acknowledges and swears by in *Clouds*.

Also prominent in *Clouds* are theories about poetry and music (636–54), and about the correct naming of things (658–93). In Plato, the character Protagoras encourages the study of poetry (*Prt.* 338e–9a) in which Hippias and Ion claim expertise (*Hippias Minor*; *Ion*), while correct naming is associated with the sophist Prodicus (*Cratylus* 384b; *Prt.* 339e–41e) and less decisively with the neo-Heraclitean Cratylus – with whom Aristotle says that Plato studied. More worrying, though not directly associated with Socrates or his fellow proprietor of the *phrontistêrion*, Chaerephon, who appears to be involved with the minutiae of biology (*Clouds* 143–66), are the two arguments, Superior and Inferior, that reside with them and have taken on a life of their own. It is not so much the strange, new, technical and cosmological ideas that threatened society, but the new interest in those using the courts and deliberative bodies of Athens in making the inferior (and amoral) argument appear superior (and justified). Plato (*Theaetetus* 172a–c) shares the worries of Aristophanes about the moral relativism that results from the application to civic life of Protagoras' theory that there are two arguments on every matter (*Antiope* fr. 189; D. L. 9.51 = A1 'DK'; *Antiope* fr. 189; cf. Euripides). Techniques include appeals to the questionable conduct of the gods and of heroes (*Clouds* 1048–82; cf. *Euthyphro* 5e–6a; *Republic* 378b).

The tragic playwright Euripides must also be placed among the intellectuals satirized by Aristophanes (*Acharnians*, *Thesmophoriazousai*, *Frogs*), for he is regularly credited with words and ideas that recall the comedian's portrait of Socrates: indeed a fragment of the first version of *Clouds* (*Aristophanes*. fr. 376K = D. L. 2.18) makes Socrates the source of Euripides' clever, tricky-talking tragedies. On Euripides and the intellectual world both Wildberg (2006) and Conacher (1998) are useful. Religious experts including Hierocles (*Peace*) are another of his comic targets, and the urban-design expert Meton appears in *Birds*. Ameipsias' comedy *Connus* (423 BC, as *Clouds*) revolves around a teacher of new music referred to by Plato's Socrates as his teacher (*Euthydemus* 272c), and also brought Socrates on stage, while Eupolis' *Flatterers* of two years later depicts the would-be intellectuals who tried to sponge off the riches of Callias, among them Protagoras (ff. 157–8) and Socrates' strange colleague Chaerephon (f. 180).

Insofar as the plays of Aristophanes gave a vivid picture of intellectual life, Plato was influenced by them, though lamenting the bad publicity that *Clouds* had given Socrates. *Euthd.* seems to allude to *Clouds* a number of times; the depiction of Callias' house in *Prt.* appears to owe something to the *phrontistêrion*, and *Clouds* is even quoted with approval (*Symposium* 221b).

EDUCATION (*PAIDEIA*)

Samuel Scolnicov

Education can be described as Plato's central concern. Since before Homeric times, Greek education consisted, on the whole, of athletic training and instillation of heroic values. The chief educational aims were manly valour (*aretê*, a word that would later be used to designate human excellence in general) and competitiveness.

Education was deemed the responsibility of the parents until the eighteenth year. From preclassical times, infants were left at home with their mothers until the age of seven.

In classical times, elementary education was provided by professional teachers, usually of low social status, thus easily affordable, to whom the children were taken by a household slave, the *paidagogos*. Education consisted mainly in the learning of reading and writing and memorizing poetry, in particular Homer. Literacy was apparently already rather widespread in Athens, and in general in Greece, before classical times (Harris 1989). Poetry was taught for its educational value, as offering role models for emulation. It was to this function of poetry that Plato was to be opposed. In addition, better-to-do families would also provide instruction in music, including singing and some basic numeracy.

The physical aspect of education was not disregarded in youth, as in adulthood, and the competitive spirit remained unabated, as evidenced by the wide appeal of the panhellenic games and the Athenian penchant for legal disputation. Education was very much the same for both sexes except in Athens where girls learned only what was adequate for the running of a household. Girls elsewhere were taught wrestling, running and javelin throwing. In some places, there were also 'finishing schools' for girls, like that of Sappho in Lesbos in the sixth-century BCE.

Sparta was apparently the first Greek city to develop an institutionalized system of education, whose aim was avowedly militaristic. Boys were taken from their mothers at the age of seven and lived in communal barracks until after military service, to which they returned periodically. Literacy was not much prized. The evidence about education in other parts of the Greek world is rather more sketchy and circumstantial

In classical times, the heroic ideal was gradually superseded by *paideia* – initially, in aristocratic circles, 'a profound and intimate relationship, a personal union between a young man and an elder who was at once his model, his guide, his initiator' (Marrou 1956) and later as an ideal of culture and education, akin to the German concept of *Bildung*. From Protagoras' speech in the Platonic dialogue named after him, no doubt voicing the current opinion, we know that education was thought of primarily as socialization and society was regarded as the chief educational agent.

In the fifth century BCE, democratic Athens attracted those that became known as the sophists (literally 'experts'), itinerant intellectuals from all over Greece who introduced the idea of higher education for those who could pay. Democracy meant the demise of aristocratic values in favour of the idea of pragmatic success in private and public life. Any free man, and eventually anyone, could become *kalos k'agathos* (fine and good), initially a denotation of aristocracy but, with democracy, coming to designate 'the good man'.

The sophists (q.v.) taught the art of a flourishing life, *eudaimonia* (generally, but misleadingly translated as 'happiness'; q.v.) readily understood as political success. They developed and perfected rhetorical and dialectical skills as tools of success in public life and in the courts. Gorgias of Leontini wrote manuals of rhetoric, now mostly lost, which included model speeches such as the extant *Encomium of Helen*. The anonymous *Dissoi logoi* (*Double arguments*) is a rather schematic textbook of exercises developing Protagoras' dictum that on every issue two opposing arguments can be developed.

The sophists' main interest was in man and in society and they were rightly described, in modern times, as the 'fifth-century humanists'. They developed the beginnings of what we would now call psychology, sociology, anthropology and political science. Some of them also dealt with mathematics, astronomy and the like, always with a view to their human relevance. Common to all was a keen interest in language and its uses.

Plato and Isocrates (q.v.) established the first institutions of higher learning. Little is known about their organization. Isocrates continued the sophistic line and taught rhetoric, as preparation for public life. Plato's Academy (q.v.) was arguably the first institution of research. An inkling of Plato's educational programme in the Academy may probably be had from the curriculum proposed by him in bks 3 and 7 of his *Republic*. Plato recognized the place of the mathematical sciences in his educational programme, yet was opposed, on grounds of principle, to the separation of disciplines within philosophy, though perhaps subordinated to the primacy of ethics. Many of his associates went on to serve as political advisors in Greek cities. Aristotle, in his Lyceum, possibly instituted division of labour in research. Higher education was later formalized in 'schools' as the Academy, the Lyceum, the Stoa, Epicurus' Garden, etc.

ELEATICS

Herbert Granger

'Our Eleatic tribe', reports Plato's Eleatic Stranger, begins with Xenophanes of Colophon, and even earlier (*Sophist* 242d). But the true founder of the school is Parmenides of Elea, whose most notable

13

disciples are limited to Zeno of Elea and Melissus of Samos. Scholars accept a date of 515 for Parmenides' birth, calculated from Plato's depiction, very likely highly fictional, of an encounter between the old Parmenides and the young Socrates (*Parmenides* 127b–c). Parmenides published his only work in the first quarter of the fifth century, a poem in heroic verse, which is remarkable for its doctrines, but above all for its deft use of extensive philosophical argumentation for the first time. Despite the poem's rational exposition of doctrines, in its elaborate proem an unnamed youth narrates his supernatural journey to an unnamed goddess lodged in some unknown place, who welcomes him warmly and tells him she shall reveal to him the 'truth' and the 'opinions of mortals', which possess no 'true trust' ('DK' B1.29–30). These two subjects make up the two expository parts of the poem.

Although no aspect of the goddess' argument is beyond dispute, plausibly she grounds her speculation on the supposition that thought, speech and knowledge require for their subject something that exists. Accordingly, what does not exist, or 'nonbeing', cannot be thought about, expressed or known, and any conception that presupposes what does not exist is as much nonsense as 'non-being' itself.

The goddess proceeds a priori to deduce the basic features of reality. 'Being', or reality, does not suffer generation and destruction, since if it came to be it must have previously not existed, and if it perished it must pass away into nonexistence. Furthermore, since the goddess takes any change to be a variety of generation and destruction, reality is free from any sort of change, 'alteration in place and exchange of bright colour' (B8.40–1). Reality is also indivisible, a single object, uniform in character and limited in extent in

the shape of a sphere. Some contemporary scholars, however, deny Parmenides' belief in numerical monism, but Plato (*Sph*. 242d), as well as Aristotle (On *Generation and Corruption* 325a13–15), do not hesitate in attributing the doctrine to him.

The goddess is not deterred by the mismatch between her description of reality and what sensation reveals to be a world of a multitude of changing, diverse objects, and she requires the youth to judge her words with his 'reason' ('DK' B7.5–6). Nevertheless, when the goddess ends her discourse on truth and takes up the 'opinions of mortals', she lays out in detail a natural philosophy that includes a cosmogony and even a theogony. She justifies her discourse by maintaining that it lays bare the fundamental mistake inherent in mortal thinking, in its positing two opposing first principles, light and night. These in mixing with one another yield the cosmos, although light and night in their eternity and homogeneity are each like the single object of reality revealed in 'truth'. The goddess explains to the youth that her cosmology has plausibility, presumably satisfies the testimony of the senses, and that armed with this knowledge no mortal opinion shall ever 'outstrip' him (B8.60–1). Zeno and Melissus indicate no interest in natural philosophy, but plausibly the 'opinions of mortals' provides the model for the fifth-century BCE natural philosophers who succeeded Parmenides.

Zeno and Melissus are the heirs of Parmenides, not merely in doctrine, but above all in their argumentative prowess. Parmenides has no such effect on the pre-Socratic natural philosophers, who venture little in the way of argument, and before Socrates and Plato it is the sophist Gorgias of Leontini who exemplifies best someone who emulates Eleatic argumentation (B3).

Zeno, the younger friend and fellow citizen of Parmenides, may be appreciated as marshalling his extraordinary argumentative skills in support of his teacher's extraordinary doctrines. Plato's Socrates prods him into confessing that his book defends Parmenides' monism from his critics by demonstrating that their pluralism yields even more absurdities than Parmenides' monism (*Prm.* 128d). Zeno largely limits himself to demonstrating the absurdities inherent in pluralism and locomotion. His arguments against pluralism proceed by deducing from its assumption of a pair of contradictory consequences. For example, a plurality of objects entails that they be both limited in number and unlimited in number. If things are many they must be just as many as they are, and thus they must be of a certain number. If things are many, they are unlimited because between any two objects there is a third, but similarly there must be objects between the third object and the two it lies between, and so on to infinity. Presumably, objects are distinct only because another object separates them. The 'stadium' is the best known of Zeno's arguments against locomotion. A moving object must first arrive at the halfway point to its goal before reaching its goal, but before it arrives at the halfway point it must first arrive at the point halfway to the initial halfway point, and so on to infinity. But no object may traverse in a finite time infinite arrival points. Zeno's argumentative dexterity prompted Aristotle to proclaim him the discoverer of 'dialectic' (D. L. 8.57), the argumentative style Socrates made famous.

Melissus, who commanded the Samian fleet that defeated the Athenians in 441, follows, but also deviates from, Parmenides. Reality remains eternal, one, uniform and changeless. If what is should have come to be, then previous to its existence it was nothing, but

something cannot come to be from nothing ('DK' B1). What exists has no temporal beginning, and thus, Melissus infers invalidly, it has no temporal end. Unlike Parmenides, Melissus describes eternal reality in temporal terms, as existing in the past, present and future, not an eternal present. Melissus infers wildly and fallaciously from the eternity of what exists to its infinite magnitude, unlike Parmenides who speaks of 'being' as limited in the shape of a sphere. Where Parmenides gives no argument for monism, Melissus argues cleverly that the infinite extent of what is requires it to be one, because if two things existed they cannot be infinite since they would have boundaries upon one another. Further, since what is is one it must be homogeneous, alike in every way, because otherwise it would form a plurality. There can be no change of any sort, be it a change in quality, size or arrangement of parts, because change would entail the coming-into-existence of what did not exist and the passing away into nonexistence of what had existed. Melissus uses the 'empty', or the void, which he identifies with 'nothing', to formulate a novel argument against locomotion. What there is is completely 'full', and thus there is no place empty of what is that would allow what is to move into it. Although Aristotle dismisses Melissus as an intellectual lightweight, he develops careful arguments, often clearly expressed, and he makes original contributions to the Eleatic school.

Plato has profound respect for Parmenides, whom his Socrates describes as 'venerable and awesome' (*Theaetetus* 183e). Outstanding in Plato's considerable debt to Parmenides are his beliefs that thought and knowledge require an existing object and that reality is discovered not through sensation but through thought alone. Plato's transcendent forms, which are beyond space and time, provide the basis of his metaphysics and epistemology, and, although Plato is committed to a multitude of forms, in much of his exposition he conceives of them individually after the fashion of Parmenides' 'being', each as being eternal, changeless and uniform in nature (e.g. *Phd.* 78d–9a; *Ti.* 27a–d). But when it comes to 'non-being' Plato cannot follow Parmenides. Plato explicitly shuns 'non-being' as the contrary of 'being' (*Sph.* 258e), and he reduces 'is not' to 'differs from' (*Sph.* 257b, 258d).

For further information, see Barnes (1979), Gallop (1984), Guthrie (1969) and Mourelatos (1970).

ISOCRATES AND LOGOGRAPHY

David Mirhady

At *Phaedrus* 278e–9b Phaedrus describes a then youthful Isocrates (*c.* 436/5–338 BCE) as a companion of Socrates. Socrates himself then both characterizes Isocrates as nobler than Lysias and prophesies a great career for him in philosophy. Since Isocrates and Plato were contemporaries and headed the most well known philosophical schools in Athens during the time, the temptation is very strong to see the passage as ironic, Plato casting an implicit criticism at his rival. According to this view, the Lysias who in the dialogue is so roundly criticized for the moral and intellectual weakness of his logography actually represents the historical Isocrates. Several works from both Plato and Isocrates suggest such an ongoing rivalry. Since Isocrates was devoted to written discourse, particularly logography, there is a fundamental difference between him and Plato on the issue of writing (q.v.), but there are other differences as well.

After his family fortune was wiped out in the Peloponnesian war, Isocrates began afresh as a logographer (or speechwriter) for others who were presenting cases in the law courts. We have six such speeches (including one for a trial on Aegina), but Isocrates later disavowed such forensic logographic activity (*Antidosis* 15.36–7). The vast majority of the more than 100 extant speeches of the Attic orators were written for the law courts, however, so that 'logography' in general is identified with them. In Plato (*Phdr.* 257c) and elsewhere (e.g. Demosthenes 58.19) the term 'logographer' is used disparagingly and identified with forensic chicanery. Isocrates' *oeuvre* actually contains several other genres of written discourse, including letters and epideictic speeches, as well as 'speeches', but none of them were intended for oral delivery.

Isocrates' early educational programme is revealed in his *Against the Sophists* (13), which shares many of the commonplace criticisms of the sophists that appear in Platonic dialogues: their unconcern for the truth, their selfishness, their aim of gratifying rather than educating listeners, and their distrust of their students (see Benoit 1991). It also reveals Isocrates' understanding of 'philosophy' – he never uses the term 'rhetoric' in reference to his teaching. For Isocrates, philosophy entails devotion to a career of political leadership, particularly as that career involves engaging in political discourse, such as his own written 'speeches'. Scholars such as De Vries (1953:39–40) have seen Platonic parodying of *Against the Sophists* (13–18) in *Phdr.* (268c and 269d), but not all are convinced.

More clearly, anti-Platonic views appear in Isocrates' mythological *Encomium of Helen*. Isocrates criticizes those who believe that there is a single *epistêmê* for courage, wisdom and justice (*Just.* 10.1) and those who pretend to do *elenchoi* (4): 'It is much better to conjecture reasonably about useful things than to have precise knowledge of what is useless' (5, Trans. Mirhady). It is hard to avoid seeing Plato as the object of this criticism. The most recent commentary on Isocrates' *Busiris* (Livingstone 2001:48–56), unlike the more widely held view, stresses similarities between it and Plato's *Republic* rather than the criticism. In both *Helen* and *Busiris* Isocrates engages in the sophistic practises of paradoxical encomia and making the weaker argument the stronger, of praising the unpraiseworthy. Ever since Homer's *Iliad* Helen's behaviour in going to Troy and abandoning her family was seen as irresponsible, and Busiris was generally characterized as a brutal Egyptian king who killed every Greek he could get his hands on until Heracles put an end to him. Isocrates' rehabilitation of Helen and Busiris seems part of a broader strategy to use mythological examples as positive and not negative lessons. Rather than rejecting and replacing traditional Greek mythology, as Plato does, Isocrates seeks to reform it, which would be a dissimilarity between them.

Plato's *Gorgias* clearly entails a thorough critique of rhetorical teaching in general, but it seems unlikely that the Gorgias of that dialogue represents Isocrates. In the dialogue, Gorgias concedes that if his students do not have moral knowledge then they will acquire it through association with him (*Grg.* 459c–60a4). Isocrates never makes this claim, although he does say that his training will be an aid to acquiring moral knowledge (*Against the Sophists* 13.31; *Antidosis* 15.274, 278). In the *Phdr.* Socrates argues that while writing speeches is not in itself a disgrace, writing them badly is (*Phdr.* 258d). Inasmuch as the theme of the speeches criticized by Socrates is erotic desire, and Helen was *the* mythological object of erotic desire, it seems possible that Plato was indirectly criticizing Isocrates' *Encomium*. Both works include criticisms of

others' works of the subject – Isocrates criticizes Gorgias' *Helen* – and both make mention of Stesichorus' palinode.

Aside from Plato and Isocrates, Alcidamas also addresses the issue of writing and logography in his short polemic *On Those Who Write Written Speeches, or On Sophists*. Scholars have debated the relative chronologies of Alcidamas' essay and the works of Plato and Isocrates without consensus (see O'Sullivan 1992:23–31). It could well be that Alcidamas is criticizing Isocrates, especially since the latter was so devoted to written composition. Alcidamas argues that a training in *ex tempore* speaking will be superior to that for logography (see esp. 6 and 13).

In Isocrates' epistemology *doxa* is approved as more practical than *epistêmê*, especially in decisions about the future (see *Antidosis* 15.271 and *On the Peace* 8.8). He appears, however, not to criticize dialectic, acknowledging that face-to-face communication is best for many of the same reasons discussed in *Phdr.* (*Letter to Dionysius* 2–3; *Phdr.* 274b–8b). He also seems to share Plato's view of the sophist's use of argumentative question and answer (*Antid.* 15.45; *Sophist* 225b–6a). For Isocrates the political aims of Greek unity and Athenian hegemony were also almost inseparable from philosophy (*Panathenaicus* 12.2). In his later writings, however, he argues that Greek unity can best be achieved under the leadership of Athens' rival, Philip of Macedon (5. *To Philip*).

ORALITY AND LITERACY

Joanne B. Waugh

Orality and literacy became topics relevant to the study of Plato with the publication of Eric Havelock's *Preface to Plato* (1963).

Havelock argued that Socrates attacked poetry in the *Republic* because from the Greek Dark Ages, if not before, the archetype for Greek *paideia* (q.v. Education) had been oral poetry – poetry that singers composed extemporaneously in performance, without the aid of writing. The evidence for the existence of such poetry in early Greece was provided by Milman Parry's analyses of Homeric epics, analyses that demonstrated how such composition was possible.

Oral composition-in-performance is a means of preserving and communicating culture. Human societies have existed without literacy for much longer than they have existed with it. The burden of proof rests not with those who assert that early Greek society was an oral culture, but with anyone who claims that it was a literate one. Making this claim is complicated by the fact that views of what constitutes a literate society differ markedly. At one extreme, a society is deemed literate if a majority of adults can write and read their names. At the other, a society is considered literate if (a) it relies on written texts to preserve and to transmit its cultural traditions and to conduct matters of government, commerce, inquiry and law; (b) to be a functioning member of that society one must be able to read and write fluently; and (c) it has a sufficiently robust material culture to support these practises, including educating its citizens and workers. What evidence we possess does not make it easy to determine the extent to which the Greeks during the classical period were literate.

Alphabetic writing was introduced into Greece in the eighth-century BCE (Carpenter 1933) and after a time performers began to use fixed texts. From the archaic until the classical periods, writing was used more widely and in the service of the *polis*, but the public performance of artfully composed speech remained a primary cultural and political occasion until well into the fourth century. This explains the persistence of meter, verse and rhythmical prose, poetic and rhetorical language and traditional themes and fanciful stories in Greek texts and inscriptions – political, philosophical or legislative – from the advent of the *polis* to its acme. Inscriptions of 'state' documents on stone were found as early as the late sixth-century BCE, but inscribing public documents on stone did not become a regular practise before the middle of the fifth century (Sickinger 1999:4; Thomas 1992:137). In any case, an inference from the existence of stone inscriptions to a substantial body of writers and readers and the material culture to support literacy is problematic. Written inscriptions often function as symbolic objects the meanings of which are not confined to the words inscribed, and thus have significance even for those who cannot read them (Thomas 1992:74–100). Still, the creations and uses of written documents proliferated during the fifth century, and in its closing decade the Athenians established the Metroön as a repository for some or all state documents (Sickinger 1999:1–3; Thomas 1992:143). Only in the fourth century, however, did written documents cease to be supplementary and subordinate to oral testimony, and begin to be accepted as proof in the courts (Robb 1994:139–41; Thomas 1992:89 ff., 148 ff.). The extent and limits of classical literacy are summed up by Harris, who observes that 'the notion that every citizen male should know how to read and write made its appearance during the classical period of Greek culture, but came nowhere near to realization even in Athens' (1989:114). He concludes that for the period in question, the percent of literates among the population of Attica as a whole probably lies in the range of 5–10 per cent (1989:114).

18

Thus we find rhapsodes continuing to recite – indeed, perform – fixed texts in the classical period, especially those purporting to be the whole or part of Homer's *Iliad* or *Odyssey* (cf. *Ion*). In the *R*. Socrates comments on Homer's popularity and importance, pointing out that some will claim that Homer and the tragic poets know all about technical matters, human conduct and religion (598d10–e2) and the admirers of Homer say 'Homer educated Hellas' and that on matters of conduct he should be studied as a guide by which one regulates one's whole life (606e2–7). According to Havelock, the persistence of these public performances of artful speech was what Plato found objectionable. The rhythm on the levels of syntax, diction, actions and events, the vivid and memorable imagery and the compelling narratives of anthropomorphic gods and heroes – the very things that made the speech artful and the performances memorable for their audiences – developed in them habits of mind inimical to philosophical modes of thought. Philosophical modes of thought, Havelock argued, are developed as writing and reading permit and encourage reflection on, and analysis of, the language and content of traditional explanations.

Questions about how, when and why ancient Greece moved from being a society that relied on oral performance in transmitting culture to one that employed writing and reading in many of its cultural affairs are now central to classical scholarship. These studies contest general claims about orality and literacy *per se* identified at various times with Havelock, Jack Goody and Walter Ong as technologies of the intellect, but for the most part support Havelock's specific claims about the oral poetic tradition in Greece and its gradual acquisition of literacy. Current scholarship provides reasons to doubt that alphabetic writing was sufficient for the emergence of Greek philosophy rather than necessary.

Still, with a few notable exceptions such as Robb (1994), the importance of orality and literacy to the study of Plato has not been as widely recognized among contemporary philosophers as it should be, the result of the widespread but waning practise of 'rationally reconstructing' arguments alleged to be implicit in texts from the history of philosophy. These arguments need not take into account the historical and sociocultural context of a text's author and audience, the occasion and medium of its presentation and the choice to write – and to read – philosophy in a particular way. Absent such considerations, philosophers from any period can be read as formulating doctrines on perennial philosophical problems.

When history and context are taken into account, the resulting interpretations may differ greatly from conventional ones. Consider passages in the *Phaedrus* (274b6–8e2) and in the *Epistles* (7.341b2–5; 2.314b10–c6) that are sometimes cited as relevant to discussions of orality and literacy. Socrates' remarks about writing in the *Phdr.* have been taken to refer to writing *simpliciter*, but a strong case has been made that Socrates is referring to the *technai* of the sophists, an innovative form of *paideia* that rivals Plato's own (Cole 1991:123). The passages in *Ep.* 2 and 7, from which some readers conclude that Plato never committed his philosophical views to writing yet subscribed to philosophical doctrines intimated in the dialogues, look different when viewed in relation to other artful speech of Plato's day. The statements from these letters underscore that the point of the dialogues is not to present philosophical doctrines but to teach their audience *philosophia*, thereby replacing other artfully composed speech that for so long had constituted Greek *paideia*.

POETRY (EPIC AND LYRIC)

Catherine Collobert

Epic and lyric poetry, which flourished in the archaic period (eighth-century BCE to fifth-century BCE), is often quoted, referred to or discussed in Plato's dialogues.

Hesiod (*Theogony, Works and Days, Shield of Herakles*) is more or less a contemporary of Solon and Archilochus (seventh-century BCE). Ancient Greek poetry, especially epic, has to be understood in the context of oral tradition, which shaped the epics in various ways. The most significant is that oral composition is based upon a formula, which allows for improvization. Moreover, a salient feature is performance: poetry is a performance rather than a 'text'. Parts of the epic cycle, the *Iliad* and the *Odyssey*, whose poet was taken to be Homer, were sung by bards and later rhapsodes, as Plato describes them in the *Ion*, in the context of festivals like the festival of the Panathenaia in Athens.

Epic poetry introduces itself as poetry of the past, that is, the Heroic Age: the *kleea proteron anthropon* (*Theogony* 100), that is to say, the heroes of the Trojan war and their return, as in the *Iliad* and the *Odyssey*, and the very beginnings of the cosmos, as in the *Theog*. However, the Homeric epics were not regarded as historical reports and they contain a mixture of elements from different time periods. Yet, the song is not only a celebration of the past but also of the future (*Theog*. 31) and the present. According to the poet of the *Hymn to Apollo*, the song bears on the gods' happiness and the miserable state of human affairs (*Hymn to Apollo* 190–3).

Thanks to the Muses, the goddesses of poetry, the poet sings human and divine deeds. Despite the doubtful etymological relation between muse and memory, there is an acknowledged parentage between the muse and memory and the song and memory: Pindar conceives of memory as the mirror of fine deeds (*Nemean* 7.14–15). The Muses' omniscience and omnipresence (Homer, *Il*. II.485) are imparted to the poet who has, therefore, access to the past and possesses a universal and divine knowledge. The divine gift of poetry does not only allow the poet to transmit knowledge to his audience but also gives pleasure. According to Hesiod, Zeus created poetry first for his own pleasure (*Theog*. 37, 51), and second, to grant mankind 'a forgetting of ills and a rest from sorrows' (55) and lighten their sufferings (98–9). Regarding themselves as masters of both truth and pleasure, the poets did not consider these two ends to be incompatible because pleasure does not necessarily address the irrational part of the soul, as Plato has it (*Republic* 603a–c, 605a–7b).

The invocation of the Muses does not lead the poet to consider himself as merely a mouthpiece of the divine. Even though the invocation is a kind of inspiration (*Od*. 8.499; *Theog*. 33) it does not equate with possession (q.v. Madness and Possession), contrary to Plato's claim in *Ion* and *Phaedrus*. The equation allows him to deprive the poet not only of a *technê* but also of knowledge. Possessed, that is, under the spell of the divine and 'out of his mind', the poet is in an irrational state of mind, contributing nothing to his poetry. However, although the human and the divine parts in the making of the song are not clearly distinguished, the poet acknowledges a kind of autonomy through the common idea that the Muses teach the poet (*Od*. 8.481, 8.487, 17.518; Solon, 1.51–2; *Th*. 22; Hesiod,

Works and Days 662). Divine inspiration does not deprive the poet of a poetic skill (*Od.* 14.131), contrary to what Plato claims (*Ion*). Pindar speaks of an inventive ability (*eumachania*) that prevents him from being merely the follower of Homer (*Pythian* 7b8–20). Comparing the poet with a seer, Pindar tells us that the skill consists chiefly of interpreting the Muses' sayings. He thus makes the art of the poet an art of interpretation (Snell *P.* 6.6, f. 94a5, f. 150), which is under attack in *Ion* (535a). The broad range of topics that poetry embraces makes it a kind of encyclopaedia, especially the *Il.* and the *Od.* (see Plato, *R.* 606e2; Xenophon, *Symp*osium 3–6). Plato's critique of Homer's and the poets' alleged *polymathia* leads him to condemn their role in education. Poetry conveys a certain ethical insight whose values, for the most part Homeric, are called into question on account of their detrimental consequences (*R.* bk 3). Heroes are poor models whose imitation perverts the soul. However, this critique of the heroic posture is not only Plato's but also that of the lyric poets, though the perspective is very different in each case. Lyric poetry (iambic, melic and elegiac poetry) is centred on the individual and the present, and expresses itself in the first person. Archilochus rejects the Homeric idealized hero and his search for *kleos* – Simonides of Ceos and Hipponax depict the triviality and poverty of life. However, harking back to Homer, the last representatives of lyric poetry like Bacchylides and Pindar define poetry as an art of immortalization. By bestowing fame on mortals who no longer accomplish warlike deeds but only athletic ones, the poet gives them immortality. Whether or not it is a criticism of heroism, lyric poetry does not renounce the aim of conveying a moral message and content. This is why the poet Theognis of Megara

(sixth-century BCE) could be the target of Plato according to whom the poet gives an inconsistent view on virtue in his *Elegies* (*Men.* 95d–6a). Inconsistency is one of Plato's favourite criticisms against the poets (e.g. *Lg.* 719c).

The sayings of lyric poets are considered to be wise and true by various characters in the dialogues and, in consequence, are subjected to Socrates' elenchus, as in the case of Simonides in *R.* bk 1 and *Protagoras*. Plato maintains on the one hand that poetry consists of an illusory, dangerous and deceitful art, and on the other hand, that it is the product of ignorance. However, even though lyric poetry is banished from the ideal city along with epic, it is not, like Homer and to a lesser extent Hesiod, the main target of Plato's attacks. The reason may be that Homer, as 'the best of the poets', embodies par excellence the figure of poetic authority against which Plato wages war (*R.* 606e–7a).

PRE-SOCRATIC PHILOSOPHERS

J. H. Lesher

Plato refers frequently to the views held by earlier thinkers, typically while lining up witnesses for or against a philosophical thesis. His characters speak approvingly of the doctrines of Parmenides and the Pythagoreans but repudiate in the strongest terms the teachings of 'atheistic materialists' – thinkers such as the Milesian inquirers into nature we today regard as the founders of Western philosophy and science. The chief failings of the materialists were not acknowledging the priority of soul over matter and not believing that a cosmic intelligence has arranged all things for the best. On occasion Plato states a view held by a thinker he has elsewhere criticized and he is not above borrowing the ideas of others without identifying his source. Thus, while Plato's dialogues are an invaluable source of information for the views of earlier thinkers, his representations must be read with caution.

Plato's Thales is the familiar combination of scientific inquirer (*Theaetetus* 174a) and practical sage (*Hippias Major* 281c; *Epistle* 2.311a; *Protagoras* 343a; *Republic* 10.600a). Thales is also credited with the view that 'all things are full of gods' (*Laws* 10.899b), which exempted him from the indictments of materialist cosmologies levelled in the *Epinomis* (988b) and *Lg*. bk 10 (886e). The story of Thales and the serving girl (*Tht*. 174a) suggests that Plato saw Thales as a prototype of the philosopher whose inquiries expose him to public ridicule and scorn.

At *Sophist* 242d Plato presents Xenophanes of Colophon as one of the early thinkers who affirmed that 'all things are one', but elsewhere Plato follows Xenophanes' lead on a number of points. For example, the proposal to censor poetic depictions of the gods put forward in *R*. bk 10 echoes sentiments Xenophanes expressed in fragments 'DK' B1, 11, 12 and 22; the call at *Apology* 36e and *R*. 5.465d to honour the city's wise counsellors more than victorious athletes tracks the language of Xenophanes B3; and the distinction between knowledge and true opinion (endorsed at *Men*. 98a and elsewhere) appears first in Xenophanes B34. Plato's unwillingness to acknowledge his indebtedness to Xenophanes may derive from Xenophanes' endorsement of the kind of materialist view (B27 and 29) the Athenian of *Lg*. bk 10 claimed warranted a minimum of 5 years of solitary confinement or the death penalty (*Lg*. 909). Plato might also have disliked Xenophanes' claim that people in different regions conceive of the gods in different terms (cf. B16 and *Lg*. 10.889e) and that god 'shakes all things by the thought of his mind' (B25) but is otherwise uninvolved in human affairs (see further, Lesher 1992).

Pythagoras of Samos appears only once in the dialogues, when (at *R*. 10.600a) Plato identifies him as 'the founder of a way of life'. But *Philebus* 16d alludes to a 'Prometheus like figure' who taught that 'all things consist of a one and many, and have in their nature a conjunction of limit and unlimited' and that 'we must go from one form to look for two, if the case admits of this, otherwise for three or some other number of forms'. Although the evidence relating to ancient Pythagoreanism (q.v. Pythagoreanism) is often unreliable, it seems certain that at some point Plato became enamoured of Pythagorean doctrine. His most extensive account of the physical cosmos is presented by Timaeus, an imaginary Pythagorean statesman and scientist. In the *R*. he describes the study of mathematics as essential preparation for philosophical dialectic and an essential component in the training of the guardians (*Ti*. 536d). His tripartite view of the soul echoes a Pythagoras anecdote about the three kinds of lives (Diogenes Laertius 8.8). The simile of the divided line in *R*. bk 6 (q.v.) embodies the same fourfold progression Pythagoras' followers identified as the *tetractys* their master had passed down to their generation (Aëtius I, 3, 8). Plato's definition of justice assumes the conception of harmony described by the Pythagorean Philolaus of Croton ('DK' 44, B6). These and other points of contact clearly indicate that Plato knew and embraced many of the Pythagorean doctrines of his own era (see Huffman 1993).

Plato credited Heraclitus of Ephesus with the mistaken (indeed, self-defeating) doctrine of 'flux' or 'radical change', that is, that all things are changing in all respects all the time (*Cratylus* 401d, 402a, 411b; *Phlb*. 43a; *Tht*. 152e, 160d, 177c). But the most likely basis for Plato's interpretation – the 'river fragments' 'DK' B12, 49a and 91b – can be read instead as affirming the unity of the opposites and the measured character of all change (see Kirk 1954). Moreover, at least one aspect of Heraclitean reality remained exempt from change, namely the *logos* that 'holds forever' (B1). Plato also expressed contempt for Heraclitus' aphorism-spouting followers (*Tht*. 180) and accused him of failing to understand his own doctrine of opposites (*Symposium* 187a). But Plato concurred in many other aspects of Heraclitus' philosophy. Plato held that the doctrine of flux holds true for all things located in the sensible realm, including human beings (cf. *Smp*. 207d). The Stranger at *Sph*. 242d has no difficulty in attributing to a 'certain Ionian muse' the view that 'the real is both many and one and is held together by enmity and friendship [and that] in parting asunder it is always being drawn together'. In addition, at *Phaedo* 65a and *R*. 6.508 Plato indicts the senses as unsuitable sources of knowledge, much as Heraclitus had indicted 'eyes and ears as bad witnesses' ('DK' B107). The contrast of sleeping with waking, a leitmotif in many of the surviving Heraclitus fragments, became one of Plato's favourite themes.

Parmenides of Elea (q.v. Eleatics) provided Plato with both the terminology and philosophical foundations for two key doctrines in his philosophy: a dualistic metaphysics and rationalist theory of knowledge (cf. Diotima's description of Beauty Itself at *Smp*. 211a, the linking of knowledge with being at *R*. 5.476, and the denigration of sense perception in the simile of the divided line at *R*. 6.508–11). On the Parmenidean-Platonic view, 'what is' cannot fail to be in any way, and therefore never changes, moves, is divided, comes into being or is destroyed. Moreover, since knowledge must be a secure possession, it must have as its objects things that remain forever in possession of their attributes, which can only be the Forms or Ideas we apprehend in thought (see further, Palmer 1999 and q.v. Eleatics).

Plato refers frequently to doctrines associated with Empedocles of Akragas, but with little approval. At *Men*. 76c Socrates draws on an Empedoclean theory of 'effluences' to define colour but disparages the resulting definition as 'pompous'. At *Tht*. 152e Socrates includes Empedocles among the earlier thinkers who mistakenly thought that all things are in the process of becoming. *Phd*. 96b contains what is probably a reference to Empedocles' view of blood as the medium of thought ('DK' A30, 86 and 97). *Timaeus* 48b introduces a geometrical improvement on the Empedoclean doctrine of 'roots' (B6 and A30). And the *Sph*. alludes to 'a certain muse in Sicily' who held that 'the real is both many and one and held together by enmity and friendship' (*Sph*. 242d, 243a; cf. B26). But Plato appears to have shared Empedocles' conception of philosophy as a guide to life as well as his view of the present life as merely one stage in the soul's long journey (cf. B111 and 115 with the myth of Er in *R*. bk 10).

Plato credited Anaxagoras of Clazomenae with four doctrines: that the sun and moon are not gods but merely stone and earth (*Apology* 26d), that the moon receives its light from the sun (*Cratylus* 409b), that 'all things are together' (*Gorgias* 465d; *Phd*. 72c) and that 'Mind produces order and is the cause of everything' (*Cra*. 413c, 400a; *Lg*. 10.886d, 12.967b; *Phd*. 98b). In the *Phd*. Socrates faults Anaxagoras for failing to stick to his hypothesis that the Mind orders all things, resorting instead to causes such as 'air, aether, water, and many other absurdities' (*Phd*. 98c). In 'DK' B12, however, Anaxagoras speaks of Mind as 'itself' and 'all by itself' (*auto* and *eph' eautou*), phrases Plato will employ in characterizing the Forms or Ideas (cf. *Ti*. 51b8). Anaxagoras would certainly have been among those 'earlier thinkers' praised in the *Philebus* for affirming 'that reason and a marvellous organizing intelligence (*noun kai phronêsin*) pilot the whole universe' (*Phd*. 28d).

The fact that the names of the founders of atomic theory, Leucippus and Democritus, appear nowhere in Plato's writings provides some measure of his animosity towards materialist cosmologies. The possibility that reality consisted entirely of material bodies jostling about in empty space, and that events could be fully accounted for in terms of physical causes, were ideas Plato regarded as anathema. So, when (at *Ti*. 53 ff.) Plato offers his own theory of matter his geometrical 'atoms' are so richly endowed with aesthetic, moral, and mathematical properties as to hardly count as material bodies at all. The silent treatment Plato gave to the atomists provides a useful reminder that his representations of the views held by his predecessors were neither disinterested nor entirely dispassionate.

PYTHAGOREANS

Carl A. Huffman

Some have thought that the Pythagoreans played a powerful role in shaping Platonic thought (Guthrie 1975:35). In late antiquity, Plato could be presented as a member of the Pythagorean School (Photius 438b17). The evidence suggests, however, that Pythagorean influence on Plato has been considerably exaggerated. Indeed, recent overviews of Plato's philosophy (e.g. Benson 2006; Kraut 1992c) make only a few, mostly passing, references to Pythagoreanism, thus suggesting that Plato is explicable with little mention of the Pythagoreans.

Plato refers explicitly to Pythagoras and the Pythagoreans only once each. Many scholars think, however, that a single sentence from the *Metaphysics* indicates that Aristotle thought Plato heavily indebted to Pythagoreanism. In the survey of his predecessors, Aristotle asserts that Plato's philosophy 'agrees with these men in most respects' (987a29–31). Although many see 'these men' as the Pythagoreans, the context suggests the reference is to all the pre-Socratics (Huffman 2008). Moreover, Aristotle explains Plato's central achievement in metaphysics, the theory of forms, in terms of the combined influence of Socrates and Heracliteans (*Metaphysics* 987a32–b10, 1078b12–30), without mention of the Pythagoreans. It is with principles that are even more fundamental than forms that he sees the closest connection between Plato and Pythagoreanism. Even here he stresses differences. Plato's one and indefinite dyad correspond to the Pythagoreans' limit and unlimited, but Plato separates his principles from the physical world, while the Pythagoreans identify theirs with it. Plato also replaces the unlimited with the indefinite dyad.

Plato's sparse references to the Pythagoreans are in accord with Aristotle's presentation. The sole reference to Pythagoras (*Republic* 600b) is positive and indicates that Plato thought of him as a private educator who left behind a way of life. There is no suggestion of any close connection to or veneration for Pythagoras. The single reference to the Pythagoreans (*R.* 530d) praises them for treating harmonics and astronomy as sister sciences but criticizes them for looking for numbers in heard harmonies rather than ascending to problems and treating numbers apart from sensibles (*R*. 531c).

Plato's clearest nonexplicit reference to the Pythagoreans is found at *Philebus* 16c–17a. Socrates describes a method that 'was hurled down from the gods by some Prometheus along with fire' and that men before his time adopted. This method regards limit and unlimited as inherent in all things and knowledge as arising when we grasp the precise number that applies to each thing. In the later tradition, where Pythagoras becomes the source of all philosophical wisdom, this Prometheus was inevitably identified with Pythagoras. Nothing in Plato's reference to Pythagoras in the *R*., however, suggests that he saw him as a divine figure and it is likely that Plato was simply referring to a revised Prometheus, who hurled down the method along with fire as gifts to humanity (Huffman 1999). The men before our time who adopt the method are undoubtedly Pythagoreans. Aristotle explicitly identifies limit, unlimited and number as basic principles of the Pythagoreans and these principles are also found in the fragments of Philolaus.

Pythagorean influence appears earlier in Plato's career in two areas, the fate of the soul and mathematics (Kahn 2001:3–4). Vivid accounts of the judgement and reincarnation of the soul, which appear abruptly in *Gorgias*, *Meno*, *Phaedo* and *R*. are often traced to Pythagorean influence arising from his visit to Italy and Sicily in 387 BCE. Pythagoras was perhaps the first to introduce the doctrine of metempsychosis into Greece (Dicaearchus Fr. 40 Mirhady). It was, however, also found in Orphism, in Empedocles and possibly in Bacchic rites (Burkert 1985:294; Burkert 1987:87). At *Laws* 870d–e, Plato presents it as something taught in religious initiations (*teletai*), which suggests Orphic or Bacchic practises. It is, thus, far from clear that Plato

was always thinking of Pythagoreans when he mentioned it.

Other aspects of Plato's account of the fate of the soul are even less securely traced to Pythagoreanism. The unnamed 'wise' man who teaches (*Grg*. 493a) that we are dead in this life and that the body (*sôma*) is the tomb (*sêma*) of the soul is not Orphic; the Orphics are assigned a competing view at *Cratylus* 400c. He might be a Pythagorean, but later sources also point to Heraclitus (Dodds 1959:300). The Sicilian or Italian mythologizer mentioned in the same passage, who made the soul a leaky jar, is also not likely to be a Pythagorean. Nor is it true that, whenever Socrates refers to 'the wise', he is referring to the Pythagoreans (Burkert 1972:78 correcting Dodds 1959:297). The wise man of *R*. (583b; cf. *Phlb*. 44b), who regards pleasure as unreal is not a Pythagorean as Adam (1902:378); suggested he was. Pythagoreans distrusted pleasure but regarded it as all too real (Huffman 2005:323–37). The 'wise men and women' of *Men*. (81a), who are 'priests and priestesses who have made it their concern to given an account of their practices' are likely to be Orphics or others engaged in mysteries, since Pythagoreans are not called priests in our sources. Women did have a prominent role in Pythagoreanism, but they were also initiated into the Bacchic mysteries (Burkert 1985:294). The view that all nature is akin (*Men*. 81d) may be a Platonic adaption of the Pythagorean view that all animate creatures are related (Dicaearchus Fr. 40, Mirhady).

The *Phd*. is peopled by Pythagoreans such as Philolaus and Echecrates, but Plato does not call them Pythagoreans and is not simply presenting Pythagorean views. Socrates assigns the theory that the body is a prison, in which the soul is undergoing punishment from which it should not escape by suicide (*Phd.* 62c), to the mysteries and not to Philolaus. The Pythagorean idea that the soul is a harmony is heavily criticized (*Phd.* 86b; see Huffman 1993:328; Huffman 2009). To argue that the *Phd.* myth follows a Pythagorean source in the smallest details (Kingsley 1995:79–171) is implausible, since the supposed Pythagorean source has not survived. There may be Pythagorean elements in the *Grg.* myth, but Dodds shows that it draws on a great variety of sources. Plato's typical transformation of his sources is clear in the case of metempsychosis. He borrows the idea that the soul goes through a series of rebirths, remembering things encountered previous to this existence. His theory of recollection grafts onto this religious idea – the distinctly Platonic notion of a separation between an intelligible world of forms and the sensible world. What we recollect is our encounter with the forms in a disembodied state, whereas Pythagoras only claimed to remember his previous physical incarnations. As an epistemological doctrine, the doctrine of recollection owes very little to Pythagoreanism.

Similarly, mere mention of mathematics is no indication that Plato is drawing on Pythagoreanism. Rigorous mathematics is Greek rather than specifically Pythagorean. The most prominent mathematicians in the dialogues, Theodorus and Theaetetus, are not Pythagoreans. In *R.* bk 7, although aware of Archytas' achievements in mathematics (Huffman 2005:385–401), Plato finds its value in the ability to turn the soul from the sensible to the intelligible realm, while he criticizes the Pythagoreans for locating numbers in sensible things. Part of the terminology used to describe the nuptial number (*R.* 546c; cf. *sunêkooi* at *Lg.* 711e (Burkert 1972:84)) is drawn from Pythagorean sources (Huffman 2005:439–42), but there is no reason to think that the number itself

was Pythagorean. The southern Italian who gives his name to Plato's *Timaeus*, has been thought to represent Archytas. The situation is not so simple. The construction of the world soul relies on the mathematics of the Pythagorean diatonic scale, but it is the scale used by Philolaus not Archytas. Moreover, features of the cosmology of the *Ti.* are in direct conflict with Pythagoreanism. Archytas argued that the universe was unlimited in extent (Huffman 2005:540), whereas Plato's universe has a limit. Philolaus makes the earth a planet orbiting around a central fire. Plato, like Philolaus, apparently has a spherical earth, but it is firmly in the centre. The moral cosmology of the *Phd.* and *R.* myths, and the conception of a heavenly music in the latter, owe something to Pythagoras' own cosmology and to Philolaus' description of the cosmos as a harmony (Huffman 2010). At *Grg.* 507e, the Pythagoreans are undoubtedly included among 'the wise', who say that heaven and earth are held together by friendship, order and justice and hence call the whole a *kosmos* (order), although Empedocles and Anaximander are probably included as well. Pythagoras' invention of the word *kosmos* is a later fabrication (Burkert 1972:77). Socrates' warning to Callicles that he is ignoring mathematical proportion (*Politicus* 508a) may be an allusion to Archytas (Huffman 2005:208–11); in the *Plt.* (284e) 'the clever who say that measure is concerned with all things' could be Pythagoreans, although the passage is problematic. In all these cases, however, as in the *Ti.*, while Plato borrows specific aspects of Pythagoreanism, he integrates them into a system that is distinctly Platonic and often profoundly un-Pythagorean. With the exception of Plato's later theory of principles, Pythagoreanism was just one among many influences on Plato rather than being central to his development.

RHETORIC AND SPEECHMAKING

Richard Marback

The term *rhêtorikê*, or rhetoric, understood as the art of using words to persuade others in assemblies and courts of law, first appears in Plato's *Gorgias*. The term is a derivation of an older, commonly used word for politicians who spoke in assemblies and courts, *rhêtôr*. The speeches given by politicians in assemblies were deliberative. Speeches given in courts of law were judicial (see Schiappa 1991:39–58). In *Grg.*, rhetoric is used to refer less to the practises of giving speeches in assemblies and courts of law and more to the art of teaching others to deliver such speeches. The passage where the term *rhêtorikê* first appears is one in which Socrates is questioning Gorgias about the identity of his art and the associated nature of the wisdom he professes to teach. The conclusions of the dialogue – that rhetoric is like cookery in that both are arts of flattery, gratification and indulgence, at the same time the sophist is like the tyrant in that both possess the power to do what they please but lack the wisdom to know and do what is best – are cynical conclusions about the roles of rhetoric and speechmaking in civic life. Many were sceptical about the teaching of speechmaking, worried about the potential created for insincerity. At the same time, rhetoric and the art of speechmaking did contribute to Athenian democracy by standardizing competence and encouraging scepticism (see further, Guthrie 1971a; also Poulakos 1995:11–46). We get a broader sense of the ancient Greek art of persuading through speeches by turning directly to the words of the sophist Gorgias himself.

In 'Encomium of Helen', Gorgias displays his flair for language at the same time as he delves into the mysterious power of words. The speech is a defence of Helen of Troy against any blame she carries for leaving Sparta with Paris and causing the Trojan War. Gorgias claims Helen could have been persuaded to go with Paris in four ways: by the gods, by force, by love or through speech. The first three means of persuasion – divine intervention, physical force and the passion of love – are, according to Gorgias, irresistible, and so leave Helen innocent of acting in a blameworthy manner. The fourth means by which she may have been persuaded, speech, is also irresistible, and so Helen is again found to be not blameworthy. The persuasive power of speech is irresistible because

The effect of speech upon the condition of the soul is comparable to the power of drugs over the nature of bodies. For just as different drugs dispel different secretions from the body, so also in the case of speeches, some distress, others delight, some cause fear, others make the hearer bold, and some drug and bewitch the soul with a kind of evil persuasion (14, trans. Kennedy 1963).

In this passage the word for speech is *logos* (q.v.), a general term that denotes word or speech or language as well as principle or reason. Here Gorgias would seem to be saying through his comparison to drugs that the effects of speech on souls is less a consequence of the idea communicated and more a result of the language of the idea's communication.

Expressing the persuasive and, at least in this case, deceptive power of words over the soul through appeal to magic and the effects of drugs on bodies is no mere flourish or imagery. As far back as the oral culture of the Homeric tradition speech was considered a divine gift. To speak well was to be inspired as well as inspiring. Not only could epic poets be inspired and inspiring speakers, speechmaking itself was a prevalent feature in epic poetry as well as in the later tragedies (Kennedy 1994:11–29). As Gorgias remarks, poetry is speech with meter and if poetry could be understood as speech with meter, then speech could draw on the stylistics of poetry to exert influence over the emotions and perceptions of an audience. Conscious arrangement of rhythm and meter could drug and trick the souls of an audience by compelling emotional responses that confuse, overwhelm and manipulate the limitations of human memory, understanding and foresight (de Romilly 1975:3–22).

The persuasive power of a speech, then, is visceral. The sounds of words were experienced and understood as more than auditory representations communicating ideas to disembodied intellects. The soul and body were inextricably intertwined. We need only recall from *Phaedrus* (246–54) Plato's myth of the charioteer of the soul to get a sense of the close relationships among reason, moral sentiments and irascible appetites. Words were indeed magical as well as medicinal. Words could and did quicken the heart, steel the nerves, inflame or extinguish the passions and mesmerize the soul. People are susceptible to the persuasive and deceptive power of speeches because they are by nature social creatures vulnerable to, and dependent on, each other.

With the realization that, through an art of rhetoric, they could manipulate words in ways that 'drug and trick the soul', sophists recognized the potential power to be had over the souls of others through the delivery of carefully crafted speeches. Teaching the powerful art of speechmaking, sophists taught the deliberative and judicial speaking that became increasingly important to the political functioning of ancient Athenian democracy. Of course such an education could not but run the risk of being seen by more traditional thinkers as more deceptive

than persuasive. Such is the view often found in the dialogues of Plato, portraying rhetoric and speechmaking as deceptive and so as an illicit drug that contributes to the diseases of soul and to the state instead of to their health and well-being. Although Socrates himself sometimes gives speeches and seems to envisage a proper philosophic rhetoric in the *Phdr.*, for Plato the speaking that cured souls was to be had less in speechmaking and more in the give and take of dialogue. The tension between dialogue and speechmaking reflects the question of how best to establish through language the bonds of philosophical friendship that hold people together in societies. An art of rhetoric that had as its explicit goal a training in the making of speeches which could have therapeutic effects on state and soul was a later historical development, most fully articulated after Plato by Aristotle (see further, Nussbaum 1994).

SOCRATES (HISTORICAL)

William Prior

(I) LIFE

Socrates, one of the greatest philosophers of the ancient Greek world and for several ancient schools an exemplar of what the philosophical life should be, was an Athenian citizen born in 469 BCE. He was the son of Sophroniscus, a stonecutter, and Phaenarete, a midwife; and he was married to Xanthippe, with whom he had three children (*Phaedo* 60a, 116a–b). His adult years coincided with the 'Golden Age' of Athens, and he was present during Athens' decline and fall during the Peloponnesian War (431–404). Socrates was a public figure during at least part of this period: the comic playwright Aristophanes made him the target of his play the *Clouds* (423; later revised). His odd physical appearance and his way of life made him a ready target for the comic poets. Socrates served as a hoplite (a heavy-armed infantryman) in at least three of Athens' military campaigns in the Peloponnesian War (at Potideia in 429 BCE, Delium in 424 BCE and Amphipolis in 422 BCE). Plato notes his courage during the retreat from Delium (*Laches* 181b; *Symposium* 221a).

(II) Philosophical Activity

Socrates seems to have spent most of his time in the agora, the public market place, discussing philosophy. He denied that he was a teacher, and he did not accept pay as did numerous other thinkers of the day, but he did attract a coterie of young followers, most importantly including Xenophon and Plato. Several of these followers made contributions to the Socratic literature, dialogues written with Socrates as the central figure (Kahn 1996:1–35). Except for the writings of Xenophon and Plato, however, only fragments of their works remain.

(III) Trial

In 399 Socrates was brought to trial on charges of impiety (lit. 'not believing in the gods in whom the city believes, but in other new spiritual things' *Apology* 24b) and corrupting the youth. He was found guilty, sentenced to death and executed by hemlock poisoning. Several reasons for his conviction and execution have been offered. At least one scholar (Burnyeat 1998) has argued that he was guilty of impiety. Others note his arrogance before the jury, or his relationship with antidemocratic elements within Athens (in

particular, Plato's uncle Critias and his cousin Charmides). Even more important may have been his association with Alcibiades, a highly controversial Athenian political leader, though a democratic one. Alcibiades and Socrates had an erotic relationship, comically described by Alcibiades in Plato's *Smp.* (217a–19d; see also, *Alcibiades I* and *Protagoras*). Socrates' status as the leading intellectual in Athens and as a central figure in the intellectual revolution that took place in the latter half of the fifth century doubtlessly aroused antipathy among many jurors.

(IV) The Socratic Problem

The above information is generally accepted concerning Socrates. He examined others in public as well as in private and he discussed ethics. The Socratic dialogue form presumably reflects the dialectical activity of the historical Socrates. Beyond this, it is difficult to be certain what, if anything, Socrates believed or taught or what kind of person he was. The problem is that we have four early sources: Aristophanes, Aristotle, Plato and Xenophon, and they do not always agree. Three of these sources were contemporaries of Socrates who knew him personally (Aristophanes, Plato and Xenophon); the other was a member of Plato's Academy who had access to eye witness accounts of Socrates (Aristotle). The discrepancies among our sources have produced the 'Socratic Problem', and its persistence in the literature may be a sign that it is insoluble.

The problem arises from the fact that Socrates wrote nothing, so that all of our earliest accounts of his views come from the sources mentioned above. Though there are areas of overlap in these sources' portraits of Socrates, there are important differences. Controversially (cf. Dover 1968),

Aristophanes portrays Socrates in the *Clouds* as a philosophical mountebank, a purveyor of doctrines in all areas, who dispenses these doctrines from a school called the *phrontis-terion* (think tank). Aristophanes' Socrates combines features of a philosopher of nature with that of a sophist. It is difficult for us to know, at this distance from the *Clouds*, how serious this portrait is to be taken (though Socrates takes it seriously enough to respond to it in the *Ap.* 18a–d, 19c–d).

For Plato and Xenophon, however, Socrates is a revered figure with the highest ethical standards. They differ to some degree on what these standards entail. For Plato, Socrates rejects the *lex talionis*, the repayment of 'an eye for an eye', whereas Xenophon's Socrates does not (Vlastos 1991a:179–99). Plato's Socrates has a developed theory of virtue, equating virtue with knowledge and denying the possibility of moral weakness; Xenophon's Socrates is more of a homespun moral philosopher offering practical, moral advice. Aristotle does not offer a complete portrait of Socrates, but he offers interesting bits of information, many of which seem to confirm the portraits in the Platonic dialogues.

Plato's portrait of Socrates has proved to be the most compelling for most contemporary scholars. Even if we confine ourselves to the Platonic portrait of Socrates, however, it is difficult, if not impossible to form a single coherent picture of his views. Socrates in the *Ap.* (23a–b) professes scepticism about the existence of knowledge in humans. In the *Theaetetus* (149a–51d) Plato portrays Socrates as a midwife who, though barren himself, elicits philosophical truths from his interlocutors. For Alcibiades in the *Smp.* (221d–2a), Socrates' barrenness is only an ironic mask for philosophical riches hidden within. Numerous scholars have seen in those

riches philosophical doctrines in the area of ethics. Other scholars (including Penner 1992) have attributed to Plato's Socrates a theory of the nature of the soul. Still others have attributed to him an early version of the theory of forms (Allen 1971; Prior 2004).

Socrates remains a mystery. His influence on other philosophers, however, is not. He was more influential on Plato than any other philosopher, as is shown by the fact that he is present in all the dialogues save the very late *Laws* and is the leading speaker in most of them. We may not know precisely where the historical Socrates ends and the Platonic Socrates begins, but we can detect his influence on Plato throughout most of the corpus.

SOCRATICS (OTHER THAN PLATO)

Menahem Luz

The term 'Socratic philosophers' (*Sôkratikoi*) is an ancient one employed to denote either Socrates' pupils or later philosophers who regarded him as their founder (Goulet-Cazé 1999:161–5). Since Plato and Xenophon are often considered his principal representatives today, modern scholars invented the terms 'Other Socratics' (Nails 2002:xxviii) or 'Minor Socratics' to denote Socrates' other followers and sometimes their pupils as well (Giannantoni 1985:1–2). Plato gives a select list of Socrates' 'inner circle' at the time of his execution (*Phaedo* 59b–c), but of these only five are examined in any detail by the ancient biographers (D. L. 2.60–105, 6. 1–19) and considered leading Minor Socratic today (Kahn 1996:1–35): Antisthenes of Piraeus, Aeschines of Sphettus, Euclides of Megara, Phaedo of Elis and Aristippus of Cyrene. By the late fourth century, 'Socratic compositions' (*Sôkratikoi logoi*) were a recognized literary genre (Aristotle, *Poetics* 1447b11; *Rhetoric* 1416a21) and sources of imitation for Socratic literature composed during the Hellenistic-Roman era when leading Minor Socratics were anachronistically considered the founders of the Cynics, Hedonists, Megarian dialecticians and neo-Eleatics (Vander Waerdt 1994a:Part II). Some of these imitations were associated with other lesser Socratics featuring in the works of Plato and Xenophon (Field 1967:133–74): for example, Crito, Simon the Cobbler, Glauco, Simmias and Cebes (Goulet-Cazé 1999: notes to pp. 202–3, 333–42). The genuine works of the leading Socratics survive only as a mass of ancient quotations supplemented by recently discovered papyrus fragments. Xenophon encapsulates many of their ideas but reformulated as conversations held between them and Socrates (e.g. *Symposium* i, iv; *Memorabilia* II. i, iii). A more reliable though selective source is Aristotle who criticizes the logic of Antisthenes and the Antistheneans (*Metaphysics* 1024b32–4, 1043b24–6), Aristippus (*Metaphysics* 996a32; *Rhetoric* 1398b30–3) and the style of Aeschines (*Rhetoric* 1417b1–2). The Minor Socratics did not form a single unified Socratic school although modern scholars have attempted to extract features common to them and Plato in order to uncover the teaching of the historical Socrates (Vlastos 1997:63n, 103, 208). Former scholars viewed them as Plato's companions (Field 1967:Part 3) while more recent research has contrasted them: for example, the non-transcendental understanding of the good in Aeschines and Antisthenes with Plato's theory of ideas (Rankin 1986:ch. 1); or the teachability of virtue in Antisthenes (Giannantoni 1983:II, f. 99) and Aeschines with Plato's *Men.* (Bluck 1964:117–18, 368). Yet others have looked

for interactions between the Socratics, Plato and Xenophon (Kahn 1994:1–35). A notable example is the question of political virtue denied in Plato's *Gorgias*, but later limited to the heroes of Athenian history in Aeschines' *Miltiades*, and ironically subservient to divine providence in the *Men.* (Bluck 1964:117–18; Dodds 1985:29–30). More provocative is the absence of Socrates' *aporia* in their work, thus questioning its historicity in the Platonic Socrates.

Modern scholarship has reassessed each of the five Minor Socratics as independent thinkers aside from the Hellenistic schools allegedly descended from them:

(1) Antisthenes of Piraeus (*c.* 445–*c.* 340 BCE) was said to have first been a paid sophist composing artificial speeches concerning the Homeric heroes (Rankin 1986:ch. 7). Even after his daily conversations with Socrates, his dialogues were characterized less by dialectic and more by imaginary speeches presented by mythological heroes as in the *Hercules* (Luz 1996:89–92) – or by foreign historical figures as in the *Cyrus* (Giananntoni 1983:II, VA, ff. 92–9). In both dialogues he showed how virtue was achieved at a universal level and through effort rather than through contemplation, a point that much influenced the early Stoa (Luz 1994:115–17). Even his definition of philosophy 'as a discussion with one's self' (Giananntoni 1983:II, VA ff. 100) stands in contrast to Plato's dialectic. Moreover, his theory of language that each word denotes one single concept to be defined only by itself – as in the new fragment 'disgracefulness is disgraceful' (Luz 2000:92–3) – recalls Prodicus' linguistic interest rather than Plato's search for universal definitions (Navia

2001:ch. 4). Much of this may be connected with his direct assault on Plato in the dialogue '*That Willy (Sathon) or on Contradiction*' criticizing Plato's metaphysics and summarized in the saying 'I see a horse but not Horseness' (Giannantoni 1983:II, ff. 147–59). Citations from his work on nature (*Physikos*) reformulate Xenophanes but are more sophisticated: there are many gods by convention, but only one in nature (ff. 179–83; Caizzi 1966:100–1). Much of his ethical theory was passed down to the Cynics and Stoa though his relationship with them was through his writings (Long 1996:28–46): virtue was a 'Socratic strength' to be grasped through reason and example rather than Academic study, but once learned it becomes a 'weapon that cannot be lost'. While he saw that true riches lay in virtue (Giannantoni 1983:II, VA, ff. 80–3), he did not reject possessions in themselves like the Cynics. Though 'preferring madness to pleasure' (ibid. ff. 118–28) he did not reject easily attained enjoyment (43–4).

(2) Aeschines of Sphettus (*c.* 435–*c.* 355 BCE) was a less original thinker than Antisthenes though his seven genuine dialogues were much admired in antiquity (Field 1967:146) for their unembellished 'Socratic character' (D. L. 2.61). Since the last publication of his fragments (Dittmar 1912; Krauss 1911), there have been substantial papyrological additions to his *Alcibiades* (CPF I 1989:120–34; Lobel 1919:no. 1608) and *Miltiades* (CPF I 1989:134–48; Patzer 1975; Slings 1975:301–8) dialogues. In the former, Socrates deflates Alcibiades' political aspirations in that he has less *epistêmê* even than his hero Themistocles (Field 1967:147–9). The dialogue also

explains how Socrates' divinely inspired *erôs* enables him to instil self-knowledge in Alcibiades. Though this theory of Socratic *erôs* has been termed 'innovative' (Kahn 1994:87), the fragments have striking similarities to Plato's dialogues as well as divergences with regard to the attainment of political *epistêmê* (Kahn 1996:19–23). In the *Miltiades*, Socrates persuades Miltiades to complete an education of the soul in addition to that of the body, turning to Euripides for advice, who refers them back to 'the wisest of the Greeks' (Socrates?) for teaching (Slings 1975:307). In the *Aspasia*, we have themes recalling Plato (*Menexenus*) and Xenophon (*Oeconomicus*) but where Pericles' mistress instructs Socrates on married love.

(3) Euclides of Megara (*c.* 450–368 BCE) allegedly sheltered Plato after Socrates' execution (D. L. 2.106). Although he composed six 'eristic' dialogues of 'question and answer' (ibid. 106–7), very little survives of them (Giannantoni 1985:49–57; Doering 1972:ff. 15–49) but his Socratic memoirs and style were allegedly used by Plato in the *Theaetetus* (143b5–6). His methodology attacked his opponents' conclusions rather than their suppositions (Goulet-Cazé 1999:366) 'in a manner Parmenidean' (D. L. 2.106), that is, Zeno (Doering 1972:83–4). His pupils in the 'dialectic school' of Megara hence developed a number of logical-dialectical paradoxes confuting claims to real knowledge (ibid. 108) while his own appearance in Plato (*Tht.* 142a–3c) is in a dialogue questioning the meaning of knowledge. Euclides may nonetheless have held positive doctrines as in his identification of the Socratic good with the Parmenidean One (Goulet-Cazé

1999:316, n. 1), sometimes seen as a sign of Platonic influence (Kahn 1996:13–14). However, it is unlikely that Euclides was in philosophical agreement with Plato seeing that his 'eristical' method of 'question and answer' (D. L. 2.106) was a sophistry Plato much criticized in the *Euthydemus* and elsewhere. Elsewhere he compared sleep and death (Doering 1972:80–1, f. 19) in almost determinist tones (ibid. ff. 12, 13), an attitude he jokingly maintained in relation to the gods (ibid. f. 11). Logicians have been interested in his use of Zeno's argumentation, wondering if it reached him directly or through Socrates (Kneale and Kneale 1964:8–9).

(4) Phaedo of Elis (born *c.* 417 BCE) returned to his native land after Socrates' execution, but we know little of his Elian School of philosophy, which was absorbed by the Eretrian school of eristics within a few generations (Giannantoni 1983:I. IIIA fr. 1–7). In his dialogue, *Zopyros*, he discussed traditional physiognomy whereby a person's character is read from his features and likely criticized as 'grandfatherly stupidity' (ibid. f. 9). His description of the effect of the wise as an unnoticed sting perceived by its later effect may contain his answer to physiognomy (Clay 1994:29, no. 11). In the *Simon* he probably discussed Socrates' conversations with Simon the cobbler (Goulet-Cazé 1999:312), a genre later to influence the Cynics. Since the anecdotes describe Phaedo's early life as a slave, it may be speculated that this dialogue presents the philosophy of the workingman in contrast to the 'executive' Cephalus (*Republic* 329e).

(5) Aristippus of Cyrene (*c.* 430–355 BCE) was much disparaged by his contemporaries as a hedonist (D. L. 2.65), believing pleasure (*hêdonê*) to be the highest good and end (Mannebach 1961, ff. 155–62). Xenophon (*Mem.* II.i.1–34, III.viii.4–10) depicts him as a sybarite corrected by Socrates, but it is clear from the argument that Aristippus sought pleasure, not luxury, and for comfort's sake, social seclusion. Perhaps in reply to the antihedonist, Antisthenes, Aristippus claimed that he learned from philosophy 'how to speak extravagantly' (D. L. 2.68). Scholars have contrasted his thought to Plato's discussions of pleasure (Gosling and Taylor 1984:42–3; Kahn 1996:17–18), but some concluded that he was a serious Socratic though much misunderstood in his time (McKirahan 1994:377–82). Since his relative Aristippus II (Mannebach 1961:ff. 163–7) developed the details of this theory, it has been difficult to draw a clear distinction between them (Giannantoni 1985:123–8, 161–70) and by the Roman period there was difficulty even in assigning his dialogues (D. L. 2.83–5). The relationship between these hedonists and the Epicureans (Giannantoni 1985:171–2) could only have occurred after Aristippus' death.

THE SOPHISTS

Richard Marback

The Greek term from which the name *sophistês*, or sophist, is derived is *sophos*, translating as wise or the wise man. Wisdom is the knowledge of an expert, knowledge in a particular art, craft or skill, such as music, navigation or sculpture. A person wise in an art such as navigation could teach that art. Such teaching was never purely practical in nature as it was more than a handing down of technical skill. To acquire wisdom in an art required learning when, how and to what effect one's knowledge should be put, it was to acquire a capacity for judgement. General instruction in moral judgement was considered the responsibility of ancient poets (see Guthrie 1971a). In the fifth century, the class of professional teachers grouped as sophists – a grouping that included Gorgias, Protagoras and Prodicus – taught not poetry but eloquence and persuasion in speaking and writing, especially the speaking and writing associated with political life. Gorgias drew from the poetry of Empedocles to cultivate a poetic style in political oratory. Other sophists, such as Protagoras, claimed that lessons in persuasion taught wisdom in statecraft as well as virtue of character (see Kennedy 1994).

The claim that someone could possess the wisdom of virtue (q.v.) and teach it to someone who did not possess it had among its supporters those suspicious of the possibility that such virtues as aristocratic excellence were not strictly inherited (see Jaeger 1939–44). In the fifth century the distinction between *nomos* and *physis*, or convention and nature, made it possible to think of wisdom as something more akin to ingenuity or cleverness, a human capacity for overcoming natural limitations. Those who were truly clever possessed a knowledge of, and so a facility with manipulating, the customs, habits and practises of an art. Such cleverness had negative as well as positive connotations (see Atwill 2009). Someone dexterous enough in an art such as rhetoric could potentially deceive others about what is and what is possible. One of the so-called first sophists, Protagoras, made great use of the distinction between *nomos* and *physis*. His observation that 'Man is the measure of all things' suggests that what can come to count as the wisdom of statecraft,

or virtue, is not what is given by nature but what people become aware of, what they invent for themselves, for it is through their interactions with each other that they create the possibility of their attaining virtues and becoming good (see Jarratt 1991). The point is developed in Protagoras' recounting of the myth of Prometheus distributing to humans the various arts by which they secure survival (*Protagoras* 321c–2d). As animals, humans are not adapted to survival. They depend for their survival not only on wisdom in specific Promethean arts such as saddle-making and metal-working but also on the more general political arts delivered by Hermes, the moral virtues of *aidos* and *dikê*, or the senses of justice (q.v.) and shame, which make it possible for humans to form bonds of civic friendship. These are not virtues that all humans possess in equal amounts at birth, although they are virtues all humans have the potential to acquire and develop through lives lived in civic friendship. The educational and political institutions created by humans cultivate the specific character that humanity achieves. To be human, then, is to be responsible for achieving virtue for oneself, independent of the dictates or limits of nature.

If to be human is to make one's self, then anything becomes possible. The sophist Gorgias exploits possibility, driving a wedge between the man-made and the naturally given when he argues: Nothing exists. If it exists, it cannot be known. If it can be known, it cannot be expressed (see Sprague 1972). While the extreme scepticism of Gorgias differs from the extreme relativism of Protagoras, their views together suggest a period of critical self-awareness and increased confidence in the power of human thought, a period that has been characterized as the Greek enlightenment. It was a period during which the Greeks cultivated their humanity by cultivating their capacities in a wide variety of technical and political arts. Prodicus contributed to the cultivation of political wisdom an insistence on precision in the definition of terms and clarity in political oratory that heightened critical self-reflection. His concern for distinguishing clearly the meanings of words may have influenced Socrates to dissect the precise meaning of what his interlocutors say in response to his questions. Certainly, Prodicus and Socrates were acquainted (see Guthrie 1971a). In the *Men.* (96d), Socrates remarks that he had been trained by Prodicus. In the *Theaetetus* (151b), he explains that he has sent pupils to Prodicus to learn his art.

Sophists such as Gorgias, Protagoras and Prodicus travelled from city to city giving performances of their persuasive and verbal skills. They also taught the arts of eristic, forensics and rhetoric to those who could afford their fees. With access to education in the arts of persuasion citizens of the ancient Greek cities could more skilfully declaim and debate the ideas of justice, statecraft and virtue. The sophistic claim to teach an art of virtue may have resonated with confidence in human ambition and the demands of a democracy, but it also aroused concern about the very possibility of ethical and political wisdom (see Solmsen 1975). Because of their verbal abilities, and because their lessons were only available to those who could pay, the sophists were often envied, disdained and ridiculed. Since the sophists charged fees for their wisdom they could, unlike their rival, Socrates, become corrupted by economic necessity, constrained to craft their lessons in excellence and virtue so as to fetch from their patrons the highest prices. Socrates, unconstrained by the pursuit of fees in his quest for wisdom, was freed to discover the unfettered truth of excellence and virtue with others who were also lovers of wisdom for its own sake.

Plato's critical presentation of the sophists as the rivals of Socrates may encourage a reading that opposes Plato and Platonism to the sophists and sophistry. Such a reading removes the drama of the dialogues from the sophistic claims to which they respond. To read Plato in this way, to read the dialogues outside the intellectual ferment regarding human wisdom, is to miss recognizing issues that most concerned the ancient Greeks, issues Plato could not consider except through earnest engagement with the sophists – the intertwined issues of appearances, being and becoming, deliberation, desire, education, friendship, justice, persuasion and virtue.

2

THE DIALOGUES

THE PLATONIC CORPUS AND MANUSCRIPT TRADITION

Harold Tarrant

Our Platonic corpus, consisting of nine 'tetralogies' (groups of four works), goes back at least to the time of Thrasyllus, court intellectual of the Roman Emperor Tiberius in the first-century BCE. The same first tetralogy is also attributed by Albinus (*Prologue* 4) to a Dercyllides of uncertain date. Tetralogies were systematically furnished with second titles based on the topic under investigation rather than the participant (Diogenes Laertius D. L. 3.57). Some second titles unsurprisingly antedate Thrasyllus, but he presumably added others for the sake of completeness. Some manuscripts preserve both second titles and each dialogue's 'character' as determined by a dichotomic classification at D. L. 3.49–51, though what standing the classification had is unclear, since most ancient Platonists from Plutarch to Olympiodorus afford little attention to characters, second titles and tetralogies alike.

In the tetralogies the multibook works (*Republic*; *Laws*) and the thirteen *Epistles* count as one item each. Many MSS preserve part of the Thrasyllan order. The two oldest date from the ninth century, Paris A (tetralogies 8, 9, and *Spuria*) and Bodleian B (tetralogies 1–6). Together they cover most of corpus, except the short tetralogy 7. Manuscript A has Armenian origins (Saffrey 2007), and MS D is an important additional witness for the *R*. MS B incorporates the scholia of Arethas, while MSS T and W are the best representatives of different families that supplement B, both preserving most of tetralogies 1–7 with some of 8. For a different part of the W-group P is the main representative, while Duke (1995:ix–xi) has afforded more weight than is customary to Q. F, which is the principal representative of a different arm of the tradition (Dodds 1959), is accordingly a valuable, if erratic, resource for selected dialogues, in addition to MSS A (Slings et al. 2005:195) and B, etc.

While not good enough to make scholarly emendation redundant, the combined MSS preserve their contents much better than MSS of most classical Greek authors. The ancient commentators, particularly Proclus, Damascius and Olympiodorus, preserve evidence of readings that have since disappeared, while occasionally being unaware of our readings. However, since ancient copyists were just as prone to making mistakes as Byzantine and medieval ones, even the earliest papyri of fragments of Plato's text, going back to Hellenistic times, are more likely to be wrong than right when deviating from the principal MSS traditions. The most recent editions make considerably more use of the indirect tradition in the apparatus, but this does not result in very much change to the printed text.

Already in the second century CE authors were aware of emendations to the text of Plato that had been inspired by doctrinal rather than scholarly concerns (Dillon 1989). Galen, in his *Commentary on the Medical Aspects of the Timaeus*, prefers to check at 77b–c a copy stemming from one Atticus, possibly Cicero's friend (Alline 1915:104–12). Whether it was possible to check superior copies of other dialogues is unknown.

It seems improbable that the Thrasyllan order, found at D. L. 3.56–61, was firmly established much before his time. Rival reading orders were promoted by other Platonists and scholars of the period, and Theon of Smyrna probably postulated different tetralogies (Tarrant 1993:58–84). In any case, it is clear that ancient Platonists generally refused to allow the Thrasyllan order any special status. Aristophanes of Byzantium (D. L. 3.61–2), at the close of the third-century BCE, had arranged 15 works into trilogies. What seems to have persisted was the belief that Plato had arranged dialogues in groupings reminiscent of tragic performances at the Dionysia, and the fact that some dialogues were intended to constitute sequences (e.g. *Theaetetus-Sophist-Politicus*) seems incontestable.

A recently published papyrus (Sedley 2009b) reveals the rationale for seeing the second tetralogy as a single coherent study. In it the *Cratylus* is seen as a prelude, while the remaining dialogues are said to deal with methods of definition and division; the *Tht.* is seen as the more tentative as it is keen to expose errors about knowledge, whereas the *Sph.* and *Plt.* are seen as confident.

It is usually assumed that some kind of important collection of texts was organized and retained in the Old Academy, and, by the time of Zeno of Citium's youth (Antigonus of Carystus at D. L. 3.66), a fee set for consulting it. It is well known that Philip of Opus, alleged author of *Epin.* (q.v.), was held responsible for the arrangement of the *Lg.* into 12 books, and the Suda also credits him with the less-than-natural arrangement of *R.* into 10. The difference in the number of books employed, 10 rather than 12, suggests that the *R.* was meant to be read with *Timaeus* and *Critias*. This evidence is plausible, not compelling, and nothing is known about other early groups, though two further groups of 12 may have been intended, omitting most of the *dubia* (q.v.). However, the early inclusion of the *dubia* in the corpus would have soon obscured the rationale behind any ordering of the scrolls. Besides Philip, early Academics known to have had some role connected with the books include Hermodorus (trading in them), Crantor (as first exegete, at least of *Ti.*, Proclus *in Ti.* 1.76.1–2) and Arcesilaus ('coming to possess' them, presumably those once available to his close friend Crantor, D. L. 4.32). The evidence suggests an important role relating to the books, separate from the scholarch's more public position.

The early history of the corpus is in fact somewhat mysterious, and inseparable from the intractable questions of (a) the state in which Plato had left his writings (especially but not solely *Lg.*; Nails and Thesleff 2003), and (b) the origin of the *dubia*. Among these was *Min.*, which Aristophanes of Byzantium already grouped with *Lg.* (plus the similarly dubious *Epin.*) in his arrangement, presumably because its proper place was by then believed to be with the corpus. The authorship of *Alcibiades II*, *Hipparchus* and *Amatores* was debated even in antiquity (Aelian *VH* 8.2; Athenaeus 11.506c; D. L. 9.37).

In antiquity, the preoccupation with understanding the full corpus seems to have been confined to the early Roman imperial period, following Andronicus' work on the Corpus Aristotelicum. Platonists from Plutarch onward concentrated on the exegesis of what we should regard as 'mature' works, and Neoplatonists from Iamblichus onward employed a reduced curriculum of 12 dialogues (plus *R.* and *Lg.*). In this the only works sometimes (if controversially) thought 'early' today are *Alcibiades I*, *Grg.* and *Cra.*

ALCIBIADES I

Harold Tarrant

The *Alcibiades I* is a dialogue of moderate length in dramatic form, between two speakers only: Socrates (in the guise of a divinely-inspired lover and educator) and the youthful Alcibiades who is slightly too old to prove attractive to men seeking physical gratification. His guardian Pericles is still alive, and he is on the threshold of embarking on a political career – prematurely in Socrates' view. It is clear that Plutarch (*Life of Alcibiades* IV) regards it as historically sound, though Attic comedy ignores any relationship between Socrates and Alcibiades, both of whom are satirized separately.

The authorship of the *Alc. I* has, since Schleiermacher in the early nineteenth century, been more hotly contested than that of any other dialogue. Conclusive arguments for settling the issue are elusive (for opposing views, see Denyer 2001:14–20; Smith 2004). Similarly there is no agreement among those who defend Platonic authorship about whether it is early or late in his output. On virtually every page there is some connection with something elsewhere in the Platonic dialogues, usually in those deemed to be early – if only because what is at issue is the Platonic understanding of Socrates, whose picture is more vivid there. These connections consciously set the work in the Platonic (rather than Socratic) tradition (cf. *Theages* 128a, 130a), a fact which some see as confirming Platonic authorship, others as undermining it. There are oddities of both language and Socratic philosophy, but such are to be found in most genuine works. It may be argued that its presence in the Corpus speaks for authenticity, or that its actual placement, in the unusually suspicious Fourth Tetralogy, speaks against it.

The work adds to the mythology surrounding the allegedly erotic relationship between Socrates and Alcibiades, and captures a brief but allegedly important episode in Athens' history, from the first word that Socrates addresses to Alcibiades until the latter's agreement to reciprocate his love. In doing so it fulfils some of Aristotle's important requirements for a tragic plot. It opens with Socrates explaining to Alcibiades why after following him about for years he is finally speaking to him, especially when no other lover has been well received. He credits the divine sign, here firmly associated with a guiding god, with having prevented him until now. He expects acceptance because Alcibiades has Alexander-like ambitions to rule the world, and he is the only one who can prepare him to achieve them – if the god allows (*Alc. I* 105e).

The dialogue naturally falls into three parts. The first, seen as employing Socrates' traditional elenchus by Neoplatonist interpreters, demonstrates to Alcibiades that he has learned nothing relevant to public policymaking, in particular that he has learned nothing of justice and injustice) *precisely* because he had supposed from childhood that he knew enough about them (110b). Accused of never seeking a credible teacher, Alcibiades suggests that he has learned from ordinary citizens, whose authority is then undermined with reference to their internal disagreement. Alcibiades claims that expediency is more germane to public debate than justice, but is forced to admit that there is no conflict between the two (116d). He remarks on his shaken confidence and vacillating ideas, which Socrates shows to be linked with his false assumption that he knows the most important things when he does not in fact know: the most lamentable form of ignorance (118b). It is then implied that Pericles' record suggests that he knew no better.

Alcibiades' tactic now changes. Thrown the lifeline that Athenians generally are ignorant, he claims that his abilities can at least prevail over them. Socrates shows that it is not prevailing over the Assembly that counts, but prevailing over the enemy. Alcibiades has to educate himself above the level of Spartan and Persian rivals (120a). In the second main part, a long, central speech, Socrates compares Alcibiades' credentials with those of Spartan and Persian kings (and imagines how unworthy an opponent for their sons the royal mothers would hold him to be.)

Now chastened, Alcibiades asks Socrates how to correct his condition (124b). Seeing that he needs self-care, he is led to search in the final part for the right kind of self-improvement, but the idea of good deliberation proves inadequate. Eventually Socrates helps with the observation that self-care requires *self-improvement*, not improvement of things we have an interest in (128e), so that, first and foremost, we must know *ourselves*. This is shown to be neither of the bodies nor the combination of body and soul, but soul alone,)

ΣΩΜΑΤΟΣ VS. PSYCHE

with the welcome consequence that Socrates loves Alcibiades alone rather than Alcibiades' attractive assets (131e).) Self-knowledge is like self-seeing, in that it requires a bright and lively mirror (133a), so that rather than gaze into the pupil of another's eye (a suitably erotic image), we must apparently gaze into the finest core of a soul, in which its wisdom and its divinity reside (133c).

Interpretation of this passage was hotly contested in late antiquity, resulting in textual difficulties (Tarrant 2007); a passage (133c8–17), absent from manuscripts, is sometimes supplied with too little caution from Christian sources. Reconstruction is uncertain. Pagan commentators assume that Alcibiades is being invited to gaze upon Socrates' mind and upon a god operating within, not upon an external god as the additional lines assume. This section from 128e, which gave the work its ancient subtitle *On the Nature of a Human Being*, also attracts most attention in modern times from proponents of authenticity and spuriousness alike.

From that point Alcibiades is easily shown that he must aim at personal excellence rather than at tyrannical power (135b), and that excellence alone is the choice for a free man. Alcibiades returns Socrates' love, and, while the ending is neither aporetic nor paradoxical, it includes an ominous warning that the power of the people may overpower their friendship.

THE APOLOGY OF SOCRATES

Thomas C. Brickhouse and Nicholas D. Smith

It is impossible to know precisely when Plato wrote the *Apology of Socrates*, although most scholars believe that it was written

39

early in Plato's career (q.v. Compositional Chronology). The work has the outward appearance of being a set of three speeches that Socrates actually made when he was tried for impiety in 399 BCE. No one thinks that Plato's *Ap.* expresses Socrates' words verbatim. Some argue, however, that Plato's version must have captured the substance and tone of what Socrates said, since Plato's intent must have been to show how unjust was Socrates' condemnation, and Plato would have defeated his own purpose had he significantly distorted Socrates' actual words. There were hundreds of witnesses to the speech itself who would have been able to identify serious distortions of the truth (e.g. Burnet 1924:63–4; more recently, Kahn 1996:88–9).

Others, impressed by the work's exquisite crafting, argue that Plato's version must be a fabrication, perhaps an account of what Socrates could have or should have said (De Stryker and Slings 1994:1–8). However, the fact that Plato's *Ap.* is undeniably the product of literary mastery is obviously compatible with its capturing both the central claims Socrates' made and the manner in which he made them. Yet another position notes the many incompatible reports about Socrates made by his contemporaries and urges scepticism regarding the historical question (e.g. Morrison 2000:235–65; Prior 2001:41–57). No one denies the importance of the work for Plato's portrait of Socrates.

According to Plato, Socrates thought he had to answer two sets of accusations, the slanders that had been spread for many years that he was an atheistic nature philosopher and an amoral sophist (*Ap.* 19b4–c1), and the newer, formal accusations that he corrupted the young, did not believe in the gods the city believed in, and introduced new divinities (24b8–c1). He flatly denies the older accusations, explaining that his reputation for wisdom comes from his failed attempts to find a counter-example to a Delphic oracle that no one is wiser than Socrates himself. He concludes that what the oracle meant is that he '. . . is aware that he is in truth worth nothing with respect to wisdom' (23b2–4). Socrates responds to the formal charges by means of an interrogation of his chief accuser, Meletus, in which Socrates shows that Meletus' own conception of his accusations is self-contradictory. There is little credible evidence that the prosecution was relying on unspoken, distinctly political charges (Irwin 2005:127–49). For the view that Socrates' was actually guilty of impiety, see Burnyeat 1997:1–12. For the view that the charge of 'introducing new divinities' was especially damaging to Socrates, see McPherran (1996:169–74).

The centrepiece of the defence speech is Socrates' explanation of why he has engaged in philosophy. He declares that he has actually been ordered by the god to do philosophy and that this is a kind of service to the god (*Ap.* 23b7–c1, 30a5–7). His mission on behalf of the god is one he must pursue as long as he 'draws breath and is able' (29d2–4). The purpose of his mission is to exhort his fellow Athenians to pursue virtue and to understand that '. . . from virtue comes money and all good things for men in private and public' (30b2–4). Since his fellow citizens have failed to grasp this truth, the god has attached him to the city 'like a gadfly' (30e5). Socrates explains that his 'divine voice', his *daimonion* (q.v.), warned him not to try to improve the city by going into politics because, were he to do so, he could not possibly survive as an honest person (31c4–2a4).

Socrates is convicted by a narrow majority – had only 30 more jurors found him innocent, he would have been acquitted (36a5–6).

The closeness of the vote is remarkable given the long-standing prejudices against him in the minds of many jurors (see 18b1–c1). Because the penalty for conviction was not set by law, Socrates had the opportunity to offer a counter penalty to Meletus' proposal that he be put to death. Socrates thinks he has been a great benefactor to Athens, and so says he deserves 'free meals in the Prytaneum', an honour reserved for Olympic victors and other distinguished Athenians (36d4–7a1). He explains why he cannot offer any penalty, including exile, which would preclude his philosophizing. In the end, he offers to pay a fine of thirty minas, a substantial sum, which he can pay with the help of four friends, one of whom was Plato himself (38b1–9).

In Socrates' third speech, he first 'prophesies' to those who voted for his condemnation that there will be others who will come after him to 'test' them as he had tried to do and they will find these others even more difficult. To those who voted for his acquittal, he says that death is nothing to fear: it is either a dreamless sleep or a transmigration to Hades, where he can converse with the other dead. A good person cannot be harmed in life or in death (41c8–d2). He closes by exhorting this group of jurors to 'trouble' his sons in the same way as he has troubled his fellow citizens (41e2–2a2).

Scholars have been divided over what Socrates, as Plato portrays him, sought to accomplish. The traditional view is that Socrates was either indifferent to the outcome of the trial or that he was actually inviting martyrdom for the cause of philosophy (e.g. Taylor 1960:156). Against this, recent commentators, noting the closeness of the vote to convict Socrates, argue that Socrates actually convinced many jurors that he deserved to be released. Moreover, if, as he claims, Socrates sees himself as divinely ordained to practise

philosophy, he could neither be indifferent to continuing this mission nor could he end his mission by seeking his own death. Trying to gain acquittal in a manner consistent with his moral commitments appears then to have been his only option (Brickhouse and Smith 1989:37–47, 210–34).

CHARMIDES

Gerald A. Press

The *Charmides* is set in a gymnasium on the day following Socrates' return from military service in a siege at the outset of the Peloponnesian War (429 BCE). Socrates narrates (to an unnamed 'friend') his discussion about *sôphrosynê* (temperance or moderation) with Charmides and Critias, Plato's uncle and cousin respectively. Our awareness of their later historical lives (as notoriously immoderate members of the tyranny that ruled Athens for a short time after it had lost the war) establishes situational irony (q.v.) and a political context. The dialogue falls naturally into three parts or acts.

A long prologue (*Chrm.* 153a–9a) introduces Plato's familiar thematic contrasts between ordinary socio-political concerns and philosophy, beauty and wisdom and body and soul. Whereas everyone in the gym wants to hear the war news, Socrates is only interested in knowing about the current state of 'philosophy' and whether any young men are notable for their beauty and wisdom (153a–d). Through the ruse that Socrates has medical knowledge and knows a cure for the headaches Charmides has been experiencing, he begins to discuss with the young and very beautiful Charmides the nature of the *sôphrosynê* that his guardian, Critias, has attributed to him.

41

In the second act, Charmides initially proposes (159b–62b) that *sôphrosynê* is quietness and that it is modesty. These are private and behavioural accounts appropriate to his age, but easily refuted. For although *sôphrosynê*, being an excellence (q.v.) must always be admirable (*kalon*, 159c), good and beneficial (*agathon*, 160e), quiet behaviours are not always admirable and modest behaviour may not always be good. Instead of thinking for himself as agreed, Charmides now proposes something he has heard, that *sôphrosynê* is 'minding one's own business' or 'doing one's own things' (*to ta heatou prattein*, 161b). The same phrase appears in the *Republic* (433a) as an account of justice (q.v.), and was a political slogan (North 1966:101f.). Here, however, Socrates calls it a riddle, because reading, writing and practicing productive arts such as healing and house building are "doing other people's business" (*Chrm.* 161e) and a city would not be governed temperately or well ordered if every citizen did everything for himself.

The shift to a social and political scope for *sôphrosynê* coincides with a shift of interlocutor from Charmides to the elder, politically active Critias from whom Charmides heard this idea. It exemplifies the "pedimental structure" (q.v.) often to be found in the dialogues, with discussion moving from an outer, behavioural to an inner, intellectual focus and from lower, existential to higher, conceptual accounts, returning later to the behavioural and existential level.

The argumentation in this third act (162c–75d) is far more complex and difficult than the earlier ones. In response to a series of Socrates' objections, Critias explains 'doing one's own' as doing or making good things (163e), then as knowing oneself (165b) and finally as knowledge of itself and other sciences or types of knowledge, "knowledge of knowledge" for short (*epistêmê epistêmês*, 166c). Responding to Critias' proud but mistaken confidence that he has knowledge and his misappropriation of Socrates' ideas, Socrates' refutation of this view has two stages. First, he argues, it seems strange, perhaps impossible, for something to exercise its specific power on itself, for example, a seeing of seeing or a hearing of hearing (169b). Second, he argues that, even if knowledge of knowledge" were possible, it would not be beneficial either to know *that* one knows something or to know *what* one knows; but if it is not beneficial, then it cannot be *sôphrosynê* since it was agreed that excellences are always beneficial. This is true even though a society in which individuals did all and only what they know might seem ideal (a utopia of knowledge or expertise, 173a–d), to which Critias agrees. Real benefit, however, would not derive from this sort of knowledge, but only from knowledge of good and evil (174d). Socrates concludes that they have failed to discover what *sôphrosynê* is (175b) and Charmides, with Critias' collusion, declares that he will continue discussing things with Socrates, even if they have to force Socrates into it (176c).

Until the last few decades, most scholars focused on a few specific questions about the last act, particularly the complexities of *epistêmê epistêmês* (Chen 1978; Dyson 1974; McKim 1985), which seemed relevant to issues in contemporary epistemology. To many, the ending suggests that *sôphrosynê* is knowledge of good and evil, consistent with the unity of the virtues thought to be Socrates' or Plato's doctrine (Santas 1973; Stalley 2000). Others have seen the *Chrm.* more generally as teaching an interrogative philosophical stance (Hyland 1985) or as a microcosm of Socratic philosophy, the life of critical reason (Schmid 1997).

Recent scholars have more diverse interests. Some investigate the psychosomatic medicine that is a recurrent Platonic theme (cp. Laín Entralgo 1970; McPherran 2002; Murphy 2000). It has been recognized that the twist given to self-knowledge by Critias contradicts the traditional sense of the Delphic admonition 'Know thyself' (Benson 2003; Tuozzo 2000). The broadly political dimensions of the dialogue and false utopias that Socrates rejects have also been noted (Landy 1998; Tuozzo 2001). Several have observed a puzzling pattern, Socrates criticizing ideas here he elsewhere champions: doing your own thing, self-knowledge, knowledge of knowledge, culminating in his paradoxical, seeming rejection of *sôphrosynê* itself as either impossible or useless (Carone 1998; Tsouna 1997).

These problems can be resolved by a more holistic and contextual approach beginning from the observation that Socrates' therapeutic educational mission with his interlocutors, like Plato's with his readers, is guidance towards recognizing their lack of knowledge and *sôphrosynê* and pursuit of them through open-ended conversational dialectic (q.v.) rather than by propounding doctrines. It is important that *sôphrosynê* was semantically rich, aligned in various contexts with individual shame, self-control, moderation, purity, personal orderliness and good political order and opposed to folly, insolence or violence, courage, intemperance or licentiousness and wantonness (North 1966; Rademaker 2005). At the dialogue's dramatic date, *sôphrosynê* was the locus of conflict between a traditional value and sophistic criticism while also politically contested as a term for Spartan identity but used rhetorically by Athenian oligarchs (Thucydides, *History* 3.82.8).

Given Critias and Charmides as important oligarchs, their use of the Spartan-oligarchic political slogan, the epistemic utopia idealized by Critias (*Chrm.* 172a, 173d), his oligarchic reinterpretation of the Delphic motto to evade its traditional sense of controlling oneself and remaining within the bounds of appropriate human behaviour (164d f.), the *Chrm.* is a broad investigation of *sôphrosynê* that subsumes ethical and political meanings both traditional and contemporary.

As is usual in the dialogues, the conceptual theme, *sôphrosynê*, is dramatized in the resonances of characters' historical lives with their dialogical words and deeds. Chaerephon, Critias and Charmides enact lack of *sôphrosynê* in different ways as Socrates enacts its possession both by his carefully described recovery from sexual arousal (155d) and by his modest, playful but rigorous philosophic inquiry. Critias and Charmides, the future intemperate oligarchs, both speak and act here in ways that are intemperate and quasityrannical. Socrates shows us the true *sôphrosynê* in contrast with them and with the 'mad' (153b) democratic Chaerephon as well.

The *Chrm.* thus canvasses many major contemporary uses of *sôphrosynê*, suggesting their limits, and the importance of a cognitive component. Given Socrates' regular role in the dialogues as representative in word and deed of an alternative way of life called 'philosophy' (q.v.), the dialogue also suggests that unreflective traditionalism, sophistic rationalism and the contested contemporary political and rhetorical uses to which *sôphrosynê* was being put are transcended by something at once more rational, critical and intellectual than tradition and more modest and self-controlled than was understood by the politicians, democratic and oligarchic alike.

CLITOPHON

Francisco Gonzalez

Lacking a setting or dramatic date, the *Clitophon* begins with Socrates reproaching the eponymous pupil for speaking badly of him behind his back. Clitophon replies that while he has been critical of some things in Socrates he has also been always ready to praise other things. Socrates asks to hear of both his positive and negative points so as to learn and become better, and then remains silent while Clitophon delivers what proves to be rather more blame than praise. Praising and even imitating Socrates' exhortations to virtue, Clitophon complains that Socrates never takes the next step of teaching us what virtue is. Clitophon claims to have been converted and to want nothing more than to be a just person, but when he has asked Socrates' companions and Socrates himself for an account of what justice is and how it is to be attained, he has received only unsatisfactory and even contradictory answers. Imagine being persuaded to become a doctor, but then finding no one who can tell you what medicine is and how it can be learned! Clitophon therefore claims to have arrived at the conclusion that Socrates either does not know what he is talking about or is keeping his knowledge from others. In either case, Clitophon has no use for him and would rather go to Thrasymachus (q.v. sophists), who does have something to say about justice and is willing to teach it. The only other time we encounter Clitophon in the Platonic corpus is in the *Republic* where he has already become a pupil of Thrasymachus and comes to his defence.

As many scholars consider the *Clit.* to be spurious, much of the scholarship has focused on the related questions of the dialogue's authenticity and its purpose. With regard to the latter issue, Slings (1999:128–34) and Gaiser (1959:30, 110–11) have both seen the *Clit.* as bringing out the protreptic character of the Socratic elenchus, even if they have interpreted this differently. Depending on one's view of the relation between the Socratic method and Plato's own philosophical method, the dialogue could also be seen as addressing the protreptic character of Plato's philosophy. At issue in the dialogue would then be whether this characteristic is a weakness (with Clitophon, as did Grote 1865: vol. 3:22–3) or a strength (against Clitophon).

Already in antiquity Plato's dialogues were criticized for having a primarily protreptic function. Cicero has Varro in the *Academica* observe that the Socratic writings of Plato and others show that 'Socrates' discourse was exhausted in the praise of virtue and in the exhortation of people to study virtue' (I.4.16). But an important early testimony of Dicaearchus, the pupil of Aristotle and Theophrastus (Dorandi 1991:125–6), shows that not long after Plato's death criticisms like Clitophon's were directed against the protreptic character of the dialogues: the very success of the dialogues in exhorting so many to the pursuit of philosophy was seen as encouraging a superficiality that does not go beyond such exhortation and its obvious truisms.

Why then would Plato write a dialogue that appears to confirm such criticisms? Even if Plato wanted to draw attention to the protreptic character of the Socratic method and perhaps of his own dialogues, why would he do so in the form of an unanswered critique? One way of avoiding this question is to deny that Plato is the author. The best recent discussion is Slings (1999:222–7), who concludes that no linguistic case can be made against authenticity. Slings also rejects arguments based on formal composition and overall style, concluding with some hesitation that the dialogue is authentic. Yet, that such arguments are subjective is confirmed by the fact that in the 1981 version of his book, Slings, on the basis of the very arguments rejected in 1999, concluded that 'the *Clitophon* was not written by Plato, but by a very close and intelligent pupil of Plato, who wished to advertise his master's ideals of philosophical literature' (Slings 1981:257).

Whether one follows Slings in 1981 or Slings in 1999, the question of the meaning and purpose of the dialogue of course remains. Even if one believes for stylistic reasons that the dialogue was not written by Plato, one could still hold that 'The *Clitophon* is written from a wholly Platonic point of view' (Slings 1999:227; see also 127) and therefore could have been written only by a student who fully understood Plato's aims (Slings 1999:231). Indeed, apparently the only reason for the switch in Slings' position between 1981 and 1999 is that he comes to find the hypothesis of such a perfect pupil too far-fetched. But then we are back to our question: why would either Plato or a faithful pupil write an unanswered critique of Socrates?

One other external solution has been proposed: the absence of a concluding response to Clitophon's criticism has led many modern scholars (though apparently no one in antiquity) to the view that the *Clit.* is unfinished. Slings (1999) documents the history of this view (Slings 1999:10–13) and then proceeds to present arguments against it (ibid.:13–18). One argument appears especially strong: through his ironic assumption that Clitophon's praise and blame will accurately describe his strengths and weaknesses, Socrates shows at the very beginning of the dialogue that he intends to make no response, but instead to listen demurely (*Clit.* 15).

If one believes that the dialogue is complete and that it was written either by Plato himself or by a faithful if perhaps somewhat clumsy student, then one is left with the following interpretative options: (a) that the 'Socrates' criticized in the dialogue is not Socrates (ibid.:3–4, 209–15); (b) that Plato saw the critique as valid against Socrates but as not applying to himself and therefore sought through the dialogue to distance himself from Socrates (Stefanini 1932:I.192–3, 204, 206–7); (c) that Plato saw the critique as unanswerable but not damning; for example, Roochnik holds that there can be no response to Clitophon because Clitophon is a radical relativist and philosophy is incapable of refuting radical relativism (1984:139–42); (d) that the dialogue implies an answer to the critique and can for some reason only imply it. Since Clitophon's case rests on a sharp dichotomy between protreptic as what turns one to the pursuit of virtue, and teaching as what provides virtue, one way of defending the fourth option is to argue that the dialogue wants us to question, weaken and perhaps even reject this dichotomy. For example, Gaiser (1959) and Gonzalez (2002) argue that Socrates' protreptic is constructive because it is capable itself of in some way providing the virtue towards which it turns one. Since virtue, as such a process, cannot be taught to someone who, like Clitophon, belittles the process, Socrates' silence at the end can be explained.

Nonetheless, even if the *Clit.* were neither by Plato nor Platonic in content, it would still be a valuable record of an ancient critique of Plato's Socrates that is undoubtedly shared by many readers of the Socratic dialogues today and hence merits serious consideration.

CRATYLUS

Robbert van den Berg

In the *Cratylus* Socrates explores the thesis of the eponymous character that the correctness of names (*orthotês tôn onomatôn*) depends uniquely on nature (*physis*) and does not involve convention (*nomos*) in any way. Names in this context include both personal names (e.g. 'Socrates') and common names (e.g. 'horse'). The issue of the correctness of names was a topic discussed in Sophistic circles, as Socrates reminds his audience (*Cra.* 384a–b), yet his own discussion of it is clearly informed by Plato's own philosophical theories, including that of the forms (q.v.). In part for this reason the *Cra.* is often considered to belong to the middle period dialogues that were written before the *Republic* (q.v.), even though some scholars tend to date it later, while it is also possible that Plato at a later time in his career updated an earlier version of the text (Sedley 2003:6–14).

The dialogue can be divided into three parts. In the first part Socrates examines, together with Hermogenes, Cratylus' riddling claim that the correctness of names depends on nature alone and that this correctness is the same for those who speak Greek and other languages alike. Cratylus refuses to clarify his position and during the greatest part of the dialogue stands by silently while Socrates attempts to make sense of his claim. Elsewhere (*Theaetetus* 179e–80c; q.v.), this behaviour is associated with the followers of Heraclitus and at the very end of the dialogue Cratylus indeed declares himself to be one. Socrates starts by refuting Hermogenes' view that the correctness of names is merely a matter of convention. Hermogenes holds that when we agree to call one type of animal 'man' and another 'horse', these are their correct names. When

we next agree to call them the other way around, 'man' will be the correct name of a horse and vice versa. Against this thesis, Socrates argues as follows. There exist stable natures of things and actions, which may be used as criteria against which to judge particular things or actions: a good knife is a knife that has been made in accordance with its nature and thus performs its function of cutting well. The same holds for an activity. Therefore, if names are tools and naming is an activity, correct names and naming correctly depend on nature, not on convention. Names are the tools of (Platonic) dialecticians, who use them to teach by dividing up reality. A correct name functions as a didactic tool since it is somehow capable of expressing the nature of its object. A name does so because of its 'form' (*eidos*). This name-form is best understood as the meaning of a word. The name-form is the same in all languages, be it that it is expressed in different pieces of phonetic matter (i.e. in the sounds of the various languages). Take the names for horse in Greek and English: the sounds '*hippos*' and 'horse' may be different, yet they contain the same name-form, that is, they both mean the same thing. Note that even though the name-form 'horse' is somehow related to the nature, that is, form of horse, these forms are not identical. The name 'horse' is after all not itself a horse (Kretzmann 1971:130).

In the second part of the dialogue Socrates shows how names may actually instruct us: when analysed correctly they reveal the reasons of the name-givers of old to name the things as they did. The gods, for example, are called *theoi* because the visible gods, that is, the heavenly bodies, can be seen to 'run' (*thein*, 397c–d). Modern scholarship frequently refers to this type of analysis as 'etymology', originally a Stoic term, and which should not be confused with etymology in the modern sense. Socrates continues to produce a massive collection of these etymologies, the function of which has been much debated in recent scholarship. In part, it is certainly intended to criticize widespread contemporary attempts to derive a deeper understanding of the nature of things by studying their names (Baxter 1992:86–163), yet Socrates' etymologies seem too good to be merely a parody (see Barney 2001:49–80; Sedley 2003:75–146).

It is only in the third and final part (*Cra.* 427d ff.), though, when he finally manages to draw Cratylus into the discussion, that Socrates openly criticizes etymology as a source of knowledge. Having seemingly vindicated Cratylus' claim, Socrates now confronts him with the fact that just as portraits allow for degrees of likeness, so names may have varying degrees of correctness. When a name is in certain respects unlike its object, however, it may still continue to function as a name, since we still understand what it refers to. Socrates puts this down to convention, which thus appears to play a role in the correctness of names after all. We judge the degree of correctness of names by comparing them to the things themselves. But if we have direct access to the things themselves, why bother about examining them indirectly by etymologizing their names? More in particular, Socrates asks Cratylus to reconsider his Heracleitean belief that everything is forever in flux. For, from Socrates' etymologies it had emerged that the ancient name-givers all subscribed to Heraclitus' flux doctrine. Yet, since they may well have been mistaken, we should investigate for ourselves the question whether Heraclitus was right or that there exist at least some unchanging entities such as beauty (q.v.) itself, a rather explicit reference to the theory of forms. Cratylus,

however, turns a deaf ear to Socrates' appeal to investigate the matter and leaves.

What, then, is the bottom line of the *Cra.*? Many scholars assume that it is the condemnation of etymology as a source of knowledge. The *Cra.*, however, is not just about the philosophical abuse of names, but also about their proper use. Dialectic is the method to investigate things for ourselves – precisely what Cratylus declines to do – and names are the instruments by means of which this is to be done, as the Eleatic visitor demonstrates in the *Sophist* and the *Statesman* (Van den Berg 2008:8–13).

CRITO

Charles M. Young

In 399 BCE, Socrates of Athens was tried and convicted of impiety, and given the death penalty. Plato's *Crito* purports to relate a conversion between Socrates and a friend and age-mate, Crito, shortly before Socrates' execution is to be carried out. After some preliminary banter (*Cri.* 43a1–4b5), at times poignant (see esp. 44a1–b5), Crito urges Socrates to take advantage of plans that Crito and others have made to secure Socrates' escape (44b5–6a8). As considerations in favour of Socrates' acquiescence, Crito first claims (a) that Socrates' execution will cost Crito an irreplaceable friend (44b6–8) and (b) that it will make Crito look bad in the eyes of the many, whether deservedly so or not (44b9–c5). He also alleges (c) that Socrates would be doing wrong in allowing his enemies to succeed in bringing about his death when he need not do so (45c5–8); (d) that it would also be wrong to abandon his children to the fate of orphans (45c8–d8); and, to sum up,

(e) that if the execution takes place, everyone – Socrates and all his friends – will have behaved badly in every stage of the business (45d8–6a4). In between these points in favour of escaping, Crito tries to defuse various points against escaping, arguing that the costs to himself and others for aiding and abetting the escape would be minimal (45a6–b7) and that Socrates will be safe in exile (45b7–c4).

Socrates responds by moving to the level of principle (46b1–c6). Ignoring (a) as irrelevant, he first disposes of Crito's opinion, explicit in (b) and implicit in (e), that it matters what other people think (46c6–7c7). He also ignores (c) and (d), except for their presupposition that it matters whether what one is doing is right or wrong. In fact, he argues, given (f) that what really matters is living well and rightly (48b3–9); the *only* thing that matters in acting is whether one is doing right or wrong (48b12–c2), with doing wrong understood to include harming people (49c7–8). Thus he reaches the conclusion (g) that one should never do wrong (49b8) and the question whether Socrates should disobey the law according to which the judgements of courts are authoritative (50b6–8) and escape comes down to the question whether it would be right for him to escape (48b11–c2).

To settle this question, Socrates advances a further principle: (h) that one should do what one has agreed to do (49e6–7). He also suggests (j) that escaping would harm those least deserving of harm (49e9–50a3) and (k) that escaping would involve breaking an agreement (50a2–3). Crito accepts (h) but pleads incomprehension in the face of (j) and (k). Socrates then at 50a8–4d1 personifies the Laws of Athens and imagines what they might say to him if he did choose to disobey the law.

The Laws' speech is dense, complex and highly rhetorical. But they do want to be understood, and so they tell us at 51e how to disentangle their various lines of thought. They say that he who disobeys them does wrong in three ways, because he disobeys us who are his parents, because he disobeys us who are his benefactors and because he disobeys the laws without persuading them that they are in some way wrong. By this they mean that they have three arguments leading to the conclusion that he who disobeys does wrong, one involving an alleged similarity between the Laws and one's parents, another appealing to the fact that the laws have benefited him and a third invoking an agreement they think he has made to 'persuade or obey' (hereafter, simply 'obey') them.

The Laws' strategy in each of these three arguments is the same. They take obligations that anyone will agree one has – that it is wrong (a) to harm or do violence to (hereafter, simply 'harm') one's parents, (b) to harm one's benefactors and (c) not to do what one has agreed to do – and argue that each applies to a citizen who disobeys the law.

(1) Since it is wrong to harm one's parents (51c2), and worse to harm the laws than to harm one's parents (51c1–2) and disobeying the law harms the laws (50a9–b5), it is wrong to disobey.

(2) Since it is wrong to harm one's benefactors (unstated), and the laws are one's benefactors (see 50d5–e1; see also 50e2 and 51c7–d1) and disobeying the laws harms the laws (50a9–b5), it is wrong to disobey.

(3) Since it is wrong not to do what one has agreed to do (borrowed from Socrates at 49e6–7), and a citizen has agreed to obey the laws (51e1–4), it is wrong for a citizen to disobey.

When Crito has no response to these arguments, Socrates decides to remain in prison and await his execution (54e1–2).

Several points about these arguments are worthy of note. First, the first argument does not depend on the idea that it is wrong to disobey one's parents (*pace* Brickhouse and Smith 1994:143–9; Kraut 1984:92–103). It rather depends on the idea that it is wrong to harm one's parents; suitably qualified, this has a chance of being true. Second, Socrates himself thinks that harming is always wrong; the Laws say only that harming one's parents or one's benefactors is wrong; their claims, suitably qualified, have a better chance of being true than Socrates'. This is one reason to think that the Laws may not speak for Socrates; for others, see Young 2006: notes 4, 8 and 11. Third, (1) and (2) depend on the idea that disobeying causes harm; (3) does not. So to win the day, the Laws need only the claim that disobeying causes harm or the claim that a citizen has agreed to obey them, but not both. Finally, the requirement to obey enters into all three arguments. But according to (1) and (2), one is alleged to have an obligation to obey because of the consequences of disobeying (the harm such failure causes), whereas according to (3), the obligation to obey is itself alleged to be a consequence of one's having agreed to obey.

Nearly everything about the *Cri.* is controversial. Perhaps the most important questions are how to understand Socrates' defence of his idea (g) that one should never do wrong (49b8) and how to understand the Laws' claim that a citizen is required to 'persuade or obey' them (51b3–4, 51b9–c1 and 51e7). For a sense of the range of interpretative options for the first question, see Gomez-Lobo (1999:chs 6–9), Vlastos (1991a:chs 7–8) and Young (1997). For the second, see Brickhouse and Smith (1994:sec. 5.2), Kraut (1984:ch. 3) and Young (1997).

DUBIA AND SPURIA

John Dillon

A notable feature of the Platonic Corpus (like some other ancient collections) is the inclusion of works the majority of modern scholars – and in some cases ancient scholars – deem spurious. Suspected works include *Alcibiades I*, *Clitophon*, *Epinomis* (often credited in antiquity to Philippus of Opus, probably correctly) and even *Hippias Major*; their authenticity has also found defenders in recent years, some strenuous. This article concentrates on two further categories to be covered here: (a) works now almost universally regarded as un-Platonic, but included by the first-century CE editor Thrasyllus in his tetralogical system (and hence classified as *dubia*); and (b) works which had in antiquity been relegated to an Appendix (and so categorized as *spuria*). The former group comprises the following: *Alc. II*, *Amatores* (or *Anterastae*, 'Rivals in Love'), *Hipparchus*, *Theages*, *Minos*; the latter: *Axiochus*, *Definitions*, *On Justice*, *On Virtue*, *Demodocus*, *Eryxias*, *Sisyphus*. They vary from the relatively well turned and interesting to the schematic and simpleminded. I will deal with them in turn, after first contributing some reflections on the composition of the corpus as a whole.

We cannot be sure whether any dubia, for example, *Epin.*, *Hp. Ma.*, *Clit.* or *Alc. I*, were already incorporated in the original edition of Plato's works, probably put together under Xenocrates (Alline 1915:46–50) and, if so, on what grounds. Xenocrates may have welcomed such documents as useful products of the Academy, compatible with what

Plato would have accepted, and thus the edition was not intentionally confined to Plato's works. We should try to penetrate the state of mind of whoever initially included these and other works that we do not deem genuine, and of whose origin they must surely have been aware. If the concept of an official Old Academic edition or collection is rejected, the next candidate will be Aristophanes of Byzantium (c. 257–180 BCE), second Head of the Alexandrian Library, who arranged at least fifteen of the dialogues into trilogies. However, since Aristophanes only arranged *some* dialogues, he hardly concerned himself with *dubia* or *spuria*, but internal evidence (both of language and of philosophical content, including antistoic themes) suggests that many of them crept into the corpus somehow during the period of the New Academy. Otherwise, prior to Thrasyllus, we have only the shadowy Dercyllides (Albinus, *Isagoge* 4) to whom one might plausibly attribute the tetralogical arrangement, but we have no idea what his contribution may have been.

We must, however, assume that during the evolution of our corpus, works which were plainly not Platonic (e.g. *Alc. II*, *Just.*, *Virt.* or *Demod.*) were admitted to the collection, albeit in a subordinate capacity, by editors aware of their spuriousness, who felt that they contributed to Platonist doctrine, perhaps as teaching aids for beginners (a role later played by both *Alc. I* and *Thg.*). At any rate, we need not imagine that ancient editors or readers, either of these or of the collected *Epistles*, were necessarily deceived concerning their status.

The topic of the short *Alc. II* is overtly (as represented by its subtitle in MSS), 'prayer' (*proseukhê*) – Socrates finds Alcibiades on his way to offer a prayer to the gods – but in reality it concerns rather the Stoic 'paradox' that all those not wise are mad, and then the subversion of this in a 'Socratic' direction. A distinctly 'Xenophontic' (i.e. rather sententious) Socrates, starting from this Stoicizing position, proceeds to argue that it is actually better not to possess 'technical' knowledge unless one also knows what is best, that is, how and when best to apply one's knowledge (*Alc. II* 146e–7d). The work exhibits echoes of *Alc. I*; so, it must postdate *Alc. I*. It is probably a product of the New Academy, designed to upstage the Stoics.

Rather different is the case of *Amat.*, the topic of which, as indicated in its subtitle, is the nature of 'philosophy'. Couched in a narrative by Socrates (on the model of *Charmides* or *Lysis*), this involves a dispute between two rivals in love whom Socrates engages over the relative merits of physical training (*gymnastikê*) or cultural pursuits (*mousikê*). The supporter of the latter, who defines philosophy as the acquisition of ever more technical knowledge (*Amat.* 133c), might be expected to find support from Socrates, but Socrates cuts him down, by dismissing this in favour of the ideal of self-knowledge. Unlike *Alc. II*, this could be a product of the later Old Academy, and embodies an attack on Peripatetic philosophy, which could be seen as encouraging *polymathia*.

Hipparch., about which doubts were expressed by Aelian (*Varia Historia* VIII.2), is a curious production, involving a disputation of Socrates with an unnamed 'companion' on the moral status of 'gain' (*kerdos*). The companion begins with a simpleminded denunciation of the money-grubber, or 'lover of gain', which Socrates then picks apart by getting him to agree that gain is useful, and so, is a good, and all men desire it. The dialogue acquires its name not from a participant, but from the Athenian tyrant Hipparchus, son of Peisistratus, who is dragged into the discussion as the author of the precept 'Do not deceive a friend'. The purpose of the work seems dialectical rather than 'ethical', which would be consistent with a New Academic date.

Thg. is more polished, centring on a request by Socrates' old friend Demodocus for advice on the education of his son Theages, who is badgering him to be allowed to study statecraft with a sophist. The employment of the Socratic elenchus is here rather ham-handed, as is usual in doubtful works, but its most un-Platonic aspect is a long speech by Socrates concerning his *daimonion*, or divine sign. The statement that its influence is always negative is Platonic enough, but Socrates' description of its power in respect of his would-be students, is quite un-Platonic. It seems designed almost to elevate Socrates to the status of a divine man. It could, from the linguistic and stylistic point of view, conceivably be a product of the Old Academy, but may be much later. Its genuineness, however, was never doubted in antiquity.

Min. is a brief discussion between Socrates and an unnamed companion, and begins with an attempt to define 'law'. There is a central digression involving the excellent education given directly by Zeus to Minos, the legendary Cretan law giver, from whom the work gets its name. Superficially it serves as a more Socratic introduction to the topic of *Laws*, but its dialectical nature and structure are reminiscent of *Hipparch.*

Among works relegated to the *Appendix* as *spuria*, *Ax.* takes the form of a *protreptikos*, calculated to dispel the fear of death, in which Socrates, at the urging of Cleinias, delivers a discourse to Cleinias' father Axiochus, who thinks that he is dying. It is well composed and quite lively, but its language is notably un-Platonic, many forms being otherwise unattested before late Hellenistic times. It also draws upon an established tradition of consolation-literature. It may be dated to the last period of the New Academy.

Def. was attributed in ancient times to Speusippus (*Anon. Proleg.* 26), and an item by that name is listed among his works by Diogenes Laertius (D. L. 4.5), but what we have seems rather to be a product of multiple authorship. It consists of a list of 185 definitions of philosophical terms, in no obvious order and often providing multiple explanations. More precisely, there is a first section (*Def.* 411a–14e), in which the terms are arranged according to the scholastic division of philosophy, first formalized by Xenocrates, into physics, ethics and logic (including epistemology), followed by a somewhat shorter section (414e–16d), exhibiting no order whatever. While it may partly originate with Speusippus, it has the appearance of a work to which anyone could add, and a number of the definitions reflect Stoic formulations.

Just. and *Virt.* are among several dialogues described as *akephaloi* ('headless') in a list preserved by Diogenes Laertius (3.57), which contained many lost works along with *Halcyon* (a lively little work, preserved in the corpus of Lucian, though much earlier). 'Headless' cannot mean simply that they lack a frame-story or conversation, since that is common. It highlights rather their extreme lack of any introductory element. The *Just.* begins 'Can you tell me what is the just?', and the *Virt.*, 'Is virtue something teachable?' In either case, Socrates is presented as addressing an anonymous interlocutor. Both dialogues last for just over three pages. In the former, we are faced mainly with a scholastic exercise in method, but the conclusion is reached that no one is willingly unjust. In the latter, Socrates concludes that virtue is neither teachable nor a gift of nature. These may be no more than student exercises, drawing respectively on such works as *Gorgias, Republic* bk 1 and *Men.*, and cannot be dated.

Demod. is also 'headless'. It falls into four parts, only the first of which explicitly involves Demodocus (father of Theages). This part comprises an argument by Socrates against the coherence of the concept of taking counsel together (*symbouleuesthai*). The other three parts address other questions of 'practical ethics': (a) is it right to condemn someone after listening only to their accuser? (b) who is at fault (*hamartanei*), he who asks unsuccessfully for a loan or he who refuses? (c) in whom is it better to put one's trust, in strangers or in friends and relations? The arguments appear to be exercises in 'equipollence', and compatible with the New Academy rather than with the Platonic tradition.

Eryx. concerns the ethical status of wealth, and the nature of true wealth, consequent on Socrates and a group of friends viewing a Syracusan ambassador – described as the richest man in Sicily, but also the wickedest. Socrates argues that only the wise man is rich, while Critias counters that without some wealth one cannot even exercise one's wisdom. Socrates, however, comes back with the argument that riches are only advantageous to those who know how to use them, viz. the wise. The dialogue is well composed and exhibits no distinctively late features. It has been argued that the examination of the distinctively Stoic thesis that 'only the wise man is rich' necessitates a New Academic provenance, but the theme of the self-sufficiency of virtue was also explored in the Academy under Polemon.

The *Sis.*, lastly, is concerned, like *Demod.* I, with the theme of 'taking counsel'. The scene appears to be set, most oddly, not in Athens, but in Pharsalus in Thessaly, where Socrates is conversing with a prominent citizen of that town, Sisyphus, who had to miss an interesting talk by the musician Stratonicus the previous day by reason of having to attend a meeting of the City Council. The wisdom of consulting with one's peers, irrespective of their expertise or wisdom, had plainly become something of a *topos* in the Hellenistic period, if not before. This would seem to be a product of the New Academic period.

EUTHYDEMUS

Monique Dixsaut

The *Euthydemus* is entirely governed by ambiguity. The Socratic art of argument, dialectic (q.v.), is introduced facing its double, the art of 'fighting with words' or eristic. The aim is to bring their differences to the fore, but the dialogue also reveals to what extent their practises are formally identical. The characters move in couples: Euthydemus and his elder brother Dionysodorus, who late in life have discovered the most refined version of pancratium, the art of refuting any assertion whether true or false; young Cleinias and his lover Ctesippus, Socrates and Crito, or Socrates (who relates) and Socrates (who dialogues). A conversation between Socrates and Crito at the beginning and at the end provides the framework of the dialogue: Socrates' long account of the discussion he had the previous day. It is divided into three eristic sections separated by two dialectical ones.

The two sophists pretend that they can teach excellence (q.v.; *aretê*) and exhort anyone to philosophize, the rules being that the interlocutor agrees to answer, that he does not answer by means of another question and that he adds no determination or qualification, thus committing a 'parapht-egm'. In order to make a demonstration (*epideixis*) of their 'protreptic' knowledge, the sophists first ask Cleinias whether those who learn are wise or ignorant, and whether they learn what they know or what they do not know. By compelling the boy to agree that in any case it is impossible to learn, the two brothers state from the outset what essentially differentiates them from the philosopher: a sophist never learns anything, whatever the length of time he spends 'rolling about among arguments' (*Sophist* 264a2). Due to his refusal to cram his memory with what he may have said, he is doomed to an indefinitely repetitive present.

Socrates explains to a perplexed Cleinias that the sophists are only preparing him to find out about 'the correctness of names', and then he questions the boy in his turn to give the conversation a more serious turn. Both agree that all men certainly wish to be happy (*eu prattein*) and believe that it means having many good things, but Socrates shows that what matters is not possessing them, for nothing can benefit us unless we make good use of it. Since nothing can bring about right use except knowledge (*epistêmê*), knowledge (q.v.) is in fact the only good worth having. But the nature of such knowledge remains unspecified.

Socrates then surrenders the conversation to the two eristics, who seize the occasion to complement a first series of paradoxes following from the sophistic theory of logos. Each single argument is cut to the familiar Eleatic pattern: 'is' and 'is not' obey a strict law of contradiction, any middle being excluded. So, to wish that Cleinias *becomes* virtuous is to wish him *not to be* (i.e. not virtuous): to be dead; similarly, knowing excludes every form of not knowing, hence the impossibility of ignorance, false statement and contradiction.

Socrates is quite familiar with the latter argument, having heard it from the followers of Protagoras, but the Socratic Antisthenes may be the target (Brancacci 2005:217–23). Since their teaching has turned out to consist in nothing but refutation, the sophists make themselves ridiculous when they argue that refutation is impossible.

Before resuming his discussion with Cleinias, so as to give an example of how a dialogue should be conducted, Socrates insists that the sophists must be listened to because, in spite of everything, they urge one to philosophize (that is probably the reason why, the day before, his *daimonion* had prevented Socrates from leaving the palestra). The highest good has been identified with a knowledge that must be both a science of production and a science of use, but now neither the art particular to the orator nor the art of leading men (strategy or politics) fulfils that demand. For just as the general does not know what to do with his quarry and hands it over to the statesman, so the geometer hands his to the dialectician, Cleinias explains (Crito doubts Cleinias could have said that, and Socrates is not quite sure he did: the story comes to us as filtered all along through 'Socrates' ironic screen') (Friedländer 1964:179). A royal art has emerged into view, but if it makes men good and useful, that will be only thanks to a knowledge which has no object but itself, that is, the art of making others good and useful (cf. *Charmides* 166e ff.). Socrates is no more a teacher than the sophist since neither of them is able to teach *something*.

The eristics make a pretence of coming to the rescue. From Socrates' admission that he knows one thing, they move on to the conclusion that Socrates knows, has always known and will always know, everything. Confounding that which is *other* with that which is *not*, and using the equivocation of words such as 'his' or 'yours', the sophists establish that any man who is a father is a father of all and that Ctesippus' father is a dog. So the reader is led to understand the necessity to introduce qualifications in the law of contradiction by specifying 'when' and 'to what respect'. Next it is the theory of participation (q.v.) which comes in for its share of derision: to say that a beautiful thing is beautiful because a certain beauty is present with it (*para*) amounts to saying that if an ox is present with you, you are an ox. Since Socrates and the ox are both physical particulars, the only possible mode of presence is a physical one, and any difference between forms and particular objects is denied. Dionysodorus' ox is the comic equivalent of Parmenides' sail (*Parmenides* 131B–C; cf. Sprague 1962:29), and both point to the danger of using spatial terms like being 'in' or 'over': here, the sophists come nearest to being philosophers.

Are those sophisms borrowed from some collection or from a treatise written by Euthydemus, or did Plato make them up himself? No one will ever know, but in any case it is clear that he groups and connects them after a strategy of his own, and in such a way as to provide a key to them. While Aristotle's *Soph. El.* proceeds according to an ordered listing of the causes of paralogisms, Plato is more interested in their content: the problems they raise. Socrates clarifies the semantic equivocation of learning (*manthanein*), 'acquiring knowledge' or 'understanding', but for him the difficulty remains and will be solved only by venturing the hypothesis of reminiscence (*Meno* 80e f.). The Eleatic denial of change and becoming, along with an eristic technique, is applied to major problems of Plato's philosophy: learning, is virtue teachable, forms and participation, capacity (*dunamis*) active

and passive, due measure, the existence of an opposite of being, sameness and difference, otherness and not being, etc. Each will prove to be dealt very seriously in later dialogues.

When Socrates suggests again that Crito and his sons should follow the eristics' teaching his friend remains reluctant. He does not seem to consider, however, that Socrates would be a decent teacher – a doubt strengthened by the conversation he just had with 'somebody' who, after listening to the debate, has concluded that philosophy 'is worth nothing'. It hardly matters whether Isocrates is referred to here (as is probably the case) or not. Socrates constructs an hybrid type who stands halfway between philosophy and politics and claims that his *sophia* betters that of those he calls 'sophists' (Dixsaut 1986), those to whom philosophy deals only with words, not realities – and that it also betters the *sophia* of those to whom politics is just a question of action. By borrowing from politics its 'great subjects', he wants to avoid the logomachy threatening any philosophical discussion, while at the same time he refrains from getting involved in the dangers and fights of public life. Socrates does not tackle the heart of the matter and seems to hold that a logic of the value of the intermediate (*metaxu*) is enough to refute this anonymous character, since it shows that what stands midway between two good things is inferior to both.

The outcome of the dialogue is the rejection of philosophy conceived as the pursuit of an eristic as well as a rhetorical *sophia*. Dialectic alone has the power of converting the souls of those who, like Cleinias, are able to learn by themselves, which is arguably the only possible meaning in Plato of the word 'protreptic'.

EUTHYPHRO

Roslyn Weiss

Plato's *Euthyphro* raises the question, 'What is holiness?', one of the many 'What is x?' questions that are central to Socrates' conversations with his interlocutors. (Other dialogues explore the nature of virtue, justice, courage, temperance and friendship.) The *Euthphr.*'s question is prompted by Socrates' indictment in 399 BCE on the charge of impiety (and of corrupting the youth), which brings him to the court of the King Archon where he fortuitously meets Euthyphro who is there to prosecute his father for murder. Euthyphro's justification for prosecuting his father relies on an odd mixture of principle and self-serving protectionism (McPherran 2005; for Weiss 1994:263–4, it is mainly the latter; so, too for Burnet 1924:23). In Allen's view (1970:23), Euthyphro is concerned for his father's purity as well as for his own). Although Euthyphro speaks of a duty to prosecute anyone who has committed injustice, he is concerned about the pollution (*miasma*) that affects the close associates of the offender. He emulates Zeus, the god he regards as most powerful, never questioning the justice of Zeus' own slaying of his father. Euthyphro's arrogant confidence in his expertise concerning the gods' ways and their likes and dislikes make him a fit target for Socrates' withering elenchus. On the pretence that only instruction in holiness or piety by Euthyphro will save him from death by hemlock, Socrates turns to him for enlightenment as to the nature of the holy.

Euthyphro tries to oblige. His first attempt to define the holy yields: 'The holy is what I am doing now' (*Euthphr.* 5d–e), namely, prosecuting anyone who commits injustice. His second proposal is that the holy is what is dear to the gods, the unholy what is not dear to them or hated by them (6e–7a). Third, he suggests that the holy is what is dear to *all* the gods (9e). Fourth, that the holy is *tendance* (*therapeia*) of the gods (12e). And fifth, that it is providing service or assistance (*hupêretikê*) to the gods through prayer and sacrifice (13d–14c).

Each of Euthyphro's attempts at definition is thwarted by a fatal Socratic objection. The first, as Socrates sees it, hardly qualifies as a definition at all: it offers an example of holiness but misses its core. Geach (1966) objects to Socrates' dismissal of Euthyphro's first definition, challenging what has come to be known as Socrates' priority of definition principle. Geach contends that there is little reason to believe that one cannot know anything, and hence that one cannot give examples of anything, before or without knowing its 'essence'. The second falls short in that it specifies a definition not exclusively of the holy but of what is both holy and not holy – since some gods may well love what others hate. The third is found lacking because even if all the gods love the same thing, that accord remains accidental or coincidental; indeed, when the gods are not themselves just, it makes little difference whether or not they all agree (Friedländer 1964:87). Moreover, unless there is something inherently holy in the object of the gods' love by virtue of which all the gods love it, their loving it is irrelevant to its status as holy. The fourth fails because the gods do not need, and do not stand to benefit from, anything human beings can provide. And the last collapses because the prayer and sacrifice involved in tending the gods reduce to a commercial exchange and ultimately to a means of pleasing the gods – and so are tantamount to a return to the first definition. The dialogue's significance and continued relevance owe much to its pivotal argument in which Socrates asks Euthyphro,

'Is a thing holy because the gods love it, or do the gods love it because it is holy?' In the hands of the ethicists and theologians who later appropriated this question, right and wrong were substituted for the holy, as follows: are right and wrong determined by god's will and command (a view known as voluntarism), or do the divine will and command reflect what is (independently) right and wrong? The *Euthphr.* strongly suggests that the latter is the case: god may apprehend what is good and just but that does not make it so.

The argument proceeds by distinguishing between a thing's being god-loved (*theophiles*) and its being holy: a thing attains its character as god-loved by the gods' loving it (just as a thing acquires the status of being a carried thing by virtue of someone's carrying it), but a thing's being holy does not await the gods' loving it; on the contrary, it is its holiness that inspires the gods' love. Some scholars – for example, Friedländer (1964:87); McPherran (1985:289) – have credited Euthyphro with successfully identifying if not the *ousia* (essence) of the holy, then at least a relevant *pathos* (attribute) (*Euthphr.* 11a–b). Yet, all Socrates says in fact is that Euthyphro has spoken in *pathos-* (as opposed to *ousia-*) terms – not that the *pathos* he has provided is a correct one. The best-known reconstruction (and critique) of this argument is Cohen's (1971). In Cohen's view, Socrates has proved not that the holy cannot be defined as god-loved, but that it cannot be defined as god-loved when the gods' reason for loving it is that it is holy. Geach (1966), too, is critical of the argument; he contends that the gods love a thing not because it is holy but because they know or believe it to be so; moreover, there is no reason that they could not love what is intended to please them. A recent and thorough discussion of the argument

and related secondary literature (Wolfsdorf 2005:32–49) faults Plato for taking being seen and being loved as states that involve change. For a defence of Plato and the ambitiousness of his project, see Judson (2010). Vlastos (1991a) sees in this central argument of the dialogue a rejection of the traditional, or 'magical', Greek religious understanding of the gods as essentially powerful and capricious beings who need to be pampered and placated.

One lingering question is whether any acceptable definition of holiness emerges from the *Euthphr.* Might holiness indeed be the assistance human beings provide to the gods in producing a noble product (*Euthphr.* 13d–14a)? If so, the nature of that product needs to be specified: a likely candidate would be human virtue. Socrates in the *Apology* (29e–30b) certainly portrays himself as the god's servant or messenger whose task it is to encourage those he encounters to care above all for prudence, truth and the virtuous state of their souls. Perhaps he is, for this reason, a paragon of piety.

GORGIAS

Harold Tarrant

The *Gorgias* is a work of ethics with important political implications. Political questions generally cause Plato to write at greatest length, as in *Republic* and *Laws*. *Grg.* is accordingly the longest of his single-book dialogues, and not unexpectedly shows considerable complexity, both in its philosophic ideas and in their literary presentation. There are three interlocutors, Gorgias the rhetorical teacher, Polus his pupil and the writer of a rhetorical handbook and Callicles, an otherwise unknown Athenian with undisguised political ambitions. Also present, and contrasted with Gorgias' understudy Polus, is Socrates' companion Chaerephon. Anachronistic references to Archelaus of Macedon obscure a setting in the 420s (Tarrant 2008).

Like other putatively 'early' dialogues, *Grg.* contains long stretches of Socratic argument known as elenchus (q.v.), but is perhaps the first to show Socrates (a) reflecting on the nature of proper elenctic practise (metaelenctic: *Grg.* 473b–5e, 505d–6a, 508e–9b), (b) going over the steps of an argument with an imaginary rather than a real interlocutor (506b–7c), (c) explaining a complicated theory of real and false crafts of his own involving dichotomic classification (464b–6a) and (d) twice assuming the role of myth-teller (493a–c, 523a–4a), while using myths to illustrate a view of his own.

The dialogue moves from polite but tough engagement with Gorgias (whose concern is the reputation of his own discipline), through somewhat impatient argument with the younger Polus (who is more intent on scoring points than on solving issues), to an urgent discussion of how one should live one's life in the real world of fifth-century Athens with the somewhat better-intentioned Callicles. The futures of Socrates (486a4–d1) and of Callicles (526e1–7a4) are both at stake. As in *Theaetetus,* the material becomes increasingly challenging as the dialogue progresses, making scholars wonder why it is named after Gorgias rather than Callicles, the dominant interlocutor for three fifths of the work (481b6–527e7).

The dialogue opens with Socrates and Chaerephon arriving too late for Gorgias' demonstration of his rhetorical skills. Gorgias agrees to answer some of Socrates' questions, and Chaerephon is told to ask what Gorgias is, that is, what profession he practises. Polus tries to answer, but even Gorgias finds it

hard to satisfy Socrates' requirements for a definition that excludes all other practises. It transpires that it is productive of mass persuasion concerning matters of justice, injustice and the like, but does not profess to impart knowledge (455a). Pointing to the walls and dockyards of Athens as examples of rhetoric's power (455d–6a) Gorgias seems to impress Socrates, who politely conceals his true evaluation of such 'defences' until 519a. Socrates pounces at 457c when Gorgias refers to people who use rhetoric for unjust purposes. Does this mean that they have not been taught regarding what was allegedly the subject matter of rhetoric, including justice? Gorgias is shamed into answering and agreeing that any pupil of rhetoric who does not know what justice is could learn it from him (460a). This Socrates finds inconsistent with the view that teachers should not be blamed for unjust uses – though it is doubtful whether Gorgias meant to imply that this 'learning' of justice involved acquiring just habits.

This infuriates Polus, who accuses Socrates of boorishness, and is in turn lured into a conversation, in which he asks questions – following Socrates' prompts. Socrates explains that he regards rhetoric as a non-scientific knack rather than an art (q.v.), since it aims at the pleasure of the listeners rather than at their benefit. It *competes* with justice, the genuine art of restoring psychic health. The disjunction of what is (for the present) pleasant and what is genuinely good is vital to the dialogue, central to the explanation of the term 'fine' or 'honourable' (*kalon*) at 474d–5a and the following argument about why doing injustice is worse than receiving it; central to the dispute between Socrates and Callicles about how life should be lived at 495a–9b; and central to Socrates' view of the shortcomings of Athenian politicians.

Polus, shocked to hear Socrates deny that rhetoric is a fine thing, resumes the theme of rhetoric's power, as evidenced by the slick-speaking tyrant's unrestrained opportunity for injustice. Distinguishing between what one (genuinely) wants and what one should do to achieve it, Socrates denies such persons' power, since they mistake for ends the means by which they can achieve them (467c–8e), so that tyrannical power is 'unenviable' (469a). Polus ultimately claims that getting wronged is worse (*kakion*), yet less fine/honourable (less *kalon*, i.e. *aischion*) than wronging another (474c). Socrates himself would normally identify 'good' and 'fine' and hence 'bad' and 'dishonourable', but suggests that Polus employs twin criteria when applying the terms 'fine' and 'dishonourable', goodness and pleasantness (474d–e). If wronging another is more dishonourable than getting wronged it should therefore be either (a) worse or (b) more painful. But it is less painful. Therefore it is better. Similarly avoiding punishment is more dishonourable than getting punished, so, being less painful, it is worse. Debate arises over whether the argument is flawed (Klosko 1984; Vlastos 1967), but being *ad hominem*, it needs *Polus* to refute it. Otherwise Socrates is free to conclude for him that orators wanting the best outcome should ensure that they and their friends are punished for any injustices they had committed (*Grg.* 480a). The underlying medical notion of injustice as disease that undermines its agent's soul, and requires the cure of punishment, fleshes out the picture.

Callicles' entry introduces the sophistic distinction between what is naturally just, good and fine, and what is conventionally so, and with it an attack on the uselessness of philosophy in the real world. He advocates pursuit of natural justice, that is, becoming better off in every respect than others, encouraging and

satisfying the desires and identifying pleasure and the good. Socrates counters with myth, didactic images and two powerful arguments against the hedonistic thesis (493a–9b). Callicles, he claims, has failed to see the importance of orderliness in the world and in the human soul, which underpins all human virtues. By vindicating the distinction between good and pleasure he renews the attack on rhetoric (particularly Athenian political rhetoric) as pleasure-giving flattery, which fails to do what is good for citizens and encourages their vices. Condemnation of Pericles and other democratic heroes presents a radical and uncompromising challenge to democratic assumptions.

The final myth (523a–4a) speaks of Zeus' introduction of the naked judgement of the soul, so that nobody can avoid punishment by deception from Hades: identified in the earlier myth with the unseen workings of the inner soul (493b). Whether the myth really concerns punishment and cure in this life or the next (Sedley 2009a), it offers an unreformed Callicles nothing to look forward to.

The *Grg.* achieves a powerful philosophic unity, underpinned by its insights into the life and death of Socrates (Stauffer 2006); in so doing it sees Socrates transformed from the tricky interrogator into an independent political thinker, armed with new tools of persuasion, the beginnings of a complex psychology and a powerful vision of the role of justice and order in the world.

HIPPIAS MAJOR

Jacques Antoine Duvoisin
Socrates meets the sophist (q.v.) Hippias somewhere in Athens and they discuss the

nature of *to kalon* (the beautiful, noble or fine).

The dialogue begins with a discussion of Hippias' achievements as a private teacher and as an envoy of his city. Socrates engages in teasing flattery as well as some quite subtle wit at Hippias' expense. This lays the groundwork for the central theme of the main argument – How can anyone praise or blame anything without being able to articulate the principle whereby one judges? – but also for the dialogue's central comic conceit. Socrates invents an alter ego who chastises him for the flaws in the positions Hippias offers so as to protect Hippias' enormous vanity from being bruised in the interchange.

This passage culminates in Hippias' account of his recent and popular exhibition in Sparta, which he intends to present 2 days later in Athens. The exhibition consists of an imaginary conversation between Nestor and Achilles' son, Neoptolemus, after the fall of Troy. Hippias, speaking as Nestor, gives a long speech outlining the noble deeds that lead to great reputation. In response, Socrates announces that he recently discovered, at the hands of an insolent questioner, that he is unqualified to find fault with speeches or to praise them as beautiful or noble, since he is unable to say 'what the beautiful is' (*Hippias Major* 286d). This introduces the subject of the rest of the conversation.

Hippias proposes several accounts of what the beautiful is: a beautiful maiden, gold and finally 'to be rich, healthy and honoured by the Greeks, to reach old age and, having buried one's parents, to be buried lavishly by one's own children' (291e). Each is more extravagant than the last, and each is rebutted with considerable comic wit. Socrates then offers several of his own: the appropriate, the useful and the beneficial. Each of these falls short as well. A final suggestion – the

pleasing through hearing and sight – leads to a lengthy digression on the meaning of the phrase 'both and each'. Can two things together be something (fair, strong, just, etc.) that each is not, or vice versa? Hippias thinks not and tries to embarrass Socrates, accusing him of dialectical hairsplitting and failing to consider 'the wholes of things' (301b). Socrates gives a series of arithmetical examples (e.g. each is one but both together are two, both together are even but each one is odd) which, while intriguing, do not further the inquiry into the beautiful. The dialogue ends, returning briefly to an earlier proposal: what is pleasant through sight and hearing, which suggests that the beautiful is beneficial pleasure. But Socrates points out that this fails for the same reason that the beneficial failed earlier. Hippias laments the tendency of Socrates' conversation to reduce everything to slivers and bits, and reminds him of the value of being able to produce a well shaped discourse in the courts or the assembly, while Socrates points out that speaking about noble deeds in public without being able to say what the noble is constantly reminds him of the wretchedness of his own condition.

In ancient Greek, *to kalon* covers a wide range of moral and aesthetic ground unlike any single word in English. The beautiful or the noble each cover part of what *to kalon* means, but neither is adequate by itself. The fine has both a moral and an aesthetic sense, but is perhaps too weak.

The *Hp. Ma.* resembles other early dialogues like the *Euthyphro*, *Laches* and *Meno*, in which a moral issue is reduced to an underlying question of the form 'What is __?' As in those other dialogues, the question remains unanswered and the conversation ends in perplexity (*aporia*). But comic inflection is much more evident in the *Hp. Ma.* than elsewhere. Also, perplexity concerning *to kalon* is not the end point of this dialogue, but rather its starting point: Socrates introduces the main question with reference to a perplexity that he was thrown into *prior* to meeting Hippias. Finally, the activity in relation to which Socrates professes to be perplexed is different. He is thrown into perplexity '. . . while criticizing things in certain speeches as ugly, and praising other things as beautiful . . .' (286c). The praising and blaming of things in speech is central to Socratic dialectic, and accordingly the dialogue might be viewed as *the* aporetic dialogue, since it examines the perplexity of dialectic itself.

In the sequence of answers Socrates proposes – the appropriate, the useful and the beneficial – each falls short, giving way to a syntactically similar successor formed out of its own failure. It might seem that this series could continue indefinitely, but here the beneficial is the end of the line. No further answer is possible. Since the beneficial is the cause or father of the good, it cannot itself *be* good. But to say that the beautiful is not good is absurd. Other early dialogues fail to define courage or piety or virtue because the interlocutors are unable to proceed further. But here the failure grows out of dialectic itself. Socrates apparently introduces the question concerning *to kalon* to discourage Hippias from holding his exhibition. But he is not persuaded to call it off even though he cannot say what *to kalon* is. By contrast, Socrates makes explicit for himself (and us) the inability of dialectic to resolve the perplexity concerning *to kalon*. The distinction between the philosopher and the sophist could not be clearer.

The comedy of this dialogue is not just an occasional witty exchange, or a borrowed phrase. The narrative structure of the *Hp. Ma.* is comic in shape. The usual stock characters of the comic tradition are here: the *eiron* (Socrates), the *alazon* (Hippias), but also the beautiful maiden of ambiguous circumstances and the wayward son. The only figure missing is the negligent father. But that may be the philosophical point. The father – a moral, educational authority – *is* absent, here as in so many other dialogues, and there is a contest to take his place. Hippias' exhibition makes his claim to the educational authority of the absent father. Socrates effectively punctures Hippias' pretensions, even if he cannot persuade him to give them up. But Socrates also cannot claim the father's authority for philosophy. The father is a guarantor of legitimacy, and in his absence everything shows itself to be inauthentic, even dialectic, since it cannot articulate the relationship between the noble and the good except in the paradoxical image of negligent paternity: the beautiful turns out to be the father of the good, but a father who does not resemble his child. If comedy is the genre most suited to inauthenticity, it may also be suitable to philosophical inquiry as Plato conceives it. The question of the generic constitution of philosophy has not received much attention in the scholarly literature, but the *Hp. Ma.* is an invitation to take it up for ourselves.

The authenticity of the *Hp. Ma.* was much debated in the previous two centuries. Arguments for rejecting it were based on judgements of its comic style and vocabulary, or on a concern that it seems to combine mature theoretical motifs with the aporetic shape of the earliest dialogues. But in the absence of decisive evidence against it the *Hp. Ma.* has quietly been received back into the canon in recent years. Ironically, however, the question of authenticity in various forms is a central concern of the text, and so the question of textual provenance should not be simply forgotten even as the text has come to be accepted.

HIPPIAS MINOR

Francesco Fronterotta and
Jean-François Pradeau

The dialogue takes place following a lecture Hippias has just given on the Homeric poems, before a large audience (Pottenger 1995–6). Socrates, who has attended the lecture, wants to question the sophist on a particular point of his Homeric exegesis: the definition he has given of the characters of Achilles and Odysseus. Achilles, more simple and sincere (or the most veridical, *haploustatos kai alêthestatos*) is supposedly better than Odysseus, who is 'double' (*polutropos*). It is thus Achilles' 'simplicity' that should reveal his sincerity, whereas the 'duplicity' (or 'multiplicity') of Odysseus, for its part, indicates an ambiguous and deceptive character (Mulhern 1984). These are the moral qualities that will form the subject of the discussion.

A large part of the text is devoted to the examination of the examples that the two interlocutors propose – and oppose – to one another in the course of the discussion; first on the basis of Homer (*Hippias Minor* 364b–5d, 369a–71e), then by examining the various domains of knowledge of the sophist (366c–9a), the activities of the body (372a–5a) and the properties of the soul (375a–6b). The sequence of arguments in the *Hi. Mi.* is rather simple, and is summarized as early as 366a–7a. The starting point is the hypothesis that all deception comes from knowledge and a capacity (or power: *dunamis*), for the deceiver must be capable (*dunatos*) of deceiving, and can be so only on the condition of having knowledge in the field in which he is to carry out his deception (*sophos kai dunatos*, 366a; Weiss 1981). It is this affirmation that collides head on with the ethical theory Plato makes Socrates

profess in the dialogues, a doctrine according to which excellence or virtue (*aretê*) is a form of knowledge or reflection (Jantzen 1989). On the other hand, if one maintains that knowledge is morally 'neutral', insofar as its application may vary according to the subject practicing it, it can no longer be identified with moral excellence. We then witness the ruin of another major thesis of Platonic ethics, according to which the freedom of an individual finds its limit, according to Plato, in the demand for a self-realization that affirms that no one can wish for his own destruction and his own death, his own 'evil', but that every individual desires to be happy, by conquering his happiness or his well-being (cf. for instance *Gorgias* 509e, *Meno* 78a, *Protagoras* 345d).

The most radical consequence of these premises, which Hippias and Socrates are obliged to accept on several occasions (particularly at 366b–c, 367a, 367e, 368b–9a, etc.), is the following: if having knowledge and being capable of something means that one is 'good' (*agathos*) at it, or that one is 'the best' (*aristos*) at it, then the man who is 'good' or 'the best' will necessarily be the one who deceives, that is, the one who 'does wrong' (366c–7a). At first glance, the *Hp. Mi.* thus ends with an admission of defeat (376b–c), for Socrates and Hippias cannot accept that it pertains to a good man to choose deception and voluntary wrongdoing; yet they cannot succeed in correcting the argument. Yet, it is possible to read the course of the discussion in another way, by asking, Do the competence and capacity that enable one to tell the truth or to deceive, to distinguish and then to practise the true or the false by exercising free choice presuppose a genuine indifference with regard to good and evil on the part of the agent? In other words, do 'knowing' and 'being able to do' evil necessarily imply that one does it? Is the knowledge that leads one to do evil genuine knowledge? As Aristotle emphasizes, alluding explicitly to these difficulties (see *Metaphysics* 5.29, 1025a2–1; cf. also *Nicomachean Ethics* 7 3, 1145b), the demonstration of the *Hp. Mi.* puts to the test a certain idea of knowledge (*sophia*), understood as the neutral possession of several items of theoretical knowledge, which are translated into technical competence and practical capacities. This conception of knowledge is characteristic of the epistemological and ethical doctrine of the sophists (q.v.), at least insofar as Plato depicts and refutes it. In this sophistic perspective, 'knowledge' indeed leads to a 'know-how', indifferent in itself to good and evil, and the choice of good or of evil, detached from knowledge, remains up to the agent. Reading the *Hp. Mi.* in this way, and imputing the *aporiai* of the dialogue to the sophistic conception of knowledge, one immediately realizes what must be opposed to the sophist, at the same time as the result of these *aporiai*: the Platonic ethical doctrine of excellence as knowledge. For, the knowledge that coincides with excellence consists, according to Plato, in the possession of a knowledge that contains its good (*agathon*) within it: that is, the element that guides and orients the agent's will and his choice. One must concede that all knowledge implies the knowledge of good and evil (with regard to its objects and with regard to its eventual implementation), so that no neutral knowledge exists, nor, consequently, does any will that is indifferent to good and evil. The *sophoi kai dunatoi*, who were to deceive intentionally, according to Hippias, turn out to be bereft of genuine knowledge: if they choose in full cognizance that they are deceiving, their knowledge lacks the indispensable awareness of the distinction between good and evil and is therefore not genuine knowledge. If, however, they deceive unintentionally, this can obviously only be through ignorance of the good.

Taking the measure of the conflict between the paradoxical ethics assumed in the *Hp. Mi.* and the Platonic doctrine of excellence (*aretê*), one is able to see more satisfactorily the meaning of the dialogue, and the direction Socrates wishes to impose upon the discussion. We are invited to do this by the discussion at 376b, when Socrates adds a restriction to his conclusion according to which 'the person who behaves and works in a shameful and unjust way . . . can only be the man who is good', adding nonchalantly, 'if a man of this kind exists. . . .' However, for the reasons that have just been indicated, this man cannot exist if *aretê* is really a form of knowledge.

ION

Christopher Janaway

Ion, Plato's shortest dialogue, is often assigned to an early Socratic period. There are two characters: Socrates and Ion. The latter (not a known historical character) is a professional rhapsode, a public reciter and commentator on poetry. *Ion* appears to contain the beginnings of Plato's philosophical reflection on the arts (q.v. Aesthetics), and has been treated as a foundational document in Western aesthetics (Schaper 1968:20–1; criticized by Stern-Gillet 2004).

Percy Bysshe Shelley's appreciation of *Ion* and his influential translation (1821) epitomize attempts to find a positive account of poetry in Socrates' evocation of inspiration (q.v.) at the heart of the dialogue (*Ion* 533c–5a, 535e–6d). In a long display speech, markedly different from the surrounding question-and-answer style, Socrates portrays poets as lacking rational understanding of the process by which they compose, and subject to powerful external influence from one of the Muses. Like rings attracted to a magnet, they acquire magnetic power themselves, inspiring a performer such as Ion, who recites scenes from the *Iliad* and *Odyssey*, transmitting the magnetism and moving his audience.

'Good poets' owe their finest productions to their being divinely inspired (*entheios*) and may even be called divine (*theios*). But this is no unequivocal praise of poetry (q.v.), or perhaps no praise of it at all, given the framing parts of the dialogue in which Socrates refutes Ion's claims to expert knowledge – *epistêmê* or *technê*, the latter term being preponderant. The main force of the divine inspiration story is to deny that poetic composition, performance and exegesis arise 'by *technê*', by expertise or skill (q.v. Art). While performing, Ion is said to be 'taken out of himself', abandoned to emotions elicited by the Homeric scene he recites: evidence of his place in the chain of sheer inspiration (535b–e).

When Ion claims he is expert on the poetic virtues of Homer, but can say nothing worthwhile about other poets, Socrates refutes his claim to master a *technê* on the grounds of his commanding no general principles that apply across all relevant subject matter (531a–3c). Later Ion asserts that he is well versed in all forms of expertise that Homer portrays well, such as charioteering and generalship, conflating knowing about the poetic representation of some expertise with possessing that expertise. Socrates elicits from him the absurd statement that he is the best general among the Greeks – 'That, too, I learned from Homer's poetry' (541b). But

Ion gives evidence of being good at nothing except rhapsody, so had better accept the epithet 'divine' on pain of appearing dishonest (542a–b).

The dialogue has been found puzzling and even contradictory, in that Socrates talks repeatedly of 'rhapsodic expertise' (*rhapsoidikê technê*), while apparently arguing that there is no such thing. The contradiction may be removed if the assumption of rhapsodic expertise is merely ironic throughout (Flashar 1958), or if Plato recognizes the possibility of rhapsodic and poetic *technai*, but denies them any role in the 'artistic success' or fineness of the best poetry (Janaway 1995:14–35; opposed by Stern-Gillet 2004), or if he allows poet and performer each a *technê*, but denies this status to the rhapsode's critical discourse about poetry (Ferrari 1989).

LACHES

Eugenio Benitez

According to the canon of Thrasyllus (see D. L. 3.59), Plato's *Laches* is about courage and employs, to borrow a term from *Theaetetus* 149a–51d, an 'obstetric' method, in which the ideas of Socrates' interlocutors are delivered into the light of day and examined. These Thrasyllan labels correctly identify the simple theme and tactic of the *La.*, but as with all of the Socratic dialogues, apparent simplicity disguises enormous subtlety of structure and composition. One thing that seems hidden from most readers is the special relation between theme and tactic, namely that the practise of Socratic dialogue requires and exhibits courage in examining what one really thinks. The *La.* seems also to be a 'proleptic' dialogue, in the sense of anticipating philosophical views presented more fully in later works (see Kahn 1998); at least, many strands of its argument are taken up in other dialogues, especially the *Protagoras*. The conversation in the *La.* itself ends inconclusively. The *La.* is a dramatically rich dialogue in the sense that its interpretation must be guided by knowledge of its characters (q.v.), setting and dramatic date. Specific behaviours of Socrates' interlocutors (such as Nicias' attempt to avoid being drawn into the conversation) display attested features of their character (e.g. Nicias' circumspection) in relation to the theme of courage. While a basic understanding can be acquired from reading the *La.* on its own, the appreciation gained from examination of historical events surrounding the dialogue is invaluable (q.v. History).

The *La.* is set during the Peloponnesian War, possibly during the Peace of Nicias, certainly after the retreat from Delium, and certainly before the Sicilian Expedition. There are possible allusions to the Battle of Mantinaea, at which Laches was killed (*La.* 193a), and the debacle at Syracuse, following which Nicias met his death (199a). The fact that two generals are chosen interlocutors is almost universally agreed to reflect their appropriateness to the topic; nevertheless, their deaths in battle may signal an intention on Plato's part to look beyond the art of war for the source of courage. Other characters of the *La.* have only a minor part in the conversation, yet their role is important in establishing the context within which an examination of courage becomes necessary. Lysimachus and Melesias, who initiate the discussion, are shadowy figures in history, although there is some suggestion that Melesias at least may have been anti-democratic (Thucydides, *History* 8.86). The pretext under which the dialogue takes place is a prearranged meeting with Nicias and Laches at a demonstration of hoplitics or 'fighting-in-armour' by a mercenary sophist named Stesilaus. Scholars have not treated Stesilaus or his art as a paradigm of courage, either for Plato or the characters in the dialogue. The pretext merely allows Lysimachus and Melesias to introduce their sons to two of the most influential men in Athens. Socrates is the spanner in the works. He is present by some chance, but he is already acquainted with the sons of Lysimachus and Melesias, and his bravery in battle, attested in the *La.* as in the *Symposium*, gives him the right to speak and ask questions about courage. Socrates' tactic of direct examination appears as counterpoint to the indirectly domineering tactics of Lysimachus.

The conversation is not initially about courage but about Stesilaus' art of fighting in armour. Lysimachus and Melesias make it clear, however, that what they want most is for their sons to become prominent. Socrates steers the conversation towards what would make them deservedly prominent. Everyone agrees that excellence (q.v. *aretê*) would do the trick, but as to what that is, they can neither say themselves nor point to anyone who can say. The theme of courage is then introduced as part of the investigation into what excellence is. Thus questions about the nature of excellence, whether it can be taught and whether the cardinal virtues are proper parts of excellence or something else lie at the foundation of the philosophical arguments of the *La.*

Socrates first discusses courage with Laches. The direct results of their discussion are not very significant, but the examination reveals three principles characteristic of Plato's approach to ethics. The first is that the cause of excellence is distinct from its effects. In this connection, the scope of courage is widened considerably. The *La.* displaces the Greek focus on military exploits, first by the reminder that even standing one's ground takes courage, and then by expanding the concept of endurance to cover bearing up under all sorts of circumstances, including cross-examination. The courage to persist in an inquiry introduces a second principle, namely, the say-what-you-think rule of Socratic conversation (*La.* 193c, 194a). This principle of openness stands in direct opposition to the assumption of Lysimachus, Melesias and Nicias that safety is to be found in cover. It is connected with a third principle introduced by Laches, namely the harmony of word and deed (188c–9c). This principle seems fundamental to explaining the failure of the *La.*: none of the characters exhibit it (193e), yet without such harmony there appears little hope of understanding what courage really is.

Socrates' conversation with Nicias adds a cognitive dimension to the conception of courage, and shows partly why the harmony between word and deed has not been attained. Even animals perform brave deeds; human courage must involve some sort of understanding, forethought or wisdom. The refutation of Nicias (who gets his idea about courage from what he has heard Socrates say) is mostly a lesson about what sort of understanding courage does not involve. It is not tactical understanding, nor is it the art of prognostication. It seems to be an understanding of value, but Nicias is unable or unwilling to look far enough into himself to find out more.

Plato does not hide the principle of word and deed in the *La.* As Chaucer pointed out, anyone who can read Plato will see it (Man of Laws Tale, prologue 741–2). The implication that comparing the characters to their words is fundamental to understanding the

La. is often forgotten, however (for further discussions, see Benitez 2000; Schmid 1992).

LAWS

Eugenio Benitez

The *Laws* is the longest and, according to tradition, the last of Plato's dialogues. It was left 'in the wax' at the time of Plato's death and brought into publication by Philip of Opus (D. L. 3.37). Whether Philip had a hand in editing the work or whether he merely transcribed it is uncertain (for one recent account, see Nails and Thesleff 2003). The most recent analyses of its style indicate significant affinities with the *Sophist*, *Politicus* and *Philebus*, though there are stark differences in places. These, however, might be explained in various ways, and there has never been any question that the *Lg.* substantially contains the thought of Plato. If we set special problems of composition aside, including admittedly serious questions about the overall coherence of the dialogue, then the chief difficulties remaining for an interpreter of the *Lg.* include (a) its dramatic date and structure, (b) its relation to other political dialogues of Plato, especially the *Republic* and the *Plt.* and (c) the extensive discussion of cosmology and theology in *Lg.* bk 10.

The *Lg.* is the only dialogue set at any distance from Athens. It is set in Crete, where three elderly gentlemen – an unnamed Athenian, a Spartan (Megillus) and a Cnossian (Clinias) – pass the day in conversation about a political constitution as they wind their way from Cnossos to the cave of Zeus on Mt. Ida. Along the way the trio frequently remind us that they are old and that despite the seriousness of their topic, their discussion is a divertissement. These two dramatic features alone (the age of the interlocutors and their penchant for mild amusement) may account for the tendency of the *Lg.* towards digression, anacolouthon and inconsistency at least as well as the uncharitable supposition of 'the failing powers of the author' (Bury 1942:vii; for a thorough recent account of amusement in the *Lg.* see Jouët-Pastré 2006). At any rate, the *Lg.* loudly trumpets the view, expressed elsewhere in Plato's dialogues, that written works are a form of play (see *Phaedrus* 276d). The choice for interpreters here seems straightforward.

A more difficult, but nevertheless significant choice concerns the dramatic date of the *Lg.* No specific date is given or determined by internal historical reference. Recently, however, Zuckert has argued that the *Lg.* is set before the Peloponnesian War (see Zuckert 2009:11–13, 51–8). Zuckert points out that the *Lg.* describes the Persian Wars and Persian culture in detail while it never once mentions the Peloponnesian War. Around this she builds a case that is circumstantial but difficult to resist. If Zuckert is right, then certain features of the *Lg.* – such as the absence of philosophy from the proposed curriculum for the fictional city of Magnesia, or the attention to habituated virtue rather than the virtue that involves genuine understanding of itself, or the separation of courage from the other virtues – need not be interpreted as signalling a change in Plato's philosophical views, or as demanded by the general practical needs of establishing a city. An alternative view of the dramatic date is that of Dušanić (1990:364–5) who notes that the Spartan ambassador Megillus was active in about 408.

Whatever choices an interpreter makes, however, it is impossible to avoid comparisons between the *R.* and the *Lg.* The two dialogues can easily and usefully be mapped, book against book, to reveal treatments of similar themes, such as education, censorship, the relation of justice to happiness, the role of women as citizens, the different kinds of constitution and the role of a philosopher or council of philosophers in providing ultimate guidance for the city. A sensitive and careful comparison of the *Lg.* and *R.* in terms of fundamental themes in ethics and moral psychology can be found in Bobonich (2002). Another point of comparison, the development of Plato's political philosophy from the *R.* to the *Lg.* has been a preoccupation of much scholarship. It is widely held that Plato gradually moves away from the rule by philosopher-kings prescribed in the *R.* and turns towards reliance on the rule of law, first in the *Plt.* and then even more emphatically in the *Lg.* The progression from personal authority to rule of law is discussed at length in Klosko (2006). Brown (2004) treats the similarities between the two dialogues' ethical implications of early childhood rearing.

In addition to the points of comparison with the *R.*, the *Lg.* discusses at length some political themes that are not given much attention in other dialogues, including the philosophy of punishment, the general conception of law (including its rationale and function), family law and the law of the marketplace. Despite the protestations of the Athenian that he can only outline a constitution, the *Lg.* provides a very thorough sketch of civil administration, including detailed discussion of executive, legislative, judicial, diplomatic, economic and religious offices, as well as arrangements for police, wardens, real estate officers and lesser functionaries. The *Lg.* also contains the only extensive example of a penal code to be found in Plato's works. The code, which includes provisions for the law of both free persons and slaves, has been thoroughly discussed in Saunders (1994).

The tenth book of the *Lg.* contains an unexpected digression into matters of philosophy, cosmology and theology. The attachment of this digression to the law of impiety seems contrived, and the philosophical level of discussion – as seen in arguments concerning the types and origin of movement in the universe, naturalism and the existence of god – is well beyond anything else in the *Lg.* The Athenian even makes excuses for the level of difficulty (*Lg.* 892d–3a). The relation of this book to the rest of the *Lg.* remains a difficult and unresolved matter. It may be that Plato was not able to integrate this material adequately before his death. (For discussion that tends to support this view, see Dillon 2003a.) For Platonists, *Lg.* bk 10 must appear to be the central book, to the exclusion of practically everything else. For political philosophers, it appears incidental. In much of the recent literature, the theology and politics of the *Lg.* are treated separately. Excellent scholarship on the *Lg.* has emerged in recent years, including the publication a very useful bibliography (Saunders and Brisson 2000). For historical context the work of Morrow (1993) remains indispensable.

LETTERS

V. Bradley Lewis

Thirteen letters (*epistulai*) are included in the traditional canon of Plato's works (q.v. Corpus). While both Aristophanes of Byzantium and Thrasyllus include the letters in their collections (third-century BCE and first-century BCE, respectively), modern scholarship has cast doubt on their authenticity. Seven of the letters concern Plato's involvement in Syracusan affairs

(*Epistles 1–4, 7, 8, 13*). Four are addressed to Dionysius II (*1–3, 13*) – two to the friends and followers of Dion (*7, 8*) and two to Archytas of Tarentum (*9, 12*) – one to Perdiccas of Macedonia (*5*) and one each to Dion (*4*), Hermias, the tyrant of Atarneus and Plato's students, Erastus and Coriscus (*6*), Aristodorus, a friend of Dion (*10*) and a Laodamas, whose identity is uncertain (*11*). Both 2 and 6 also contain, like 7, some material of a cryptic, metaphysical nature.

The lengthiest and most significant letter is the well known seventh, which purports to have been an answer to a request by Dion's friends for advice in the wake of Dion's assassination in 353 BCE, but which also has the apologetic character of an open letter. It contains an autobiographical passage in which Plato recounts his early political ambitions, which were disappointed by the degenerate character of Athenian politics but especially by the judicial murder of Socrates. Plato concluded that real reform could only be accomplished from the perspective afforded by true philosophy and with the aid of virtuous and philosophical comrades under the right circumstances. He accordingly drew away from politics (324b–6b). His later Syracusan intervention is explained largely by reference to his friendship for Dion, whom Plato had befriended on his first visit to the island between 390 and 387. Dion wrote to Plato of Dionysius II's passion for philosophy and suggested that Syracuse could provide a kind of proving ground for Plato's political ideals. While there is some dispute about just what Plato's hopes were in Syracuse, *Ep.* 7 provides little evidence that he aimed to establish a government there like that described in the *Republic*; rather it emphasizes Plato's attempts to persuade Dionysius to abandon tyranny, give Syracuse a proper legal code and establish the city as a bulwark in the defence of Hellenic civilization in the west against the Carthaginians (see Morrow 1935:140–5). The letter also contains a famous but controversial discussion of knowledge and learning, the so-called philosophical digression (342a–4e).

Ep. 8 picks up from the seventh explaining in somewhat more detail the application of Plato's political principles to the erstwhile reform of Syracuse. The content seems to closely track the proposals contained in the *Laws*. Of the other letters concerned with Syracuse, *Ep. 1–3* are addressed to Dionysius II: *Ep. 1* portrays Plato as a kind of vice-regent with Dionysius and is certainly spurious; *Ep.* 2 presents advice about both governing and philosophical study that is similar to that in *Ep. 7*; *Ep. 3* purports to have been written between Plato's second and third visit (although some suggest that, if authentic, it may have been written after Dion's coup) and offers a defence of his conduct as well as of the then-exiled Dion. *Ep. 13* concerns the same time period, but it is more personal and suggests that Plato hoped to influence the tyrant in a way favourable to Dion's interests. *Ep. 4* is addressed to Dion and claims to have been written between Dion's victory over Dionysus and his assassination. It supports Dion's work and advises political moderation. Among the remaining letters are the two brief missives to the Pythagorean mathematician-statesman Archytas and relatively brief letters to associates and letters of introduction and recommendation for others.

Most scholarship on the letters has concerned the question of authenticity. While the antiquity of the letters is impressive, the ancient practise of pseudonymous composition – especially of letters – is well known and doubts about some of Plato's *Epistles* (especially the first, but also the twelfth) long predate modern textual criticism. No recent scholar has accepted all thirteen of the letters. Brisson's 1987 survey shows that among 32 authors since Ficino in 1484 *Ep.* 7 and 8 have enjoyed the greatest support, with 26 scholars defending the authenticity of 7 and 25 that of 8. *Ep.* 6 was defended by 18 of Brisson's authors; *Ep.* 3 has had 14 defenders. Most scholars have rejected the rest although all save the first has had a number of advocates (Brisson 1987:72). An earlier and somewhat less systematic tabulation by Guthrie (1978:401) yielded similar findings.

The modern debate on the authenticity of the letters has focused mainly on three issues: the coherence of the content of the letters with the content of the dialogues; stylometric comparison of the letters and the dialogues; and agreement between the content of the letters and other ancient historical sources, especially but not exclusively concerning the Syracusan affairs in which Plato was involved. Not surprisingly, given its potential value, most of the controversy has concerned *Ep.* 7, which critics have argued contains important contradictions with Plato's established views about the theory of knowledge and about politics (see especially Edelstein 1966). Others have argued that the content of the letter does fit with Plato's views about both matters (see Lewis 2000; Morrow 1935:61–79). Some have also suggested that the 'philosophical digression' in particular could be an interpolation in what is otherwise an authentic letter of Plato (see Brisson 1987:145–58). Ledger's comprehensive 1989 stylometric analysis argues strongly that *Ep.* 7 was the product of the same author as the *Lg.*, and also supports the authenticity of *Ep. 3, 8* and *13*. The other main approach to the authenticity question has focused on external evidence. Here, the strongest case can be made for *Ep.* 7 with the other letters facing more and more serious objections. Overall the balance of recent scholarly opinion has tended towards acceptance of *Ep.* 7 as either genuinely Platonic or the product of a contemporary with intimate knowledge of Plato's thought and deeds (Brunt 1993:312–25), but the matter remains controversial.

LYSIS

Francisco Gonzalez

The dialogue opens in front of a newly constructed wrestling school where Socrates learns, in response to his usual inquiry after 'the beautiful', of the beautiful boy Lysis and his quite maladroit and fruitless pursuit by the hopelessly enamoured older youth Hippothales. Offering to show Hippothales how such a boy can be won, Socrates enters the school and engages Lysis along with his friend Menexenus in a discussion concerning the nature of friendship (q.v.; and, more broadly, love). After humiliating Lysis (by arguing that his parents do not entrust their things to him and therefore cannot love him as their own because of his lack of wisdom), he humiliates the combative Menexenus (by catching him in the dilemma of whether friendship is a nonreciprocal relation (as seemingly attested by the possibility of being a *philos* of wisdom) or is necessarily reciprocal (as seemingly attested by the absurdity of calling yourself the *philos* of someone who hates you). Socrates then shows the two friends how difficult it is to give an adequate account of friendship. Arguing that neither opposites, nor those who are alike, (specifically, alike in goodness) can be friends, Socrates suggests that perhaps the relationship exists between what is neither good nor bad (which would appear to describe the human condition) and what is good or

beautiful. But because we clearly love some good things as a means to other good things, this account threatens to produce an infinite regress unless we postulate a 'first beloved' for the sake of which everything else is loved, but which is not itself loved for the sake of anything else. But this creates another problem: *why* is the 'first beloved' loved if not for the sake of something else? The suggestion that it is loved as a means of eliminating what is bad, is rejected because not all desire appears to depend on the existence of something bad. The final suggestion is that we love the 'first beloved', that is, the good, because in being lacked by us, it also naturally *belongs to us*. But is not claiming that the object of friendship is what is akin to us the same as claiming that it is what is *like* us: an account already refuted? With this *aporia*, their guardians forcefully take the two boys home.

For a long time the *Lysis* was, especially in English language scholarship, either ignored, dismissed as a failure (Guthrie 1975) or judged spurious (Tejera 1990), though it had a few defenders (e.g. Bolotin 1979; Glaser 1935). Some interpreters have been repelled by its seemingly 'utilitarian' conception of love (Vlastos 1973). In recent years, scholarship on the dialogue has grown exponentially and has proven nearly unanimous in judging it successful and indispensable to Plato's thought. In what follows I will note the problems that originally led to the dialogue's neglect and how these problems have been addressed in the recent literature.

The main problem was not its dubious arguments or inconclusive ending, which characterize other dialogues as well, but that while in other aporetic dialogues the argument could be easily seen as at least making progress, the argument of the *Ly.* seemed particularly disjointed and inclined towards

[handwritten margin note: ? ERISTIC = DISPUTATION; WHERE DOES AMBIGUITY ENTER?]

preying on verbal ambiguities, that is, eristic (Annas 1997; Guthrie 1975:143; Price 1989). This problem has been addressed in the recent literature in three ways. First, more careful analyses of the argument have shown that it actually builds towards an increasingly better account of the subject. Second, in line with a more general trend in recent Platonic scholarship, the dramatic richness of the dialogue has been shown to provide an indispensable context for understanding the direction and point of the argument. (see Gonzalez 1995a, 2000, 2003; Penner and Rowe 2005:204–5). Third, this more careful analysis of the argument that also situates it in its dramatic context has found the dialogue suggesting a positive solution to the problems it raises; that we, as neither good nor bad, love that ultimate good of which we have been deprived but which belongs to us (Penner and Rowe 2005:182–4) and that this shared erotic "affinity with the good "grounds that affinity between two people that characterizes *philia* (Bordt 1998:89–92; Gonzalez 1995a, 2000, 2003; Penner and Rowe 2005:167–9). Justin (2005) and Rudebusch, on the other hand, interpret *philia* in the dialogue as only an instance of desire for the good that depends on finding something good in another person.

Without denying the utilitarian character of the friendship described in the *Ly.*, scholars have been able to give this characteristic a much more positive interpretation (see Bordt 1998:139–40, 214; Gonzalez 2003; Penner and Rowe 2005:280–91).

Another debated question is the seemingly basic one of the dialogue's *topic*. Those who think the dialogue is about *philia* (e.g. Annas 1977; Guthrie 1975:154; Hoerber 1959; Price 1989:9–10; Robinson 1986) could argue that this is the concept explicitly addressed and that the two boys, Lysis

and Menexenus, are *philoi* and are explicitly described as instantiating, at least in appearance, what the discussion is about. Those claiming the discussion is about *erôs* (e.g. Bolotin 1979:206; Friedländer 1958–64:1:50–1, 2:102; Haden 1983) could point out that the impetus for the discussion is Hippothales' erotic pursuit of Lysis and Socrates' offer of showing that young man how to conduct such a pursuit properly, as well as pointing out that the discussion explicitly returns to *eros* at the very end. Ironically both interpretations of the dialogue's topic only encouraged its neglect. If taken to be about *erôs*, then it was largely overshadowed by the much more exhaustive and seemingly positive treatments in the *Symposium* and *Phaedrus*. If taken to be about *philia*, then it was overshadowed by the much more thorough, systematic and conclusive treatment of the topic in Aristotle's ethics. Scholars have recently vindicated the independence and unique contribution of the *Ly.* by recognizing it to be about both *erôs* and *philia* together (Penner and Rowe 2005:270). It differs from the *Smp.* and the *Phdr.* in applying, through its emphasis on *philia*, their metaphysical interpretation of *erôs* to interpersonal relationships. And it differs from Aristotle's treatment of *philia* in grounding this relation on the erotic drive towards some transcendent good.

Another disputed question has been the place of the *Ly.* in the Platonic corpus. The metaphysical content of the dialogue has created problems for dating: while in terms of topic and form it appeared to belong to the 'early' dialogues, its sophisticated metaphysical distinctions appeared to place it at least among the 'middle' dialogues. The question of dating has ceased to be pressing given the growing abandonment of any attempt to establish a chronology of

Plato's dialogues. The recent literature has also shown the dialogue to contribute to Plato's metaphysics and thus to differ from other 'Socratic' dialogues. Whether due to its distinction between two kinds of being-present-in (see Bordt 1998:105, 191–2) or its analysis of how something can be 'ours' without being possessed or its elaboration of the notion of 'real reference' (Penner and Rowe 2005:210), the *Ly.* has become a reference text for understanding the Platonic forms and their relation to us and the sensible world. (And the long debate about whether forms are present or not in the *Ly.* appears to be settling towards the former alternative. See Bordt 1998:203–4; Penner and Rowe 2005:278.) The *Ly.* has thus gone from being at best a marginal and negligible text in the Platonic corpus to being now one of the key texts for understanding Plato's philosophy as a whole.

MENEXENUS

Nickolas Pappas

The *Menexenus* is almost entirely a sample of funeral rhetoric (q.v.) whose purpose remains fundamentally controversial.

(I) CHARACTERS AND SETTING

Socrates meets Menexenus, who wants to speak at the annual public funeral for Athenian soldiers (*Mx.* 234b). Socrates says such rhetoric is magical (234c–5c) but not difficult. His own rhetoric teacher Aspasia (courtesan, companion to Pericles) taught him a fine example (235e–6c). Socrates delivers a speech in the manner of Pericles' famous funeral oration (Thucydides, *History* 2.35–46; Monoson 1992).

(II) THE FUNERAL SPEECH

Socrates' speech endorses the custom of such speeches (*Mx.* 236d–e), then praises Athens. The praise begins with a myth (q.v.) about the first Athenians' birth from the earth (237b–8b) and continues with a synopsis of Athenian history (239a–46a). The history tracks Athens' dominance from the Persian Wars (490 BCE) until the King's Peace (386). Next, the speech turns to moral instruction. In the voice of the dead soldiers, it exhorts their survivors to moderation and courage (246d–8d). A dismissal follows.

(III) PARODY OR IMPROVEMENT?

One sentence from the *Mx.* (235d) is quoted twice by Aristotle (*Rhetoric* 1267b8, 1415b30); if not for this evidence of authenticity, the dialogue's peculiarity might have caused it to be classed as spurious (q.v. Corpus). Instead, readers debate whether Plato meant the speech as serious rhetoric (Huby 1957; Kahn 1963) or as parody (Long 2003; Loraux 1986; Pownall 2004; Salkever 1993).

Certain features of the dialogue suggest a joke is afoot: the playful opening conversation, the claim that Aspasia wrote this speech (Bloedow 1975; Henry 1995), Socrates' exceeding praise for Athens, with a history wiped clean of Athenian misdeeds (Trivigno 2009), and the anachronism in Socrates' account of events down to thirteen years after his death (Rosenstock 1994). Instead of countering this interpretation with unprovable appeals to 'seriousness' of tone, one can argue that Plato intends the speech to be *better* than Pericles' on the grounds that the differences between the speeches harmonize with other Platonic criticisms of Pericles.

The speeches differ in how they praise and how they characterize moral education.

Moreover, the *Mx.* speech differs from Thucydides' *History* in the form of macro-historical narrative it offers. Pericles' speech stinted on praise and ignored the possibility that the city might improve its citizens. He disparaged rhetoric, elevating *ergon* 'deed' above *logos* 'speech'. The *Mx.* deliberately raises *logos* to the status of *ergon* in recognition of how one inculcates virtue. Its report from the dead soldiers urges moral improvement; its myth of autochthony includes aboriginal divine instruction within the city's founding (*Mx.* 238b). Again, unlike Pericles, Socrates praises Athens unrestrainedly. Praise is excessive language proper to magnificent objects and bespeaks moral elevation and exhortation.

Plato's *Gorgias* (q.v.) and *Protagoras* (q.v.) take Pericles to task for neglecting to improve either his sons' souls or his fellow citizens' (*Grg.* 503c, 515e; *Prt.* 319e–20b). And in all the ways indicated, the *Mx.* speech aims at the educational function for rhetoric that Pericles declined to attempt. It can be called an attempt to produce something better than its original: rhetoric in a philosopher's hands.

Finally, the speech reads as a rebuttal to Thucydides. Socrates recounts a history powered by psychodynamic forces. The world order deteriorates depressingly but coherently along lines reminiscent of the city's decline in *Republic* 8–9 (q.v.), an order that Thucydides would not give to world events.

MENO

Roslyn Weiss

The *Meno* is a dialogue whose ethical and epistemological concerns are bridged by the question, 'can virtue be taught?' Although the dialogue begins with an exploration of the nature of virtue, the notion of teaching inevitably raises questions about knowledge or expertise and its relationship to belief or opinion.

The dramatic date of the dialogue is widely put at some time during 403/2 BCE, since it is thought that the Meno character of the Platonic dialogue is the same Meno who, according to Xenophon's *Anabasis*, was employed as a mercenary in Cyrus' unsuccessful attempt on the Persian throne, and who would therefore have been in Asia Minor by the year 401 and executed by the king of Persia in 400 BCE. The appearance of Anytus in the dialogue provides another clue: if Anytus currently holds office as a democrat, the dialogue must take place after the democracy was restored in Athens following the fall of the Thirty in 403.

The dialogue begins as Meno, a wealthy and well born Thessalian, young enough still to have suitors but not too young to command a company and head a household, confronts the older Socrates, now in his late sixties, with the question whether virtue can be taught or whether it comes by practise, is learned, is possessed by nature or has some other source (*Men.* 70a). The abruptness with which the dialogue begins precludes any proper setting of the scene; we learn only later (90b) that Meno's host in Athens is Anytus, a democrat who is nevertheless staunchly conservative and who is known to have been one of Socrates' three accusers at the infamous trial at which Socrates was sentenced to death.

Socrates swiftly turns Meno's question concerning the manner of virtue's acquisition into the more basic one with which he is more at home: what is virtue? A confident Meno, having studied with the prominent fifth-century rhetorician Gorgias, is certain that he knows: there is a distinct virtue for each kind of person – for men in their prime, for women, for children, for slaves and for old men. As Socrates presses Meno for a definition of virtue, for the specification of that which all the virtues have in common, a somewhat more diffident Meno ventures, first, rather obtusely, that virtue is the ability to rule men (70c), and second, that virtue is justice (70d).

Meno's definition of virtue as justice launches an extended foray into the matter of definition. Since justice is agreed to be only a part of virtue, it cannot define virtue any more than roundness can define shape. Once Socrates has supplied models of definition that are acceptable to Meno (particularly the Empedoclean definition of colour in terms of effluences), it falls to Meno once again to define virtue. No more successful this time around – relying on a poet, he defines virtue as desiring fine things and having the power to attain them – Meno becomes belligerent, attacking Socrates for deliberately confounding those with whom he engages, for numbing them much as a sting ray does. He then produces his notorious 'paradox', in which he contends, first, that it is impossible to search for what one does not already know for one would not know what one is searching for and, second, that even if one were to happen upon that for which one searched, one would not know it (80d). Scholars have been divided in their views of how seriously Plato takes Meno's paradox. Some think he regards it as an unworthy attempt to obstruct the discussion (Ritter 1933:102; Shorey 1933:157; Taylor 1926:235–6), particularly given its strikingly ad hominem form (Bluck 1961:272; Moline 1969:153–61; Thompson 1901:116–17; Weiss 2001:52n12); others think Plato takes it quite seriously, if not in Meno's formulation of it, then at least in

Socrates' reformulation (Moravcsik 1970:57; Scolnicov 1976:51).

Socrates counters the paradox with a myth of recollection, which is intended to establish that inquiry into what is not yet known will succeed if one is sufficiently dogged, since one's soul contains all that it has learned in previous incarnations. The myth has spawned much controversy, with some scholars convinced that what the soul 'recollects' are Platonic forms (Gulley 1954:195; Guthrie 1975:253–4; Taylor 1926:130) and others remaining far more sceptical (Ebert 1973:180, n2; Ross 1951:18n3, 22; Sharples 1985:14; Weiss 2001:75). One reason that scholars have come to believe that it is forms that the myth's soul 'sees' is that Socrates chooses the nonempirical subject matter of geometry for his demonstration of how recollection works. He has Meno summon a slave untutored in geometry and, by means only of asking questions, appears to elicit from the slave the correct answer to the puzzle he has posed, namely, on which line of a square is a second square whose area is twice that of the original square constructed? Since Socrates asks the slave rather leading questions, however, it is unclear how much 'recollecting' is actually going on as the slave pursues the puzzle's solution, and how much he is in fact being taught by Socrates. For some scholars (Bluck 1961:13; Guthrie 1975:255), all is recollection; for others, recollection ends at the demonstration's final stage (Klein 1965:107; Vlastos 1991a:119); for still others, there is only teaching (Anderson 1993:135; Weiss 2001:98). Scott (2006:102–9) hopes to salvage recollection by deflating its sense: recollection is the ability to follow a demonstration. Yet, Socrates contends that the only explanation for the slave's achievement is that true opinions were always in him (*Men.* 85c–6b).

As the dialogue proceeds, Meno revives his initial question: how is virtue acquired? Socrates introduces a new method, the 'method of hypothesis', as a fruitful way to approach questions whose answers are not yet known. Employing this new method, Socrates establishes that virtue is teachable: virtue is teachable if and only if it is knowledge; all good things are associated in some way with knowledge; and virtue is a good thing. No sooner, however, does Socrates confirm virtue's teachability than he challenges his own conclusion by citing the empirical fact (if it is a fact) that there are no teachers and students of virtue.

The dialogue concludes with an important distinction between true opinion and knowledge. Socrates associates knowledge once again with recollection, recasting recollection as the 'tethering' of true opinion (97e–8a). Interestingly, Socrates in the *Men.* applauds true opinion for its capacity to guide aright, faulting it only for its tendency to take flight. Having determined, then, that virtue, since it has neither teachers nor students, is not knowledge, Socrates supposes that it is a kind of true opinion (or good repute – *eudoxia*), and settles finally on the rather unsettling insight that virtue must come to human beings by 'divine dispensation without intelligence' (99e).

How seriously one takes the dialogue's conclusion may turn on one's view of the sudden appearance of the term *eudoxia*, 'good repute', in place of the expected true or right opinion (compare Thompson 1901:225 for whom it is insignificant with Klein 1965:253): does the shift intimate that for Socrates good statesmen succeed not because they think well but because they are well thought of? Or does Socrates hold that there are in principle (Bluck 1961:39–40) or even in fact (Scott 2006:186–92) good leaders whose virtue depends not on knowledge but on true opinion? Or, in the end, is Socrates, for all his talk of true opinion, committed to the view that there can be no genuine virtue without knowledge (Wilkes 1979)?

PARMENIDES

Samuel Scolnicov

Interpretations of *Parmenides* have ranged from reading it as an introduction to the whole of Platonic – and more often Neoplatonic – metaphysics (e.g. Dodds 1928), sometimes in an esotericist variation (e.g. Migliori 1990), to viewing it as a record of unsolved (and perhaps unsolvable) 'honest perplexities' (Vlastos 1954), as protreptic 'mental gymnastics' (Grote 1875), as a collection of sophistic tricks (e.g. Owen 1970) or even as an elaborate (though admittedly tedious) joke (e.g. Taylor 1934). Logical reconstructions of the dialogue have been offered by Brumbaugh (1961) and recently by Rickless (2007).

The first problem in the interpretation of the dialogue is the relation between its first, aporetic part (*Prm.* 130a3–7c3), following the proem (126a1–30a2), and the longer second part, containing a set of ostensibly self-contradictory arguments (137c4–66c5). Ryle (1939b) followed Apelt (1919) and Wundt (1935) in surmising that the two parts were composed at different times and are only loosely connected. Cornford (1939) practically ignores the first part. More recent interpretations (Gill 1996; Meinwald 1991; Scolnicov 2003) have tried to present a unified view of the dialogue. For a useful summary of previous interpretations, see Migliori (1990).

The structure of *Prm.* is not unknown from other dialogues (*Meno*; *Republic*):

a relatively short aporetic first part and a longer euporetic part aimed at solving the problems raised in the first part. As usual with Plato, whatever is said in it is to be understood from the point of view of the speaker who says it. In the first, aporetic part of the dialogue, the Platonic Socrates' proposal of ideas (or forms (q.v.), as they are sometimes termed in English) and participation is criticized by Parmenides from an Eleatic point of view. In Parmenidean terms, participation (q.v.) is impossible. It requires not only two types of entities, rational and sensible (something the historical Parmenides was prepared to consider, albeit only in his Way of Opinion, f. 8.52–9), but also two modes of being, being in itself and being in relation to something else (which Parmenides did not accept, cf. f. 8.56 'apart', 58 'in itself'). Types of entities are categories and are, as such, mutually exclusive: cats are not dogs, and sensible things are not ideas. Modes of being are different ways in which the same thing can be: a portrait is, in itself, without reference or relation to anything else, colour on canvas; in relation to its sitter, it is *his* or *her* portrait.

The second part of the *Prm.* proceeds in eight arguments (commonly, but erroneously called 'hypotheses'). Neoplatonists and interpretations of Neoplatonic inspiration have seen in it nine 'hypotheses', counting IIa (see below) as a separate argument. But this goes against the method set out at *Prm.* 135c8–6e4. There, the method yields four arguments. The entity under investigation, the 'one', viz. any one thing but in particular the idea, is hypothetized to be or, alternatively, not to be. The consequences of the resulting propositions are considered for that one and for the others than it. But, in each case, the one is taken either in itself (Arguments I,

IV, VI, VIII) or in relation to something else (Arguments II, III, V, VII).

The first Argument (137c4–42a8) reiterates and expands, in formal terms, the aporia of the first part. Let us take the Parmenidean view of being as being in itself. This constrains us to recognize that the one (whatever it is) cannot be in relation to anything else. Hence, it cannot have any properties, cannot be named, spoken about, thought, perceived, etc., and any participation is impossible (142a1–6). But if participation is impossible, thought too is impossible, as any relation between ideas or between them and he who thinks them is ruled out. The aporia, however, is pragmatic, not logical. The impossibility of thinking and speaking about the one poses a problem only for the person who is actually engaged in inquiry about it.

According to the method (q.v.) introduced by Plato in the *Men.*, such a *reductio ad absurdum* does not block the way to a conclusion intuitively accepted (such as that true opinion and knowledge are possible) but requires a change of hypothesis, self-evident as the original one may be. Instead of accepting as the main premise that what is one cannot be many (137c4–5) – according to the strong, Parmenidean principle of noncontradiction (f. 7.1), that opposites must be mutually exclusive – an alternative premise is proposed, that what is one can be many, but not in the same respect. Thus, what is one *can* have different, even opposed, attributes. The whole of the second part of this dialogue is hypothetical, that is, its conclusions depend on the premise of each argument and refer to possibilities rather than to actualities. (Note the subjunctive or optative throughout this part of the dialogue, with the exception of *Prm.* 146a6–8, for stylistic variation, as recognized by

Aristotle, *Metaphysics* 5.7; 1077a35). The list of properties potentially ascribed to the one in the various arguments, and especially in argument II, can be seen as Plato's list of categories, culled, in fact, from Parmenides' f. 8. Argument IIa (*Prm.* 155e3–7b5) is an appendix on entities that are specifically in relation to time, that is, sensible beings. Argument III (157b6–9b1) establishes the same consequences for the others than the one, showing that each of the others is also a one. Argument IV (159b2–60b2) demonstrates that if the one is only in itself, the consequences true of it in Argument I are true also of the others.

Argument V (160b5–3b6) gives us a detailed analysis of participation as restricted to those aspects of the idea that make it *this*, rather than *that*, idea, not those, such as atemporality or oneness, that are common to all ideas and establishes the interdependence of being and not being as a requisite of participation (162a4–b8). Argument VI (163b7–4b4) establishes that nothing can be true of the one that is not in relation to anything, Argument VII (164b5–5e1) presents a purely perspectival ontology, in which to be is to be only in relation to something or to someone, and merely to be different for something else. From Plato such an ontology is not impossible, but is epistemologically unsatisfactory. This conclusion leads directly to Argument VIII (165e2–6c2), to the effect that if the one is not in itself but only in relation to something or someone else, there can be no truth. The general conclusion (166c2–5) is that the one has to be, paradoxically but necessarily, both in itself and in relation to something or someone else so as to be able truly to bear all attributes, even contradictories, under different aspects.

PHAEDO

E. E. Pender

At the height of his powers as a composer, Plato presents a masterpiece. Phaedo responds to Echecrates' opening question – how did Socrates die? – by narrating his account of the philosopher's final conversations and death. The choice of Phaedo as narrator reflects the historical circumstance of his presence at Socrates' death but also the possibility that he was the absent Plato's actual informant on the events (*Phaedo* 59b). In addition, Phaedo's life story, as a former prisoner of war liberated from slavery by Socrates and now practicing philosophy, gives further point to the main theme of death as liberation for the philosopher, a theme prominent in the dramatic scenario of the imprisoned Socrates, whose soul is about to be freed from the final bonds of the body. The frame dialogue between Phaedo and Echecrates is set in Phlius in the Peloponnese, where Echecrates is a member of the Pythagorean community (D. L. 8.46; q.v. Pythagoreans). Within the reported dialogue Socrates' interlocutors are Simmias and Cebes – both Socratics but also familiar with Pythagorean thought (*Phd.* 61d). The setting and characters thus establish a Pythagorean complexion for a debate which has at its centre the, notably Pythagorean, claim that soul is immortal and able to survive the death of the body.

The first main argument is Socrates' defence of his confidence in the face of death, which rests on his conviction that, as a philosopher, he will enter the presence of gods and gain a welcome release from the body (63b–9e). The argument that death is a blessing for the wise man motivates the four arguments for immortality of soul which in turn demand the exposition of forms (q.v.) as causes. In this way Socrates' defence structures the dialogue and the final metaphysical account is revealed as the underlying cause and guarantee of Socrates' hope and gladness at death, as the fulfilment of his purpose to gain *phronêsis* (68a2).

The first argument for immortality is that from cyclical processes (70c–2e) life and death are opposites and there is balanced reciprocity between dying and coming-back-to-life. Since living people are born from the dead, the souls of the dead must exist to allow this cycle to continue. The second argument, from recollection (72e–7a), maintains that our understanding of abstracts such as 'the equal itself' (74a10) depends on knowledge which must have been gained *before* our first sense-perceptions and therefore that our souls must have existed and been able to learn before birth. The third argument, from affinity (78b–84b), turns to the nature of the soul itself and rests on the principle that 'like knows like'. Socrates distinguishes the naturally composite from the naturally non-composite: the former liable to change and dissolution, visible, apprehended by the senses and mortal; the latter constant, invisible, known only to the intellect and divine. The body's greater affinity to the composite and the soul's to the noncomposite is then established dialectically, with Cebes accepting wholeheartedly (81e11) the conclusion that the purified soul is stronger and more independent than the body and so is able to depart after death to the invisible, with which it shares affinity. Within this argument Socrates explains how contact with the body contaminates the soul while philosophy provides its *only* means of freedom and purification through detached reasoning (82e–3b). When this apparently climactic argument

ends, there is silence (84c). But Cebes' critical objection and demand for proof that the soul will definitively exist after death (86e–8b) forces a radically new approach: the final argument, from opposites (102a–7b). Socrates now recounts how he rejected explanations of the world deriving from physical causes and instead turned to theories as the only way to find truth (99e). To explain his new method of reasoning, he speaks of different entities each of which exists 'itself by itself' (100b) – the forms. Discussion of largeness and smallness leads to the key principle that opposites cannot admit opposites (102e–3a). Following various examples of opposition, the dénouement is reached at *Phd.* 105d as soul is identified as the principle of life and its opposite as death. Since soul as life-force cannot admit its opposite, death, then soul is necessarily immortal and imperishable.

Given the difficulty of the issues raised, it is not surprising that *Phd.* continues to occupy much critical attention. Scholars disagree on the purpose, details and validity of each one of the arguments and advance differing interpretations on every key aspect of the text: soul-body dualism (Pakaluk 2003), recollection (Dimas 2003; Franklin 2005); how the non-composite soul relates to tripartition; how reincarnation can be reconciled with an immortality deriving from contact with the Forms; whether continuity of experiences and consciousness across different lives is feasible; the hypothetical method (Rowe 1993:227–49); the nature of forms – as causes (Sedley 1998), reasons or explanations; the question of immanence, and their precise role in sense-perception and recollection (Osborne 1995).

In contrast, within the text at the conclusion of the four arguments, Cebes' objections to the immortality of soul have been met and his doubts overcome. Simmias too is satisfied 'as far as the arguments go' but admits that he remains doubtful due to the nature of the discussion and his low esteem of human enquiry (Sedley 1990). Socrates has thus led an investigation that is a model of cooperative dialectic. He has stimulated reactions and challenges, probed responses and welcomed admissions of doubt. He has offered encouragement and reassurance, and, crucially, at the close guides his followers towards the further testing of hypotheses necessary to reach a definitive account (*Phd.* 107b).

It is only at this conclusion that Socrates turns to myth: the story of the afterlife is presented not as confirming or superseding the arguments for immortality of soul but as simply taking a different approach. The myth offers a detailed geographical account of the regions of the afterlife and the journeys of the souls after death. It provides a teleological perspective of the universe as a place of intelligent design where goodness is rewarded. While the mass of souls after death remain bound in the physical realm, the philosopher's soul alone gains its freedom to live 'bodiless' forever, in beautiful dwelling places beyond the earth (114c). The myth therefore justifies the gladness of the philosopher at death and, for the rest, calls attention to the urgent need to philosophize in the here-and-now in order to seize this brief chance to escape from the horrors of the underworld and eternal reincarnation (Pender 2011).

While the grandeur of the myth opens an eternal perspective, the spell is broken as Socrates turns to the practical need to bathe before drinking the poison – to save the women the trouble of washing a dead body (115a). This detail intensifies the growing divergence between Socrates as an eternally living soul and Socrates as a corpse (see

also 115c–d). While the narrative attention is fixed on the physical experiences of taking the poison, Socrates' own thought lies elsewhere. So the dialogue ends with its main message played out in the dramatic action: the increasing detachment of the philosopher's soul from body, and his *consequent* serenity.

The huge scope of the dialogue provides Plato's comprehensive response to his philosophical predecessors: to the mystery-religions on the true nature of imprisonment and purification (62b, 67c–d, 69c–d); to the natural scientists on coming-to-be and passing away (96a–c); to Anaxagoras on what *nous* as a cosmic force really entails (97b–9d); and to the Pythagoreans on why their theories of immortality and reincarnation need revision in the light of the forms. Since Plato presents his distinctive metaphysics and teleology as a development of Socrates' principles, *Phd.* asserts his position in the Socratic succession (Most 1993) and their shared preeminence in the Greek philosophical tradition.

PHAEDRUS

Alessandra Fussi

The dialogue (dramatic date: 418–16; cf. Nails 2002:314) can be divided into a prologue, three speeches on *erôs*, love (q.v.) and a discussion of good and bad speaking and writing. In contrast with the *Symposium* (a narrated dialogue on *erôs* whose main scene takes place at night, in a private house, with many speakers) the *Phaedrus* is a performed dialogue with only two characters, who converse during the day and mostly in the countryside. Phaedrus is the dramatic link between the two dialogues: the 'father of the logos' in the *Smp.* (177d5) plays a similar role in the

Phdr. (cf. Socrates' comment to this effect at 242a7–b4). Socrates and Phaedrus walk along the Ilissus River and exchange speeches while lying under the shade of a plane tree, with the sun reaching its zenith at the end of Socrates' second speech (Griswold 1986:34). In the highly refined cultural setting of the *Smp.*, the speakers compete to deliver the best encomium of *erôs* (*Smp.* 177d2–5, 198c5–9b5; on encomiastic discourse in the two dialogues, cf. Nightingale 1995:110–13, 138–9, 154–7). Not the positive, but the negative sides of *erôs* are highlighted in the first two speeches of the *Phdr.* (cf. Rosen 1988:78–101). It is only as an afterthought that Socrates decides to pronounce a speech in praise of *erôs*, the so-called palinode, because, if *erôs* is a god or something divine, the previous accusations were shameful and blasphemous (*Phdr.* 242de).

Glaring light, extreme heat, the chorus of the cicadas (230c3, 258e6–9d8) are carefully marked off as a background to the conversation, and central themes of the dialogue emerge from the characters' response to their natural surroundings. Socrates emphatically highlights the beauty of the place (230b2–c5), while Phaedrus, a valetudinarian, finds the surroundings only fit for physical exercise (cf. Ferrari 1987:4–9). Phaedrus' insensitivity to natural beauty matches his philosophical insensitivity: when Socrates' palinode is over, he fails to raise any questions and rushes to imagine how Lysias, the rhetorician, might compete (*Phdr.* 257c).

The relationship between beauty (q.v.) and *erôs* is central in the dialogue (Hyland 2008:64–90). In the first speech in defence of the non-lover (a written text by Lysias read aloud by Phaedrus) lovers are criticized for their fickleness: attracted by the beautiful body of the beloved, as the bloom of youth fades they abandon the boy and break all their promises (*Phdr.* 234ab); in the second speech, delivered by Socrates in competition with Lysias, the fictional speaker is a concealed lover who passes as a non-lover. Here the relationship between *erôs* and beauty is more complex, because envy enters the scene (Fussi 2006). The lover is initially allured by the beauty of the boy (*Phdr.* 238b7–c4), but, being a slave to pleasure, he 'will turn his boy into whatever is most pleasing to himself' (238e; trans. Nehamas and Woodruff 1995). Since, however, 'a sick man takes pleasure in anything that does not resist him, but sees anyone who is equal or superior as an enemy' (238e–9a), the lover (older and uglier than the beloved: 240d8–e1) comes to resent the beauty of the boy. Rather than honouring and protecting the beloved, he degrades his physical beauty (239c3–d8), and hampers his potential for mental growth (239a2–c2).

This view of *erôs* derives from the concealed lover's thesis that two principles fight for rule in the soul: when acquired opinion rules through reason, it aims at the best, but when the innate desire for pleasure prevails, the person becomes sick and completely unreliable (whether this conception exemplifies Plato's previous theories is a matter of debate: cf. Nussbaum 1986; Price 1989). In the palinode, however, Socrates presents a tripartite image of the soul (q.v.). He likens the human soul to a winged chariot composed by a charioteer (reason) and two horses (spiritedness and appetite). Arguably, the soul's wing symbolizes *erôs* (Griswold:94–9), as it mediates among the parts of the soul, transforming the natural run of the horses into upward movement to the hyperuranian region, where the soul can contemplate the forms (q.v.). Socrates' reflection moves from the nature of the divine soul to that of the human soul, and from the condition that the latter enjoys before incarnation, to the travails encountered during its worldly life. When a soul loses its wings, it falls and takes on an earthly body. Only those souls which contemplated true being, however, can take on human bodies, and, of these, only that soul which was nourished on the forms long enough will take the body of a man who will become a 'lover of wisdom or of beauty or who will be cultivated in the arts and prone to erotic love' (248d). Philosophy, *erôs* and beauty are, therefore, closely linked together. Only the form of beauty, among the beings that truly are, can be perceived by the senses. The process of recollection (q.v.) from earthly beauty to beauty itself can be set in motion in a philosophical soul through falling in love (250d). The beautiful face of the beloved allows the wings of the soul to grow back, radically transforming the behaviour of the person who, as both Lysias' non-lover (231d4–6) and Socrates' concealed lover (241a4b3) had pointed out, when in love acts as if he was no longer himself. The sight of beauty, however, can have different outcomes, since it initiates a struggle among the three parts of the soul. When reason loses, behaviours like those criticized in the first two speeches are likely to ensue, and love can become a shameful affair. Paradoxically, reason wins the struggle with the bad horse not when it tries to control its team, but when its concentration shifts from the team to beauty itself, that is, when the beauty of the beloved reminds the lover of his 'prior' experience of divine beauty. Controlling the two horses, thus, is not the goal, but the outcome of recollection (Ferrari 1992:266).

Different kinds of souls react differently to beauty: when the palinode is over, Socrates and Phaedrus turn to discuss which kinds of speeches and writings are beautiful, which are shameful, and why (*Phdr.* 258d1–5; 259e1–2; on the supposed lack of unity of the dialogue, Burger 1980; Griswold 1986:157–201; cf. Hackforth 1972:136–7). Rhetoric, present in the first half of the *Phdr.* in the form of a written speech and two extemporaneous ones – all aimed at persuading a young beloved – becomes thematic in the second half, where those speeches are analysed in light of their being artfully composed or not (*Phdr.* 262c5–6b1). True rhetoric (q.v.) is distinguished from artless practise (259e4–60e5), and defined as the art of 'directing the souls by means of speech' (*psychagogia tis dia logon*, 261a6–7, cf. 271c10). According to Socrates, rhetoricians ought to know the truth concerning the subjects they want to address (259e4–6, 273d1–3), since a good composition mirrors in its structure the natural structure of its object, exhibiting the organic unity of a living creature (264c2–5). Good rhetoricians, therefore, are also dialecticians (266c1), capable of mastering the art of collection and division (263b6–c, cf. 273e1–4). Indeed, in Socrates' account, only philosophers can become good rhetoricians (cf. 261a3–5, 273d–e), since rhetoricians ought to acquire knowledge concerning not only the subjects they discuss but also the souls of those they strive to persuade (271a1–2). The ideal rhetorician will study the nature of the soul in general – whether it is uniform or composite (270d1, cf. 230a) – as well as the different kinds of souls and characters in particular (271b1–d8). Furthermore, he will be able to detect in practise which speeches are best suited to whom (271d8–2a8), and to grasp the right occasions for speaking and being silent (272a4). The *Phdr.* ends with a critique of writing (274–9), which has attracted much discussion among scholars, especially in light of Plato's choice to write dialogues (Derrida 1972a; Hyland 2008:115–35; cf. Szlezák 1999).

PHILEBUS

Verity Harte

The *Philebus* is one of Plato's later works. Among these, it is unusual in featuring Socrates as lead speaker. This return of Socrates goes with the Socratic character of the dialogue's topic: the nature of the good and of the good human life in particular. The dialogue stages a contest between pleasure and a family of intellectual candidates including reason and knowledge to determine which, if either, is 'that state or disposition of soul capable of providing the happy life for all people' (*Phlb.* 11d4–6). It concludes that neither pleasure nor the intellectual candidates win first prize: a life containing a mixture of pleasure and reason is better than a life containing pleasure or reason alone. But the intellectual candidates are more highly ranked in an evaluation of what contributes to the value of this victorious mixed life.

The *Phlb.* is a 'direct dialogue', a direct conversation involving the principal interlocutors without introduction or narration. It purports to begin in the middle of a conversation. Outside the frame of the dialogue, Socrates has been defending the claim of the intellectual candidates in this competition with pleasure against the hedonism of one Philebus. Philebus, however, 'has withdrawn' (11c8), leaving one Protarchus to be Socrates' interlocutor in defence of pleasure's claim. This pointed offstage placement of Philebus may itself be part of an argument against an extreme form of hedonism as defending a life removed from the human rational sphere (Frede 1997:94–5; McCabe 2000:128–34).

Given its topic and vivid presentation, one might expect the dialogue to be among Plato's more popular works. That it is not so is largely due to the interruption of the otherwise smooth flow of its contest by apparent digressions into abstruse matters of methodology and ontology. A principal challenge for interpreting the *Phlb.* is making sense of its structure.

The first digression follows Socrates' and Protarchus' disagreement over whether or not pleasure – and Socrates' intellectual candidates also – come in various kinds, kinds that make a difference to their value. Socrates' insistence that they do leads to his more general claim that such structural complexity is omnipresent in objects of systematic investigation. Socrates proposes a general method for systematic investigation based on a claim about the nature of things: that everything is composed of one and many, having within it both limit (*peras*) and unlimitedness (*apeirian*) (*Phlb.* 16c9–10). Given this ontology, Socrates' method proposes serial division and enumeration of each complex unity into its constituent kinds, ceasing – 'letting each one of them go into the unlimited' (16e1–2) – only when every component has been enumerated.

Protarchus baulks at applying such systematic investigation to pleasure and asks that Socrates do so. Instead, Socrates conjures one of the swiftest and most important of the dialogue's arguments (20b–2c). Faced with a choice between two lives – a life in which there is pleasure, but none of the intellectual candidates and an intellectual life with no pleasure – Protarchus rejects not only the purely intellectual life, but also the life containing pleasure alone, concluding that a life in which both are present is better than either. Protarchus rejects the life of pleasure alone because a life in which one constantly experiences maximal pleasure, but does not know one is doing so nor remember one has is not a life that he – or any person – would rationally choose to live. This 'Choice of Lives' argument could, in principle, mark the end of the contest between pleasure and the intellectual candidates, giving victory to neither. In fact, it leads to a version of the promised systematic investigation of pleasure and the intellectual candidates in the service of a second contest – as to which of these competitors is responsible for the value of the victorious mixed life – and to a more detailed description of this victorious life.

Socrates does not immediately embark on the systematic investigation of pleasure and the intellectual candidates, but starts further back, dividing beings in general into four kinds (23c–7c). Two – 'unlimited' (*apeiron*) and 'limit' (*peras*) – pick up the claim about the nature of things that underlay his earlier method, although it is disputed whether these terms are used consistently in the two different passages. (Contrast Striker 1970 and Frede 1997:202–5 with Gosling 1975:186 and Meinwald 1998. For my own view, see Harte 2002:78–208). Third is the mixture of limit and unlimited, to which the victorious mixed life is assigned. Pleasure is agreed, on somewhat dubious grounds, to be of the kind, unlimited. Socrates' intellectual candidates are assigned to a fourth kind, the cause of mixture, in an early version of the argument from design (28d–38d), according to which the order apparent in the universe is explicable only by appeal to an intelligent cause or designer. (See Frede 1997:213–21 for appropriate caution in drawing this comparison. For the history of 'design arguments' in antiquity, see Sedley 2007a.)

This assignment of the intellectual candidates presages the way in which, in the ensuing examination of pleasure, Plato's most detailed psychology is used to show how pleasure is dependent upon Socrates' candidates. Pleasure is identified with perceived processes of restoration of optimal conditions

of body or soul (*Phlb*. 31c–2b). Deprived of such optimal conditions, an animal can, through perception, recognize this deprivation as painful; through memory, identify and desire what would restore its optimal condition; and, through human imagination and reason, derive pleasure from the confident expectation of its restoration. When these mechanisms err – in particular, when our confident expectations about future pleasure are wrong or exaggerated – we experience one or another kind of 'false pleasure'. (Plato's understanding of the falsity of false pleasures has been the subject of much dispute, for which see Evans 2008; Frede 1985; Harte 2003–4.) By the same token, even realistically appraised restorative pleasures are mostly irretrievably mixed up with pain: mostly – Socrates identifies as 'true' certain perceptual and intellectual pleasures that replenish painless lacks of which we are unaware (*Phlb*. 51a–3c). Nevertheless, all such restorative pleasures are dependent for whatever value they have on the value of the optimal condition they restore. Hence, this – not pleasure – must be the locus of value.

Brief by comparison, Socrates' investigation of the intellectual candidates (55c–9d) also uses truth as a criterion to evaluate different intellectual activities, based on the use therein of forms of measurement. This appeal to measurement foreshadows its role in the final awarding of prizes in the dialogue's contest. Though noteworthy for its inclusion of both pleasure and practical crafts in its victorious, mixed life, the dialogue's 'practical' turn is offset by the abstract character of first and second prize-winners in its fivefold prize giving (66a–c). These go to geometrical features of the life's construction: proportion, measure and so on. Third and fourth prizes go to Socrates' intellectual candidates. Fifth prize goes to true pleasures, the only kind of pleasure to make it into the prizewinning components of the winning life.

The *Phlb.* – its discussion of pleasure especially – was influential in antiquity, for example, providing important background to the psychology developed by Aristotle in *de Anima* and *Parva Naturalia*, as well as to his treatment of pleasure in *Nicomachean Ethics*.

POLITICUS (STATESMAN)

Kenneth Sayre

Plato's *Politicus* is introduced (*Plt.* 258a) as third in a projected quartet of dialogues: the *Theaetetus* (a discussion of knowledge between Socrates and the young mathematician, Theaetetus), the *Sophist* (a conversation between Theaetetus and a master dialectician from Elea on the art of verbal deception), the *Plt.* (between the Eleatic master and another young mathematician named Socrates) and a fourth dialogue on philosophy between the two Socrateses which was never written.

The *Plt.*'s ostensible topic is the art of statecraft (kingship). At the very middle of the dialogue (283c–5c), however, there is a succinct analysis of normative measurement on which statecraft is said to depend, immediately following which we are told explicitly that the conversation's primary concern is not with statecraft but with making its participants better dialecticians. Statesmanship is the subject with reference to which the dialogue teaches its dialectical lessons.

One tactic followed by the Eleatic master is to make mistakes deliberately for instructional purposes. Statesmanship is defined initially as a self-directive kind of theoretical knowledge dealing with care for living subjects, specifically with herds of humans as distinct from beasts. This definition is judged erroneous because human herd-rearing is only a small part of herd-rearing generally and does not by itself comprise a form (*eidos* 262b; q.v.). There follows a tutorial on proper definition in which Young Socrates (YS) is advised to divide according to forms (*kat'eidê* 262e) by cutting things 'through the middle' (*dia meson*).

After testing YS with a few less-than-serious definitions of human being (including 'featherless biped'), the Eleatic observes that they have not yet distinguished the statesman from other human care providers like farmers, bakers and doctors. Making that distinction, he says, requires a new beginning. He then recounts a myth contrasting the age of Zeus (the present age) with the age of Cronus (for detailed commentary on the myth, see Lane 1998; Miller 2002; also q.v. Myth).

Under Cronus the universe runs backwards and order is maintained by divine control. Human beings spring full grown from the earth and become increasingly younger until they disappear. All needs are satisfied by a bountiful earth and animals live without preying on one another. When Cronus releases control, however, the world becomes increasingly disorderly, creatures fend for themselves at each other's expense and humans require god-given gifts of fire and craft for sheer survival. At the chaotic end of this sequence the universe reverses direction and the age of Zeus begins.

The express purpose of the myth is to show that the paradigm of shepherding, epitomized by Cronus, is a mismatch for civic leadership in the age of Zeus. This paradigm gives rise to the confusion between statesmen and care providers like farmers and doctors, and it provides no help in studying the manner of kingly rule. Another paradigm is needed. After a brief examination of the use of paradigms in learning grammar (a 'paradigm of paradigms', *Plt.* 277d), the Eleatic proposes weaving as a more helpful paradigm for statecraft under present conditions.

Weaving is defined first as a skill of fabricating woolen garments for protective wear. Like the initial definition of statecraft, however, this attempt fails to distinguish its definiendum from related arts (e.g. carding and fulling). A revised definition classifies these associated arts as merely contributive and singles out weaving as the manufacture of woolen clothing by intertwining warp and woof (283a).

Both weaving and statesmanship, like all other arts, depend upon due measure (*to metrion* 284a). The same holds for dialectic (q.v.) itself. In a brief discussion at the very heart of the dialogue (283c–5c), the Eleatic contrasts two kinds of measurement. One compares excess and deficiency (also termed the great and the small 283e) with respect to each other, the other measures them with respect to normative standards (the mean, the fitting, the timely and the requisite 284e). The latter (normative measurement) is prerequisite not only for art (q.v.) but for the difference between good and bad in human affairs (283e). If 'due measure' did not exist, there would be no arts, no products of arts and no difference between good and bad.

This key passage on measurement employs terminology characteristic of Plato's late (post-*Parmenides*) ontology. Both excess and deficiency and great and small are designations of the principle which, according to Aristotle's rendition of Plato's views, cooperates with unity in producing forms and with forms in generating sensible things. The *Plt.* is one of several dialogues expressing such views, sometimes referred to as Plato's Unwritten Doctrines (q.v.) (for details, see Sayre 2005, 2006).

In beginning the final definition of statesmanship (*Plt.* 287b), the Eleatic cautions that the divisions will not always be dichotomous. Nor will they be confined to the right hand side. Indeed, nondichotomous division along the left was previously introduced in the definition of weaving, a departure from the format followed earlier in the dialogue.

The final definition begins by separating civic arts into direct and contributory causes, which later are then subdivided into seven parts (e.g. tool making, vehicle manufacture). Direct causes are divided into governors and servants, the latter further divided into classes typified by slaves, merchants, clerks and priests. Here the Eleatic expresses concern that the statesman might become hidden in a group described as 'the greatest enchanters among the sophists' (291c). This danger is forestalled by dividing governors into leaders of genuine and imitative (303c) polities, including kingly and tyrannical monarchies, aristocracies and oligarchies and lawful and lawless democracies. Among leaders of genuine polities, the statesman is finally divided from his governor subordinates, notably generals, judges and rhetoricians.

At the end of this formal definition (305e), statesmanship emerges as the civic art controlling all other arts involved in the life of a genuine polity. After this paradigmatic illustration of dialectical procedure, the Eleatic returns to matters of practical statesmanship.

The paradigm of weaving is brought to bear once again at *Plt.* 305e with a discussion of the statesman's practical task of weaving opposing temperaments into an integrated social fabric. 'Warp' and 'woof' for this fabric are provided by the polity's more courageous and more peaceable characters, respectively. When these groups interbreed and are imbued with civic virtue (true opinion about the beautiful, the just and the good 309c), the result is a unified and prosperous state (311c).

PROTAGORAS

Daniel C. Russell

Protagoras, a so-called Socratic dialogue, features conversations between Socrates and the sophist Protagoras, a self-professed teacher of virtue (q.v.). The focus of the dialogue is whether virtue can be taught, and along the way Plato also examines several other issues: whether virtue is a unity; whether virtue is knowledge; the possibility and nature of *akrasia* (q.v.); and the value of pleasure (q.v.). The dialogue falls roughly into five sections.

Prt. 309a–17e. Socrates narrates how he was awakened early by a young friend, Hippocrates, eager to meet and study with Protagoras, recently arrived in Athens. Socrates suggests that they meet Protagoras to see whether he is a fit teacher, and this sets the tone of the dialogue: sophists profess to alter their students' very souls, and students have reason to be cautious. They find Protagoras at the home of his Athenian patron, where he has been giving presentations of his rhetorical prowess before several prominent Athenians (the extended family of Pericles), other sophists (Hippias and Prodicus) and his own 'chorus' (315b) of hangers-on.

Prt. 317e–28d. Socrates questions Protagoras about whether virtue really is teachable. Protagoras replies with a long, eloquent discussion – often called his 'Great Speech' – on the nature and the teaching of virtue. He argues that while virtue is

something common – and offers a myth to illustrate how virtue binds civilized society (see Shortridge 2007) – still virtue is teachable: for example, punishment of criminals and naughty children alike aims to instil virtue in them. Moreover, some people even excel in virtue, which can be taught by specialists. This issue is very important to Plato, since if virtue is teachable, then it should be some kind of knowledge (q.v.). It is also important in his assessment of the sophists (q.v.): they claim to teach virtue, but can they explain what sort of knowledge virtue is?

Prt. 328d–4c. In order to understand whether virtue is teachable, Socrates says, he needs to know how the several virtues are related to each other. As the dialogue unfolds, Socrates' concern becomes clear: if virtue is teachable, then it must be a unified body of knowledge; but does Protagoras think virtue is knowledge, or a unity? Socrates first asks questions about unity, and in reply Protagoras says that the virtues are not the same but all distinct parts of virtue; moreover, these parts are heterogeneous, like the parts of the face, separable from each other and dissimilar to each other. Socrates then asks Protagoras about three pairs of virtues – justice (q.v.) and piety (q.v.), wisdom and temperance, and temperance and justice – in each case suggesting that Protagoras accepts more cohesion within these pairs than his previous statements suggest.

The heart of this discussion is Protagoras' view as to whether to have any one of the virtues is to have them all, what scholars often call the 'reciprocity of the virtues' or the 'unity of the virtues' (see Manuwald 2005). Plato takes up this thesis in several other dialogues, but it is significant here for the connection that Plato clearly draws between it and the very idea that virtue is teachable.

Prt. 334c–49a. Protagoras soon tires of giving short answers, preferring to make speeches instead, and the conversation breaks down. After a struggle over how to proceed, Protagoras questions Socrates, focusing on an apparent inconsistency in a poem of Simonides, viz. that it is both hard to become good and not hard (rather, impossible) to be good. Thus begins what is sometimes called a literary digression, in the middle of the dialogue. Socrates discusses the poem briefly with the sophist Prodicus, and is eventually persuaded to make his own speech, which includes a good deal of humour and irony. To eliminate the apparent inconsistency, Socrates distinguishes between the process of *becoming* good and the state of *being* good (see Baltzly 1992 for discussion). But what is most significant about Socrates' speech is his insistence there that no one does wrong willingly – the so-called Socratic paradox. Plato revisits this provocative idea throughout his career, and there is enormous scholarly controversy over how to characterize the progression of his thought on this issue. This idea is also a central issue in the dialogue's final arguments, which follow immediately.

Prt. 349a–62. Socrates finally steers the discussion back to the relations between the virtues. Protagoras now says that while there may be connections between some virtues, 'courage is completely different from all the rest'. In reply, Socrates focuses on Protagoras' view that the knowledge he imparts is something fine and powerful. Socrates suggests presenting this knowledge as a skill – the 'art of measurement' – for measuring the quantities of pleasure and pain an action produces (see Nussbaum 1986:ch. 4; Richardson 1990). This is because laypersons would accept that an action is right when there is preponderance of pleasure over pain, and

that pleasure and pain are the fundamental motivational drives. In that case, they would agree that the 'art of measurement' guarantees right action: right action, on this view, is also one that there is most motivation to do, and the 'art of measurement' identifies such action. Such an advertisement would both appeal to Protagoras' audience and portray virtue as both teachable and immune to wilful wrongdoing. However, it also makes courage a form of knowledge, like the other virtues (and wisdom in particular), contra Protagoras' earlier assertion. Protagoras then breaks off the discussion, and in parting, Socrates says that whereas originally Protagoras affirmed and Socrates doubted that virtue is teachable, their positions have now reversed. Like many Socratic dialogues, *Prt.* is 'aporetic', ending apparently without solving its central puzzles.

This passage is among the most controversial in the corpus (see the commentaries of Denyer 2008 and Taylor 1976). On one hand, it puts forth normative and psychological hedonism, as well as a quantitative model of virtue, but such ideas seem to conflict with Plato's other dialogues; on the other, it also defends such Socratic theses as the reciprocity of the virtues and the Socratic paradox (on the latter see Wolfsdorf 2006). Much controversy surrounds the relation between *Prt.* and *Gorgias* particularly, since in *Grg.* Socrates is highly critical of hedonism. This controversy has not been conclusive: some deny that these dialogues actually disagree on this point (e.g. Rudebusch 1999); and even if they do, perhaps Plato simply changed his mind. Yet others argue that *Prt.* itself gives no evidence that Plato endorsed hedonism, other dialogues aside (e.g. Russell 2005). But at present, there is little reason to anticipate scholarly consensus on these points.

REPUBLIC

Nickolas Pappas

The *Republic* is among Plato's greatest works and likely his most controversial. Its subject is *dikaiosunê* 'justice' (q.v.), both as an individual human virtue (q.v.) and a feature of political existence. The dialogue also ranges over topics in metaphysics, education (q.v.) and aesthetics (q.v.); but its proposals for political reform have inspired both the most enthusiastic revolutionary thinking and the most horrified anti-utopianism.

Whether Plato wrote the *R.* all at once or in stages, it was later editors who divided it into 10 books, those divisions sometimes registering turns in the conversation (beginnings of bks 2, 5, 8, 10). The change after bk 1 separates its rendered scene and characters from the drier constructive argumentation that takes up bks 2–10. Bks 2–10 rarely acknowledge that their conversation is unfolding anywhere special; bk 1 sets the stage in Piraeus, the port of Athens, at the home of Polemarchus, the son of Cephalus, a noncitizen who has grown old and wealthy. It is summer, the year perhaps around 422 BCE, although scholars have debated this consensus, many arguing for a dramatic date a full decade later (Nails 1998). If it is 422 the Peloponnesian War has paused in a truce; Socrates is about 50. (Plato wrote the *R.* decades later, when its active participants were dead.)

Socrates spends bk 1 trying to define and defend justice (Lycos 1987; Sparshott 1966). His host's father is a pious man possessed of virtues but no skill at justifying them. Polemarchus represents the new ideas of Sophists and poets. Socrates reduces him to silence too. Then Thrasymachus mounts an attack on morality: 'Justice' refers to nothing but what benefits those in power (*R.* 338c). For that reason behaving justly is never in anyone's interests (343c).

Bk 2 replaces these interlocutors with Plato's brothers Glaucon and Adeimantus. They restate Thrasymachus' challenge systematically, asking Socrates not merely to silence one critic but to defend morality against all critics (357a–b). Thereafter they let Socrates lead them through the thicket of the *R.*'s argument. They are civilized, even placid; they want to learn.

The *R.* thus represents two genres of Platonic dialogue, bk 1 resembling those contentious, inconclusive dialogues called 'early' or 'Socratic' while the remainder belongs with 'Platonic' dialogues about Forms, soul and other positive doctrines. Some scholars believe Plato wrote bk 1 earlier as a freestanding dialogue, revisiting it later to expand and improve its argument. More often it is thought he wrote bk 1 deliberately in the style of his own shorter dialogues, to contrast their negative and personal cross-examinations with another mode of philosophizing, something less embattled and therefore less exciting, but with the promise to issue in conclusions – something closer to teaching philosophy (Kahn 1993).

The *R.* as a whole is powered by an analogy that Socrates introduces in bk 2: *A soul is like a city* (*R.* 368e–9a). Justice and other virtues in a human soul (q.v.) share structural characteristics with the justice and other virtues of a state. The parallel between individual and collective virtues emerges from an underlying tripartite organization of functions common to city and soul. This analogy lets the *R.* explore ethical and political matters together (Cooper 1977; Ferrari 2005).

(I) POLITICAL THOUGHT

As a document of political philosophy the *R.* is sometimes called utopian. But it makes concessions to economic and political realities (abandoning the simple town Socrates first proposes to examine a sophisticated city that Glaucon considers more widely attractive: 372d–e); and it worries how to implement its reforms (e.g. 471c–d). The city it proposes is meant to follow from axioms applicable to every society: A1: People come together to create a new social unity (369c). A2: In a well-run society people specialize their labour (369e–70a). The R. appeals to A1 when mandating policies that promote concord, while A2 keeps each citizen assigned to a single task. Indeed, since Platonic justice is cooperation among disparate groups in a city (433a), justice combines the axioms.

A2 also yields Plato's class analysis, when 'labour' means very broadly the three *civic functions*. People serve their society by producing goods and services. Citizens perform another civic function by fighting in the military. And they serve to the extent that they participate in governance. So Plato divides the city into three classes: a small group of rulers, a selective army and the productive mass of the population (414a–b). This is not a simplification of class divisions in Athens but the invention of new classes. The Greek cities' *mesoi* 'middle ones' were farmers who worked their land, wore armour to serve in the infantry and voted in the assembly. Thus, Plato's stratification divides the hoplite-farmer-assemblyman into three, signalling that the idealized citizen of classical Greece was untenable in a philosophical city.

The functional analysis may make trouble on Plato's own terms. Athenian citizens had to exercise their reason in the assembly, fight courageously in the army and work as self-interested producers on the farm. They had to have the complete souls described by Plato's psychology (see below). But those complete humans disappear from the Platonic city.

Will the best city contain the best individuals after all?

The R. focuses on the rulers and soldiers, collectively 'guardians'. They live communally, sharing meals and sleeping in barracks without privacy (416d–17b). Men and women (q.v.) rule and fight side by side (452a; Bluestone 1987); 'marriages' are temporary breeding assignments, orchestrated by the rulers so that the fittest guardians reproduce (459a–60a). Their children are reared in nurseries not knowing who their parents are (460b–d).

The abolition of the family leaves children attached only to fellow guardians. Their identity is their public identity. Athenian tragedy worried how to coordinate family loyalties with loyalties to the state; Plato undoes this problem at a stroke by eliminating families.

Finally the rulers must be philosophers – 'philosopher-kings' as they are popularly known – though it is important to remember that they are both men and women (473c–d). If the R. creates its classes by dividing actual Athenians into two or three functions, then the philosopher-kings and -queens reflect the forcible concatenation of two types, the executive and the contemplative. Scholars debate whether this figure violates A2, and how philosophers might be persuaded to be governed, when by their natures they have something much better to do (Brown 2000; Mahoney 1992).

Plato's solution to the tensions inherent in the philosopher-king recalls his earlier solution to a lesser tension. When Socrates proposes a standing army he specifies that these guardians be gentle to fellow citizens but fierce towards enemies (R. 375c). How to produce a gentle fierce soldier? Education (410e): Socrates launches into a treatment of poetry and other arts, followed by extensive physical education (376c–412b).

Analogously, those higher-flying birds, the philosopher-kings, need intensive intellectual education. They study the forms and 'the good' (503e–6a; Sedley 2007b). Their education also covers mathematics (q.v.) and dialectic (q.v.) (521d–34e; Burnyeat 2000).

(II) Psychology and Ethics

Socrates discovers a tripartite structure within the soul: reason, spiritedness, desire (440e–1a). Examples of internal conflict show that these are distinct elements or motives (437b–40a; Lorenz 2006).

The most innovative of the three is *thumos* 'spirit' or 'anger' (439e), the element that engenders shame and indignation. Without some such element the soul would only possess reason and desire, the outcome always threatening that desires can overpower the quiet voice of reason. The spirited part of the soul possesses irrational energy and therefore the strength to resist desires, yet it stands near enough to reason to take instruction from it. If the body is a cage and reason is the little human trapped inside with desire, a many-headed monster, spirit is the lion that this homunculus tames to keep the monster at bay (588b–9a).

Desire (q.v.) first appears simple, a self-gratifying wish that moves without thinking (437c). But desires vary from sexual desire, the maddest of all (329c, 458d), through desires for food and drink, to the most rational seeming among them, money love. Most desires coexist: one eats, sees a play. But sexual desire tyrannizes the others (572e) until the sexual obsessive seeks nothing but forbidden intercourse (572c–d). At the other extreme, love of money imparts self-discipline (554c–d).

Reason is differently ambiguous. First it is the motive that governs other motives, the soul's executive branch. Later reason's function expands to include desire for knowledge (475b); so possessing a soul governed by reason means *both* coordinating your motives *and* practicing philosophy. Reason knows two native activities, as the philosopher-kings have two jobs to do.

Socrates argues that the soul is immortal (608d–11a). He recounts a myth (q.v.) of otherworldly judgement and reincarnation (614b–21b). However religious this argument sounds, it accords with the *R*.'s pattern of removing 'body' from accounts of motive (411e, 518d). All actions can be accounted for in terms belonging exclusively to soul; no wonder the soul persists without a body.

The city and soul work together, rather than in parallel, in the *R*.'s overarching argument. They also join in one subsidiary argument.

(III) The Benefits of Justice

The *R*.'s overarching argument says that the just life is preferable to the unjust life. Justice in the city denotes an establishment in which rulers and ruled respect each other's functions and interests, and cooperate in running the city (433b–d). The many kinds of injustice are presented as a sequence of decline in constitutions, from the best state to an honour-loving martial aristocracy (timocracy), then downward through oligarchy and democracy to tyranny (bks 8 and 9).

Meanwhile, the just soul possesses the appeal of a balanced mental state (443a–b). This sounds intrinsically desirable. But alongside his history of worsening regimes Socrates recounts the decline among souls, naming the ever-worse souls after the regimes they resemble. Each unjust soul makes the just type look better off, as bad cities enhance the appeal of the good city.

Socrates lingers over the contrast between a tyrant and a philosopher. Focusing on the superiority that intellectual pleasures enjoy over unnecessary bodily pleasures – all lust and illusion – Socrates concludes that the best person's life is far happier than the worst person's (587e; Parry 2007).

(IV) POETRY AND THE OTHER ARTS

The R.'s politics and psychology combine differently in its attacks on poetry (q.v.). The first treatment (bks 2–3) emphasizes politics and the young guardians' education. Socrates evaluates the content of epic poems and Athenian tragedies: What do they say about gods and heroes (377a–91e)? His assessment becomes formalist when it banishes drama and narratives containing direct speech by characters. *Mimêsis* 'representation, enactment' amounts to inauthenticity or deception (392b–4c). Anyone who acts out the part of an inferior person will pick up bad habits (395d).

The arguments in bk 10 view mimêtic poetry from the soul's perspective (595a), understanding *mimêsis* as representation or imitation (q.v.; Nehamas 1982b). Like painting, mimêtic poetry is the imitation of appearance (598b); therefore it strengthens the worst part of the soul, the part that feeds on illusions (602c–d; cf. 585d). Tragedy stirs up pity and grief and weakens the soul's capacity to govern itself (606a–d).

Bk 10 extends the claims of bk 3. Not only children but nearly everyone risks being corrupted by mimêtic poetry. Not only the depictions of bad characters corrupt but depiction as such, for it trades in appearance alone, not truth.

(V) METAPHYSICS

A digression from the tight analogy between city and discussion of the ruler leads the R. to its central metaphysical subject: the forms (q.v.), objects of greater being than ordinary things.

Philosophers, who love learning, differ from 'spectacle-lovers' thanks to the difference between forms – what philosophers pursue in their studies – and the sights and sounds of particular objects that a fan of entertainment rushes to see and hear: tragedies, music and paintings (475e–6b). Individual things can only be objects of *doxa* 'belief, opinion' (479d–e). Forms are objects of knowledge (476d).

Often, as here, Plato's Socrates introduces forms as if his interlocutor knew what they were. He speaks of those objects that philosophers love to learn about as 'the beautiful itself', for example, Glaucon acknowledges them (476a). Then (as elsewhere) the R. follows an argument for insiders with one directed to open audiences, in this case the experience lovers being differentiated from philosophers (479a–e). This argument says: Particular objects hold their properties equivocally, being beautiful in one respect and ugly in another; likewise both large and small, good and bad. What *is and is not F* (for any property F) cannot be clearly known as a form can be. For, by hypothesis a form simply *is* F. Largeness is large, not large and small (Nehamas 1979; Patterson 1985). One knows what is and has opinions about what is and is not.

If Socrates is right that non-forms cannot be known, the argument offers a pragmatic consideration in favour of forms' existence. Without them there is no knowledge. If anyone knows anything, the philosopher knows forms. The lover of spectacles, sensations and things possesses mere opinions about the visible world.

(VI) THE GOOD

The form of the good (q.v.) is the conscious goal and consummation of the philosophers' education (504a–6a). The good is not one form among many but in some way a greatest form. To show how they are related Socrates uses a simile (*sun*), a geometrical image (*line*) and an allegory (*cave*).

What the *sun* (q.v.) is among visible objects the good is among things understood by intellect (508a–9b). The sun is the cause of other objects and also provides the light by which those who see can see those objects. The good causes the existence of the forms and makes it possible for those who can reason to know forms. As the eye is guided by sunlight to see what the sun has caused to be, the mind is guided by the good to know what *it* has made.

The *divided line* (q.v.) complicates this analogy (509d–11e). Socrates divides a line into two segments of unequal length, then subdivides each segment. The main division separates visible from intelligible; within the visible domain the subdivision sets objects against their shadows and reflections. As a tree has greater reality than its reflection, so too does the intelligible world as a whole compared to the visible world (Denyer 2007; Smith 1996).

Within the intelligible realm the opposition between being and image (q.v.) distinguishes forms from mathematical objects. As an object of thought, the circle deserves a place in the world known to thought. But because mathematicians use such objects in a way that Plato calls 'hypothetical' – he seems to mean: without defining their terms – imagistic cognition remains mixed into their understanding (*R.* 510c–11a). Mathematicals stand below those objects of dialectic that philosophers know through rigorous definitions, the forms (511b–d).

Are there four different grades of objects on the line, each causing a distinct type of cognition; or do different ways of understanding a single object let it be more than one type of thing? The text is tempted by both possibilities. Socrates ranks mental states according to their objects' reality (511d–e). But mathematical and empirical people look at the same round bowl and the mind of one goes to bodiless circles while the other stays focused on the material bowl (510d). How one thinks determines what one thinks about.

The *allegory of the cave* (q.v.) brings politics back into the metaphysics. The sun again represents the good; trees and animals stand for forms; the visible world is symbolized by the inside of a huge sunless cave. Within the cave, shapes of trees and animals correspond to three-dimensional things. Those shapes cast shadows on the cave wall and the shackled prisoners experience only these shadows. Socrates tells of one prisoner unchained and turned to see the shapes whose shadows he had been watching, then the fire that cast those shadows (515c–e). Finally he leaves the cave and truly sees. But he has to return to lead his former fellows, despite the ridicule awaiting him (516e–17a).

Why should the prisoner feel obligated to go back into the cave; why should the philosopher deign to reign? Socrates addresses that problem (519d–20c) but passes over another: If this returning figure is the good city's philosopher, the jeers that greet him sound like the abuse that Socrates endured in Athens. After all the improvements that the good city promised, are *these* its citizens, the same know-nothings who shouted Socrates down in court?

SOPHIST

Noburu Notomi

Plato's late dialogue, the *Sophist*, starts with the reference to 'yesterday's agreement' of reunion (*Sph*. 216a), made at the end of the *Theaetetus* (210d), and thus dramatically succeeds that dialogue, by introducing a new speaker, the visitor from Elea.

When Theodorus introduces the Eleatic visitor as a 'philosopher', Socrates raises a question about the confusion between *elenchus* and *eristic*; he says that it is difficult to discern many appearances of the philosopher, for the philosopher is like a god and sometimes appears to be a sophist, a statesman and even a mad person (*Sph*. 216a–d). On the general assumption that the philosopher, sophist and statesman constitute three separate kinds, the speakers agree to define these three one by one, starting with the sophist. This setting of the inquiry may be taken as indicating a tripartite project to define the three figures in three dialogues, namely the *Sph*., the *Politicus* and the *Philosopher*. But the last one was never written, so many commentators conjecture about various reasons why Plato gave up the project. On the other hand, some argue (Frede 1996; Notomi 1999) that, as far as the initial purpose is to distinguish the philosopher from his appearances, the extant two dialogues suffice to *show* the philosopher by defining the other two. If this is the case, Plato had no intention to write an independent dialogue, but *Sph*. is expected to provide a key to defining the philosopher as distinct from the sophist. For an alternative view, see Davidson (1985).

A definition is pursued by dividing a genus into species. This method of division is originally proposed in *Phaedrus*, and fully used in *Sph*. (see Brown 2010; Gill 2010). The sophist is first defined as a hunter for rich young men, but then other definitions follow: a merchant, a retail dealer and a manufacturing trader of learning, an eristic, who fights and earns money in private arguments and a purifier of wrong opinions in

the soul by means of refutation. These definitions show the aspects of the sophist's activity, which were depicted in earlier dialogues (*Protagoras, Gorgias, Euthydemus*, etc.).

However, the sixth definition called 'sophist of noble lineage' looks like Socrates, and this resemblance casts a strong doubt upon the whole inquiry of definition. Also, the plurality of definitions causes a serious problem because each object must have a single definition of its essence. A new attempt at a final definition then reveals that the essence of the sophist's art lies in the very act of making such appearances. But when the art of image making is divided into the making of likenesses (correct images) and that of *phantasmata* (wrong images), the inquirers face a series of difficulties, as if the sophist counterattacks them. From this point, a long digression of the middle part of the dialogue (*Sph*. 236d–64b, which modern scholars see as central and most important) starts.

The difficulties are concerned with appearance, image, falsehood and *not-being* (*to mê on*): 'appearing without really being so' and 'stating a falsehood' presuppose that '*not-being* is', which was strictly forbidden by Parmenides (236d–7b). The inquirers now have to prove, against Parmenides, the proper combination of *not-being* and *being* (*to on*), as if committing a 'parricide' (241d–2a).

Examinations are made in a parallel way concerning *not-being* and *being*. First, it is shown that self-contradiction results from any attempt to treat '*not-being*' in isolation: it is totally unspeakable or unthinkable, but this conclusion already involved the speaker in speaking of it. Next, it is also shown that various attempts to define '*being*' fail. First, both pluralist and monist positions turn out to be inconsistent and contradictory. Then, the materialists, who maintain that only bodily things *are*, and the idealists, called 'friends of forms' (whose theory resembles the earlier theory of forms in *Phaedo*), are made to accept that *being* is both things changing and things unchangeable. However, since this definition does not properly grasp being as distinct from change and rest, all the attempts fail. Now the inquiry needs 'joint illumination' or 'parity assumption' of *being* and *not-being* (250e–1a).

The second half of the middle part seeks a solution of the difficulties of *not-being* and falsehood. To prove the correct relation between *not-being* and *being*, the inquirers have to secure the proper combination of kinds in general. They demonstrate how the greatest kinds (change, rest, identity, difference and *being*) relate to each other. This demonstration itself belongs to the art of dialectic (253c–e), and therefore it *shows* what the philosopher should do, in contrast to the sophistic argument that confuses these concepts so as to produce falsehoods, contradictions and refutations.

After proving the proper combination of *not-being* and *being* (as principles of separation and combination), and thus by securing the possibility of *logos* in general, the inquirers next show that a false statement combines a statement (*logos*, as the combination of a subject and a verb) and *not-being*. Thus, the inquiry of the middle part of the dialogue defends the definition of the sophist as a maker of false statements.

The topic discussed most in the latter half of the twentieth-century scholarship was whether, and how, Plato distinguishes different uses of the verb 'to be'. Does he distinguish between copula and existence or between identity and predication, or not at all? (see Brown 1986; Owen 1971) However, recent studies focus more on the nature of *logos* (q.v.; discourse, argument or statement)

rather than the verb 'to be' (see Brown 2008; Notomi 2007).

The final inquiry succeeds in defining the sophist as the imitator of the wise without really being wise (*Sph.* 268b–d). This dialogue thus settles a crucial issue and a long concern in Plato's philosophy, that is, what the sophist is, and how Socrates' true philosophy differs from sophistry. It provides a basis of 'logic' for Aristotle, who makes a full use of its fruits in his logical treatises, especially *De interpretatione* and *Sophistici elenchi*.

SYMPOSIUM

Angela Hobbs

The *Symposium* tells of a drinking party in which a variety of characters meet to celebrate the tragedian Agathon's victory in a dramatic contest; they decide to forgo the customary sensuous entertainments and give speeches instead on *erôs*, erotic love. Plato explores questions about the origins, definition, aims, objects and effects of *erôs* both through what the symposiasts say in their formal speeches and by how they interact; he thus gives an indication of what sort of life and moral character a particular view of *erôs* might promote and reflect. The distance between the date of composition (*c.* 384–379 BCE) and the dramatic dates of the symposium and the framework conversation (416 BCE and *c.* 405 BCE) allows Plato to make ironic references to future events known to his readers, such as the downfall of the soldier-statesman Alcibiades, the death of Socrates, and the connection between their two fates.

The choice of a relaxed symposium setting enables Plato to reveal different facets of Socrates' complex personality, such as his ability to drink without becoming drunk (*cp. Laws* 633c, on the importance in a state of regular drinking parties as a means of testing self-control). The occasion also allows the beautiful Alcibiades to recount how Socrates resisted all his youthful attempts to seduce him; in this respect at any rate, Plato implies, Socrates did not corrupt the young.

The tale of the drinking party is intricately nested: Apollodorus, a follower of Socrates, recounts it to a group of unnamed businessmen, having heard it himself from Aristodemus, another Socratic acolyte who was actually present; one of the central speeches, that of Socrates, relates Socrates' purported conversation with a priestess named Diotima. Furthermore, Aristodemus cannot remember all the details clearly (*Sym.* 180c) and admits to having fallen asleep towards the end. Plato thereby creates even more distance than usual between himself as author and the content of the speeches and compels his readers to participate in interpretation; we are also invited to reflect on the crucial but unreliable nature of intermediaries – a central theme of the dialogue – and how best to get at the truth of different kinds of subject matter. What is the relation between *mythos* (q.v. Myth) and *logos* (q.v.)? Can there be a *logos* of love?

Considerable emphasis is placed on the order of the speeches, which anticipates the importance of an orderly rational and emotional progression up the rungs of the ladder of love in Diotima's speech; in general, order, not disorder, is seen as the more creative force in the dialogue (note the banishment of the *aulos*-girl at 176e; q.v. *Women*).

The first speaker, Phaedrus, gives an encomium to romantic love of a particular individual. We want our beloved to admire us and we thus behave at our best in their

presence; the gods will in turn reward us after death for self-sacrifice inspired by love. Phaedrus believes he is portraying love as entirely desirable and beneficial; the reader, however, may feel that his lovers tend to die young. A more pragmatic view is taken by Pausanias, who distinguishes between 'heavenly' and 'popular' *erôs*; he anticipates Diotima to the extent that the quality of *erôs* depends on the nature of its object, and the manner in which it is performed. 'Popular' love is concerned with the body and can be directed by the male lover (Pausanias envisages a male subject) towards either women or boys; 'heavenly' *erôs* occurs when a man is attracted to a boy's intellect, and is concerned to further his cultural and political education. Pausanias depicts heavenly love as perfect, but its time limit (the passive role of the boy 'beloved' was not considered appropriate for a man) means that it contains inherent tensions.

The doctor, Eryximachus, continues the distinction between good and bad *erôs*, but, in a further anticipation of Diotima, the concept of *erôs* is widened. It is now a cosmic force, the attraction of one element for another, and has both physical and moral dimensions: the right kind of attraction leads to harmony and health, the wrong kind to conflict and disease. The good *erôs* reconciles opposites in fields as diverse as medicine, music and the climate; it is, critically, the force that mediates between humans and gods. Eryximachus assumes that erotic love, properly conducted, is essential for our physical and mental well-being. The comic playwright Aristophanes expands on this, claiming that to understand love we need to know first about the nature of human beings (189d). Plato thereby invites us to consider which speaker (and which kind of expertise) gives the most accurate account of our human needs. According to Aristophanes' myth of our origins, humans were once spherical beings (some all male, some all female and some hermaphrodite), but were split in two when they challenged the gods. Bereft, they search the world for their missing half, and this desire for and pursuit of the whole is what we call *erôs* (192e): the lost half does not have to be good or beautiful, but simply one's own. Those that find their other half yearn to accept Hephaistus' offer and be fused into one.

Aristophanes' myth raises profound questions. If love is defined as a search, then would not the completion of this search cancel out the conditions that make love possible? Do lovers perceive and love each other as unique, separate individuals or simply as the missing part of themselves? The host Agathon's speech, in contrast, self-referentially depicts the god *Erôs* as a beautiful, winsome and perfectly good youth, but Plato's intentions in including his anodyne poetics become clear when Socrates subjects them to an elenchus, arguing (*pace* Aristophanes) that as love is of the beautiful and good things that it lacks, love itself cannot be beautiful or good – an argument that depends on beauty being homogeneous and coextensive with equally homogeneous goodness.

These conclusions form the basis (201d) of Socrates' account of Diotima's teachings on love (q.v. Love, Women). Diotima claims that *erôs* is a daimonic intermediary between god and humans. Its object is permanent possession of what is good (206a), and it achieves this 'through giving birth in the beautiful, in relation to both body and soul' (206b); as personal immortality is not available for mortals, these creations are the best substitutes we can achieve. There are different grades of creation, and physical offspring are the lowest; the highest are the products of

reason. We begin by loving a beautiful body, but, if we are guided aright, we will re-channel this erotic energy onto beautiful souls, laws and sciences, until finally we come to apprehend and love the form of beauty itself, in which blessed state life is truly 'liveable' (211d). Whether this ascent up the 'ladder of love' requires us to give up our risky attachments to individual humans is vigorously debated: what does contemplation of the form of beauty actually involve? And can it still accurately be described as a state of *erôs* or has *erôs* transformed into something else? Furthermore, if the form of beauty is itself beautiful, then would it not be vulnerable to the Third Man argument?

The counter claims of love for a unique and irreplaceable individual are movingly put forward by Alcibiades, who declines to give an account of *erôs*, offering instead a history of his personal (and sexually unrequited) love for Socrates. Both the creative and destructive possibilities of such an attachment are manifest both in his speech and in his interchanges with Socrates and Agathon. Here too there is keen debate as to how seriously Plato views Alcibiades' challenge: he is allowed to be glamorous and charismatic, and to give the last speech; on the other hand, his chaotic and clouded exit perhaps provides the dangerous *cômus* to Plato's own symposiastic entertainment. Socrates then debates with Agathon and Aristophanes whether the same man can write both tragedy and comedy – maybe Plato believes that in the *Smp.* he has achieved both feats with Alcibiades' help – and, after they too fall asleep, leaves for the Lyceum to begin a new day of philosophical inquiry.

For further information, see Ferrari (1992), Hobbs (2000:ch. 9; 2006), Hunter (2004), Lesher et al. (2006), Murray (1990), Price (1989) and Santas (1988).

THEAETETUS

Ronald Polansky

Shorey (1933) considered *Theaetetus* 'arguabl[y] . . . the richest in thought of all the Platonic dialogues'. The dialogue opens the dramatic series surrounding Socrates' trial and death: *Tht.*, *Euthyphro*, *Sophist*, *Statesman*, *Apology*, *Crito* and *Phaedo*, by raising the fundamental question, 'What is knowledge?' Two great mathematicians, Theodorus and the young Theaetetus are Socrates' interlocutors. A frame dialogue set outside Athens, like the *Phd.*, has Euclides and Terpsion probably in 369 BCE recalling Socrates' death and linking it with the impending death of Theaetetus. Far from corrupting the youth Theaetetus, Socrates seems to have contributed to his intellectual success and bravery in battle.

The dialogue seeks knowledge of knowledge. The elderly Theodorus resisting philosophical conversation, the young Theaetetus becomes the main interlocutor led through four progressively stronger accounts of knowledge. Theaetetus first names what Theodorus teaches and the productive arts as knowledge (*Tht.* 146c–d), which only offers instances of knowledge rather than disclosing *what* knowledge is. Theaetetus is provoked to recall earlier mathematical insight that may be pertinent (147c–8b). He had divided the integers into 'square numbers', for example, 4, 9, 16 ($=n^2$), with the other integers being 'oblong numbers'. When squares are made with areas equal to 'oblong numbers', their sides will be incommensurable with the sides of the squares of 'square number' area, but the areas of the squares are all commensurable. Yet, Theaetetus cannot fashion an account of knowledge like this mathematical work, so Socrates encourages him by professing to practise midwifery that detects youths fertile with conceptions, and delivers and tests their conceptions (148e–51d).

Theaetetus then suggests that knowledge is some sort of perception (*aisthêsis*, 151e), as he has 'perceived' the two sorts of numbers project into squares. Since Theaetetus is vague about 'perception', Socrates delivers the conception by identifying as its 'parents' Protagorean relativism and Heraclitean flux. These parents are necessary and sufficient conditions for the conception to be viable. Extreme individual relativism based on removing any unity and being leaves only relational becoming so that whatever appears to any sentient being seems 'knowledge'.

Much of the dialogue is Socrates delivering the conception by linking it with its 'parents' and countering each part of the conception (151e–86e). Thus he introduces and undermines some classic arguments for relativism and scepticism, such as whether we are now dreaming (158b–d), nothing universal exists except names (157a–c) and only shifting aggregates, rather than wholes, truly are (159c). Protagoras is imagined back to life in the dialogue. Forced to defend his own claim to wisdom if each sentient being measures what is true for it, he argues that the wise change perceivers so that they have better, though not truer, perceptions (166d–7d). But this Protagorean wisdom presupposes superior insight into the future, so not *all* appearances are true (177c–9b). Protagorean relativism also refutes itself by conceding that those disagreeing with him are correct, for they think themselves absolutely rather than just relatively correct (170a–1c). Heraclitean flux makes things change so much that no statement such as 'knowledge is perception' has stable truth (181b–3b). And Theaetetus' proposal that perception is knowledge fails since each sense perceives only its own sort of object, yet we make judgements about objects of all the senses (184b–6e). Either perception can make no judgements at all and does not get to any truth, or perception cannot get to the essence of things to know what they really are. In what he calls a 'digression' at the dialogue's centre, Socrates contrasts the hustling Protagorean courtroom orator with a philosopher, holding it wisdom to escape this realm and to liken himself to god (176a–d).

The account of knowledge as perception rejected, Theaetetus suggests that knowledge is true judgement (187b). But unless there can be *false* judgement, *true* judgement adds nothing to judgement. Several efforts to account for false judgement explore the obstacle of non being, define thought as silent internal conversation, depict the soul as wax receiving impressions (191c–5b), and introduce levels of actuality and potentiality in the aviary image (196c–200a). Inadequately accounting for false judgement, which might be ignorance, they can reject true judgement as knowledge since judges in court might be persuaded to make the right decision, but do not know as a firsthand witness (201a–c).

Theaetetus proposes that knowledge could be true judgement supported by an account (201c–d). Socrates explicates this 'dream theory' (201–6) to mean that 'simple' elements permit no further account but the 'syllables' they compose have an account through these elements. This applies to mathematicians who make demonstrations from unaccountable hypotheses and other sorts of positions based on beliefs taken to be self-justifying or self-evident. Since Theaetetus is dissatisfied with unaccountable elements, Socrates works out three further accounts of 'account' that might convert true judgement into knowledge. Account giving might be: (a) vocalizing the true judgement (206d–e), (b) going through all the elements of the whole

about which the true judgement is made (206e–8b) or (c) saying what is uniquely different about what we would know (208c–10a). But none of this helps. Anyone can vocalize a true judgement, which does nothing to supplement it. Going through all the elements still does not guarantee knowledge since a child may spell his entire name but be unable to spell the same syllables within other names. And adding the difference to a true judgement that must already have the difference to be about just this thing adds nothing.

They are left with no account of knowledge. But if the four accounts they have considered are all the really likely accounts of knowledge, and the accounts of account offered are all the plausible accounts of account or justification, then this dialogue has engaged in comprehensive reflection. Moreover, the four accounts of account at the end can be seen in one-to-one correspondence to the four major accounts of knowledge through the dialogue. Thus, they may manage to overcome the incommensurability of true judgement with knowledge since the last part's reconsideration of all that preceded is 'squaring' that raises true judgement to commensurability with knowledge, as suggested by Theaetetus' mathematical work. Merely *adding* an account as additional judgement does little, but reviewing perspicuously all they have gone through they get beyond true judgement. This interpretation has the dialogue enacting just what it is about, human understanding.

Other prominent interpretations seek to explain the dialogue's apparent failure. Some suppose we should see that without introducing the forms knowledge could not be understood (e.g. Cornford 1935). But though unchanging objects are needed for knowledge, this hardly tells what knowledge is. Burnyeat

97

(1990) suggests that Plato leaves the reader to pull the dialogue together, which is compatible with the large interpretation offered, though the offered interpretation already pulls it together. Sedley (2004) supposes that the *Tht.* has the late Plato reutilizing Socrates to show how Plato came to be dissatisfied with some of his earlier positions, and hence Socrates serves as midwife for Plato's later thought. This version of chronological interpretation has the attraction or limitation of all such interpretation.

THEAGES

Mark Joyal

The dialogue's setting is the Stoa of Zeus in the Athenian agora. Demodocus and his son Theages have travelled to Athens from their rural home in order to consult Socrates. Inspired by reports from his friends, Theages wants his father to put him under the tutelage of a sophist who will make him 'wise' (*sophos*; *Theages* 121cd). Through probing from Socrates, Theages is driven to acknowledge reluctantly that the 'wisdom' he seeks is really the desire to become an absolute ruler. An inquiry follows whose goal is to identify the ideal teacher for Theages. Several possibilities are discarded; both Theages and Demodocus then turn to Socrates himself to assume this role. Socrates protests, alleging his near complete lack of knowledge (apart from expertise in matters of *eros*, 'love' or 'desire'; *Thg.* 128b). Theages, however, thinks that his educational progress depends upon Socrates' willingness to associate with him. Not so, says Socrates; the progress which his 'associates' make results from the willingness and participation of his 'divine sign' (*to daimonion sêmeion*; 128d). Socrates

tells a series of stories to illustrate the behaviour of his sign. These do nothing to dissuade Theages, who even proposes that he will placate the divine sign with prayers and sacrifices, if he must.

Most discussion about this work has focused on its authenticity, its depiction of Socrates' divine sign and its purpose. The three issues are interrelated, since judgements about authenticity have usually depended in large measure on the character of the divine sign (q.v. *daimon*) as it appears in *Thg.*, and many interpreters have seen the dialogue's purpose as tied to the prominent role that the sign seems to play (more space is devoted to it in *Thg.* than in any other Platonic dialogue). The divine sign differs here from its presentation in other dialogues whose authenticity is generally unchallenged. Above all, in *Thg.* it is given a wider and more active role than the purely personal and inhibitory character that it displays elsewhere in the Platonic Corpus: the sign occurs to Socrates not only when he should desist from an act on which he has embarked but also when a companion of his should desist; it provides Socrates with the ability to foretell the outcome of future events; and it is said here to participate in the improvement which Socrates' companions make through their association with him. This portrayal raises doubts about authenticity not simply because of its differences from representations of the divine sign in indisputably genuine Plato, but also because it anticipates emphases that we find in much later conceptions of the sign (Joyal 1995).

There is no unanimity about the authenticity of *Thg.*, but the majority opinion is against its Platonic authorship. There is likewise no consensus on the dialogue's date of composition (q.v. compositional chronology): proposals range from the early part of Plato's literary career to the half-century or so after his death.

The dialogue's value, however, is not necessarily diminished by doubts about authorship: even if the dialogue is un-Platonic, it is important as a relatively early expression of the intellectual preoccupations of an otherwise unknown Socratic writer. Accordingly, several interpreters in recent years have made sincere attempts to understand the dialogue on its own terms (e.g. Bailly 2004; Döring 2004; Joyal 2000). There now seems widespread agreement that the theme and purpose of *Thg.* are not simply to describe one author's understanding of the nature of Socrates' divine sign. Instead, the sign is viewed as an important element in Socratic 'association' (*sunousia*) (e.g. Joyal 2000:48–9, 59–61; Tarrant 2005). In *Thg.* the nature of this remarkable association serves to distinguish Socrates from other candidates for the role of Theages' teacher (e.g. Friedländer 1965).

TIMAEUS AND CRITIAS

Thomas Johansen

The *Timaeus* and the *Critias* are the first two parts of an unfinished trilogy, presented to Socrates as a single project (*Ti.* 17b) in return for his account of an ideal state much like that of *Republic*. The speeches are thematically linked: Timaeus' cosmology (q.v.) shows how goodness is represented in nature (q.v.), while Critias' Atlantis story further shows how citizens of Socrates' ideally just city will conquer evil, given the support of Timaeus' natural order. The *Ti.-Criti.* as a whole presents a world in which goodness prevails, from the planets down to the human sphere.

Timaeus argues that the cosmos is a likeness of the eternal forms (q.v.) and that an account of such a likeness can at best be 'likely' (29b–d) (Burnyeat 2005). The reason why there can be no certainty about the likeness seems to be that its features are not the same as those of the original but only analogous. So, for example, the cosmos is spherical as an analogue to the completeness of the shapeless forms (Johansen 2004:49–60).

Timaeus characterizes his account alternately as *logos* and *muthos*, 'reason' and 'myth' (q.v.). It may be that the qualifier 'likely' cancels out the customary *logos/muthos* contrast (Vlastos 1965). Alternatively '*muthos*' may serve to downgrade the account available to humans compared to one obtainable by a god (Johansen 2004:62–4).

Cosmology relies on two causal principles (Johansen 2008): the desire of a divine craftsman to make the world as good as possible and 'necessity', that is, necessary conjunctions or consequences of properties that are, as it were, brute facts of nature. So, for example, fire is necessarily mobile because it is composed of small pyramid-shaped parts (*Ti.* 55e–6a). Necessity can be employed to further the good, as a 'co-cause' (*sunaition*, 46d–e), but intelligence cannot alter the way necessity itself works.

'Necessity' relates to the nature and motions of the simple bodies and these depend on the so-called receptacle. The simple bodies appear fleetingly in the receptacle without any substantiality. It is unclear whether Timaeus is characterizing bodies as they are now (cf. *Theaetetus* 156a–7c) or as they were before the cosmos. According to whether it enters into composition of bodies, the receptacle may be seen as matter, the stuff bodies are made of or as that 'in which' bodies occur, that is, the place or space (*chôra*) that bodies occupy.

The cosmos is an ensouled body, composed according to geometrical principles that ensure order and unity. The soul is made from a mixture of the divisible and indivisible kinds of being, sameness and difference. The composition explains both (cf. Aristotle, *De Anima* 406b28–31) the soul's ability to move (57d) and its ability to make judgements about sameness and difference, on the principle that 'like is known by like'. The mixture is structured according to the harmonic scale, and then divided and bent to form seven circular hoops, which move the seven planets according to different ratios.

To fit the world-soul its body is spherical. Its constituents, earth, water, fire and air, are proportionately ordered in the same way as the soul (Cornford 1937:49). Each body is composed of one of two sorts of triangle, which combine according to geometrical principles (53c–7c) (Vlastos 1965:401–19) and allow the bodies (with the exception of earth) to change into each other (54b–c).

The human, immortal soul (q.v.) is created in the same way as the world-soul, albeit with less pure ingredients. When embodied, the soul is disturbed by irrational desires. But because the soul is in origin rational, it can, through the study of the cosmos, assimilate its motions to those of the world-soul, thereby again becoming orderly and temperate (47b–c, 90c–d) (Sedley 2000).

To help us in this task, god's assistants in creating human nature, the 'lesser gods', have divided the soul into the three parts familiar from *R.*, the rational, the spirited and the appetitive. This arrangement allows for each part to perform its proper function without interference from the others. The human body has three distinct regions, head, heart and lower abdomen, which service the three parts of the soul. The entire human organism is thus designed for the promotion of our good while embodied (Johansen 2004:142–52). Those men who fail will be reincarnated as women or as the various lower animals, according to their degree of irrationality. Thereby the cosmos becomes complete with all the kinds of living beings.

Criti. sets out to show how ancient Athenians, with Timaeus' nature and Socrates' education, prevailed against Atlantis. Where Athens is a projection of the intellectually spirited, Atlantis is from its inception appetitive. So, the virgin Athena founded Athens to produce philosophy-warriors like herself (*Criti.* 24c–d), while Poseidon instituted Atlantis to protect his mistress. While originally virtuous, its luxurious, variegated designs and its location by the sea (cf. *Laws* 705d) make Atlantis susceptible to vice. Its dynastic constitution recalls Asian tyrannies, while also resembling fifth-century democratic Athens (Vidal-Naquet 1981), not a contradiction given that both tyranny and democracy, according to *R.* 571a ff., are political manifestations of the appetitive soul. If Atlantis looks like a utopia, it is an *appetitive* utopia, and so, in Plato's eyes, a *dystopia*. While various historical events (such as the volcanic eruption at Thera) may have inspired Plato (Gill 1979:viii–xii), Atlantis was clearly conceived by him as a foil for his ideal city.

Criti. ends with Zeus about to announce his punishment of Atlantis. One theory is that the work was left incomplete to reflect Critias' limited abilities or devious character (Welliver 1977:44). However, Critias (*Ti.* 26a–b) had already delivered his speech to his companions the same morning. Another suggestion is that Plato abandoned the project in favour of the *Lg*, whose third book tells of the near destruction of civilization by a deluge and its subsequent history down to Plato's day. This further suggests that Hermocrates might have spoken about the different kinds of constitution now also contained in the *Lg*. (Cornford 1937:7–8; Gill 1979).

3

IMPORTANT FEATURES
OF THE DIALOGUES

ANONYMITY

Gerald A. Press

Paradoxically, Plato is silent and almost completely absent in the dialogues. This Platonic anonymity constitutes a problem for those who read the dialogues expecting to learn Plato's philosophical doctrines. The most common solution is the assumption that Socrates and other characters are Plato's mouthpieces, that the views and arguments they put forward are Plato's own. But the assumption contradicts the evident character of the dialogues and Plato's many strategies of self-concealment. Although anonymity is often ignored, in recent decades scholars have proposed various alternatives that involve rethinking Plato's approach to philosophy (q.v.) and philosophic writing (cf. Press 2000).

Plato 'never speaks in his own name' (Edelstein 1962:1). There is no character called Plato who speaks in any dialogue. Plato is named only twice: as present, offering money for Socrates' penalty, in the *Apology* (38b) and as absent, 'sick', the day Socrates died (*Phaedo* 59b). Although we assume that Plato wrote all of the authentic dialogues (q.v. Corpus; Dubia and Spuria), in some dialogues he takes pains to render the narrative

less reliable (*Symposium, Parmenides*) or to conceal himself as their author (*Prm.; Phd.; Theaetetus*). The *Letters* purport to be Plato speaking in his own name. However, all but the seventh are widely considered inauthentic and the seventh, whatever authority it may have, includes the puzzling statement 'There is no writing of mine about these matters [*viz.*, "with which I am concerned"], nor will there ever be one. For this knowledge is not something that can be put into words like other sciences' (*Ep.* 7 341c).

We expect philosophers to tell us what they think and we want to know what Plato thinks. He is one of the most influential philosophers, inspiration of various 'Platonisms' (q.v. Academy) and Neoplatonism (q.v.). It seems natural to suppose that Plato had doctrines or definite views that he propounded in his writings. But this reflects a modern historical interest (Tigerstedt 1977). Ancient readers were often more interested in the truth and wisdom to be found in the dialogues than in what exactly Plato's views were (Tarrant 2000). Plato's authorial absence and silence, his denial that he ever did or will write his views down and Socrates' recurrent devaluation of writing (especially *Phaedrus* 275d–8b; cp. *Protagoras* 347c–8a) suggest it may be futile to read the dialogues seeking explicit statement of Plato's philosophical doctrines in any strong sense of that term.

The most common response to this, already recognized by Diogenes Laertius (3.52), has been to assume that Socrates and other characters are Platonic mouthpieces (Kraut 1992a:25–6). Thus, in most dialogues what Socrates says represents Plato's own views, whereas elsewhere the Eleatic visitor (*Sophist*, *Politicus*), Timaeus (*Timaeus*) and the Athenian visitor (*Laws*) have this role. The assumption seems natural, since most major philosophic texts try to prove theories directly. It is convenient, since it provides an easy way to get what readers want: an authoritative statement of Plato's views. And, after 2,000 years it has become traditional.

But it is incompatible with the dialogues' obvious character as literary fiction, rather than didactic treatises or discursive history (q.v.). It also requires explanation why Plato would switch mouthpieces from a dominant one, Socrates, to an unnamed Eleatic, a character named Parmenides, and an Athenian Stranger, whose views and practises do not seem consistent with those of the Socrates of the Socratic dialogues. Moreover, indications in the dialogues and other ancient testimonies suggest that Plato was tireless in his writing and editing habits (q.v. Compositional chronology). He took care to conceal his own views and to avoid presenting himself as an authority, as his character Socrates (q.v.) usually avoids it in the dialogues.

Instead of taking Platonic anonymity and the literary character of the dialogues as problems to be solved, many recent interpreters have taken them as guidance to different ways of understanding what Plato is trying to do and how the dialogues work. Anonymity along with Plato's use of myth (q.v.), irony (q.v.), characters (q.v.), play (q.v.) and the writing (q.v.) of dramas rather

than treatises indicates that his model of the practise of philosophy is unlike the doctrinal model of philosophic writing.

Several twentieth-century pragmatists saw the dialogues as dramatizations of the life of reason rather than assertions of philosophic doctrine (Woodbridge 1929:54 followed by Randall 1970 and Tejera 1984). This approach troubles some interpreters because it seems to reduce philosophy to 'mere' literature. Slightly more dogmatically, the dialogues have been seen as 'presentations of a possible philosophical standpoint . . . which [Plato] acknowledges conditionally' (Merlan 1947:415) and their purpose as to induce in us a 'sense of being at a loss' (ibid 430). Plato's refusal to dogmatize may look like scepticism, as it did to the 'New Academy' of Arcesilaus (q.v., Academy, history of), but this seems inconsistent with the fervour of Plato's Socrates about learning the truth. On more mitigated approaches, Plato is not a sceptic, but merely withholds the certitude desired by dogmatists, as for Philo of Larisa. Thus Stefanini (1949, v.1:xxxii–xxxiv) suggested that Plato's view is a 'constructive skepsis'. A quite different response to Platonic anonymity is taking the dialogues to withhold Plato's true doctrines, because those were made available only orally and esoterically (q.v., Esoterism, Tübingen approach).

These proposals assume that propounding doctrine is somehow the essence of the philosopher's task. But Plato may have had a quite different, non-dogmatic view of philosophy. It has been argued that Plato saw himself as a moral guide, in the manner of the pre-Platonic poets (cf. Edelstein 1962:9). More specifically, the dialogues can be viewed as working in a way essentially different from that of a treatise, as something 'pedagogical' rather than doctrinal (Gordon 1999; Sayre 1995a; Thesleff

1999), providing the reader guided acquisition of the habit of philosophic thought rather than specific doctrines. The dialogues' 'double open-endedness' – both conclusions reached and their premises remain tentative – has been taken to show that for Plato as for Socrates, philosophy consists in oral dialectic (Nails 1995:218–31), which shifts intellectual responsibility to the audience or reader. The dialogues can also be viewed as generating enactments of Plato's principles, orientations and vision of reality within the reader's mind rather than seeking to gain rational adherence to propositional truths (Press 2007).

ARGUMENT (see Logos (Ch. 4))

CHARACTER (FEATURE)

Ruby Blondell

Plato's dialogues present us with dozens of characters, most of them (loosely) based on historical figures (for a full prosopography, see Nails 2002). They range in social status from the nameless slave who learns geometry in the *Meno* to members of the gilded aristocracy; but most are drawn from the educated male elite of Athens and other Greek cities. Their social class is often reinforced by the dramatic settings, which typically represent such cultural institutions as gymnasia, festivals, the court and prison system, sophistic education and the symposium. On the margins of the dialogues, as of Athenian public life, can be found female entertainers, craftsmen, children, slaves and non-Greek-speakers, all of whom are mentioned frequently in passing. Married women and citizen girls are not represented, with the notable exception

of Xanthippe, Socrates' wife, who laments his imminent death in *Phaedo* and is thereupon escorted away at her husband's request (*Phd.* 60a). The only female characters who speak at length are a courtesan (Aspasia) and a foreign priestess (Diotima), both of whom are licensed to associate with men by their special status and neither of whom is directly dramatized.

Characters other than Socrates (q.v.) fall loosely into three types, marked by conventional wisdom, youthful enthusiasm and professional expertise respectively. Members of each type are individuated along a number of axes, whether social, characterological or intellectual. They vary, for example, in age (from adolescents to very old men), the size of their speaking role (from the minimally scripted slave of Meno to the voluble Athenian Stranger), their activity or passivity (from silent bystanders to the aggressive Thrasymachus), the specificity with which they are characterized (from nameless ciphers to the colourful Alcibiades), their philosophical acumen (from the talented Theaetetus to the manipulable Hippias) and the degree of sympathy with which they are presented (from the endearing Lysis to the obnoxious Callicles). Employment of such variables serves to locate each character somewhere on a scale between the generic and the uniquely particularized. Yet, some of Plato's most memorable characters embody generic and individual identities simultaneously. Hippias, for example, is a 'representative' sophist, but at the same time retains a distinctive identity easily distinguishable from Thrasymachus, Gorgias or Protagoras. This paradox is most fully embodied in Socrates, who is simultaneously the ideal type of the philosopher and a detailed, concretely imagined and richly embodied idiosyncratic personality.

In the vast majority of the dialogues Socrates plays a privileged role. The function of other characters tends to vary along with his persona and methods. When he employs the elenchus (q.v.), Socrates examines not just arguments but individual people in ways that cast doubt not merely on their beliefs but also on the personality, way of life and social roles that condition those beliefs and are in turn conditioned by them. This method is thus intrinsically ad hominem in a peculiarly personal way. If its force is to be fully appreciated, the interlocutor's particular character – those aspects of his life and personality that make him respond as he does – must be made present to the reader. Most of these respondents are either more or less promising young men – usually Athenians of good family – or mature claimants to wisdom, especially professionals, patriarchs and representatives of traditional education. Sophists are prominent for various reasons, including their role as educators, their public availability, their agonism (which both invites and legitimates verbal confrontation), their role as professional intellectuals and the importance of their cultural influence. In each case Plato uses 'literary' characterization in conjunction with Socratic questioning to bring out the limitations of the interlocutor's point of view, often showing how this is rooted in his particular social status and personality. The respondents' various reactions bring out the strengths and weaknesses of Socrates' elenctic method as an educational tool. Some seem inspired to embrace philosophy but others grow angry, give up or fall silent, without any sign of changing the way they live.

In other dialogues Socrates plays a more constructive role, airing substantive and challenging ideas, often at considerable length. This Socrates uses his interlocutors largely as a sounding board for his own ideas. Their primary (though not exclusive) responsibility is to understand what they are told and help to develop it constructively. This Socrates needs interlocutors who are at once more sympathetic and more open-minded than his elenctic victims tend to be. This can be seen clearly in the transition from bk 1 of the *Republic* (which is elenctic in style) to bks 2–10. In the latter books the respondents are Glaucon and Adeimantus (Plato's brothers), who exemplify the kind of respondent Socrates needs if he is to move towards a more positive kind of dialectic: they are intelligent, cooperative, good-humoured, encouraging, committed to Socratic values and open to new ideas. Their sympathetic support enables him to run the risk of exposure entailed by positive discourse.

To many readers these interlocutors seem bland and generic compared to the vivid characters of bk 1. This makes them less entertaining, but gives them a more universal mimêtic function (q.v. Character as a Topic). Moreover the traits in Plato's brothers that are linked to their dialectical promise overlap substantially with the qualifications for guardianship, and ultimately for rulership, in Callipolis. This exemplifies Plato's tendency to explore issues of character on dramatic and discursive levels simultaneously: ideas about character aired within the dialogues are explored obliquely through the portrayal and interactions of the very characters who are engaged in the discussion (see further, Blondell 2002).

In several late dialogues Socrates' role is much smaller or even non-existent: he is replaced by dominant speakers with few individual character traits beyond an ability to hold forth authoritatively at considerable length. The interlocutors are also minimally characterized, and have little to do besides agree with the dominant speaker. As a result, the characterization in many of these dialogues often seems dull and lifeless compared to the Socratic works. This shift is often seen in terms of a Platonic literary decline; but it represents, rather, a different set of 'literary' choices, including a move towards the generic that reflects ancient ideals about both literary and ethical character (q.v. Character as a Topic).

DRAMA

Andrea Nightingale

Plato drew on the genres of tragedy and comedy in creating his dialogues. At times, Plato offers pure 'dramatic representation' (*mimêsis*, q.v.) in his dialogues; in other cases, he has a narrator describe the speech and action in the dialogue, thus using the combination of 'simple narration' (*haplê diêgêsis*) and 'dramatic representation' (*mimêsis*), categories that are outlined in *Republic* bk 3. In both cases, however, we find dramatic exchanges over issues central to human life. Of course, Plato attacks comedy and tragedy in *R.* bk 10 for fostering emotions at the expense of reason; he certainly did not want his own dialogues to evoke the audience responses that the Greek dramatists did. Even in the seemingly tragic case of Socrates' execution in the *Phaedo*, Plato portrays Socrates as someone to be admired rather than pitied. Socrates is not a tragic figure but a heroic martyr.

Plato uses both comic and tragic discourses in his dialogues in part as a philosophic attack on Greek drama (q.v. Poetry in Chapter 4). But Plato did not simply overturn comedy and tragedy: his own dramatic dialogues reveal Plato's debt to these genres. In the *Symposium*, for example, the comic poet Aristophanes delivers a very humorous speech on love. And, in the same dialogue, Alcibiades' claim that he chose 'the crowd' over Socrates – political power over philosophy – has a tragic resonance. Alcibiades had convinced the Athenians to send the disastrous expedition to Sicily and he himself turned traitor to Athens after being recalled to stand trial for profaning the Eleusinian Mysteries. Indeed, the very presence of Alcibiades in the *Smp.* reminds us that the Athenians suspected Socrates of teaching Alcibiades and other Athenian aristocrats the wrong political views – a suspicion that led, in part, to Socrates' trial and execution. In the *Smp.*, then, we find a blend of comedy and tragedy. As Socrates says at the end of the dialogue, the 'skilled' playwright should be able to write both tragedies and comedies (in ancient Greece, tragedians only wrote tragedies and satyr plays and comedians only wrote comedies). Plato implicitly identifies himself as the one man who can write in both genres. In short, Plato created an entirely new kind of genre – a dialogue that was at once philosophical and dramatic. He thus creates urgent situations in which characters' hopes rise and fall and which convince readers that the issues need to be resolved.

In the *Laws*, Plato distinguishes between genres concerned with the 'ridiculous' (*geloios*) and the 'serious' (*spoudaios*; q.v., Play and seriousness). He places Homer, Hesiod and the tragedians in the latter category (indeed, Plato often conflates epic with tragedy) and iambic poetry and comedy in the latter. But what is truly 'ridiculous' and 'serious'? In *R.* bk 10, Plato banishes the seemingly 'serious' tragedy from the ideal city: tragedy wrongly portrays 'good' men becoming worse men (ethically and emotionally) when they confront pain or loss. The philosophic individual, in contrast, remains good and virtuous even when he is harmed or in pain. Yet, Plato did not simply dismiss the genre of tragedy. In *Lg.* bk 7, the Athenian contrasts the 'so-called serious' creations of the tragedians with the 'most beautiful and finest tragedy' that he and his interlocutors have produced in their construction of the city of Magnesia with its unique law code. In the *Lg.*, then, Plato denies that tragedy is truly 'serious' and confers upon his own creation the title of 'serious tragedy'. Clearly, this new mode of 'tragedy' is 'serious' and deals with 'noble' characters, but does not feature unhappy individuals. Indeed, the educational system in Magnesia is designed to train the citizens to be 'truly virtuous' and to resist emotions such as fear and lamentation. Plato's new 'drama' borrows from tragedy its presentation of serious, noble and ethical characters while abandoning the tragic plot line.

In *R.* bk 10, Plato also lashes out against low or 'ridiculous' poetry; here, he clearly targets the genre of comedy. Yet, Plato himself chose to defend a number of ideas that find direct parallels in Aristophanes. For example, Aristophanes' *Ecclesiazusae* set forth an upside down world in which women have the capacity to rule and the citizens jointly share property and even their children. In *R.* bk 5, Plato adopts these very ideas for his own ideal city: women can serve as 'philosophic' rulers, and the ruling class will raise their children in common and own no private property. While borrowing these ideas from Aristophanes, Plato nonetheless attacks the comedian for presenting these ideas as 'ridiculous:' in fact, he says, we should take these ideas seriously. Here and elsewhere, Plato makes it quite clear that he considers comedy a force to be reckoned with in the Athenian democracy. Indeed, in the *Apology*, Socrates suggests that a comedian turned the people against him and thus prepared the ground for his eventual trial (he refers here to Aristophanes' *Clouds*, which offered a very negative portrayal of Socrates).

Plato also uses powerful and 'dramatic' myths that take the form of mini narratives within the dialogues. These myths reflect scenes from the genres of epic, tragedy and comedy. In the allegory of the cave (q.v.), for example, we find a scene from the 'underworld': Plato in fact compares the world we live in here on earth to Hades. Clearly, Homer's depiction of Hades in the *Odyssey* was used by many tragic and comic playwrights. But Plato transforms the traditional literary notions of the underworld by comparing the 'shades' in Hades to people on earth. In the *Statesman*, moreover, Plato creates a myth where people live in a world which moves backwards in time: in the 'Age of Cronos', people are born old and get younger and younger until they die as infants. This myth borrows from Hesiod's myth of the Golden Age, yet it suggests that this age was not at all 'golden'. The people living in the 'Age of Cronos' cannot practise philosophy or become virtuous because they are getting younger all the time. Of course, Plato's myths are embedded in a larger dialogue that deals with philosophic issues. These 'literary' creations take on philosophic meaning when interpreted in the context of the dialogue as a whole.

In sum, Plato borrowed from literary genres even as he attacked their traditional use. In order to place his mode of philosophy on the map, Plato had to reckon with the public and authoritative voices in democratic Athens: epic, tragedy and comedy. In using (and abusing) these genres, Plato offered a new 'philosophic voice' in fourth-century Greek culture.

HISTORY

Gerald A. Press

First-time readers often take the dialogues to be historical; but Plato is not a history writer and the dialogues are not history. With caution they may sometimes provide evidence about historical persons or events, but, for understanding Plato, the important point is that he *uses* historical material for philosophic purposes.

Some older scholars (e.g. Burnet 1920) took the dialogues as historical accounts. Gregory Vlastos influentially argued that the historical Socrates' philosophy could be extracted from a group of dialogues he considered 'early' and 'Socratic' (q.v. Vlastosian approaches). However, scholars now generally agree that the dialogues are not historical records of actual Socratic conversations. Many take place before Plato was born or was old enough to have heard them, and for the rest, no plausible account explains how Plato could have learned such detailed conversations (Sayre 1995a:1–4). In context, they are part of an ancient literary-philosophic genre called 'Socratic accounts' (*Sokratikoi logoi*) that was also practised, less famously and influentially, by Antisthenes, Aeschines, Xenophon and others (q.v. Socratics).

Although Plato's characters sometimes refer to events that have happened in the recent or more distant past (e.g. a specific battle is mentioned *Charmides* 153a), he does not write *about* that event, attempting to ascertain exactly what happened or why. Instead, he uses it to construct a plausible but fictional representation of the aristocratic intellectual world of the last half of the fifth century BCE and, in this case, to give a political context to the discussion of a politically charged excellence.

The 'illusion of historicity' (Sayre 1995a:2) derives from the dialogues' independently known (often important or influential) characters (q.v.), real world settings and references to specific known events. They contain so many such characters and details and are so internally consistent that generations of students and scholars have conflated Plato's Socrates (q.v. Socrates character) with the historical Socrates (q.v.). Even though Plato's Socrates is a literary construct (however much he may have been based on the Socrates Plato knew), he has dominated our understanding of the historical Socrates until recently, a richly ironic measure of Plato's success as a writer.

When a reference in a Platonic dialogue coheres with external evidence, it may be used for historical purposes (e.g. Taylor 1976:78–9), but this requires caution for Plato is not an historian and he regularly redeploys historical material for philosophic purposes. On the other hand, the mention of established historical events is used to give dialogues what modern scholars call 'dramatic dates' which enable us to read the dialogues in relation to Athens' political and cultural history as well as in relation to the philosophic biography of the character Socrates (Zuckert 2009).

Nearly all Plato's characters – their names, families, interests and deeds – are modelled on historical figures (Nails 2002:xxxvii). Fluidity in the representation of historical characters was common among ancient writers and Plato exploits the resulting 'tension between abstraction and embodiment' (Blondell 2002:34–6). By being precisely who they are, they more powerfully symbolize Platonic character assessments and philosophic points. Socrates discusses piety (q.v.) with a religious zealot in the *Euthyphro*, temperance with notoriously intemperate oligarchs in the *Chrm.*, and rhetoric with sophists and orators in the *Gorgias*. Settings also add vividness, depth and complexity. The *Apology* is in the courtroom where Socrates gives his defence speech. The *Phaedo* is in his prison cell, culminating in his death. The *Republic*'s discussion of justice is set in the home of Polemarchus, who was later put to death and his family property unjustly confiscated by the oligarchs.

Plato's frequent and complex use of historical characters, settings, dates and events heightens the reader's intellectual interest, intensifies the thematic focus and elicits the close attention to arguments and ideas in which all philosophic teaching and learning consist. It also subtly evokes the reader's emotional and imaginative involvement, generating a commitment to orientations and ideas expressed that transcends the intellectual persuasiveness of the arguments alone. As in great fiction, paradoxically, the specificity and plausibility of Plato's dramas enhances the universality of their meaning and the effect on readers of their philosophic message.

HUMOUR

David Roochnik

Despite their profound seriousness, the Platonic dialogues are often quite funny. To illustrate, consider the following scenes: (a) A group of older men are sitting on a bench, when a half naked, gorgeous young thing approaches. In their eagerness to make room for the young beauty the men start pushing each other, and the two on the end fall off the bench. (b) A philosopher is arguing against a position held by a distinguished rival, one who is now dead. In order to represent his

opponent's views fairly, the philosopher summons him from the earth. The dead man emerges, but only up to his neck. The conversation continues in the presence of his protruding head. (c) A philosopher proposes a theory that so shocks his interlocutor that he responds as follows: imagine, he says, that the men hearing your theory become so enraged that they rip off their clothes, grab whatever weapon is available and attack you. Unperturbed, the philosopher begins explaining his ideas to the naked men attacking him. (d) Two dim-witted lawyers are practicing their skill in cross-examination on a younger man. Like tag team wrestlers they take turns jumping into the ring to pelt their hapless opponent with arguments like this: since you have a dog, the dog is yours. Your dog is the mother of some puppies. Since the dog is both yours and a mother, you must be a son-of-a-bitch.

These scenes were all conjured by Plato. The first paraphrases the opening of the *Charmides* (153c), when young Charmides enters the room. The second comes from the *Theaetetus* (171d), when Socrates summons the dead Protagoras. The third is Glaucon's response to Socrates' announcement in the *Republic* (473e–4a) of the philosopher-kings. The fourth depicts, with some liberties, the sophists Euthydemus and Dionysodorus in the *Euthydemus* (298d–e). What is striking is that all four are situated in a serious philosophical context. (a) The *Chrm.* scene triggers Socrates' remarkable discussion of 'moderation' (*sôphrosunê*). (b) In the *Tht.* Socrates is refuting Protagorean relativism. (c) The naked men imagined by Glaucon force Socrates to discuss the nature of philosophy in the central books of *R*. Note that Socrates says, 'we must distinguish for them [the naked attackers] whom we mean when we venture to say that philosophers must rule' (*R.* 474b4–6).

(d) With their absurdly fallacious arguments the sophistic brothers unwittingly raise the issue of the nature of predication. In sum, Plato both takes these issues seriously – most important, he provides a great deal of suggestive material for the serious reader to pursue and develop on their own – and leavens their treatment with stunning humour.

Plato's humour is not designed simply to provide a respite from the toil of conceptual labour. Instead, it is itself serious. For Platonic humour suggests that every human pursuit, even philosophy, is partial, precarious, of limited value and therefore deserving of criticism. As the Athenian Stranger puts it in the *Laws*, 'human affairs are not worthy of great seriousness'. We are neither wise nor divine and so none of our 'affairs' can ever be entirely flawless. Nonetheless, he continues, 'we must be serious about them' (*Lg.* 803b). We are constrained by our own humanity to take seriously what is not truly serious, namely, ourselves. As a result, we are often ridiculous.

From the above one might infer that Platonic philosophy is itself comedic. But this would be a mistake. Plato explains why in the *Symposium,* when he has Aristophanes tell the following story. Briefly put: we were once spherical double beings with eight limbs, two faces, two sets of genitals and so on. We were terribly arrogant and attacked the gods. Zeus punished us by cutting us in half. As a result we spend the rest of our lives seeking our lost other half. This seeking is known as love. As Aristophanes puts it, 'love (*erôs*) is the name of the desire and pursuit of wholeness' (192a10–11).

The image of the spherical beings is funny. But what makes the story truly comedic is that, given the logic of Aristophanes' myth, love or human striving itself is doomed to fail. For him, the human impulse towards wholeness is paradigmatically expressed in sexual intercourse, an activity we take with 'great seriousness' (*megalês spoudês*:192c7). The problem is that the original wholeness to which this activity aspires was neither sexual – in the earliest stages of human history we procreated like cicadas by depositing egg and sperm on the earth (see 191c) – nor was it truly satisfying. Even when we were whole we felt the need to attack the gods. On this account, our love lives, our very selves, are largely ridiculous. As Aristophanes puts it, the soul of every lover wants something more than sex, but 'cannot say what it is' (192d1). Underneath its hilarious veneer, then, Aristophanes' story is grim. For it offers no prospect of human transcendence. The best we can do (through sex) is attempt to recover a wholeness that in fact is inaccessible. But Plato himself, despite being almost as funny as Aristophanes, does not share this view. For the *Smp.* moves beyond comedy, first to Agathon's praise of beauty (see 197b), and then to Diotima's description of the erotic ascent towards philosophy (see 210a–12b). In other words, comedy expresses only one side of the human condition. Despite their limitations and, perhaps, the ultimate impossibility of fully attaining wisdom, philosophers should nonetheless be serious in their quest to articulate the beautiful, the good and the true. But they should always consider the possibility that they might be making fools of themselves. The *Smp.* urges the reader to pursue this form of self-criticism by ending not with Socrates, but with Alcibiades, who condemns the philosopher for being too serious about ideas and thereby oblivious to the flesh and blood human beings who are standing before him (or lying beside him; see 216e and 219c.)

Plato's humour is expressed in a variety of guises. He is an inveterate punster.

(Note his play on *tokos*, both 'interest' and 'offspring' at *R.* 507a1.) He can conjure up wild images. (Consider *Phaedrus* 247e where the disembodied soul is said to munch on the eternal forms.) He can poke fun, sometimes painfully, at Socrates' opponents. (Note that he has Critias, famous as an excessively cruel tyrant, defend the definition of moderation as 'self-knowledge' at *Chrm.* 165d.) His Socrates is often wonderfully ironic (q.v. Irony) and he can be immensely playful in his writing (q.v. Play). Indeed, there are a vast number of examples of Platonic humour. All are serious and perhaps are finally designed to give voice to what Socrates in the *Philebus* calls 'the tragedy and comedy of life' (*Phlb.* 50b). (For more on Plato's use of humour, see Press 2007 and Rankin 1967.)

IRONY

Samuel Scolnicov

In Attic comedy, the *eirôn* is the character who gets the upper hand by subterfuge, feigning weakness. *Eironeia*, in this context, before Cicero gave it the milder, urbane tone it has today, had always had a negative connotation, which it still carries in Plato's use of the term. Socrates' most bitter opponents accuse him of *eironeia* (Callicles, *Gorgias*; Thrasymachus, *Republic* 1); or else the term refers to such accusations (*Apology* 38a1). Alcibiades, with a touch of bitterness, describes Socrates as speaking ironically (*Symposuim* 219a). At *Euthydemus* 302b3, in a nice ironical inversion, Socrates imputes irony to Dionysodorus. *Cratylus* 384a1 is a special case of Cratylus being accused by Hermogenes of being ironical, with a possible oblique reference to Socrates.

Irony is not deceit. Deceit depends on the speaker being believed. Irony always involves an element of double talk: the speaker says what he says and hopes, without saying as much, that his interlocutor (or a third party, present or presumed) will see the disparity between what is said and the context in which it is said.

Three types of irony should be distinguished. The first is simple irony, when the 'opposite of what is said is to be understood' (Cicero, *de or.* 2.67; Quintilian, *Inst. or.* 6.2.5, 9.2.44; cf. *Rhetoric Alex.*, 134a17). When Strepsiades describes his son as 'this excellent boy', he wants the audience to understand that the son is a good-for-nothing (Aristophanes, *Clouds* 8). In the second, 'complex' type of irony (attributed by Vlastos (1987) to Socrates), the hearer is left undecided between the two opposing poles. When Socrates says that he is aware of knowing nothing, great or small (*Ap.* 21b), it is unclear whether we are intended to believe him or not. Cf. *Hippias Minor* 376b–c: Can we trust the argument that the good man is he who does wrong of his own accord?

Typically, however, Socrates' irony is 'open' irony. We are made aware of what is not the case; but we are never told what the alternative is. Socrates uses the same words as his interlocutors, but with a different meaning. But the Platonic dialogue is not an exercise in disambiguation, as if there were two meanings of the term under consideration and Plato's task was to tell them apart. Before Plato's Socrates, 'learning' did not mean 'recollecting' (*Meno* 81d ff.) and courage was not equated with knowledge (*Laches*; *Protagoras* 360d).

For Plato, following Gorgias ('DK' f. 3), language is basically incommunicative, at least insofar as critical terms, such as 'justice' or 'good' are concerned. It is always context dependent (e.g. *Euthd.* 277e ff.). Thus, all speech is potentially ironical between speaker and hearer, and only the pragmatic context can tell irony from serious talk – or so one should hope. In advocating an ethics in which the good is identified with knowledge arising from one's own soul and in which ethical concepts can only be expressed by existing terms, with peculiar, at least arguably idiosyncratic meanings, Plato's Socrates can only use irony to try to arouse in his interlocutors the intuition of what is, for him, the real meaning of those terms. There is no manner in which that meaning can be straightforwardly conveyed by words. One has to see for oneself the truth, to be *reminded* of it, without actually being told (*Men.* 85b–e). Socrates hopes the disparity between the accepted meaning of the terms used and their epistemic or pragmatic context will disabuse his interlocutors of their unreflective opinions. He can make one aware of the contradictions aroused by the usual meanings of these terms, but he cannot go any further.

Plato's Socrates is bound to proceed dialectically. All his arguments proceed from premises accepted by his interlocutors, on pain of not being understood and by Socrates himself arguably only for the sake of the argument. The irony of the Platonic dialogues is double. On the one hand, Socrates is ironical towards his interlocutors; on the other hand, Plato is ironical towards his readers. What he writes cannot be taken unquestionably at face value as representing his own views, or one will often find oneself being led astray, as notoriously happens in the aporetic dialogues, and not only in these. Even in the nonaporetic dialogues, in which Plato is supposed to propose positive doctrines, one has to be careful in ascribing such doctrines to Plato. There is in his writings hardly a passage that has not been hotly disputed as to

whether or not it is ironical. Plato's use of myths is similar (cf. *Men.* 86b; *Phaedo* 114d; q.v. Myths).

Plato's use of myths is intrinsically ironical. In an obvious sense, they are not to be taken as literally true. Yet, in another sense, not specified, they do express some ethical truth. Even if this truth is given at the end of the myth, it is clear that its formulation in mythical terms is not unproblematic, and Plato says so expressly (cf. *Men.* 86b; *Phd.* 114d). But for open irony to be at all effective, it must have a definite anchoring point from which the intended meaning can be derived. Nothing within the dialogues can serve as such a point, free of every context. Socrates' death, however, is an absolute point of reference, an event outside the dialogues. Socrates did not die in jest. From this event one can learn that his saying that 'the unexamined life is not worth living for human beings' (*Ap.* 38a) was not ironical. Against this sentence, establishing the absolute, unconditional value of *logos* (q.v.), all other doctrines proposed in the dialogues should be measured. Plato cannot prove the value of living an examined life; such a proof would presuppose the very value of examining one's opinions. Those present at the death of Socrates were convinced of it with no need for argument. For those who were not there, Plato tries to reconstruct that occasion in the hope that its emotional impact will lead us beyond his inevitable ironical dissimulation.

LANGUAGE

Holger Thesleff

Plato's fourth-century BCE Attic Greek is unproblematic, as such, to today's specialists; and the text tradition is on the whole reliable. His linguistic choices, however, are often remarkable and highly relevant to a more subtle interpretation. The stylistic nuances (Thesleff 1967) and allusions offer considerable difficulties for us.

Translations are in various ways defective; the reader is recommended to compare different modern translations (preferably in different languages).

It is important always to keep in mind that Plato wrote 'literature' even in philosophically argumentative parts of his dialogues. His writings are imitations or enactments (Press 2007:137–40) of oral discussions with a wide range of allusions and emotional and imaginative appeal (cf. McCabe 2008:96–8 'philosophical fiction'). The artistic components of his dialogues are sometimes very significantly interwoven with their explicitly cognitive content. Plato's often deplored lack of esteem of arts and poetry (q.v.) and other emotional aspects of human life, is somewhat compensated by his indulgence in linguistic expression.

Ancient literary critics were well aware of Plato's quite unique artistry (cf. Rutherford 1995), though they do not seem to have studied it systematically. The rhetorical breadth and force of his language in some sections of his works was noted more often than his play with colloquialisms or poeticisms. Aristotle compared his prose to poetry.

Except for some late works, Plato uses linguistic means to characterize persons and moods. Since the persons are often seen as types, rather than as historical individuals (q.v. Character), we very seldom find strict imitations of idioms or dialects (as in *Phaedo* 62a); but the tenor of the text very often reflects the personality of the speaker (Thesleff 1967:160–4). Plato is a good imitator of conventional rhetoric and other public manners of speech, as can be seen

in *Menexenus, Protagoras, Symposium* and *Phaedrus*. Plato's Socrates stands in a category of his own, also linguistically. He may imitate others, but he is most at home with a vivid, fluent colloquial Attic with playful ingredients, avoiding vulgarisms. It is impossible to distinguish linguistically the historical Socrates from Plato's character Socrates, but in passages with pathos or otherwise strong emotionality we may hear Plato's own voice (notably in the latter part of *Gorgias*, and in *Republic* bks 5, 6 and 9).

A rough categorization of the different styles used in different dialogues and different passages may be of considerable help for our interpretation (Thesleff 1967). Changes in the structure and technique of the dialogue bring with them shifts of style (q.v. Pedimentality). In fact, linguistic criteria can to some extent be used for determining shifts between ambivalent play, irony or serious emphasis (q.v. Play).

The all-pervading importance of dialogue for Plato is reflected in his notorious denunciation of written texts (except for memoranda) which are 'unable to answer' when questioned (*Phdr.* 277de; q.v. Orality, Writing).

The proper meaning of words was a question of profound interest to some sophists (notably Prodicus, in *Prt.* 337a–c; *Cratylus* 384b) and, apparently, to Socrates as well. This issue affected Plato's use of language in various ways. The play with etymologies in *Crat.* (q.v.) has, besides its philosophical aim, to find a way through the debate about the conventional versus natural meaning of words (q.v. Language (topic)). Plato takes a delight in the semantics and connotations of words and neologisms. Such etymological or ambiguously allusive wordplay (q.v. Play) is more common in most dialogues than is normally realized. To take just one example, in *Meno* (85c–6c) there is some suggestive play with *alêthês* 'true' in the sense of 'not forgotten'. Ambivalent wordplay is also applied to the old search for the 'true' meaning of poetry (*Prt.* 338c–47a; *R.* 1.332b).

The Socratic/Platonic search for definitions grew from the commitment to the 'proper meaning' question (q.v. Forms). The fact that the answers are often or even normally left open *aporetically* is a sign of Plato's deeply felt sense of the ambiguity of spoken or written words.

In Plato's view, language does not carry truth in itself, but a spoken or written 'argument' or 'discussion' conveys more of rationality (*logos*, q.v. Dialectic; cf. Desjardins 1988:110–25) than various other suggestive ways of expression such as poetry or oratory or myths.

Typically, Plato avoids the coining of philosophical terms, though his language appears to be at times quite sophisticated. The most notorious example is his flowing terminology for the so-called theory of forms (q.v., also Thesleff 1999:50–90). Translations are easily misleading here.

One aspect of Plato's semantics is his method of 'division and collection' (q.v. Dialectic), which has to follow the 'natural joints' of concepts and things (cf. *Phdr.* 265de; *Politicus* 287c). One of its aims is a classification of things into genus and species, though the playful analyses in *Sophist* and *Plt.* only approximate to consistency. Its ultimate end is, rather, to reach the upmost ideas and forms of the universe (see *R.* bk 6; *Phdr.*). The linguistic expressions of the parts and wholes discussed tend to be abstract denominations; concrete objects do not seem to have been systematically analysed in Plato's circle (though the examining of a pumpkin is ridiculed in a comedy fragment, Epicrates f. 11). For his large use of abstractions, Plato was aided by the Greek tendency to formulate abstract nouns by means of suffixes and the article.

Since the 1860s, Plato's linguistic practise has been studied more consistently in order to determine the chronology and authenticity of his writings (Thesleff 1982). It was noticed that a group of dialogues, called 'late dialogues' because of their stylistic affinity with the posthumously published *Laws*, displayed characteristic mannerisms such as heavy and rare words, archaisms and a twisted word order. Possibly, the most typical characteristics of Plato's 'late style' reflect a mannerism, not of Plato himself, but of younger assistants who contributed to the formulation of the written texts.

LITERARY COMPOSITION

Jill Gordon

Greek literature left a distinctive mark on Plato's works, as he employed a variety of literary forms and devices. The literary forms Plato used included letters, dramas in which characters speak directly in their own voices, and dramas in which a narrator recounts for the reader what each character said (q.v. Letters, Drama). To great effect Plato used the literary devices of character development, irony, puns and plays on words, metaphor, mythmaking, detailed dramatic settings and powerful imagery (q.v. Characters, Irony, Myth, Myths and Stories, and Image). He was extremely talented in crafting various speaking and writing styles among his characters. And he evoked both laughter and pathos, sometimes together in a single dialogue.

A small but illustrative set of examples of Plato's literary achievements would include the following. The *Republic* presents arguably the best known philosophical image in all of Western thought: the analogy of the cave (q.v.), which continues to have power and relevance. It is a detailed metaphor for the emergence from ignorance to enlightenment. Socratic irony (q.v.) pervades Plato's dialogues, most notably, though not exclusively, in Socrates' praise of the intelligence of interlocutors who, the reader is able to see, remain unaware of their own ignorance. Though Plato uses this device in many dialogues, it is particularly accessible in *Euthyphro* and *Meno*. Aristophanes' speech in *Symposium* (q.v.) contains a myth, which is Plato's original creation, but which is nevertheless traditional in feel. The myth contains imaginative and vivid descriptions of human *erôs*, and it has distinct comic and tragic elements. Several dialogues also include myths depicting the fate of the soul (q.v.) in the afterlife (e.g. *Gorgias*, *Phaedo* and *R.*). Socrates' final hours before he drank the hemlock, depicted in *Phd.*, are quite moving, despite Socrates' admonitions to his friends not to cry about his imminent death. *Phaedrus* contains a critique of writing, a paradoxical and provocative critique since it appears in a written work. *Phdr.* also provides a speech that mimics the style of fifth-century Attic speechwriter and orator, Lysias. The *Smp.*, in which several characters give extensive speeches, is perhaps the best single example of Plato's ability to mimic and create in the style of various other writers and speakers. And finally, the profound effect of Plato's ideas on Western philosophy emerges in part from his detailed and powerful literary characterization of Socrates across the dialogues (q.v. Characters and Socrates as Character).

Despite Plato's extensive use of these and other literary devices, there is a common belief that he was an enemy of the poets and poetry (q.v.). This belief is based primarily on passages in *R.* in which Socrates raises concerns about the effects of poetry on the soul and the role of poets in the ideal city (377a–83c, 386a–95b, 598d–608b); Socrates even refers to an 'ancient quarrel between philosophy and poetry' (607b). Ancient philosophy and what we would now call 'literature', however, cannot easily be separated – by form or content – into distinct categories. Several figures who are considered philosophers wrote in metered verse (e.g. Xenophanes and Parmenides): Heraclitus wrote in cryptic oracular aphorisms, many tragic and comic poets addressed philosophical issues, the sophists (q.v.) engaged important epistemic and metaphysical issues in their books and public speeches, and Plato wrote philosophical dialogues that are among the best works of literature to emerge from the classical period. Plato's dialogues leave us therefore in a quandary: how to understand his broad use of literary techniques and devices, a trait he shares with other philosophers of the time, against the backdrop of Socrates' criticisms of various aspects of poetry and writing in the dialogues. Plato appears to be crafting literary works that at the same time interrogate the literary project deeply and critically.

With this enigma in mind, modern scholars approach the dialogues with a variety of interpretive strategies. In the twentieth century in some Anglo-American philosophical circles, the literary aspects of the dialogues were mostly ignored in order to focus on the arguments, which could be formalized and whose validity and soundness evaluated (e.g. Vlastos 1978a, 1978b). The implicit assumption in this scholarship was that the arguments were philosophical, but the literary aspects of the dialogues were not. By contrast, Leo Strauss and his students (q.v., Straussian approaches), paid careful attention to dramatic details, looking there for signs of esoteric meaning (q.v., Esotericism), although some scholars say that the Straussians imputed disproportionate importance to them. Yet others focus on Plato's literary composition in the historical context of the Greek transition from oral to literate culture. They aim to explore facets of both Plato's inheritance from and tensions with the older, oral poetic traditions from which his dialogues emerge (e.g. Havelock 1965; Hershbell 1995; Waugh 1995, opposed by Harris 1989 and Knox 1968). Still others turned to stylometric analyses of Plato's dialogues to determine the order in which they were composed. The belief was that by exploring the compositional style of each dialogue and differences between dialogues, one could determine whether they were written earlier or later in Plato's career, or at the very least, determine which dialogues were written in close proximity to one another. These studies, however, have been somewhat discredited as relying on faulty assumptions and as delivering inconsistent results (Nails 1993, 1994). Gradually and more extensively, English speaking scholars have studied the arguments and the dramatic and literary aspects in more synthetic, holistic ways (e.g. Gonzalez 1995b; Press 1993; Scott 2007). There is now an extensive body of secondary literature exploring the relationship between Plato's dialogues and ancient tragedy (e.g. Nussbaum 1986), comedy and mime (e.g. Clay 2005; Howland 2007; Miller 2008) and other ancient literary genres (e.g. Nightingale 1995). Scholars also investigate how Plato uses various literary techniques to accomplish philosophical ends (e.g. Blondell 2002; Gordon 1999).

While Plato's dialogues are deeply embedded in, and indebted to, Greek poetic traditions, they also make innovative literary contributions of their own and they provide a critical perspective on the cultural, ethical and philosophical function of literature.

MUSICAL STRUCTURE OF THE DIALOGUES

J. B. Kennedy

Recent research suggests that Plato may have inserted symbolic passages in his dialogues at regular intervals to give them a musical structure. Struck (2004), Ford (2002), Sedley (2003) and others have shown that ancient Greek symbolism and allegory were common themes of discussion in the late fifth century and especially in the circles around Socrates. Plato's musical structures are another kind of symbolism and fit within this context.

The musical structures shed new light on some well known puzzles about the structure of Plato's narratives. Plato mocked his contemporaries for failing to organize their compositions (e.g. *Phaedrus* 264a4–e4), but his own dialogues can seem disjointed and meandering. The structure of the *Republic* is thought by some to be a hodgepodge of tracts written at different times (Annas 1981; Lear 1992; Rutherford 1995). The conclusions of many of the dialogues have also puzzled Plato's readers. Some end without propounding a definite doctrine, which has led a minority in ancient and modern times to suppose that Plato had no positive, philosophical programme. Musical structures give the dialogues an underlying unity and coherence and provide an explanation for Plato's aporetic conclusions.

Plato had strong motivations for using such symbolic structures. The dialogues often discuss the idea that 'forms' lie beneath appearances and give the objects we observe their properties and structures. Students of philosophy are urged to compare, count and measure objects to find the general forms they instantiate. The *Philebus* suggests that identifying musical scales, for example, is a paradigm of this search for the forms (*Phlb.* 17c11–e1). The philosophy ascribed to Pythagoras provides another motivation. Pythagoras taught that every object, and even the whole cosmos, has an underlying musical and mathematical structure (Burkert 1972; Kahn 2001). Although the dialogues hardly mention Pythagoras, many believe that Plato was influenced by him (q.v. Pythagoreans). Giving the dialogues an underlying musical structure thus conforms to the core doctrines of both Platonism and Pythagoreanism.

Introducing a few ideas from Greek music (q.v.) theory will clarify Plato's musical structures. Notes harmonize when their frequencies form simple ratios such as $1 : 2$, $2 : 3$ and $3 : 4$. In fact, these ratios are the most important musical intervals. The $1 : 2$ ratio, for example, is called an 'octave' (Barker 2007; West 1992). Since the number 12 has many factors, it was common even before Plato to illustrate these musical intervals with the numbers 6, 8, 9 and 12. Thus the octave was said to be a $6 : 12$ ratio. Music theorists would demonstrate these intervals on monochords or instruments with many strings. Some theorists 'divided' their string or a ruler alongside it into 12 equal parts, which made it easy to sound the major musical intervals (Creese 2010). The lowest note on a monochord is sounded by the whole string. If the other notes are compared with this ground note (say by playing them successively), some will harmonize with it and some will not. The Greeks therefore distinguished the more harmonious notes (3, 4, 6, 8 and 9), which formed low whole number ratios with 12, from the more dissonant notes (5, 7, 10 and 11). Music theorists also held that the smallest useful musical interval was a 'quarter-interval' (from say eight to eight and a quarter). These musical ideas lead to a natural interpretation of the structure embedded in the dialogues (Kennedy 2010, 2011). Plato divided each of his dialogues into 12 parts. At each twelfth he inserted a passage which was a symbol for a musical note.

In a given dialogue, the 12 passages each describe a species of some given genus. In the *Symposium*, for example, they describe a species of 'harmony', which in Greek meant 'attunement', 'blending', 'fitting together' or, more narrowly, 'mode' or 'musical harmony'. Plato also divided each twelfth into four parts and inserted similar passages to mark the quarter intervals. The conversations in Plato's dialogues were organized around the underlying musical structure. Episodes or arguments tend to fill out one or more quarter intervals. Major concepts or major turns in the narrative tend to be lodged at the locations of musical notes. Generally, passages about virtue, truth, goodness and other Platonic ideals mark the harmonious notes; dissonant notes are marked by vice, lying, evil, Hades, etc.

To insert these musical symbols at the proper places Plato or his scribe probably counted the number of lines in his dialogues. Classical Greeks counted lines in book scrolls just as we count pages in a book or words in a file. Scribes were paid by the line and this determined the costs of book scrolls. The standard line, even for prose, contained the same number of syllables as a line in Homer's poems (Ohly 1928). That Plato is aware of line counting is indicated by *Laws* 958e9–9a1. (The lengths of the Stephanus pages in modern editions of Plato are irregular and cannot be used as an accurate measure of location.) Moreover, classical Greek had little or no punctuation and no spaces between words or sentences. A word processor can strip out the punctuation and spaces from modern, scholarly texts and return them to a format with accurate line counts.

Plato's musical structure can be seen in the *Smp*. The locations of its twelfths are listed below and Kennedy (2011) includes a close reading and commentary on all its symbolic passages. The philosophical climax of the dialogue is the vision of the form of beauty (q.v.) at the top of Diotima's ladder. The description of beauty's unity occurs nine-twelfths of the way through the dialogue and so coincides with the very harmonic ninth note. The extreme unity of the form of beauty is a kind of extreme 'harmony' in the Greek sense, and so appropriately marks this harmonic note. The eighth note, which is also very harmonic, is marked by a vivid passage describing copulation with beauty (another species of blending or mixing). The dissonant notes, however, are marked with failures to 'harmonise'. The eleventh note is marked by the extreme sense of shame felt by Alcibiades when Socrates rejected his romantic overtures. The tenth note is marked by the comparison of Socrates to an ugly satyr. Thus, these dissonant notes are marked by strikingly negative passages which describe conflict and emotional dissonance in a relationship.

The lengths of the speeches show that Plato used the musical structure as a kind of outline. Pausanias finishes speaking a few lines after the third note. Eryximachus finishes before the fourth note. Aristophanes finishes at the fifth note. Agathon's noisy peroration precedes the sixth note. Socrates begins his speech at the quarter note just after note six (*Smp*. 199b4) and finishes at the quarter note just after note nine (212c2) and so speaks for a fourth of the entire dialogue. Many species of 'harmony' are used to mark

the locations of the musical notes: the envisaged fusion of true lovers (third quarter note after four-twelfths), Eryximachus' discussion of musical harmony (second quarter note after three-twelfths) and so on. The quarter intervals in the opening frame provide a particularly clear introduction to the nature of Plato's symbolism. The *Lg*. says that music has two components: 'rhythm' is a motion through time and 'harmony' is a blending of high and low frequencies to produce some intermediate pitch (*Lg*. 664e8–a2; cf. *Smp*. 187a8 ff.).

The *Smp*.'s first four musical notes are marked by passages describing motions like walking. Moreover, in each passage, a wiser character like Socrates *agrees* with an ignorant character, which is a kind of harmony between high and low. These descriptions of motion and harmony are symbols marking musical notes. The frame's narrative is also shaped by the musical notes. The opening episode, in which the narrator recollects an earlier request to recite the speeches, lasts for one quarter interval. Socrates' famous 'fit of abstraction', in which he remains stationary in a neighbour's porch, also fills out one quarter interval. (Locations of the 12 musical notes in the *Smp*. using the OCT edition: 1/12 = 176c5, 2/12 = 181e3, 3/12 = 185b6, 4/12 = 189d5, 5/12 = 193d8, 6/12 = 198a8, 7/12 = 202c7, 8/12 = 206e1, 9/12 = 211b4, 10/12 = 215c2, 11/12 = 219d6, 12/12 = 223d12. The quarter intervals in the frame end at 1q: 173c3, 2q: 174c8, 3q: 175c7.)

In sum, these musical structures can resolve many puzzles, if other dialogues are composed by the same principles. They could show that each dialogue is given a coherent organization by a musical form which is embedded in the surface narrative and, like other forms, is accessible only to those who count and make comparisons. They also explain why the dialogues end negatively. The final tenth and eleventh notes are dissonant. The philosophical climaxes of the dialogues are at the ninth, more harmonic note.

MYTH

Luc Brisson

For Plato, myth has two defects. It is an unverifiable discourse, which must often be considered false when it departs from a doctrinal point defended by Plato. And it is a story whose elements are linked together in a contingent way, unlike argumentative discourse, whose inner organization features a necessary character. Yet, this does not mean that Plato renounces traditional myths, which he uses abundantly in his work. What is more, he adapts some of them, and he sometimes even creates new ones, as a function of circumstances. Why? There are two reasons, one theoretical in nature, and the other practical. Plato recognizes the indispensable efficacy of myth in the fields of ethics and politics for the large number of people who are not philosophers and in whose soul the desiring part (*epithumia*) predominates. Plato knows, moreover, that he can only speak in mythical terms of the soul, and hence of certain subjects of a metaphysical and epistemological nature (see further, Brisson 2004; Havelock 1963).

The characters who appear in myths, as enumerated in bks 2 and 3 of the *Republic* – that is, gods, demons, heroes, the inhabitants of Hades and the men of the past – cannot be the subject of a discourse that could be declared to be 'true' or 'false' in a Platonic context. Myths recount the exploits accomplished in a very distant past by men living in the sensible world, of whom tradition has retained the memory. Gods, demons, heroes and inhabitants of Hades are situated between the world of intelligible forms and the world of sensible things, at the level of the soul and all that is immortal about it.

The gods, demons, heroes and immortals are either living beings in the full sense of the term, or the offspring of immortalized mortals. Man is endowed with a soul (q.v.) of which one part is immortal, and is thereby akin to the gods, who must use it as a puppet (*Laws* 1.644d–5c), and hence it is also akin to the demons and the heroes. The destiny of this immortal part must be described before it falls into a body (*Phaedrus* 259b–d), and especially after it has left this body, that is, according to popular belief in ancient Greece, when it is in Hades. Such myths as those found at the end of the *Gorgias*, *Phaedo* (107d–14d) or *R.* (10.614a–21d, the Myth of Er) have precisely the destiny of the immortal part of the soul as their subject.

Moreover, the domain of myth that evokes men of the past covers roughly the same territory that was later to be claimed by the historians, as can be observed in the myth of Atlantis (*Timaeus* 21e–6d; *Critias*), and in bk 3 of the *Lg.*, which evokes the beginnings of human life. Quite naturally, it is with the help of a myth that Plato evokes the various origins: of writing (*Phdr.* 274c–5b, the myth of Theuth), of human nature (*Symposium* 189d–93d, Aristophanes' myth of double beings), of the cicadas (*Phdr.* 259b–d) and even of the universe (*Ti.*). The idea that the soul has an existence separated from all bodies, in the course of which it has acquired a particular knowledge that it must recall in its subsequent existences, is explicitly tied to religious traditions in the *Meno*, the *Phd.*, the *Phdr.* and the *Smp.* The idea that its previous behaviour is subject to retribution is affirmed in several eschatological myths, particularly at the end of the *Grg.*, the *Phd.* and the *R.* Finally, the idea that it is incarnated in various bodies, human or animal, is formulated in the *Phdr.* and the *Ti.* In addition, everything concerning the intelligible is associated with myth through the intermediary of these beliefs about the soul: the myth of the cave (*R.* 7.514a–17; q.v.), prolonged by the 'allegory' of the sun (*R.* 6.506d–9b; q.v.) and that of the line (*R.* 6.506d–9b; q.v.). It follows that myths constitute a terrain on which fundamental philosophical speculations take root: those concerning the soul and the intelligible forms. Myths thus constitute a reservoir of axioms or premises for the philosopher in the fields of metaphysics and epistemology.

Myth also plays an essential role in ethics and politics. In the *R.*, the myth of autochthony (*R.* 3.414d–e), also evoked in the *Lg.*, along with that of the metals, serves to convince the inhabitants that the city is one and indivisible, although it is made up of diverse groups. The myth of Gyges (*R.* 2.359d–60b) provides a marvellous illustration of the thesis rejected by Socrates, according to which injustice is something naturally good. In the *Lg.*, myth plays a considerable role in legislation. In bk 4 (*Lg.* 719c–24a), Plato enquires into the practise of the legislator, comparing him to the poet and the doctor. Unlike the poet, who does not hesitate to develop contradictory discourses on the same subject, the legislator must maintain a coherent discourse. Although he maintains one discourse on one and the same subject, however, the legislator need not necessarily limit himself to a simplistic discourse. He must have the prescription of a law preceded by a declaration that tries to substitute persuasion for the fear of punishment. It is thus persuasion that must obtain, right from the outset, an

obedience to the law that is, as it were, automatic. For Plato, therefore, myth has a twofold function, practical and theoretical.

On the level of ethics and politics, myth leads the individual to obey the moral rules and the laws established by persuasion, without the necessity of involving coercion. On a properly speculative level, myths constitute the starting point for a reflection on the soul and the intelligible forms, the two themes that were to impose themselves upon tradition as the characteristics of Platonic philosophy.

PEDAGOGICAL STRUCTURE OF THE DIALOGUES

Kenneth Sayre

Plato could have written in the form of verse, like Parmenides, in that of orations, like Isocrates, or even that of philosophic essays. Instead he chose the form of dramatic conversations (dialogues). Reasons for this choice are not immediately apparent.

One possible explanation is that the dialogues are records of actual Socratic conversations which themselves occurred in dialogue form. Commentators generally consider this unlikely, however, since (among other reasons) many dialogues depict conversations which Plato could not have attended (compare Kahn 1981).

Another possibility is that Plato wrote primarily to present his own philosophic views and chose this form to make his presentation more engaging. But this too seems unlikely. Among reasons are (a) that conflicting views are expressed in different dialogues (e.g. the soul is incomposite in the *Phaedo* and tripartite in the *Republic*), (b) that protagonists in the dialogues often speak disingenuously (consider Socratic irony) and (c) that several dialogues contain arguments that appear deliberately faulty (see Sprague 1962).

A further argument against this second possibility is found in the *Epistle* 7, which most Plato scholars today accept as genuine (q.v. Letters). In this document the author states that philosophic understanding cannot be conveyed in language and that he has never undertaken to commit his knowledge of the subject to writing. Taken at face value, this statement precludes reading the dialogues as repositories of Platonic teaching. But if the dialogues are neither records of actual conversations nor engaging expressions of Plato's own philosophy, what then?

Hints towards a more plausible explanation come with further reading of the *Ep.* 7. After stating that philosophic understanding cannot be conveyed by words, the author observes that it comes with hard work, persistence and discipline, along with repeated conversations with a master that employ 'friendly elenchus' and 'well intentioned question and answer'. For the successful learner, the outcome is a 'sudden (*exaiphnês*) flash of insight' bearing knowledge of the subject concerned. Subjects mentioned include 'the good, the beautiful, and the just' (*Ep.* 342D).

Similar accounts of philosophic training appear in several dialogues. In developing the midwife analogy in the *Theaetetus*, Socrates speaks of the 'many beautiful discoveries' (*Tht.* 150c) engendered in the minds of students who maintain conversation with him and benefit from his inquisitive art (elenchus). In the *Phaedrus*, he talks about 'lessons on what is just, beautiful, and good' (*Phdr.* 276c) that result in knowledge impressed as discourse 'in the soul of the learner'. And in the *Symposium*, he extols the 'wondrous beauty' that appears suddenly (*exaiphnês*;

Smp. 210e) in the mental vision of someone well trained in love.

In these dialogues, as in *Ep.* 7, the path to philosophic understanding is portrayed as laborious, involving sustained conversation with a master of elenchus and culminating in a spontaneous flash of insight within the mind of the learner. The metaphor of illumination 'at the end of the path' is also prominent in *R.* (508d), *Phdr.* (250b) and *Philebus* (16c). One thing this imagery signifies is that philosophic enlightenment is induced in the mind of the learner, rather than being conveyed from without by demonstrative argument.

This portrayal of philosophic fulfilment probably was based on Plato's own experience in conversation with the historical Socrates (q.v.). Such fulfilment also must have been a major factor underlying Plato's adoption of the conversational format for his writings. What Plato got from Socrates, first and foremost, was not a set of doctrines subsequently recorded in written form, but rather an ingenious method of guiding students along a path to philosophic enlightenment. Plato's dialogues, in effect, are teaching instruments structured to provide his readers the kind of learning experience that he himself received in conversations with Socrates.

To drive the point home, we may look at various features of the dialogues that help them play this pedagogic role. Primary among such is that the Socrates of the dialogues (q.v. Socrates as a character), like his historical counterpart, is a master of enticement (flattery, irony and innuendo) as well as probative refutation. The actual Socrates engaged listeners by sheer power of personality. Countless readers have been inspired subsequently to a life of philosophy by the charismatic character in Plato's dialogues.

Another factor is the way Plato uses dramatic markers to highlight crucial moments in a pedagogical conversation. In the *Meno*, for example, the theory of recollection is introduced in conversation with a new respondent (the slave replaces Meno), and the method of hypothesis is dramatized by the arrival of Anytus. And both the nadir (*Phd.* 89a) and the zenith (*Phd.* 102a) of the philosophic drama in *Phd.* are punctuated by the re-entry of Phaedo and Echecrates from the outer dialogue. The purpose of signposts like these, presumably, is to focus attention on key developments as the conversation progresses.

Other pedagogical devices involve the use of distinctive characters (q.v.) to set the stage for the conversations ensuing. Thus, the story of *Smp.* is recounted by Aristodemus (a participant in the party who fell asleep before it ended) and Apollodorus (self-described as crazy), which imbues the main conversation with a dreamlike atmosphere. Similar contrivances are used in other dialogues (*Euthydemus, Protagoras, Parmenides*), with the effect of establishing a unique context in which the conversation can be read most fruitfully.

Also worth mentioning is Plato's knack for imparting momentum to his dialogues, which carry the reader forward once the conversation has 'officially' ended. At the end of *Tht.*, for example, alert readers will realize that several senses of *logos* especially relevant to knowledge have not yet been examined and will be motivated to test these senses on their own. Similar effects are found in *Men., R.* and *Phlb.* By pointing to things never explicitly stated, these dialogues invite readers to continue the investigation by themselves (for further discussion, see Sayre 1992).

Most noteworthy pedagogically, however, is the way Plato's more successful dialogues are structured in layers ready to be unpacked in successive readings. An example is the *Sophist*, which invites being read progressively as (a) a mundane attempt to define sophistry, (b) an exploration of the semantics of falsehood, (c) an examination of the nature of not-being and finally, (d) an explication of truth and falsehood themselves. This accounts for the experience many readers have of learning more from a dialogue each time they read it (see Sayre 1995a for more detail).

An alternative account of Plato's pedagogical use of dialogic structure may be found in Miller (1986). Also instructive in this regard is Frede (1992b).

PEDIMENTAL STRUCTURE OF THE DIALOGUES

Holger Thesleff

Most of Plato's dialogues, including many *dubia* (q.v.), are carefully composed (q.v. Literary composition). They have a 'literary' stamp. This is interesting, since they were not on the whole meant for presentation to general anonymous audiences used to public performances of poetry, drama or oratory, the main genres of 'literature' in Plato's days. The refinements of the compositional patterns of the dialogues, like the philosophical contents, the language and style (q.v. Language) and the irony (q.v.) and allusive play (q.v.), are rather adapted to small groups of relatively well informed persons and their friends who appreciated such moves.

One can easily detect a certain rhythm or pulse in the composition and technique of the dialogue. There is normally an introduction, sometimes in two or more stages, gradually leading 'into' the place where the philosopher meets his interlocutors. Then there are variations between argumentative passages and interludes with different types of dialogue. At the end there comes a comparatively brief conclusion which, interestingly, tends to leave the discussion somehow open. Even explicitly 'aporetic' conclusions suggest that something is bound to follow. A study of the compositional rhythm of the texts may, like the study of shifts of style (Thesleff 1967), contribute to our understanding of where and how the author wants to place the emphasis.

It has sometimes been noticed that the majority of Platonic dialogues follow a general pattern which can be termed 'pedimental' (Thesleff 1993) or 'ring composition' (Douglas 2007), the archaic compositional principle of returning to the beginning at the end. Plato's pedimentality, however, is a refinement of classical ring composition since the central section of dialogues often rises to a higher intellectual or conceptual level before returning to the mundane level where the conversation began. The central parts or sections of a dialogue often form a core where essential thoughts or new aspects or a crucial phase are introduced. As in the triangular 'pediment' or tympanum of a Greek temple, symbolically important ideas are placed in the centre. More peripheral or more ordinary facts and suggestions, and less significant circumstances, are pushed towards the beginning and the end. Reflections of similar principles can be found in other classical Greek genres of literature, notably in tragedy (the peripety) and old comedy (the parabasis). Plato was influenced by drama (q.v.), though a direct dependence is unlikely.

A closer consideration of the character of the central sections and their function within the pedimentality may give useful clues to the interpretation of the dialogues.

The most manifest example, easily understood by every reader, is the pyramidally central place of Diotima's speech in *Symposium* (q.v.). There is a gradual rise to it, and then a slope beginning with Alcibiades' joining the company. Other very obvious cases include Socrates' musings on inspiration in *Ion* (q.v.), and the first part of his palinodic speech on the cosmic flight of the soul in *Phaedrus* (q.v.), an illustration of true 'psychagogy' (*Phdr.* 271c), so different from myths and oratory.

The relevance of pedimentality in the *Republic* (q.v.) is worth specific notice (Dorter 2006:3–8; cf. the challenge by Roochnik 2003:4–7). The beginning and the end concern rather concrete human realities or myths seen from a human perspective, but from the opening onwards, and backwards from the end, we find ever more abstract philosophical themes which culminate in the three, mutually interdependent analogies in the centre of the work (bks 6, 7), the sun, the line and the cave (qq.v.). These are actively illuminating symbols pointing to the fact that metaphysics and its application to the education of philosophers constitute the central nucleus of this work. The other themes are arranged around it in a kind of descending order.

Metaphysics is often more prominent in the central sections than in other parts of the dialogues. Pedimentality can make a push, as it were, towards the higher level of Plato's two-level universe (Thesleff 1999). The discussion on the whole concerns human matters, but the central sections give glimpses of the (metaphorically) 'divine'.

The pedimental composition is seldom as spectacularly evident as in the examples just mentioned, yet it may offer an important aid to the interpreter. In the *Phaedo* (q.v.), where innumerable generations of readers have sought towards the end for the 'definite' proof of the immortality of the soul, the resumption of the frame dialogue at the centre (*Phd.* 88c) in fact indicates a retardation and a concentration on an idea which is emphasized in various ways: whatever hopes or myths or arguments there are for the survival of the human soul, dialectic ought not to be rejected and Socrates' *logos* with its metaphysical reach will live on even if he does not do so as a person. But at the beginning and the end of the dialogue, the perspectives of living human individuals are in the foreground.

A similar framing of the central section occurs in *Euthydemus* (q.v.) where Clinias unexpectedly hints that the Royal Art will give a lasting solution to the problems at hand. This probably refers to the schooling of philosophers, treated with banter at the beginning and the end. In *Protagoras* (q.v.), the two-level contrast of 'becoming' or 'being' good, an implicit clue to the entire dialogue, is playfully alluded to in Socrates' sophistic answer to Protagoras' speech in the centre. *Meno* (q.v.), again somewhat playfully, introduces the recollection doctrine in the pedimental central section. And *Theaetetus* (q.v.), to take a last rather obvious example, has a digression on the two paradigms of human life in its centre: one of the implications seems to be that an orientation towards the upper level is essential in epistemology, in spite of all the different perspectives opened by the discussion. Some scholars regard the provocative 'philosophical digression' in the *Seventh Letter* (342a–4d) as a sign of its authenticity; others, the sure sign of a practised imitator.

The aspect of pedimental composition ought to be observed in almost all Platonic dialogues. Occasionally, however, it is not very easily traceable. Notably in *Gorgias*

and in *Crito* (less obviously in *Philebus*), the rhetorical principle of 'climactic' arrangement is dominant. In both dialogues Socrates is intent on persuading his interlocutor and his listeners by consistent argumentation, an approach not normally used so explicitly by Plato. The principle of pedimentality is better suited to the reflective mood of most dialogues.

PLAY

Holger Thesleff

Since a solemnly serious Plato has dominated the picture of Platonism since antiquity, it is particularly important to note his use of playful wit and humour (q.v.). Indeed, this general feature, taken in a very large sense, is essential not only as a literary device in the dialogues but basic for the interpretation of his philosophy.

Awareness of the aspect of play is a primary challenge for readers of Plato, even if they do not feel Platonic play is amusing. Though Plato often hints that he is jesting, his playfulness (*paidia*, derived from the word for child, like English 'kidding') involves various degrees of seriousness: it is always ambiguous to some extent, but normally with an earnest point. '"Play" . . . combines interested detachment with cautious engagement and enables the philosopher to give both the rational and sensuous worlds their due' (Plass 1967:359). Like most kinds of humour, Platonic play has two significant constituents, distancing or perspective, on one hand, and a simultaneous confrontation with two different paradigms, a double exposure, on the other. The latter corresponds to his non-dualistic two-level model of thought (Thesleff 1999). Play and earnestness belong together (e.g. *Symposium* 216e, 223d), but suggestive play may reach higher than mere statements of facts (see Press 2007:104–29).

The two-level approach is manifestly present in the Platonic irony (q.v.), which is normally a gently ambivalent reference from what appears to be the case to what is really true. Most of Socrates' apparent *aporiai* are understatements of this type. Plato's philosopher has nothing of the cynic's laughing scorn from below, and his moral polemics are seldom explicitly bitter (as in *Gorgias* and parts of *Republic*; note the regret 7.536c). Occasional overstatements may involve some playful disdain, such as the profuse praise of the sophist in *Hippias Major*. Sometimes Socrates' self-irony clearly includes the author (e.g. *Theaetetus* 174ab).

Ambivalent word play is an integral part of Plato's reasoning. This is indirectly reflected in his notorious lack of consistent terminology: language can be played with. He plays semiseriously with the belief that words have a covert meaning (q.v. Language), and this belief somehow lies behind his two-level *dihaeretic* method (q.v. Dialectic), pedantically overplayed in the *Sophist* and *Politicus*. But other kinds of word play also abound in the dialogues, sometimes boisterously as in *Euthydemus*, very often with cognitive allusions, as the musings about what might be forms in *Meno* (72a–5c). Translations usually miss such points.

A humorous distance from everyday trivialities and duties is implied in the concept of 'leisure' (*scholê*, in *Tht.* 172cd), necessary for play and the pursuit of philosophy. Plato has a delicate sense of the bizarre in human behaviour. Though he perhaps lacks a humorously warm understanding of ordinary people, he makes his chosen dialogue characters (q.v.) subject to intellectual wit.

It is reflected in much of his two-level play in mime-like or even farcical confrontations of his always odd Socrates (who has more truth inside him than others, see *Smp.*, especially 215ab) with his interlocutors. Good humoured banter often creates an everyday background to more serious elements of thought. While others may laugh, Plato's philosopher rather smiles (Rankin 1967). In the *Phaedo* such play is reduced to quiet gentleness, but reflections of oral banter occur in the late works (see *Sph.*; *Philebus*).

Oral communication can be deeply serious even if writing is play or pastime (q.v. Writing; Guthrie 1975:56–66). Plato's famous censure of poetry (q.v.) has traits of active mockery motivated both morally and epistemologically; but his appreciation of artistic qualities notable in poetry is beyond doubt (e.g. see *R.* 10.607b–8b). His satirical handling of rhetoric (q.v.) indicates the same ambivalence. More one-sidedly extreme is the censure of ridicule in *Lg.* (e.g. 7.816de; cf. *Phlb.* 48a–50c). Playful seriousness can be recommended (*Lg.* 7.803d), and all learning ought to be accompanied by play (e.g. *R.* 7.536e; note the pun on *paideia* in *Lg.* 1.643bc).

The play inherent in parts of Plato's powerful imagery also illuminates the ambivalence of his two-level thinking. His well known myths (q.v.), which can be regarded as constructive thought-play (below), often contain some bizarre ingredients (e.g. *R.* 10.607b–8b). The tentative, partly comical similes in *Tht.* (191a–200d) of how epistemic memory works perhaps reflect some frustration on Plato's part. Numerous other similes are humorously suggestive, such as Socrates the gadfly (*Apology* 30e) or the torpedo fish (*Men.* 80a). Even in the naturally earnest *Epistle* 7 there is vivid imagery, and the notorious 'digression' has a touch of irony. Mathematical passages may be playfully complicated (as the Nuptial Number in *R.* 8.546c–7a). However, the three central allegories in the *R.* 6–7 (see Pedimentality) are primarily serious with very slight touches of humour (e.g. 509c). The modern reader has to listen very carefully to the tone of the wording, which was made clearer by the original oral delivery.

A particular challenge to all interpreters of Plato comes from an attitude that can be generally called 'thought-play'. He rarely gives explicitly unambiguous 'proofs' for the position his philosopher takes (but cf. *Grg.* 509a; q.v. Account). The attentive reader will often find signs in the context to indicate a thought experiment (or 'abduction') or a provocative step without firm ground in the author's convictions. Given Plato's sense of wit and amusement, we have to be aware of the playful aspect of such instances. Sweepingly generalizing claims such as the remarks on recollection as the basis of true knowledge in *Men.* (81b, etc.) and *Phd.* (72e–6c, but not really followed up elsewhere), or the utopian vision of the ideal state (cf. *R.* 9.592ab; *Lg.* 5.739a–e), or the implications of the kingly art at the centre of *Euthd.* (291cd), or perhaps the so-called unwritten doctrines (see Thesleff 1999:104–7) are worth considering as thought-play. Sometimes there is less humour than human hope and belief in Plato's thought experiments, notably in the main lines of his eschatological myths and in Socrates' personal expectations in the *Phd.*, too often interpreted as Platonic doctrines.

It has been occasionally suggested that perhaps there is more play than consistently serious thinking in Plato's dialogues. It is better to describe his attitude, generally, as playful seriousness open to much ambivalence.

PROLEPTIC COMPOSITION

Hayden W. Ausland

Proleptic composition is a concept used in the modern literary criticism of ancient poetry that has been adapted for understanding the relation between what is held to have been composed earlier and later in Plato's dialogues. The literary category has distant origins in ancient grammatical and rhetorical theory, where 'prolepsis' denotes a deliberately partial anticipation of something greater yet to come (Ausland 2008). The notion was first extensively brought to bear on the development of poetic imagery in the tragedies of Aeschylus, notably by A. Lebeck (1971), following whom Charles Kahn has, since the late 1960s, sought to use it in associating a number of apparently doctrinal passages in Plato's dialogues that have for some time been held instead to reflect a less than deliberate development in their author's thought (1968). In a subsequent series of articles and one book, Kahn argues (e.g. 1988 with 1996) that partial or otherwise inchoate allusions to acknowledged Platonistic views in aporetic dialogues normally held to be early compositions do not in themselves show that Plato was himself experiencing perplexity, while in the process of forming such theories, since they may be read as deliberately designed to point only partially to fuller expositions found in dialogues normally held to belong to a middle period in Plato's literary activity.

The relation of *Republic* bk 1 to its remaining books constitutes a special case of the same general phenomenon. By allowing for such philosophical anticipation, Kahn would appear to revert to the approach to the dialogues characteristic of the early nineteenth century, inaugurated by Friedrich Schleiermacher, who held the dialogues constituted a series in which the earliest elements already aimed methodically at the expositions found in the dialogues Plato produced at the end of his literary efforts (cf. Kahn 1993:137–8f. with Schleiermacher 1828:11). His approach would thus appear to call into serious question the romanticizing and idealizing style of interpretation later inaugurated by K. F. Hermann, according to which a reconstructed chronology of the dialogues reflects their author's specially representative spiritual and personal development (q.v. Nineteenth-Century Platonic Scholarship).

While revolutionary in principle, Kahn's approach does not go far enough to cohere with readings positing an unstated, inner meaning to the dialogues (Griswold 1999, 2000; Kahn 2000). It has at the same time gained but limited credence with the mainstream (e.g. Gill 1998), and has at length approximated once more to the biographically developmental approach conventional for the twentieth century (e.g. Kahn 2007). The tension within the approach thus reflects alternative attitudes towards the possibility that Plato practised esotericism (q.v.), or, more generally, that his writings were written with a view to some end beyond merely documenting their author's philosophical doctrines, for instance as flexibly philosophical dramas, or 'enactments', irreducible to a systematic exposition.

Desultory results of further application of a notion of proleptic composition to the interpretation of Plato's theories, as these are understood within the conventional approach, have been disappointing (e.g. Wilson 1995), with otherwise parallel dramatic readings showing greater promise (e.g. Rudebusch 2002), raising a question regarding the validity, not of some category of proleptic composition per se, but of its

service to received views about the content of Plato's philosophy. A possibility comes into view that the units of Platonic expression to which it is best applied might better be conceived in the first instance along the same lines as the artistic anticipation found in Aeschylean tragedy, allowing the theoretical results of such a reading to emerge independently of any prior assumption of a personal Platonic development.

SOCRATES (THE CHARACTER)

Jill Gordon

Because the historical Socrates (q.v.) did not write anything, our impressions and knowledge of him come through depictions of him in other ancient authors' texts, Plato's dialogues being arguably the best-known among them. Other Socratic texts, written by authors who were directly acquainted with the historical Socrates, include the comic poet Aristophanes' *Clouds* and three of Xenophon's works, *Apology*, *Symposium* and *Oeconomicus*. Aristotle implies (*Poetics* 1447b8–9) that several ancient authors wrote Socratic dialogues, and some corroborating textual evidence survives (q.v. Socratics other than Plato). Some Platonic scholars believe they can separate the historical Socrates from his characterization in Plato's dialogues, but this is disputed (e.g. cf. Kahn 1998; Vlastos 1991a). The various depictions of Socrates are consistent in many respects, although each is, at least to some degree, a literary characterization of the historical Socrates (q.v. Literary Composition). Socrates is not even characterized by Plato entirely consistently across the dialogues. Blondell (2002) discusses various avatars of Socrates in Plato's dialogues, and Plato's possible reasons for writing some dialogues that do not feature Socrates in a primary role.

The profound influence of Plato's Socrates can be attributed in part to the character's utterly compelling, and even strange (*atopos*), singularity (see *Ap*. 31c4; *Gorgias* 494d1; *Smp*. 221d2), and to the alluring vision of philosophical activity that he enacts. Plato's character, Socrates, has become definitive of the 'Socratic', both popularly and philosophically. He is the paradigm of principled martyrdom in the face of illegitimate political power; he informs our understanding that philosophy consists in asking questions, what is popularly called the 'Socratic method', and he voices a unique and powerful type of irony that also bears his name (q.v. Irony). Intensifying his already profound array of extraordinary attributes, Socrates is characterized by paradoxes and extremes, both in body and in soul.

In his bodily persona, Socrates tries to live unconcerned with bodily matters, separating body from soul as far as is possible (*Phaedo* 64a–8b). And yet his body is physically strong and resistant to many exigencies that would affect a normal person's body, including extreme cold, hunger and sleep deprivation (*Smp*. 219e–20b, 223d). Socrates typically wanders in his bare feet (*Phdr*. 229a3; *Smp*. 173b2, 220b6). He is characterized as impervious to the effects of wine (*Smp*. 176c, 220a) and more resistant than most humans to pain and discomfort, a contributing factor to his valour in battle (*Smp*. 219e ff.). Capable equally of physical vigour and corporeal stillness, he sometimes stands perfectly still for long periods of time, apparently lost in thought (*Smp*. 174d, 175a–b).

Socrates is ugly by Greek standards (*Men*. 76c; *Smp*. 218d–e; *Theaetetus* 143e–4a), with bulging eyes, a broad, flat nose and a corpulent body. He is compared to a satyr, the over-sexed, half human, half goat mythological figure (*Smp*. 221e1), a creature also depicted with bulging eyes and wide nose. Despite his ugliness, however, Socrates is erotically linked to Alcibiades (*Alcibiades I*; *Grg*.; *Protagoras*; and *Smp*.), the most beautiful young man in Athens, who declares a strange attraction to Socrates' special kind of enchanting beauty (*Smp*. 218c ff.). Socrates describes himself as an expert in erotic matters (*Smp*. 177d–e) and others agree (*Phdr*. 227c). He always seeks out the most beautiful, in body and soul, among the Athenian youths (e.g. *Alc. I*; *Charmides*; *Lysis*; *Smp*. 216d; *Tht*.), and yet it is unclear whether he ever consummates his erotic relations physically with these young men (*Smp*. 216b–19d).

Socrates' inner, psychic character is also the locus of contradiction and extreme. He is intellectually precocious (*Parmenides*), and characterized by great wisdom, if nothing else. And although the Oracle at Delphi declared that no one was wiser than he, Socrates comes to understand this pronouncement to mean that his wisdom resides in his ignorance, or rather, that whereas others think they are wise when they are not, Socrates does not think he knows what he does not know (*Ap*. 20d ff.).

Socrates exhibits human excellence (q.v. *aretê*) to a greater degree than most human beings, having a robust soul to complement his robust body. The Athenians convicted Socrates of corrupting the young, and yet the young Phaedo describes him as 'the best, and also the wisest and the most upright' of all the men he has known (*Phd*. 118a). And even with regard to Socrates' excellences, Plato plays with paradox. In a dialogue focusing on the excellence of *sôphrosunê*, or self-control, for example, Socrates describes his sexual arousal at the moment when young Charmides' cape falls open and Socrates gets a glimpse inside (*Chrm.* 155d). Socrates emphasizes the importance of self-knowledge in this dialogue, a theme that also appears in *Alc. I* and *Phdr.*

Socrates was also charged with impiety, or not believing in the gods that the city believed in (*Ap.* 24b), and yet Plato's Socrates constantly and provocatively invokes the divine, and his entire life is devoted to fulfilling a divine mission (*Ap.* 29a–d). He even scolds the Athenian jury that convicts him, saying he is literally the god's gift to Athens (*Ap.* 30d–e). He is also distinct for his unique communication with the *daimon* (q.v.), indicating his special connection to the divine. Plato's Socrates is both playful and serious; he is an ironist and a gadfly. He devotes his entire life to improving souls, but claims not to be a teacher. He exhorts interlocutors to live well, but he eschews acolytes.

Socrates' manner of death is most definitive of his character, especially as it is portrayed in the dialogues *Ap.*, *Crito* and *Phd.*, and Plato wraps even these events in paradox. By stridently opposing the Athenian democracy and refusing to live anything but the philosophical life to which he is committed, he puts an end to his philosophizing – at least in his embodied life. For both interlocutors and readers, he is an object of love, admiration, irritation, fear, esteem, hatred, wonder and misunderstanding. Plato's characterization of Socrates' life and death has ensured the Socratic legacy for 2,500 years.

4

TOPICS AND THEMES TREATED
IN THE DIALOGUES

ACCOUNT (see *Logos*)

AESTHETICS

Eugenio Benitez

Many of Plato's dialogues explicitly discuss matters that today fall under the umbrella of aesthetics. Literary criticism occupies a prominent place in the *Ion, Menexenus, Symposium, Republic, Phaedrus* and *Laws*. Arguments about the standard of aesthetic judgement occupy most of the *Hippias Major*, as well as portions of the *Smp.* and the second book of the *Lg.* Some dialogues even venture into territory that we might describe as 'pure aesthetics', in that they discuss specific perceptible properties of form, colour or sound (*Hp. Ma.* 298 ff.; *Philebus* 51c), the manner by which art objects appear as they do to spectators (*Sophist* 236a), the characteristics of an artwork purely in terms of art (*Lg.* 667d) or the ontological status of art objects (*R.* 596a ff.). A few dialogues incidentally discuss painting, sculpture or music (narrowly construed), by way of illustrating a more general topic (*R.* 472d ff.; *Phlb.* 17d; *Critias* 107b), and some dialogues, such as the *Gorgias* and *Timaeus*, delineate or at

least prominently display the aims, conditions and principles of art (*technê*, q.v.). Thus it can be said that aesthetic themes are prominent throughout the works of Plato. There are two dimensions of Plato's aesthetics, however, that are arguably more fundamental to his philosophy than any of the specific themes just mentioned. They are the dimensions of *mimêsis* (q.v.), or representation, and the dimension of *mousikê*, or 'music' in the broad sense that includes all the arts (q.v. music). When these are taken into consideration it becomes plain that aesthetics is not just prominent in, but central to Plato's thought.

According to several dialogues, *all* writing, and indeed *all* art, is a form of *mimêsis* (e.g. *Criti.* 107b; *Lg.* 668b). It is not always appreciated how comprehensive this claim is for Plato. It includes even philosophical writing, which is admitted to be a form of poetry (*Lg.* 817a), and so it applies both to the dialogues themselves (811c), and to their function (*Phdr.* 276d). We should therefore expect that Plato's dialogues are composed according to their own explicit ideas about aesthetic representation. The most important of these ideas is the distinction drawn in the *Sph.* between two ways that an image might represent its original. One way is by really being like the original. Such images are called 'likenesses' (*Sph.* 235d6). Another way is by *seeming*, but not really being like the original. Such images are called 'phantasms' (236c3). To be genuinely philosophical, the dialogues must attain the standard of likenesses. Yet, even if the dialogues attain that standard, they remain distinct from their originals. The inability of an artwork ever to copy its original perfectly has implications for the interpretation of Plato in general, since it seems unlikely, based on the aesthetics of original and image, that Plato would ever suppose that his dialogues stated the truth simply and exactly. The best they might do is to disclose truth to one who could see them from the right perspective. On this view, doctrine would be avoided in preference of a variety of convergent likenesses.

There is an even more comprehensive implication of the view that all art is mimêtic. In the *Ti.*, we are told that the world itself is a work of art, that it is in fact 'a moving image of eternity' (*Ti.* 37d5). Because the relationship of the world to eternity is one of likeness, the status of the world as image implies that the appearance–reality distinction is, for Plato, an aesthetic one. Reality does not underlie the appearances like some sort of primary substance; it is represented in them, as in a work of art. On this view there is not any fundamental difference between the way one discovers reality through art or through natural science – in either case one is finding the real in a reflection. As a result, musical skills (in the broad sense) become an all-inclusive conduit to reality. Music, when genuinely harmonious, provides the pattern for discovering anything true. In this sense all music is philosophical, and philosophy is 'the greatest music' (*Phaedo* 61a3).

Once we see that for Plato all disclosure occurs by means of images, we can better understand his deep concerns about music and musical education. Music is for him not merely cultural study, it is a matter of ontology. As the Athenian Stranger puts it, 'anyone who would not err about a poem must recognise what it is (*hoti pot' esti*); he must recognise its reality (*ousian*) – what it wants to be and what it is really a likeness of (*ti pote bouletai kai hotou pot estin eikôn ontôs, Lg.* 668c4–7)'. The skills basic to education in the arts are the very same skills that appear in more developed form in the philosopher. In that case images that fail to resemble how things really are, in particular images that present an attractive but skewed perspective of things, are not only deceptive but mentally distorting. They warp mental processes so that it becomes hard to see correctly. A child whose mental processes were warped by long exposure to distortions would have difficulty in acquiring the skill to see what is reflected in images (cf. *Lg.* 653a–c). An adult whose mental processes were so distorted would be like someone chained to the way of mistake (cf. *R.* 514a).

Fortunately, thinks Plato, the intellectual appeal of beauty, symmetry and truth far outweigh the hedonistic attractions of a false perspective (*Phlb.* 65b–e). Moreover, the natural desire for all things beautiful is capable of being trained and focused (*Smp.* 210a ff.). Anyone who has once caught a glimpse of what is truly fair will be eager to behold it again. That is the motivation to philosophy. Considered from the point of view of beauty and symmetry, it seems like a fundamentally aesthetic motivation. Considered from the point of view of truth, it seems like a fundamentally epistemological motivation. At the deepest level, however, it is nothing more than a motivation for the good (*R.* 504e).

AKRASIA (INCONTINENCE, WEAKNESS OF WILL)

Daniel C. Russell

Although Aristotle (*Nicomachean Ethics* VII) made *akrasia* the standard term in ancient (and modern) discussions of acting against one's better judgement, Plato more often writes of doing wrong willingly or knowingly (*hekôn*) as opposed to doing so unwillingly or unknowingly (*akôn*). Like Aristotle, though, Plato recognized a problem in explaining how such a thing is possible.

Plato characterizes *akrasia* (or rather *akrateia*, as he calls it at *Timaeus* 86d) as voluntarily acting badly against one's better judgement due to being overcome by a desire, despite being able to do otherwise. Consider someone who voluntarily overeats despite meaning to stick to a diet. One might characterize his behaviour as akratic – a breakdown between judgement and choice – and then explain how such breakdowns occur. Alternatively, perhaps this characterization is mistaken and the behaviour should be explained in some other way. Plato appears to have taken each of these approaches in different places.

In some dialogues Plato rejects the possibility of *akrasia* on the grounds that there is no opposition between such motivating forces as practical reason and desire (q.v.). In the *Protagoras*, Socrates puts forward the thesis that no one does wrong wittingly. Whereas most people think that knowledge is often 'dragged around' by desire 'as if it were a slave', Socrates suggests that 'knowledge is a fine thing capable of ruling a person' and that 'if someone were to know what is good and bad, then he would not be forced by anything to act otherwise than knowledge dictates' (*Prt.* 352c). Socrates' argument for this thesis focuses on pleasure: what we desire

is pleasure, and to judge that something is better or worse is to judge that it is more pleasant or less pleasant, respectively; so since practical reason (in the form of either knowledge or belief, 358b–c) and desire have the same targets, they do not oppose each other. Apparent cases of *akrasia* must really be cases of ignorance that one is doing the worse thing.

Since desire has the same target as practical reason, desire must always seek what is good, that is, beneficial for one. That is, no one does wrong willingly:

> Now, no one goes willingly toward the bad or what he believes to be bad; neither is it in human nature, so it seems, to desire to go toward what one believes to be bad instead of to the good. And when he is forced to choose between one of two bad things, no one will choose the greater if he is able to choose the lesser. (358d)

Earlier in *Prt.* Socrates declared it 'uneducated' to suppose 'that any human being willingly makes a mistake or willingly does anything wrong or bad'; rather, educated persons know 'very well that anyone who does anything wrong or bad does so involuntarily' (345d–e). Similarly, in *Meno* (77a–8a) Socrates argues that if people did bad things knowing them to be bad, then they would know that such things were harmful for them and thus would make them miserable and unhappy. But since nobody desires to be miserable and unhappy, anyone who desires what is in fact bad must mistakenly believe that that thing is beneficial for him. Likewise, responding to Callicles who espouses *akrasia* in *Gorgias*, Socrates says that 'no one does what's unjust because he desires to', but that 'all who do so do it unwillingly' (*Grg.* 509e). This, he says, is because we desire to do only those things that benefit us: 'when one desires some act for the sake of some end, that end must be something beneficial for one, since when one learns that an act would be harmful for one, one stops desiring it' (467c–8c). The denial of *akrasia* – often called the 'Socratic paradox' – rests on the idea that what desire seeks is also what practical reason seeks, so that there can be no opposition between them.

Elsewhere, however, Plato argues that desire does not seek what practical reason seeks. In *Republic*, Socrates famously divides the soul (q.v.) into 'reason', 'spirit' and 'appetite', and argues that whereas reason and spirit seek what is beneficial, appetite (not distinguished from desire) does not (*R.* 437b–41c). Indeed, Socrates compares spirit and reason to a lion and a tamer united against appetite, depicted as a hydra (588b–90d). On this view, one can desire to do what one judges to be bad, as when Leontius succumbed to a desire to look at corpses (439e–40b). Likewise, in *Phaedrus* (237d–8c) Plato depicts reason as a charioteer with one noble and obedient horse (spirit) and one ugly, disobedient horse (appetite/desire) that is deaf to reason and occasionally gets its way. And in *Sophist*, Plato distinguishes going wrong out of ignorance from going wrong out of vice, that is, a 'discord' between 'beliefs and desires, anger and pleasures, reason and pains' (*Sph.* 228b). In these dialogues, apparently one can desire what reason judges to be bad for one, making *akrasia* possible.

However, in yet other dialogues Plato seems to hold *both* that *akrasia* is possible *and* that no one does wrong willingly. In *Laws*, the Athenian says that there can be discord between one's 'feelings of pleasure and pain and [one's] rational judgment' (*Lg.* 689a), and that while some people are 'immoderate' due to ignorance, some are so

due to 'lack of self-control' (734b). (Although 644d–5b also seems to suggest that the soul is divided into parts, Bobonich 1994 has challenged this; see Gerson 2003 for a reply.) Yet the Athenian also says that 'every unjust man is unjust against his will', since no one willingly embraces things that are harmful for him in his 'most precious part' (731c; see also 860d–4c; *Philebus* 22b). The Athenian brings these two thoughts together by saying that succumbing to *akrasia* is succumbing to doing what one does not really desire to do (*Lg.* 863d–e; see also *Clitomachus* 407d). But this is puzzling: if to act against practical reason is to do what one does not really desire to do, then how can desire also lead one to act against practical reason?

Some help may come from *Ti.*, where it is said that a corrupted person has excessive desires but is not willingly in such a condition (*Ti.* 86b–7b). Perhaps Plato's thought is that in its uncorrupted condition desire seeks what practical reason seeks, and that 'willingly' must be understood in terms of desire in its uncorrupted condition. So *akrasia* is the result of a corrupted condition, which is bad for one, and no one is 'willingly' in that corrupt condition. Moreover, since wrongdoing is bad for the one who does it, it follows that no one does wrong 'willingly'.

Many scholars believe that Plato denied the possibility of *akrasia* (when he did) on the grounds that desire is a species of practical reason (e.g. Penner 1991), a view often called 'Socratic intellectualism'; but there is no consensus on this point (e.g. Brickhouse and Smith 2007; Devereux 1995). Moreover, the apparent shifts in Plato's thinking on *akrasia* and the nature of the soul have been central to modern debates about the unity (or otherwise) of Plato's philosophy across his career (e.g. Annas 1999:ch. 6; Vlastos 1991a:48, 86–91).

ANTILOGY AND ERISTICS (ERISTIC)

Menahem Luz

Antilogy (*antilogia*) is an ancient concept mentioned as early as Herodotus (VIII.77, IX.88) and etymologically corresponding to the English term 'contradiction' (*anti* = contra, *logia* = diction), but broader in scope with a secondary meaning of 'dispute' or 'gainsay' where no formal contradiction is implied. Although the art of antilogical contradiction (*antilogikê technê*) was occasionally employed by Socrates in order to disprove a mistaken opinion (*Theaetetus* 197a), the art of 'antilogy and disputation' was chiefly employed in competitions for profit by the sophists as part of their art of eristic (*Sophist* 226a).

The word Eristics is derived from the term 'rivalry' (*eris*) since the sophists competed against one another or a prospective client in disputation (*Lysis* 211b) employing any verbal trick or captious 'sophism' even if reached through false assumptions as exemplified throughout Plato's *Euthd.* (Kneale and Kneale 1964:12–15). Plato thus did not regard eristic 'rivalry' as serious philosophy but 'a game' in disputation (*Sph.* 237b–c) – that is, argument for argument's sake – and employing antilogy for this purpose (216a, 232b). Although there are many cases where antilogy and eristics should be distinguished (Kerferd 1989:62–5), antilogical eristics were also employed as part of a sophist's training in order to enhance expertise in the art of persuasion. They were also employed in public rhetorical displays (*epideixeis*), in which a sophist would give a public lecture contradicting or disputing conventionally accepted norms – for example, Gorgias' *Encomium to Helen* defends the immorality of Helen of Troy. Since the search for the truth was often secondary to the art of persuasion in antilogical eristics, the conclusions were often based on an ambiguous, if not on a relativistic, understanding of the goals of philosophy (Guthrie 1971a:176–81). Although many scholars have followed the ancients in denigrating Eristics, some have considered it and antilogy more objectively as the first tentative steps towards logical thinking (Kneale and Kneale 1964:12).

The relativistic sophist Protagoras was said to have been the first to develop antilogy as a principle of argumentation: 'there are two arguments (*logoi*) on every theme contraposed (*antikeimenoi*) to each other' (D. L. 9.51.13–5). This was probably discussed in his lost work: '*Antilogies* vols.1, 2' (54.19; cf. 9.38) and a surviving text of his school reads:

There are two *logoi* cited by the philosophers in Greece concerning the good and bad, for some claim that the good is one thing and the bad another while others [claim] that they are the same thing for something is good for some but bad for others – and even for the same person it is sometimes good and sometimes bad. (*Dissoi Logoi* 2.90.1.1)

In this quotation from the *Dissoi Logoi* not only are 'good' and 'bad' relative, but even the arguments for and against this claim are relative in that they comprise two *logoi* in the form of an antilogy. Plato later criticized the sophists who wasted their time in 'antilogical arguments (*logoi*)' in that they lacked 'the art of *logos*' to distinguish between truth and the falsehood (*Phaedo* 90b–c; cf. 101e). Since Protagoras maintained that the individual is the sole 'measure' of truth not only for the phenomena but also for the truth of a *logos* or its *antilogos*, the decision on which of them is to become the accepted norm depended on a speaker's power of persuasion rather than the objective truth of his arguments (D. L. 9.51.14–16). While Protagoras might contradict (*antilegei*) accepted social norms and *logoi* by democratic persuasion, an extreme sophist like Thrasymachus would use antilogical eristic to justify tyranny through the use of fallacy and ambiguous argument (*Republic* 343b–4c). The antilogical method was also used in eristic exercise whereby rival students vied with each other to justify the case of either one of the two antilogies. However, as early as Plato (*Phaedrus* 261d–e), it was also used in forensic training, juridical theory (one must hear both sides prior to judgement) and later in sceptical enquiry (for every *logos* there is an *antilogos*).

Conservatives like Aristophanes (*Clouds* 889–1104) and philosophers in the Socratic circle viewed this relative and nonnormative approach as undermining belief in *logoi* that supported accepted morality since in their view only one of the two antilogies could be true by nature or reason at any one time. Nonetheless, it has been claimed that Socrates' method of dialectic refutation (*elenchus*; q.v.) can be seen to be derived from the antilogical methods of the sophists in that he too sought for inconsistencies in the arguments of his conversants (Gulley 1968:31).

A method of countering the Sophists was formulated by Antisthenes (q.v. Other Socratics) that each definition and statement (*logos*) can denote only one thing (e.g. 'gold is gold') and statements in other terms (e.g. 'gold is a yellow metal') are contradictions referring gold to something else (Luz 2000:92). Thus, Antisthenes concluded that it is impossible to contradict (*antilegein*) since each *logos* refers to a separate entity. Plato recognized that the art of contradiction (*antilogikê technê*) can intrude itself into serious dialectic as well as false eristic especially when the conversants

make generalizations that do not distinguish between the different species of subject (*R.* 454a–b). Besides Plato's criticism of sophistic contradiction (*antilogikos*) as having no part in true philosophy (*Tht.* 164c–d), he also includes philosophical questioning that contradicts the opponents' conclusions rather than their hypotheses (*Sph.* 225b–d). This has been plausibly interpreted as a reference to Euclides' Megarian school (Cornford 1964:176–7) where antilogical paradox was employed precisely for this purpose.

Like Plato, who incorporated the principle of antilogies into his method of diairesis (q.v. Method) whereby each species could be divided into a class that is like and unlike, Aristotle's early logical work '*On the Opposites*' (*peri enantion*) established that it is not contrasting (*antikeimena*) subjects that are syllogies (e.g. wisdom and ignorance) but their definitions that are (Ross 1970:108, f. 3). This however was to be replaced by his doctrine in the *Categories* where substance has no opposite itself and while the other categories (quality, quantity, etc.) may contain opposites (black and white, heavy and light) they are not opposites in themselves. Just as he treated the examination of sophistic rhetoric in an objective, nonmoralizing way, so Aristotle turned to sophistries, eristics and antilogies in his work *Sophistical Refutations*, where he drew the distinction between different forms of logical reasoning ('syllogism'), for reasoning can be either true or false, but it is the duty of the true reason not only to prove something but also to refute false reasoning (*Sophistical Refutations* 176b29–31). In the *Topics*, Aristotle carefully worked out rules by which the dialectical syllogism can avoid this and confute the antilogy (*Topics* 105a:18–19). His answer to the Protagorean antilogy (*Metaphysics* 4; 1011b23–24) is found in his principle of the Law of the

Excluded Middle (*metaxu antiphaseos*): it is impossible to maintain (*phanai*) and contradict (*apophanai*) the same thing in the same relationship at the same time (*Metaphysics* 4; 1005b.19–20, 26–34n). However, he did find a use for antilogies in *Metaphysics* 2: in order to understand a problem we have to list all of its quandaries (*aporiai*) and arguments *pro et contra*. There he set forth 14 quandaries of metaphysics, each by *thesis* and *antithesis*, but strictly avoided any formal solution for either side. Aristotle, however, did not believe that each *thesis* and *antithesis* had equal weight in the end, but that we must attain positive knowledge of a subject by weighing both sides beforehand. In this way he clears the table for his positive *apodeictic* discussion of metaphysics in the following books. Without the antitheses of bk 2 we would not know which arguments to set aside.

APPEARANCE AND REALITY (REALITY)

Christopher Moore

Plato's dialogues prompt reflection on at least four related questions about reality. Ethical: how does living well take apprehending what is real? Epistemological: in what ways does apprehending what is real differ from believing what is merely apparent? Metaphysical: what does accepting a distinction between reality and appearance mean for the nature of things? Methodological: by what means might one come to know what is real?

Plato's characters distinguish diverse kinds of appearances from reality:

- *eikos*: 'plausible', 'probable', 'reasonable'; what is persuasive in a speech, in contrast to what is true (*alêtheia*)

- *doxa*: a 'belief', an 'opinion', a 'thought'; what seems (*dokein*) so to someone, in contrast to what really is the case, for example, knowledge (*epistêmê*) or understanding (*nous*)
- *ta legomena*: 'things said'; what a community of speakers accepts (compare *muthoi*), in contrast to what really is so
- *to phainomenon*: 'what appears so'; how things received by the senses (*aisthêseis*) are perceived or thought about, in contrast to what is or exists (*to einai*)
- *to mê on*: 'what is not'; what some people mistake for what really exists (*to on*)
- *to genomenos*: 'what comes to be'; what changes and has changing appearances, in contrast to whatever is unchanging (and may be invisible)
- dream-appearances, shadows, reflections, paintings and mimêtic activity

(I) ETHICS

In the dialogues, understanding a virtue may start in, but cannot stop at, specifying either those people who appear to exemplify that virtue or those sets of traits which seem typical of those people who exemplify that virtue. Many of Plato's characters come to accept that understanding a virtue requires proposing an abstract definition and then testing it against counter-examples. That the reality of a virtue or some other object of moral reflection may be discovered through conceptual analysis seems likely to be a cultural presupposition preceding Socrates but elaborated by Plato's Socrates.

People act on their thoughts about their moral obligations, circumstances and resources, but their thoughts may not reflect reality. Protagoras sees himself as a completely capable educator; Crito worries he will be seen as a shameful friend. Yet the dialogues suggest that they fail to know what they really can, and thus ought, to do. They lack self-knowledge (q.v.). This has bad consequences for their students, the city (*Phaedrus* 277e1–3), their associates (*Theaetetus* 201c) and themselves, either at present or hereafter (*Gorgias* 524d).

Rather than emphasizing the 'depth' of self-knowledge when writing about getting to the reality of one's nature, Plato uses the tropes of matching inward with outward (*Phdr.* 279b9; *Symposium* 215b), comparing oneself to ideals (*Phdr.* 230a), working with others (*Alcibiades 1* 133b) and being able to say what one means (*Laches* 194b).

(II) Epistemology

The myth of the cave (q.v.) in *Republic* bk 7 suggests that what we now accept as real we may later reject as mere shadow, reflection or image. The myth does not tell us how to assess the match between our beliefs and the world. But bk 1 depicts refutative exchange, the revelation of beliefs and their (inconsistent) consequences to show that some of what one thought cannot be true. Bks 2–3 and 10 dwell on the effects of attending to imitations of reality (*mimêsis*) (cf. *Sophist* 267e1; *Grg.* 462b–5d). Bk 6's divided line image (q.v.) gives a symbol of the distinction between reflections, material objects, hypothetical knowledge and grounded knowledge. Bk 7's system of education identifies the way a person might become practised at acquiring knowledge of immutable things (universal forms), particularly through mathematics and deliberate conversation.

The *Tht.* discusses the nature of knowledge, in particular how to distinguish it from (mere) perception, (mere) true belief and (mere) true belief with an account, but does not conclude with any explicit agreement

about what makes our apprehension of reality distinctive (Burnyeat 1990).

(III) Metaphysics

Degree of reality seems proportional to explanatory scope: whatever most explains the order of the universe is the most real; how things appear to us is less real (though not entirely unreal).

In the *Tht.*, Socrates impersonates a Protagoras who argues that the world is just as it seems to each of its perceivers. The bulk of the dialogue goes to undermine (some version) of this relativistic thesis, thus supporting the view that something constant underlies everyone's perceptions. Talk about appearance or seeming or opinion makes sense only against an assumption that there is something more real.

It is traditional to call Plato, in contrast to Aristotle, an idealist, someone who suspects or is committed to the belief that the really real is not the changing particulars but something imperceptible, immutable and intelligible. While Plato likely did not pioneer distinguishing between appearance and reality with 'form' (*eidos*, *idea*) language, his dialogues did draw implications from such talk. It may be impossible to articulate a *theory* of forms from these dialogues, either because Plato did not have one; or if he did, did not use the dialogues to set out and defend it, or because his views changed over time. Nevertheless, the dialogues might show the value of thinking about what *could* explain how the world seems to us (Moravscik 1992; Thesleff 1999).

(IV) Methodology

In the *Ion*, Socrates wonders how Ion could know what Homer really thought. Socrates suggests he has no rational skill but is served instead by 'inspiration' (q.v.). Whether Plato believes any aspect of reality could be apprehended via inspiration, prophecy or direct intuition, is hard to say, but it is doubtful he thinks such means could verify their own accuracy.

What seems clearer is that in that dialogue Socrates removes the appearance of Ion's great wisdom and reveals that Ion really just has a knack with Homeriana. Socrates finds this out by asking Ion questions (*erôtesis*), examining the things he says (*exetasis*), and refuting him (*elenchos*). These three revelatory activities together calls 'philosophizing' (*Ap.* 29de). What Plato thinks this kind of talking can establish is uncertain.

The dialogues offer many more candidate methods (q.v.) for discovering reality amid appearances. One might remember what the wise have said (*Men.* 81a5; *Phdr.* 260a5–6), study with those who know (*Lg.* 186c–d), run deductions (*Phdr.* 245c6–6a2), look at a diagram (*Men.* 82b9), hypothesize (*Men.* 86e7–7b7; *Phd.* 100a3–8; *Parmenides* 136a1–2) and practise dividing and collecting (*Sph.* 218c; *Phdr.* 277b5–9). The *R.* appears to encourage 'dialectic' (q.v.) as a way to knowing how things really are (*R.* 454a, 511b–c), though it is not clear what this term means beyond deliberate, reasonable and sustained examination (cf. *Prm.* 135c2). To be a philosopher on the model of Socrates involves trying to live on the basis of good reasons, reasons based in what is real and true, on facts and valid inference. (It is debatable whether the other philosophers in Plato's dialogues stand for this.) Many of our reasons are good, but our accepting them is insufficient reason for continuing to accept them. Yet, deciding which to keep involves a conceptual difficulty. Since beliefs are checked only against other beliefs – our

resource is always what seems so to us (*Tht.* 171d3–5) – we may seem caught in a web of appearances. Plato's Socrates seems to have responded by (tentatively) taking as real those theses that survived continuous testing. Plato may further have thought that mathematics or similar practises could reveal significant parts of reality, though which parts, and with what significance, remains a difficult question.

APPETITE (see Desire)

ARGUMENT (see *Logos*)

ART (*TECHNÊ*)

David Roochnik

Technê, typically translated as 'art', 'expertise', 'craft' or 'skill', is a word used widely and with great significance in Plato's early dialogues, for example consider *Laches* 184e–5e. Here Socrates is faced with the question of how to educate a young man in 'virtue' or 'excellence' (*aretê*). He insists that only 'an expert', someone who is *technikos* (*La.* 185a1) – that is, has mastered a *technê* – in the matter under deliberation is qualified to provide an answer. To convince his interlocutors that this is the case he deploys an analogy: if one wished to know what physical exercise the boy should practise in order to develop an excellent body, he would consult an expert or technical 'trainer' (*paidotribê*:184e3). In an analogous fashion, when the question concerns the excellence of the young men, someone who is 'expert (*technikos*) in the care (*therapeian*) of the soul (*psuchê*)' (185e4) is required.

Apology 20a–c presents a second example. If, Socrates argues, Callias' two sons were colts, he would hire an experienced, well-trained and well-regarded professional to supervise their upbringing, for only such an expert would be able to cultivate the excellence 'appropriate' (*prosêkousan*:*Ap.* 20b1) to horses. His sons are young men but no less, Socrates suggests, do they require someone 'knowledgeable' (*epistêmôn*:20b5) to educate them in their specific excellence; namely, in 'human and political excellence' (20b4–5). Again, the analogy is manifest: as the technical horse trainer is to the excellence of colts, so the technical educator is to the excellence appropriate to young men.

Since an 'expert', or *technitês*, has mastered his subject thoroughly, his knowledge can be readily identified. He can, in many cases, simply point to the results of his work to give evidence of his skill. For example, after months of training by someone knowledgeable in *hippikê*, the *technê* of horsemanship, the young colt will be visibly improved. For this reason its owner is willing to pay the expert horse trainer for his services. (Indeed, at times '*technitês*' can even be translated as 'professional'.) In general, it is reasonable for 'laymen' (*idioteis*) who are not knowledgeable in the field – and every *technê* has a specific or determinate field – to defer to the expert's judgements. Even though the colt belongs to a wealthy aristocrat, its owner, if he truly wants an excellent horse, will rigorously follow the regimen prescribed by the horse trainer.

With this in mind, consider the consequences of a strict reading of Socrates' use of the *technê*-analogy. On the simplest level, if there were a *technitês* in human excellence then the endeavour to live a good life would become a question that could be answered, a problem that could be solved. Second, if the analogy holds strictly, it would be reasonable for other human beings to subordinate themselves to the one who possesses such answers: to what Jenks calls the 'moral expert' (Jenks 2008:xv). As a result, it is arguable that there is a direct connection between Socrates' use of the *technê*-analogy in the early dialogues and the political authoritarianism that he seems to defend in the *Republic* where 'philosopher-kings' are firmly in control of the lives of the citizens. In other words, a political implication of a strict reading of the analogy is that it becomes reasonable for citizens to obey an epistemically authoritative ruler.

Many scholars such as Parry (1996) read Socrates' use of the *technê*-analogy in this fashion. In other words, they take *technê* to be a positive model for Plato's early attempt to develop a moral theory. (See Irwin 1977a:71–5 for a clear summary of this position.) For at least three related reasons this view must be challenged. First and most generally, the notion of a 'moral expert' implied by a positive reading of the analogy conflicts with the *aporetic* or interrogative character of so many of Socrates' dialogues. Second, if it is the case that as the horse trainer is to horses, so the expert in human virtue is to human beings, then human *aretê* must, like the specific excellence of horses, be a determinate epistemic object. It must constitute a bounded conceptual field that can be thoroughly mastered. Again, the *aporetic* character of the dialogues should call this into question. Third, if the field of expertise is, as the *La.* passage cited above suggests, the human soul, then the *psuchê* must also be determinate, for it must be capable of becoming a subject matter of an expert's *technê*. It is arguable on the basis of a reading of the *Symposium* such as that presented in Hyland (2008:39–41), for example, that the *psuchê* is not such an object. As a result, a strict reading of the analogy becomes problematic.

The above does not imply that the analogy is without philosophical significance. Instead, it suggests that it should be read as quite limited. Virtue may indeed be analogous to *technê* but only in the minimal sense of being some kind of knowledge, even if not a technical one. In fact, it is conceivable, as Roochnik (1996) argues, that Plato has Socrates deploy the analogy precisely to develop a conception of virtue as non-technical knowledge. To clarify, consider Vlastos's distinction between 'knowledge$_c$', a rigorous form of knowledge whose hallmark is 'infallible certainty' (Vlastos 1985:14) and 'knowledge$_e$' (Vlastos 1985:15), 'elenctic knowledge' that Socrates derives through his familiar argumentative strategies. Even though it does not invoke the *technê* model this distinction is useful. The 'elenctic knowledge' Socrates both encourages and may even possess is not strictly technical. Instead, it emerges only from dialogue with others.

BEAUTY (*KALON*)

Gabriel Richardson Lear

The notion of beauty (*to kalon*) is surprisingly pervasive in Plato's dialogues (ugly = *aischron*). Whereas modern philosophers tend to treat beauty as the special concern of aesthetics, Plato finds a significant role for it in his metaphysics, cosmology, epistemology and ethics. For example, Socrates argues that beauty, along with proportion and truth, is the cause of the good life and, more generally, of good mixtures (*Philebus* 65a). The beauty of the cosmos (q.v.) marks it as formed in the image of eternal models (*Timaeus* 28a–9a). Love of genuinely beautiful poetry and people is a necessary, or at least useful, preliminary for the development

of reason (*Republic* 401d–2b). Erotic experience of a beautiful body can turn one's life towards the pursuit of wisdom (*Symposium* 210a–12a; *Phaedrus* 250d–6e). And all the interlocutors assume that virtue is *kalon*, including the great amoralist Callicles, who is presented as claiming against Socrates that pleonectic power is more genuinely *kalon* – and thus more truly virtuous – than the traditional moral virtues (*Gorgias* 482c–6d, 508c–e; cf. *Sophist* 228e, 230d–e). Plato does assume that good art will be *kalon* (*R.* 377b, 401c; *Laws* 668a, 669a) and establishes a criteria of poetic beauty, but he does not make the modern assumption that art provides an especially pure or philosophically illuminating case of the experience of beauty. *That* experience in Plato's view is the experience of love (q.v.).

The Greek term *kalon* can be translated by a number of English words: beautiful, fine, admirable, noble and good. In its adverbial form, *kalôs*, it is typically used as the equivalent of the adverbial form of *agathos* (good). Some scholars doubt that Plato's discussion of the *kalon* really concerns beauty at all, especially in moral contexts (Irwin 1979:154). But although the two concepts are not exactly the same (Kosman 2010), it is unlikely that Plato's *kalon* is simply the praiseworthy in general, only sometimes referring to what is admirable in a specifically aesthetic way (i.e. by eliciting a special sort of pleasure in an observer). For example, Plato often has characters assert that things are *kalon* when their parts are well-proportioned, harmonious and measured (*Phlb.* 64e; *R.* 402d; *Sph.* 228a, 235e–6a; *Ti.* 30c, 87c–8c). This analysis coincides with one traditional account of beauty. Furthermore, he emphasizes the way we are 'struck all of a sudden' by *kala* people and ideas, suggesting that the *kalon* is distinguished in part by the way it affects our receptivity (*Smp*. 210e; *Phdr*. 250b–d). The *kalon* forces itself on our awareness, either through our eyes or on the mind. Since this experience of being struck is vital to Plato's story of how *erôs* can be channelled into a process of intellectual development – the *kalon* object of love is, at each stage, a 'summoner' of philosophical thought (Ferrari 1987:144–6) – we should take care not to disown the *kalon*'s kinship with beauty in this respect.

In the *R*. Socrates claims that the form of the good (q.v.) is the cause of 'all that is correct and beautiful in anything' (*R*. 517c; cf. 452e; *Ti*. 30a). If this were true, it would justify his claim that all beautiful things are good (*Alc. 1* 115a–16c; *Meno* 77b; *Protagoras* 358b; for the converse, that all good things are beautiful: *Lysis* 216d; *Smp*. 201c, 204d–e). In the *R*., he is especially concerned with the beauty of things with a proper work or function. We can see why goodness in such things would cause them to be *kalon*. For the goodness of such a thing is whatever it is that enables it to perform its proper function well, but that is precisely what will determine what it is for that thing to be well-proportioned and internally harmonious. And proportion and harmony are the hallmarks of beauty (*R*. 601d, 452e; *Ti*. 87c). This functional account of beauty fits well with one of the definitions of the beautiful proposed in *Hippias Major*: that it is the appropriate (*Hp. Ma*. 290c–1d). It also makes sense of the intuition that the beautiful is beneficial (*Grg*. 474d; *Hp. Ma*. 296e–7a; *Laches* 192d; cf. *R*. 364a). Though genuinely *kala* things may not suit the desires we happen to have, if they are human artefacts, actions or souls, they *will* be useful from the point of view of the human function (*R*. 589c; *Ti*. 87e). It is less clear how beautiful things without

functions – numerical proportions, patches of pure colour might be examples – can be explained in terms of their relation to the good. This raises the question of whether and how to distinguish beauty and goodness (Barney 2010; Hobbs 2000:222–7; Lear 2007; Price 1989:16; White 1989).

Insofar as we experience something as beautiful, we feel pleasure (q.v.). Sometimes the pleasure is pure (*Phlb*. 51c–d), other times it is 'mixed' with pain (*Phdr*. 251c–d). This connection between pleasure and beauty reveals another aspect of Plato's view: beauty is a feature of the way things appear or manifest themselves to a subject. In the *Phdr*. Socrates claims that the beautiful alone among the forms 'shines out' through the sensible objects which participate in it (*Phdr*. 250b–e). In the first instance, this means that it is a form whose images we can literally see. But the 'radiance' of beauty seems also to refer to our mode of access to it. Although we may work out later why something is beautiful, *that* it is beautiful is something of which we are immediately aware.

Beauty is therefore the power of appearing, that is, manifesting oneself as, perfect and internally harmonious. This does not imply that whenever we experience something as beautiful, it is in fact beautiful. Our own defective perspective (perceptual or ethical) may cause a false appearance of beauty or ugliness (*Sph*. 235d–6a; cf. *Hp. Ma*. 294a–e; *R*. 602b). And as with other illusions of appearance, one can experience something as beautiful without believing as a matter of rational conviction that it is perfect. In this case, a conflict would occur between the part of the soul to which the object appears beautiful and the part which believes that it is not.

Genuinely beautiful things are therefore truthful in the sense of communicating to a spectator an accurate appearance of perfection. This is especially important for Plato's discussions of *kalos logos*, beautiful speech, a topic that covers rhetorical persuasion (*Hp. Ma.*; *Phdr.*), poetry (*Ion*; *R.*) and, by implication, philosophical discourse (*Smp.* 198b–9b; *Lg.* 817b). Since speech conveys an image both of the world it describes and of the person describing it, beautiful speech must be truthful both in the sense of being authentic and in the sense of imprinting in the listener beliefs which are correct, or at least likely in outline. Truly beautiful speech is, therefore, either wise or philosophical.

The experience of beauty is pleasant. Pleasure, according to Plato, is a qualification of awareness attendant upon 'being filled with what is appropriate to our nature' (*R.* 585d; *Phlb.* 31d). In other words, pleasant objects and activities seem good for us (*Lg.* 657c). The implication, though Plato does not say so explicitly, is that the experience of beauty is not only the experience of a thing's manifest perfection but also the experience of the thing's perfection as good for the subject. It is no wonder, then, that the experience of beauty excites *erôs*, that passionate desire for 'intercourse' with the beautiful thing.

Plato's faith in the transformative power of beauty may seem overly optimistic, but he does not think it is guaranteed. In the *Phdr.* Socrates depicts all aspects of the soul as responsive to the *kalon* boy, but their responses conflict. The life of philosophical conversation is only one way the struggle may be resolved (*Phdr.* 256a–c). Thus, it would be unfair to accuse Plato of sentimental blindness to the danger of beauty. Beauty has a beneficial effect only on souls innately capable of improvement and only if they have a 'leader to lead them aright' (*Smp.* 210a).

BEING AND BECOMING (*ON, ONTA; GIGNESTHAI*)

Sandra Peterson

Several passages in Plato contrast being, using the Greek infinitive 'to be' (*einai*) or participle 'being' (*on*) and becoming (*gignesthai*). The contrast, tailored in each dialogue to its particular interlocutors, resists tidy packaging into a single stance of Plato's.

I discuss passages from *Timaeus, Theaetetus* and *Republic*. Other relevant passages are: *Phaedo* 78c–9a, 102b–3c; *Cratylus* 439b–40e; *Symposium* 207d–8b; *Parmenides* 152b–e, 163d; *Sophist* 248a–9d; *Philebus* 26d, 27b, 54a–d, 59a–d, 61d–e; and *Laws* 893b–4.

(I) TIMAEUS

At *Ti.* 27d–8a Timaeus strongly contrasts (a) what always is and never becomes, and (b) what always becomes and never is. What always is 'is grasped by understanding, which involves a reasoned account. It is unchanging'. What becomes is 'grasped by opinion, which involves unreasoning sense perception. It comes to be and passes away but never really is'. The latter apparently includes all perceptible items in our world. Accounts of being are more reliable than accounts of becoming, which are merely likely (*Ti.* 29b–c). 'What being is to becoming truth is to belief (*pistis*)' (*Ti.* 29c).

According to Timaeus (*Ti.* 28a–9a), a craftsman who made the universe could use only an eternal (*aidion*) model because a beautiful work requires an eternal model.

As an example of what is grasped by understanding alone and not perceived by the senses Timaeus (*Ti.* 51b–e) gives 'intelligible forms' such as fire itself, of which the fiery stuff in space that we perceive is an image.

Timaeus further explains at *Ti.* 37e–8b that we should not apply future or past tensed forms of the verb 'to be' to what is everlasting. We cannot say that it was and will be, but we can say that it is. We can use 'was' and 'will be' of what becomes, but cannot accurately say even that what becomes *is* what becomes. Timaeus does not dwell on this linguistic point.

To illustrate Plato's contrast between what *becomes* round and what *is* round, consider: when a lump of dough gets round after continued rolling, a doughy sphere gets generated or comes-to-be (*gignetai*). Sphere-shape, however, always is (*esti*) round: the shape, sphere, did not ever become round. What a sphere is, the sphere itself, is, permanently, round.

(II) THEAETETUS

Socrates at *Tht.* 152d finds Theaetetus receptive to a view that elides the contrast between being and becoming. This view, which Socrates calls 'not a paltry account' of Protagoras, Heracleitus and Empedocles, declares that nothing ever is:

> . . . nothing *is* one thing itself by itself, and you would not correctly call something some sort of thing, but if you label it great it shows itself small . . . – and everything that way, nothing *being* one thing or of something nor any sort of thing. But from movement, change, and mixture with one another, everything that we say *is* – not labeling it correctly – gets generated. For nothing ever is but always gets generated. (152d2–e1)

Socrates subsequently gives the example (154a) that colour gets generated or comes to be between an eye and an object when they (each a complex of motions and changes) collide. He says:

nothing is hard, hot, or anything, just by itself; . . . but in their intercourse with one another things get . . . qualified in all ways, as a result of their change. (156e)

[T]hings are always getting generated for someone. We should exclude 'be'; from everywhere . . . Nor ought we to admit 'something', 'someone's', 'my', 'this', 'that', or any other word that brings things to a standstill. (157b)

Socrates introduced the view that things never are, but always get generated or come to be, to bolster Theaetetus' proposal that knowledge is perception. On this view when we incorrectly say that something is, we should most properly say that it is getting generated for someone. (Or we could less properly say that it is for someone.) Socrates explains the connection to Theaetetus' proposal:

> 160c: Since what acts on me is for me and not someone else, it's also the case that I and not someone else, perceive it? . . . So my perception is true for me – because it's always of the being that's mine and as Protagoras said, it's for me to decide . . . Well then . . . how could I fail to have knowledge of the things I'm a perceiver of? . . . So you were quite right to say that knowledge is nothing but perception.

At *Tht.* 183b, however, Socrates and Theaetetus agree that in our current language one cannot state the theory that everything constantly changes, unless perhaps one simply utters 'not so' endlessly – which, presumably, reduces the theory to absurdity. Socrates drops it from the ensuing conversation.

(III) REPUBLIC

What purely is contrasts with what rolls about or wanders between what purely is

142

and what is not (*R*. 475c–80b). What purely is, including such items as the beautiful itself, is always the same in all respects and is an appropriate object of knowledge (477). It is the special interest of philosophers (480). Certain items roll about in that if they may be called, for example, just or beautiful, they may also be called unjust or ugly (in some respect). Only later at 485b does the word 'becoming' occur: philosophers love the learning that makes clear to them 'the being that always is and does not wander around between becoming and decaying'. At 521–32 we read that study of mathematics draws us from becoming to study being (521d). The study of being leads us to the final item of study, good itself (532b).

The secondary literature disputes whether such passages suggest (a) every perceptible change in every respect at all times (Cherniss 1957:356 responding to Owen 1953a), or suggest at most that there is (b) at each time every perceptible change in some respect or other (Irwin 1977b:3 note 5). There is also dispute whether Plato believed (a) at some time: Irwin (1977b:6) says no. Cherniss (1957:349–60) says yes.

CAUSE (*AITIA*)

Fred D. Miller, Jr.

Plato's terms *aitia* (n.) and *aitios* or *aition* (adj.) are traditionally translated as 'cause', although 'reason' and 'explanation' are also used. The correct translation is controversial, as will become clear.

The concept of cause helps to distinguish reliable from unreliable beliefs: although true opinions are valuable as long as they remain, they tend to escape from our souls, so that they are not worth much unless tied down by an 'account (or working out, *logismos*) of the cause (*aitia*)' (*Meno* 97e–8a). This is also suggested by *Timaeus* 27e–8a, which makes two points: first, that belief is concerned with that which comes to be, in distinction from knowledge which is concerned with that which is, and, second, that everything that comes to be comes to be through the agency of some cause (cf. *Philebus* 26e).

In the *Phaedo* Plato makes Socrates interrupt his attempt to prove that the soul is immortal by turning to an inquiry into 'the cause of generation and destruction' (*Phd*. 96a). Although earlier scientists speculated about the causes of a wide range of natural phenomena, Plato was the first to consider critically what it meant to speak of a cause of something. According to Plato earlier scientists took causes (e.g. of thinking) to be bodily processes involving stuffs like air or fire or blood.

Socrates says that he was intrigued by Anaxagoras' claim that intelligence (*nous*) is the cause of everything, but disappointed when he found that Anaxagoras actually tried to explain things in terms of material processes like other earlier scientists. It is as if one were to say that Socrates' actions are due to his mind but then to explain why he was sitting in his prison cell in Athens rather than escaping to another city as due to the position of his bones, sinews, flesh and skin. This indicates a failure 'to distinguish the real cause from that without which the cause would not be able to act as a cause' (99b). What Anaxagoras calls the cause is merely a necessary condition of what he purports to explain. The cause of X should explain why X in fact exists and not some contrary state of affairs. Ideally it would explain 'what was the best way for it to be, or to be acted upon, or to act' (97c–d).

The best causal explanation would explain how the universe is held together by the good and what ought to be. After confessing that he has not found such a cause, he offers a second best method of explanation based on the theory of forms, which involves the following claims: There exist forms such as the beautiful itself, and particular things are beautiful only because they partake of the beautiful itself. The forms typically have opposites which they cannot admit, for example, tallness cannot be short, and shortness cannot be tall (102d). Moreover, there are two types of forms – for example, tallness 'in nature' versus tallness 'in us' – which some commentators call transcendent and immanent forms (102d–3b). For example, the immanent form of shortness is itself short and cannot be tall, and it also compels whatever it enters to share in shortness. Socrates is short because he shares in the immanent form of shortness, while Phaedo is tall because he is occupied by the immanent form of tallness. This useful distinction also explains the paradoxical fact that a particular can in a way partake of opposite forms: Simmias can have the immanent form of tallness in relation to Socrates and the immanent form of shortness in relation to Phaedo. Finally, in order to support more sophisticated explanations, the theory recognizes a special bearer of a form, which is distinct from the form but brings the form with it whenever it occupies a particular and will not admit the opposite of the form that it brings. For example, an object becomes hot when it is occupied by fire, the special bearer of heat; and if the object is occupied by snow, the special bearer of cold, the fire retreats or ceases to exist. Likewise three brings oddness with it and excludes evenness. (It is noteworthy that Plato includes a mathematical example.) The *Phd*.'s final proof of the immortality of the soul presupposes this theory of causality, for the soul is the special bearer of life which cannot admit of death.

In the later dialogues perhaps Plato adumbrates the causal explanation of the cosmos envisioned in the *Phd*. The *Phlb*. distinguishes four factors – the unlimited, limit, the mixture that comes to be from the foregoing and the cause or productive agent that brings this mixture about (*Phlb*. 27b–c). Further, it recognizes intelligence (*nous*) or soul as the fundamental cause of the universe (*Phlb*. 30d; cf. *Ti*. 46d; and *Lg*. 10.891e). However, the *Ti*. recognizes two kinds of causes: intelligent and unintelligent (*Ti*. 46c–e, 68e). The former is identified with intelligence, personified as the cosmic demiurge (29a), while the latter is necessity, which is called 'the straying cause' (48a). The latter is evidently postulated to explain the pervasive resistance to orderliness. Plato's search for the first cause of cosmic order, especially in *Lg*. bk 10, is a precursor of cosmological arguments for the existence of god by Aristotle and later theorists, though lower levels are dependent on higher in the *Republic*'s divided line (q.v.) as well.

Against the theory of the *Phd*. Aristotle objects that Platonic forms cannot be causes because causes produce their effects intermittently, although the forms exist perpetually and continuously. Again, health seems to be produced by a doctor rather than by the form of health itself (*Gen. & Corr*. 2.9.335b17–24). Aristotle assumes that Plato's *aitia* is a rival to his own theory of four causes: for example, a particular statue has four causes, a particular sculptor (efficient cause) imposes a particular shape (formal cause) on particular bronze (material cause) for a particular purpose (final cause). He complains that Plato recognizes the formal and material causes of things, but overlooks the efficient and final causes (*Metaphysics* 1.6.998a8–10).

Recent commentators disagree over Plato's understanding of *aitia*. Does he have in mind what many moderns would understand as a *causal* explanation of a natural phenomenon, or does he intend instead a *logical* or *metaphysical* explanation of phenomena? The causal interpretation is suggested by Socrates' statement in the *Phd.* that he is seeking an 'investigation of the cause of generation and destruction' (*Phd.* 96a) and that he is concerned with problems like those discussed by the pre-Socratics such as why the earth has the shape it does and why it is located where it is (97d). If Plato is seeking a cause, what sort is it? Is it a formal cause (see Sedley 1998) or a final cause (see Taylor 1969)? Or does the *Phd.* anticipate the sort of comprehensive causal explanation found in the later dialogues, which arguably accommodates all four Aristotelian causes (see Hankinson 1998)? However, the causal interpretation has trouble with other examples in the *Phd.*: for example, Socrates is shorter than Simmias because he has smallness compared with Simmias' tallness (*Phd.* 102b–3a), and three bringing oddness with it and excluding evenness (104d). These examples suggest that Plato is concerned with a logical or metaphysical explanation, such as a conceptual analysis of essences (see Vlastos 1969) or an account of truth-making conditions (see Sharma 2009). These interpretations would lead off into very different directions, but, arguably, Plato's account of *aitia* shares features with both causal and metaphysical explanation.

CAVE, THE ALLEGORY OF THE

D. C. Schindler

The allegory of the cave that Socrates presents after the images of the sun (q.v.) and

the divided line (q.v.) is an image of education (*Republic* 514a; q.v. Education), which Plato says elsewhere is the only acquisition one retains after death (*Phaedo* 108d). This cluster of images serves to unpack in detail the dense series of claims Socrates makes about the 'greatest study', which provides the measure for all other studies, namely, the idea of the good (*R.* 505a–6a). The cluster occurs in the middle of a discussion of the nature of philosophy and towards the end of the long interruption that occupies the central books of the *R.* (bks 5–7), and so falls between the 'peak' of the city as a kingship or aristocracy (445c–d) and its decline into increasingly less perfect orders. It can be said to represent a paradigm outside of the whole discussion that stands as the ultimate reference point for the city described within that discussion (cf. 472c–3a) just as the idea of the good explicated in these images represents the ultimate standard for all thought and deed. The argument regarding the good and the soul's relationship with it that comes to expression in these passages is, among other things, the basic response to the challenges presented to Socrates by Glaucon and Adeimantus at the beginning of the main body of the dialogue.

Socrates insists the allegory must be connected with 'what was said before' (517a–b), that is the images of the sun and the line. If the sun image introduced the epistemological and ontological significance of the good, drawing a distinction between the realm of the sensible, which is mixed with darkness, and the realm of the intelligible illumined by the light, the line image subdivides the realms and articulates their relationships to one another mathematically. The cave image draws on the epistemological and ontological role of the good illustrated in the sun and on the notion of levels of reality and stages of the apprehension of truth illustrated in the line, bringing these together in what may be called a 'moving image', that is the mini-drama of education as a liberation from the slavery of ignorance. The various parts of the cave image symbolize an order of life (ethics and politics) based on the nature of reality and the soul's apprehension of it (metaphysics and epistemology). Scholars have rejected any simple one-to-one correspondence between the segments of the line and the stages of education in the cave, but the inference that the cave allegory ought therefore to be read independently of the previous images, and in some cases independently of the dialogue as a whole, is unwarranted.

The sun in the cave image represents the idea of the good, which Socrates calls the 'cause of all that is right and beautiful' (517c), both of the sun and its light in the visible realm and of truth and understanding in the intelligible realm. The things outside of the cave are intelligible objects – presumably the forms (q.v.) – and the artefacts inside the cave presumably represent visible, that is physical things. While Socrates does not explain the significance of the shadows cast upon the cave wall, we may interpret them, in light of Socrates' general discussion of the problem of education in the *R*., as the 'imitation' of reality in the poets' (and the sophists') speeches, and perhaps also as a reference to the 'noble lie' used to impose political order on the ignorant (cf. 414b–c, 459c–d).

The cave image presents three basic conditions of our nature in its education: first, we begin as bound at the bottom, so that the shadows and sounds reflected off the back wall constitute the whole of our experience (514a–15c); second, we may be turned around while still in the cave so that we may see the fire light and the artefacts that cast their shadows; third, we may be dragged out of the cave into the world illuminated by the

sun. This last level unfolds gradually in five steps (shadows, reflections in water, things themselves, the heavens and heavenly bodies at night and the sun). Socrates explains that education is a 'turning around of the whole soul' (518c) – that is, not the introduction of intelligence, but a directing of this already extant power *along with* our soul's spirited nature and appetites (cf. the 'parts' of the soul, 436a–b) towards the good. The educated and uneducated soul prove to be polar opposites: the latter measures everything it encounters against its 'truth', namely, the 'shadows of artificial things' (515c) and so experiences confusion in relation to reality; the former measures everything by the good, the most complete standard (cf. 504c) and so finds itself at a loss when it faces, once again, the darkness of the cave.

Because education involves a fundamental reordering of desire (q.v.), the prisoners must be released by someone outside of themselves and be forced out of the cave (since they would be able to liberate themselves only if their desires were already properly ordered). This, however, entails an infinite regress problem that Plato does not explicitly address. Socrates suggests that the prisoners would resist their liberator, and would in fact kill him if they had the chance (517a – a reference to Socrates?). When the prisoners are first released, they become dazzled by the firelight and so lose the ability to make out the shadows. What appears to be a state of confusion, however, is in reality an advance towards truth. The confusion intensifies when the prisoners enter out into the light of day, that is, the realm of the intelligible. However, once their eyes grow accustomed to the light at its source, they in turn come to pity those who are still inside the cave, and would 'prefer to undergo everything rather than live that way' (516d–e). The reason for the philosopher's return to the cave, which Socrates insists is necessary (519c–d), remains controversial; the stated explanation is that, in the city, private interest must ultimately be subordinated to the common good (519e–20d). Thus, it is the universal truth of the idea of the good that requires both an ascent out of the cave and then a descent back into the cave, in both cases against one's apparent desire.

CHARACTER (TOPIC)

Ruby Blondell

The English word 'character' may denote – among other things – both (moral) character and a theatrical dramatis persona. In the former sense it approximates to the Greek *ethos*, which embraces both moral qualities and the social and personal features that help to construct, embody and convey these qualities (such as age, status, social relationships, gender, way of life, deportment, physiognomy and manner of speaking). *Ethos* also covers intellectual traits, that is, the rational and rhetorical skills and attitudes that are used to reach and convey moral choices. For character in the latter sense – the theatrical or literary – Greek normally uses a different word (*prosopon*); yet the two concepts remain intimately linked. Literary characters are conceived of, and represented, in the first place as embodiments of moral qualities, while philosophers show a strong concern with character types and their external expression both in actual people and in the arts, especially theatre.

In English, 'character' often refers to moral character as detached from physical circumstances, or as opposed to individual quirks of 'personality', which are often viewed as 'non-moral', or irrelevant to assessing a person's character. But in ancient Greek terms all such features have potentially ethical implications, since they are viewed as constituting, expressing and/or representing *ethos*. Characteristics that might now be seen as quirks of personality tend to be viewed as simultaneously *formative* and *indicative* of both social identity and moral character. Yet, the human ideal remains one of simplicity and harmony. In literature, philosophy and the visual arts, idiosyncrasy, whether physical or psychological, tends to denote not special beauty or appeal but a departure from some ideal and more homogeneous ethical and/or aesthetic standard.

There is a close relationship in Greek culture generally, and Plato in particular, between character in both the above senses and education. Almost all ancient Greek writers assume that the representation of persons exerts on its consumers (actors, audience, readers or listeners) an emotional effect that tends to assimilate them to the characters represented (on this 'mimêtic pedagogy;' see Blondell 2002:80–112). Traditional educational models, such as Homer's heroes, may have certain positive traits, but in general, their impact is presented as overwhelmingly negative. Plato's characters, especially Socrates, often criticize the educational use of such poetry; in addition, Plato as author defuses the threat of traditional character models both by co-opting them for his own purposes and by supplanting them in his own works. In *Hippias Minor*, for example, he uses Socrates to challenge the educational value of Achilles and Odysseus, but also appropriates these heroes for his own use (Blondell 2002:113–64). The most important positive character model in Plato's works is Socrates, who is marked, paradoxically, by an unparalleled degree of physical and intellectual idiosyncrasy.

Plato's pervasive concern with human character, its formation and representation, is central to the *Republic*, which provides a fully developed picture of the character required for the philosopher-rulers of Callipolis. This ideal incorporates a long list of admirable qualities, which may be summarised as vigour and gentleness in mind and body. It is to be achieved through three stages of character formation. First, the young guardians must have the right *natural inclinations and capacities*. Second, these traits must be fostered from infancy by *cultural education*, including poetry and the visual arts as well as physical training; at this stage the young guardians' characters are to be 'molded' by the right kind of poetry and storytelling, which will use appropriate literary role models to 'dye' their souls indelibly with right opinion (429c–30b). Finally the guardians are subjected to many years of *higher education* (519c), largely mathematical in nature; this culminates in dialectic, which eventually allows the truly superior soul to reach the vision of the forms.

The resulting ideal character is uniform and homogenous since, as Socrates puts it, 'there is one form of virtue, but the forms of vice are unlimited' (445c). This means not only that there are many more ways of being bad than being good, but also that within each individual complexity and variation of character are to be frowned upon in contrast to the simple and homogeneous. The belief that the virtuous *ethos* is simple, the complex inferior (604e), is one important reason for Socrates' famous disapproval of imitation (q.v.), since sympathetic identification with a range of characters is expected to fragment the guardians' own *ethos*. This quest for a single perfect character-type is a central aspect of the dialogue's pervasive concern with stability, homogeneity and unity, and hostility to

plurality and change. The philosopher-rulers are defined by their ability to see beyond the distracting multiplicity of the phenomenal world to the homogeneous unity of the forms (474b–6d). The same vision informs their characters. Like the statue of the perfectly just man (361d), the undifferentiated model of the philosopher-ruler lacks distracting personal detail, providing an abstract, impersonal ideal of philosophical perfection. Only their level of progress on a linear scale differentiates the guardians.

This ideal is developed still further in the *Theaetetus*, where 'likeness to god' (176b) – an idealized state of epistemic, ethical and personal self-consistency and stability – is presented by Socrates as the ultimate human ideal. Ironically, however, this ideal remains unattainable as long as we are, in fact, embodied human beings. Plato seems well aware of this. The ideal philosopher in the Theaetetus is paired with his anti-ideal, the orator, who is fully engaged in the messy business of Athenian social and political life. We are left to infer that the best any real human being can do is to negotiate between these two poles, striving for 'likeness to god' while acknowledging her inescapable embeddedness in the material and social world that makes such a goal ultimately unattainable. The ever-paradoxical Socrates models this mediating role for us.

CITY (*POLIS*)

Richard Stalley

In his political and moral philosophy, Plato takes it for granted that he is dealing with life in the Greek *polis* (plural *poleis*), a small independent city state. His two longest works, the *Republic* and the *Laws*, both describe imaginary cities. While they are in many respects different from each other, they arguably embody very similar conceptions of the nature and purpose of the *polis*. The underlying principles are brought out most clearly in the *R.*, which describes an ideal that is unlikely ever to exist. The *Lg.* shows how they might be embodied in a more practical form.

The city comes into being because individuals in isolation cannot provide all they need for survival (*R.* 369b7–73d). But its main function is certainly not to accumulate wealth. The ideal location for a city is one that will provide all the necessities of human life without producing a surplus to permit trade and luxurious living (*Lg.* 704a1–5c7). There are, in fact, three main kinds of functions which must be fulfilled effectively if a city is to survive and prosper. The first is to provide for the production of food and manufactured articles and for the buying and selling of these. The second is to wage war and the third is to govern itself wisely. A distinctively Platonic idea is that each of these roles should be performed exclusively by people with the appropriate training and aptitudes and that confusing them can undermine and even destroy the city (*R.* 412b9–15d3).

To avoid this confusion of roles, the ideal city of the *R.* would be based on a division of the citizens into three classes: (a) those involved in farming, manufacture and trade; (b) the soldiers or guardians (*phulakes*); and (c) the rulers (*R.* 373d–4e). Those destined to be soldiers would be selected in early childhood and undergo a long training. The rulers would be chosen from the best and wisest of the guardians to undergo a philosophical training that would ultimately enable them to achieve a rational understanding of the good and the just (*R.* 502c–41b). In the more

practical city of the *Lg.* the confusion of roles is avoided by different means. Citizens will be forbidden to engage in trade and manufacture – those tasks will be left to resident aliens (*Lg.* 846d1–7b6, 918a6–20a4). All citizens will serve in the army and take some part in government but the latter is still conceived as a work of reason. The city is therefore controlled by a strict code of law (q.v.) established by a wise legislator and the most important positions are assigned to the oldest and wisest citizens.

Plato believes that the good of the city requires that its citizens possess the virtues of wisdom, courage, temperance and justice. A central concern of the city is therefore to provide an education (q.v.), which will develop the right kind of character in its citizens. In the *R.* there is a long account of the training in poetry, music and gymnastics that will inculcate the virtues and a similar education is prescribed in the *Lg.*

Plato also assumes that whatever makes for the unity of the city is good, while anything that pulls it apart is bad (see Schofield 2006:212–33). Unity requires shared feelings and friendship (q.v.) among the citizens. One major obstacle is the pursuit of wealth. In existing cities rulers use their power to pursue their own economic interests and to exploit their fellow citizens (*R.* 416d–17b). Differences in wealth also create conflict between the rich and the poor (*R.* 421d–3b). To avoid these outcomes soldiers and rulers in the ideal city of the *R.* would have no homes or property of their own but would live together like soldiers in a camp. In the *Lg.*, a different, and presumably more practical, solution is suggested. Each citizen family will have its own farm, which will be inalienable. The farms will be of equal size and the amount of wealth that can be accumulated in addition to the farm will be limited (*Lg.* 737b5–d8, 739e7–41a5, 744d2–5b2). The disruptive effect of differences in wealth will thus be kept to a minimum (see Morrow 1960:95–152; Stalley 1983:97–111).

Another threat to the unity of the city is that citizens may feel loyalty to their family rather than to the city as a whole. In the ideal city of the *R.*, this danger would be avoided by the abolition of the family. Mating among the guardians would be arranged by the rulers and the children resulting from this would be brought up in common. No one would be able to identify their biological parents or offspring (*R.* 457b7–66d7). This would ensure that citizens share feelings of pleasure and pain. There is no such proposal for the city of the *Lg.* Indeed, its citizens would be legally required to marry (*Lg.* 772c5–4d2). The point seems to be that, in practise, the unity of the city will be preserved by the careful regulation of the family and by institutions such as common meals and shared religious rites.

In the *R.* Plato uses the tripartite structure of his ideal city to elucidate the structure of the human soul. This, together with the emphasis on the unity of the city and abolition of property and families for the guardians, has led some commentators to suppose that Plato is concerned for the good of the city as opposed to that of its citizens. The latter are seen merely as parts of a larger whole, having no independent value. Other commentators have argued that, when Plato speaks of the good of the city, he really has in mind the happiness of all the citizens (see Taylor 1986). Plato would probably see a false antithesis here. On his conception a worthwhile life requires membership of a city. The good of the individual consists in possessing the very virtues that are needed for the survival of the city and cannot be acquired outside it.

CONVENTION (see Law)

COSMOS (*KOSMOS*)

Gretchen Reydams-Schils

The *Timaeus* is the principal dialogue for studying Plato's view of the cosmos, though relevant comments are also found in several other dialogues.

The cosmology of the *Ti.* (26c) draws on the fundamental distinction between 'being', or intelligible reality, grasped by understanding and the object of truth, that is, unchanging versus 'becoming', or sensible reality, grasped by sense-perception and the object of opinion that is always in flux (Brisson 1994; Johansen 2004; Zeyl 2000). That which 'comes to be' presupposes a cause of its coming to be. In the case of the universe – which falls under the heading of becoming because it is visible, tangible and corporeal – the cause is a good god, or divine artisan and demiurge who knows no envy, and makes the world as good as possible, introducing order in a state of disorder (*Ti.* 30a), by using being as his model, not becoming. The demiurge's model for the universe is also referred to as the 'living thing' that contains all different kinds of intelligible living things. Given that things that have intelligence are superior to those that do not, the world soul, which gives life to the entire universe, is endowed with a mind.

Timaeus also stipulates two types of accounts that have the same characteristics as their respective objects. The account of being shares as much as possible in being's stability and truth-value. The account of becoming as an image, or likeness, of being, can at best be only 'likely' and convincing. Plato's point here turns on the verbal pun in the connection between 'likeness'/*eikôn* and 'likely'/*eikôs*. This is a first epistemological restriction applying to any account of the universe: given what the universe is, it cannot be an object of true knowledge. A second epistemological restriction follows from the limitations of human nature in its attempt to speak of things divine and the origin of the universe.

Mathematics plays a key role in the structure of the universe, as a vehicle for the transfer of order from being to becoming. Both the world body (*Ti.* 31b–2c) and the world soul (35b–6d) are governed by proportional ratios. The traces of the elements in the receptacle have different regular solids, made out of triangles, assigned to them. These triangles and solids also account for the elements' transformations into each other and formations into things. The fixed stars belong to the circle of the same in the structure of the world soul, and the planets to the circle of the other.

Timaeus' account has three main parts: (a) the works of intellect (29d–47e); (b) the works of necessity (47e–69a); and (c) the combined works of intellect and necessity (69a–92c). The second part, on necessity or the wandering cause, introduces a third principle, in addition to being and becoming, namely the receptacle. Plato's account of this 'third kind' reveals fundamental tensions (Algra 1995; Sayre 2002). A first tension exists between the receptacle as some kind of space or medium or as a constituent component of sensible things. The most likely hypothesis is that the receptacle constitutes the condition for things in the phenomenal world appearing as corporeal and sensible. A second tension occurs between the two accounts of the receptacle as being, on the one hand, completely neutral, and as being endowed with traces of the elements in disorderly motion, on the other.

The ending of the *Ti.* has its own version of the 'becoming like god' theme (90a–d; Sedley 1999). Whenever a human soul enters a human body, the rational component of its soul, modelled after and made of the same ingredients as the world soul, becomes disrupted (42e–4c). This order, however, can be restored by realigning one's soul with the world soul, both through thinking and the contemplation of the revolutions of heavenly bodies that follow the revolutions of the world soul. Hence, the order of the cosmos becomes directly relevant for an ordered and happy human life.

The speech which the demiurge addresses to the younger gods (who will create the human body and the irrational parts of the human soul), and the rules he gives the rational human souls (41a–2e) have several themes in common with the afterlife and soul myths of the *Republic* (the Myth of Er, 614b–end), the *Phaedo* (107c–15a), the *Gorgias* (523a–7a) and the *Phaedrus* (246a–57b). These accounts display a judgement of the soul's first or previous life, with rewards and punishments, and reflections on the consequences of earlier choices for subsequent lives, in the process of reincarnation. They also present a view of the cosmos, least developed in the *Grg.* myth, that reflects this moral order, with clear distinctions between a higher realm more or less close to intelligible reality and lower realms for souls weighed down by corporeal and sensible reality.

The myth of the origin and governance of the world in the *Politicus*, as told by the Stranger (*Plt.* 268d–74e), posits an ongoing alternation between two phases of the universe: one governed by the supreme god, who delegates the supervision of parts of the universe to other gods and demons, and another in which the world is left to itself. The governance of god represents a blissful state, whereas the other phase leads to a gradual decline until the god eventually takes matters in hand again. Corporeal entities such as the world cannot remain in an immutable state, but inherently contain a factor of disorder.

Based on the principle that self-motion presupposes soul, bk 10 of the *Laws* (896c–9d) posits the existence of a disorderly soul as a counterpart to the rational and beneficial world soul that governs the heavens and the universe as a whole. The exposition emphasizes that the universe is ordered and governed by providence, rather than chance. The *Philebus* (23c–31b) assumes as the basic components of reality limit, the unlimited, a mixture of these two, and a divine maker called Zeus as cause; it restates key claims about the order of the universe, the world body and the rational nature of the world soul (Kahn 2010). Finally, the *Epinomis*, wrongly attributed to Plato and probably by Philip of Opus, assigns all levels within the universe their own kind of demons, according to a principle of plenitude.

CROSS EXAMINATION (see *Elenchus*)

DAIMÔN

A. A. Long

Daimôn is one of the terms employed to designate supernatural beings by Plato, and is used in a number of different, but related, ways in the dialogues.

The polytheistic religious beliefs of ancient Greece were remarkably fluid (q.v. Religion). They conformed to subsequent Western notions in regarding divinity as exponentially more powerful than every human capacity or possibility, but beyond that, how one conceived of the divine was susceptible to great variation. Plato made a virtue of this fluidity in two related ways. From his literary and philosophical predecessors he selected attributes of divinity that discounted or discarded the anthropomorphic and often fearsome features represented in mythology and civic cult. Second, and more significantly, he emphasized the idea that divinity is always providential and never responsible for any harm to human beings or to the universe. In advancing this thesis, Plato chiefly employs the singular or plural of the term *theos*, which is the standard Greek word to apply to Zeus and other leading gods. But in his late work, *Laws*, he often combines *theos* or *theoi* (plural) with the term *daimôn* (singular or plural) and sometimes adjoins to these terms the word *heros*, producing the providential triad 'god(s), divine spirit (s), and hero(es)'. The point of this complex expression was to be as comprehensive as possible in reference to everything in Plato's culture that could be deemed divine, ranging from the most exalted divinities to those former men worshipped after their deaths as deified heroes. By this token a *daimôn* was a divine being of lesser status than a *theos*.

Although Plato generally marks that difference, he also employs 'god or *daimôn*' or 'god and *daimôn*' as a hendiadys (e.g. *Cratylus* 438c6; *Lg.* 730a, 906a). Such fluidity in the use of these terms goes back to the earliest Greek literature. Homer sometimes calls Olympian gods and goddesses individually or collectively *daimons*, but he chiefly uses *daimôn* to refer to divine power impersonally – as we might say 'the divine' or 'divinity'. In an important extension of this usage, *daimôn* stands for the fate or lot allocated to mortals, which they are powerless to withstand. 'Oh *daimôn*', cries Oedipus in Sophocles' tragedy, when he learns that he has fulfilled his terrible fate; and the Persian King

Xerxes uses the same expression in Aeschylus' *Persians* at the point of his total defeat by the Greeks. Such pessimism was due to the belief, widely reflected in early Greek literature, that the Greek gods, far from being providential, were often ill-disposed to human beings. Plato rarely uses *daimôn* in this impersonal or negative way. His *daimons* are most typically guardian spirits attached to particular persons. As such, they may be compared with the function that Plato and Xenophon applied to the divine sign or divine voice that Socrates experienced from time to time, and which these authors (and very likely Socrates himself) called *daimonion*. However, that was a special usage of this term, signifying Socrates' peculiar claim to be the object of an individual providential concern.

Hesiod, who was more or less contemporary with Homer, foreshadowed Plato's providential conception of *daimons* in his account of the *post mortem* destiny of the blissful people from the Golden Age: 'Because of the plans of mighty Zeus they are good daimons, earth-dwelling \ guardians of mortal men, who keep watch over court judgements and \ wrongful acts, clad in mist, roaming all over the earth, and givers of wealth' (*Works and Days* 122–6). Plato drew directly on this passage in the *Cra.* (398b) where he has Socrates say:

> Hesiod and the other poets are right, who say that, when a good man dies, he has a great dispensation and honor, and becomes a *daimôn*, which is a name given to him because it accords with wisdom. Accordingly, I myself propose that every good man is *daimonios*, whether dead or alive, and rightly called a *daimôn*.

In spite of its spoof etymology (deriving *daimôn* from *daëmon*, meaning 'wise') this is a seminal text for the ways Plato uses the term *daimôn* to signify a guardian spirit, whether in life and/or after death.

He does this most elaborately in the eschatological myths (q.v. Myth) that conclude the *Phaedo* and *Republic*. Common to both contexts is the allotment to souls of a *daimôn* responsible for watching over persons during their embodied life. In the *Phd.* (107d–8a), the *daimôn* 'allotted to each person' conducts the *post mortem* souls to the underworld's place of judgement, but in the *R.* (617e, 620d) the story is more complex. There the narrative starts from souls that are awaiting rebirth. After drawing lots, to determine who goes first, the souls are required to choose their next lives from a vast selection of lives (animal as well as human), and then, having made that choice, make the further choice of a *daimôn* 'to watch over their life and fulfil the choices made'.

Guardian spirit is Plato's exact expression, but in using it he does not anticipate the modern, entirely protective or kindly sense of a *guardian* angel. What Plato's *daimons* 'guard' or secure is the *necessity* that embodied souls conform to the lives they have chosen. When the mythological trappings are removed, his guardian spirits are tantamount to personifications of each person's inevitable destiny as determined by their prenatal choices. A hundred years earlier Heraclitus had expressed this idea in his lapidary statement: 'Character is a human being's *daimôn*'. As to the mythology, Plato was influenced by eschatological ideas associated with Orphic mystery cults, which are diffused in earlier literature and thought, especially Empedocles, Pindar and Euripides.

Does Plato's conception of a guardian spirit fit the notion that divinity is always providential and never harmful to human beings? It is quite consistent with that idea, when qualified by the following Platonic assumptions – first, that human beings, not divinity, are entirely responsible for the choices they make and the outcomes of these, and second, that divinity is always just. Accordingly, human beings are justly rewarded in the afterlife for good conduct and punished for the reverse.

Plato interprets the concept of a guardian *daimôn* most creatively in the context of the *Timaeus* (90a–d) where he expounds the anatomy of the soul:

As regards the most authoritative form of soul present in us, we should think of it thus: that God has given it to each person as a *daimôn*, that thing which we say dwells at the top of our body and elevates us from earth to our celestial kinship.

Here Plato uses *daimôn* to refer to what he elsewhere calls the 'rational' part of the tripartite soul. As the passage continues, Plato describes the truly philosophical person as someone who, by always keeping his cohabiting *daimôn* well-tended, must be supremely prosperous (*eudaimôn*). *Eudaimonia* (often translated by 'happiness') is the standard word for prosperity. In everyday Greek it connoted material well-being or good fortune, and was thus taken to be subject to the arbitrary dispensation of gods rather than under a person's control. Plato, by contrast, makes *eudaimonia* (q.v. Happiness) depend primarily on the virtues of a rationally governed character. In the *Ti.* passage he plays on the etymology of *eudaimonia* (literally, 'a god-favoured condition') by associating it with both the traditional idea of a guardian deity and his entirely nontraditional conception of reason as a human being's normative guardian.

Plato's principal uses of *daimôn* have now been covered. Two further well known

contexts remain to be discussed. According to Diotima in the *Symposium* (202d), Eros (q.v. Love) is not a god (*theos*) because, rather than *having* good and beautiful things, he is in need and desirous of them. Is he then a mortal? The answer is negative because Eros, being 'in between mortal and immortal', is a great *daimôn*, 'for everything *daimonion*' has this intermediate status. Categorical though this sounds, it should not be taken to be Plato's theological axiom. As already stated, he likes to use phrases such as '*theos* and/or *daimôn*'. But, though he generally treats *daimons* as lesser beings than that which he signifies by *theos*, his concept of the divine is sufficiently capacious to include *daimons* as well as more exalted deities. This finding is borne out by the passage in the *Apology* (26c–8a) in which Socrates refutes his accuser Meletus' charge that he does not believe in gods at all. Socrates' argument, in summary, runs thus: Belief in divine matters (*daimonia pragmata*) entails belief in *daimons*. Socrates, by Meletus' admission (referring to the indictment of his introducing 'novel *daimonia*'), believes in divine matters. Therefore, Socrates believes in *daimons*. *Daimons* are either gods or children of gods, from which it follows that Socrates believes in gods.

Did Socrates take his divine sign to be the voice of a *daimôn*? No firm answer to this question can be given, but the word *daimonion* (literally 'divine thing') is just as appropriate to a visitation from a fully fledged god, in which case its most likely source for Socrates would be the god Apollo whose oracle initiated his interpretation of his mission to the citizens of Athens.

For further information on *daimôn*, see Burkert (1985), Greene (1944), Long (2004), McPherran (1996) and Vernant (1980).

DEATH

E. E. Pender

Plato understands that the fear of death (*thanatos*) afflicts humankind in waking hours and in the terrors of dreams (*Republic* 330e; *Laws* 904d). He observes the abhorrence of the underworld familiar in Greek culture from Homeric poetry onwards (*R.* 386c–387a) and captured in Achilles' famous lament at the loss of life (*Odyssey* 11:489). He also offers sensitive and moving reflections on grief, where the advice to those mourning the 'calamity' of death is to bear such sorrows as lightly as possible (*Menexenus* 247c–d; *R.* 603e–4d). Both Aspasia and Socrates refer to the need for 'healing' (*Mx.* 247d2; *R.* 604d1–2), but where Aspasia counsels gentle consolation through social practise, Socrates' prescription for grief is reasoning and proper training of the mind. While both of these responses to death speak in familiar cultural terms, Socrates' articulation adumbrates the greater achievement of the philosopher explored elsewhere: the realization that death is to be welcomed.

Plato's redefinition of death is accomplished over various dialogues but key texts are *Apology*, *Phaedo* and *Timaeus*. In *Ap.* Socrates' judgement is that death is one of two things: either it is 'like being nothing', with no perception of anything, or it is a sort of migration (*metoikêsis*) of the soul (*Ap.* 40c6–10). The former state, likened to a dreamless sleep, would be a 'marvellous benefit'. And the latter experience, likened to travelling abroad to a place of good company, would also be a good thing. Indeed, if a person arriving in the other world is to find true judges and more blessed men, 'as people say', then Socrates is willing 'to die many times' (*Ap.* 40c–1c). The idea of migration

is taken up in Plato's fuller examination of death in *Phd.*

The crux of the *Phaedo*'s account of death is that it is 'nothing other than the separation (*apallagê*) of soul from body' (*Phd.* 64c4–5). The state of being dead is therefore where soul and body have come to be apart (cf. *Gorgias* 524b). Socrates explains (*Phd.* 64a–7d) that since the body causes desire for physical pleasure and hinders the gaining of wisdom, the philosopher gladly welcomes this 'release' (*lusis*) of his soul. Socrates then presents four individual arguments on the immortality of soul, culminating in the conclusion that due to its essential nature as life force, the soul cannot admit death and so cannot die (*Phd.* 102a–7b). Socrates' various arguments recall earlier views on the afterlife, including the poetic conception of Hades and the 'ancient doctrine' of reincarnation held by the mystery religions and the followers of Pythagoras (q.v., *Phd.*). But Plato radically transforms earlier ideas in line with his own teleology and account of abstract reality.

Plato's thought on death is founded upon his arguments for immortality and his commitment to the forms as the basis of existence, knowledge and goodness. For while all souls will necessarily exist after death, the incarnate and discarnate periods of their eternal lives are revealed as determined by their level of knowledge of the forms and their consequent virtue. When soul is fully rational it will be as separate as possible from the corrupting influence of the physical and will achieve its true nature as an immaterial entity. During human life degrees of separation can be attained through contemplation of abstracts (Pakaluk 2003) but full and permanent withdrawal requires death as the removal of the last obstacle to uninterrupted contact with the forms. This ability of soul in human life to withdraw into itself gives rise to Plato's striking claim that the life of philosophy is the practise of death (*Phd.* 64a).

The *Ti.* shares with *Phd.* the view that death can allow the soul to return to its primary state, separated from physical matter, and provides a closer account of the process of death itself. While the language of liberation is dominant in *Phd.* (e.g. 67d, 82e), there is also a more neutral presentation of soul as an object bound in the body (e.g. 81e, 92a1), a dual perspective continued in *Ti.* The gods create the human being by binding together the parts of the body (*Ti.* 43a), and then binding the soul within it (69e, 70e, 73c). Conversely, natural death is identified (81d, 89b) as the breaking apart of the bonds of the body which in turn loosen the bonds of the soul. The theme of liberation is recalled as the unloosened soul is said to 'fly away with pleasure' (81e). On the inverted perspective of the philosopher, death is to be welcomed as the freeing of soul – the source of the person's identity. In contrast, the body is to be disposed of as a mere 'bulk of flesh' (*Lg.* 959a–c; *Phd.* 115d–16a) and funerals are to be conducted with modesty and restraint (*Lg.* 959d–60a).

Plato's account of death is extended through his various eschatological myths – *Phd.*, *Grg.*, *R.*, *Phaedrus* and *Lg.* bk 10 (see Stalley 2009:188–94) – which depict the afterlife rewards and punishment of souls and support the convictions that the gods are good and the universe just. Plato uses established terms and story patterns in his afterlife myths (Edmonds 2004) but each is subtly crafted to fit its specific dialogic context. Although the myths do not form a composite whole and individually continue to pose significant hermeneutical challenges (Ferrari 2009; Halliwell 2007; Kingsley 1995 on

Phd.), nevertheless, they consistently support Plato's insistence that the consequences of our human behaviour are not to be escaped along with the body (e.g. *Phd.* 107c5; *Lg.* 959b). For, each myth depicts how the event of death initiates different experiences depending on the soul's condition. The souls of philosophers, who have spent their human lives contemplating the forms, will be rewarded by transport out of the physical realm altogether, to an eternity in blessed, divine regions where they will enjoy even greater access to truth (e.g. *Phd.* 114c; *Phdr.* 247b–e; *Lg.* 904e; see also *Ti.* 42b). Less virtuous souls who are nevertheless 'curable', the majority (*Phd.* 90a), will pass through a series of bodies, experiencing not one but multiple deaths. The death events of these souls cause the afterlife periods during which they pay the penalty for misdeeds, periods which will be followed by new incarnations as opportunities for improvement. Therefore, while physical death is the same for philosophical and other souls, their respective states of being 'dead' are very different. Plato's accounts of death necessarily stretch the normal life/death polarity, a point particularly borne out in the case of evil people.

In his famous image of the cave (q.v.), Plato suggests, in a further striking inversion, that the unenlightened life is itself a state of 'death' (Laird 2003; O'Connor 2007). Incurably corrupt people in their Hades-on-earth will then find their souls, upon their actual death event, separating from their bodies and departing to an afterlife of punishment, imaged in the myths as in Tartarus, the place of retribution (*Phd.* 113e; *Grg.* 523b; *R.* 616a). These evil souls, beyond all hope of reform, have experienced their final death in bodily form and will gain no further incarnation. Tartarus is then to be seen as an end state: the souls here remain alive but their death experience is more like a cessation of life, the 'nothing' envisaged at *Phd.* 91b2. Thus, in their lack of any fulfilling life, evil people suffer a more intensive set of 'deaths'. Moreover, if their incurable vice is recognized during their civic lives, their woes may be compounded by the death penalty (*Lg.* 735e, 957e). For execution will hasten their physical dissolution and the transition of their soul to Tartarus. However, while it is permissible for the journey to Tartarus to be expedited by human judges, Plato is careful to point out that decisions on the timing of other people's departures must be left to the gods. Thus suicide – even for a philosopher – is forbidden (*Phd.* 62a–c).

DESIRE (APPETITE) (*EPITHUMIA*)

Antonio Chu

There are two theories of how desires bring about intended actions in Plato: one the intellectualism (q.v.) of the Socratic dialogues, the other a theory that makes room for irrational desires bringing about actions in the *Republic* and other dialogues.

The intellectualist account takes it as a psychological fact that all humans desire the good (i.e. happiness) as our ultimate end (*Euthydemus* 281c–e; *Symposium* 204d–5a). This common desire of ours is egoistic: it is our *own* happiness that we each seek to realize in life. In a given situation, this fundamental desire for the good will naturally give rise to the general desire for whatever is the best means to the agent's happiness in the given circumstances. Through the agent's judgement as to what specific action in the given circumstances is the best means to

happiness, an indefinite desire for *whatever* is the best means becomes the executive desire for the particular action which is judged to be the best option available. Executive desires so generated all have a means-ends structure, aiming at a particular action that has the agent's happiness as its ultimate end (*Gorgias* 467; *Lysis* 217). Since these executive desires are shaped jointly by the agent's general desire for the good and the agent's *judgment* concerning which action in the given circumstances will maximize happiness, they are all *rational* desires for the good (Penner 2005). And given that *every* executive desire is fashioned in this manner, it will follow that all desire is for the good (*Meno* 77b–c). Moreover, since it is the real objective good and not the apparent good which we desire (78a), it will further follow that we never desire bad things. Due to misjudgement as to what is the best option in the given situation, the desire generated from this intellectual error may bring about an action that is in fact bad. This action, however, is *not* the action the agent really wants to do. This explains why tyrants, despite their enormous political power, only manage to do what seems best rather than what they want (*Grg.* 467a–b). In virtue of their political power, tyrants undoubtedly can bring about whatever action seems best. Unfortunately, by downplaying the relevance of the science of the good in determining what is the best option in a given circumstance, there is little hope that they will ever do what they want, that is, do what will in fact maximize their true happiness (Penner 1991).

Given the egoistic nature of our desires, it is no surprise that no one errs willingly (in securing their own happiness) (*Protagoras* 357–8). This also rules out any straightforward *akrasia* (q.v.): acting intentionally contrary to what one judges to be the best option. It is impossible to form an executive desire for an action that the agent does not at the time judge to be the best. Insofar as the agent has an executive desire for the problematic action, it will indicate a momentary lapse in judgement or a desire that results from a temporary change of mind as to what is best (*Prt.* 356d–e; *Men.* 97–8). Failure to maximize one's happiness in one's action is due strictly to ignorance of what is best. Hence, an unexamined life is not worth living (*Apology* 38a). For unless we regularly examine and reexamine the web of beliefs we utilize in determining what is the best option in a given situation, it is unlikely that our rational desires will result in actions that actually maximize our happiness. It is therefore important to engage regularly in the type of intellectual conversation made famous by the Socrates of the Socratic dialogues.

The intellectualist account of desire is both a form of psychological egoism and a form of intellectualism. It is the former because it explains every intended action in terms of the agent's fundamental desire for personal happiness. It is the latter because it maintains that bad actions are not the result of bad motives or the agent's desire for bad things but the result of intellectual errors and ignorance of what is good.

The theory of desire developed in the *R.* proceeds on the assumption that, in addition to rational desires which reside in the rational part of the soul (q.v.), there are irrational desires (residing in the appetitive part and the spirited part of the soul). In fact, it is this assumption which enables Plato to divide the soul into parts without committing himself to there being indefinitely many parts (Penner 1971). Since irrational desires are blind to all considerations concerning the good, their strength varies independently

of reason's estimation of the good that will result from their realization. In situations where an irrational desire is in conflict with an opposing rational desire (e.g. the appetitive desire to drink *simpliciter* opposed by the rational desire *not* to drink given the belief that not drinking is best for the entire soul), a clear-eyed *akrasia* will occur whenever the irrational desire is strong enough to overwhelm the rational desire. Consequently, intellectual training alone will not suffice to direct most individuals towards good actions. Nonrational trainings will be required to tame irrational desires and bring their strength in line with the good expected from their realization. See, for instance, the education programme in physical training and music outlined in *R.* bks 2–3 where habituation replaces intellectual conversation as the means for shaping our desires (at least as far as our irrational desires are concerned).

In the late dialogues, Plato's sympathy is usually with the theory of desire developed in the *R.* (although *Laws* is an exception). Whether this is indeed a superior account of human desire will depend in part on whether it provides a plausible and coherent account of our psychology of action. That this is so has been challenged (see Penner 1990). And given the richness of Plato's language, there are alternative interpretations of his views on desire (see Anagnostopoulos 2006; Annas 1981; Bobonich 2002; Cooper 1984; Irwin 1995; Price 1995). These alternative interpretations generally see Plato's postulation of irrational desire as providing (a) a more adequate account of the complexity of human psyche and (b) a more plausible psychology of action. In addition, they generally take his argument for irrational desire in *R.* bk 2 to be compatible with the attribution of some limited form of means-ends reasoning to the appetitive part of the soul.

DIALECTIC (*DIALEKTIKÊ*)

Dirk Baltzly

As a method for discovering important philosophical truths, Plato's dialectic has a degree of fame that is inversely proportional to our evidence for what it actually amounts to. Heidegger confidently pronounced it a 'philosophical embarrassment' in a tone that suggests that he thought he knew just what dialectic was. I think he was overconfident. Dialectic is hard to pin down.

The noun 'dialectic' (*dialektikê*) is formed from an adjective (*dialektikos*) whose broader sense is 'conversational'. The associated verb can mean 'to converse', as well as 'to sort things' – an etymological connection noted in Xenophon's account of Socrates (*Mem.* IV.5.12). The term seemingly acquired an association with philosophy early on. A fragment from Aristotle credits its discovery to Zeno of Elea (f. 65). Yet we should be cautious in assuming that this means that there is a single philosophical method – dialectic – found in the works of both Zeno and Plato. Indeed, we should be cautious in assuming that when Plato himself writes about dialectic, he always has in mind one and the same thing. The give and take of argument was, and remains, characteristic of philosophy and that give and take can resemble a conversation, even when written and there is but a single author who takes both parts (as in Aquinas' *Summa Theologica*). So it is unsurprising that the method that is peculiar to philosophy should be called dialectical or conversational. But this uniformity of terminology may hide a diversity of opinion about what conversational activities are best suited to reveal philosophical truth.

At one time scholars used the term 'dialectic' to describe the method of philosophizing that one finds in all Plato's dialogues – those called early, as well as the middle or later dialogues (Robinson 1953). It is common now to call the method putatively employed by Socrates in the early dialogues the elenchus (q.v.). Perhaps the most influential characterization of Socrates' method has been Vlastos (1983) (see, however, Scott 2002). It has also become customary to distinguish the 'method of hypothesis' that is described or illustrated in *Men.* 86e–7b and *Phaedo* 99e–100b (Benson 2003; Van Eck 1994). Currently, when scholars talk about Platonic dialectic it is typically the philosophical method described by Socrates in *Republic* 531d–9e that they have in mind. The relation of dialectic as it is described in the *R.* to the method of division illustrated in dialogues such as the *Sophist* and *Statesman* is unclear. Plato certainly uses the term 'dialectic' in these contexts (*Sph.* 253d–e; *Plt.* 285c–6b), yet it is not easy to see how the divisions illustrated in these dialogues' search for an account of the sophist or the statesman conform to what we are told about dialectic in the *R.*

The nature of the dialectician's inquiry in the *R.* is contrasted with the manner in which mathematicians pursue the truth in the divided line (q.v.) at *R.* 511a–c. Not only are the methods different, but so too are the mental conditions that result from following them. Let us examine the latter first.

Exercise of the methods characteristic of mathematics results in a cognitive state called *dianoia*, while the practise of dialectic yields a superior cognitive condition called *noêsis*. Translations of these terms vary across different authors, for the contrast drawn between them answers to no convenient distinction in English. In the subsequent Platonist tradition (q.v. Neoplatonism), however, *dianoia* is associated with discursive reasoning which is secondary to *noêsis*. The latter is a kind of direct, intellectual insight that results from the exercise of the faculty of intellect (*nous*). In keeping with the conversational sense of *dialektikos*, Socrates insists that the person who masters dialectic is able to give an account (*logos*) of the essence (*ousia*) of each thing, and especially of the good (*R.* 534b–c).

The method of dialectic is contrasted with that of mathematics on two grounds. First, mathematical reasoning allegedly makes improper use of hypotheses. While dialectic treats hypotheses as hypotheses, using them as steps to ascend to an *unhypothetical* starting point or first principle (*archê*), mathematics proceeds from hypotheses to a conclusion (510b4–9, 511b3–c2). Moreover, we are told that dialectic ultimately 'does away with' these hypotheses (533c8). Second, mathematical reasoning involves the use of images and things that are visible, while dialectic does not (510d5–11a1, 511b8–c2). It is for this reason that Socrates describes mathematical studies as merely a 'prelude' to dialectic (531d7) and they are often referred to as '*propaedeutic*'.

It is not easy to know what dialectic is given this very abstract description. The notion of an unhypothetical first principle is particularly vexed. Is the form of the good, which clearly occupies a special role in the metaphysics of the *R.*, the unhypothetical first principle (Adam 1902)? *R.* 532a–b describes dialectic as the soul's journey from visible to invisible, intelligible reality – a journey that ends with the grasp of the good itself. This requires that we assume that dialectic's end point is also its unhypothetical starting point.

Another related question is whether the method that is *described* in the middle books of the *R.* is *practised* in any of the Platonic dialogues. Some interpreters think so. Consider, for example, that the *R.* implies that dialectic could turn the unquestioned hypotheses of mathematics into knowledge (533b6–c5). Consider also that in the *Parmenides*, Parmenides appears to deduce the existence of numbers and the kinds into which they fall from some abstract considerations about what follows if we take up the hypothesis 'if one is' (*Prm.* 143b–4a). One suggestion is that an unhypothetical starting point is a proposition that is established by showing that its denial is self-refuting in a certain sense (Baltzly 1996, 1999; criticized in Bailey 2006).

Roughly, the first strategy that identifies dialectic's unhypothetical first principle with the good is ontological and equates the unhypothetical aspect of the *archê* in dialectic with the ontological supremacy of the form of the good (*R.* 509b6–10). The second strategy is epistemological and treats the unhypothetical character of the dialectician's *archê* as a matter of the kind of argument used to establish it.

The dialectician's avoidance of images or visible things is perhaps easier to understand. In the *R.*, Socrates repeatedly contrasts forms with sensible things and we have seen that he treats dialectic as part of the soul's turning away from the realm of sense objects or the 'coping stone' of such studies as lead the soul upward (*R.* 534e).

Other puzzles about dialectic in the *R.* include the relation of what is said there to descriptions of dialectic given in other works. One example is *Sph.* 253d–e. Here again dialectic is the distinctive method of the philosopher. However, now the dialectician is likened to the grammarian or musician who knows which letters or notes are which, and also which can combine with one another (cf. *Philebus* 16c–17e). Similarly in *Phaedrus* 266d, Socrates describes the person who masters the art of collecting particulars into their proper kinds and dividing those kinds 'along nature's joints' as a dialectician. Here, perhaps, the sense of the verb *dialegein* that means 'pick out' is relevant. In neither dialogue, however, do we find mention of an unhypothetical first principle. Moreover, the kinds of dichotomous division practised in dialogues such as the *Sph.* or the *Plt.* readily lend themselves to forking diagrams, at least as an aid to memory. Finally, it is unclear how far the method of division concerns itself with forms (Trevaskis 1967).

In spite of these apparent differences, there are also some important commonalities between the description of dialectic in the *R.* and Plato's remarks on dialectic and the illustration of the method of division in later dialogues. First, there is the fact that dialectic deals with something intelligible and not with sensibles (*R.* 531e; *Plt.* 286a), though it is disputed whether what is divided in the later dialogues are the same things as middle period forms. Second, the dialectician can give an accurate account that can be defended in question and answer (*R.* 511c; *Cra.* 390e). The latter point seems to militate against an understanding of dialectic as a state of mental fitness that permits one to simply *see* a philosophical truth without being able to communicate or defend it in argument (cf. *Epistle* 7, 341c).

Here, then, are the threads that interpreters attempt to weave together to arrive at an account of Platonic dialectic. If there is a uniform and explicit picture of Platonic philosophy's distinctive method in the dialogues, then it has remained well hidden for over two and half millennia. In my view, students of Plato do well to treat authoritative pronouncements such as Heidegger's on 'Platonic dialectic' with great caution.

DIVIDED LINE

Nicholas D. Smith

The divided line passage begins at *Republic* 509d6 by comparing the relative 'kind and place' (trans. Grube and Reeve) of the form of the good and the sun to a divided line. All but one of the manuscripts say that the line is to be divided unequally. Contemporary editions and translations prefer 'unequal', given the emphasis on proportions throughout the passage.

But scholars have disagreed about the orientation (vertical, horizontal or diagonal) of the line and also about which of the subsections described in more detail in the passage should be supposed to be represented, and by which lengths. The literature on the line is perhaps more extensive than on any other passage in Plato's works. Lafrance (1986) provides a 275-page annotated bibliography (in French) of everything published on this single passage from 1804 to 1984. Many new articles and sections of books have been added to this literature since then. For detailed discussions with citations of all of the scholarly debates about this passage, see Smith (1996). As for orientation, it seems decisive that some subsections are said to be higher than others (see *R.* 511a6 and 511d8), which rules out a horizontal line, and since no right–left distinctions are made, most representations depict the line as vertical, rather than diagonal.

The relative lengths of the different sections are still debated. Plato first claims that the lengths of the line represent different degrees of clarity and obscurity (*saphêneia kai asapheia*:509d9) and also truth and untruth (*alêtheia te kai mê*:510a9), which is compatible with the longer sections representing more of the positives but also

161

with representing more of the negatives of these comparisons. See the debate between Proclus and Plutarch, as reported in Denyer (2007:293); Denyer himself thinks that the choice is 'arbitrary'. In Plato's concluding remarks (at 511e3), however, only the positives are mentioned, so the proportions appear to indicate degrees of clarity and truth represented by each section of the line.

Immediately after the first division, Plato subdivides the original sections in the same proportion as in the first division (509d6–7). Let the line be AE (with A at the top), the original division at C, and subdivisions at B on the top section and D on the bottom section; the overall proportions of the line will now be (in algebraic notation) AC/CE = AB/BC = CD/DE, with AB the highest and longest of the subsections, and DE as the shortest at the bottom.

A mathematical consequence of this construction is that the two middle subsections (BC, CD) are equal in length. Scholars debate whether this equality is significant. On one hand, the same sorts of objects (particular sensibles) are mentioned in relation to both of the relevant subsections: as the originals at CD of the images at DE (509e1–10a3) and as the images at BC of the originals at AB (510b4–5, 510b7–9, 510d5–6, 510e1–11a1, 511a6–7, 511c1, 511c7–8). Moreover, given Plato's own proficiency in geometry, it would be strange to see him perform an operation that (surely he knew) would *require* the middle subsections to be equal – but this is precisely what happens at 533e7–4a5, in which Plato recalls the earlier proportion in such a way as to switch the two middle terms in the proportion (which would now be, in algebraic notation: AC/CE = AB/CD = BC/DE). However, there are also good reasons for resisting making the equality a significant feature of the line's construction. For one

thing, Plato never explicitly mentions this consequence. But also recall that the proportions are supposed to represent differences in the degrees of clarity and truth in the different subsections of the line. Even if we grant that the same objects belong at both of the middle segments, it is clearly not the case that Plato thinks that what is represented at BC (assigned to thought (*dianoia*) at 511d8) is no more clear than the segment (assigned to belief (*pistis*) at 511e1) immediately below it. Indeed, Plato later (at 533d5) explicitly says that *dianoia* is clearer than *doxa* which, according to 510a9, would appear to be represented by either the higher only or else both of the lower two subsections.

Still others have claimed that the second highest level (BC) should be associated with images, but not sensible ones; instead, some scholars claim that the 'mathematical intermediates' of the sort Aristotle says (at *Metaphysics* 1.987b15–18) Plato included in his philosophy were intended for BC. Though still defended by many scholars, this view has the defect of basing an interpretation on something that Plato himself fails to mention in the text itself. Complicating this debate further is the interpretive business of how exactly the image of the cave is supposed to 'map' onto the distinctions made in the line passage, and how many sets of objects are to be found in that subsequent simile, and in the theory of higher education that follows it in bk VII. At any rate, the highest subsection represents the practise of dialectic, which is associated only with forms and reasoning up to a first principle and only then down to conclusions (511b3–c2); the second highest represents the mathematical disciplines, which use images and hypothesize forms, drawing conclusions directly from these hypotheses, but failing to link them with an unhypothetical starting point (510c1–11a1, 511c3–d5).

The second lowest subsection is associated with visible particulars (510a5–6), and the lowest subsection is associated with shadows and reflections of the sensible particulars (509e1–10a3).

In the closing sentences of the divided line simile, Plato arranges each of the subsections in the proportion and now associates each one with a distinct 'condition in the soul' (*pathêma en tê psuchê* – 511d7). Scholars remain unresolved on the exact relation of these to the cognitive powers (*dunameis*) discussed at the end of bk 5. Of these powers, ignorance seems not to be represented on the line at all, whereas knowledge (*epistêmê*) is associated either with the highest subsection (associated at 511d8 with understanding (*noêsis*)) or with both of the top two subsections, and opinion (*doxa*), as I have already said, with either the higher or both of the lower subsections.

EDUCATION

Samuel Scolnicov

Education, as a direct consequence of his ethics, is, implicitly or explicitly, the central concern of Plato's thought. Plato aimed at providing the epistemological and metaphysical basis for his Socrates' educational convictions, as he interpreted them. Traditionally, the aim of Greek education (q.v. Education as background) was *aretê* (human excellence, often somewhat misleadingly translated as 'virtue'), which the Sophists claimed to teach as a technique. Socrates opposed this view, since any technique is double-edged: the best doctor is also the best poisoner and the best guardian is also the best thief. But *aretê* cannot be misused and cannot be passed on from master to pupil. Plato's Socrates insists

throughout on the personal character of learning. 'Answer as you think', he demands (*Gorgias, Meno, Euthydemus*). Even a wrong answer is preferable to an insincere one (*Men., Tht.*) Thrasymachus, Socrates' bitter adversary in *Republic* bk 1, complains that Socrates always asks and never answers; and when he does, he is always suspect of speaking ironically and dialectically.

Plato's Socrates summarized his educational aim in one sentence: 'The unexamined life is not worth living for a human being' (*Apology* 38a). This he called 'the care of one's soul' (*Ap.*), cleansing the soul of contradictions in thought and deed (*Grg.*). Socrates' main educational tool was the *elenchus*, the confrontation of his interlocutor with the logical and, more often, emotional consequences of his received opinions. The horror of contradiction is natural to the soul, but is seldom immediately felt. Once the soul is rid of its inner contradictions, the truth will follow of itself, so Socrates believed. (Objective) reality is in the soul, but in an indistinct manner, distorted by false and muddled opinions.

In *Grg.*, the crucial distinction is explicitly made between *pepisteukenai* (having been persuaded) and *memathekenai* (having learned). To have learned is to be able to give a proper account of the matter at hand; to be persuaded is to be convinced of it for reasons extraneous to the matter. In *Men.*, the parallel distinction is drawn between *doxa* (opinion) and *epistêmê* (knowledge, in the strict sense). The 'geometry lesson' in *Men.* and the simile of the midwife in *Tht.* demonstrate this distinction. The interlocutor is enjoined to recollect what he somehow already knows in an indistinct manner. In recollection (*anamnêsis*, q.v.), the content arising in the mind is not perceived as something new, but gradually recognized as if it had been in the mind beforehand, like remembering something that has been forgotten and is recognized as such. *Anamnêsis*, however, is not in the proposal of answers. These can, for example, be suggested by Socrates, quoted from poets, presented as dreams. *Anamnêsis* involves working through the reasons for or against the view entertained, until it is abandoned or else transformed from opinion into knowledge. (Cf. *Men.* 82e12: 'Mark how he will go on remembering', *Tht.* 160e3: 'Shall we then say this is your newborn?')

Education as a personal project is necessarily a product of *erôs* (q.v., Love) in all its manifestations. Aristophanes in the *Symposium* introduces the theme of man's incompleteness, his awareness of it, and his longing for what he lacks. Socrates transfers Aristophanes' insight from the natural to the metaphysical plane: a person is not incomplete, but imperfect. Education is the process of helping someone to reach the perfection that is his, but not yet grasped.

The *R.* and the *Laws* see the state as primarily an educational institution, whose function is the promotion of *eudaimonia*, human flourishing (not quite the modern concept of 'happiness', with its subjective connotations), as a result of *aretê*. Human excellence or perfection is his rationality. But reason will arise only in those souls that are already predisposed to it (*R.*). Early education is the nurturing of reason by irrational means: gymnastics and music (including poetry). Much importance is given to the educational role of myth and art. But Plato is also wary of the force of poetry, and of art in general; hence the necessity of careful censorship (*R.*; *Lg.*).

Higher education in the *R.* is for the future guardians and philosophers, in the *Lg.* for all, in the measure of their capacities. It is education in the five mathematical sciences

(arithmetic, plane geometry, stereometry, kinematics ('astronomy') and acoustics ('harmonics')). Mathematics is the paradigmatic science, the science of structure. It leads to the idea of the good, viz. the idea of the nontemporal, well ordered, self-contained teleological system of ideas, of necessity imperfectly exhibited in this sensible, moving world.

Plato sets himself in *R.* bk 2 the task of showing that justice, as hierarchy under reason, is desirable for the soul and for the state not only for its consequences but also, and foremost, for itself. Hence, *eudaimonia* is not in the consequences of one's actions, for these are beyond one's control. But *aretê* itself has no masters and the god is not to blame (*R.* bk 10 617e3–5). *Aretê* is in the *êthos*, one's moral character and the *locus* of one's moral responsibility, not in what happens but in one's relation to what happens. The end of education is the development of this *êthos* informed by reason.

In the famous simile of the cave (q.v.), education is a long and arduous process. The prisoner is taken out of the cave against his will and complains that the shadows were much clearer than what he is now shown. Education is not 'like putting sight into unseeing eyes'. It is turning the eye of the soul, together with the whole soul, from the sensible to the intelligible, a *Gestalt* switch from everyday, instrumental to ideal, normative rationality.

In the final myth of *R.* bk 10, the first soul to choose its new life had lived a life of demotic *aretê*, by custom, without *philosophia*. In matter of overt behaviour, demotic *aretê* is not different from true *aretê*. But it has no true moral worth. No one in that myth achieves true *aretê*. Perhaps only Socrates could, in Plato's eyes. Thus, in *Lg.*, Plato must satisfy himself with leaving a detailed prescription for the good life in the good city, like the itinerant doctor of the *Politicus*. These laws are introduced by preambles, so as to achieve obedience through understanding of their instrumental civic advantages, insofar as possible. Even the well intentioned rulers will not be the philosophers of the *R.* and will have had neither their vision of the good nor their understanding of the normativity of reason. They will, at most, be able to imitate the good order of the heavens and educate their citizens according to it.

For further reading, see Jaeger (1939–44), Nettleship (1935), Scolnicov (1988) and Stenzel (1928).

ELENCHUS (CROSS-EXAMINATION, REFUTATION)

Harold Tarrant

Elenchus is a name now applied to the arguments most characteristic of Socrates in the so-called early dialogues. Indeed, its presence has been used as a developmentalist criterion for a dialogue's inclusion in this group (Vlastos 1994:29–37). The word derives from the Greek *elenchos*, meaning a 'test' to determine how sound something or somebody is, and is closely related to a verb for 'refute' *exelenchein*. The simple verb *elenchein* may be found in this meaning, though more often as 'put to the test'. While it is unclear whether Socrates preferred to characterize his philosophic activity as elenchus, Plato's dialogues show that such terminology was in widespread use in his intellectual world for a variety of verbal challenges to somebody considered to be an opponent in a debate.

Regardless of Plato's use of the term, it is clear that his Socrates adopts a distinctive approach to refutation that merits some technical name to describe it. The approach

is directed at both the moral views held by opponents and their moral integrity. In the words of Plato's Nicias at *Laches* 187e, Lysimachus does not know that whoever joins in a close discussion with Socrates, regardless of the original topic of conversation, must necessarily 'not cease to be dragged around and around by him in argument until he is drawn into giving an account of himself – both how he now lives and how he has lived his past life'. Plato regularly shows Socrates manoeuvring an interlocutor first into some kind of moral discussion, and then into revealing – and indeed seeing problems with – the false moral assumptions upon which his life is founded. The procedure is founded on Socrates' conviction that 'the unexamined life is not worth living' (*Apology* 38a), and the falsehoods standardly relate to areas in which interlocutors were highly regarded, whether a professional area (e.g. rhetoric, sophistry, 'musical' performance), or a socially prized quality such as one of the virtues. Though Socrates may deny that he can improve upon another's account (e.g. *Charmides* 175e; *La.* 200e), he compares favourably not only because his own image does not rely on claims to moral virtue or moral knowledge but also because it is obvious that he has long been scrutinizing the issues as they apply to him. Conceived as I have described it so far, 'elenchus' does not apply to all Socratic questioning, only cases involving claims to social or intellectual standing, so the slave in *Meno* or young men in *Lysis* and *Euthydemus* are not seen as targets of 'the elenchus'. Once an interlocutor has been engaged in debate Socrates elicits a premise that he challenges. The challenge comes not by direct confrontation but by eliciting from the interlocutor unforced admissions that serve as further premises, and which, taken together, can be shown to entail the contrary of the premise challenged. The consequences are usually spelled out clearly and politely, so that the person being refuted is given no good reason to attack Socrates for hostile conduct and is more likely therefore to blame himself, as Socrates points out on Protagoras' behalf at *Theaetetus* 167e–8a. As the *Alcibiades I* (112e–13e) fully argues, free and honest admissions leading to the refutation of an interlocutor reflect his own views, not those of Socrates. While it is not necessarily the challenged proposition that is refuted, since any one of the premises might be faulty, all admissions are assumed to coincide with the interlocutor's beliefs, so that his total set of moral beliefs is found wanting and any special claims to moral expertise are thereby undermined.

Since Vlastos' seminal article (1983) much of the discussion about the elenchus centres on whether Socrates is committed to its use as a vehicle for the refutation or demonstration of moral theses. Central to this question are the arguments with Polus in the *Gorgias*, where Socrates claims that (a) the truth is never refuted (*Grg.* 473b) and (b) it has been demonstrated that his claim was correct (479e). The former would not in itself justify certainty that anything left unrefuted must be true, and for Socrates it justifies only the *assumption* that it is so (509a–b). The latter would be more meaningful if it were clear that demonstration were used in its modern philosophic sense, but Polus has already used the verb at 470d2 for what history can 'demonstrate'. Besides, the demonstration-claim is followed by 'So if this is true . . .', a conditional clause that would be redundant if the truth had indeed been demonstrated. Similarly, at 509b, the conditional clause 'so if it is so' confirms that Socrates is not making a knowledge claim, and that there remains scope for challenging positions that

have survived all attempts to refute them. *Grg.* has less to do with the irrefutable truth or falsehood of moral propositions than with which of them may be rationally adopted as the foundations of our public lives. Conversely, outside *Grg.* where philosophic and rhetorical refutation compete for legitimacy, Socrates gives little hint that he has reflected deeply on precisely what the elenchus achieves or the conditions that enable it to work (Vlastos 1994:34–6). The consequence of the paucity of what one might call 'meta-elenctic' outside the *Grg.* means that articles on individual elenchi (several examples in Scott 2002) are often more rewarding than those offering an overall theory.

One constant, however, is the conviction that the truth is best approached in discussions involving at least two good minds, as *Protagoras* 348c–e demonstrates. When two perspectives are brought to bear on an issue it is far less likely that conclusions reached will be fatally flawed by false admissions arising from an individual's personal viewpoint (Tarrant 2006). That people view things differently in the heat of the moment is argued at *Prt.* 352d–8e, where moral lapses are explained as temporary misjudgements. We know from Thucydides, *History* 3.82 (Price 2001) that pressures led to radical misuse of moral vocabulary in Socrates' time. Such misuse is reflected in the extreme positions adopted by some interlocutors, for example *Euthyphro* 4a and *Grg.* 482e–95d. The temporary nature of moral mistakes (unlike moral knowledge) is underlined by such passages as *Euthphr.* 11b–c, *Alc.* 1. 116e–17a and *Men.* 95c–6b.

Hence, Socrates sees himself as offering the divine service of reawakening people to their moral selves through *elenchos* and close examination (*Ap.* 29d–31a), as if restoring their minds to the natural condition.

Vlastos (1983:52–5) accordingly saw not only Socrates as having access to the moral propositions required to negate an interlocutor's mistake but also the interlocutor himself. The systematic manner in which he built such requirements into his theory finds little support today, but the *naturalness* of moral knowledge is implied by the metaphors of recollection and giving birth that are applied to Socrates-induced discovery in dialogues that Vlastos placed later. If moral awareness is the default position for human beings, and ignorance an aberration, then one might indeed expect an interlocutor to recognize *some* moral truths unsystematically, and the seasoned philosopher to recognize most of them, seeing them more as an organic whole.

EPISTEMOLOGY (KNOWLEDGE)

Mi-Kyoung Lee

Nowhere in Plato's writings does he articulate and unequivocally endorse a theory or definition of knowledge. Admittedly, the *Theaetetus* is devoted to the question, what is knowledge? Yet, because the dialogue is aporetic – that is, contains a rejection of all three conceptions of knowledge considered – it is controversial what, if anything, Plato intended us to conclude from that dialogue. Even so, there are indications in the *Tht.* as well as in earlier dialogues, especially the *Apology, Meno, Phaedo* and the *Republic*, of Plato's views about knowledge. The following theses about knowledge are found in these dialogues: (a) knowledge is, above all, *expert* knowledge, which allows its possessor to give an explanatory account of things, and which gives one the ability to withstand critical examination; (b) coming to acquire

knowledge is a kind of 'recollection' (q.v.); (c) the primary objects of knowledge are the forms (q.v.); (d) knowledge ideally comes with an understanding of the full causes of things, which would require a teleological explanation of why things came to be for the best, or for some good; (e) finally, some scholars believe, Plato defines knowledge as a state involving true judgement with an explanatory account; others however think that he reserves for knowledge of the forms themselves a different, self-certifying kind of knowledge.

In the 'Socratic' or aporetic dialogues, very little is said about methodological or epistemological matters; Plato's character, Socrates, does not explain what he is doing, or explain what is needed for success in the inquiries about virtue and happiness he undertakes. Nor does Socrates take any pains to spell out what knowledge is, and how it differs from true belief. What we get, instead, is Socrates' keen interest in coming to have knowledge – something he denies possessing – about how one ought to live. He displays little interest in asking, for its own sake, what knowledge is; rather, he is interested in finding out whether anyone has knowledge of what the good life is (*Ap.* 20e–4a, 29b–30b). As he makes clear in dialogues like the *Euthyphro, Men.* and *Laches*, he expects that one should be able to give an account of concepts like virtue, piety, courage and justice, one that can survive scrutiny, that is, Socrates' *elenchus* or 'testing' of his interlocutors (q.v.). Typically, the dialogues end with the interlocutors giving up, and admitting puzzlement and confusion.

In the *Men.*, however, Plato has Socrates address the question whether coming to have knowledge is really possible: if we do not know a thing, why should we think that we will be able to discover anything about it? The puzzle has the following form: if one does not know what one is looking for, how will one know what to look for? And how will one know it, if one should find it? The answer is that the inquiry is guided by one's conception and understanding of what one is looking for. These fall short of knowledge, but are sufficient to guide one nonetheless, and help one to recognize the correct answer, when one finds it. To demonstrate how successful inquiry occurs, Socrates offers a demonstration using a slave boy, who, asked questions by Socrates, is prompted to consider and reject two incorrect answers to a geometry problem, and then arrives at and recognizes as correct the true answer. Socrates calls this 'recollection', by which he seems to mean that we possess innate knowledge or true beliefs.

The *Men.* also explores the distinction between knowledge and true belief. Socrates compares true beliefs to the statues of Daedalus, a famous sculptor: like Daedalus' statues, true beliefs 'are not willing to remain long, and they escape from a man's mind, so that they are not worth much until one ties them down by (giving) an account of the reason why', that is, why they are true (*Men.* 97e–8a). Whether Plato means to endorse Socrates' claim that knowledge is true belief 'tied down with a reckoning (or account, *logismos*) of the reason why' is not clear – since in the *R.*, Socrates seems to think that knowledge is not a species of true belief at all.

In the central books of the *R.*, Plato has Socrates argue that knowledge is only possible if one has a grasp of the forms. With this argument, Plato makes an attack on the 'sight-lovers', who deny that anything universal can be said about what makes things beautiful, just or good, and insist on the multiplicity of beauty, justice or goodness. They cannot have knowledge, because knowledge

requires a grasp of the forms, that is, minimally, of what all things of a kind have in common, and what it is to be a thing of that kind. Plato illustrates the contrast between knowledge and reality in a series of famous analogies: the sun (*R.* bk 6.507a–9c; q.v.), the line (*R.* bk 6.509c–11e; q.v.) and the cave (*R.* bk 7.514a–21b; q.v.). Scholars disagree about whether Plato endorses, in these analogies, the idea that knowledge is foundational, that is, that there is a special kind of certain or self-certifying knowledge (concerning the form of the good and other forms) upon which all other knowledge is based. It is clear, however, that Plato retains Socrates' idea that knowledge derives from dialectic – an idea present already in the *Men.*, endorsed in the *R.* and more fully developed in the rich conceptions of dialectic and division in the *Sophist* and *Politicus*.

Finally, in the *Tht.*, Socrates and his interlocutors Theodorus and Theaetetus examine and ultimately reject three accounts of knowledge: (a) perception, (b) true judgement and (c) true judgement with an account. Knowledge as perception is linked with Protagorean relativism and a thesis of Heraclitean flux and variability, both of which Socrates proceeds to reject. Knowledge as true judgement is quickly dispatched by means of the example of a jury that is correctly persuaded of the truth by a good lawyer, but still lacks *knowledge* of the truth since they are not eyewitnesses. Knowledge as true judgement with an account appears to some scholars identical with the thesis put forward in *Men.* (97e–98a); however, Socrates and his interlocutors are here unable to find a kind of account which, when added to true judgement, would transform it into knowledge, because one falls into the problem whether this account is knowledge or opinion, and hence into infinite regress.

Thus, the *Tht.* presents an interpretive puzzle about whether Plato thinks knowledge is something besides these options, or whether he has left clues for the astute reader about why Socrates rejects an option which should continue to be taken seriously as a definition of knowledge. Solving the puzzle most likely requires, as Cornford suggested, that one take into account the ways that the *Tht.* looks forward to the *Sph.* and other late dialogues.

Despite the lack of clearly endorsed doctrines, Plato's dialogues are full of rich and imaginative ideas about the nature of knowledge and are the source of the following seminal ideas, whether endorsed by Plato or not: that knowledge might be innate, that knowledge can only be of universals (i.e. of forms), that knowledge is foundational, that mathematics and geometry offer a paradigm of what knowledge might look like, that knowledge must be a science that offers teleological explanations, and finally, that knowledge is true belief or judgement with an explanation or justification.

For further readings, see Benson (2000), Fine (1990), Fine (1992), Lee (2005), Lee (2008), Matthews (2008), Polansky (1992), Scott (2006), Sedley (2004), Taylor (2008) and Vlastos (1983).

ERISTIC (see Antilogy and eristics)

ERÔS (see Love)

ETHICS

Richard Foley

Plato's ethical theory is eudaimonist, for he, like most ancient philosophers, holds that all good actions aim at happiness (q.v., *eudaimonia*) or its Greek equivalent, faring well (*Meno* 87c–8d; *Republic* 621c–d). He additionally believes that the human virtues (or excellences, *aretê*; q.v.) govern the attainment of happiness, and consequently much of his ethical and pedagogical writing passionately advocates cultivating virtue. The precise relation between virtue and happiness is disputed (Brickhouse and Smith 1994:103–36), although many take Plato to believe that the virtues are necessary and sufficient for happiness (Irwin 1977a; Vlastos 1991a). Plato's further view on the relation between happiness and pleasure is more controversial. Plato does reject hedonism if pleasure is identified with the satisfaction of the appetites, but it is challenging to harmonize his opposition to hedonism in the *Gorgias* (500d) with its endorsement in the *Protagoras* (351b–4e). Irwin (1995:78–126) offers an important discussion of this topic, and advocates distinguishing two versions of hedonism.

Beyond this basic commitment to eudaimonism, Plato's ethical theory frustrates attempts at systematic, unified, comprehensive treatment. Scholars often divide his work into two distinct groups. This division generally correlates both with the division of Plato's works into earlier and middle periods, but also with the exegetical and theoretical methodologies that are brought to bear on the dialogues. It is also often cast, though unproductively, as a distinction between the historical Socrates (q.v.) and the mature, emancipated Plato.

Plato's early dialogues present his readers with some important challenges regarding the reconstruction of his ethical theory. These dialogues contain a welter of historical, biographical, dialogical and literary details that substantially complicate their ethical message. Additionally vexing is that although many end aporetically, these conversations are richly insightful and guided with skill, which suggests that they may contain an implicit ethical doctrine. There is widespread speculation that one element of Plato's early ethical theory is 'intellectualism' (q.v.), the doctrine that the virtues are a type of knowledge. The further assumption that Plato thinks virtue is knowledge of the good specifically leads some to argue that the virtues are not just necessarily coincident, but in fact identical (Ferejohn 1982; Penner 1973).

The ethical position of Plato's early works is distinctive for advocating a method (q.v.) which it prioritizes above any specific moral tenets. Plato depicts philosophy as simultaneously a process of critical self-examination and an investigation into the definitions of central moral terms like 'piety', 'courage' and 'temperance'. Socrates repeatedly contrives to shift the conversation to an evaluation of the life led by his interlocutors (*Laches* 187e–8c). The ensuing Socratic elenchus usually results not only in the refutation of proposed definitions but also in the erosion of the putative expert's original self-confidence. In contrast, Socrates appears as a paragon of virtue, perhaps because he has thought critically about his actions (Vlastos 1983), though such direct self-examination on Socrates' part is rarely depicted by Plato. Socrates asserts that this examination is necessary (*Apology* 38a) and sufficient (*Ap.* 41c–d) for happiness, which offers confirmation for intellectualism: philosophical activity yields knowledge, which is identical to virtue, which is itself necessary and sufficient for happiness.

It must be stressed, however, that the emphasis for Plato is on Socrates' method. Plato himself raises doubts about the desirability or even possibility of deriving moral practise from philosophical theory, but this is not to say that Plato is a moral sceptic (Kraut 1992c:3). Instead, he is an ethical reformer, seeking to liberate normative terms from an earlier aristocratic tradition that valorizes wealth, strength and power, to something we would recognize as genuinely moral. Some of the tenets of this new ethical theory are so surprising that they are often labelled paradoxical: the virtues are unitary (*Prt.* 329b–d; *La.* 198d–9e), virtue is a type of knowledge (*La.* 199c–e), *akrasia* (q.v.) is impossible (*Grg.* 459c–60b; *Men.* 77a–8b), it is better to suffer than to do injustice (*Grg.* 469c), it is never just to mistreat another, even in retaliation (*Cri.* 49c–d) and a worse person cannot harm a better (*Ap.* 30d).

Progress in ethics can perhaps be made through Socratic inquiry into ordinary moral beliefs. Pursuing a strategy similar to one Rawls later named 'the method of reflective equilibrium', Socratic dialogues seek to expose and diminish inconsistencies between our general moral principles and our ethical convictions in specific cases (Rawls 1971). Many dialogues make progress in this regard, since early definitions are improved in compelling ways over the course of the conversation. Yet puzzlingly, all end aporetically, progressive trajectory notwithstanding (*Charmides*; *Euthyphro*; *Hippias Major*; *La.*). The reader should build on this preliminary work by adopting the Socratic method, in which case the aporetic conclusion conceals the hortatory aspect to Plato's writing. It should be noted, however, that Socrates defends his ethical views more explicitly in some early dialogues (*Ap.*; *Cri.*).

The ethical works of Plato's middle and late periods reveal a shift to a more assertive style, although Plato will sometimes employ contrasting speeches or intermittent use of the Socratic method (*R.* bk 1; *Symposium*; *Phaedrus*). This transformation also correlates with an alteration in the techniques of exegesis and evaluation used by the scholarly community. Theoretically minded ethicists object that the Socratic method of striving for consistency is inappropriately deferential to one's starting point. Instead, normative questions require a philosophical account of the good (q.v.). This approach to Platonic ethics emphasizes *R.* above other dialogues. Bks 6 and 7, specifically the analogies of ship, sun, line and the allegory of the cave (q.v.), explain the source from which ethical claims derive their authority. On this theory, the good is prior to virtue (Santas 1985:223), which means that aporetic discussions can be resolved through the study of the good. Some argue that the problems encountered in the earlier dialogues led Plato to this new theory of the good (Irwin 1977a:132–76; Kraut 1992c:10). However, any understanding of the good itself presupposes elaborate metaphysical and epistemological theories (Kraut 1992:6; Santas 1985:223). The allegation that this ethical theory is empty for failing to show how to derive ethical maxims from abstruse metaphysics spans the history of philosophy (Aristotle *Metaphysics* 1096b8–7a13; Popper 1962:274–5n32).

Reconciling Plato's diverse writings on ethics thus continues to pose challenges. Although developmentalism (q.v.) provides one avenue for thinking about this issue, it is difficult to accept that the lively debates of the early works could have been supplanted by the abstract and relatively uncritical theorizing of the later works. Plato's enigmatic shift from moral critic to dogmatic theoretician thus endures as one of the most compelling topics in Plato scholarship.

EUDAIMONIA (see Happiness)

EXCELLENCE (VIRTUE) (*ARETÊ*)

Naomi Reshotko

'Excellence' is one of the two most common English translations of the Greek word *aretê*. In translating Plato's dialogues, the English word 'virtue' is also used. Translators tend to use the two English words 'excellence' and 'virtue' in distinctive, although not unrelated, contexts and their different uses can be understood to capture a primary and a more derivative notion of *aretê* for Plato. There is discussion of the excellence of a tool or a craft in many dialogues. The excellence of a tool or craft is that which enables it to do what it alone is designed to do and also that which it does best. This task of a tool or craft is also distinguished as its proper function (*ergon*): the excellence of a knife is the sharpness that enables it to cut (i.e. to perform the function of cutting) and the excellence of cobbling is its ability to make shoes. The rationale would seem to be that the tool or craft becomes excellent when it can excel at its proper function.

The proper function of a human being, which can in turn be honed and perfected, is that person's *aretê* – human excellence – and which concerns the soul (q.v.). In *Republic* 1 (353a1–4a4), the function of the soul is ruling, deliberating and living. Justice (q.v.) is that excellence of the soul by which it rules well, and insofar as it does so, it lives well and is happy. The word 'virtue', as the translation for *aretê*, would, in the case of the human being, point to that aspect or part of the human being – the soul – that can be honed and by the improvement of which a human becomes excellent or virtuous. The good human being is the excellent one and is the virtuous one – but the good human being, we would also say, 'has' virtue.

Some dialogues, as just seen, are marked by the character Socrates' preoccupation with the relationship between *aretê* and *eudaimonia*. Plato seems here to make an effort to isolate the relationship between virtue – understood as the excellence of the function that is particular to humans – and human flourishing. There is, to his mind, a very important connection between being virtuous and flourishing or, to state it more boldly, between being virtuous and *being happy*. There has been extensive debate over what exactly this relationship is. That virtue is sufficient for happiness, that it is necessary for happiness, that virtue and happiness (q.v.) are identical, that, not virtue, but, virtuous *behaviour* is sufficient for happiness, and that the pursuit of virtue, while it does not guarantee happiness, is the only way to purposefully pursue happiness are all claims that have been attributed to Plato or to the historical Socrates via the exegesis of Plato's texts.

Since 'virtue', a burdened and storied Latinized term taken to be a moral term often stands in for the Greek *aretê*, it is evident that *aretê* is understood by many to be a moral term as well. But, it is not obvious that Plato always (or, some would say, ever) uses *aretê* with a moral tone. It is widely agreed that a subgroup of dialogues, often referred to as 'Socratic' on the assumption that they represent the views of either the historical Socrates or Plato during a period in which he was under the influence of Socrates, use the word *aretê* to refer only to knowledge. Socrates, who asserts that the only thing that ever benefits us is wisdom (*Euthydemus* 281e2–5; *Meno* 87d4–8, 88c6–d1), says that *aretê* always benefits us (*Men.* 87e3) and even

says that *aretê* is wisdom (*Men.* 88c4–d3; Ferejohn 1984:107). While it is argued that Plato intended to single out a particular kind of knowledge that might be associated with consequent moral behaviour, there is also support for the notion that, according to Plato, all knowledge is equally important and equally a component of virtue.

Plato discusses several human character traits under the umbrella of *arête*. While he singles out five 'virtues' (*sophia* or wisdom, *sôphrosynê* or temperance, *andreia* or bravery, *dikaiosunê* or justice, *hosiotês* or piety), and addresses them individually in particular dialogues, in the *R.*, he narrows it down to four 'demotic' virtues (omitting piety). One central doctrine of the Socratic dialogues (particularly *Protagoras* and *Laches*) is known alternatively as 'the unity of virtue' or the 'the unity of the virtues', depending on one's reading of the text. Those who adopt the 'unity of the virtues' find Socrates claiming that a person cannot have only one of the virtues, but each person is, for example, if brave then also wise, etc. (Vlastos 1972). 'The unity of virtue' finds the claim to be that all of these are names for one and the same thing (Penner 1973). That thing is taken to be the psychological state that causes virtuous behaviour. These virtuous behaviours are then distinguished by context: bravery is what virtuous behaviour looks like on the battlefield, temperance is what virtuous behaviour looks like at the banquet table, etc. Thus, the unity of virtue thesis resonates with the notion that virtue is all knowledge and that virtuous behaviour is simply knowledgeable behaviour and wise people on the battlefield act bravely while wise people in the courts act justly.

It is widely recognized that Plato brings the notion of *aretê*, here best understood as 'excellence', into his conception of justice and the structure of his republic. The *kallipolis* – the fine city proposed in the *R.* – is just because in it each person does that to which he or she is best suited and that at which he or she excels. The people are, in turn, placed into three classes according to their interests and abilities and each of those classes as a collective does that at which it excels. Here, rather than there being some generic human excellence that is the function of humans generally, Plato is looking upon the function and excellence of individual people in the same way he looks at the function and excellence of tools. Knives are made of certain materials that promote their function and allow them to be excellent at cutting. Likewise, retailers have specific physical and mental abilities that make them suited to and allow them to excel as retailers whereas farmers have a different and complementary set. Those who should become auxiliaries and guardians are distinguished by their mental and physical abilities as well. Thus, the republic fails when its individual members do jobs to which they are not well suited but most of all when the classes no longer interact according to their excellences. It is central to the guardians' excellence that they look out for the interests of the republic as a whole, while it is central to the craftspeoples' excellence that they concern themselves with their own affairs and trust the guardians to deal with larger issues.

FORMS (*EIDOS*) (IDEA)

Kenneth Sayre

Perhaps the best known doctrine associated with Plato is his so-called theory of forms. Yet that theory is never fully articulated in his extant writings. It has even been questioned whether Plato's thoughts about forms constituted an actual theory (Sayre 1995b). A consequence is that there is considerable disagreement about the contents of the account in question. This article summarizes the account's main features without attempting to arbitrate disputed issues.

Aristotle reports (*Metaphysics* 1078b12–15) that Plato was led to his theory of forms by being persuaded that knowledge requires permanent objects and that sensible things are always in flux. To meet this requirement, Plato posited eternal and incomposite forms as proper objects of thought. Forms thus are both immutable and entirely what they are, without parts to admit opposing features. A plausible example is the form justice (q.v.), which (setting aside for now the problem of self-predication) is wholly just and in no respect otherwise.

Another consequence is that forms can be presented immediately to thought or intellect, whereas particular things are presented only in sense perception (q.v.). Thus forms can be known as they are, in and by themselves, independently of their relation to sense particulars.

Forms and sense particulars are related by participation (q.v.), whereby particulars take on determinate properties. Thus, sense particulars (otherwise in constant flux) become beautiful (just, large, etc.) by participating in the corresponding form (beauty, etc.). Whereas forms are what they are independently of other things (are absolute), features of particulars are caused by participation.

As a result of this causal dependency, sensible things also share names with forms in which they participate. In effect, forms serve as paradigms for naming sense particulars that participate in them. Thus we find Socrates in the *Euthphro* saying he must know what the form holiness is in order to tell whether a particular act should be called holy (cf. Allen 1971).

These several tenets comprise what is often described as a 'two world ontology'. On one hand are forms which are absolute, wholly real (nowise other than they are) and knowable by thought. On the other are sense particulars which are dependent on forms for their properties, are subject to opposing properties and can be apprehended by sensation but not by intellect. Due to these differences, forms are said to be ontologically *separate* from the world of sense experience.

These are the main tenets of the account associated with Plato's so-called middle dialogues, notably in the *Phaedo*, *Republic* and *Symposium*. As it stands, this theory raises various problems which have been subject to extensive debate. One is the issue of what participation amounts to. This shows up in the question of what things have corresponding forms.

The theory maintains that things are called by the same name (or described by the same predicate) by virtue of participating in the same forms. Conversely, a single form is involved whenever we assign the same name to (*R*. 596a) or predicate the same property of (*Parmenides* 132a) many things. But we apply the same name in the case of dirt and other such paltry things. Does this mean that there are forms in which such objects participate? If so, this deviates from Plato's practise in the dialogues of emphasizing preeminent forms like goodness, beauty and justice.

A related question pertains to self-predication. At *Protagoras* 330e, for instance, Socrates says that holiness is holy, and at *Phd.* 100c that beauty is beautiful. But is the form oddness (*Phd.* 104d) odd, or the form largeness (*Prm.* 132a) large? Not only do self-predications like these seem senseless, but they give rise to the notorious third man

argument attacking the notion of participation itself. Although entire books have been written about such issues (see Allen 1971; Cohen and Keyt 1991), the debates they raise will probably continue indefinitely.

Perhaps the biggest anomaly affecting the theory of the middle period, however, is that several of its key tenets are challenged in later dialogues. Questioning the youthful Socrates in his namesake dialogue, Parmenides attacks in rapid sequence the theses that forms are incomposite, causes of sensible properties, knowable by thought, paradigms for naming and separate in and by themselves. Although commentators disagree on the seriousness of these attacks (for a classic disagreement, see Cherniss 1957; Owen 1953a), they clearly call attention to aspects of the original theory that require rethinking.

Apart from Parmenides' problems, the *Sophist* contains an account of forms (or kinds) that directly opposes certain tenets of the original theory. Forms here admit opposing characters, inasmuch as sameness is different from difference and difference is the same as itself. Forms in the *Sph.* also are no longer changeless, since a form's status alters when it becomes known.

Another departure from the original theory appears in the *Timaeus*. Participation initially was a two-term relation between forms and sensible objects. In *Ti.*, it is represented instead as a three-term relation involving forms (or paradigms), a characterless receptacle and sensible copies ('reflections') of the forms in the latter. Another innovation here is that forms take on geometrical features, enabling a mathematical description of the makeup of physical properties.

An even more radical departure appears in the *Philebus*, where the forms and receptacle of *Ti.* are replaced by the ontological principles of limit and unlimited respectively.

Forms here become limits in the sense of measures or numbers (terms used synonymously in Aristotle's *Physics* 4.11). In this late dialogue a wide array of sensible things are said to derive from the imposition of limit on the unlimited, ranging from grammatical phonemes and musical scales to good health, fair weather and an orderly universe.

Recent scholarship has indicated that the conception of forms at work in the *Phlb.* may correspond to claims Aristotle makes about Plato's forms in the *Metaphysics* (see Sayre 2005, 2006). One claim is that forms are numbers. Another is that forms come from participation of the indefinite dyad in unity. Equivalent claims, in the language of the *Phlb.*, are that forms are measures and that they arise from a mixture of unlimited with limit.

If this correspondence holds true, yet another tenet of the original theory is rejected in the later dialogues. A key provision originally is that forms are incomposite, whereas in *Phlb.* they are composed of limit and the unlimited. In other respects, however, the initial theory holds firm. Forms still are knowable by intellect, paradigms for naming and responsible for determinate properties of sensible things.

FRIENDSHIP (*PHILIA*)

David Konstan

A discussion of friendship in Plato encounters two major problems. The first pertains to Greek terminology: for *philia*, the word normally translated as 'friendship', has a far wider range, embracing almost all that English includes under 'love' (q.v.), and more (e.g. social concord and foreign alliances). When the adjective *philos*, 'dear' or 'loving', is accompanied by the definite article and thus nominalized ('the dear one'), it usually means 'friend', although in the plural it occasionally includes kin ('dear ones'). Rather than distinguishing sharply between friendship and other types of affection, such as familial, Greek employed a single inclusive term. *Philia* was, however, clearly differentiated from *erôs*, 'erotic love', which a man typically felt towards a woman (in amatory rather than domestic contexts) or an adolescent boy. Thus, to determine Plato's views of friendship, one must distinguish it both from *erôs*, which Plato discussed imaginatively, and love or *philia* in general.

The second difficulty is specific to Plato: for Plato was not much interested in analyzing friendship as such, though friendships, like that between Socrates and Crito, are illustrated in his dialogues. The dialogue commonly read as Plato's treatment of friendship, namely the *Lysis* (sometimes subtitled 'On Friendship'; cf. Bolotin 1979), has as much to do with *erôs* and other kinds of affection as with friendship. Plato was chiefly concerned with the nature of desire or attraction in general, of which friendship is one type. Erotic desire in particular seemed to him a better emblem of the philosophical aspiration to pass beyond the world of changing appearances to the timeless realm of 'ideas'.

Although the *Ly.* does treat *philia*, it is not a typical 'dialogue of definition' (Sedley 1989). It opens with Socrates advising a young man named Hippothales on the right way to court Lysis, the boy with whom he is in love; indeed he claims that his only skill is detecting 'who loves and who is loved' (*erônta te kai erômenon*, 204B8–10). Note that these are two roles, lover and beloved; *erôs* is typically an asymmetrical relationship (the age difference between Hippothales and

Lysis is relevant). Hippothales hopes Lysis will feel affection for him (*prosphilês*, from *philia*), not *erôs* (cf. Plato *Phaedrus* 255d; Aristotle *Nicomachean Ethics* 8.4,1157a6–9; *Eudemian Ethics* 7.3,1238b36–9; Dover 1993:197; Halperin 1993:418). By contrast, the relation between friends (*philoi*) was understood to be mutual. As Socrates puts it, 'unless both parties love, neither is a friend' (*Ly.* 213A; cf. Aristotle *Nicomachean Ethics* 8.2, 1155b31–6a5; Hutter 1978:6). The frame of the dialogue concerns *erôs*, not friendship.

Engaging Lysis in conversation, Socrates asks whether his parents love him: the term is *philein* (*eran*, the verb corresponding to *erôs*, would be inappropriate, though *stergein*, referring mainly to parental affection, would have been possible). Socrates argues that they love him for what he knows and is good at. Nothing prevents affection on this basis from being mutual, but Socrates is interested here in the cause of affection, not in friendship per se. Socrates then inquires what kinds of things are dear (*philon*, neuter), and proceeds to argue that friendship resides neither in one party loving another or being loved, nor again – and this is surprising – in both parties mutually loving each other. Having overturned his own earlier description of friendship, Socrates considers whether we love those who are similar or different, and rejects both options; again, the focus is on the reasons for loving. In a series of subtle arguments, Socrates demonstrates that we love or desire something for the sake of something else, for example, medicine for the sake of health, but this leads to an infinite regress – there must be some first or primary object of love (*prôton philon*). Socrates finally suggests that we desire (*epithumein*) what we lack or have been deprived of, and this must somehow belong to us (*oikeion*);

thus, Socrates declares, '*erôs* and *philia* and *epithumia* [desire] are for one's own' (*Ly.* 221E3–4; on the conflation of the three terms, cf. Cummins 1981; Robinson 1986:74–5). But this too turns out to be a false lead, and the dialogue ends in aporia. At all events, friendship is clearly of interest only as one species of affection (cf. Penner and Rowe 2005; contrast Nichols 2009:169).

Plato touches on *philia* again in the *Laws*, here too in association with erotic love and desire (*Lg.* 8.836E). He explains that we call 'dear' (*philon*) what is similar in respect to virtue, and also what is dissimilar when one party is in need of the other; in either case, when it is intense we dub it *erôs* (837A). Plato's attention is on *erôs* here, and more particularly on pederasty (q.v., paiderasteia); *philia* is incidental.

Like ancient Greeks generally, Plato often contrasts friends and enemies (*ekhthroi*). But because the disjunction tends to be exhaustive, the class of 'friends' may become so wide as to include (absent civil dissension) all fellow citizens (cf. 694–5, 708); indeed, taking to an extreme the adage that the possessions of friends are in common, Plato concludes that in an ideal state there will be no private property at all (*Republic* 424A, 449C). In Greek one could speak of such solidarity as *philia* (cf. Aristotle's *politikê philia*, *Nicomachean Ethics* 8.11; *Eudemian Ethics* 1241a32–3), but rendering the term as 'friendship' is misleading. In the *R.* (335), Socrates ventures the definition that a *philos*, properly speaking, is anyone who is good, an *ekhthros* one who is bad, but he goes on to affirm, against common wisdom, that it is not just to harm anyone, since that is to make a person worse. Plato is clearly undermining the conventional opposition of friend and enemy.

Of course, the Greeks recognized more intimate degrees of friendship, and Aristotle denied that one could have many close friends (*Nicomachean Ethics* 9.10). But unlike Aristotle, Plato did not investigate such friendship systematically, though he no doubt appreciated it: Socrates much admires, for example, the bond between Lysis and his agemate Menexenus. When he visits Socrates in jail, Crito affirms that he will never again find such a companion (*Crito* 44B), and tries to convince Socrates to let him bribe the jailer, since it is shameful to value money more than friends. But for Socrates evading the law is wrong, and so he refuses the aid proffered by his friends. So too, Phaedo assures Echecrates that Socrates died in the presence of many friends (*Phd.* 58C), but he is amazed that Socrates conversed with them unsentimentally, as on any other day (58E–9A). Though Socrates may have described himself, tongue in cheek, as an expert in *ta erôtika*, when it came to *philia* what most interested him, and Plato, was the love of wisdom or *philosophia*.

GOODNESS (THE GOOD, *AGATHON*)

Rafael Ferber

The good is for the Platonic Socrates that for which everything is done (cf. *Gorgias* 468b). This is an 'axiom' to which Plato seems to adhere during his whole writing career (cf. *Symposium* 205e–6a, *Republic* 505d–e, *Philebus.* 65a). But the Socratic good becomes for Plato in the R. the idea of the good, which is also the 'greatest thing to be learned' and the 'greatest lesson' (*megiston mathêma*, R. 505a, 519c).

We may find a first allusion to this idea in the *Lysis* in 'what we like in the first place' (*prôton philon*, Ly. 219d), cf. Penner and Rowe (2005:278–9). The *Politicus* may touch

on this idea under the title of the 'exact itself' (284d; cf. Ferber 2002:190). But the idea of the good is treated explicitly only in the sixth and seventh book of the R. in the course of three similes, though caution is warranted: the Platonic Socrates gives in these similes only his 'opinions without science' (R. 506c) and even these opinions are incomplete (506e1–3). First, he distances himself from existing philosophical conceptions of the good, where the good consists in pleasure or in knowledge (cf. 505b–c). Both conceptions are refuted, one because there are also bad pleasures (cf. *Grg.* 499c6–7), the other because this conception would be circular (cf. *Euthyphro* 292e3): knowledge would be knowledge of something, namely, the good. Second, the Platonic Socrates says positively three things about the good: (a) it is not sought like 'just and beautiful things' (505d), where we may be satisfied also with the appearance, but as something which really is good. So we may be conventionalists concerning the 'just and beautiful things', but we are realists concerning the good. We want not the apparent, but the real good. (b) It is the final cause of all that is good in desire and action (517b7–c4). (c) The knowledge of the idea of the good is the condition of the knowledge of just and the beautiful things, that is, the ideas of justice and beauty (506a). This means that if the ideas of justice and beauty were not also good, they would not be ideas of real but only of apparent justice and beauty. Since without knowledge of the idea of the good no other knowledge is of any use to us (cf. 505a2–3), knowledge of apparent justice and apparent beauty would not be of any use to us. Therefore knowledge of the idea of the good is required to know the goodness and usefulness of just and beautiful things.

These two negative and three positive (formal) determinations are supplemented by the substantive description which the Platonic Socrates gives in the three similes. Common to them is that the idea of the good figures as cause (q.v.; *aitia*, 508e3.517b2) or principle (*archê*, 510b7). In the simile of the sun (q.v.), it functions as the cause of knowledge, truth and being, although it is itself not being (*ouk ousias ontos tou agathou*, 509b8–9), but 'surpasses the being in dignity and power' (*epekeina tês ousias presbeia kai dynamei hyperechontos*, 505b9–10). Thus Plato seems to found his ontology and epistemology on a supreme principle which – if the cause is not the same as that which is caused – must be 'something else and more beautiful than knowledge and truth' (508e5–6) and being (but cf. Baltes 1997; Ferber 2005; Seel 2007). We can see in this description of the good the inauguration of the problem of the third between and above being and thinking: As light and its master, the sun, functions as a third item (*R.* 507d.e), so the idea of the good functions as a third item between and above thinking and being. In the simile of the line (q.v.), the idea of the good, though not mentioned there, functions as an unhypothetical principle (*anhypothetos archê*) of the mathematical 'presuppositions' (*hypotheseis*, 510c6), that is, the four arts of the *quadrivium* (on the text of the simile cf. Lafrance 1994; on interpretations between 1804 and 1984, Lafrance 1987).

The image of the cave (q.v.) shows us what education means for Plato. It is 'a leading of the soul' (*psychês periagogê*, 521c1) that is also a return of the soul's attention to the really good. But the idea of the good functions also as a principle of Plato's politics so that not only every soul in her private life, but 'anyone who is to act sensibly in private or public must see it' (510c). Because the philosopher-kings and -queens know the really good, they will also, in the sense of the

Socratic paradox that virtue is knowledge, realize the good in the city (on all three similes cf. Ferber 1984:49–166, 1989:49–219; Schindler 2008:139–75).

The *Phlb.* starts with the search for a certain state of the soul which can render the life of all human beings happy (cf. *Phlb.* 11d4–6). But it asks nevertheless the Socratic question '. . . what in fact is the good . . .' (13e5–6) and holds on to a 'single form' (*mia idea*) of the good (65a1), which Socrates tries to hold down with the conjunction of three qualities (*poia*): 'beauty, symmetry and truth' (65a2; cf. Ferber 2010). In his old age, Plato seems to have held a public 'lecture on the good', although this lecture may go back to earlier 'seminars' or '*synousiai*' 'on the good'. (cf. Simplicius, *in Aristotelis Physica commentaria Phlb.* 542.1012, 545.24). After an anecdote reported by Aristoxenos about Aristotle, the hearers of the lecture expected to be told

> . . . something about one of the recognized human goods, such as wealth, health or strength, or, in sum, some marvelous happiness. But when it appeared that Plato was to talk *on mathematics and numbers and geometry and astronomy*, leading up to the statement that there the good is one (*hoti tagaton estin hen*), they were overwhelmed by the paradox of the whole matter. Some then thought little of the thing and others even reproved it. (Aristoxenus, *The Elements of Harmony* II)

In this lecture, Plato may have presented the idea on the good in a dialectical way, where unity as we find it in the abstract structures of mathematics may have played a significant role (cf. Burnyeat 2000). From this lecture, only fragments from notes taken by his hearers, especially from Aristotle, survive (cf. the collection of fragments in Gaiser 1963:441–557; Isnardi-Parente 1997:406–84, 1998:5–115; Krämer 1990:203–17). But we find in Aristotle's *Metaphysics* a 'short and principal' summary (987a27, 988a17) of the public lecture whose content Plato may have already communicated earlier to his advanced students (cf. Ferber 1989:211–16).

HAPPINESS (*EUDAIMONIA*)

Rachana Kamtekar

In contemporary usage, 'happiness' is sometimes taken to be a feeling, as temporary or permanent as feelings are. In ancient Greek usage, in contrast, *eudaimonia*, the term translated 'happiness', characterizes a whole life and not just a moment of feeling, and has an objective dimension: the happy life not only feels good to the one who lives it, but is good. Sometimes translators use 'flourishing' instead; one ground for this is that not only humans, but other species as well, are said to flourish when they are in a good condition relative to their capacities, but it was for the ancients a philosophical issue whether *eudaimonia* ought to be conceived this way, and indeed whether a life of pleasure not only feels good to the one who lives it but also is the best life; the same philosophical issue arises today about happiness, and it cannot be settled by a translation (see Kraut 1979).

Plato takes it as uncontroversial that all of us wish to be happy, that is, to live well (*Euthydemus* 278e; *Meno* 78a–b; *Symposium* 205a). He does not mean by this that we wish that our desires, whatever they are, be satisfied; rather, happiness requires possessing, and correctly using, genuinely good things (*Euthd.* 280d). But happiness is not divorced from desire-satisfaction either, for

we all do in fact desire the genuinely good things obtaining which will make us happy (*Gorgias* 468b; *Men.* 77b–8b; *Republic* 505d–e); evidence of this includes our pursuit of what appears good, our loss of desire for things once we learn they are not good, and our efforts to determine what really is good.

What are the genuinely good things the possession and correct use of which make us happy? In the *Philebus*, Socrates argues that the good or happy human life contains a mixture of knowledge and pleasure (*Phlb.* 20d–2a). In the *Grg.* (470e) and *R.* bk 1 (354a), Socrates says that our happiness depends entirely on whether or not we are virtuous, but at other times he makes the weaker claim that having virtue makes one happier than any of those who lack virtue, no matter what else they have and one lacks (*R.* 360e–2c, 387d, 392cd, 580b). The comparative claim allows nonmoral goods, such as health and wealth, to contribute to the virtuous person's happiness. (The case that the *R.* makes only this 'comparative' claim about happiness' relationship to virtue is made in Irwin 1995:191–3 and contested in Annas 1999:84–7; the alternatives for relating happiness and virtue are canvassed in Vlastos 1999.) To explain *how* virtue contributes to happiness, the *R.* (443d–4e) describes justice as a harmonious condition of soul, analogous to health for the body and wisdom as the perfection of our best capacity, reason, in knowledge of the forms and especially of the form of the good (*R.* 518c–d, 504e–5a). In both cases, the happiness described involves both the satisfaction of desires and the possession of some genuinely good thing(s).

On the grounds that happiness consists in contemplation of the forms, an activity which is interrupted by our bodily condition, Plato sometimes (e.g. *Phaedo, Phaedrus*) seems to restrict true happiness to life after death for philosophers.

The universal desire for happiness serves as the cornerstone of a number of arguments in Plato: in the *R.*, the (presumed) desire of his interlocutors for happiness enables Socrates to justify being just on the grounds that being just is (at least) necessary for our happiness; in the *Euthd.*, Socrates wins Clinias over to philosophy on the grounds that wisdom is the condition for benefiting from any other goods (*Euthd.* 278e–82d); in the *Protagoras*, Socrates convinces a hypothetical majority that what we call being overwhelmed by pleasure is actually ignorance on the grounds that no one knowingly goes for anything other than what they judge best, viz., most pleasant (*Prt.* 352a–8d). Many scholars take the desire for happiness to be a foundation that structures Plato's ethics, committing him to 'ethical eudaimonism', according to which to be rational, action must aim at one's own happiness (e.g. Irwin 1995). Some also take Plato to be committed to 'psychological eudaimonism', the descriptive thesis that our actions in fact aim at our own happiness (e.g. Penner 1991). Yet Plato does seem to consider some noneudaimonistic reasons for action: the desire to reproduce, and thereby approximate, the immortality one desires (*Smp.* 207a–9e); the love of beauty (*Phdr.* 249d–56e); the debt philosophers owe to the city that educated them (*R.* 520a–e; White 2002 discusses this and other noneudaimonistic passages in Plato).

Happiness is important to Plato's political thought as well as his ethical thought. Thus, legislation should aim at the happiness of the citizens (*Laws* 743c; the *R.* uses the language of aiming at the happiness of the *city* in order not to beg the question of whether the citizens, who are virtuous, will thereby be happy, see Kamtekar 2010), and political justification consists in showing that the government is competent to make citizens good or happy (*Politicus* 293a–e). (Kamtekar (2006) and Reeve (1988) offer alternative accounts of how happiness figures in political justification).

IDEA (see Forms)

IMAGE (*EIKÔN*)

Richard Patterson

Images (*eikônes*) are of great importance to Plato for several reasons. For one, the traditional Homeric and tragic images of gods, heroes, humans and the afterlife had for many generations exercised a corrupting influence on all of Greek society, and the reform of these images was of fundamental importance for Plato's vision of proper religious, civic and moral education (see esp. *Republic* bks 2–3; cf. bk 10 for further criticisms of epic and tragic imagery). Second, in that same general spirit of harnessing the power of images to positive effect, Plato casts his own philosophical writings as verbal images of encounters among philosophical ideas and theories, and of diverse choices concerning how one ought to live, all fashioned so as to reveal to the receptive reader their true nature and value. Third, the relation of images to the 'real things' of which they are likenesses furnishes Plato's principle illustration of his radically counterintuitive views about reality, understanding and value. This brief article will focus on the second and third of these points.

Although the Platonic Socrates appears in different roles – refutational gadfly, barren midwife of ideas, planner of the just city – he remains a philosophical counterweight to the great Homeric images of heroism and excellence: in philosophy lies the greatest *agôn* (struggle, contest) – that to discover and lead the best life. This requires not only wisdom and self-control, but also the traditional heroic quality of *andreia* ('courage', 'stout heartedness'). For the philosopher must take on powerful advocates of false conceptions of excellence and happiness (Homer, Thrasymachus, Callicles, Protagoras), defend the truth even if his views meet with scorn and ridicule (*R*. bk 5), persevere in the most protracted and difficult of investigations and, if need be, choose death rather than abandon philosophy (*Apology; Phaedo*).

The philosophic hero does not cease to become an image of justice itself or wisdom; rather she becomes a true and accurate enactment or imitation (*mimêsis*; q.v. Imitation) of wisdom and justice. By contrast, the reputedly wise Homer, along with the legendary fifth-century sophists (literally, 'wise men') are not only distorted but deceptive imitations of wisdom. As the *Sophist* suggests, the latter appear wise only to the unwise, who are in no position to judge – just as colossal sculptures have their proportions cleverly altered so as to look right to those who must view them from an inferior perspective (*Sph*. 235d, ff.). The philosophic *mimêsis* of wisdom is a genuine likeness (*eikôn*) rather than a semblance (*phantasma*), and so can help convey, to those adequately equipped to respond appropriately, the true nature of wisdom. Indeed, the philosophic life becomes an 'imitation of god' (*Theaetetus* 176b), where divinity is invested not in scandal-ridden Olympians, but in eternal, purely intelligible standards of goodness.

These imperceptible but intelligible 'forms' (q.v.) provide standards of excellence not only for individual lives but also for human communities, and even for the cosmos as a whole. In all three spheres goodness lies in correct imitation or enactment (*mimêsis*) of standards that obtain whether or not anyone or anything ever discovers or lives up to them. A philosopher can shape her own life in the image of wisdom, can fashion an image of a just city in words, and might, if put in charge as philosopher-king, create an actual city in the image of justice itself (*R*. 472, 540a, 592a–b). Analogously, the divine craftsman-creator of the world makes the best possible likeness (*eikôn*) of his good, intelligible, model (*paradeigma, Timaeus* 29b), bringing rational order into an initial disorderly motion in the 'receptacle' (*hypodoche*; something like 'place', *chora Ti*. 49a–52c).

If a truly good life requires apprehension and *mimêsis* (imitation, enactment) of eternal, immutable, world-independent standards of goodness, this requires in turn that Plato's new and radical metaphysics of forms and worldly imitations be itself coherent. But this has been in dispute since Plato's own day. Putting aside a host of thorny subordinate issues, the central question is this: did Plato think of forms as perfect or complete exemplars of various kinds of things, and their worldly images as imperfect or incomplete examples? Or are forms abstract entities that are not in general instances of themselves – something like properties themselves (e.g. equality, justice, humanity) – with worldly images being things that embody or possess those properties? Both approaches have advocates dating back to antiquity. (For two modern influential versions of the first interpretation, see Vlastos and Owen in Allen 1967; for defence of the second, see Allen and Cherniss in Allen 1967; Patterson 1985; Prior 1985).

On a 'perfect/complete exemplar' reading of forms, worldly imitations are imperfect copies or duplicates of forms. But this makes most forms into impossible objects. For example, humanity itself is both the perfect human being and a bodiless, imperceptible, purely intelligible thing. Or (on another version of this first type of reading) equality itself becomes a thing whose equality is 'complete' in and of itself; equality is equal without being equal to anything. Either way, the theory is plainly incoherent. It also gives rise to an infinite regress of forms rather than a single form for a given property, as first explained by Plato himself via the eponymous protagonist of his *Parmenides* (132a–b; 132d–3a).

But the image analogy in fact strongly supports a reading on which forms are abstract natures and worldly imitations are embodiments or enactments of those abstract natures. The form of human itself, for example, and its worldly images are related in the way that paintings, reflections, dreams and verbal images of a human being are related to a living human being. Although the painting or reflection is rightly labelled 'human' (rather than 'ox') it is not a second human being at all, perfect or imperfect. Similarly, the flesh-and-blood human being is not a more-or-less imperfect copy of the intelligible form of human; on the contrary, it is not an intelligible (or eternal, immutable, bodiless) thing at all. Rather, it is an enactment or embodiment of the intelligible nature common to all earthly humans. Both are rightly called 'human', but they are very different kinds of 'human' (*R.* 597b) – one the unique, nonspatial, immutable, intelligible form of human, the other a spatial, changing and perceptible embodiment of the form. It is precisely this combination of a critical kinship between image and model on the one hand, with the absence of garden-variety resemblance between the two on the other,

that Plato emphasizes repeatedly by use of the image analogy. On this second sort of interpretation, then, the problems discussed above for the 'image/model' theory of the relation between forms and worldly things do not arise. And one may safely and quite sensibly say that being a just person is not a matter of trying to be, or almost being, another form of justice, but of exemplifying or enacting in one's life the eternal and objective nature of justice.

IMITATION (see *Mimêsis*)

INCONTINENCE (see *Akrasia*)

INSPIRATION

Kathryn A. Morgan

Plato uses the concept of inspiration flexibly, although it plays a major role only in *Ion* and *Phaedrus*. The vocabulary of what we call 'inspiration' was expressed in Greek in various ways, as being 'held' by a divine force, 'breathed upon' or (mostly) as having a god inside you, being *entheos*. As had been recognized for centuries, this was the force that motivated prophets and poets, and made their gifts 'divine'. There does not seem, however, to have been a consistent or systematic theorization of inspiration prior to Plato. Even within his corpus we still find the vocabulary of inspiration being used loosely. Phaedrus in the *Symposium* can speak of being 'inspired' by love to acts of courage (*Smp.* 179a7–8). Socrates in the *Philebus* says that one who has been seduced by the pleasures of discourse is also 'inspired' (*Phlb.* 15d4–e2) and in the *Cratylus* he has himself been 'inspired' to etymologize by Euthyphro of Prospalta (*Cra.* 396d2–5). By this assertion he attempts to disclaim responsibility for the material he presents. This strategy is central to more developed treatments of inspiration elsewhere in the corpus.

As Murray (1981) has shown, early Greek literature drew no dichotomy between divine empowerment and individual skill; inspiration was thus not irrational. Plato, however, bases his entire theory of inspiration as ecstatic possession on this dichotomy and develops it in the *Ion*. There Socrates suggests that poets are moved by a 'divine force' (*Ion* 533d3) and that the Muse makes them 'inspired' and 'divinely possessed' (533e3–8), but then expands the notion, suggesting that a poet cannot compose until 'his mind is no longer in him' and that god does this so that mortals will know that it is not the poet (or prophet) who is speaking, but the god himself (534b3–d4). Socrates here deploys the strong contrast between human skill and divine force as a way of explaining Ion's inability to provide any rational basis for his talents in reciting and explicating Homeric poetry. As many commentators have seen, however, this view of inspiration, while couched as a compliment, is intended to disqualify poets from intellectual pretensions and discredit them as cultural authorities. Far from transparently reflecting his society's beliefs, Plato has pushed them to a tendentious extreme.

The significance of this contrast stretches beyond poetry and has political and philosophical implications. In the *Apology* Socrates again contrasts poetic inspiration with knowledge, and (as he did in the *Ion*) connects poetry with prophecy (*Ap.* 22b8–c4). Here, crucially, his comment that poets compose not by knowledge but by inspiration is closely juxtaposed to his similar

discovery about politicians: they are reputed to be experts but speak without knowledge (21b9–c7, 22a8–9). This connection is made explicit in the *Meno*, where he concludes that politicians succeed not through knowledge but by a kind of right opinion and in this respect are just like prophets:

> We could say that politicians, no less than these, are divine and have a god in them; they have been breathed upon and are possessed by a god when they speak successfully about many great matters although they do not know what they are talking about. (99d1–5)

The focus in these passages is not so much on divine encroachment on an individual but on success achieved despite lack of knowledge. The notion of inspiration thus gives Plato a way of critiquing poetic and political accomplishment. It can even be deployed in an attack on Heraclitean philosophers, among whom there are no teachers and pupils, but who 'arise spontaneously wherever each of them happens to catch his inspiration, and none of them thinks the others know anything' (*Theaetetus* 180b8–c3).

Plato was an important figure in the development of an abstract vocabulary of inspiration. The noun *enthousiasmos* appears first in Plato and Democritus ('DK' 68B18), while the adjective *enthousiastikos*, the noun *enthousiasis*, and verb *enthousiazô* are first preserved in the Platonic corpus (q.v.). This reflects a general concern with the technical analysis and criticism of poets in the second half of the fifth century, but also reveals how suggestive Plato found the concept.

Phdr. marks the culmination of this interest, where the model of inspiration found in the *Ion* recurs and is superseded by a philosophical counterpart. Inspiration is prominent in the first part of the dialogue. Socrates' two speeches on love are presented as inspired by various powers: the Muses, the Nymphs, Pan (among others). Moreover, the content of Socrates' great palinode is concerned with inspiration, insofar as the speech starts with the observation that certain traditional manifestations of madness (q.v.) may be connected with the divine realm and are beneficial. Among these are prophetic, ritual ('telestic'), poetic and erotic madness. Poetic madness, in particular, is said to come from the Muses and be a form of possession (*Phdr.* 244a6–5a5). So far, the model is the one familiar from the *Ion*, but once Socrates describes the fate of the soul before and after embodiment, things begin to change. Now we learn that the philosopher, when recollecting the forms seen while disincarnate, is often thought to be out of his senses because the many do not see that he is 'inspired'. Similarly the lover is 'inspired' to recollect the form of beauty by seeing earthly beauty, and this is the best of all types of 'inspiration' (or 'enthusiasm') (249c4–e4). Enthusiasm or inspiration is now seen as a psychic reaction to a likeness of a form that carries one to the divine realm. We thus move from a notion of inspiration as possession and incursion, where the poet is a passive instrument of the god, to a philosophical mode where inspiration is associated with recollection (q.v.). In the best-case scenario of the *Phdr.* philosophical inspiration is married to reason and the philosopher uses contact with the divine to engage in systematic reflection. In the *Phdr.*, then, Plato has returned to the coexistence of reason and divine experience that characterized earlier notions of inspiration, but this idealized combination exists not in the poet, but in the philosophical lover.

INTELLECTUALISM

William Prior

Intellectualism is a view attributed to Socrates in several of Plato's Socratic dialogues that treats certain mental states, in particular virtue and vice, as states of the intellect alone, and which, as a result, denies the existence of moral weakness (*akrasia*; q.v.). Intellectualism is especially prominent in the *Laches*, *Gorgias*, *Euthydemus*, *Protagoras* and *Meno*.

(I) VIRTUE IS KNOWLEDGE

Perhaps the most prominent mental state that receives an intellectualist treatment at the hands of Plato is virtue. In the *La.*, while attempting to define courage, Laches comes up with a definition of what Socrates calls 'virtue entire': knowledge of all goods and evils (*La.* 199c–d). Why is virtue knowledge? The *Men.* provides the following argument: virtue is good, makes us good and is thus beneficial. Other goods, such as health, strength, beauty and wealth, or the psychological qualities moderation, justice, courage, intelligence, memory and munificence, are sometimes beneficial and sometimes harmful. What renders them beneficial is right use; what produces right use is knowledge (understanding, wisdom). Thus knowledge, as the only intrinsically beneficial quality a person can possess, is virtue (*Men.* 87b–9a). A similar argument occurs in the *Euthd.* (278e–82d).

The *Prt.* offers a detailed account of what is meant by happiness and wisdom, one that is unique to the Socratic dialogues. In an argument with the many, Socrates leads them to admit that they regard pleasure as good and pain as bad (*Prt.* 354c). Given this account of happiness, Socrates argues that wisdom is an art of measurement of pleasure and pain (358a–b).

(II) Vice Is Ignorance

If virtue is knowledge, it is easy to understand vice as ignorance. In the passage of the *Men.* discussed above Socrates states, 'all that the soul undertakes and endures, if directed by wisdom, ends in happiness, but if directed by ignorance, it ends in the opposite' (*Men.* 88c). The *Euthd.*, in the same vein states, 'with respect to all the things we called good in the beginning, the correct account is not that in themselves are they good by nature, but rather as follows: if ignorance controls them, they are greater evils than their opposites' (*Euthd.* 281d). The analysis of vice in the *Prt.* yields the following account of ignorance as vice:

If, then, I said, the pleasant is good, no one who either knows or believes other things are better than the things he is doing, and possible, then does those things if he is capable of the better; nor is the 'being worse than oneself' anything other than ignorance and 'being stronger than oneself' anything other than wisdom. (*Prt.* 358c. Tr. Prior)

This ignorance is identified as false belief; the belief in question is a miscalculation of the magnitude of pleasure and pain involved in a particular course of action, an error in perspective (356c–e).

(III) No One Does Wrong Willingly

Perhaps the most paradoxical claim in the intellectualist position is the denial of *akrasia* (q.v.), moral weakness. The phenomenon of moral weakness is alleged to occur when one, in full possession of knowledge of the best course of action, nevertheless chooses an inferior course, under the influence of some other mental state. 'The many' think of

knowledge 'as being utterly dragged around . . . as if it were a slave' (352c). The position shared by Socrates and Protagoras, in contrast, is that:

knowledge is a fine thing, capable of ruling a person, and if someone were to know what is good and bad, then he would not be forced by anything to act other than as knowledge dictates, and intelligence would be sufficient to save a person. (352c)

The most elaborate Socratic argument against *akrasia*, of which the above claim is a part, occurs in the *Prt.* and relies on the assumption of hedonism (354b–d). The many believe in *akrasia* because they believe that a person knowing full well that a given action is more beneficial than another, will nonetheless perform that other action because of being overcome by pleasure (352d–e). On the assumption that pleasure is the good, Socrates shows that this view of the many does not make sense by substituting 'good' for 'pleasant' in their position. The difficulty with this argument is that it only works on the assumption of hedonism, and the *Prt.* is the only dialogue in which Plato advocates hedonism, even for the sake of argument.

(IV) Later Developments

The intellectualist position described above is prominent in the 'Socratic' dialogues, though it is also present in *Laws*. The *Republic* offers a different moral psychology and a new theory of virtue. For some scholars (e.g. Penner 2002) this change marks a transition between the view of the historical Socrates and the view of Plato. The major development in the *R.* that gives rise to the modification or abandonment of intellectualism is the introduction, in bk 4, of the tripartite conception of the soul. The soul is divided into three distinct parts: reason, spirit and appetite. Whereas the intellectualist picture identified virtue as a whole with knowledge, the new theory allocates the virtues to different parts of the soul. Closest to the intellectual conception of the soul is reason, to which is assigned the virtue of wisdom. The spirited part of the soul is assigned the virtue of courage, while the virtues of temperance and justice are allocated to the three parts in combination (*R*. bk 4.442c–d). The *Prt*. had described wisdom as a powerful force, capable of ruling a person; the *R*., in contrast, describes reason, the seat of wisdom, as requiring the aid of spirit if it is to prevail over the appetites (441e). Further, whereas the Socratic dialogues had insisted that every desire was for the good (cf., e.g. *Grg*. 468b; also Kahn 2008:4 and Penner 2002:195), the *R*. defines thirst in terms of drink and warns against adding 'good' to the object of desire (*R*. bk 4.437d–8b). Despite this new theory of the *R*., aspects of intellectualism reappear in the dialogues generally considered late, in particular in the *Lg*. (5.731c; 9.860d) and *Timaeus* (86d; cf. Kahn 1996:72n). This renders doubtful the claim that Plato ever abandoned the central tenets of intellectualism.

See also: Brickhouse and Smith (2009), Irwin (1977a), Nehamas (1999), Segvic (2002) and Shorey (1903).

JUSTICE (*DIKAION, DIKAIOSYNÊ*)

Richard D. Parry

Justice is the overarching theme in the *Republic*. If people are to live in a political community, they must share equitably in such goods as wealth and personal security.

However, in bk 2 of the *R*., Glaucon presents the common opinion that humans have a strong motivation to take more than their equitable share. Since all are equally vulnerable to suffering if each acted on such motivation, a community adopts rules to assure respect for persons and property (*R*. 358e–9a). However, there is a problem with this account of justice. After all, if someone – because of, for example, intelligence or strength – can act unjustly without being caught, he enjoys a significant advantage over the just person, who follows the rules. So, why should anyone want to be just who is intelligent or strong enough to act unjustly with impunity?

To answer the question, Socrates undertakes to show that justice is beneficial to the just person himself (357b). In developing his argument, Socrates' goal is to show that justice is beneficial for one's soul. This significant move relies on an idea, known in other moral systems, that the true value of justice is psychological; it affords an internal good that outweighs whatever external advantage one can obtain by acting unjustly.

In order to make this kind of argument, Socrates needs an account of the soul (q.v.), which up until this point in Greek thought has been conceived of as simply the principle of life. Socrates does something unprecedented by analyzing the soul as a structured whole of differing parts. In order to make such an account accessible, he compares the soul to the city, with its organization of differing parts (368e). Nevertheless, when Socrates begins we realize that he is talking about an ideal city, profoundly unlike Athens. In the organization of this city there are three chief functions; providing for the material life of the city, ruling and war-making. The first compromises such crafts as farming, weaving, cobbling, house building, animal herding and commercial trading, undertaken by those naturally suited to such work (369b–71a). Ruling is carried out by people with a philosophical nature; war-making by those with an aggressive and honour-focused nature but gentle to those they know (374e–6c; 412c–e). Justice in the city consists in each class sticking to the function for which its members are suited by nature and not interfering with that of another (433b–d).

This account of civic justice may seem strange in that it entails not a distribution of goods but a distribution of functions. Further, the distribution does not depend on a value like equality but rather on one's natural ability to fulfil the function. In this account, justice is rendered to an individual when he is given the function for which he is suited by nature; justice is rendered to others when he fulfils that function. It is clear that, in this account, justice does not recognize or guarantee individual rights in the modern sense. For starters, no one has the right to decide for himself about his natural function. For Plato, however, individual rights are not so much suppressed as unknown.

After this account of justice in the city, Socrates turns to justice in the soul. He argues that the soul also has a tripartite structure with analogous functions for the parts (436a–41c). Reason (q.v.) is the part suited by nature to rule in the soul. The part corresponding to the producers is appetite (q.v.), primarily bodily appetites for food, drink and sex. The part corresponding to the military is called the spirited part (*thumos or thumoeides*). While contemporary readers will recognize reason and appetite, the spirited part is not so familiar. While it is the source of anger against others, it also becomes angry against appetites when they urge wrongful action. Finally, justice in the soul, like justice in the city, is constituted by each part doing its particular function and not interfering with that of another. The function of reason is to rule in the soul, exercising forethought for the whole soul. The function of the spirited part is to be the ally of reason. Together they keep guard over the appetitive part so it does not try to rule (441e–2a). Justice also respects the various functions. Guided by wisdom, reason is a benevolent dictator, looking out for the welfare of the other parts (442c). Thus, if reason tried to enforce a policy of asceticism on the appetites or of passivity on the spirited part, it would not be treating them justly because it would be frustrating their respective functions.

Justice in the soul, then, entails a healthy integration of various interests or tendencies – reason, spirited part and appetite. While a soul so well organized enjoys a great psychological good, there still needs to be an argument linking justice among the parts of the soul to the common notion of justice as respect for persons and property. Socrates argues that injustice committed by an individual against another arises from injustice among the parts of his soul. Unjust acts (forbidden by law or custom) such as embezzlement, betrayal of the city or of friends, breaking oaths and adultery are impossible for someone whose soul is justly ordered (442e–3e).

Not only does justice in the soul beget lawfulness, the law of the city should have a role in establishing virtue. In the *Gorgias*, Socrates argues that lawmaking and judging aim at what is best for the soul (*Grg.* 464b–d, 501a–c). Indeed, the good orator seeks to establish virtuous order and harmony in it; when the soul is disordered by undisciplined desires, his speech must curb them (503d–5c). Finally, judicial punishment can relieve the vicious soul of its injustice (478a–80b). The novel idea that punishment has a function other than retribution is developed in the *Laws*. The Athenian Stranger argues that punishment for serious crimes should aim to cure the soul of the criminal. However, if the judges determine that a cure is not possible they should pass a sentence of death, which will rid the city of an evil doer and deter others (854d–5a, 862c–3a).

The *R.* begins with the common idea that justice is a relation among individuals, defined by rules and the actions prescribed by those rules. However, by making this kind of justice the effect of what justice is really, that is, a hierarchical structure among parts of the soul, Plato has shifted the focus from justice understood as kinds of right action to justice as a psychological disposition, that is, the way the parts habitually interact, from which appropriate actions flow. Finally, by making justice primarily a psychological disposition, Plato is then able to make another argument, that is, that it is a more valuable disposition to have than any of its rivals. A soul with the disposition that results in its acting justly is simply finer as a soul than one with the disposition that results in its acting unjustly.

For further reading on justice, see Cooper (2004), Irwin (1995), Kosman (2007), Kraut (1992b) and Vlastos (1971b).

KNOWLEDGE (see Epistemology)

LANGUAGE

Susan B. Levin

Plato's reflections on language engage substantially with predecessors in philosophical, sophistic, and literary traditions. When revising existing views in more promising directions, his concern is ever with the merit of ideas, not their source. While pre-Socratics and Socrates notice language in defending views of nature and thriving, Plato is the first to devote sustained, systematic attention to it. Many deem familiar linguistic usage misleading, but only Parmenides repudiates it altogether. Stopping short of his Eleatic forebear, Plato's metaphysical discovery of forms and their spatiotemporal participants leads him to acknowledge a pronounced gap between optimal and commonplace deployments of terms, particularly those corresponding to mathematical concepts and values.

Through recollection (q.v.; *anamnêsis*) philosophers attain a grasp of reality wholly independent of language, thereby returning as fully as possible to the clarity attending forms' initial discernment by souls alone. Plato's treatments of ontological, epistemological and linguistic issues are deeply intertwined: the fact that reality is comprised of natural, stable unities enables understanding, and this insight in turn powers philosophers' deployment of language.

Plato's own theorizing on this topic emerges with force in *Cra.* (q.v.), the first work of Western philosophy devoted to language, which investigates the claim that the descriptive content of words or names (*onomata*) reveals their referents' natures (*phuseis*). While controversy persists over what view of terms' correctness *Cra.* envisions, many conclude that it rejects naturalism based on descriptive content as an adequate determinant of whether *onomata* are fittingly assigned. One requires a prior, independent grasp of reality to assess terms' semantic (or phonetic) constitution since otherwise one can interpret even the most salient terms – for example, *epistêmê* ('knowledge', *Cra.* 412a, 437a) – through antithetical, ontological prisms. Precisely that awareness, however, renders otiose the quest to grasp natures through such linguistic study.

While *Cra.* targets an etymological approach to *orthotês onomatôn* (the correctness of words or names), *Phaedo* debuts a revamped version of eponymy, prominent in Greek literature, to provide the semantics of the form-participant tie (see Levin 2001:101–18). The primary referents of terms for mathematical concepts and values (e.g. triangular, beautiful) are transcendent, separately existing forms (*eidê*). Their secondary referents are forms' participants, for example, Helen of Troy and Phidias' statue of Athena, possessing a measure of beauty through participation in the corresponding form (q.v. Participation, Forms), and are thus properly named 'beautiful' (*Phd.* 102b, 103b). The limits on participants' beauty (they are such in one regard but not another, at one time but not others, etc.) ground the restricted application of 'beautiful' to them. The form's unblemished standing, in contrast, ensures that the term 'beautiful' applies to it eternally, without constraint (*Phd.* 103e). Far from being tied to the form, hence nature-disclosing, through descriptive content, on the view of many the link to *phusis* is via the *onoma*'s unique descriptive force. Though Plato is solidly committed to terms' legitimate twofold application, *Phd.*, *Symposium* and *Republic* underscore just how far philosophical awareness and linguistic usage diverge from the ordinary. While some, holding forms to be universals, assume that eponymy offers a general theory of predication, the fact that not all common nouns and adjectives have *eidê* corresponding to them (*R.* 523a–5a; *Parmenides* 130c–d) means that eponymy cannot function in this capacity.

How far, if at all, the third man argument (q.v. *Prm.*) calls the metaphysics and accompanying *onoma*-based semantics of these dialogues into question remains hotly contested. On one interpretation, the challenge to forms' explanatory power stems from the fact that *F*-ness, too, is *F* (e.g. Beauty is beautiful, *Phd.* 100c), with some claiming that the theory of forms emerges unscathed only if their *onomata* do not carry unique descriptive force, serving instead as proper names or indications of identity. At this juncture, however, it is individual forms' being what and as they are that warrants the relevant terms' application to them, and it is only because forms' *onomata* do so apply that participants' appellations may derive therefrom.

While Plato's linguistic focus thus far is *onomata*, the late writings evince a fascination with *logoi*. As before, his pursuit of linguistic concerns takes its compass from ontology. Whether or not Plato now sees a problem with the metaphysics and accompanying semantics of earlier dialogues, his late writings take the weight off self-predication to mark forms off from one another (see Moravcsik 1973). This transpires in part through the method of division (*diairesis*, q.v. Method) – debuted in *Phaedrus* (265e–6c) and elaborated in *Sophist* and *Statesman* – according to which the natures of *eidê* are disclosed through *logoi*, more than mereological sums, whose component *onomata* join to distinguish each explanandum (e.g. sophistry) from the rest. Though descriptive content may be relevant, as in *Cra.*'s conclusion terms merit does not hinge on their constitution's illumining natures (see Levin 2008). Again, philosophers' reflectiveness equips them alone to assess and deploy language reliably. Dialectic qua division may uncover what is wrongly thought to constitute elements of reality; such parts (*merê*) that are not also kinds (*genê*) are undeserving of *onomata*, which must therefore be excluded from a true, or philosophical, lexicon. The centrality of *onoma*-deletion and -construction to Plato's late philosophical method is yet another indication of the distance separating philosophical deployment of language from ordinary, nontheoretical usage.

Plato's handling of falsehood in *Sph*. has received tremendous attention. The sophist eludes the charge of speaking falsely if so doing involves speaking of 'what is not', construed as synonymous with 'what in no way is'. Plato's defence of false statement's possibility rests ontologically on a discussion of forms' interweaving, particularly the role of the different (*heteron*), and linguistically on a stipulation of statements' divergence, qua bearers of meaning, from names. The referents of both *onomata* (here, 'subjects' or 'agents') and *rhêmata* (variously rendered by scholars as 'verbs', 'actions', 'affections' and 'predicates') are assumed to exist outside the mind (261d–2c); Plato's account therefore excludes formulations taking unicorns or Narcissus as subjects.

Interpreters diverge on key points, including whether Plato distinguishes two or more uses of *esti* (existence, identity, predication). To those who (a) deem the third man argument worrisome when forms' *onomata* apply with descriptive force and (b) contend that *Sph*. disentangles identity and predication, this distinction is a welcome innovation. Scholars who conclude that awareness of different uses of *esti* is lacking in Plato disagree on whether he confuses existence and predication, or predication and identity. Certain commentators (e.g. Kahn 1966) stress that Greek does not demarcate existential and predicative uses of 'is' and that the absence of differentiation is a boon to Plato's account. Scholars even diverge on suitable terminology for the conduct of discussions (cf. Owen 1971 and White 1993).

In *Sph*.'s framework, difference supplants not being, allowing Plato to refute the view that 'what is not' (*to mê on*) and 'what in no

way is' (*to mêdamôs on*) are synonymous. Since the difference is key to his handling of false statement, much hinges on how *heteron* is construed. *Sph*. 256a–b is often taken to focus on *to mê on* qua nonidentity (e.g. change is not the same). In contrast, *Sph*. 263a–b, citing 'Theaetetus sits' versus 'Theaetetus flies', appears (with 257b–8c) to involve negative predication. Yet, notoriously, this discussion purports to recur to the line of thought set forth in *Sph*. 256a–b. Persistent queries abound: (a) Does the earlier reference not involve nonidentity after all? (b) Does nonidentity somehow remain Plato's focus or (c) does subsequent discussion expand to include negative predication while taking nonidentity for granted? (d) If *heteron* simply means separate things at the two junctures (e.g. 'other than' versus 'incompatible with'), is Plato's account of false statement unsuccessful? To those answering (d) in the affirmative Plato is confused, not realizing that he has made a switch; to those denying jeopardy, the difference is innocuous or even philosophically apposite.

Despite divergent constructions and assessments, many acknowledge the importance of Plato's distinguishing *onomata* and *rhêmata* as functionally different and essential components of statements. Plato's move away from using *onoma* to encompass 'nearly all categories of words' (Smith 2008:148) allows him to distinguish meaningfulness from truth value and hence jettison decisively a name based, either or model of statements' correctness. Plato's insistence that genuine statements bear meaning even when false is widely viewed as a salient innovation, as is his distinction of true and false *logoi* from positive and negative ones.

Scholarly debate on right terminology for discussions of *esti* in *Sph*. reflects in microcosm, a worry voiced by some that we go awry in our grasp of Plato by taking as the touchstone of interpretation modern discussions of logic and language. Though not everyone would agree where historical faithfulness left off and anachronism began, it is salutary to distinguish between what suffices as a response to Plato's critical targets and the merit his inquiries might or might not have from our perspective. As these orientations are not mutually exclusive, some maintain that Plato's theorizing succeeds admirably on both counts. Regardless of one's stance on its degree of proximity to modern concerns, the observation of Frede (1992a:423) is apt: We must not forget that 'in his day Plato was dealing with almost entirely unexplored issues for whose discussion even the most rudimentary concepts were missing'. Against this backdrop, Plato's investigation of false statement – along with other semantic milestones gracing his dialogues – is a 'singular achievement', indeed.

LAW (CONVENTION) (*NOMOS*)

Richard Stalley

The Greek word *nomos* (plural *nomoi*) is standardly translated as 'law', but has a wider meaning than the English word. It may refer not only to what we would call a 'law' but also to any kind of custom or convention. So, Greek authors, including Plato, do not distinguish sharply between law and social customs or between law and morality (Ostwald 1962:20–54; Stalley 1983:23–4).

In the fifth century BCE some thinkers began to emphasize the contrast between human laws or conventions (*nomoi*) and what happens by nature (*phusis*). They argued that laws or conventions do not exist by nature but result from agreements made

by human beings (see Guthrie 1971a). Some evidently took this to imply that law or morality has no real claim on us and would be ignored by wise individuals if they could do so with impunity (*Republic* 343c1–4c9). Others argued for something like a modern social contract theory. In order to avoid a situation in which people can injure each other at will, human beings have agreed to establish laws. They call what accords with the law 'just' and what contravenes it 'unjust' and punish those who transgress (358e2–9b5). Plato rejects such views. He argues that justice (q.v.) is a fundamental value and is not simply the product of human decisions.

In the *R*. Plato argues at length that being just is worthwhile in itself and is in our interests even if it brings us poverty, derision or death. He elucidates this conception by describing an ideally just city. In doing so he does not emphasize law, and focuses more attention on the education of the philosopher-rulers who will govern the city. He even suggests that people who have been properly educated will not need laws to govern the minutiae of personal relations or the details of commercial transactions (*R*. 425a8–6a4). Some commentators take this to mean that an ideal city with truly wise rulers would need no laws at all. But Plato uses the word *nomos* in referring to the ideal city and even makes Socrates refer to himself and his companions as legislating (*nomothetein*) for the city they are constructing in words (e.g. *R*. 417b8, 456c1). Plato's position may be that citizens who have been thoroughly educated in the principles on which the city is founded will not need detailed directions as to how they should lead their daily lives. Equally, there may be little need for mechanisms of enforcement. But that does not mean that there will be no laws.

In the *Laws* Plato describes what seems to be a more practical ideal city. It does not depend on philosopher-rulers but is, rather, founded on the principle of the sovereignty of law. Genuine law is seen as the work of reason (*Lg.* 713a9–15d6). In the city of the *Lg.* it is embodied in a detailed code laid down by a wise legislator. The constitution is designed to ensure that law, thus understood, is always supreme. In particular, a complicated system of checks and balances ensures that those who hold office always conform to the law. The ultimate aim of legislation is the common good of the city, which is understood as requiring citizens to possess the virtues of wisdom, temperance, justice and courage. The wise legislator will ensure that all the city's institutions and laws are directed towards this goal (631b2–2d7). This means that education is a central concern but it also applies to every other aspect of life. These points are illustrated with a detailed law code, covering matters such as marriage and the family, property, agriculture and trade, religious belief and practise, and crimes such as homicide and assault. A distinctive feature is that laws are accompanied by persuasive 'preambles'. The idea here is that it is better if people are persuaded to obey the law voluntarily rather than coerced into doing so by fear of punishment (718a6–23d4). There are many examples of such preambles, some quite elaborate. It is a matter of controversy among scholars whether these should be seen as appealing primarily to reason or to emotion (see Bobonich 1992; Stalley 1994).

Plato rejects retributive accounts of punishment and sees it as serving primarily to cure criminals of their wickedness (*Protagoras* 323c3–4c5; *Gorgias* 472d6–80b5; *R.* 380a 6–c3; *Lg.* 933e6–4c6). He suggests, therefore, that judges should pay close attention to the state of mind and circumstances of the individual (*Lg.* 862b1–3a2). But his code draws heavily on Athenian practise and prescribes punishments of a conventional kind with little apparent scope for variation (see Saunders 1991; Stalley 1995).

Plato's treatment of law in the *Politicus* has proved particularly controversial (e.g. Lane 1998:146–63, 197–201; Rowe 1995:15–18). In that dialogue the Eleatic stranger likens law to instructions left behind by a doctor who has gone away or is otherwise unable to give individual advice to his patients. On one line of interpretation, Plato is arguing that ideally the expert politician should rule without constraint but, where such a person is unavailable, rule by law is a second best. Indeed, a city without an expert ruler should stick rigidly to its laws, even if the processes by which those laws are chosen are not particularly rational. The *Plt.* has thus been regarded as marking a transition between the *R.* (seen as demanding the untrammelled rule of philosopher-kings) and the *Lg.* Recent scholarship has cast doubt on this view. A key point here is that the account of law in the *Plt.* seems to stand apart both from that of the *R.* and from that of the *Lg.* It is possible, therefore, that Plato sees the views he puts into the mouth of the Eleatic stranger as significantly defective. As he sees it, genuine law is not simply a substitute for the decisions of an expert ruler and should not be applied mechanically. It requires the right institutions and a properly educated populace to preserve and apply it.

LOGIC

Charles M. Young

Logic (following Quine 1986) is the systematic study of logical truth (or, equivalently, valid argument). A logical truth is a sentence that is true in virtue of its logical form. Logical form is relative to a set of grammatical categories, and logical systems may be classified by the categories assumed to matter for logical form. Since Frege (1879) the set of categories thought to matter begins with sentence and sentential operator, definitive of sentential logic and goes on to include term, predicate and quantifying expression, definitive of predicate or quantificational logic. From there one may go on, in various ways, to develop temporal, modal, conditional, relevantist and intuitionist systems of logic. (See Burgess 2009 for a helpful survey and sharp assessment of such developments.)

Plato has the ideas of logical form and logical truth. *Republic* 4.436b9, for example, affirms:

> *Exclusion*: It is not possible for the same thing to do or to suffer contraries in the same respect, in relation to the same thing, or at the same time.

This is a kissing cousin of our:

> *Non-Contradiction*: It is not possible for both a sentence and its negation to be true.

But whereas Non-Contradiction appeals to the grammatical category of sentences to tell us, for example, that if 'Helen is beautiful' is true, then 'It's not the case that Helen is beautiful' is not. Exclusion appeals to the grammatical category of contrary to tell us, for example, that if 'Helen is beautiful' and 'Helen is ugly' are both true, then she is beautiful and ugly in different respects (appearance vs. character, say), in relation to different things (Quasimodo vs. Aphrodite, say) or at different times (youth vs. old age,

say). The divergence between Plato and Frege emerges sharply if we note that the sentence 'If justice is a virtue, then injustice is a vice' is presumptively a logical truth in the logic of contrariety, but not in modern sentential or predicate logic.

Plato wrote dialogues and not treatises, and he does not engage in any systematic study of logical form and truth, in the manner, say, of Aristotle's *Prior Analytics* (or even the *Topics*), and thus cannot be said to have a logic in the sense specified above (and hence 'logic' does not appear in the index of Kraut 1992a). What we get instead is a congeries of insights and speculations about what might matter for logical form and logical truth, often expressed in difficult Greek, that may or may not be capable of systematization. To give a sense of what we have and the problems we face, I take up three texts that deal in abstract and in various ways with predication.

Socrates says at *Euthyphro* 6e3–6 that if he learned what the idea of piety is, he would be able to use that idea as a standard and say that an action or person that is *such as [it is]* is pious. Here *such as [it is]* is a stab at translating the Greek *toioutos*, a combination of the indefinite pronoun *toios* (= *of some sort*) and the demonstrative pronoun *houtos* (= *this*); other tries include *of that kind* (Grube 2002), *resembles [it]* (Cooper 1974), *agrees [with it]* (Fowler D. H. 1999). Whatever the translation, the idea seems clear enough. Socrates thinks that if:

(1) Piety is (say) doing what the god wants done,

and if Socrates is *such as [it is]* – that is, if

(2) Socrates is doing what the god wants done,

then it follows that

(3) Socrates is pious.

If we note that 'is' marks identity in (1) and predication in (2) and (3), and that 'doing' is a gerund in (1) and a participle in (2), then it follows that:

(4) If piety is doing what the god wants done, and Socrates is doing what the god wants done, then Socrates is pious.

This evidently expresses a logical truth connecting noun phrases that mention properties with terms mentioning things that have those properties.

So far, so good. Consider *Charmides* 169e1–5, where Critias, with Socrates' endorsement, states that '[one] is *such as* what he has: he who has quickness is quick, and he who has beauty is beautiful, he who has knowledge will know, and he who has knowledge that is of itself will know himself'. Here '[one] is *such as* what he has' is very close to a generalization of the logical truth of the *Euthphr.* But two points might give us pause. First, the inference from '[one] is *such as* what he has' to 'he who has quickness is quick' arguably presupposes 'quickness is quick', not unlike this English exchange: 'You'll have to be quick to do that' – 'Quick? I'm quickness itself!'. Second, we might balk, though again Socrates does not, at the inference to 'he who has knowledge that is of itself will know himself'.

Anyone still on the bus at this point will surely get off faced with *R.* 438a7–b2: 'Regarding things that are *such as* to be *of something*, those that are of certain sorts are of something of a certain sort, and those that are just themselves are of something that is just itself', a principle that appeals to the grammatical category of a relative term to support the thought that thirst as such is for drink as such, and not for good drink, even though all desire is for the good. Shorey's translation 'But I need hardly remind you' (of the particles *alla mentoi* with which Socrates introduces the principle) anticipates the incomprehension that Glaucon immediately expresses. The principle requires over forty lines for its elucidation.

Whether Plato's various scattered remarks on contrariety, predication and relation can be brought under control and organized into a coherent logical system remains to be seen. Some worthwhile work has been done – for example Robinson 1966, Lloyd 1992a and, most recently and most systematically, Dancy 2007. But there is still much to do.

LOGOS (ACCOUNT, ARGUMENT) (DEFINITION, STATEMENT)

Kenneth Sayre

The term *logos* in Attic Greek carries dozens of meanings, many of which occur routinely in Plato's writings. There are several occurrences, however, in which the term conveys meanings with particular philosophic significance. Sometimes the significance is relatively transparent, while in other cases it poses substantive problems. We begin with a few transparent cases.

One unproblematic sense of *logos* is that of reasoned argument or account. When Socrates asks Protagoras for an explanation of how virtue can be taught, the latter decides to respond not by a reasoned account (*logô Protagoras* 329C) but by telling a story (the myth of Prometheus). Yet Socrates eventually wins the disputation with an elaborately constructed argument (*logon* 361A).

Another philosophically significant sense is statement or judgement. In the *Sophist*, statement (*logos* 262A) is defined as a combination of names and verbs and said to possess both reference and truth value. And in his conversation with Phaedrus, Socrates examines what a true statement (*alêthês logos Phaedrus* 270C) would say about the soul's nature.

There is also the standard mathematical sense of ratio or proportion (*Republic* 509D, 511E) where Socrates describes the ratio (*logon*) on which the divided line is based.

A further straightforward meaning is that of definition. Thus at the beginning of the *Theaetetus*, Socrates invites the young mathematician to formulate a single *logos* that applies to the many varieties of knowledge. In Theaetetus' subsequent conversation with the Eleatic stranger, likewise, the two embark on the project of capturing the nature of the sophist in a clear definition (*logô Tht.* 218C) Other occurrences of *logos* in this sense can be found in the *Phdr.*, the *Laws* and the Seventh Letter.

Closely related is the sense at *Phaedo* 99E–100A where Socrates is describing his so-called second best method of *logos*. The method consists of hypothesizing what appears to be the soundest judgement (*logon*) on a topic and then testing other statements for agreement with it (for detailed analysis, see Sayre 1995a:ch. 5). This use of the term is comparable to that at *Tht.* 151E, where Socrates expresses appreciation for Theaetetus' initial account equating knowledge with perception. In such contexts the term *logos* can be understood to mean conjecture or hypothesis.

We turn next to senses that are philosophically significant but more problematic. A noteworthy case comes with the final hypothesis of *Tht.* (knowledge is true opinion plus *logos*) where the problem is explicitly stated. The problem is to specify a sense in which *logos* might convert true opinion into knowledge. Senses examined and found wanting are (a) mere speech, (b) enumerative account and (c) distinguishing characteristic. A striking feature of this list is that none of these three is a serious contender for the role, whereas more promising candidates (explanation, reason, ground) appear to be deliberately avoided.

Nonetheless, we find Socrates acknowledging at *Tht.* 202D that knowledge requires both logos and true opinion. Basically the same requirement is stated in several other contexts including *Meno* 98A, *Symposium* 202A and *R.* 533C (see also *Timaeus* 51D–E). Although the sense in question remains elusive, Plato seems to treat *logos* as a necessary ingredient of knowledge.

Another problem associated with the final hypothesis is what to make of the 'dream theory', which Socrates examines at length before taking up the three senses of *logos* mentioned previously. The theory in a nutshell is that every composite thing consists of elements that can be named but not described, and that a description (*logos*) can be given of a composite object by combining the names of its elements. While this sense of *logos* is more sophisticated than the other three, its relevance to the rest of the dialogue is not apparent. For one thing, it is not obvious how true opinion about an object could be converted to knowledge by adding a description in terms of its elements. Other puzzles debated by commentators are the source of this 'theory' and why Plato used so much space (four-and-a-half Stephanus pages) at the end of the dialogue in discussing it (for a detailed discussion, see Bluck 1956; Burnyeat 1970; Fine 1979; Sayre 1969).

Beyond these puzzling occurrences in *Tht.*, appearances of the term *logos* in other writings pose problems of a seemingly more basic nature. Following his discussion of the mathematical curriculum in *R.* bk 7, Socrates attributes to dialectic the power to grasp forms through the exercise of *logos* (*R.* 532A). Proceeding thus, Socrates continues, the dialectician is able to reach the limit of the intelligible world and to grasp the nature of the good itself. This description of dialectic occurs against the background of three famous images depicting various aspects of the philosopher's quest: (a) the sun (q.v.) as the visible analogue of the good which is the ultimate source of being, (b) the divided line (q.v.) representing the soul's ascent to the intelligible forms and (c) the cave (q.v.) dramatizing the attainment of knowledge and the philosopher's responsibility to the state. This background makes it clear that the philosopher's quest is consummated with a grasp of the good through *logos*, which accordingly might be designated the '*logos* of dialectic'.

Moving beyond the gorgeous rhetoric of *R.*, however, we find other texts that seem to deny *logos* this exalted power. One is the *Ep.* 7, where the author explains why philosophic understanding cannot be conveyed in language (*logôn Ep.* 7 343A). In this explanation, the author states explicitly that *logos* is inadequate to express the mind's grasp of the good (342D). Whatever the dialectical *logos* of *R.* might be, it cannot be communicated verbally.

Another Platonic writing disclaiming the ability of language to convey philosophic understanding is the *Phdr.* One legitimate use of written discourses (presumably including the dialogues) nonetheless, as Socrates remarks, is to provide reminders of another kind of *logos* (*Phdr.* 276E) inscribed in the soul of the budding philosopher. This 'soul-ingrained' *logos* has potential not only of growing into fully fledged philosophic knowledge but also of spreading to other souls through the medium of dialectical discourse. Perhaps the dialectical *logos* of *R.* coincides with the soul-bound *logos* of *Phdr.*, in that both mature in a mental grasp of the eternal forms.

One sense of *logos* not found in Plato (as in Heraclitus and the Stoics), however, is that of ordering principle in a rational universe. Plato's closest approximation to such a principle is the world soul of *Ti.*, which is not described as a kind of *logos*.

LOVE (*ERÔS*)

D. C. *Schindler*

Love (*erôs*) – one of the only things Socrates claims to fall under his expertise (*Symposium* 177d–e; cf. *Theages* 128b; *Lysis* 204c) – represents the primary theme in the two so-called erotic dialogues, the *Phaedrus* and the *Smp.*, though it also plays a significant role in the *Republic*.

Love appears as essentially ambiguous in the *R.* On the one hand, Plato calls it a 'tyrant', presenting it as the most intense of the soul's base desires (*R.* 403a, 439d). On the other hand, Socrates identifies love for knowledge of unchanging being as the defining characteristic of the philosopher (485a–b, 490b). In the one case, then, love is what imprisons us in a lawless dream world (576b), while in the other case love is what draws us to the real. Plato typically uses the plural when speaking of the tyrant's 'loves', and calls philosophical love, by contrast, 'true *erôs*' (490c), but he does not explicate the precise nature of the difference thematically in this dialogue.

Greater light is shed on this ambiguity in the *Phdr.*, in which Socrates presents two speeches on love as a response to Phaedrus' reading of a speech by Lysias. In the first, Socrates reformulates, with more order and clarity, the view of love presented in the prior speech by Lysias, and in the second, a 'palinode' or recantation, he corrects the first, directly stating, 'There is no truth to that account' (*Phdr.* 244a). Socrates begins the first speech by defining love as a 'desire for beautiful things' (237d) – or, more specifically, the 'beauty of bodies' (238c) – and goes on to associate it with a desire for pleasures that runs counter to our 'acquired opinion that strives for the best' (237d–e). This love is similar to the 'tyrant' that appeared in the *R.*, insofar as it is a force that seeks to dominate its object; it always leads to excess, and it is essentially opposed, as a 'madness', to the order and unity of reason.

The palinode, which is one of the literary gems in the Platonic corpus, begins with the claim that madness can be beneficial if it is a 'gift from the gods' (244a) – that is, 'madness' need not be sub or anti rational, but may also be supra rational, and so in principle able to include reason. This view of love requires a revision of both its subject and object: the soul is interpreted as having a transcendent origin and destination, and the beauty that provokes *erôs* is no longer a merely physical object, but now an essentially transcendent reality that distinguishes itself from all the other intelligibles by being *also* accessible to bodily sight (250d–e). Socrates memorably expresses love, thus understood, as the 'wings' that carry the soul from its mundane state to the sphere 'beyond the heavens', the realm of 'really real reality' (247c). Love, in this case, is not simply one of the soul's desires, but is in fact the movement of the whole

soul – which Socrates depicts as a winged chariot, with a charioteer (reason), an obedient horse (noble passions) and an unruly one (base passions) – towards its proper end. Because it thus serves to 'bridge' the difference between the transcendent and the bodily, the notion of beauty and its correlative love, that Plato presents in the *Phdr.* is seen by some as the hinge concept of his philosophy in general.

The most elaborate exposition of the nature of love in Plato's work can be found in the *Smp.* It contains six speeches on love, followed by a speech by Alcibiades on Socrates (who thus seems to personify *erôs*). Scholars do not agree whether it is legitimate to identify Plato's own view of love with any particular account, though a certain priority is generally accorded to Socrates'. The most famous speech is no doubt that given by Aristophanes, who expounds a myth to explain the origin of love: originally spherical beings were divided by Zeus because of their haughtiness, and each fragment now seeks his or her other half in order to recover the original unity. Socrates' speech – in which he recounts a conversation he had with the prophetess Diotima and so sneaks in, as it were, the only woman 'present' in the group (cf. *Smp.* 176e) – is nevertheless the most comprehensive, insofar as it takes up elements from the other speeches, ordering and correcting them as it proceeds. In contrast to Agathon's view of love as the supreme beauty, Diotima begins by showing that, as a desire, love is essentially constituted by a need or lack (200a–b), though she distinguishes this from complete absence. Instead, in line with the account in the *Phdr.*, love appears as a 'spirit' that mediates between the human and divine and so connects them (202d–3a). It is identified with neither complete fullness nor complete emptiness, but is the child of Penia and Poros (poverty and plenty) (203b–c).

Also like the account in the *Phdr.*, the (efficient) cause of love is beauty, though Diotima redescribes its object as goodness in order to provide its final cause (204e). As a desire for the good, love thus turns out to be the truth of any desire whatsoever, since all desires aim at their objects insofar as they are good. Whereas Aristophanes explained *erôs* as a desire for completion, and thus as essentially relative to the needy soul, Diotima shows that this need itself must be defined in turn by the good in itself (205e–6a). But the desire for the good in this complete sense is in fact a desire for eternal goodness, so that Diotima is able to specify the purpose of love further as 'begetting in the beautiful, both in body and in soul', for reproduction is a mortal image of immortality (206b–7a). This allows her to explain a variety of phenomena in the animal and human worlds, which had been alluded to in the previous speeches, in relation to the single desire for immortality.

Before elaborating what has come to be known as the 'ladder of love', Diotima confesses to Socrates that the 'final and highest' mystery of love is one that might exceed his capacity (210a). Some scholars have read this as Plato's indication of where his philosophy departs from that of his teacher. Diotima presents an itinerary for the achievement of love in its purest sense: one begins by loving beautiful bodies, first one and then all bodies insofar as they are beautiful; then, one forgets bodies and learns to love souls and their deeds in noble actions and laws; and thirdly one comes to love knowledge of various sorts. In other words, there is a movement from physical, to moral, and then to intellectual beauty (which corresponds to the three parts of the soul elaborated in the *R.*).

Finally, one encounters beauty in its absolute existence, that is, not as relative to anything at all. This beauty in itself is presented as the cause of all the foregoing instances of beauty, and described as completely transcendent of any beautiful thing, no matter how noble, as beyond what appears to the senses and to reason, and as incapable of diminution or change (211a–b).

Scholars have claimed that this description of beauty contradicts the beauty in the *Phdr.*, which is an intelligible object that is also physically visible – but there is no reason in principle why it cannot *both* lie beyond the mind and senses *and* be accessible to them (for the transcendent form of beauty presents itself in the *Smp.* at every level up the 'ladder'). Nevertheless, Plato does not himself address this problem directly. Scholars also complain that Plato's account in the *Smp.* excludes the possibility of love for individuals, though others have argued that Diotima's speech can be read as describing an increasingly nonpossessive love, which can in principle still be had for individuals.

MADNESS AND POSSESSION

Silke-Maria Weineck

The theme of madness serves several distinct functions in Plato's dialogues. When linked to poetry, as in *Ion* and *Phaedrus*, madness as divine inspiration or possession (*theia mania*, *enthousiasmos*) allows Socrates to develop a distinction between poetry and philosophy. While poetry appears as a unique utterance the production of which is neither the result of specialized knowledge nor subject to the poet's conscious control, philosophy emerges as the controlled, repeatable and teachable labour of thought.

At the same time, madness provides a corrective to overly rationalist thought. Thus, Socrates' 'inspired' second speech in the *Phdr.* refutes the cynical argument of the first one. In the *Republic*, the example of madness serves to undermine the definition of justice as the habit of paying one's debt and speaking the truth:

> [I]f a man takes weapons from a friend when the latter is of sound mind, and the friend demands them back when he is mad, one shouldn't give back such things, and the man who gave them back would not be just, and moreover, one should not be willing to tell someone in this state the whole truth. (*R.* 331c–d, trans. Bloom)

In the *Ion*, Socrates persuades the eponymous rhapsode to recant the mercenary account of his craft ('if I set them to crying, I shall laugh myself because I am making money, but if they laugh, then I shall cry because of the money I am losing', *Ion* 535e) in favour of a model of divine inspiration, for 'to be held to be divine is far finer' (*Ion* 542b, trans. Bloom).

Third, the question of divine – or quasi-divine – possession is at stake in Socrates' *daimonion* (q.v.; *Apology* 31d, 40b–c; *Phdr.* 242c, 242b), the enigmatic inner voice that at times is said to negatively guide his speech and actions and further complicates the notion of Socrates as the philosopher of self-possessed reason (Burkert 1985:178–81; Destrée and Smith 2005; Gall 2009).

In general, Plato shows little interest in madness as an illness; in the *Phdr.* he distinguishes between 'two kinds of madness, one resulting from human ailments, the other from a divine disturbance of our conventions of conduct' (*Phdr.* 265a, trans. Hackforth), and as in *Ion*, it is only the nonsomatic kind that is of interest. The madness that matters, then, is nearly always a form of divine interference or possession, an intervention into what we might call conventional human subjectivity, and Plato's two most important dialogues on madness, *Ion* and *Phdr.*, take considerable care to distinguish it both from various forms of *technê* of speaking (e.g. rhetoric, dialectics, *psychagogia*).

Ion struggles to preserve an understanding of rhapsody as a skill or craft (*technê*) that necessarily presupposes knowledge (*epistêmê*) of the poetic product he delivers. Socrates contends that the accomplishments of rhapsody rest on divine inspiration, and that the rhapsode performs in a state devoid of knowledge, sovereign skill and reason (*epistêmê*, *technê*, *nous*). He develops that theory in the famous monologue about the magnetic chain of divine inspiration linking poet, rhapsode and audience. This speech contains the *Ion*'s most quoted lines: 'For the poet is a light thing, winged and sacred, unable to make poetry before he is enthused and out of his mind and intelligence is no longer in him' (*Ion* 534b). Though long neglected as a minor piece – Pangle (1987) calls it one of the 'forgotten dialogues', and Goethe (1796) called it a 'persiflage' of enthusiasm – the *Ion* nonetheless presents interpretative challenges worth exploring (Tigerstedt 1970), particularly when read as a disquisition not on poetry but on rhapsody. In this light, the central concern of the dialogue is not the nature of poetry but the question of poetry's guardianship. If the possessed poet is himself dispossessed of reason and knowledge, the meaning of poetry needs to be mediated by those who are not poets themselves. As Ion loses his argument, philosophy emerges as the first form of a practise that will eventually become known as literary criticism (Weineck 2002:19–31).

While *Ion* operates with a notion of poetic inspiration that may be an already well worn cliché, the *Phdr.* develops a far more complex account of various forms of madness: prophetic, ritual, erotic and poetic *mania*, sent, respectively, by Apollo, Dionysus, Eros and the Muses. The dialogue is notoriously complex, consisting of three speeches that weigh the benefits that lovers and nonlovers provide to boys or young men. In the third speech, Socrates revokes the praise of the ostensibly rational nonlover and extols the virtue of erotic madness as a path to the recollection (*anamnêsis*) of the forms – provided that the mad lover can restrain his physical desire and thus transform the relationship into one of shared discourse.

Socrates' account of madness reverses the steadiest assumptions of madness held in modern times. As ritual it is a remedy instead of an ailment; as prophecy it imparts the most reliable intelligence instead of the most unreliable; as erotic madness it leads to perfect attachment instead of perfect solitude. Madness is neither excluded from nor an episode in or a footnote to history. In fact, *mania* seems to hold a central place within what we might call the different orders of history – the history of the individual, of the great families, of the state, of the nation, of the human soul. In the *Phdr.*, all of them, in various ways, *depend* on the interlude of madness – just as they depend on madness to be nothing but an interlude. At the same time, *mania* interrupts the usual progression of things and terminates the course of causality: in the *Oresteia*, clearly the backdrop of Socrates' example of Dionysian *mania*, only madness can stop the self-perpetuation of ancient pollution.

This is not to say that the *Phdr.* breaks with the *Ion*'s tendency to privilege philosophy over inspiration as intellectual and rhetorical *technê*, but certain forms of madness emerge not only as compatible with philosophy (*Phdr.* 278c–d) but perhaps as philosophy's necessary precondition (Weineck 2002:32–44). In other words, the *Phdr.*'s philosophy of madness solves, if ambivalently, the problem of the origin of meaningful discourse.

Neither written nor spoken, the prohibitions of the *daimonion* (q.v. Daimon) constitute a genre of its own that escapes the various taxonomies of *logoi* Plato proposes. It is the *daimonion* that prevents Socrates from leaving after his first speech and prompts Socrates' recantation or palinode of cynical reason (if we can call it that): 'This story is not true' (*Phdr.* 243b). Truth, or more precisely the recantation of nontruth, then, depends in its origin on the event of words without a speaker, an event as unforeseeable and incalculable as the event of divine madness.

MATHEMATICS (*MATHÊMATIKÊ*)

Christine J. Thomas

Plato's 'encounter with geometry was to prove no passing infatuation, but a love match, a lifelong attachment as deep as it was intense' (Vlastos 1991b:130). Plato's fascination extended to number theory, harmonics and astronomy. Though the degree to which Plato was himself an accomplished, practicing mathematician is disputed, he is credited in antiquity with facilitating mathematical progress and even directing major lines of research (Cherniss 1951; Fowler 1999; Proclus 1970; Simplicius *in De Caelo* 488.20–4). Famously, the entrance to Plato's Academy is said to have borne the inscription, 'Let no one who is ungeometrical enter'. The exact nature and details of Plato's attachment, however, are difficult to discern. The precision, methodical rigour and intellectual authority of successful mathematical proofs surely appeal to Plato; but it is not easy to identify the features of particular mathematical strategies or results that impress him most. Moreover, although mathematical education is regarded as propaedeutic to philosophy, any effort to determine exactly how or why mathematics is assigned this role quickly becomes an attempt to solve a provocative mystery. At best, we can confidently say that Plato deems mathematics a rich resource for pursuing his first love: dialectic (q.v.).

Plato often looks to mathematics for inspiration. Philosophical attempts at definition are to emulate the account of 'the even' as 'the part of number that is not scalene but isosceles' (*Euthyphro* 12d8–10) or the definition of 'powers' (i.e. incommensurable lengths) as 'the lines that square off oblong numbers' (*Theaetetus* 148a7–b2). Indeed, some of the dramas played out in Plato's dialogues constitute historical evidence of developments and struggles in the geometry of incommensurability (*Men.* 82b–5c; *Tht.* 147c7–8b2), stereometry (*Tht.* 148b2; *Republic* 509d6–8, 528a6–b5; *Timaeus* 53dff), and harmonics and astronomy (*R.* 528e3–31c4; *Ti.* 32c5–40d5; *Laws* 821b5–2c9). Though the full import of Plato's appeals to mathematical accomplishments is often difficult to unpack, he clearly aims to illustrate the sorts of approaches and results he hopes for in philosophy (Burnyeat 1978, 2000; Heath 1981; Knorr 1989; Lloyd 1992; Netz 2003).

As for mathematical method, Plato most explicitly calls on geometry. A successful geometric analysis either discovers premises required to complete a proof of a purported conclusion or it identifies construction procedures to solve an articulated construction problem (Menn 2002). Geometric synthesis reverses the direction of investigation and moves from given principles to conclusions. Plato self-consciously mimics both geometrical analysis (*Men.* 86e3ff.) and geometrical synthesis (*Phaedo* 100a1–1e7) in philosophical inquiries that proceed 'from hypotheses' (Mueller 1992).

Of particular interest to Plato, however, is the idea that an investigation might ultimately light on something 'unhypothetical'. For although rigorous investigations from hypotheses might gain some epistemic entitlement to their results, those results are nevertheless conditional. Even the most successful mathematical proof fails to yield the highest kind of understanding (*noêsis*) so long as it begins from hypotheses which are not themselves sufficiently epistemically secure (*R.* 533b6–c2). For Plato, a consistent mathematical science is not guaranteed to yield truth, and convincingness is not sufficient for genuine understanding (*Cratylus* 436c8–d8; *R.* 510c1–d3, 533b1–d1). Ultimately, a nonmathematical (or metamathematical), dialectical inquiry must discover 'the unhypothetical first principle (*archê*) of everything' thereby providing epistemic foundations for mathematical and philosophical investigations at once (*R.* 511b5–7).

What, then, is the relation of mathematics to philosophy? For dialectic discovers epistemic grounds for mathematics, but mathematical study appears to be an essential element of any educational curriculum that aims to produce dialectically capable individuals (*R.* 522c–31d, 533a8–10). Like the most important philosophical objects and truths, the objects and truths of mathematics are discovered, for Plato, not constructed. Mathematicians do not 'make their figures, they simply discover those which already are' (*Euthydemus* 290c1–3). In the *R.*, Socrates comments on the absurd, though unavoidable talk of practicing geometers who speak of 'squaring', 'applying' and 'adding' as if they are actually making and acting on their figures (*R.* 527a6–b6). In fact, mathematical arguments are for the sake of apprehending eternal, unchanging entities by means of thought alone. Number theory, geometry, pure harmonics and pure astronomy facilitate the soul's cognitive contact with being or 'what always is'. In the ideal case, then, mathematical study turns an inquiring philosophical soul away from the changing perceptible realm towards the realm of unchanging, imperceptible, eternal beings. Ultimately, the *R.*'s mathematical curriculum prepares a soul for cognition of the most important beings available to thought alone, Plato's forms (q.v.; e.g. justice, beauty and goodness).

On the one hand, Plato is not alone in taking mathematics to supply paradigmatic examples of cognitions that are significantly independent of sense experience. Like many in the so-called rationalist tradition, Plato regards the mind or soul as having cognitive capacities through reason alone to grasp purely intelligible objects or truths, to recognize that such objects or truths are eternal or necessary and to see *why* eternal or necessary truths are true (i.e. to recognize what a priori justification or entitlement to such truths might be available). On the other hand, for Plato, mathematical study has a particularly important and surprising role to play. For, the ultimate aim of mathematical education is successful apprehension of a particular form, the form of the good (*R.* 526d8–e1). For Plato, the form of goodness (q.v.) itself plays the role of the unhypothetical first principle of everything; and mathematical study, along with dialectic and practical political experience, somehow make cognition of this form possible (*R.* 531c6–d4).

Some of the surprise perhaps diminishes in noting that the one who masters the educational curriculum of the *R.* comes to understand the governing principles of the richly mathematically constituted cosmos described in Plato's *Ti.* The truths of the pure mathematical sciences are also the metaphysical truths grounding the unity, structure and motions of the cosmic soul and body, and of every soul, body and ordered entity in the cosmos (Burnyeat 2000). Grasping ultimate mathematical truths is, then, to grasp ultimate physical and metaphysical truths; it is to begin to understand how the cosmos has been mathematically structured by a divine, intelligent craftsman. Moreover, where the imposition of mathematical structure produces unity, order, concord, harmony and intelligibility, it also produces goodness (*Ti.* 29d7–30a6, 53a7–c1, 68e1–6; *Phlb.* 64d9–5a5). The study of organizing mathematical principles is, in some sense then, the study of goodness (Burnyeat 2000; White 2006).

Finally, for Plato, any soul that is capable of understanding cosmic structure and motion must be like the cosmos; it must itself be mathematically structured. Insofar as a soul's motions can become assimilated to cosmic psychic motions, it can become intelligent. The flourishing human soul is the one that has (among other things) studied geometry, astronomy and harmonics, thereby making possible the alignment of its motions with the divine motions of the cosmic soul (*Ti.* 47b5–e2). To become so aligned is to become like god, to become intelligent and happy (*Ti.* 90b6–d7).

MEDICINE (*IATRIKĒ*)

Mark L. McPherran

Plato's attention to the craft of medicine, which is conceived of as a paradigmatic instance of expert knowledge that lesser fields should imitate (*Gorgias* 464a–7c), is evident throughout his work (e.g. *Phaedrus* 268a–70d; *Republic* 403d–10b; *Politicus* 292d–300a; *Timaeus* 64a–92c; *Laws* 889b–e). This is made particularly clear by his various uses of the analogy of soul to body, of psychic health to somatic health (e.g. *Crito* 47a–8b; *Grg.* 463e–5d; *Phdr.* 270a–e; *Sophist* 223e, 226e–30e; *Plt.* 292e–3c) and the microcosmic and macrocosmic conception of human nature found in the *Ti.* – a conception that parallels the similar one found in the Hippocratic work *On Regimen* (Jouanna 1998:70). Indeed, some take the frequency and force of the analogy to show that Socrates (s.v.) and Plato were the inventors of 'scientific verbal psychotherapy', beside whom 'Gorgias and Antiphon are mere prehistory' (Laín Entralgo 1970:137; cf. 126; cf. Moes 2000).

In Plato's day medicine was just emerging as a science from its religious, magical roots. Hippocrates started off as an Asclepiad – born ten years after Socrates on Kos, the site of one of the four major healing temple-hospitals of Asclepius. The clinical work and success of the Hippocratic school, however, dates for the most part from the time *subsequent* to Hippocrates' departure from Kos and its temple (Jouanna 1998:27, 30–1). Plato understands Hippocratic medicine to hold that illnesses result from an imbalance in the body of the four humours – fluids that are equal in proportion in healthy individuals (*Timaeus* 82a–6a). When these humours (blood, black bile, yellow bile and phlegm) are not in balance, sickness results. Hippocratic treatment focused on restoring a proper balance (see further, and on medicine in philosophy, Pellegrin 2009).

Two prominent uses of a medical analogy are found in the *Cri.* and *Grg.* Here Socrates'

theory of the soul (q.v.) is fairly minimal: it is that in us, separate from our bodies, that is the subject or agent of moral judgement, choice and action – that wherein vice and virtue reside (*Cri.* 47e–8a). It is the entire, *real self*: the 'I' of consciousness and personality, and the part of us that engages in intellectual activity. It is also more important than the body, and, like the body, can be harmed to so great an extent (by false moral beliefs or wrong acts) that one might no longer have a life worth living (*Cri.* 47d–8a; *Grg.* 479b–c). To care for this entity in the manner of a physician – that is, employing an analogous expert knowledge (*technê* (q.v. Art)) – is to endeavour to make it as good and happy as possible by improving it in respect of virtue and guarding it from the harm of vice, a task accomplished through correct philosophical training, elenctic testing and virtuous action (*Cri.* 48a–8d; *Grg.* 467c–81b). Although medicine is an important *technê* in comparison to the 'knack' of cookery, since the soul is more important than the body, philosophy is a more important field of knowledge than medicine in the final analysis (*Grg.* 464a–6a).

The medical analogy also shows up in the *Charmides*, where Socrates is presented to young, beautiful Charmides as a 'physician' with a cure for his morning headaches. Aroused by the youth, Socrates claims to know a medicinal leaf, a *pharmakon*, but one that is only effective if accompanied by the singing of the charm (*epôidê*) that goes with it. Socrates then endorses the view of those successful holistic Greek physicians who do not attempt to cure eyes by themselves, but '. . . try to treat and heal the whole and the part together' (*Chrm.* 156c). Socrates next reports that he learned his charm while with the army, from one of the physicians of the Thracian king Zalmoxis (156d–7c).

He tells Socrates that Greek physicians are acceptably knowledgeable, but that they often forget that just as one ought not to attempt to cure the eyes without the head, or the head without the body, so neither ought one to attempt to cure the body without the soul . . . for the part can never be well unless the whole is well. One should begin by curing the soul, something done by using words that produce moderation in the soul (*Chrm.* 156d–7c; cf. *Phdr.* 269e–70e on this and Hippocratic method). Some have identified these charming words as those spoken by Socrates during his subsequent elenctic examination of Charmides and Critias; but in any event, by the end of the dialogue, Socrates emerges as a subtle diagnostician of both men's lack of moderation, character defects so deep that neither of them can profit from further association with Socrates. The dialogue has also communicated the idea that philosophical 'treatment' is more central and more valuable than mere physical treatment.

It is natural to suppose that at least one of Plato's purposes in employing the character of the physician Eryximachus in the *Symposium* is to convey the import of his own understanding of medicine insofar as it bears on the central topic of that dialogue: *erôs*. Although some have taken Eryximachus to be a bombastic dogmatist who serves primarily as a target of Platonic satire, others argue that his speech 'is not a caricature but rather an historically correct picture of a [Hippocratic] medical man of that time', Edelstein 1945:91). He does indeed give a Hippocratic medical account – but also a grand universalizing account of *erôs* – one that takes in both the realm of nature and that of the gods. Moreover, it is a theory supported by such stars of pre-Socratic science as Heraclitus (*Smp.* 187a–c). Here, it has been argued that Plato subsequently uses

Diotima to insist that true physicians – unlike Eryximachus – must be philosophers who are pious by accepting the primacy of a philosophical *erôs* that will lead them towards the Platonic project of 'becoming like god' (*Tht.* 176a–7c; see further McPherran 2006; q.v. Piety; Religion; Love). Socrates seems cast as such a physician when he is likened to a midwife who helps deliver beautiful ideas in the *Tht.* (148e–51d).

The *Philebus* also employs Hippocratic notions (emptying, repletion and *homonoia*) in its analysis of pleasure (*Phlb.* 31a–3c; 44b–9a) in order to address its central topic, namely, the search for that 'state or condition of the soul that can render the life of every man a happy life' (11d). It has even been argued that if we follow this medical suggestion by construing the dialogue to offer a diagnosis of the 'disease' of hedonism, followed by an account of the philosophical cure for it, we can understand how its puzzling transitions and digressions actually contribute to a coherent overall unity (Moes 2000:113–61). Whether or not that is so, it has also been observed by scholars such as Dorothea Frede that the dualistic account of *erôs* as a physical, medical phenomenon we find outlined in the *Smp.* at 185e–9d makes a brief cameo appearance towards the end of the *Phlb.* account of the fourfold division of all beings (23c–7c), where there occurs what is arguably an allusion to the goddess Aphrodite (26b–c; Frede 1993:23, n. 1; see further Dorothea Frede 1992; McPherran 2010).

Besides using medical analogies, Plato is interested in medicine per se in determining how the medical theories of his day might be squared with his own theories of nature and the human constitution, and what role physicians would play in the idealized states of the *R.* and *Lg.* In his *R.*, for example, Plato employs his health analogy once he has established that justice is good in itself, by claiming that justice and injustice are 'in the soul what the healthful and diseaseful are in the body; there is no difference' (*R.* 444c). But here Plato seems less willing than he was in, say, the *Grg.* to view medicine as a standalone *technê*. By arguing for a tripartite soul of intellect, spirit and appetite in *R.* bk 4, Plato is led to see the 'intertwining of soul and body in the cases of spirit and appetite' (Levin 2007:147). The result is that the practise of medicine must come under the purview of the philosophical rulers of his Kallipolis, who will guide physicians in their treatments so as to maximize the overall goodness of this ideal polis (Levin 2007). Here, as in the *Smp.*, the primacy of philosophical treatment in comparison to medical treatment for Plato is made clear. Meanwhile, Hippocrates laboured to free medicine 'from the yoke of philosophy' (Pellegrin 2009:667).

METAPHYSICS (see Ontology)

METHOD

Hugh H. Benson

For Plato, philosophy is the love of wisdom. It is the search for and attempt to acquire knowledge of the most important things. Following Plato, I will be using 'wisdom' and 'knowledge' interchangeably. To engage in such a search methodically is to systematically – purposively and repeatedly – attempt to acquire such knowledge. Clearly, Socrates is not always engaging in this sort of behaviour. Sometimes, for example, he is simply attempting to persuade the jury of his innocence. Nevertheless, Plato often depicts Socrates as attempting to acquire knowledge and to do so in a systematic way.

If we look at both Plato's depiction of Socrates and Plato's explicit description of his method, we notice three distinct phases of Plato's account – the elenctic phase, the hypothesis phase and the collection and division phase – each of which corresponds to a common division of the dialogues into early, middle and late, whether or not these phases indicate a development in Plato's thinking on method (q.v. Developmentalism).

(I) The Elenctic Phase

In dialogues like the *Euthyphro*, *Laches*, *Charmides* and *Protagoras*, Plato depicts Socrates as engaging in a series of short questions and answers with various interlocutors. In every case, these interlocutors have some claim to knowledge of some relatively important matter. Euthyphro, for example, claims to know both that prosecuting his father is a pious action and what piety itself is. Socrates' questioning is aimed at testing the reputed knowledge of these interlocutors. This questioning method (the *elenchos*) has the following structure:

(1) Socrates asks the interlocutor a question the answer to which, p, is meant to exhibit the interlocutor's wisdom, usually, but not always, concerning the definition of some moral concept.

(2) The interlocutor provides answers, q, r and s to a series of other Socratic questions.

(3) Socrates goes on to show that these answers entail the negation of the original answer.

(4) Thus, the conjunction (p & q & r & s) is false.

The *elenchos* is not aimed at acquiring knowledge, but at testing the reputed knowledge of another. Moreover, its conclusion asserts only the falsity of a conjunction (i.e. that

p, q, r and s are inconsistent) and not the falsity of one of the conjuncts. If Socrates is to come to know that one of these conjuncts is false (and so that its negation is true) by means of the *elenchos*, he must take the other conjuncts to have some special epistemic status. Unfortunately, Socrates' descriptions of this method suggest that the conjuncts all have the same epistemic status. The only property the conjuncts must have is that the interlocutor believes them. As a method for acquiring the knowledge one lacks the *elenchos* looks ineffective (perhaps confirmed by Socrates' profession of ignorance near the end of his life in the *Apology*, despite a lifetime of searching). (For a famously different interpretation of the Socratic *elenchos* see Vlastos 1981.) As a method for eliminating one's false conceit of knowledge, a necessary first step in seeking the knowledge one lacks, the *elenchos* plays an important role in Plato's philosophical method.

(II) THE HYPOTHESIS PHASE

In the *Meno*, Socrates asks how it is possible to acquire knowledge (Meno's Paradox, 80d–e). In various places in dialogues like the *Men.*, *Phaedo*, *Republic* and *Parmenides* Plato also depicts Socrates as describing and practicing the hypothetical method as an answer. This method consists of two stages in attempting to come to know the answer, p, to some important question (e.g. 'Is virtue teachable?').

Stage 1: find a second proposition, q, whose truth is necessary and sufficient for the truth of p, and show how q entails p.
Stage 2: confirm the truth of q:

(1) by finding a third proposition r whose truth is necessary and sufficient for the truth of q, and

(2) by examining the consequences of q to determine their coherence.

In the *R.*, Plato explains that the first part of the second stage, which is simply the application of the first stage on the 'higher hypothesis', q, is to be repeated on successively 'higher hypotheses' until one reaches the 'unhypothetical first principle'. This latter appears to be the form of the good. In addition, Plato describes the second part of the second stage in terms strongly reminiscent of the *elenchos*. Only when one pursues both of these confirmation procedures to their limit can one genuinely be said to have acquired the knowledge sought.

(III) THE COLLECTION AND DIVISION PHASE

In the *Phaedrus* and the *Philebus*, Plato describes a further method known as collection and division, which he depicts at length in the *Sophist* and the *Politicus*. It too consists of two stages.

Stage 1: collect together a scattered plurality into a unity.
Stage 2: divide the unity one has collected along its natural divisions.

In some dialogues, Plato appears to require that the division that takes place in the second stage be done dichotomously. In other places, however, he appears to allow for a more open-ended division.

It has sometimes been thought that the method of collection and division was intended by Plato to replace the hypothetical method of the so-called middle dialogues. But the appearance of the former method in the *Phdr.* makes such a view difficult to sustain. As a consequence, Plato's method of collection and division must be understood as an alternative method to the hypothetical method or as an extension of or an addendum to the hypothetical method.

(IV) DIALECTIC

Plato's philosophical method is often referred to as dialectic (q.v.), a kind of working through in words; but this should not be understood as indicating a distinct method from those we have just described. Rather, Plato tends to call 'dialectic' whatever method he is recommending at the moment. It is better to take Plato's philosophical method (his dialectic) to be the combination of the three phases we have outlined, although how they are to be fitted together into a single method for acquiring knowledge is a matter of continued controversy.

MIMÊSIS (IMITATION)

Stephen Halliwell

The vocabulary of mimêsis, conventionally but often inadequately translated as 'imitation', is found in numerous Platonic contexts, applied to matters ranging from everyday life to speculative metaphysics. Its most significant use occurs in a series of dialogues from *Cratylus* to *Laws* in connection with two philosophical topics: first, questions relating to the representational and expressive capacities of poetic, musical and visual art; second, the epistemologically problematic relationship (construed in terms of image and original) between representation in general and reality. Mimêsis is a hallmark of certain Platonic habits of thought. There is no such thing, however, as a single Platonic theory of mimêsis.

In *Cra.* Socrates calls language itself mimêtic (*Cra.* 414b, 422e–7d): the 'primary names' of things were putatively based (by the hypothetical name giver) on natural likenesses between individual sounds and aspects of reality. But mimêsis embedded in semantics is differentiated from mimêsis in musical (including poetic) and visual art: the latter is taken, not without simplification, to represent only the sensory properties of things, whereas the former captures their essence (*ousia*). Socrates allows visual images to be 'correct' or 'incorrect', but not, unlike discourse, true or false (430a–1d). Correctness here denotes something like basic resemblance, a qualitative not a mathematically exact relationship to objects (432a–d). *Philebus*, by contrast, gives the idea of an image quasipropositional force by characterizing thought itself as inner discourse (*logos*) accompanied by 'paintings in the soul' (*Phlb.* 39b–40b), a sort of illustrated book (38e–9b). Here the terminology of mimêsis is not used for mental images themselves, though it is used to describe the 'false (i.e. ethically mistaken) pleasures' associated with misconceived mental states (40c). Such pleasures are hardly 'imitations' of true pleasures, more like defective surrogates (cf., e.g. *Politicus* 293e, 297c for comparable usage).

The *Republic* approaches questions of artistic mimêsis from shifting angles. Socrates categorizes all visual, musical and poetic arts in the 'city of luxury' as kinds of mimêsis (*R.* 2.373b); they form a cultural fabric of image-making and dramatic pretence. Later, however, he temporarily restricts poetic mimêsis to one particular mode of discourse, that is, first person, direct speech, as opposed to third person narrative. He dwells on the psychic assimilation ('self-likening') which this requires of performers of such poetry (3.392d–8b), stressing the ethically destabilizing consequences of intense imaginative identification. The concept of mimêsis is applied (again) to music at R. 399a–400a, where Socrates acknowledges a debt to Damon in positing the expressive power of rhythms and melodies to convey equivalents to states of soul/character and even the ethical qualities of 'a life' (399e–400a).

Although mimêsis is glossed at R. 393c by appeal to vocal or bodily impersonation, the various stages of the argument entail more than a concept of imitation. Mimêsis involves ways in which material media (shapes and colours, musical sounds, speech, the body) can communicate meaning through correspondence to, or simulation of, objects or states of affairs (real or imagined). But the extension of the concept fluctuates; its conditions are never clearly defined. Moreover, the limitation of artistic mimêsis to purely sensory properties at Cra. 423c–d is ignored; music's expression of emotions and character traits demonstrates that point; and there is a broader hint of mimêsis qua embodiment of ethical values in artistic form at R. 399e–401a.

Fluidity in the scope of mimêsis helps to explain why in R. 10 Socrates returns to the subject and now asks what 'mimêsis as a whole' consists in (595c). But bk 10 adds new puzzles. Socrates develops an analogy between poetry and painting; the notorious mirror analogy at 596d–e seems to restrict mimêsis to mere replication of appearances. The idea of mirroring clashes, however, with depiction of gods and Hades at 596c, as well as with earlier references to idealized painting (e.g. 5.472d, 6.500e–1c). Moreover, a tripartite scheme of unchanging reality ('forms', q.v.), material particulars and mimetic simulacra (596–7: influenced, though not precisely matching, the metaphysics of the middle books) apparently relegates mimêsis

to ontological emptiness. Yet the tragic poet, disparaged with other mimêsis artists at 597e, is later said to produce works which overcome the souls of 'even the best of us' (605c–d): mimêsis remains psychologically powerful. Rather than diagnosing a crude flaw in the argument, we can read the rhetorically provocative critique of mimêsis in bk 10 as exposing art's own deeply paradoxical combination of imaginative pretence with emotionally compelling seductiveness. Socrates admits nostalgia for the latter (607c–d); he leaves open the question whether it can be harnessed, as 3.401a–e suggested, to ethically beneficial ends.

In the Sophist, 'the mimêsis' is a large, diverse class of activities (Sph. 234b). But in order to trap the sophist himself as an impostor, the argument imprints mimêsis in general with suspicions of the false and fake: the production of 'simulacra' (eidôla, 265b). Visual mimêsis in particular is used as an analogy with which to construct a dichotomy between 'original' and 'image' (q.v.). But Sph. complicates matters by distinguishing between 'eicastic' (objectively accurate) and 'phantastic' (perspectivally adjusted) mimêsis (235c–e); it even contemplates mimêsis informed by knowledge (267b–e). While condemning the sophist as a 'counterfeiter of reality' (235a), therefore, the dialogue allows for superior and inferior forms of mimêsis (cf. e.g. Plt. 300c–d).

Variation between positive and negative paradigms of mimêsis occurs throughout Plato's work. If the sophist consistently marks the second pole, the status of mimêsis art wavers between mere 'play' (e.g. Plt. 288c, R. 602b) and a power to change the soul. Lg. (esp. 2.653c–71b, 6.764–7.817) contains intricate attempts to appraise artistic mimêsis with multiple criteria, including those of artistic form, 'correctness' of depiction, and a mixed psychology of pleasure and ethical judgement. Plato's own writing has a mimêtic dimension and can figure itself as a rival to poetry (*Lg.* 817e; cf. Critias' remark, *Criti.* 107b–d). Some passages go further (providing a cue for Neoplatonists like Plotinus; q.v. Neoplatonism) and gesture towards the thought that all reality may be built on mimêtic correspondences: see the relationship between bodily and transcendent beauty at *Phdr.* 251a, or the notion (influenced by Pythagoreanism: cf. Aristotle *Metaphysics* 987b11–12) of the entire cosmos as mimêsis of a timeless model of being (e.g. *Ti.* 38a, 39e, 50c).

MUSIC

A. Gabrièle Wersinger

Plato's philosophy is concerned with music not only as a metaphor (*Phaedo* 61a3; *Republic* 531d8–9) but as a model for physics, psychology, education, politics and dialectics.

Harmonics, as in the curriculum of the rulers (*R.* 531a1), applies a mathematical method (*logistikê*) to music based on numerical relations (*logoi* and *analogiai*). Musical concords are *epimoric* (n+1:n) or double ratios (2n:n), though not all *epimoric* ratios are concordant; discords are *epimeric* ratios (nm:n) (*R.* 531c3–4). These ratios play a central role in the generation of the cosmos in *Timaeus*. Plato knew from Archytas that one may supply a missing geometrical mean, G, in the ratio of an octave (2:1) by using the fifth and fourth as arithmetic mean, A, and harmonic mean, H, that is, $G^2 = A \cdot H$ (*Ti.* 31c5–2a7, 36a1–4). He gives the world's soul the structure of a 'musical proportion' (*Epinomis* 991a5–b5; Heath 1921:86–90). But this method does

not work for concords smaller than the octave, so Plato divides the ratio of the fourth (4:3) diatonically, that is, into two tones and a semitone: 9:8, 9:8, 256:243 (*Ti.* 36a8–b5; Wersinger 2008a:171–4). Harmonics takes account of the ratios of intervals in scalar systems (*Phlb.* 17d1–4) corresponding to notes (*phthongoi*, *R.* 443d7–e1); in the conjunct system (*sunêmmenon*), two fourths are interwoven in the middle, producing a seventh (9 : 8, 9 : 8, 256 : 243, 9 : 8, 9 : 8, 9 : 8, 256 : 243). In the disjunct system (*diêzeugmenon*) the two fourths are separated by a disjunctive ratio (9:8) yielding a fifth within an octave (Wersinger 2008b:288–96). Such a system (9 : 8, 9 : 8, 256 : 243, 9 : 8, 9 : 8, 9 : 8, 256 : 243) structures the world's soul (*Ti.* 36a).

Harmoniai, or patterns of tuning (often translated 'modes') attributed to Damon (West 1992:174) were initially irregular scales with ethnic names (*R.* 398d11–9c3). The notes and intervallic ratios of the Dorian *harmonia*, for example, exceeds the octave:

re	mi	mi⁺	fa	la	si	si⁺	do	mi
9/8	28/27	36/35	5/4	9/8	28/27	36/35	5/4	

(The + indicates a note raised by less than a semitone.) Theorists tried to reduce the *harmoniai* to a system at the end of the fifth-century BCE (Barker 1989:15), and Plato criticizes one such attempt (*R.* 531a4), perhaps that of Eratocles (described by Barker 1982:189).

In Plato's *own* system, his model for dialectics (*Phlb.* 17c11–d4), four notes comprising a diatonic fourth delimit four *harmoniai* (Dorian, Phrygian, Lydian and Mixolydian) that give rise to four others (*R.* 400a7), fourths to fourths: Dorian-Hypodorian, Hypophrygian-Phrygian, Hypolydian-Lydian

Plato's Systems of *Harmoniai*

	Hypodorian	Hypophrygian	Hypolydian	Dorian	Phrygian	Lydian	Mixolydian	Hypermixolydian
nêtê								fa
9:8								
paranêtê							fa	mi♭
9:8								
paramesê						fa	mi♭	re♭
256:243								
mesê					fa	mi	re	do
9:8								
lichanos				fa	mi♭	re	do	si♭
9:8								
parhypatê			fa	mi♭	re♭	do	si♭	la♭
256:243								
hypatê		fa	mi	re	do	si	la	sol
9:8								
nêtê	fa	mi♭	re	do	si♭	la	sol	fa
9:8								
paranêtê	mi♭	re♭	do	si♭	la♭	sol	fa	
9:8								
paramesê	re♭	si	si♭	la♭	sol♭	fa		
256:243								
mesê	do	si♭	la	sol	fa			
9:8								
lichanos	si♭	la♭	sol	fa				
9:8								
parhypatê	la♭	sol♭	fa					
256:243								
hypatê	sol	fa						
9:8								
proslambanomenos	fa							
intervallic ratios	9:8	9:8	256:243	9:8	9:8	9:8	256:243	9:8

and Hypermixolydian-Phrygian (Ptolemy in Barker 1989:336). Those fourths build a diatonic conjunct octave (9 : 8, 9 : 8, 256 : 243, 9 : 8, 9 : 8, 256 : 243, 9 : 8) organizing eight systems of *harmoniai* from Hypodorian to Hypermixolydian. In the illustration of Plato's system below, notes and intervals are listed vertically, and *tonoi* are horizontal. The systems generate one another by cyclic reordering of the intervals, moving up from the bottom. The highest pitch of the Hypodorian octave coincides with the lowest pitch of the Hypermixolydian octave so that in the *nêtê* all pitches are similar (*homotonon*, *Phlb.* 17c4 and *R.* 617b7).

When *harmoniai* are heard, they generate emotions in the mortal soul, corresponding to the heart's being stressed or relaxed (*Ti.* 69c1, 70d5). The tuning of the strings of the lyre (*Phd.* 86c3–4; Wersinger 2010) influences the 'strings' of the soul (*R.* 411b4). Spiritedness (375b8) is softened by music (411b1; *Protagoras* 326b2–4), but too much music excessively slackens it, producing cowardliness (411a9–b5; Wersinger 2007:58–9).

To compose a melody (*melopoiia*) one has to select the rhythms and *harmoniai* (*Smp.* 187d1–2) appropriate to the specific genres of song (*Lg.* 700b1–c1), for example, the Syntonolydian for tragedies (*R.* 398e1). The aim of music is to show the image (*theama*, *R.* 402d4) of the character (*êthos*, *R.* 400d8–e3) of the soul, as in the verbal pictures of the virtuous man in war and peace by which Socrates illustrates selected *harmoniai* (399a5–c3). Only Dorian and Phrygian *harmoniai*, with their corresponding rhythms (400b1–4), are suitable in education (*R.* 399a; cf. *Smp.* 187d3; *Lg.* 673a3) because the city's future guardians must imitate a character whose moderation and courage are prominent. Socrates disallows instruments (*R.* 399d3–4) that modulate continuously

among the *harmoniai* because they accustom the soul to all emotions, including harmful ones (*R.* 395b9–7c6; *Lg.* 800d3). The so-called new music introduced by composers of dithyramb or tragic poets such as Agathon, Euripides or Timotheus (Wersinger 2001:78–82; West 1992:356–66) leads to the decay of the state (*Lg.* 700a3–1c5).

Although audible music is inferior to harmonics (*Ti.* 47c8–9; *R.* 522a), it helps to correct the disharmony inherent in sensation (*Ti.* 43a5–3d8, 47d5–6). In the choral city of *Lg.* (664c4–d4, 665b5), expert musicians, probably members of the nocturnal council, are able, thanks to numbers, to adapt harmoniai and rhythms to rational forms of virtue (670b2–6, 963c7, 964d2, 967e2–3). Elsewhere, however, if harmonics helps the soul in its conversion (periagôgê, *R.* 518d3) towards intelligible reality, dialectical knowledge of the good (*R.* 534e2–5) remains inaccessible to harmonics.

MYTH (*MUTHOS*)

Luc Brisson

In ancient Greek, *muthos* first signified 'thought that is expressed, opinion'. This meaning was then modified in the course of the transformations affecting the verbs expressing 'saying' and the nouns designating 'words' or 'speech'. This historical evolution found its final development in Plato, who is the first author to use the term *muthos* in the sense that we still give it. By using *muthos* in a nonmetaphorical way, Plato describes a certain type of discourse, fashioned by the poets of his society, with a view to substituting for it another one, the *logos* produced by the philosophers. Yet although he shows himself to be highly critical with regard to

211

myths, Plato must admit that philosophers cannot do without them. Thus, he takes his inspiration from the poets to develop certain points of his doctrine, and he goes so far as to fabricate myths, thereby recognizing their efficacy in the fields of ethics and politics.

Plato presents myth as a message by means of which a given collectivity transmits from generation to generation what it keeps in memory of its past, considering it as part of its history. The past of which myth speaks has the origin of the gods as its starting point, and its lower chronological limit is a period distant enough for it to be impossible for the narrator to validate the discourse he holds, whether through having been a witness to the events he recounts, or by basing his story on the accounts of eye witnesses.

In ancient Greece, this transmission of the memorable initially took place exclusively from mouth to ear. And when, according to what Plato recounts in the *Timaeus*, Solon went to Egypt to refresh the failing memory of the Greeks, he was informed by a priest of Sais who did not decipher the characters engraved on the walls of the temple of Neith, for he knew the contents of the message he was transmitting by heart. For Plato, writing can only play the part of a 'counter-role', in the etymological sense of the term, with regard to *muthos*: 'a double-entry register'. Yet this function remains important, for in view of the catastrophes that periodically fell upon ancient Greece, exclusive recourse to orality (q.v.) naturally entailed a progressive impoverishment of the information transmitted.

In an oral civilization, the fashioning of a message is inseparable from its emission, whereas in a written civilization, these two spheres are clearly distinguished. The ambiguity of the Platonic vocabulary on this point testifies to the gradual passage to writing around this time in ancient Greece.

Nevertheless, Plato distinguishes, frequently and fairly clearly, between the fashioning of a myth and its narration.

Thus distinguished from its fabrication, the narration of a myth becomes the task either of such professionals as the poets (*Republic* 2.377d4–6) and their subordinates (rhapsodes, actors and choreutes, *R.* 2.373b6–8), or of nonprofessionals. Professionals recount myths primarily on the occasion of festivals, and particularly in the context of contests (*Ti.* 21b1–7; *Critias* 108b3–7; cf. 108d3–6). We recall that rhapsody contests took place at Athens during the Panathenaea, and tragedy contests during the urban Dionysia. Most of those who recounted myths, however, were necessarily nonprofessionals, who expressed themselves in all circumstances, and outside of any competitive context. In Plato, these nonprofessionals feature two characteristics: advanced age and feminine gender. Why is this?

In a civilization of writing, the accumulation of messages is independent of individuals: it is equivalent to the preservation of traces on material support. In a civilization of orality, by contrast, the accumulation of messages can only be individual. Consequently, advanced age appears as a necessary, if not sufficient, corollary of the amplitude of the reservoir of knowledge in a given individual: the more elderly the individual, the more memories he must have. In addition, the narrator's old age allows a reduction of the degradation that affects every message transmitted in an exclusively oral way for a long period of time, a degradation that results from the transformation every story undergoes at each stage of its transmission. Between grandparents and grandchildren, one stage is skipped. The second feature is the femininity of the narrators: mothers (*R.* 2.377c2–4, 381e1–6; *Laws* 10.887d2–3),

212

nursemaids (*R.* 2.377c2–4; *Lg.* 10.887d2–3) and old women (*Gorgias*, 527a5–6; *R.* 1.350e2–4). Thus, it is primarily women who tell myths, and this is simply because of their privileged relationships with those for whom myths are primarily intended: children. In sum, as far as the current description is concerned, it is old women who obviously present the greatest interest, for in them our two characteristics, advanced age and female gender, are combined.

The reception of myth, which in an oral civilization cannot be separated from its emission, and hence from its fabrication, is fundamentally a matter of listening for the audience addressed by both professionals and nonprofessionals. For instance, in the dramatic contests of the Dionysia, the audience was made up of Athenians and foreigners, rich and poor, accompanied by their wives and children; there may even have been slaves attending. Those who told myths occasionally, by contrast, had a much more limited audience, essentially consisting in children younger than seven years old (*Lg.* 10.887d2–3; *R.* 2.377a6–7), the age at which boys usually began to frequent the gymnasium in ancient Greece. In both cases, however, the narrator's need to capture his audience's attention and to maintain it constituted a formidable instrument of censorship. The narrator is always afraid of a hostile reaction from the audience.

In short, myth is a discourse by which all information concerning the distant past of a community is communicated, and preserved in the collective memory. It transmits orally the story of this past from one generation to another, whether this discourse was elaborated by a technician of the collective communication of the memorable, such as the poet, or not (see further Brisson and Naddaf 1999; Partenie 2009).

NATURE (*PHUSIS*)

Thomas Johansen

The Greek word '*phusis*', like the English 'nature', was used in a range of different ways. Prominent among these in Greek philosophy is the notion of *phusis* as a principle of growth and change. Aristotle in *Physics* bk 2 develops a theory of nature as an inner principle or cause of change and rest (q.v. Causality). Aristotle saw many of the pre-Socratic philosophers as concerned with *phusis* in this sense, referring to them (e.g. at *Metaphysics* 986b14) as 'natural philosophers' (*phusiologoi*). Plato, too, presents Socrates as concerned with a tradition of studying nature in terms of causes of change (see Naddaff 1995). So, in *Phaedo* Socrates says that as a young man he was keen on 'the wisdom which they call the inquiry into nature' (*phusis*): 'for it seemed to me to be magnificent to know about the causes of each thing, why each thing comes to be and why it is destroyed and why it is' (*Phd.* 96a). Socrates, however, raises a fundamental objection to the way this study has been pursued: Socrates thinks the real cause of natural phenomena should be the good because of which they happen, just as the real cause of Socrates' continued imprisonment was the good he intended to achieve. In contrast, the causes that have been offered by earlier philosophers – material processes such as coolings and heatings – make no use of the good and cannot be said to be real causes, at best they are necessary conditions for the real cause. While Socrates in *Apology* (19c) had indicated a general lack of interest in natural philosophy, *Phd.* thus suggests a positive view of the study of nature, as a study of the causes of change and being, as long as this inquiry focuses on the good (q.v.) as the cause. Plato pursues just such a project in the *Timaeus*. The aim of Timaeus' speech is to offer an account of the nature of the universe, from its creation down to the nature of man (*Ti.* 27a). He shows how a divine craftsman, the 'demiurge', created the world for the best by imposing order on some chaotically moving materials. As his model, the creator used the eternal forms (q.v.), in particular the form of a complete living being, comprising within it all the other kinds of living being. Using mathematical structures, he made the world as a perceptible likeness (q.v. Image, Imitation) of this model. While subject to change and corruption, the natural world has, as a likeness of the eternal forms, a degree of intelligibility and goodness. It represents a paradigm of embodied order by imitating which we can become more intelligent and virtuous. This view of the cosmos as an ethical paradigm is echoed elsewhere in Plato's works: *Gorgias* 508a; *Republic* 9.592b; *Philebus* 28d–30c.

Does the *Ti.* account really amount to a study of *nature*? First of all, since the world of change is only a likeness of eternal being, it might be objected that the natural world is not an object of study in its own right but only a means of indirectly studying forms (see Rowe 2003:30). However, Timaeus is clear that the study of the world as a likeness is distinct from that of the forms (*Ti.* 59c–d). To see why, it is important to distinguish between Plato's notion of a likeness and that of a mere copy: for Plato the world has not been worked out so as to have the same properties as its original only in an inferior way. Rather, the cosmos is a likeness in the sense that it has attributes that are different from but analogous to those of the original. For example, the demiurge makes the cosmos (q.v. Cosmology) spherical so as to make it complete like its paradigm (33a–b, cf., 30c–d), but the paradigm has no spatial shape. Similarly, time, composed of past, present and future as its parts, is created as a moving likeness of an eternal, changeless paradigm without parts. To study the world as a likeness of the forms, then, means to work out which analogous features in the medium of change would best represent the eternal paradigm, a study that cannot be reduced to reasoning about the forms, but requires a different kind of practical or productive reasoning.

Another worry is that the world as an artefact is not properly natural. The Greeks commonly distinguished between nature and the products of human agency. Aristotle articulated this distinction by saying that nature is an inner principle of change, while craft makes and moves artefacts from without. So since the cosmos depends on an external maker, we may object that it does not exemplify nature (see Lennox 1986). In *Laws* bk 10 (889a), the Athenian argues against the view that nature and chance, not art, are responsible for all the significant and fine things in the cosmos. So the four elements and the planets 'moved at random, each impelled by virtue of its own inherent properties' (*Lg.* 889b). The view of nature here seems to involve the notion of what can move itself. The Athenian counters by arguing that matter is not capable of moving itself, while soul is (cf. *Phdr.* 245c8–9), so it is soul as the first moving cause that, properly speaking, is nature. A similarly view of the soul is present in *Ti.* (34b10–5a1, 36e2–4), which stresses the way in which the soul can transmit its motions to the world body by being interwoven with it (*Ti.* 36d–e). Even if the soul was first created by god, it could be argued that the cosmos now qualifies as natural by being ensouled. By the same token, individual living beings within the cosmos might be natural in having within them a soul similar to the world soul (41d–e). This leaves the question in what way, if any, inanimate bodies such as the four elements could be said to participate in nature.

NOMOS (see Law)

NON-PROPOSITIONAL KNOWLEDGE

Hugh H. Benson

For Plato, knowledge at least sometimes appears to be understood as a (cognitive) relation between a person and a proposition or set of propositions. For example, Socrates famously professes to know that it is wrong to disobey a superior (*Apology* 29b), that knowledge is different from true belief (*Meno* 98b), and even (perhaps somewhat paradoxically) that he knows nothing important (*Ap.* 21b and 23b). Such knowledge is often referred to as propositional knowledge. Nevertheless, Plato also appears to recognize other kinds of knowledge that cannot readily be understood as a relation between a person and a proposition. For example, Plato sometimes characterizes knowledge as more like a relation between a person and an object (*Republic* 476d–80a), or as skill or expertise (*Ap.* 22c–e), or even as some kind of non-discursive self-awareness (*Seventh Letter* 344b). Such characterizations indicate a commitment to non-propositional knowledge.

Perhaps the most significant feature of nonpropositional knowledge is that knowing something nonpropositionally cannot be completely described. Any attempt to describe what it is to know something nonpropositionally will be incomplete. For example, a skilled cobbler will no doubt possess considerable propositional knowledge. She/he will need to know that a specific type of leather is long-lasting, or that another type is particularly supple. But no list of such propositions will completely capture what an expert cobbler knows how to do. Again, someone who knows Meno will again no doubt know a variety of propositions, for example, that he is handsome and that he is well born. But one's knowledge of all such propositions will never amount to Socrates' knowledge of Meno, in virtue of Socrates' actual acquaintance with the man.

This fundamental feature of non-propositional knowledge is importantly connected to its two other traditional features. Unlike propositional knowledge, the object of non-propositional knowledge does not admit of propositional truth and falsity. For example, the object of a cobbler's knowledge, perhaps the discipline of cobblery or shoes, is not something that can be true or false, nor is the object of Socrates' acquaintance knowledge, that is, Meno. It must be conceded, however, that Plato is quite willing to treat *alêtheia*, which is often correctly translated as 'truth', as a property of objects. In these circumstances *alêtheia* may be better translated as 'reality' and the adjective *alêthê* as 'real'. In addition, non-propositional knowledge admits of degrees, again allegedly unlike propositional knowledge. One can know cobblery to a better or worse degree, as anyone who has taken shoes to an incompetent cobbler is well aware. Moreover, Socrates, while he knows Meno considerably better than any of us, does not know him as well perhaps, as Meno's mother.

Given this rough characterization of the nature of non-propositional knowledge, the question arises whether Plato ever recognizes knowledge of this sort. And here the answer would seem to be that he does. In the so-called early dialogues, for example, Plato appears to take the paradigm of knowledge to be *technê* (craft or expertise). In the *Ap.*, after examining the professed knowledge of the politicians and poets and finding it wanting, he discovers that the craftsmen did know many fine things; although they also thought they knew many things that they did not. Again, in the *Laches*, the dialogue in which Socrates seeks to determine which of the two Athenian generals (if either) knows what courage is, the inquiry is initially described as an examination of the expertise of the generals. But characterizing knowledge as craft or expertise is apparently to view knowledge as the sort of thing that cannot be completely describable, as being directed towards an object that does not admit of truth or falsity, and as being the sort of thing that can admit of degrees.

Again, in the middle books of the *R.*, Plato is commonly thought to distinguish between knowledge and belief or opinion in virtue of the fact that knowledge is in some way restricted to forms, while belief is restricted to ordinary objects. These books indicate a willingness on Plato's part to characterize knowledge as a relation between a person and an object (*pace* Annas 1981 and Fine 1990). Indeed, in dialogues like the *Phaedo* and the *R.* Plato often characterizes the knowledge of a form as analogous to a person seeing an object (q.v. Vision). Other passages throughout the dialogues indicate a similar propensity. As a result, Plato is sometimes thought to think of knowledge as some sort of cognitive vision or knowledge by acquaintance – a kind of direct and unmediated intuition between a person and an object (like a form). Again, this knowledge cannot be completely describable; its object does not admit of truth and falsity, but does admit of degrees.

Finally, in a famous passage from Plato's *Ep.* 7, knowledge appears to be characterized as a kind of non-discursive intuition that follows a lot of hard intellectual work – the sort of thing whose content by its very nature cannot be expressed in words. This ineffable or indescribable experience might also be suggested by the failure in the definitional dialogues of anyone managing to pass the alleged Socratic test for knowledge, viz. providing a verbal account of Socrates' 'What is F-ness?' question. Plato's use of a geometrical question whose answer is an irrational number in the *Men.* like that of powers or square roots in the *Theaetetus* has also been thought to be suggestive of Plato's willingness to characterize knowledge as non-discursive and so again incompletely describable.

It is, of course, one thing to see that Plato was tempted to characterize knowledge in these two apparently distinct ways, and quite another to suppose that Plato took one of these ways of characterizing knowledge as fundamental or even that he recognized the distinction between them. At least one reason for wondering whether Plato saw much moment to this distinction, if he recognized it at all, is the following.

In dialogues like the *Men.*, *Phd.* and *R.* Plato appears to endorse a method of knowledge acquisition known as the hypothetical method. Whatever the precise details of this method turn out to be, the method itself appears to resemble the axiomatic-deductive method of the geometers being explored in the fourth and third centuries BCE (even in Plato's Academy) and coming to expression in works like Euclid's *Elements* in about 300 BCE. Such an axiomatic deductive system presupposes a logic of propositions (whether syllogistic (see Aristotle, *Prior Analytics* and *Posterior Analytics*) or otherwise) in which the premises of the deductions are propositions. Nevertheless, in describing this method in *R.* bk 6, Plato characterizes the starting points of this method non-propositionally, giving as examples of such starting points things like the odd and the even, the various figures, and the three kinds of angles. The reader is left to wonder whether Plato is being deliberately obscure, unaware of the distinction between propositional knowledge of the premises and nonpropositional knowledge of objects, or is simply unconcerned with the distinction.

THE ONE (*TO HEN*)

James Wilberding

In the Platonic tradition a systematic philosophy is ultimately developed in which the one (*to hen*) comes to refer to the single, highest principle of all things both sensible and intelligible. The Neoplatonist Plotinus (d. 270 CE) is the first in whom we find a clear and comprehensive exposition of the one and its production of other things. Briefly, the Plotinian one *qua* the first principle of unity transcends all plurality and thus all predicates, including that of existence; since Plotinus identifies true being (the forms; q.v.) and intellect, the one is also beyond all understanding, though some form of suprarational unification with the one is possible; finally, the one timelessly generates all things by a process of emanation. This process may be said to consist of two moments: from the one's activity of, as it were, being itself, a secondary, indeterminate principle is produced, and this principle is then given definition by the one. In this way Plotinus accounts for the timeless generation of, first, intellect and the forms, then soul, and ultimately the sensible world (see O'Meara 1993 for an accessible introduction). This raises the reasonable question of just how much of this doctrine is already to be found in Plato, which is effectively to ask to what extent Neoplatonistm (q.v.) is in fact just Platonism.

There is no denying that Plato was interested in the problem of unity. The forms themselves are introduced in order to account for the so-called one over many problem (*hen epi pollôn*), viz. that many sensible things can share one property (*Euthphro* 5c–6e; *Meno* 72c; *Phaedrus* 249b; etc., cf. Aristotle *Metaphysics* 990b13–14, 1040b29–30, 1079a7–9, etc.), and the relation obtaining between unity and plurality is central to his discussions of collection and division (q.v. Method). But of course positing the one as a completely transcendent principle of forms is another matter entirely, and our primary evidence that Plato might have done this comes from the so-called indirect tradition, and in particular from Aristotle (e.g. *Metaphysics* 987a28–8b16), who gives us reports of Plato's 'so-called unwritten doctrines' (*Physics* 209b14–15) and who also composed a report of Plato's oral lecture on the good, to which Alexander of Aphrodisias (*fl. c.* 205 CE) appears to have had direct access but which was not accessible to earlier Middle Platonists nor to later Neoplatonists (Dörrie 1987:74– 90, 275–308; see Gaiser 1968:441–557 for a collection of the *testimonia* and Erler 2007:406–16 for additions and a brief, more up-to-date and objective discussion). Aristotle tells us that Plato posited two principles as the 'elements' of the forms – the one as a determining principle and the indefinite dyad (also called the great and the small) as a material principle, and identifies this one with the good (e.g. *Metaphysics* 1091b13–15; Aristoxenus *Elementa harmonices* 2.1–2). Additional support is found in the reports on Plato's immediate successors in the Academy, Speusippus and Xenocrates, who are also described as advancing systems involving the one and the dyad (Dillon 2003b).

A central issue here is whether this material can legitimately help us to better understand the dialogues and conversely whether the dialogues can help us unpack these indirect reports. There are wildly different responses to this issue. At one extreme Harold Cherniss (1944 and 1945) attempted to explain away this material as Aristotle's misunderstanding of Plato's dialogues. At the other are the somewhat speculative efforts of the Tübingen school (q.v.; Gaiser 1968; Krämer 1959 and 1964; among Anglophone scholars, Sayre (1983) notably goes in the same direction). They see the doctrine at work in the background of the middle and late dialogues and, by invoking both the *testimonia* and critical passages from the dialogues, claim to be able to reconstruct the Platonic doctrine, which turns out to be remarkably Plotinian.

Critical here is above all the interpretation of the second part of Plato's *Prm.*. In a classic paper E. R. Dodds (1928) showed the striking parallels between the first hypothesis (*Prm.* 137c–42a) of the *Prm.* and Plotinus' description of the one that transcends all predication including existence (as well as between the second hypothesis (142b–55e) and Plotinus' intellect), but whether Plato intended such a metaphysical interpretation (as defended most thoroughly by Halfwassen 1993:265–405; more briefly in 2004) was a matter of contention even in antiquity(Proclus *On Plato's* Parmenides 630, 15–645, 8) and is still more so today (see Erler 2007:227–9 for a brief overview of interpretations). The transcendence of the one is also seen by some (e.g. Halfwassen 1993:220–64) to be indicated in the *Republic*'s account of the good (q.v.). In the simile of the sun (*R.* 506e–9c; q.v.) the good is said to be 'not being, but superior to it in rank and power' (509b8–10). This might be taken to indicate transcendence, but it need not be. After all, the form of the good is repeatedly described as a *form* (505a2, 508e2–3, 517b8–c1, etc.) and

as belonging to the realm of being (518c9, 526e3–4, 532c5–6), which strongly suggests that the good, if it is to be identified with the one at all (Hager 1970:102–56), is not a principle that transcends being and the forms but is rather the highest member of that class (Baltes 1999). Other aspects of the Plotinian one have been gathered from other passages, for example, emanation, the characteristic first moment of activity of the Plotinian One, has been thought to be lurking behind Plato's light imagery, especially *R.* 508b6–7, and the interplay between the one and the dyad has likewise been thought to be at work in the *Philebus* (esp. 14c–18d, 23c–7b) and the *Sophist* (esp. 242c–53e).

The reconstructions of the Tübingen School have not been met with wide acceptance, and not just for hermeneutic reasons. Philosophically, this approach to the dialogues is seen by opponents to saddle Plato with an unfashionably systematic philosophy at the cost of other interpretations that are not only exegetically possible (and in some cases much more so) but also of more philosophical relevance to us today. Yet, Cherniss' deflationary account of the testimonies has also failed to hold sway. The truth surely lies somewhere in between these two extremes.

ONTOLOGY (METAPHYSICS)

Allan Silverman

Of all the doctrines ascribed to Plato, perhaps the most (in)famous is what we would label a metaphysical thesis, namely that the real, or most perfect beings, are forms (q.v.). Of course the various subdisciplines of philosophy, for example, ethics, epistemology and metaphysics, and arguably philosophy itself, do not predate Plato and his student,

Aristotle, from a later edition of whose writings the term 'metaphysics' actually comes. In thinking about Plato's metaphysics, then, one should keep in mind that forms are the foundation of Plato's whole synoptic vision. It is not unlikely that he comes to postulate forms (in the *Phaedo*) in order to support his teacher Socrates (q.v.) in countering challenges posed by ethical relativists such as Protagoras, and it is almost certain that one fundamental purpose of forms is to serve as the (objective, i.e. mind-independent) objects of knowledge.

What then are forms? Forms are properties or universals. A universal property is, typically, common to many things. A form is a 'one' over many. The many things are, typically, ordinary particulars. For instance, Shaquille O'Neal and Mt Everest are tall, a basketball and a penny are circular, Socrates and Mother Teresa are pious, and Plato and Aristotle are human. (It is disputed whether there are, in addition to forms and particulars, property instances or tropes, for example, the tall-in-Shaq, as distinct from both the tall-in-Everest and the form of tallness.) Plato, unlike Aristotle, is thought to have held that forms or properties exist regardless of whether there are any instances of them. Thus, even if there never has been, is not now, nor ever will be a truly wise person, nonetheless the form of wisdom is what it is, or exists. Plato's forms are thus transcendent, as opposed to immanent or Aristotelian, universals. They are 'separate' from their particular instances.

Plato characterizes the difference between forms and particulars through several distinctions. Forms are perfect and independent beings; particulars are imperfect and dependent participants, getting (some of) their properties by having a share of forms. Forms are unchanging, immaterial and outside of space and time – they are abstract entities. Particulars change, are material, and exist in space and time. Forms are indivisibly simple (or ones); particulars are divisibly complex (have many properties). Forms are grasped by knowledge, particulars by perception or belief. Forms do not, whereas particulars do, suffer from 'the compresence' of opposite properties: whereas the form of equality is always equal and never unequal, particular sticks or stones, say, are at once equal and unequal, perhaps because a given stick is equal to a second stick but unequal to a third.

What precisely the perfection, simplicity, separation and nature or being of forms amounts to is controversial (Cherniss 1944; Silverman 2002). Relatedly, there is controversy over the range of forms, at least in the *Phd.* and *Republic* (where scholars think Plato introduces it). Looking at (many of) the forms mentioned in the arguments, scholars have argued that forms are limited to incomplete or relational properties, perhaps with special provision for ethical properties (Irwin 1977a; Owen 1957). So beauty (q.v.), goodness (q.v.), largeness, equality and justice (q.v.) are forms, because anything that is good, say, is good for a . . . diet, or a man, or whatever 'completes' the thought that X is good. Usually, the chief philosophical reason for positing forms of this sort is that particulars suffer compresence of opposites with respect to these properties; Socrates is larger than Simmias but smaller than Cebes. Since, or so it is argued, there must be entities that do not suffer such compresence, Plato posits forms that are simply and solely or perfectly and completely beautiful or large, and so on (Fine 1993). Other scholars think that the range of forms is not limited in this manner. Rather, there are forms for all the natural joints, forms corresponding to all the properties actually had by particulars. (One can also maintain that there is a form corresponding to every linguistic predicate, thus further expanding the range of forms.) How one understands the nature or being of forms varies, in part, with one's view of their range. The starting point for questions about the nature of forms is the self-predication statements sprinkled throughout the dialogues, for example, piety is pious, justice is just. Some think that justice is just in the same way as Socrates is just – it is characterized by justice (Vlastos 1981). (Since forms are 'causes' (q.v.) of the way particulars are, some think that forms transmit (via participation; q.v.) the property they respectively have to the particulars.) Others, approximationists, think that forms are perfect instances of the property whereas particulars are defective instances, say in the manner in which no physical circle is perfectly circular (Malcolm 1991). Finally, others think that forms are different kinds of beings from particulars: forms *are* simply and solely what they are, whereas particulars get all of their many properties via participation, a special ontological relation (Silverman 2002).

In other dialogues, many of the metaphysical issues involving forms and particulars are given closer scrutiny. So, many, who think that initially forms are limited, concede that later works reveal a much broader range of forms. In the *Parmenides*, Plato seems to call into question the foundations of the theory in what is known as the Third Man argument. If forms have the property in the same way as particulars, and if forms cannot 'explain' why they have the property they have, then it seems a regress of forms threatens. Some scholars think that Plato abandons forms (Ryle 1939a). Others think that he makes them immanent in particulars, and (thus) allows that particulars can both have some

properties essentially and others accidentally (Frede 1967). Others think that Plato's account of forms is not subject to the Third Man regress because forms and particulars do not have properties in the same way, or that forms are self-explainers (Code 1986). Finally, in the late dialogues Plato seems to distinguish some forms, for example, being, sameness, difference, as greatest kinds. These are what, in the tradition, are syncategorematic or transcendental properties had by all beings, as opposed to substantial forms such as greenness, or cat.

While most of his efforts are devoted to forms, especially in the late *Philebus* and *Timaeus* Plato develops a sophisticated, mathematical account of material particulars, including the cosmos, and perhaps even of matter. The key elements are geometrical forms, ratios and the receptacle, an item very similar to space. In the *Ti.*, particulars are, at bottom, materially composed of triangles and are occupants of space and time.

Finally, Plato's metaphysics also includes immaterial souls. These are primitive beings that are essentially self-movers. As such, they are ultimately responsible for all physical and psychological motion.

PAIDERASTIA (PEDERASTY)

Luc Brisson

In the *Symposium* as a whole, which should be associated with the *Phaedrus*, and particularly in the speech Socrates places in the mouth of Diotima (*Smp.* 198a–212e), *philosophia* (q.v.) is opposed to *paiderastia* on the level of education (209e–12a, and especially 211b–c). What does this mean? First of all, *paiderastia* must not be confused with what we now call 'pederasty'. In order to understand the originality of what was called *paiderastia* in archaic and classical Greece, which had almost the status of an institution among the wealthy circles of Athenian society, the following five particularities should be mentioned.

(1) *Paiderastia* implies a relationship not between two adult males, but between an adult 'lover' (*erastês*) and his 'beloved' (*erômenos*), a *paîs*. In this case, *paîs* designates a boy in the age class that begins around the time of puberty, until the appearance of the first beard, between approximately ages 12 and 18.

(2) The appearance of fuzz on a boy's cheeks represents the summit of his sexual attractiveness, which lasts until the growth of his first beard. In a transitional period, a young boy may play both an active and a passive role in a sexual relationship, but with different partners.

(3) Since it is limited to one period of life, and is not associated with an inclination towards one individual in particular, *paiderastia* is not exclusive. Adult males are expected to marry, after having played a passive role in the context of a homosexual relationship, and even while still playing an active role in them. Nevertheless, in the context of *paiderastia*, the *erastês* was often a relatively young man between twenty and thirty, who was not yet married or whose wife was very young. Moreover, in his speech (*Smp.* 189c–93d), Aristophanes insists on the existence of very strong, long-lasting bonds between individuals of the same sex. Agathon and Pausanias are a good example, since they remained together for more than 30 years.

(4) Even when pederastic relationships are characterized by mutual love and tenderness, an emotional and erotic asymmetry subsists, which the Greeks distinguish by speaking of the lover's *erôs* and the beloved's *philia*. An older man, inspired by love, pursued with his advances a younger man who, if he yielded, was led to do so by affection, gratitude and admiration, feelings united under the term *philia*; pleasure was not to be taken into account in his case (for a contrary view, see Dover 1989:204).

(5) The older male is qualified as an *erastês*, whereas the younger one is called his *erômenos* (the passive participle of *eran*) or his *paidika* (a neuter plural that literally means 'what concerns young boys'). The amorous language found in Greek literature of a certain level and particularly in Plato always remains modest, but the reader should not be fooled. Such terms as *hupourgein* 'perform a service' (*Smp.* 184d) or *charizesthai* 'accord favour' (182a–b, 182d, 183d, 185b, 186b–c, 187d, 188c, 218c–d) must be interpreted in a strong sense: the service expected or the favour requested by the older male is ultimately equivalent to a sexual relation.

Outside of the desire for sexual satisfaction and the search for a certain affection or tenderness, of what use might *paiderastia* have been in ancient Greece? Whereas marriage constituted the privileged institution that enabled an adult male to transmit his 'genetic', economic, social and political patrimony, the relations between an adult and an adolescent can serve only to ensure the transmission of an economic, social and political patrimony. Indeed, it seems that in classical Athens, the goal of *paiderastia* was to facilitate the adolescent's entry into the masculine society that ran the city economically and politically.

221

Paiderastia thus had a social and educational role. This is the origin of all the remarks and developments on the utility (*chreia*) of homosexual relations that we find in Plato, particularly in the *Phdr.* and the *Smp.*

However, despite the institutionalized form assumed by *paiderastia*, and despite the praise received by sexual relations among men, which occupy the first place, particularly in the context of the banquet given at the home of Agathon (and described in Plato's *Smp.*), this type of relation inspired resistance and censure. It is worth noting that Socrates favours avoiding homosexual coitus in *Phdr.* and the Athenian Stranger condemns it in *Laws*.

In his speech (180c–5c), Pausanias is obviously thinking of Agathon (who answers him in his speech, 194e–5a), who was first his 'beloved' in the context of *paiderastia*, when he underlines the quiet mistrust of Athenian society with regard to this practise, and even its open hostility. We find an example of this hostility in the *Thesmophoriazusae* (130–67), a comedy produced in 411 BCE, in which Aristophanes violently targets Agathon. The scene in which a relative of Euripides debates with Agathon constitutes a particularly violent condemnation of the homosexuality of the tragic poet, who must have been famous at the time.

By opposing *paiderastia* and *philosophia* on the level of education, the *Phdr.*, and especially the *Smp.*, encourage broader reflection on sexuality. Relations between the sexes are constructed as a function of social representations that vary over time and space. At the end of the fifth century BCE, certain oppositions manifest themselves in a context that is very different from our own. The opposition (active/passive) does not coincide with the polarity (man/woman), for the latter becomes confused for young men during the time of their adolescence. It does not always correspond to the contrast between adolescent and adult, for there may be interference between these terms. Finally, the couple heterosexuality/homosexuality, in so far as these terms are used with a great deal of caution, is not identical with a clear division between norm and deviance as it has been in other times and places, for homosexuality inspires both praise and blame. Indeed, the practise of *paiderastia*, which has almost the status of an institution in the upper classes of archaic and classical Athens never ceases to inspire a quiet mistrust that is sometimes transformed into hostility (see further Brisson 2006; Dover 1989; Halperin 1990).

PARTICIPATION

Fiona Leigh

Participation (*methexis*) is the relation that subsists between forms (q.v.) and things – 'participants' – in virtue of which things come to have as an attribute the property the form is named after. Thus participation has a causal or at least an explanatory role in Plato's thought. Not being overly fond of technical language, Plato describes the relation by way of various terms: sharing, participating, communing and possibly even mixing (*metalambanein, epikoinônein, metekhô, koinônein, mixis*). So, for example, if a person or a city is just, this is because of its participation in the form justice (*Republic* 443e–4d, 472b, 479e–84d), if two things are a duo they share in duality itself (*Phaedo* 101c), if anything is beautiful it is because of sharing or partaking in the beautiful (*Phd.* 100d–e; *Symposium* 211a–b), the many large things participate in the form large (*Parmenides* 132a–b), and being a different thing involves a sharing in difference (*Sophist* 256b–e). In the *Sph.*, at least a select few forms share other forms: Motion is the same as itself through participation in the same in relation to itself, and is different from the same because of sharing in difference in respect of the same (256a–b). So what exactly is participation?

What, according to Plato, the participation relation consists in is a vexed question for the student of Plato's metaphysics. No character in the dialogues offers an adequate explanation of it, and in the *Phd.* (100d), Plato makes Socrates deliberately vague on the details. Some have even doubted that Plato himself understood it.

Broadly speaking, two interpretive trends are discernable in the secondary literature. Some see participation as reflective of or reducible to the apparent defect of sensible particulars as compared with forms; others see it as playing a role in the causal connection between forms and their participants. Sensibles are characterized in desultory terms as inferior, base and merely temporary (*Phd.*; *Timaeus*; *Smp.*; *R.*). The reader gets a strange picture of sensibles, as 'striving' to be like the forms in which they participate, but always falling short (e.g. *Phd.* 74d–5d), suggesting that they are at best approximations of them (cf. *Ti.* 29b–c; *R.* 472b–3b). They are sometimes said to possess mere 'becoming', being resemblances of the forms, which are more true (*Ti.* 50d–1c; *Smp.* 211a–2a), suggesting to some that they are like reflections in a mirror, or, alternatively, are copies or imitations (q.v.) of forms, as a chair may be said to imitate a craftsman's blueprint, or a pattern (paradigm) in nature (*R.* bk 10 596a–7e; *Prm.* 132d; *Ti.* 29a–b; cf. *Ti.* 48e–9a). Such images naturally give rise to suggestions that the participation relation is one of copying, mirroring (or reflection), imitating or

approximating. Note that not all, perhaps none, of these relations are necessarily identical. One way of copying something is to be an image or visual representation of it, another way is to imitate it by causing oneself to come to share a feature in common with it (typically not all features), another is to bear a likeness in a number of essential features to it, another is to be a wholesale reproduction (fair or otherwise) of it, and yet another is to roughly resemble it as one might resemble a pattern.

Several key differences exist between forms and nonforms. While forms are purely intelligible – accessible to the mind (soul) alone – nonforms are in space and time, and are enmattered or bodily (*Ti.* 30a–1b, 48e–9a; *R.* 507b–c). Such stuff is impermanent, and is characterized by opposite properties. None of the many physically beautiful things that the vulgar crowds adore is simply beautiful, says Socrates, but each is such as to also be ugly (*R.* 5.479a–b). If the defect of sensibles lies in their matter, perhaps participation is a relation of rough resemblance in which the resemblance is limited in exactness by the imperfection of the material. However, this does little to explain possession of a property. For example, Helen of Troy is not beautiful, but ugly, relative to the goddess Athena (cf. *Hippias Major* 289a–b; cf. *Smp.* 211a), and so is both beautiful and not beautiful (compresence of opposite characters). Perhaps the thought, on the approximation view, would be that humans are made of baser stuff than gods, and so Helen does not approach the ideal of beauty (q.v.) as closely as Athena, who herself is not perfectly beautiful, but only approximates, however closely, the beauty of the form beauty. But if beauty admits of a scale, as this view implies, then either Helen, Athena, or the rest have a precise measure of beauty, not an approximation, or else Plato thought that participation admits of degrees. On the first alternative, Plato appears to have confused being a precise measure with being a dim copy or approximation; while a problem for the second alternative is that degrees of participation do not figure prominently in the dialogues (but see *R.* 472b–c). Finally, if the form embodies the ideal standard, then we must ask in virtue of what it possesses the property. If it is a further form, then as Plato himself saw, the infamous 'Third Man Argument' threatens to undermine the explanatory value of forms (*Prm.* 132a–b).

Perhaps Plato characterizes participants as mere copies of forms because they belong to a different ontological category. So, they are not deficient as mere approximations of forms made from inferior stuff, but because they are different sorts of things entirely. Only forms really exist, whereas sensibles have a more tenuous reality, rolling about in the realm of 'becoming', not true being (*R.* 479d). Consider the following analogy: a reflection of a red scarf in a mirror resembles the original, really existing scarf, of which it is a copy. But since it is merely a visual image of it, only an imitation, it is incapable of, say, keeping one warm in winter. Despite handling Socrates' talk of sensibles as shadowy reflections well, however, it is not clear that the analogy is ultimately workable. For, as the example makes clear, a reflection of a scarf is in an important sense not really a scarf at all, whereas the tallness in Simmias does seem to be a case of really being tall. Moreover, Plato himself apparently worried that an account of participation as similarity or likeness was inadequate. For, if a participant is like the relevant form, then the form is also like its participant, and it seems that this common property, in virtue of which they are alike, must in turn be explained in terms of a further form (*Prm.* 132d–3a). If

the second form is like the original form and the participant, the regress will be infinite.

If Plato's forms are universals (q.v. Ontology), as often thought, then the participation relation would be perhaps best thought of as an instantiation relation. The repeated characterization of sensibles as inferior could then be construed as an indication of Plato's fondness for his conceptual innovation of forms, as compared to the mundane things of the sensible realm. But since this is hardly a philosophical reason to privilege forms, in the absence of solid textual evidence, it is an undesirable reading of Plato (but see Harte 2008).

Alternatively, one might attempt to understand participation by focusing on the causal connection between forms and their participants. A form of F is the cause of all the F-things being F, in the sense of being the thing responsible, by Plato's lights, for them being F. No cause of something's being F can also be the cause of its being the opposite of F, and similarly, no cause of something's being F can be the opposite of F, which principles rule out other candidates for being the cause, such as material composition. Participation could, therefore, be construed as the causal relation that holds between forms and their participants. If so, however, it seems it will have to be one of the small classes of causal relations that is at the same time the state of affairs identified as the effect brought about by the cause. At least, participation seems to be temporally coextensive with the participant bearing the relevant property – it is not conceived of in the dialogues as a discrete act or event that happens at some time, which then ceases, leaving the participant as the property bearer at a later time. This suggestion raises several questions: Is participation then identical with, and reducible to, having a property as an attribute? Is the suggested view compatible with thinking of forms as universals, given that universals are not generally understood as causes of their instances?

PERCEPTION AND SENSATION (*AISTHÊSIS, AISTHANOMAI*) (SENSATION)

Timothy Chappell

One day at dawn, [Socrates] started thinking about some problem or other; he just stood outside, trying to figure it out. He couldn't resolve it, but he wouldn't give up. He simply stood there, glued to the same spot. By midday, many soldiers began to notice (*êisthanonto*) . . . (Plato, *Symposium* 220c)

They say that when [Babylon] was captured, three days later much of the city was still unaware of it (*ouk aisthesthai*). (Aristotle, *Politics* 1276a)

As these two quotations show, the classical Greek words for perception, *aisthêsis* and *aisthanomai*, normally have a straightforward nontechnical meaning: 'be aware', 'notice', 'detect' (as in Edward Lear's 'I perceive a large bird in this bush'). Furthermore they can have this nontechnical meaning even in the two Greek authors who, in their different ways, do most to refine specialized philosophical concepts of *aisthêsis*.

It is a nice question how refined their concepts are, and how closely their concepts align with any modern concept, given that, for example, Aristotle uses the same *aisthêsis*-vocabulary to discuss both sense-perception (*de Anima* 2) and moral intuition (*Nicomachean Ethics* 6). Modern philosophers often

distinguish sensation (the physical transaction) from perception (the conveying of information by means of sensation). While Plato is keenly interested in both, and indeed has separate theories for the two (for his theory of sensation see *Timaeus* 45b–6c, 67c–8d; cf. *Meno* 76c–d; *Theaetetus* 155c–7c), he is undeniably hampered by having no terms to mark this and other key distinctions.

In such famous passages as *Phaedo* 72e–7b, *Republic* 475e–80a and *Ti.* 51d–e Plato develops a critique of *aisthêsis* which tightens and sharpens not just his concept of *aisthêsis* but also the accompanying and contrasting concepts, especially knowledge (*gnôsis, epistêmê*). By a simple piece of 'ordinary language philosophy' (see especially *R.* 477a1 ff.) Plato argues that the content of knowledge is 'what is', whereas the content of *aisthêsis* (or rather *doxa* – see below) is 'what is and is not'. By definition, whatever I know is true (or real); so knowledge is about sure, stable realities. By contrast, whatever *aisthêsis* is about is unstable, ambiguous and uncertain.

Why is *aisthêsis* unstable, knowledge stable? Since *aisthêsis* constitutively depends on changeable physical processes, whereas knowledge constitutively depends on explanations (*logoi*). For Plato, to know something is actively to grasp a full (or approaching full) understanding of it; such an understanding will necessarily be stable if it is present at all. By contrast, to perceive something is to be affected, passively, by the physical world; being so affected is what sensation is, and there is no perception without sensation. But the physical world is itself unstable and unreliable, and its effects on us are particular and perspectival. So an epistemic state of being affected by the physical world must be a state of becoming what the physical world is – unstable and unreliable – and of becoming this at a particular time and from a particular perspective. If knowledge exists at all, knowledge will have to be an epistemic state which consists in being affected by 'what is' – by some reality that is *not* unstable in the way the physical world is. But knowledge does exist. Therefore knowledge is not of the physical world; it is a nonperspectival grasp of some realm of stable and unchanging realities beyond it. (Our apparent knowledge of mathematical truths is, perhaps, a clue to what such true knowledge might be like.)

However, there is a twist of paradox in the tale. The ultimate aim of the *R.*'s dialectical education is itself a sort of direct, revelatory perception, acquaintance or intuition: 'True Being . . . is visible (*theatê*) only to *Nous*' (*Phaedrus* 247c8; cp. *theôrôn* at *Smp.* 210d4). Hence we find Plato apparently denouncing this-worldly perception in almost the same breath as he exalts the perception of the forms (*R.* 517b1–9). Knowledge, as the *Tht.* insists, is not perception in any ordinary or mundane sense. And yet at the end of the philosopher's laborious ascent, by way of reasoning and hard thought and logical work, what we find is that the ultimate knowledge is itself something so like perception in its directness, immediacy and nondiscursive simplicity that Plato never finds a better or more illuminating image to describe it by.

This line of thought is central to the *R.* But Plato never expresses it just thus. In particular – as noted above – the *R.* speaks mostly of *doxa*, not of *aisthêsis*. Usually the natural translation for *doxa* is 'belief', which seems a very different thing from 'perception', still more from 'sensation'. However, the *R.*'s uses of *doxa* (see, e.g. *R.* 476b–d) show clearly that for Plato it is a technical term: *doxa* means, roughly, 'sensation-based belief', and that is not far at all from one possible sense of 'perception'.

This helps us see why, in Plato's *Tht.*, the three would-be definitions of knowledge rejected in turn are these: (a) knowledge is *aisthêsis*, (b) knowledge is true *doxa* and (c) knowledge is true *doxa* with a *logos*. Plato is well aware of the apparent discontinuity between (a), about *aisthêsis*, and (b) and (c), about *doxa*. The *Tht.* does not skate over this difference; it explores it. How can the surd, unstructured happenings of mere sensation carry the sort of informational content worth dignifying with the names *perception* or *belief* – let alone the name *knowledge*? Can someone who thinks, as Heracleitus does according to the *Tht.*, that there is nothing more to knowledge than the ebb and flow of such separate sensations, give any convincing account of the precondition of belief formation that we today call semantic structure? These are the questions that drive the argument of the *Tht.* The terrain between bare-sensation *aisthêsis* and informationally loaded *doxa* is precisely what they are designed to explore. And though he leaves his own positive doctrine implicit in the *Tht.*, it is possible to see how Plato would answer these questions; without the kind of structure for understanding that the forms provide, he sees no route at all from *aisthêsis* to knowledge. Perception on its own is – for Plato as much as for his great contemporary Democritus, whom throughout his life he seems to have ignored – merely *deception*; where Plato and Democritus differ is on what needs to be added to perception, in order for it to be something more than deception.

The *Tht.* is consistent with Plato's fundamental claim that the forms are the necessary precondition of all understanding. Nonetheless, the implicit lesson of the dialogue's explicit argument – that not just knowledge, but belief and perception too, are necessarily structured by the forms – is that there is a way for Plato to 'liberalise' his view away from the hardline 'two-worlds' Platonism that can be read into the *R*. Knowledge may be the 'highest' and purest epistemic state, but that does not mean – Plato comes to think – that there is simply *no* value in *doxa* or *aisthêsis*: these epistemic states, 'lower' though they may be, can help us too (*Philebus* 58d–62d). *Pace* the *R*., the physical world is not such that the only epistemic states we can be in about it are ignorance and *doxa*: knowledge of it is possible too, if we come to see how the changing world approximates unchanging goodness. To explain how this can be done is, of course, the project of Plato's greatest work of applied physical science: the *Timaeus*.

For further reading on Plato on perception, see Burnyeat (2000), Chappell (2005), Frede M. (2000), Modrak (2006) and Sedley (2006).

PHILOSOPHY AND THE PHILOSOPHER

Monique Dixsaut

Plato did not create the word *philosophia* (its coinage is ascribed by a later tradition to Pythagoras; Burkert; Dixsaut 1985:43–83), but he completely changed its meaning. In the texts that have been preserved, the only pre-Platonic occurrence of the word is to be found in the Hippocratic treatise *Of Ancient Medicine*, in the course of a polemic against some doctors more desirous of cosmic speculations than of true science and efficacy. The adjective *philosophos* (Heraclitus f. 35; D.K.; Antiphon 44a; Gorgias; *Encomium of Helen* 11, 13), and the verb *philosophein* (Herodotus I.30 and Thucydides 2.40–1) refer to any form of intellectual curiosity or exercise, not to a specific subject to which

some men would devote themselves. Plato sometimes retains this meaning of *philosophia* as opposed to physical and specialized activities, for instance in *Hippias Minor* (363a), *Charmides* (153e), *Protagoras* (335d) or when he describes 'the democratic man' as able to engage in 'philosophy', at times (*Republic* 561d).

The departure from this loose meaning is staged in *Gorgias* (481c–5e): the philosophy referred to by Callicles, when he says that it is a fine thing, provided one applies oneself to it with moderation and in one's youth, is not the philosophy Socrates has just said he is in love with, which demands constant self-examination and rational self-justification: to love philosophy is to be a philosopher through and through. Those who pursue this kind of knowledge, or wisdom (*sophia*), are neither wise nor ignorant (*Lysis* 218a; *Symposium* 303e–4b; *Phaedrus* 278d), but like Socrates they are wise enough to be aware that they are ignorant (*Apology* 29b). This negative wisdom is opposed to that of the *sophoi*, the experts, able to master either one particular material or a whole range of phenomena (cf. Aristotle, *On Philosophy*, f. 8 Ross), and whose *sophia* refers to a degree of excellence in performance which must be fêted. The philosopher aspires to no *sophia* of this sort. What he calls philosophy is the quest for a universal knowledge that might give birth to flawless wisdom: but as such, it seems that it can be a science belonging to the god only, or no more than a purely formal verbal *passophia*. According to Plato, the sophists are endowed with a wonderful power of appearing to be 'wise on all subjects' (*panta sophoi*, *Sophist* 233a–c, cf. scholium ad 251C), thanks to their art of controversy, but all imitators have this same ability to seem to know everything (to be *passophoi*, *R*. 598d): Prodicos (*Prt*. 315e), Protagoras

(*Theaetetus* 152c), and also Homer (194e) and Hesiod (*Ly.* 216a), or Parmenides and Melissos (*Tht.* 181b). Neither conception of *sophia* can be ascribed to Plato: for even if his Socrates sometimes seems to share the view that calling oneself *philosophos* is a token of humility, when summoning the 'divine part' of his soul, he claims that the philosopher becomes akin to the realities to which 'the gods themselves owe their divine nature' (*Phdr.* 249c; cf. *Tht.* 176b).

The *Phaedo* is the only dialogue belonging to the first period (before the *R.*) in which the adjective *philosophos* is preceded by a definite article and becomes a substantive, this new substantive being defined in contrast with other words based on *philo-*: the philosopher is not obsessed with the care of his body (*philosômatos*), he does not crave for money (*philochrêmatos*), honour (*philotimos*), power or glory (*philarkhos, philonikos*), and he is finally identified with a *philomathes*. The latter is not specified by its object but by a kind of activity or learning, whose deep signification will be revealed by the argument of reminiscence. In order to gain what he claims he loves, 'thought and truth', the philosopher must 'be dead', that is, recall through the soul alone what is really existent and fully intelligible, the invisible 'obscure to the eyes but to be seized by philosophical thought' (*Phd.* 81b7). Contrary to a commonly accepted etymology (but missing in the *Cratylus*), Plato does not give as an object to the philosopher's desire a *sophia* as impossible to obtain as it is ill defined. The meaning of the thing he calls 'philosophy' cannot amount to the sum of the two elements making up its name.

R. stresses the point: sticking to etymology leads to defining not the philosopher but the *philodox*, the lover of opinion. To sustain his proposal for the rule of philosopher-kings,

Socrates begins by wondering if one must say of the philosopher, as must be said of all those who love something (*philein ti*), that he loves not this or that particular aspect of *sophia*, but loves the whole (*R.* 474b–80a): he would have a voracious appetite for all learning. Glaucon objects that on the basis of this description, all the lovers of sights and hearing would be considered philosophers, and mighty strange ones too, for undiscerning greed, particular to appetite, and indetermination, particular to *sophia*, characterize those who only resemble philosophers. The philosopher proper is not one who likes looking at everything new, but one who likes looking at the truth. He is not curious of the many things that participate in one idea (*eidos*), but he is always trying to get at what each being truly is in itself, at the permanent and intelligible entity (*ousia*) these things participate in. Ideas are the justification of the philosopher's search, and the only science he wants to acquire is dialectic (*Philebus* 58a–e). As Parmenides asks Socrates: if, owing to the number of difficulties encountered, you give up assuming ideas, 'what will you do with philosophy?' (*Parmenides* 135c).

If the power to love the true prevails over every other kind of desire (in *R.* 581b–c, the highest part of the soul is called *philosophos*), we are dealing with a philosophical nature in which the love of truth, taken to its highest pitch, must not be called *philia* but *erôs*. It takes very little for its violence to be perverted: when he is not a philosopher, *erôs* is a tyrant, and the same can be said of a philosophical nature. Plato scholars (e.g. Annas 1981) generally find little or nothing to say of its definition in bk 6 (485–90), since it seems to offer a colourless model of human perfection. In fact, far from aiming at endowing the philosopher with every possible virtue, it is meant to remind us that it is only in him that virtues truly are virtues (cf. *Phd.* 69a–b), just as it is only in him, because truth 'leads the chorus', that the unity of virtues is fulfilled.

The philosophical nature is all the more endangered as it is sturdy and exceptionally gifted. A philosophic education must turn this nature towards its only fitting occupation, which is philosophy – failing at which, it will prove most dangerously harmful. From this passage (*R.* 491d ff.), we get a clear impression of the double-edged character of the force in human nature with which Plato is dealing (Nettleship 1929:211). The problem of the selection, education and perversion of these natures is the greatest political problem, since the philosopher is an indispensable agent when it comes to stamping a right direction on the life of the soul and of the state. His task is to recall that being a man means being able to understand oneself in all one says and does, and to remind the cities that they can only be saved if ruled by intelligence.

Making the existence of philosophy depend on the birth and preservation of philosophical natures is to make its extinction possible, which is why one must diagnose the causes for their perversion and expose the usurpers. Since there can be no philosophy without philosophers, since nothing can warrant that new philosophers will be born or that 'the best natures' will devote themselves to 'the best occupation', it follows that nothing can guarantee that philosophy will always exist. Its essence is eternal, not its existence. Philosophy is a rare plant, one which has flourished only in the West, and it is always in danger and always in need of a defence (Bloom 1968:390).

If sophists find refuge in the darkness of not being, philosophers are difficult to see because of 'the dazzling brightness of the region where they reside' (*Sph.* 254a). That is why the sophist may claim that *he* is the philosopher, and the statesman hold that public affairs demand a realism the philosopher is devoid of. When it comes to those three 'kinds', the difference between them is not to be found in a definition (that may be why Plato never wrote the dialogue of the *Philosopher*, alluded to in *Sph.* 254b), but ever again in Socrates, who is not a philosopher but *the* philosopher, a subject eluding the predicate. He might have been no more than a disinterested, slightly eccentric sophist, if his bite had not startled Plato awake and opened the history of Western philosophy.

PHUSIS (see Nature)

PIETY (*EUSEBEIA, HOSIOS*)

Mark L. McPherran

One of the central concerns of Plato's dialogues is the true nature of the cardinal virtues, piety, justice (q.v.), wisdom, courage and moderation (q.v. Excellence). Socrates and Plato inherited the everyday Greek conception of piety, which designates those things that are in accord with the norms governing proper relations between humans and gods. What marked a fifth-century BCE Greek city or person as pious, for example, was not so much a matter of having a certain set of beliefs as it was the correct observance of ancestral tradition, especially the correct performance of sacrifices and the celebration of festivals in honour of deities, minor and major. No ancient text such as the *Iliad* had the status of a Bible or Koran, and there was no organized church, trained clergy or systematic set of doctrines enforced (although there were officially recognized priests and priestesses with clearly demarcated public duties).

Plato's most sustained and famous treatment of piety is found in the *Euthyphro*. There Socrates interrogates the self-professed religious expert, Euthyphro, from whom he elicits five accounts of piety ('piety' naming the one characteristic that makes all pious actions and persons pious; *Euthphr*. 5c–d, 6d–e): (a) prosecuting whomever does injustice (5d–6e), (b) what is loved by the gods (6e–9d), (c) what is loved by *all* the gods (9e–11b), (d) the part of (generic) justice that assists the gods to produce their most beautiful product (*pagkalon ergon*; 11e–14b) and (e) the knowledge of prayer and sacrifice (14b–15c). Subjected to the Socratic *elenchos* (q.v.), Euthyphro is forced to withdraw his assent to all five proposals. However, many scholars have argued that a positive and Socratically acceptable partial conception of piety can be reconstructed on the basis of Socrates' leading hints in the *Euthphr*. concerning his fourth account, and his claims to be pursuing a god-ordered mission in the *Apology* as he defends himself against a charge of *impiety* (*Ap*. 20e–3) (e.g. McPherran 1996; Taylor 1982; see Brickhouse and Smith 1989 on Socrates' defence; McPherran 2003 has argued that the fifth account can also be interpreted in Socratically acceptable terms).

This 'Socratic piety' would be defined as 'that part of justice that is a service of humans to gods, assisting the gods in their primary task to produce their most beautiful product' (McPherran 1996:ch. 2). Socrates holds that we cannot have a precise or complete account of this product, but since he also holds that the gods are wholly good and do not quarrel like Homers' gods, their chief project must be superlatively good. Next, the Socratic view that the only or most important good is virtue/wisdom (e.g. *Ap*. 30a–b; *Euthydemus*

281d–e) makes it likely that the only or most important component of the gods' chief product is virtue or wisdom. But then, since piety as a virtue must be a craft-knowledge (q.v. Art) of how to produce goodness, *our* primary service to the gods – the one we are best suited to perform – would appear to be to help the gods produce goodness in the universe *via* the protection and improvement of the human mind/soul. Since philosophical examination of oneself and others is for Socrates the key activity that helps to achieve this goal *via* the improvement of consistency among our moral belief and the deflation of human presumptions to divine wisdom (e.g. *Ap*. 22d–3b), Socratic philosophizing is a preeminently pious activity.

This appropriation and reconception of piety as demanding of us philosophical self-examination is not wholly at odds with tradition: Socrates' antihubristic mission is very much in line with Delphic Apollo's insistence that humans obtain the self-knowledge that they and 'human wisdom' fall short of divinity. Socrates also does not appear to reject conventional religious practises *in general*, but only the narrowly self-interested motives underlying their common observance (cf. Xenophon, *Memorabilia* 1.2.64; *Ap*. 10–12). This activity can also be explained as being compatible with the demands of piety reconceived as philosophizing (see McPherran 2000).

In his later, more constructive and less aporetic work, Plato moves beyond this deflationary sense of philosophical piety when he becomes more optimistic than his teacher regarding the capacity of human beings to cross the traditional gap separating the human from the divine in respect of knowledge, wisdom and power. Plato's philosophical theology offered the unsocratic hope of an afterlife of intimate form contemplation by our souls in the realm of divinity (*Phd.* 79c–84b; *R.* 490a–b; *Phdr.* 247d–e). It was influenced on the one hand by Socrates' new intellectualist conception of piety as elenctic 'caring of the soul' (*Ap.* 29d–30b) and the success of the methods of the mathematicians of his day that he took to overcome the limitations of Socrates' elenctic method (Vlastos 1991a:ch. 4) (q.v. Method), and on the other by the aim at human-initiated divine status (especially immortality) as expressed by some of the newer, post-Hesiodic religious forms that had entered into Greece. Self-knowledge on Plato's scheme leads not so much to an appreciation of limits, then, as to the realization that we are ourselves divinities: immortal intellects that already have within them – if only we can but recollect it – all the knowledge there is to be had (*Men.* 81c–d; *Phd.* 72e–7e; *Smp.* 210a–11b) (q.v. Recollection). Platonic piety is now marked by its insistence that we engage in the intellectual project of 'becoming like god' (e.g. *Tht.* 176a–7c; *Smp.* 209e–12b; Laws 715e–18a; see further McPherran 1996:ch. 5; Morgan 1990) (q.v. Theology; Religion).

In such a scheme, the central task of human existence becomes less a matter of assisting gods and more a matter of becoming as much like them as one can. This fact, plus the more complex psychology Plato develops in *R.* bk 4, may explain Plato's decision to no longer count piety as a cardinal virtue (*R.* 427e–8a). For, it seems that prior to this text Plato had come to the view that there is little internal difference between the knowledge of how to do what is just towards gods (piety) and the knowledge of how to do what is just towards mortals (secular justice); as a result, piety as a form of psychic virtue seems to be nothing other than an aspect of generic psychic justice. So, although Plato continues to speak of pious actions in *R.*, and after piety

as a virtue is subsumed under the virtue of justice (and wisdom) as a whole, the phrase 'just and pious' is assumed to refer to generic justice.

PLEASURE (*HÊDONÊ*)

Dorothea Frede

Plato treats pleasure (*hêdonê*) as the generic name of any kind of positive state of mind (perception, emotion, experience or insight). The same is true of its counterpart pain (*lupê*). Depending on the context, translations vary between pleasure, delight, amusement or lust (cf. *Philebus* 11b). From the early and middle to the late dialogues the conception of pleasure undergoes quite some development, with a significant differentiation of the evaluation of pleasure's role in human life (Gosling and Taylor 1984).

In the so-called early Socratic dialogues pleasure is not addressed except in passing but in later Socratic dialogues, especially, the *Gorgias* (493d–500d), it is associated with desire (*epithumia*) and explained as the compensation of a lack. This leads to a fundamental critique of pleasure: desire as such is insatiable, pleasure is necessarily mixed with pain and includes bad physical and psychological states of excitement. In addition, pleasure is experienced by both good and evil persons alike so that criteria of differentiation are needed if pleasure is to be regarded as a good at all. The *Phaedo* (especially 64c–6d) associates pleasure and desire with the body and blames them for all evils to humankind such as sickness, discord and war, so that true philosophers avoid such disturbances of the mind. The exception among the early dialogues is the *Protagoras* where Socrates in his final argument for the unity of the virtues forces the famous sophist to accept the definition of virtue as the 'art of measuring pleasure and pain' (351b–7e). Whether or not Plato is serious about this argument is still a matter of debate, but 'enlightened hedonism' of this type remains unique in his work. It is hard to see how Socrates could combine his concern for the care for one's soul (q.v.) with the advocacy of an undifferentiated hedonism where the size of pleasures and pains is all that counts.

The dialogues of Plato's middle period from the *Republic* to the *Phaedrus* retain an overall critical attitude towards pleasure as long as it is associated with the lowest part of the soul. Education (q.v.) through music and gymnastics is to lead to better forms of pleasure (*R.* 3.403d–4d), and the members of the ruling class can reach a harmonious equilibrium with respect to pleasure and pain (*R.* 6.462a–4d). While pleasure and knowledge are at one point presented as unsatisfactory rivals for the title of the highest good (*R.* 6.505c–d), in bk 9 Plato stages a competition between different kinds of pleasure and finally assigns first prize to the philosopher's pleasures (*R.* 583c–5a). In that argument Plato provides an explanation of the nature of pleasure and of the difference between 'real pleasures' and 'bastard pleasures.' Between pleasure and pain there is a neutral state, free from either pleasure or pain; the motion from pain to the neutral, middle state is a mere semblance of pleasure, in contradistinction to the motion from the neutral state to that of true pleasure, which is at the same time explained as a 'filling with what is really real' – that is, with what is true and pure, uncontaminated by the body. The value of pleasure therefore depends on the quality of the respective 'filling' (*R.* 585a–7c). The *Symposium* and the *Phdr.* are not explicitly concerned with pleasure, but their incisive

treatment of love (q.v.) for the beautiful as an incentive to the higher and better shows that Plato no longer maintains a rigid separation of soul and body (cf. *Smp.* 210a–12b; *Phdr.* 253d–6e).

The *R.* gives some indications concerning the nature of pleasure as a filling or motion. For example, in bk 9, the nature of the filling depends not only on the nature of the 'filling' (of soul vs. of body) but also on the nature of what each is being 'filled' with (forms vs. sensible object); but this does not lead to a proper definition (Frede 1985). This question is finally addressed and settled in the *Phlb.*, by general consensus one of Plato's last works. Pleasure is there presented once again as the rival of knowledge (q.v.) in a contest for the highest good in human life (*Phlb.* 11a–c). But this time pleasure and its different kinds are subject to a careful investigation that leads to a definition of both pleasure and pain: while pain is the disturbance or disruption of the natural equilibrium in an organism, pleasure is its restoration (31b–6e). Such disturbances and restorations can affect both body and soul, separately and in combination, and hence there is a host of different types of pleasures and pains. In addition, in his critique of pleasure Plato gives a systematic treatment of the possibility of truth and falsity that had been left in a less than satisfactory state in *R.* bk 9. The discussion points out four quite different types of falsehood (*Phlb.* 36c–50e): (a) pleasures that have a propositional content – enjoying something that is not the case; (b) overrated pleasures; (c) the confusion of pleasure with freedom from pain; and (d) pleasures inextricably mixed with pain. This distinction permits Plato to pinpoint as true and pure all those pleasures that are free from those flaws, and to justify the conclusion that the best human state consists of a mixture of knowledge and pure pleasures (59d–64b). If the *Phlb.* ends the long-standing tug-of-war between knowledge and pleasure in Plato's work, it does not justify the conclusion that he should thereby be regarded as an enlightened hedonist. Pleasure, in its best form, represents only a second-rate good, because even its true and pure kinds are only the filling of an 'unfelt lack', and is due to the necessarily deficient status of human beings and its constant need of supplementation and replenishment in both soul and body (Harte 2004).

This clarification of the nature of pleasure and pain may be presupposed but is not explicitly addressed in Plato's last work, the *Laws*, where pleasure and pain are assigned an important role in the education of the second best city's inhabitants (*Lg.* 1.631a–2b). The importance of handling pleasure and pain in the right way is symbolized by the comparison of the human soul with a puppet that is controlled by pleasure and pain as if by iron strings, which in turn ought to be directed by the golden thread of reason and law (*Lg.* 1.644c–5d). Thus pleasure and pain remain important forces of motivation in Plato's conception of human nature; they stand in need of careful orchestration by the means of education and legislation.

POETRY (*POIÊSIS*)

Elizabeth Belfiore

Socrates' statements at the beginning of *Republic* bk 10 sum up the ambivalent and complex attitudes towards poetry represented in Plato's dialogues. After claiming that *mimêtic* poetry is harmful to all who do not know the truth, Socrates says that he must speak about this harm 'even though a certain affection (*philia*) and reverence for

Homer that has possessed me from childhood opposes my speaking' (*R.* 10.595b–c). Socrates later uses the stronger word *erôs* to refer to his love of poetry (607e7). Plato's own intense love for the poetry his Socrates condemns is evident throughout the dialogues, in which poetry is frequently quoted, and poetic language often used.

In the *R.*, Socrates first condemns the use of poetry like that of Homer and Hesiod to educate the young (bks 2 and 3), arguing that it misrepresents the gods as deceitful and harmful, and provides bad role models in the form of heroes who lack courage and self-control. He then claims, in a context not restricted to education (bk 10), that poetry and other forms of *mimêsis* (imitation, q.v.) misrepresent the truth, and appeals to an inferior part of the soul. Socrates' 'greatest accusation' is that poetry corrupts even 'the best of us'. According to Socrates, we think it right to endure our own sorrows as calmly as possible, but we do not believe that it is shameful to enjoy poetry in which someone acts in ways that we would condemn in real life. For this reason, we 'let down our guard' when we hear poetry, pitying and sympathizing with someone who grieves excessively. By thus feeding and strengthening the wailing part of our soul, we make it harder to restrain our own sorrows (605c–6d; Belfiore 1983). Socrates concludes that the only kinds of poetry that should be accepted into the city are 'hymns to the gods and encomia of good people' (607a). In *Laws* bk 2, the Athenian adopts this same rule when he states that the lawgiver must persuade or compel the poet to compose poems about 'men who are self-controlled, courageous and good in all ways' (*Lg.* 660a). Indeed, he says, tragic poets must not be allowed to speak in opposition to their rivals, the lawgivers, whom he calls 'poets of the best tragedy', because they are creators of the polity that is a *mimêsis* of the best life (*R.* 7.817a–d). In these dialogues, then, poetry is given a positive role within the city only when it conforms to rigorous ethical and religious standards. Little of traditional Greek poetry, especially that of Homer, Hesiod and the tragedians, is acceptable.

The *Ion* has sometimes been thought to express a more positive view of poetry, especially that of Homer. In this dialogue, the rhapsode Ion, a professional reciter of Homer's poems, claims that he has access to more than human knowledge because he is possessed by the same divine inspiration (q.v.) under whose influence the poets themselves compose. However, the way in which Ion arrives at this claim gives us reason to doubt that Socrates himself is represented as agreeing with it. Ion first claims that he has skill (*technê*, q.v.) concerning chariot racing, generalship and other matters about which Homer speaks. Socrates then questions Ion, casting doubt on the truth of his claim, and suggesting that Ion may be deceiving his audience about his skill and knowledge. Socrates finally forces Ion to choose between being considered an unjust deceiver or a 'divine man'. Only at this point does Ion say that he prefers to be considered 'divine', that is, divinely inspired (*Ion* 542a–b). Indeed, the view of the inspired poet in this dialogue is just as negative as it is in *Phaedrus* 248d–e, where the life of a poet is ranked only sixth in a hierarchy of nine, and in *Apology* 22a–c, where Socrates says that poets are 'enthusiastic', that is, divinely inspired, rather than wise, and that they not only know less about their own poems than anyone in their audience but also falsely believe that they are the wisest of all people in other respects as well.

Nevertheless, Plato's own love for poetry, especially that of the poets his Socrates most strongly condemns, is apparent throughout the dialogues, which contain, for example, 117 quotations from Homer and 13 from Hesiod (Brandwood 1976). These quotations serve a variety of functions (Halliwell 2000; Vicaire 1960:76–192). Some illustrate ethical points (*R.* 3.390d, quoting *Odyssey* 20.17–18, where Odysseus restrains his anger against the maids); others demonstrate Socrates' superior knowledge of poetry (*Protagoras* 338e–47a, where Socrates quotes and interprets Simonides); some serve to characterize interlocutors (e.g. the speakers in the *Symposium* quote poetry in support of their ideas (Belfiore, forthcoming)). The dialogues also contain many poetical passages of Plato's own invention, and even some metrical phrases (e.g. *Phdr.* 241d1; and *Smp.* 197d1–e5; Dover 1980:124). Most of Plato's own poetical passages are used, like the quotations, for philosophical purposes. For example, at the end of his speech containing the myth of the chariot, Socrates says that he spoke 'in poetic words' in order to turn Phaedrus towards a philosophical life (*Phdr.* 257a–b), and he states that the myth of Er might persuade his interlocutors to pursue justice and wisdom (*R.* 621c).

Plato's dialogues, then, invite us to consider ways in which love for poetry can be safely indulged, even leading to philosophical insight. Not all of traditional poetry is harmful, and Plato's own myths (q.v.) present philosophical ideas in poetic language. Moreover, by critically questioning even potentially harmful poetry, as Socrates does, we can acquire the countercharm that will allow us to listen to it without being deceived (*R.* 10.608a). Moreover, Socrates' treatment of one particular tragic poet, Agathon, suggests that it may also be possible to reform the poets themselves. After Agathon gives an encomium of Eros filled with poetic quotations, Socrates subjects him to an *elenchus* (q.v.) that demonstrates that Agathon, like Ion, does not know what he is talking about (*Smp*. 199c–201c). Unlike Ion, however, who takes refuge in the unexamined claim that he is divinely inspired, Agathon readily admits his ignorance (201b11–12). Socrates responds with a punning compliment, stating that Eros lacks (or needs) 'the good' (*agathôn*), and refers to Agathon as 'beloved' (201c). That Agathon is willing to learn from Socrates is also apparent at the end of the dialogue, when he is eager to be praised by Socrates once again, even though he thereby risks receiving a kind of 'praise' that Agathon called '*hybris*' (insolence) in an earlier encounter (175e, 223a). Significantly, Agathon is the last of the symposiasts to remain awake talking to Socrates (223d). The example of Agathon, then, suggests that a poet may be able to acquire the kind of wisdom that Socrates has, that of knowing his own lack of wisdom, if he is willing to question and examine his ideas rather than merely attempting to give pleasure to an ignorant audience. His poems will then convey this kind of wisdom, as well as giving pleasure by means of poetic language and meter. Indeed, Plato's dialogues show that if poetry is used philosophically, that is, subjected to examination, it can contribute to the search for wisdom.

POLIS (see City)

POLITICS AND THE FIGURE OF THE POLITICUS

Melissa Lane

Politicus, or 'statesman', is the Latinized form of the Greek *politikos*, a term which 'may well ... be a Platonic innovation' (Rowe 1995:1).

Certainly Plato is the first ancient Athenian author to make the *politikos* central to his account of politics. To appreciate the significance of Plato's formulation of this figure, we must begin by observing how different it was from prevailing figures in Athenian politics. Athenians at the time spoke of their political leaders primarily as the *rhêtores kai stratêgoi*, 'orators and generals', so naming those men who regularly swayed the Assembly or were elected annually as military leaders (Hansen 1991:266). In the fifth century, these two circles tended to overlap, with Pericles, for example, owing his influence both to his prowess in swaying Assembly deliberations and to his regular reelection as a general. If Athenians wanted to speak of these men in another way, they called them *dêmagôgoi*, which is best translated not by the modern pejorative term 'demagogues' but simply as 'political leaders' (see Finley 1985:69 for the neutral use, though elsewhere he accepts a pejorative use). Notice that 'orators and generals' is a description of a plurality, a small group. Political leadership in Athens was understood as consisting in a small group of sometime rivals, sometime collaborators. If the Athenians sought the image of a singular political leader elevated in kind above all others, they found this in the historical figure of the lawgiver (*nomothetês*) Solon, who like Lycurgus in Sparta had established fundamental laws for his city. Yet, having done so, these lawgivers did not take part in its daily political life: Solon voluntarily left Athens for 10 years, while Lycurgus left Sparta never to return.

With the legendary lawgiver on the one hand, and the rivalling groups of orators and generals on the other, the Athenians would have found the conception of a 'statesman' who was unique, yet who played a part in ordinary political affairs, to be alien. Yet this was the figure of the *politikos* whom Plato developed, in a direct challenge to the norms of the Athenian democracy. Plato did this in at least two ways. The first draws on his discussion in the *Gorgias*, which both criticizes the leading fifth-century orators and generals and proposes Socrates as a rival to them; the second, on the *Euthydemus* and the *Plt.*, in which the notion of a *politikê technê* ('political art' or 'political craft') and of the figure of the *politikos* defined by his knowledge of that art or science (*epistêmê*) are developed respectively. In refuting the aggressive and ambitious Callicles in the *Grg.*, Socrates undertakes an examination of the admired fifth-century orators and generals who had succeeded in winning the power in the city which Callicles argues one should seek. In line with the amateur character of all Athenian political leaders, as democratic citizens who achieve a temporary and mainly informal influence among their peers, he begins by considering simply whether Pericles, Cimon, Miltiades and Themistocles were 'good citizens' (*Grg.* 515d). The argument against their being so hinges on their having failed to make the Athenians virtuous, a failure demonstrated in the censures and rebukes which each of them suffered at least once at the hands of the people. Socrates then generalizes this point to propose by contrast a 'true political craft' (*hôs alêthôs politikê technê*; 521c7). Such an art would consist in making speeches aiming not at what is pleasant but at what is best (521d8–10). The standard of the good (q.v.) as the aim of the true statesman links the fundamental orientation of this account to the standard of the good as the aim of politics developed in the *Republic*, even though that dialogue does not refer to its (plural) philosopher-rulers by the singular term *politikos*.

A striking feature of the *Grg.* is Socrates' reference to himself within it. The proposed account of the 'true political art' quoted above is actually embedded in a Socratic self-diagnosis: 'I believe that I'm one of a few Athenians – so as not to say I'm the only one, but the only one among our contemporaries – to take up (*epicheirein*) the true political craft and practise the true politics (*prattein ta politika*)' (521c6–8). The verb *epicheirein* has the connotation of trying to do something rather than necessarily succeeding at it. In other words, Socrates sees himself as alone among his contemporaries in adopting the correct orientation for politics, in aiming at the good rather than the pleasant, but he does not here claim to have the knowledge or skill necessary to succeed in doing so.

The idea that the *politikê technê* must consist in full knowledge, rather than intention alone, is underlined in other dialogues, most notably the *Euthd.* There, between battles with a pair of shameless sophists, Socrates discusses with the young Clinias knowledge as the only art which can make a man happy and fortunate (*Euthd.* 277d–82e). What kind of knowledge is that? Socrates first dismisses the art of speechwriting (an identification which the *Grg.* reference to 'speeches' might unwisely suggest) or that of generalship: in other words, with the very arts exercised by the Athenian orators and generals. Instead, it is the 'statesman's art', also described as the 'kingly art' which makes the citizens it governs 'wise and good' (292b4, 292c4–5).

Although the *Euthd.* ends without resolving exactly what 'wise and good' here means, or how the statesman's art can cultivate these virtues in the citizens, the idea of a kingly art which defines the figure of the statesman is the central topic of the *Plt.* There, a stranger from Elea leads a discussion which eventually distinguishes the statesman from his closest rivals: identified as the orators, the generals and the jurors (these last exercising an office which any male Athenian citizen could occupy). Statecraft – now articulated as the distinctive knowledge of the *politikos*, rather than simply a generic 'political art' – is not to be identified with the knowledge of any of the practical arts, but rather as controlling the exercise of those forms of knowledge (*Plt.* 305d1–2). In particular, its role is to distinguish the 'right time' from the 'wrong time' to 'begin and set in motion the most important things in cities'. The statesman's knowledge is essentially temporal (*Plt.* 305d2–4; Lane 1998).

The Eleatic stranger goes on to define statecraft even more broadly as the art 'that controls all of these [the arts of oratory, generalship, and judging], and the laws, and cares for every aspect of things in the city, weaving everything together in the most correct way' (*Plt.* 305e2–6). Here, he draws on his earlier use of weaving as a model for statecraft, and will go on to suggest that the statesman's peculiar task is to weave together two rival groups of citizens, characterized by opposing tendencies to misidentify the correct time for initiating action. By binding together these two groups through appropriate intermarriages and shared opinions, the statesman can engender in them the ability to identify the right time for action and so embody his political art in the polity as a whole (305e–11c).

It remains a question whether the statesman must remain present in the city and what his function in doing so would be. The Eleatic stranger earlier compares the statesman to an athletics trainer who issues written instructions to his charges to cover his periodic absences. Certainly, the statesman's function is extraconstitutional, in that he does not occupy any of the ordinary offices or magistracies, but exercises his art at one remove, shaping the conditions in which the citizens exercise the magistracies (and so connecting to the political structure of the *Laws*, another dialogue which does not speak of the figure of the *politikos*). Plato's figure of the *politikos* embodies – in certain dialogues – his fundamental claim which remains consistent across the dialogues as a whole: that politics must be based on the rule of knowledge, aiming at the good.

REALITY (see Appearance and Reality)

REASON

Fred D. Miller, Jr.

The idea of reason is fundamental throughout Plato's philosophy. His terms *logos, nous, dianoia, phronêsis* and related words often correspond to 'reason' as understood by modern philosophers.

Socrates is depicted as the champion of reason. Rather than accepting other people's opinions, Socrates professes to listen only to the argument (*logos*) that seems best to him on reflection (*Crito* 46b). He would rather disagree with the majority than to contradict himself, even though he is only one person. Making no claim to wisdom he is grateful to anyone who can refute him because this will only bring him closer to the truth (*Gorgias* 482c, 506a–c). In his quest for wisdom Socrates employs the method of elenchus (q.v.). In *Meno* and *Phaedo* he supplements it with the hypothetical method and theory of recollection (q.v.). The main focus of the present article will be on the account of reason in *Republic* and later dialogues.

Throughout Plato's dialogues reasoning (*logismos*) and thought (*dianoia*) are ascribed to the soul (q.v.) as opposed to the body. For example, in *Phd.* the soul reasons (*logizetai*) best about true reality when it is unimpeded by bodily perceptions and desires (*Phd.* 64c–7e). In *R.*, however, reasoning belongs to the soul's rational faculty (*logistikon*), which is distinguished from the spirited and appetitive 'parts' of the soul (*R.* bk 4.435e–41c). This tripartite psychology is present in other dialogues: in *Phaedrus* 246a reason is compared to a charioteer guiding a winged soul-chariot; in *Timaeus* 69c–71e the rational soul is located in the head while the spirited and appetitive souls are consigned to the chest and abdomen; in *Laws* 1.644e–5a in the comparison of a human beings with a 'puppet of the gods' reasoning (*logismos*) is a 'golden and holy' cord which pulls us towards certain actions in opposition to other cords.

In Plato's epistemology (q.v.) thought (*dianoia*) involves two powers: knowledge (*epistêmê*) by which one knows a form such as the beautiful itself, and opinion (*doxa*) by which one opines about perceptible objects such as beautiful sights and sounds (*R.* bk 5.476d; *Ti.* 27d–8a). Knowledge has superior epistemic status (i.e. infallibility) because its objects are more intelligible due to their higher ontological status: the objects of knowledge are eternal and unvarying, while objects of opinion are perishable and mutable. Light is also shed on the different modes of reason by the metaphor of the divided line (q.v.) in *R.* bk 6.509d–11e. Opinion is subdivided into belief (*pistis*) concerning visible objects like animals and plants, and imagination (*eikasia*), which concerns images (e.g. reflections) of these visible objects. Knowledge also has two subdivisions: intelligence (*noêsis*), which is concerned with the

forms and ultimately the form of the good, and discursive thought (*dianoia* in a narrow sense). With discursive thought the soul uses perceptible objects as images of the forms and starts from unexamined hypotheses to derive conclusions, as in the case of geometry or arithmetic. With intelligence the soul eschews images and derives first principles from hypotheses using forms themselves.

Reason (*logos*) itself grasps the intelligible object by the power of dialectic, treating these hypotheses not as first principles but really as hypotheses, in order to go up to what is non-hypothetical and reach the principle of everything. After grasping the principle, reason, reversing itself and holding on to what follows from it, in this way descends to a conclusion making use of nothing visible at all, but, instead, of forms themselves, through them and into them, and it ends in forms. (*R.* bk 6.511b; cf. *R.* bk 7.533c–d)

Intelligence thus has two stages: ascent to a first principle through dialectic (q.v.), and descent from principle to conclusion. This leaves open important questions. For example, can Plato's sharp distinction between knowledge and belief be defended without positing a two world ontology? (for contrasting interpretations, see Cherniss 1936 and Fine 1990) Can reason achieve genuine knowledge independently of perception? Is the distinction between reason and perception all that clear since reason is required to make judgements about perceptible objects (*Tht.* 186c–d; see Burnyeat 1990:52–65 and Cooper 1970)? Further, even though *logos* can be translated as 'speech' and 'account' as well as 'reason', how closely are the three notions connected for Plato? Does knowledge always require giving an account? *Men.* 98a states that belief falls short of knowledge unless we can give an account, but *Tht.* 210a finds fault with the definition of knowledge as true belief with an account (see Taylor 2008). Again, *Sph.* 263e describes thought (*dianoia*) as silent discourse (*dialogos*), but *Ep.* 7.343a complains of the weakness of words (*logoi*) and declares that nobody with intelligence (*nous*) will be so bold as to place his thoughts in them, especially unalterable written symbols. Must the deliverances of reason have the form of propositional knowledge (q.v.)?

In Plato's psychology and normative theory the rational faculty opposes the other psychic faculties, for example, when someone wants to drink yet is unwilling to do so, because he reasons that it would be harmful (*R.* bk 4.436a–9d). It does not merely deliberate about how to satisfy one's appetites, but has its own desires for knowledge of the truth and its own pleasures taken in learning (*R.* bk 9.580a–1c). The rational part ought to rule, 'since it is really wise and exercises foresight on behalf of the whole soul' (441e). The rule of reason is the basis for the four cardinal virtues (442b–3e). Again, questions arise (see Annas 1981): Is the rational part a sort of agent or homunculus or is it merely a nexus of capacities? And is reason in fact the 'natural ruler', or is Hume right to rejoin that 'reason is, and ought to be, the slave of the passions?'

The rule of reason also has political import. Like the soul the city has a tripartite structure, with guardian, auxiliary and ruling classes. The guardians should be guided by reason; indeed, they should be philosopher-rulers: 'unless political power and philosophy coincide, there will be no respite for cities from evils' (*R.* bk 5.473c–d). Conceding the impracticality of philosopher-rule, in *Politicus* and *Lg.* the linchpin of rational rule becomes the statesman or legislator: 'opposing the greatest desires and having no human ally, all alone he will follow reason (*logos*) alone' (*Lg.* 8.835c). The rule of reason implies the rule of law: 'reason (*logos*), striving to become law', commands the citizens to avoid the desires that drag them down (*Lg.* 8.835e). This dialogue notes the linguistic similarity between *nomos* (law) and *nous* (intelligence). But this again raises questions (see Miller 2005). In particular, granting the need for rationality in politics, is the rule of reason compatible with the practises of democracy?

Plato suggests that out of all the human faculties reason has the greatest claim to immortality. At *R.* bk 10.611b–2a, the pure state of the soul is compared to the sea god Glaucus whose primary nature cannot be easily made out because he is so mutilated by waves and encrusted by shells, stones and so forth. The soul's true nature is distinguished by its love of philosophy, the hallmark of the rational faculty (cf. *R.* bk 9.581b). More explicitly *Ti.* 69c–70b (cf. *Ti.* 42e) describes the rational soul alone as 'immortal', the other 'mortal' souls being created later.

Plato also explores the role of reason on the cosmic scale, in the myth of *Ti.* the god (demiurge) who created the perceptible universe, wanting to make it as like himself as possible (*Ti.* 30b). If the cosmos (world order) does not exhibit perfect order it is because it resulted from 'the conjunction of necessity and intelligence' (48a). Similarly *Lg.* 10.893b–9b argues that the heavenly motions are due to immortal self-moving souls, and the motions are orderly if the souls are intelligent. Orderly cosmic motion involves continuous revolution around a central point, a physical motion which most closely resembles the cyclical motion of intelligence (*nous*) or understanding (*phronêsis*) itself (*Lg.* 10.898a; *Ti.* 34a).

Although Plato's radical claims on behalf of reason were challenged by his successors, starting with Aristotle, they continued to have a profound influence, notably on early modern rationalism (q.v.).

RECOLLECTION *(ANAMNÊSIS)*

Dorothea Frede

Given the importance that is attributed in the secondary literature to the notion that Plato explains learning as the recollection (*anamnêsis*) of prenatal knowledge that needs to be retrieved, because it has been covered up at the moment of the soul's embodiment, newcomers to Plato will be surprised to learn that explicit discussion of this doctrine is confined to two of Plato's works, the *Meno* and the *Phaedo* (with a brief reminder in *Phaedrus* 249c). When recollection is referred to elsewhere (mostly in verbal form, but occasionally as a noun, *Philebus* 34b–c), it means just what corresponding terms mean in English, that is, reminders of ordinary experience, most of all concerning previous agreements in the discussion.

In the *Men.* recollection is introduced as Socrates' solution to Meno's 'paradox of learning:' How one is to search for something one does not know at all, for even if one came across it, one would not recognize it as the thing one did not know (*Men.* 80d). Socrates does not directly challenge the paradox but resorts to the mythical explanation of 'wise men and women, priests and priestesses' that the soul (q.v.) is immortal, has undergone many deaths and rebirths and has therefore 'seen all things' so that it needs only to recollect what has once been known (81a–e). To illustrate how such recollection works Socrates conducts an experiment. A slave without training in geometry manages, thanks to careful questioning and a drawing

in the sand that makes use of Pythagoras' theorem, to solve the problem of how to double the area of a given square (82b–5b). As critics never tire of pointing out, the experiment proves only that with the help of suggestive questions and a drawing a layperson can be made to recognize certain basic geometrical truths (Scott 2006:99–112). In addition, it presupposes a Socrates who not only possesses the art of questioning but also knows the problem's solution beforehand. Against this it should be objected that Plato himself actually claims no more than that Socrates' questioning has stirred up opinions 'like in a dream' that only with further practise will eventually turn into knowledge (*Men.* 85c–d). It is unclear whether Plato wants to limit such 'recollectable' knowledge to mathematical truths. Nor is it clear to what extent he wants to support the myth of successive births and deaths, for in his subsequent distinction of true opinion and knowledge (q.v.) he remarks that true opinions are elusive goods 'until one ties them down by an account of the reason why. And that is recollection, as we previously agreed (98a)' (Scott 2006:182–5). Plato may therefore limit recollection to the soul's innate capacity to comprehend nonempirical truths, like those of mathematics (q.v.), that will first emerge as true opinions and through further reflection turn into knowledge proper. In addition, mathematical geniuses can and do 'find' such truths without outside help, so that the most gifted among us seem to be 'born' with the requisite knowledge.

Whether or not Plato saw the limitation of his account in the *Men.*, the explanation of recollection in *Phd.* (after a reference back to the model in the *Men.*; *Phd.* 72e–3b) takes a different turn. Instead of a recollection of mathematical theorems prompted by suggestive questions, recollection is now triggered by sense-perceptions and concerns single objects, the objects' intelligible concepts or forms (q.v.). Their sensible reminders need not be like them: just as in everyday life both things that are like and unlike can cause the recollection of something that is absent. The point of such recollection is explained by simple examples such as sticks and stones and their seeming equality and inequality (74a–5c). The point, in a nutshell, is that merely looking at two sticks and stones does not provide certainty that they are really equal to one another; sometimes they appear so, sometimes they do not. With the equal itself there is no such ambiguity, it never appears unequal, and hence it is not possible that the knowledge of the equal itself is derived from experience of sensible objects in this life, but humans have an innate knowledge of the equal or equality. In contradistinction to the form their earthly representatives 'are eager to be like it (the equal itself), but are merely *like* it' and always fall short of it. If such knowledge cannot be caused by experience of deficient objects it must have been acquired before birth and exists in a latent form that is subsequently recalled by an encounter with imperfect earthly specimens. This argument lets Plato conclude that the forms, as perfect beings, must really exist and with 'equal necessity' that our souls must have existed before birth (75c–6e). There is no determination of the types of things that have forms, but enumerations show that they are of quite different sorts: there is the equal as well as the greater and smaller, the beautiful itself (q.v. Beauty), the good itself (q.v.), the just (q.v. Justice), the pious (q.v. Piety) and 'all those things which we mark with the seal of 'what it itself is' (*auto ho estin*), both when we are putting questions and answering them' (75c–d). Earlier in the *Phd.* Socrates had added health, strength and tallness to his

catalogue of virtues (65d–e); thus, forms are not confined to concepts of moral or mathematical perfection but include physical properties, as well as relative terms.

In the *Republic*, the central work of Plato's middle years, recollection is not resorted to, and this is no accident; for the careful design of higher education that takes 15 years to complete seems to replace the notion that humans are born with the requisite knowledge. The senses in the *R.* do not provoke recollection, but instead conflicting impressions act as incentives to the higher learning that is ultimately crowned by dialectic (q.v.), the enigmatic discipline that is the hallmark of the philosopher-kings and -queens. The only dialogue that mentions recollection in the sense presupposed in the *Men.* and the *Phd.* is the *Phdr.* (249c). But that reference serves as a mediator between the mythical depiction of the soul's travel to a 'superheavenly' place in the wake of the gods and the subsequent demythologized explanation of the dialectical method of collection and division, the uncovering of the generic unity of the objects of a given field and the subsequent division into its different species. If there is a place for recollection in Plato's later work, it must consist in the ability to discover the relevant unities at the different levels of universality that is sometimes addressed as a 'divine gift' (*Phdr.* 266b; *Phlb.* 16c).

REFUTATION (see Elenchus)

RHETORIC (*RHETORIKÊ*)

Marina McCoy

Plato's *Gorgias* succinctly defines rhetoric as the 'art of persuasion' (*Grg.* 452e), but in several Platonic dialogues, the question as to rhetoric's scope and value is a topic of considerable debate. To understand the nuances behind the Platonic understanding of rhetoric, it is helpful to look at both the cultural context for rhetoric's practise and the philosophical issues that Plato raises regarding rhetoric's definition and value. The Greek term for rhetoric, *rhetorikê*, is derived from the word *rhetôr*, or speaker. In democratic Athens, the democracy consisted of an assembly at which any Greek citizen could both speak on matters of legislation and vote. Those who were known for speaking regularly and with influence were known as 'rhetors'. Thus, the term from its inception has a political as well as an oratorical significance. In his dialogues, Plato examines not only the relationship between rhetoric and philosophy but also between rhetoric and politics, and whether rhetoric might have a corrupting influence on politicians.

Some commentators have suggested that Plato may have coined the term *rhetorikê*, as the word appears in no extant works prior to the Platonic dialogues (Schiappa 1994), with the exception of Alcidamas. Not only Plato, but also intellectuals such as the sophists, Isocrates (q.v.) and Alcidamas wrote about the value of speech in political, forensic and private arenas. But the Platonic dialogues most forcefully and directly undertake the examination of rhetoric's value and its relation to philosophy and sophistry.

In Plato's *Grg.* Socrates sets out one of the strongest critiques of rhetoric in the dialogues, raising at least two important questions in talking to Gorgias: whether rhetoric is a *technê* (art); and whether rhetoricians teach justice as part of that art (Roochnik 1998). Socrates implies that Gorgias is careless about whether his students are made more just or unjust by the course of his teaching. Socrates also argues that rhetoric is not a

technê, but a mere 'knack' (*Grg.* 463b). Just as a cook might entice children with sweets, while a physician recommends healthy food, the rhetorician appeals to his audience with the aim of gratifying them, instead of speaking about what is best (464–5e). Socrates describes rhetoric as the 'counterpart of cookery in the soul' (465e). Later parts of the *Grg.* associate the practise of rhetoric in politics with the corruption of justice, as with the character of Callicles, who recommends the life of unbridled appetites as the best.

Plato's *Phaedrus*, on the other hand, presents the possibility of a philosophical rhetoric in contrast to that of sophistic oratory. After critiquing the orator Lysias' paradoxical speech on love, Socrates offers a myth in defence of love that surpasses Lysias' speech in style and content, suggesting the legitimacy of a mythological mode of speaking as a way to present philosophical ideas. Socrates then describes a positive form of rhetoric that uses a method of collection and division (q.v. Method) that draws together what one wishes to explain into a common category, and then divides it again according to its 'natural joints' (*Phdr.* 265d–e). Ideally, a speaker's discourse should be well ordered, like a 'living being' (264c). Later, the *Phdr.* takes on the question as to whether the spoken or written word is more rhetorically and philosophically valuable. On the one hand, Socrates suggests that written speech cannot address its audience with attention to their specific needs, and can easily be misunderstood when it is 'orphaned' with its 'parent' unable to defend it. On the other hand, this critique of writing takes place within the context of a written dialogue, leading some commentators to suggest that Plato may have understood the dialogue form as overcoming some of the limitations of writing (Annas 2002; Gonzalez 1995b; Griswold 1998).

Subsequently, some commentators have taken up the question of how dialogue itself functions as a rhetorical practise (Blondell 2002; Gordon 1999; Michelini 2003; Scott 2007). We also find that many Platonic dialogues feature Socrates using well known rhetorical techniques, often with the apparent aim of upsetting his interlocutor's conventional views, or as an enticement to practise philosophy (Gonzalez 1995b; McCoy 2007). Plato's critique of rhetoric is also closely linked to his criticism of poetry in works such as the *Ion* and *Republic* (Griswold 2009). As with the rhetoricians, the poets often represent and imitate reality in ways that are opposed to a philosophical orientation to the world (Rosen 1988). Again, this picture is complicated by Plato's own practise of writing dialogues that themselves frequently use myths, images and diverse forms of argument that overlap with the practise of rhetoricians and poets. Indeed, one might even suggest that the Platonic 'voice' of the dialogues is found not only in Socrates' claims about rhetoric, but also in the ideas of his opponents, who raise important objections to Socrates' practise, such as whether it is politically expedient (*Grg.* 486a–c).

Perhaps one way to reconcile the difficulty is to suggest that Plato's polemic is against those who use rhetoric to flatter and to manipulate, while the use of persuasive and beautiful language to question, to arouse discomfort about our own views and to entice us into further inquiry allows philosophy and rhetoric to go hand-in-hand. While sophistic rhetoric seeks only to gratify its audience, philosophical rhetoric seeks to lead the soul to further inquiry and reflection, and to the good itself. By including both advocates and critics of rhetoric in the dialogues, Plato encourages his readers to seek to understand more deeply the question of how one ought to live one's life.

SELF-KNOWLEDGE

Andrea Tschemplik

Concern for self-knowledge recurs in Plato's writings, although no single dialogue deals exclusively with it and it is often introduced indirectly (Annas 1985).

The ancient Delphic inscription 'Know Thyself' (*gnôthi s'auton*) was widely understood as a reminder to know one's limits as a human being; humans, after all, are not gods. It then comes as no surprise that Socrates proclaims the limits of his own knowledge at the end of his life: 'when I do not know, neither do I think I know' (*Apology* 21d). This awareness of one's ignorance can be understood as a kind of self-knowledge, and the *Ap.* shows that such knowledge also informs a way of living. Self-knowledge can be an ethical as well as an epistemological quest. The *Charmides* illustrates the difficulties of seeing self-knowledge strictly as a problem of knowledge, not involving the good. *Alcibiades I* on the other hand analyses self-knowledge as the activity of caring for the soul. In the *Phaedrus* we see the most complex formulation, where the erotic exchanges between lover and beloved ultimately lead to recognition of the self in the other. If the knowledge of ignorance is our guide to understanding self-knowledge, then all the conversations that end in an impasse, the aporetic dialogues, can be viewed as guideposts on the way. The interlocutor does not always acknowledge his debt to Socrates, however, for guiding him to that precipice; some respond to the experience of *aporia* with an arrogant shrug (*Meno*) others by running away (*Euthyphro*). One notable exception is Theaetetus, who is specifically told by Socrates, the midwife, that his philosophical mission has been accomplished, once Theaetetus recognizes that he does not know what he previously thought (Tschemplik 2008). The *Theaetetus* is doubly puzzling because knowing that one does not know what knowledge is has paradoxical implications.

The *Alc. 1* states most directly what to make of the Delphic Oracle's pronouncement (*Alc. 1* 129a, 132c). Throughout the dialogue Socrates discusses the things which we should care for and be concerned about (*epimeleîsthai*) before we enter the public realm and care for others. He guides Alcibiades (127–31) towards the understanding that care for the soul, above all else, is a fundamental expression of self-knowledge (for an interesting interpretation of this point, see Foucault 1988:23–6). In addition, Socrates points to the need for a mirror (*Alc. 1* 132c–3c) to be able to inspect oneself, offering the analogy of the pupil of the eye, in which one can see a reflection of the self. He applies the analogy to the soul, concluding that the soul must look to the most divine region of another soul, that is, knowledge and prudence (*to eidenai te kai phrôneîn*), to come to know herself. Socrates identifies this construction of self-knowledge as "soundmindedness" or "moderation" (*sôphrosynê*). Alcibiades pledges to become Socrates' attendant in pursuit of becoming virtuous.

The *Chrm.* ostensibly focuses on learning the nature of soundmindedness; it provides another approach to self-knowledge. In the first part of the dialogue Socrates converses with Charmides and, after momentarily losing himself (*Chrm.* 155d) when overcome by Charmides' beauty, offers a lengthy and exhaustive genealogical account (157e–8b)

of Charmides' provenance, as if knowing one's ancestors is a possible way of knowing oneself. In other dialogues, too, Socrates introduces parentage as an important indicator of the nature of his interlocutor, for example, in the *Tht.* he recognizes Theaetetus through his knowledge of his father; in addition, Socrates reveals who he is with reference to his mother; and in the *La.*, Laches says that he trusts Socrates because, among other reasons, he knew his father (*La.* 181a–b); whereas the character of the children of famous fathers is precisely at issue in this dialogue. Socrates provides another way of gaining self-knowledge through introspection (*Chrm.* 159a), when he insists that Charmides should look within himself to find out whether he possesses soundmindedness. But neither genealogy nor self-inspection lead to a satisfactory answer, and Charmides hands over the discussion to his cousin Critias, who equates soundmindedness with self-knowledge (165a). What follows is a complex examination of various ways self-knowledge can be construed, working through to the formulation that it is the knowledge of itself and of all other knowledges as well as the knowledge of ignorance (166e). Self-knowledge thus understood is the ability to discern what one knows and does not know and to be able to judge the same in others. Socrates calls into question the usefulness of the knowledge of knowledge, since it appears that it has no content: In this case I know that the shoemaker knows how to make shoes, but I myself do not know how to make shoes. The obvious question is why Critias, who will later be a leader of the Thirty Tyrants, offers this particular construction of self-knowledge as the definition of soundmindedness (Stern 1999). Clearly, the concern for the care of the soul evident in the *Alc. I* has been left aside; instead we have an epistemological account of self-knowledge.

In the *Phdr.* Socrates raises the importance of self-knowledge and connects it with his need for the polis and the interlocutors that a polis provides. Phaedrus seduced Socrates to take a walk in the countryside by promising him an account of Lysias' speech. When Phaedrus wonders whether Socrates believes in the mythological or the scientific accounts of various natural phenomena, Socrates responds that until he has obeyed the Delphic inscription (*Phdr.* 229e–30a) and comes to know himself, it makes no sense to investigate these other matters. He makes explicit that he cannot fulfil the injunction of self-knowledge by communing with nature; instead he requires other human beings to help him examine whether he is simple and divine or monstrous and typhonic. As the dialogue unfolds we are presented with different accounts of *erôs* and in Socrates' second speech, the palinode, self-knowledge is addressed again. After having presented the soul in the metaphor of the charioteer and two horses, Socrates characterizes the erotic encounter between the lover and the beloved (255c–6c) in terms that had already been used in the *Alc. I*:

> Then the boy is in love, but has no idea what he loves. He does not understand, and cannot explain, what has happened to him. It is as if he had caught an eye disease from someone else, but could not identify the cause; he does not realize that he is seeing himself in the lover as in a mirror. (255d)

The *Phdr.* offers an erotic encounter as a way to self-knowledge: Once each of the lovers recognize himself in the other through the recollection of the god they both followed, they can exchange philosophical speeches and live a life of virtue and friendship. The discussion of writing and logos in the second half of the dialogue can also be linked with the theme of self-knowledge, since we reveal ourselves to another and come to know ourselves through dialogue (Griswold 1986). That at least is Socrates' hope.

At the end of his life, as depicted in Plato's *Ap.*, Socrates displays the same commitment to the task of self-knowledge. He opens his defence (*Ap.* 17a) with a caveat about the power of speeches because his accusers had spoken so eloquently that they almost caused him to forget himself (*epelathomên*). In response, he offers to tell the truth about himself, including an appeal to Apollo, the god at Delphi, who is responsible for Socrates' conclusion that human wisdom is worth little or nothing (23b), that it amounts to awareness of his ignorance (21d). Socrates also took it upon himself to persuade his fellow citizens that care of the soul should be everyone's primary concern (30a–b), so that they can live the best possible life. Because he has taken care of his soul, as he tried to persuade Alcibiades to do, Socrates faces death without any fear.

The greatest obstacle to self-knowledge and the most dangerous activity we can engage in is lying to or deceiving ourselves about who we are. Another way to approach the question of self-knowledge is by examining Socrates' discussion of self-deceit and self-ignorance in the *Republic* (382a) and *Philebus* (49a–50a).

SENSATION (see Perception and Sensation)

SOPHISTS

Marina McCoy

In the Platonic dialogues, the term 'sophist' refers to any number of intellectuals who travelled from city to city and offered to teach the youth of the city a variety of topics ranging from rhetoric (q.v.) to politics, linguistics or even natural philosophy.

'Sophist', or *sophistês*, had a broad range of meanings in the Greek world. From the fifth century onwards, 'sophist' meant a 'wise person' as its root, *sophia* (wisdom), indicates (Kerferd 1981:24). Wise men such as Thales or Solon, as well as many poets, were thought to be 'sophists' because they possessed political or moral wisdom. Gradually, however, the term came to be more ambiguous, and often meant someone who had pretensions to wisdom, rather than genuine wisdom. This transition took place around the time of Plato's writing. Not only Plato, but also other authors, such as Alcidamas and Isocrates (q.v.), criticized those with a fundamentally different understanding of the 'good life' by naming their opponents as sophists. Isocrates (q.v.), for example, in his 'Against the Sophists', speaks of the sophists as those who enjoy disputation for its own sake, and who waste their time proving themselves to be clever at argument in useless topics instead of applying themselves to significant political problems (Mirhady and Too 2000). Alcidamas, in contrast, calls those who spend all their time writing, instead of learning how to speak well, by the term 'so-called sophists' (Alcidamas 1, in Muir 2000). The term 'sophist', we find, is often used to contrast some better, different practise or person.

Plato's criticism of the sophists is varied and complex. In some dialogues (e.g. *Gorgias*; *Protagoras*), he confronts the views of specific sophists. In others, such as the *Sophist*, the topic of the sophist's identity is explored more abstractly and linked to philosophical problems of metaphysics and the nature of being. The *Republic* considers the sophist primarily in terms of the difficulties with persuasive rhetoric in democracy; there, the 'many' are called the 'biggest sophists' (*R.* 492a). However, a few brief themes recur in the dialogues.

Plato's dialogues frequently use the sophists as a foil, or a contrast to philosophy (q.v.). Perhaps this distinction was significant because Socrates seems to have been tried and executed partly on suspicion of being a sophist; Aristophanes' *Clouds* portrays Socrates as a sophist as well (though Dover 1968 disputes its accuracy). Plato, in his *Apology* (*Defence*) of Socrates, carefully distinguishes Socrates from the sophists. While the sophists taught students for money, Socrates claims that he never accepted money and had not students, but only followers. While the sophists claim to know, Socrates claims that his greatest wisdom is not thinking he knows what he does not know (*Ap.* 21d).

Plato's *Grg.* begins with a conversation between Socrates and Gorgias, who claimed that he could speak persuasively on any topic (for a fee). Socrates questions Gorgias, asking whether Gorgias cares for his students if he does not teach them justice as part of the study of rhetoric. He also suggests that Gorgias' students might become unjust as a result of studying with Gorgias, if their rhetorical skill is used for unjust purposes. Later, the *Grg.* contrasts sophistry to a legitimate political art that seeks the good of the city.

Some of the sophists also seem to have written about topics that today would be considered within the realm of philosophy (Kerferd 1981). For example, Protagoras wrote works with titles such as *Truth*, *Antilogic* and *On the Gods*. While these works do not survive, fragments passed down to authors such as Sextus Empiricus indicate an interest in intellectual problems. Protagoras' best known statement is 'Man is the measure of all things: of things that are, that they are, and of things that are not, that they are not'. In the *Theaetetus*, Socrates uses this idea to explore and to further define a view of knowledge as perceptual relativism. Although it is rejected as philosophically inadequate, Protagoras here is not merely a rhetorician, but rather an intellectual concerned with articulating a particular intellectual doctrine. In the *Prt.* we find a different view of the sophist, one that pokes fun at an overly majestic self-presentation and an intellectual understanding of the good that does not seem coherent when pressed. Hippias and Prodicus (though less) are also mocked for their intellectual deficiencies and lack of humility.

Plato even uses the concept of sophistry as an entryway into difficult metaphysical issues. In the *Sph.*, the Stranger begins by attempting to define the sophist, whom Socrates says is not easy to separate from the philosopher and the statesman (*Sph.* 216c–d). However, by the dialogue's end, the main focus of the discussion is on the nature of non-being, a topic that arose in the course of understanding image-making and dissembling. Again, Plato features the sophist as much as an entryway into understanding philosophy (and later in the *Politicus*, politics) as for the purposes of rejecting sophistic discourse.

While it is tempting to seek a single central difference between sophists and philosophers, a deeper examination at times shows some overlap between them (Zuckert 2000). For example, Plato's *Ap.* features Socrates using some methods of rhetorical argumentation familiar in the courtroom by that time (McCoy 2007). Plato's dialogues often raise important critical questions for philosophers, such as whether rhetoric might have a political value. For example, Gorgias points out that he is more effective at getting medical patients to undergo treatment than his brother, a doctor, is. Such dialogues between sophists and Socrates raise questions about the value of rhetoric that are not fully answered within the dialogue itself. Instead, the term 'sophist' is used both to criticize those intellectuals who stood in opposition to Socratic and Platonic goals, and to challenge Plato's audience to reflect on the value of rhetoric and its relation to philosophy.

SOUL (*PSYCHÊ*)

T. M. Robinson

In a well known lecture John Burnet called 'the care of the soul' the core of Socrates' teaching (Burnet 1916:235 ff.), and it was undoubtedly that of Plato as well. But what exactly they meant by soul is less easy to describe (for bibliographies on soul in Plato, see Robinson 1995:166–76 and Wagner 2001:363–9). That it is distinct from the body is beyond doubt, but its relationship to what we would call the person is less clear. At *Charmides* 156e7–8 the body is an integral part of personhood; at *Phaedo* 115c and elsewhere it is simply the soul which is the person. Sometimes this is refined to suggest that the 'person' who is the soul is such in two senses: the person who exists for a while on earth, and is characterized by reason and impulse, and the person who survives physical death and lives on everlastingly, who seems to consist simply of reason. The matter is complicated further by talk in the various myths, where the person who survives death is spoken of in a way suggesting that she/he continues to be characterized by both reason and impulse, and differs from the person who once lived on earth only by having cast off materiality.

If the soul is the person, how does it relate to the body? At times it is described as what one might call an 'inner person', like a body in a tomb, or a prisoner in a prison (*Phd.* 82e3), or an oyster in a shell (*Phaedrus* 250c6). At other times, it is described more positively as the 'possessor' of a body, which it 'uses' and 'controls' (*Gorgias* 465d1). Either way, the doctrine seems to be one of numerical dualism (in contrast with what one might call the 'mitigated monism' of the *Chrm.*); soul and body seem to be distinct substances (*Grg.* 464b3), such that their numerical addition would apparently add up to two, though soul is clearly stated to be the more important and valuable of the two (*Protagoras* 313a1–c3). They are also in a tense, if not actively inimical, relationship with each other, and operate almost as independent persons, with the body possessing desires of its own that can run counter to the good of the soul if allowed free rein (*Phd.* 66b6 ff.). Each can also be 'sick' or 'healthy'; the appropriate food the soul needs for health is *mathêmata* ('pieces of knowledge') *(Prt.* 313c7), which needs to be implanted in it by reputable sources, not by sophists.

The reference to 'pieces of knowledge' points, crucially, to the fact that soul is thought of as being in its most important manifestation an intellectual principle. So much so that, as we have seen, it is on occasion apparently *equated* with reason (see *Phd.* 67c2–3, *dianoia*). It is, however, that whereby we are moral agents too, such that we/our soul can be characterized by such terms as 'righteous' and 'depraved' (*Grg.* 313a3, a4). The 'health' of the soul will consist of a right balance between reason and impulse within it. If reason is in control, the soul will manifest the virtues 'temperance' and 'justice'; if folly is in control, and impulse allowed free rein, the soul will be a sick one, 'intemperate and unjust and unholy' (505b2–4, c7–d3).

In the *Phd.* significant efforts are made to prove that the soul survives our bodily death and lives on everlastingly. But, disconcertingly, several senses of the word soul that are not easily reconcilable are used in the dialogue, and no attempt is made to reconcile them, rendering what are already a set of dubious proofs of immortality even more so. The most important sense is that of soul as being the whole person, the true or genuine self (*Phd.* 115d8–e4, *R.* 469d6–9); as such it effectively duplicates in its actions what most people take a person (= a soul/mind and body combined in some way) to be doing (see especially 94b7 ff.). Though, even this notion is not a little obfuscated by talk which apparently distinguishes a soul and the person who *possesses* that soul (66b5–7, 67e6–8). But the soul is also, for purposes of various attempts at proving immortality, seen as a life-principle or life-carrier (69e–72d, 102a ff.), and, as we have seen, as reason too. In one passage it is furthermore clearly thought of as being indestructible because it is immaterial (80b1 ff.), whereas in another it is apparently quasi-physical in nature (81c4 ff.).

This somewhat confusing situation is clarified in important ways in the *R.* Moral conflict is now affirmed to be conflict within the soul rather than between soul and body, and the 'bodily' desires (for food, drink and sex) are now affirmed to be part of the soul itself (the body being simply their instrument), and fully acceptable to the degree that they are controlled by reason. Such reason is now described as the controlling element in a soul which is not bipartite but tripartite. The soul consists, like its analogue, the state of a ruling part (reason), a soldier/police part ('spiritedness', *thymos*) and a desiderative part. The goodness of the soul like the justice of the state consists of a balance between all three parts, such that each plays the role appropriate to it and only the role appropriate to it.

This view of soul as tripartite is repeated in detail in the *Timaeus*, though now there is added to it the remarkable view that the universe itself, being a living thing, also possesses a soul. Differently from human soul, however, this soul is simply rational; there are no two 'lower' parts to it. And a major clarification of the doctrine of immortality comes with the affirmation that the universe's soul and the (rational) human soul are everlasting (i.e. with a beginning in time but without an end), all of them having been formed by a divine fashioner (the Demiurge) at a point in time which was the beginning *of* time. In the same dialogue we are also introduced to the view that there is a difference between male and female souls, the female having an inbuilt tendency towards immoral conduct (*kakia*) that the male lacks. This is little noticed by commentators, and would be disconcerting if it reflected Plato's own thinking.

In the *Phdr.*, we find an apparent reference to a tripartite soul in the famous myth of the charioteer. The first statement in that same dialogue, however, of soul's being immortal because it is a 'source of motion/change' and itself everlastingly '*self*-moving/changing' suggests that Plato may now be moving towards a different vision of its nature; certainly its supposed tripartition never appears again with clarity in any dialogue after the *Phdr.*

The *Philebus* repeats the notion (seen in detail in the *Ti.*) that soul depends for its existence upon an intelligence that performs the task of 'fashioning' and 'making' things (*Phlb.* 27b1, 26e6), reaffirming that all soul is of its nature contingent, with the exception, perhaps, of the soul of the Demiurge if the Demiurge is to be understood as a reality and as something more than simply intelligence.

In the *Laws*, Plato repeats the *Phdr.* doctrine that soul is the source of movement/ change and forever self-moving/self-changing, while still being of its nature contingent, but (influenced possibly by the view of Aristotle) he seems to have come round to the view that the world we know is sempiternal, not everlasting, so that soul's self-moving/ self-changing nature will be such across sempiternity (i.e. with neither temporal beginning nor end) rather than being characterized by everlastingness once it has been formed. Apart from this, the *Lg.* is a work in which he returns to the bipartite vision of soul that was prominent in early dialogues; only the *disiecta membra* (*pace* Saunders 1962:37–55) of the theory of tripartition seem now to remain. And till the end his basic psychophysical dualism remains a problem for him; in this, his last work, he is still unclear as to whether the soul of the sun, for example, carries it from within, pushes it from without, or guides it along its path 'by virtue of possessing some other prodigious and wonderful powers' (*Lg.* 898e8–9a4).

Two paths, however, towards a possible mitigation of the problem posed by psychophysical dualism which are mentioned in other dialogues, but ultimately not taken, are worth mentioning. Early on, in the *Chrm.*, he had looked with interest if not, in the final analysis, conviction at the possibility that the body too, not just the soul, was integral to the concept of a person. And his view, in the *Ti.* (35a), that the soul has in its very structure something of both the form world and the world of *matter* suggests that, at one time at any rate in his lifetime of research into the nature of the soul, he might have believed that the gap between soul and body might possibly be bridged if it could be shown that the soul was not as close to being wholly immaterial as he had believed it to be when he wrote the *Phd.*

THE SUN SIMILE

Nicholas D. Smith

At 504e4–6 in the *Republic*, Glaucon asks Socrates to say what the 'most important subject' will be in the future ruler's studies. This subject, declares Socrates, is the form of the good (*R*. 505a2), for it is 'by their relation to it that just things and the others become good and useful' (505a3–4, trans. Grube and Reeve). But Socrates then goes on immediately to insist that 'we have no adequate knowledge of it' (505a5–6). He criticizes 'the majority' who identify the good with pleasure, on the ground that there are bad pleasures (505c7–8), and also the 'more sophisticated' who claim that it is knowledge, on the ground that when pressed to say what sort of knowledge it might be, they can only answer that it is 'knowledge of the good' (505b8–10). Glaucon then challenges Socrates to state what he thinks the good is (506b2–4), and though Socrates first chastises him for seeking just another opinion on the subject (506b5–d1), when Glaucon persists in his request (506d2–5), Socrates carefully stipulates that he will not even attempt to articulate a theory of the good, but is willing instead to 'tell you about what is apparently an offspring of the good and most like it' (506e3–4).

So begins the first of what have been called the great 'similes of light' – the sun and divided line (in that order) at the end of *R*. bk 6, and the cave at the beginning of *R*. bk 7. Simply put, the simile of the sun compares the relative positions and roles of the good, in its domain, to that of the sun, in the sensible world. Socrates begins by reminding Glaucon of the distinction (introduced at the end of *R*. bk 5) between forms and particulars (507b2–10). Socrates then asks how we see visible things, and Glaucon answers that it is by sight (507c1–2). But unlike other varieties of perception, Socrates continues, sight requires some additional 'third kind of thing' in order to occur: light, without which even those with good eyesight cannot see (507d11–e2). The sun, they agree, is the 'cause and controller' of light (508a4–8). These observations provide the groundwork for the simile to the good, according to which, 'What the good itself is in the intelligible realm, in relation to understanding and intelligible things, the sun is in the visible realm, in relation to sight and visible things' (508c1–2).

In brief, then, the details of the simile are these:

realm:	Being	becoming
highest entity and cause:	the good	the sun
applicable power:	knowledge	vision
medium required for power to operate:	truth	light
objects effected:	forms	visible particulars
organ by which power operates:	mind	eye(s)
defective condition:	relative absence of truth	relative absence of light
results of defective condition:	opinion	poor eyesight

Several features of this simile have created interpretive discussion and controversy. First, a vital element of the simile is the comparison of truth (*alêtheia*) to light (*phôs*). But this entails that truth cannot be two-valued, as it is in sentential logic, but must come in degrees. Some translators (e.g. Shorey 1935) have tried to remediate this puzzling feature by translating '*alêtheia*' as 'truth and reality', but modern readers may find degrees of reality no less puzzling than degrees of truth. In a famous essay, Gregory Vlastos (1981), noting that the application of '*alêtheia*' here is not to propositions, but to entities, proposed conceiving of *alêtheia* as more or less like the conception of truth at work in expressions such as 'true friend' or 'real friend' where there are plainly also people who qualify as friends in some lesser way. But as Vlastos carefully notes, this requires (but also facilitates) what has come to be known as the 'predicative' reading of Plato's use of the verb 'to be' (*einai*), since neither existence nor sentential truth (as the 'existential' and 'veridical' interpretations of '*einai*', respectively, would have it; see Smith 2000) can make sense of degrees of being. An entity, accordingly, may be said to be more or less F, and would thus have the appropriate degree of *alêtheia* (as an F-thing).

Also unfamiliar to modern readers is Plato's comparison of knowledge to eyesight as a 'power' (see R. 508b6), though this conception was also explicitly at work in the epistemology provided at the end of R. bk 5, by which the philosopher was distinguished from the nonphilosopher. Contemporary epistemology conceives of knowledge not as a cognitive power, but rather as the state that may – in the best cases, at any rate – be produced as a result of the successful or proper use of our cognitive powers. Various interpretations have been offered for how we may compare Platonic to contemporary epistemology, but this subject continues to be controversial among scholars (see Smith 2000).

Finally, there has been some discussion of Plato's startling claim that the good in some way 'transcends' (Shorey 1937:107), 'exceeds' (Bloom 1968:189), 'surpasses' (Ferrari 2000:216), or is 'beyond' (White 1979:180) or 'superior to' (Grube and Reeve) being (at R. 509b9, translating Plato's '*epekeina*'). Some earlier interpretations held that we cannot even attribute being to the form of the good, but now most scholars maintain that the language of transcendence here simply emphasizes the causal primacy of the good, relative to the rest of 'what is', in the same way that the sun is claimed to be the ultimate source of causation in its realm, while still being (very visibly!) a part of that realm.

THEOLOGY

Harold Tarrant

Later Platonism (q.v. Academy), from the time of Plutarch, seems to have regarded Plato as a supreme theologian, who postulated a limited number of distinct divine powers – a very small number of gods in authors such as Alcinous (*Didascalicus* 10 etc.) and Numenius, but rather a large one in Proclus' great *Platonic Theology*, which extended to six books. Proclus assembled this theology primarily from the *Parmenides* and *Timaeus*, and secondarily from a range of passages, many myths among them, from other works. Theology was a huge issue in late antiquity, and in Platonism this was especially so because 'assimilation to god as far as possible' had become entrenched as the very goal of human life. Furthermore, the struggle for or against Christianity necessarily involved matters of theology, and the protagonists vied for the authority of Plato by offering rival interpretations, particularly of the demiurge in the *Ti.* If Plato believed in a father figure creating the world at a given point, attended by a host of lesser supernatural beings who acted for him in the physical world, then it was clearly easier for Christians to admire him and to point to him as a predecessor.

However, to consider Plato as a theologian may seem unnatural today. His leading speaker is frequently indifferent to the identity of the god of which he speaks, and sometimes even to whether he uses the singular (god) or plural (gods), regularly leading readers to wonder whether he is a polytheist or monotheist. This is not unnatural. His 'Socrates' is clearly attracted to the basic Anaxagorean idea of a controlling intelligent power, single but wide ranging in its operation (*Phaedo* 97b–8b; *Cratylus* 400a). Intelligence was assumed to lead always in the same direction. Any Platonic god will behave in accordance with intelligence, and Plato seems to have considered that this would eliminate fundamental disagreement among the members of a pantheon. For this reason Plato rejects the kind of god depicted in Hesiod and Homer in *Republic* bk 2. Where intelligence rules, as most obviously perhaps at *Philebus* 28d–30e, no real divisions need be postulated – except perhaps a division between intelligence itself and soul, both integral to the concept of 'Zeus' as cause at 30d.

It is therefore natural that Plato must reject any notion of a universe controlled by two gods of opposing intent (*Politicus* 270a). The tendency of the world to slip backwards at times must therefore be explained in terms of the temporary relinquishing of divine control. In this dialogue the controlling god is therefore compared with a helmsman, who occasionally takes a rest from his duties at the rudder.

At the end of Plato's life there seems to have been a major step towards astral theology, where not only an intelligent cosmic motive power, or soul, is postulated (as at *Ti.* 35a and *Laws* 10.896d–7c) but also unerringly intelligent souls of the heavenly bodies. Perfect intelligence that is not subject to decay is not unnaturally held to be the sign of divinity. This kind of astral theology, which involves the earth too being treated as a god, is present at *Ti.* 38c–40d, but it reaches its climax only with the *Epinomis*, and it continues in the work of later Platonists.

As for the gods of mythology, *Ti.* 40d–1a seems very reluctant to say much about them, regarding the subject as difficult, and, like *Phaedrus* 229c–30a, an unnecessary distraction. It is therefore best to go along with tradition. *Cra.* 395e–410d gives etymologies for very many gods and godlike entities, etymologies that also attempt to have the names explain their divine function. However, the whole passage, in which Socrates is said to have been inspired by the rather ambiguous figure of Euthyphro (*Euthyphr.* 396d–e), while not to be dismissed as mere trivia, seems to undercut itself regularly enough to make it unclear how seriously it is all meant. One should be similarly cautious of Plato's willingness to employ the traditional gods in some of his myths (*Gorgias* 523a–4a; *Protagoras* 320c–3a), since it was natural for him to compose them mainly from traditional materials.

Much of the discussion relating to Plato's theology has concentrated on trying to reconcile the evidence of different dialogues, particularly regarding the supreme divinity. Is it the demiurge of the *Ti.* for instance? Or the idea of the good from *R.* bk 6? Is the idea of the good closely related to the One (q.v.) as discussed in *Prm.*? And if so, how are they related to the demiurge, assuming his portrait is to be taken seriously? The problem lies with those brought up under the influence of modern world religions that make salvation depend on worshipping the right god and believing in the right creed. For Plato the most important thing in the political context was belief in gods, and in gods who have some concern for matters of this world, as *Lg.* bk 10 demonstrates. At a more personal level, happiness depends on getting our inner selves in tune with the divine by raising our own souls to the highest level of rationality that is attainable (*Theaetetus* 176a–c; *R.* 613a–b; *Ti.* 90a–d). This is the process of assimilation to god, central to later Platonism, but never explored at length or established by dialectical argument in Plato himself.

VIRTUE (see Excellence)

VISION

Michail Maiatsky

Plato's interest in vision and the visual is multifaceted, and complex. Visual words and images are frequent in the dialogues along with many direct and indirect discussions of physiological, intellectual and social vision. The increased emphasis in recent scholarship on the importance of visuality in Plato is a part of a 'scopic turn', the effect of which was to ground interpretations of the history of western European philosophy and metaphysics in its entirety in certain optical premises. On this view, the Ancient Greeks, as the founders of the European thinking tradition, were said to be ocular people in contrast to the verbal/acoustic Jews. A particular reading of Plato played a key role – both positive and negative – in this. Studies published in the

last decade have, in a sense, replayed debates of the early twentieth century, when a hyper-rationalizing neo-Kantian interpretation of Plato gave way to a reaction, for example, by the Platonists of the 'George-Kreis', as well as by Julius Stenzel (1883–1935), Bruno Snell (1896–1986) and Martin Heidegger (1889–1976). Today, scholars disagree about Platonic visuality: some believe that for Plato, the most authentic cognition is dialectic (q.v.), and thus the cognition/vision comparison is merely a figure of speech; others draw various serious conclusions from Plato's multiple and extensive use of visual motifs. Some (e.g. Press 1995) even use the term 'vision' to define the polyphonic and dialogical character of Plato's philosophy as a whole.

Platonic visuality poses a number of problems. Though historians of science consider him an important and comprehensive source, physiological representations (e.g. of vision as two opposite streams, one from an object and one from the eye meeting half-way, *Timaeus* 45a–6c, 67d) merely attest that Plato was well informed about the science of his time (Hippocrates of Chios, Democritus and even Empedocles). The study of optics, which drew on the fields of geometry, physics or ophthalmology, actually developed later on. Thus, Plato tended to treat it as the subject of a 'likely story' (*eikos logos*) and part of a wider ensemble, which could be called *scopics*.

Plato's *scopics* involves optics, the psychology of visual perception, theories of light, colour and optical illusions, theories of the image and of the sun (which in the *Republic* is a metaphysical being), together with studies of *mimêsis* (imitation; q.v.) and *sêmeiôsis* (the relation between signs and things signified). Social visibility is also important for Plato as attested by comments on the psychology of observation, testimony, ocular witnessing and judgement (*Laches passim*, *Symposium* 194bc, 218d; *R.* 442bc, 537c), the problem of (in)visibility of virtue and justice (*Meno* 72cd; *Phaedo* 65d; *Phaedrus* 254bc; *R.* 577a, 368c–9a, 402de, 445bc, 501b, 611bd), the aesthetics of theatre (etymologically linked to 'theory') and performance in general (*Laws* 659b, 701a), as well as the theory of beauty (*Phdr.* 249d–50d). Statements related to this broad scopic interest belong to different but closely related categories, among which one can distinguish: (a) visual situations: visual exchanges between participants of the dialogues, condensation of the visual lexicon and word games, *mise-en-scènes* implying observation, performance and the visual aspect; (b) myths: of the cave (*R.* bk. 7), of the Ring of Gyges (*R.* 359c sq., 612b), of the charioteer and his horses (*Phdr.* 246b sq.), of the Demiurg and his paradigm (*Ti.*); and (c) statements or doctrines that raise various philosophical questions linked to vision:

(1) The main problem of interpretation lies in the tension between what might be considered Plato's 'doctrine' and his language. In order to show the importance of the dialectical grasp of the invisible, he frequently uses visual vocabulary and images; but the analogy between vision and knowledge often encountered in his work seems at odds with the invisible character of objects of genuine science. This tension culminates in the designation of invisible paradigms with words such as *idea* and *eidos* (q.v. forms) derived from the verb *idein* (the meaning of which, however, was 'to know', before narrowing to 'to see'). The traditional expression 'theory of ideas' turns out to be an oxymoron, meaning the contemplation of the invisible.

(2) Plato expressed the distinction between the sensible and the intelligible through the opposition of two types of vision (e.g. the two visions of the soul, *Phd.* 65–79; *R.* 523–4), although corporeal vision can impede or on the contrary favour 'real' vision (the intellect looking upwards, *Tht.* 174a) by the invisible soul. This problem is connected with a Platonic imperative of knowing the similar by the similar, since the invisible object can be 'seen' only by an invisible 'seer', that is, soul.

(3) The relationship between cognition and recognition (*Philebus* 38cd; *R.* 376ac, 484cd; *Tht.* 189b sq.) is both interesting and important. One can attribute to Plato a certain *opsodicy* (coined after Leibniz's theodicy; cf. its platonic antecedent in *R.* 617e), whereas vision is summoned to the trial that will reveal its participation in the creation of illusions and distractions from what is true, and justify it partially.

(4) The problem of illumination or sudden knowledge (*Epistles* 7 341cd, 344b; *Smp.* 210e), implying that the dialectical process climaxes in a vision-like revelation of the truth.

(5) The problem of the relation of 'being' to 'seeming' on the ethical and political level (*Apology* 21c, 41b; *Hippias Major* 294d; *Lysis* 217cd; *R.* 360e–1d, 362a, 365c) as well as on the epistemological in terms of the opposition between truth and opinion (*Tht.* 188a and *passim*; *R.* 475d, 479e–80a, 527de).

(6) Discussions of the participation of the eye in vision (*Tht.* 184c sq.) are inserted in philosophical reflections on the soul, on the role of mind (*nous*), on the question of its unity and its relation to sensation or perception (*aisthêsis*; q.v.). The mind itself becomes a supervisor of all active

sensation, taking on the function of the inner eye, or the eye of the soul.

(7) The relationship of eyesight with the other senses, for example, the competition between the senses (*Ti.* 45b–7b). Eyesight is sometimes considered as one of the senses (*Tht.* 163d), at others, it is representative of all the other senses, a model sense. Primarily, however (*Phd.* 79a; *Ti.* 30cd), it features in asymmetric oppositions such as the 'sensible' versus 'invisible', or the 'thinkable' versus 'visible'. Plato's rational ethics (q.v.) and moral epistemology (q.v.) suggest that one should prefer the invisible to the visible, and that this preference is precisely what distinguishes the philosopher from any other person. Plato was the first to compare and clearly distinguish eyesight and thought. He created the vocabulary of visual metaphors, which he deployed as a pedagogical strategy for selecting and educating people towards philosophy and the pursuit of truth. Whereas for those starting out on their ascent towards philosophy, the visual operated as a metaphorical tool enabling them to 'see' the truth, for Academy initiates vested with the eye of reason (e.g. *R.* 533de), the metaphor contained a different message: it is not a 'physiological' vision at all.

WEAKNESS OF WILL (see *Akrasia*)

WOMEN

Angela Hobbs

The significance of women in Plato can be gleaned from four main sources: explicit statements about the capabilities of women, casual remarks about women, female characters, both real and fictional, and the use of imagery involving female functions and traditional female activities.

At *Meno* 73a–c Socrates counters Meno's traditional belief (*Men.* 71e) that a man's virtue is very different from that of a woman by arguing that all humans are good in the same way. The spheres in which men and women operate, however, may still be different: Socrates does not commit himself. *Republic* bk 5 addresses this issue: at *R.* 456b we are told that the nature (*physis*) of women is 'akin' or (somewhat confusingly) 'the same' as the nature of men. The only difference is that the female bears and the male begets (454e) and this difference is not relevant when considering what jobs each can do. In consequence, the more able women are capable of being trained to be guardians, either as military auxiliaries or (540c) philosopher-queens. These guardian women are to live in camp communes with their male counterparts, and their eugenically bred children are to be taken away at birth and raised in nurseries, thus releasing them for military and political duties.

These proposals have provoked heated debate. Is it really necessary to abolish the family to allow women to take part in political and military life? Is Socrates only allowing women education and power on condition that they become parodies of men, hunting, wrestling and going to war? Or does this view say more about the prejudices of the modern critic than of Socrates (or Plato)? It is certainly true that Socrates is not interested in the 'rights' of women, *qua* women, or in enabling individual women to fulfil their potential; his concern, just as with the male citizens, is to harness their abilities and energies for the overall good of the state. For these reasons, and to avoid anachronism, it may be inappropriate to describe his agenda as 'feminist'; we may also note that the possibility of female guardians depends on the domestic support of women from the producer class.

Elsewhere in the *R.*, however, women are casually disparaged, such as at 469d where plundering a corpse is said to be a mark of 'feminine small-mindedness'. Some of the apparent anomalies can be dissolved if we consider that Plato distinguishes between women as he currently perceives them in Athens, ill-educated and confined and women as they could be if properly trained. But this distinction, though important, does not explain away the fact that Socrates sometimes appears to forget that there will be female guardians too: at 395d, for instance, trainee guardians are forbidden from taking the parts of women when acting or reciting 'because they are men'. But who are to be the role models for future philosopher-queens? The Platonic corpus is notably short of female ideals, although Alcestis is praised for sacrificing her life for her husband Admetus at *Symposium* 179b–c. Even in *R.* bk 5 women and children are said to be held in common by the guardians (*R.* 461e), and at 455d Socrates claims that in general the class of men surpasses the class of women in everything. There are also a number of references (e.g. 451e) to women being weaker than men, and although Socrates probably only has physical weakness in mind, it is just possible that he intends intellectual inferiority as well.

Similar tensions apply to the *Laws*. On one hand, at *Lg.* 805a the Athenian Stranger says it is foolish for men and women not to share a common education and thus enable the state to double its achievements, and in consequence women in the *Lg.* take part in military activities up to fifty and may hold political office after forty. Yet, at 781b a

woman's natural capacity for virtue is said to be inferior to a man's, and at 781a women are said to be 'secretive and crafty' owing to their weakness. The *Timaeus* is even more problematic. At *Ti.* 42a the male sex is said to be superior (*kreitton*: this may just imply physical strength, but could also connote moral superiority), while at 90e–1a we hear that men who lived cowardly and unjust lives were reincarnated as women. In 91c the womb is spoken of as an internal creature, desirous of child-making; if this desire is thwarted it becomes ill and wanders through the body, creating havoc. For those who want to reconcile the *Ti.* with the more progressive views expressed elsewhere, the best option is to emphasize that it is Timaeus, not Socrates, who makes these claims.

In three dialogues Socrates claims to have received wise instruction from women, although they never appear in person and in each instance Socrates' tone is difficult to gauge. The most notable is Diotima in the *Smp.*, a priestess who instructs Socrates in *erôs* and to whom is given a key speech. Yet she is also called a 'perfect sophist' (*Smp.* 208c) – a highly ambivalent term in Plato's hands – and is credited only with delaying the arrival of the plague in Athens; she could not avert it altogether. Similar ambiguities apply to Aspasia, whom Socrates claims in the *Menexenus* to have trained him, Pericles and many others in the art of rhetoric, and to whom are attributed both Pericles' funeral speech and another recounted by Socrates. It is difficult to assess the level of irony here: certainly Menexenus is sceptical that a mere woman could have performed such feats (*Mx.* 249d), but this may say more about him than about Plato's view of Aspasia. Finally, at *Men.* 81a Socrates says that he learnt of reincarnation and the doctrine of recollection from certain wise priests and priestesses, though he later (*Men.* 86b) expresses uncertainty on these teachings.

Actual women are sometimes present in the dialogues, but none speaks apart from Xanthippe, Socrates' wife, who laments his impending death at *Phaedo* 60a. However, Socrates immediately banishes her; her cries would presumably disturb their enquiries on the immortality of the soul. Similarly, at *Smp.* 176e the *aulos*-girl is sent away so that the men can discuss *erôs* without distraction; it is notable that when Alcibiades arrives escorted by an *aulos*-girl at *Alc.* 212c–d, this is the point at which orderly discussion disintegrates.

But while women are largely absent, imagery drawn from female bodily functions and traditional female activities is not. Diotima claims at *Smp.* 206c that all humans are pregnant in both body and soul, and that falling in love with a beautiful person or object enables us to give birth; while at *Theaetetus* 148e–51d Socrates refers to himself as a midwife to other men's thoughts. In the *Politicus*, true statesmanship is said to be the expertise which correctly weaves together opposing human characteristics and character types (*Plt.* 305e–11c). There is keen debate as to whether such imagery elevates or denigrates actual women. Whatever the answer, the use of 'female' imagery needs to be considered together with Plato's depiction of philosophy in terms of 'male' imagery drawn from war, hunting and athletics (though, as the female guardians show, these activities need not be exclusively the provenance of men).

If Plato's views on women are complex, this may partly be because he sees the ultimate human goal as ascension to the realm of the nongendered forms. Nevertheless, it is clear that he thinks the state will benefit if some women at any rate are educated – a belief he supported (if Diogenes Laertius 3.4 is to be believed) by allowing at least two women to attend the Academy (q.v.).

WRITING (TOPIC)

David Blank

Athens in the late fifth and fourth centuries was home to a public enthusiastic for both oratory and instruction generally. Speech writers (*logographoi*; q.v. Isocrates) composed political and forensic orations for others to give, and some of those who gave their own speeches or lectures also wrote manuals of arts such as rhetoric, as well as books on scientific and philosophical subjects. Plato's Socrates, in contrast, insists that the way to do philosophy is through a dialectical question-and-answer conversation in a discourse (*logos*) 'written with knowledge in the learner's soul' (*Phaedrus* 276a5) and guided by one who can divide reality at the joints, a 'dialectician' (266c). While a rhetorical speech can be attractive, stimulating, entertaining and persuasive, its author may not be truly knowledgeable and able to 'aid' (*boêthein*) his discourse by answering questions and expanding upon it. The same holds for written discourse, and one criticism of those who make speeches is that, when questioned, they are as silent as books or keep sounding the same note, like a bell (*Protagoras* 329a).

The *Phdr.* expands on this critique (*Phdr.* 275d4). Written words seem to be alive and to speak from understanding, yet when questioned, only repeat the same thing. This dialogue contains Plato's only extended discussion of writing (274b–8b); in it he has Socrates put some of writing's disadvantages in the mouth of Thamus, an ancient King of

Upper Egypt: it induces forgetfulness; it gives the reader both the impression he has knowledge, and the boorishness that comes with that impression. Socrates not only accepts these strictures, he adds that it is folly to believe that written instructions for an art – rhetoric, say – can actually teach, and not merely remind those who already know what they say. One who actually knows what is just, fine and good, however, will instruct a pupil personally; he will take this kind of instruction seriously; he will view writing as an amusement, storing up reminders for his old age and for his successors. Like writing, lecturing does not permit genuine, productive instruction (*didachê*). Further, a written discourse reaches those who do not understand it and so have no business with it, and when it is attacked it cannot defend itself without the aid of its father, who wrote it.

The helplessness of written discourse is prominent in the main body of the dialogue, when Phaedrus reads aloud to Socrates a speech he admires written by Lysias, a *logographos*. Socrates conjectures that Phaedrus has secured the speech in a book roll, so that he could practise his own version of it; but instead he is pushed by Socrates to read the original – whereupon Socrates gives his own, better speech on the same subject, and adds both a 'palinode' in which the opposite point of view is maintained, and a critique of Lysias' speech (264b). Clearly, in the absence of its father Socrates is free to handle the speech roughly, although Lysias would perhaps not have been able to aid it, even had he been present. The same may hold of Protagoras' book *Truth*, which in the *Theaetetus* finds various defenders, including even an imagined Protagoras *redivivus*, who briefly pops his head out of the earth, only to dash off again (*Tht.* 171d) – while in fact no one comes successfully to its aid.

Written discourses are subjected to interpretation and criticism in other Platonic dialogues too. Protagoras (*Prt.* 339a) cites an ode of Simonides in order to point out a contradiction in it: Socrates defends it, but by a probably specious interpretation of its language. In the *Phaedo* Socrates recounts (*Phd.* 97c–d) how, impressed by a reading from a book of Anaxagoras, he bought it, but was disappointed when he learned that Anaxagoras did not actually explain how 'mind' made everything for the best.

In addition to its portrayal of the unsuccessful defence of Protagoras' book, the *Tht.* is the only dialogue to call attention to the process of recording a dialectical conversation in writing. Euclides has called on his memory of what Socrates told him and also asked Socrates himself to fill in the gaps in his memory, in order to write down a conversation Socrates had had with the young Theaetetus. Decades later, when Terpsion wants to hear the conversation, Euclides has his slave read it aloud (*Tht.* 143b–c). The book is therefore read in the presence of its author; but far from being its 'father', or even a participant in the original conversation, Euclides was merely an amanuensis and, beyond his introductory statement, he does not intervene in its telling in any way. The real authorship of the dialogue belongs to others. This reading of the conversation from a book roll, then, is like Antiphon's telling of what he heard from Pythodorus about the conversation between Socrates, Aristotle, Zeno and Parmenides (*Parmenides* 126a–7a) or Apollodorus' narrative of the symposium at Agathon's house, which he heard from Aristodemus, who was there, and checked with Socrates (*Symposium* 172a–3e). The *Phd.*, in contrast, is a first-person recollection of Socrates' last hours by Phaedo, who also intervenes at a crucial moment, when his listener, Echecrates, has interrupted his narrative, dismayed like the participants themselves at the fate of some of Socrates' arguments (*Phd.* 88c–9a). Phaedo's intervention, like Socrates' intervention at this point in the conversation, respects the audience's reactions, as recommended for didactic conversation in the *Phdr.*

Zeno's book, read at the beginning of the conversation reported in the *Prm.*, is the only book defended in a Platonic dialogue by its author: when Socrates begins to question Zeno about his motive for writing it, he explains he intended to support Parmenides' famous argument (*Prm.* 128c6), but that it was written out of youthful ambition and stolen by someone else before he could decide whether or not to publish it – perhaps an indication that he is disowning his work;

and in fact later it is Parmenides who comes to the aid of his own thesis. In a model of the superiority of personal instruction over writing, he carefully takes Socrates through his challenges to the theory of forms, and then, by questioning the youngest person present, through a very challenging set of eight deductions, a process he qualifies as 'training' (135d7).

In the pseudo-Platonic *Ep.* 7 there is a critique, partially overlapping that in *Phdr.*, of any attempt to write about the subjects that occupy Plato. The author argues (*Ep.* 341b–5c) that writing can be of little use about these serious matters, *viz.* the highest and first things of nature, which can only be grasped after a lengthy practise of the philosophical life and once their names, definitions and qualities have been tested between teacher and apt pupil in question and answer.

5

LATER RECEPTION, INTERPRETATION AND INFLUENCE OF PLATO AND THE DIALOGUES

Section A: The Interpretation and
Influence of Plato in the Ancient World

ANCIENT HERMENEUTICS

Catherine Collobert

Hermeneutics, the art of interpretation, derives its name from Hermes, the messenger god. Ancient hermeneutical practises provide the context in which Plato interprets the poets (q.v. Epic and Lyric Poets) and may also help in understanding how later ancient writers interpreted his dialogues (q.v. Academy).

Hermeneutics originates from a specific view on the relationship between the poet and his or her works. That the poet's speech is prophetic and oracular on account of its connection with the divine is first claimed by Pindar (*Pythian* 6.6, f. 94a5). The analogy of the muse with the Pythia and, consequently, of the poet with the seer illustrates the conception of poetry as an interpretation of the Muses' speeches. In fact, the oblique quality of divine oracles expresses the idea of a hidden meaning in need of decipherment (*Odes* 2.83–8). The poet thus appears

as a decipherer retrieving a meaning not explicitly expressed by the divine. Along the same lines, poets conceive of poetry as being oblique. This conception rests ultimately on a gap between the literality of a speech and its meaning, which is only accessible to wise people (Bacchylides, *Ep.* 3.85).

Both the poets, because of their puzzling way of writing, and philosophers like Xenophanes and Heraclitus, because of their critique of Homeric poetry, give rise to a need for interpretation. There are basically four types of interpretation: (a) non-historic, in which the historical context is ignored and the focus is on perennial questions, (b) historic or exegetic, whose purpose is to retrieve the authorial intention identified with the meaning, (c) pseudo-historic or allegorical, which is not necessarily defensive, that is, meant to defend Homer from his detractors and (d) intrinsic, in which the meaning is viewed as exceeding the authorial intention (Tate 1939).

Allegorical interpretation (*allêgorêsis*) rests on the idea that the poet purposively hides his intention. *Hyponoia*, which is usually translated into 'hidden meaning', that is, intentionally hidden, means literally a thought that lies under *la lettre du texte*. Plutarch maintains that *allêgoria* substituted for the obsolete *hyponoia* (*Moralia* 19E). However, although *allêgoria* entails *hyponoia*, the converse does not hold. Not all *hyponoia* consists in *allêgoria* according to which, for instance, the Trojan War comprises a physical or an astronomical theory. Theagenes of Rhegium, Pherecydes of Syros and Metrodorus of Lampsaca ('DK' 61A4) practise *allêgorêsis* by transposing the poetic meaning into a philosophical framework, thus translating the poetic meaning into a philosophical one. According to ancient testimonies, Anaxagoras and his school practised physical and ethical *allêgorêsis* ('DK' 59A1). The practise of *allêgorêsis* by philosophers often has the aim of validating their doctrines. The *Derveni Papyrus*, which might have been written by a student of Anaxagoras or Diogenes of Apollonia, is a case in point since it is a translation of the Orphic theogony into cosmology. On the other hand, the exegetic interpretation is based on what is taken to be the necessarily ambiguous nature of language. This is why the exegetic interpretation as practised by Anaximander, Stesimbrotus of Thasos (Xenophon, *Symposium* 3.6) and Protagoras includes grammar analysis ('DK' 80A29) and ways of structuring a speech ('DK' 80A30), that is, also, stylistic analysis (*Protagoras* 344b1–2).

All interpretation is committed to the idea that as a vehicle for underlying truths, poetry has a double language. In fact, Plato seems to take for granted that poetry conveys hidden thoughts (*Republic* 378a–d) and speaks through enigmas (*ainittetai*: *Alcibiades* II.147b). However, the examples of physical *allêgorêsis* (e.g. *Theaetetus* 153c) are meant to be ironic insofar as for Plato the poets are not hidden philosophers, as

most practitioners of *allêgorêsis* claim. In this regard, although Plato's *allêgorêsis* does not appear much different in practise from that of the pre-Socratics (q.v.) and sophists (q.v.), there is a significant difference, which is the absence of the idea of implicit philosophical truths purposively hidden by poets. The poet is definitely not a philosopher (q.v. Philosophy and Philosopher) and therefore not able to provide philosophical truths. Belonging to the realm of opinion and belief (e.g. *R.* 331d5), poetry has no truth-value. In consequence, interpreting poetry has four purposes. (a) The first is to emphasize Plato's apparent philosophical stances (*Men.* 81a–b). This allows Plato to give a philosophical truth the authority and the persuasiveness of poetry. (b) A second purpose is to undermine other philosophical theories, for example, the flux theory (*Tht.* 152d–e). Plato can thereby point to the errors of the poets' sayings, which allegedly embody philosophical doctrines. These two purposes are mostly rhetorical. (c) A third purpose is to refute *doxa*, opinion and 'elenchic interpretation', as in the case of Polemarchus' interpretation of Simonides (*R.* bk 1). Interpreting poetry is here tantamount to refuting *doxa*. (d) A fourth purpose is to demonstrate that poetry has no philosophical content, therefore, no meaning to be retrieved. In this case, interpreting poetry for the sake of finding the truth is merely a vain and naïve undertaking. This is the conclusion that Socrates reaches after he tries to interpret Simonides' poetry in *Prt.* Belonging to the nonhistoric, his interpretation implies anticontextualism whereby several lines are interpreted with no relation to the whole, and decontextualization whereby a sentence is transposed into a philosophical framework, that is, translated to become an assertion; hence the anti-intentionalism that this interpretation entails (*Phaedrus* 275c2).

Before completing the process of translation, Socrates tests various interpretations that he rejects on the ground of their falsity, and concludes by giving the only interpretation possible on account of its truth (*Prt.* 345d). The exercise, whether or not a parody, demonstrates a conflict of interpretations due to the impossibility of retrieving the authorial intention and, consequently, the necessity for reaching the truth through dialectic (*Hippias Minor* 364d; *Prt.* 347c). Poetry consists of an open text in the hands of an interpreter who manipulates it at will and who therefore becomes, to some degree, the author of the text, as Socrates exemplifies.

One may ask how Plato avoids this pitfall in the case of his own dialogues. In other words, does Plato find a way of circumscribing the various ways of interpreting his own work, that is, of circumventing the inherent weaknesses of writing, as expounded in *Phdr.*? Let us first note that in the case of narratives such as myths (q.v.), Plato discourages his reader from a literal interpretation (e.g. *Phd.* 114d) by having Socrates give the lesson of the story and practise exegesis (*R.* 618c–19b). Plato thus provides us with an interpretative framework on the basis of which he invites us to further elucidate the myth, that is, to lend ourselves to the practise of hermeneutics. The difference between an open text such as poetry and a Platonic narrative such as myth is that in the latter there is an underlying philosophical truth (*Phdr.* 278c), which under the guidance of the narrator Socrates the interpreter retrieves. A complementary means consists of a narrative's arousing in the reader the desire to understand her/his emotional experience, such as the fear of being mistaken about how we ought to live, in the case of eschatological narratives.

In *Phdr.*, Socrates argues for the superiority of a living dialogue over writing because, on the one hand, a text cannot defend itself (275e5) and, on the other hand, the former implies understanding (276e). As a simulation of a living dialogue, a written dialogue could have, however, the same effect on the soul. Some interpreters suppose that Plato endorses the polysemic nature of a text. If so, he may not have seen it as a handicap for the philosopher but rather as a trigger for understanding, that is, interpreting. The puzzles that Plato asks us to solve are philosophic and involve a philosophic confrontation along the same lines staged in the dialogues. He therefore guides and compels, to a certain extent, the reception of his work. This may have been Plato's goal: to help us become philosophers and improve our philosophical capability by having us interpret his dialogues.

ARISTOTLE

George Karamanolis

Aristotle was born in 384 BCE at Stagira in Chalcidike in northern Greece, as a son of Nicomachus, court physician to Amyntas II, king of Macedonia. In *c.* 367 Aristotle moved to Athens to study in Plato's Academy, where he stayed for 20 years, until Plato's death in 347. The evidence concerning Aristotle's study in the Academy is various anecdotes either aiming to illustrate Aristotle's supposed animosity towards Plato (Aelian 3.18–19; Düring 1957:320–6) or Aristotle's genius (*Vita Marciana* 6–7; Düring 1957:98, 109). Some of Aristotle's early works, such as the dialogues and the *Topics*, must have been written when Aristotle was a student of Plato in the Academy. It is unclear why Aristotle left the Academy; it may have been the anti-Macedonian sentiment in Athens after the victories of Philip II (Düring 1957:459), Aristotle's disappointment at not being chosen Plato's successor in the Academy (Jaeger 1962:111; Lloyd 1968:4–5) or Aristotle's disagreement with the Academy's new head, Speusippus; but it may also be that Aristotle was mature enough to conduct his own research and have a circle of students. Moving away from the Academy and initiating one's teaching circle does not necessarily amount to a break with it. Academics such as Eudoxus (D. L. 8.87) and Heraclides of Pontus (Philodemus, *Index Academicorum* col. VII Dorandi) held such circles. Aristotle left Athens to go to Assos in Asia Minor to join the circle of Hermeias, consisting mainly of Academics, and then moved to the island of Lesbos, where he carried out biological research. In 342, invited by Philip II to undertake the education of Alexander, Aristotle moved to Macedon, to return to Athens once again in 335, where he stayed until 323. This is the most prolific period of Aristotle's life, and the time he established his own school, the Lyceum (D. L. 2–3). Being indicted for impiety (D. L. 5.5), Aristotle went to Chalcis in 323, where he died a year later.

Aristotle's acquaintance with Plato's work and thought is manifested in numerous references to Plato and his dialogues. Aristotle commits Plato to specific doctrines, such as on the forms (q.v.; *Metaphysics* 1.9, 13.4–5, *Nicomachean Ethics* 1.4, 6), the first principles (*Metaphysics* 1.6), recollection (q.v.; *Prior Analytics* 2.21, *Posterior Analytics* 1.1), the creation of the world (*De caelo* 1.12, 3.1–2, 7, *Physics* 1.9, 4.2), matter (*De Generatione et Corruptione*. 1.2, 8), the soul (q.v.; *De anima* 1.2–3), the happy life (*Nicomachean Ethics*. 1.4, 2.3), the role of pleasure (q.v.; *Nicomachean Ethics*. 10.2), the political life (*Politics* 2.2–6, 5.12), let alone Plato's unwritten doctrines (q.v.; *Physics* 209b15).

Aristotle further distinguishes within Plato's dialogues between Socratic and Platonic views. On the issue of virtue or excellence (q.v.), for instance, Aristotle reports that Socrates identified virtue with knowledge and that he denied the possibility of incontinence (*akrasia*), implying that this was not Plato's position (*Nicomachean Ethics*. 1116b3–26, 1144b17–30; *Eudemian Ethics* 1229a14–16, 1230a6–8, 1246b32–7).

Aristotle takes a critical attitude towards the reportedly Platonic doctrines, approving some and, more often, criticizing others. Aristotle's testimony has been considered valuable by those ancient and modern Platonists who view Plato's philosophy as a system of doctrines. The scope of Aristotle's testimony regarding Plato's philosophy has been debated, however. Some narrow it to Aristotle's reports about Plato and the Old Academics, others extend it to the Aristotelian arguments and views which are ostensibly similar to those presented in Plato (e.g. the *Nicomachean Ethics*. vis-à-vis the *Republic*), and yet others extend it to those Aristotelian views which can qualify as developments of Platonic ideas (e.g. Aristotle's logic; Karamanolis 2006:16–28).

Based on Aristotle's evidence suggesting that Plato had doctrines, Antiochus (first-century BCE) distinguishes between Socratic/aporetic and Platonic/doctrinal dialogues (Cicero, *Academica* I.17–18) and uses Aristotle, especially his ethics (*De finibus* V.12), and the Old Academics as guides for the articulation of Plato's presumed doctrines. Aristotle's report in *Metaphysics* 1 on Plato's first principles and the forms attracted much attention from the time of Eudorus (end of the first-century BCE), who relies on *Metaphysics* 1.988a7–17 for a reconstruction of Plato's doctrine of the first principles (Alexander, *In Metaphysica* 58.31–59).

In this passage, Aristotle argues that Plato accepts two causes, a formal one, accounting for being, and matter, and he suggests that the former includes the forms and the One (q.v.). Eudorus corrects the passage to the effect that Plato admits only one cause, the One, thus crediting Plato with the metaphysical monism ascribed to Pythagoras (*Metaphysics* 1.987b21–8a7), an interpretation adopted later by Pythagorean Platonists, such as Moderatus (first-century CE) and Numenius (second-century CE). Regarding Plato's *Timaeus*, Aristotle construes the dialogue to the effect that the world was created at a certain point in time from the mixture of forms and matter (*De caelo* 1.12, 3.1–2) and criticizes Plato for committing the logical fallacy of maintaining that something generated can escape perishing. Platonists since Xenocrates set themselves in dialogue with Aristotle's interpretation of the *Ti.*, assuming much of it, while they set out to refute Aristotle's criticisms. They adopt Aristotle's terminology that the world is *genêtos* (the term does not occur in the dialogue), while arguing for a nonliteral interpretation of the dialogue; they assume Aristotle's interpretation (*Physics* 1.9, 4.2) that the receptacle (*chôra*) is identical with matter (e.g. Alcinous, *Didascalicos* 8), which is far from clear from the dialogue itself. Similarly important for the interpretation of Plato's conception of the soul in the *Ti.*, is Aristotle's *De anima* 1. Aristotle suggests that Plato considered the soul as a spatial magnitude and criticizes this view accordingly (*De anima* 407a2–19), while earlier on (*De anima* 404b16–30) he refers to the work 'On Philosophy'. It is unclear whether this means his own or Plato's lectures on philosophy, but he reports that Plato conceived of soul as a mathematical magnitude with its powers being assimilated to numbers (intellect is identified as 1, knowledge as 2, opinion

as 3, etc.). Some ancient Platonists adopted the latter interpretation, assuming Aristotle's access to Platonic doctrines (e.g. Xenocrates and Crantor, in Plutarch, *On the generation of the soul in the Timaeus* 1012E–13A).

Aristotle's critical appreciation of Plato's philosophy raises the question of how much of a Platonist he is. Seminal in this regard has been Jaeger's (1962) view that Aristotle developed himself from a faithful Platonist in the Academy to progressively non-Platonic views, until he abandoned Platonism completely at the end of his career. Against this it may be replied that Aristotle was never a faithful Platonist in the sense of not criticizing Plato, given the evidence of early works such as the *Categories* (Lloyd 1968:28–41). Besides, in a late work such as the *Nicomachean Ethics.*, Aristotle both criticizes Plato (1.6) while he also approves of and develops views defended in the *R.* and the *Philebus* (cf. 2.3, 10.2). Nevertheless, Aristotle arguably remains a Platonist in terms of his methods, standards, philosophical concerns and aims in philosophy (Gerson 2005; Owen 1986).

ACADEMY OF ATHENS, ANCIENT HISTORY OF

George Karamanolis

The Academy was a grove in the outskirts of Athens, sacred to the hero Academos, 1.5 km west of the Dipylon gate, in which there was also a gymnasium (Diogenes Laertius 3.7; Cicero; *De finibus* V.1). According to Diogenes Laertius, Plato acquired property in the Academy after his return from the first visit to Sicily in 387/6 (D. L. 3.20). The term used by our sources for this property is 'garden' (*kêpos*; *kêpidion*), but, as John

Dillon (2003:5) has rightly argued, there was more than a garden. Plato may have owned a house there (Aelian 3.19), and we also hear of a promenade (*peripatos*; Aelian 3.19), and a hall (*exedra*; D. L. 4.19), possibly a lecture hall (Cicero; *De finibus* V.4; Philodemus; *Index Academicorum* col. 29, p. 100 Mekler), close to which the students (*hoi mathêtai*) lived in little huts (D. L. 4.19). We do not know when Plato started using the place for teaching, but a turning point in the transformation of the place into a regular meeting point for Plato's associates may have been the erection of a shrine of the Muses (*mouseion*) in the Academy (D. L. 4.1). The place soon became sufficiently well known, however, to attract students from far away, such as Xenocrates from Chalcedon in the Propontis around 374/5 and Aristotle from Stagira in 367.

Our information about the activities in Plato's Academy is scarce. A number of testimonies from ancient comedy playwrights state that Plato and his pupils were walking and conversing about issues such as the good and the soul-body relationship (D. L. 3.26–32; Riginos 1976:123–9). The most significant of those testimonies is a fragment from Epicrates (third-century BCE), who presents a bunch of Academics debating about the division of the pumpkin (f. 10 Kassel-Austin). The fragment alludes to the method of division discussed in Plato's late dialogues (such as the *Sophist* and the *Politicus*; cf. D. L. 3.81–108), suggesting that some central features of Plato's thought were sufficiently defused to become subjects of parody presented to nonphilosophers. Apparently membership in the Academy was free for anyone, including women (D. L. 3.46, 4.2), but Speusippus allegedly introduced a fee (D. L. 4.2–3). Plato's circle of students was considerable (D. L. 3.46), including eminent scientists, such as Philip of

Opus and Eudoxus; the latter was appointed acting head of the Academy while Plato was in his second trip to Sicily (367–5; *Vita Marciana* 11).

The case of Eudoxus is instructive. Aristotle testifies that Eudoxus maintained a view on pleasure according to which pleasure is the highest good and man's final end, because all beings seek it and try to avoid the opposite, pain (*Nicomachean Ethics* 1172b9–25). Aristotle contrasts Eudoxus' view with the allegedly Platonic view, namely that pleasure is not the good (see *Philebus* 20e–2b, 60a–c; q.v. Pleasure). On the same issue, Speusippus is credited with an argument against the identification of pleasure with the good (q.v.) and also with the view that pleasure is not good even accidentally, on the ground that it has a sensible nature (*aisthêtê physis*), which is why he advised avoiding any pleasure (*Nicomachean Ethics*. 1152b8–10, 1153b1–9).

This evidence suggests that there was no doctrinal uniformity but rather an ongoing debate in the Academy on the role of pleasure. Evidence for this debate we have in Plato's dialogues *Protagoras*, *Phaedo*, *Phlb.* and in a series of writings on the same topic by Speusippus (D. L. 4.4), Philip of Opus (Suda s.v. *philosophos*), Xenocrates (D. L. 4.12), Heraclides (ff. 55–61 Wehrli) and also Aristotle (D. L. 5.24), which are no longer extant. The surviving evidence of the work of Plato's students and immediate successors point to a similar lack of doctrinal uniformity within the Academy also with respect to other topics, such as the first principles, the forms (q.v.), the status of the soul (q.v.), emotions (q.v.) and happiness (q.v.). Speusippus and Xenocrates, Plato's loyal students and successors in the Academy are interesting in this regard as they deal with the same issues but their answers vary, sometimes considerably.

Speusippus (*ca.* 410–338/9; scholarch 347–39), Plato's nephew, son of his sister Potone, is credited with a theory of first principles, arguably preserved by Iamblichus, *De communi mathematica scientia* ch. 4 (Dillon 2003:40–2; Merlan 1960). According to this theory, which is largely inspired by the *Timaeus* and the *Phlb.*, there are two principles, the One (q.v.), which accounts for order and identity, and a principle of multiplicity and division (*plêthos*). The two principles produce both non-spatial and spatial multiplicity, that is, numbers and geometrical objects. Speusippus' attempt clearly was to have the two principles account for all kinds of being, although it is not clear how exactly. Aristotle (*Metaphysics* 1085a31–b34, 1092a21–b8) gives an unclear and highly critical picture, and he is actually confusing us when he suggests that Speusippus abandoned the forms and replaced them with mathematical entities (*Metaphysics* 1086a2–5). Speusippus may have revised Plato's theory of forms but with a view to strengthen it. The revision may be caused by the difficulty of squaring the theory with Plato's method of division, since abstract entities, such as the form 'living being', resist division into species, for example, man or cat (Cherniss 1945:41–3). Speusippus probably maintained that the two principles produce mathematical and geometrical entities, including the world soul itself, which he defined as 'the form of omni-dimensional extended' (f. 54 Tarán). This soul serves as principle (*Metaphysics* 1028b15–27) of souls and of the sensible realm; it hosts the forms of sensible objects and eventually produces sensible reality (Dillon 2003:51–4). Given the role of intelligible entities in producing reality, Speusippus considers them essential for cognition. This can take the form of cognitive reason (*epistê-monikos logos*) or cognitive perception

(*epistêmonikê aesthesis*; Sextus, *Adv. Math.* 7.145–6; f. 75 Tarán).

Xenocrates follows Speusippus in assuming a principle of unity, order and identity, the One, and a principle of multiplicity, the Dyad (Aristotle, *Metaphysics* 1087b4–21). The One is identified with the intellect of the highest god, while the Dyad with the receptacle of the *Ti*. The contact of the two principles produces the world soul, which produces sensible reality (Plutarch, *De animae procreatione in Timaeo* 1012D–E). Unlike Speusippus, however, Xenocrates identified the forms with mathematical entities, arguing that forms and numbers have the same nature (*Metaphysics* 1028b24–7). Xenocrates characterized the forms as 'paradigmatic' (Proclus, *In Parmenidem* 888.13–15 Cousin; f. 94 Isnardi-Parente), which suggests that he maintained the eternal existence of the forms as models of the immanent counterparts in sensible entities (Alexander, *In Metaphysica* 819.37–41 Hayduck; f. 116 I.–P). Xenocrates' views, especially on the forms, appear to have been crafted as a response to Aristotle's objections, which reflects a tension in the Academy and a tendency towards systematization. Such a tendency is supported by Sextus Empiricus' testimony (*Against the Logicians* I.16), which credits Xenocrates with the division of philosophy into three branches: logic, physics and ethics.

Our knowledge of Xenocrates' successor in the Academy, Polemon (314/313–270/269) is very limited. He focused on ethics, arguing that virtue is sufficient for happiness and that the end (*telos*) must be a life according to nature (Cicero; *De finibus* IV.4). His most notable pupil was Crantor, who worked in ethics and on the *Ti.*, being the first to write an exegetical work on it (Proclus, *In Timaeum* I.76.1–2). With the election of Arcesilaus as scholarch, the Academy changed its philosophical point of view significantly enough to mark a distinct phase in its history, the 'Middle Academy' (D. L. 1.14, Sextus, *Outlines of Pyrrhonism* 1.220) or 'New Academy' (Cicero, *Academica* I.46). Arcesilaus was inspired by the Socratic practise of examining a thesis without committing himself to it; he rather withheld assent (*epochê*) as the only way of avoiding error, and criticized the Stoic doctrine of cognition (*katalêpsis*). The Stoic criticism that withholding assent leads to inaction was countered by Carneades (scholarch 156/5–137/6) who argued that plausible impression (*pithanon*) suffices for deciding and acting. This line of argument comes to an end with Philo of Larissa (scholarch 110–*c.* 83), who rejected withholding assent, arguing that knowledge is possible but not of the Stoic kind. His pupil Antiochus abandoned scepticism altogether, advocating a return to the early Academy. Antiochus maintained that Plato had doctrines, from which early Academics and Aristotle were inspired, and set out to reconstruct them, a project that was met with criticism in antiquity (*Academica* I.46, II.15). In one sense the Academy ceases to exist with Antiochus; when Cicero visits it in 79 BCE, he witnesses no philosophical activity (*De finibus* V.1–4; see Glucker 1978:242). In the following centuries Platonists teach their circles of students in their own schools.

The existing evidence about the Academy raises the question of the nature and the content of Plato's teaching. Apart from individual differences, the history of the Academy and of Platonism in general hosts two opposing interpretative strategies, the doctrinal and the sceptical (Tarrant 2000:10–19). These strategies determine two poles in the scholarly appreciation of Plato. The one assumes that Plato was teaching specific doctrines through

his dialogues, which contain some long monologues, but also his oral communications, the so-called unwritten doctrines (Aristotle, *Physics* 209b15). The opposite scholarly pole emphasizes Plato's methodology, especially the dialogic form, as a means of avoiding commitment and authority, and the revision in which Plato subjects his own theories. Several suggestions cover the middle ground between the two poles. In this falls also the position of the anonymous author of a commentary on *Theaetetus* (first-century AD?), who preserves two testimonies regarding Plato's teaching in the Academy. According to one of them, 'Plato was an Academic philosopher since he did not have any doctrines' (*Anon. in Tht.* 54.38–42), while according to the other 'Plato points to the view he likes to those who are familiar with his method' (*Tht.* 59.8–17). The Epicurean Philodemus (first-century BCE) finally argues that 'there was much teaching activity at the time [of Plato], with Plato being the architect who was presenting problems' (*Index Academicorum*, col. Y Dorandi).

JEWISH PLATONISM (ANCIENT)

David T. Runia

There is no mention of Judea or the Jewish people in Plato and there is no reference to Greek philosophical ideas in the Hebrew Bible. The history of Jewish Platonism begins when contact was established between the expanding Hellenistic world and the Jews. This process first occurred in a significant way in the bastion of Hellenism founded by Alexander the Great in Alexandria.

A foundational event for Hellenistic Judaism was the translation of the Hebrew scriptures into Greek. It has been argued that the Septuagint translation reflects the influence of Platonic terminology in some key texts, for example, *aoratos* in Gen. 1.2, *eikôn* in Gen. 1.26, *paradeigma* in Exod. 25.40 (Rösel 1994). This remains controversial, but the terminology certainly aided later thinkers in locating Platonic doctrines in scripture. The Septuagint also contains some late books originally written in Greek. The *Wisdom of Solomon* clearly shows the influence of Middle Platonism (Winston 1979:34), particularly in its doctrine of creation and the immortality of the soul. It was probably written in Alexandria in *c*. 50 BCE.

But by far the most famous ancient Jewish 'Platonist' was Philo of Alexandria (15 BCE–50 CE). Indeed, the fourth-century Church father Jerome in his brief biographical notice on Philo mentions a saying in circulation among the Greeks that 'either Plato philonizes or Philo platonizes, so great is the similarity in doctrines and style' (*De vir. ill.* 11).

Philo lived all his life in Alexandria and was a member of a wealthy and highly influential family in the Jewish community. In a famous passage (*De congressu* 73–80) he states that he received an excellent education in the subjects of the Greek *paideia*, enabling him to place his knowledge of philosophy in the service of God. He wrote in Greek and about fifty of his treatises are extant. Most of these focus on the interpretation of scripture and the promotion of Jewish causes, but five treatises treat philosophical themes and show an impressive knowledge of Greek philosophy. It may be assumed that Philo was acquainted with contemporary developments in philosophy as they occurred in the Alexandria of his day, but unfortunately he gives us no detailed information. It has to be gleaned from his writings.

Philo's basic method is to interpret the Greek Bible, and in particular the five books

of Moses, with the aid of the doctrines of Greek philosophy. He assumes that these doctrines are present in scripture and that later philosophers derived them from the great Jewish sage (or perhaps reached them independently). It enables him to demonstrate the superiority of Jewish thought and the reasonableness of the injunctions of the Jewish law. It is not surprising, therefore, that Philo only names Plato 13 times in all his writings, and almost all of these references are in his philosophical or apologetic writings (seven in the treatise *De aeternitate mundi* alone). Plato's name is never mentioned in his allegorical treatises. But Philo does twice quote passages from *Theaetetus* 176a–c in *De fuga* 63 and 82, introducing Plato as 'a person highly esteemed among those admired for their wisdom'. In *Quod omnis probus* 13 he appears to refer to 'the most holy Plato', but the reading is contested and more likely should read 'the most clear-voiced Plato', that is, a reference to *Phaedrus* 237a7. A negative note is struck in *De vita contemplativa* 57–63, where Philo sharply criticizes the eroticism of Plato's *Symposium* as compared with the sober feasts of the Therapeutae, a group of Jewish contemplatives living outside Alexandria.

Plato's philosophy had a profound effect on Philo's thought. The following doctrines are the most significant. (a) God is conceived as being and often called *to on* (based on the crucial biblical text Exod. 3.14). (b) Philo accepts and frequently uses the division into the noetic and the sense-perceptible realms. (c) He regards the doctrine of the ideas as indispensable and is the first author to speak of the *kosmos noêtos*. (d) Negative theology is commonly used to express human knowledge of God as supreme Being. (e) He closely follows the *Timaeus* in expounding the doctrine of creation, with particular emphasis on the role of the ideas and unformed matter (*hulê*). (f) The cosmos is created (taken literally as the commencement of time), but will not be destroyed. (g) The Platonic doctrine of soul is not used in cosmology, but has a strong influence on Philo's anthropology. The human being is a duality consisting of soul and body. The soul is immortal and is often described in binary and tripartite terms. (h) In ethics Philo combines Stoic and Platonist doctrines on the virtues and the passions. He is greatly attracted to the formulation of the *telos* as 'becoming like God' (*homoiôsis theôi*).

The prominence of the above doctrines shows that Philo's appropriation of Plato's thought is strongly influenced by the interpretative developments of Middle Platonism (Dillon 1996:139–81). This influence also explains his attraction to dialogues such as the *Ti.*, *Phaedo*, *Phdr.*, *Republic*, *Laws* and *Tht.*, with less use made of the early Socratic dialogues and later works such as the *Sophist* and *Politicus*. See further the detailed analyses of Méasson (1986) and Runia (1986). The further influence of Eudorus of Alexandria (q.v.) and early neo-pythagoreanism (q.v.) has been postulated (Bonazzi 2008) but cannot be proven in detail.

It would be wrong, however, to regard Philo himself as a Middle Platonist (Runia 1993b). He is attracted to the doctrines of Platonism and they play a central role in his thought. His first loyalty, however, is to his ancestral religion and its sacred writings. He uses Platonic doctrines (and also those of other philosophers) for his chief goal, to demonstrate the superiority of the philosophy of Moses.

Philo's thought exerted a strong influence on early Christian writers, especially in Alexandria (Runia 1993a), and they took over many of the Platonic themes that he located in scripture. But the Rabbis in Palestine rejected his positive attitude to Hellenism and were not interested in Platonic thought. Jewish Platonism does not recommence until the medieval period (q.v. Medieval Jewish Platonism).

NEOPLATONISM AND ITS DIASPORA

Francesco Fronterotta

(I) PLOTINUS

Regarded as the founder of Neoplatonism (Cleary 1997; Lloyd 1990; Wallis 1972), Plotinus (*c.* 205–70 CE) was born in Egypt and around the age of 27 became a disciple of Ammonius Saccas. He took part in the Emperor Gordian III's expedition to the East, but on the Emperor's death (244), he took refuge in Antioch and then in Rome. Plotinus lived in the capital of the Empire from 244 to 269 among members of the Roman aristocracy linked to the Emperor Gallienus, upon whose assassination in 269 he left Rome for Campania, where he died more or less in solitude in 270. During his period in Rome Plotinus united a large group of followers, the most important of whom were Amelius (from 246 to 269) and Porphyry (from 263 to 268), both of whom attended his lessons, which were mainly devoted to commenting on the works of Plato. He began to set his teaching down in writing in 254, and from then to 263 produced 21 treatises; between 263 and 268 Plotinus composed 24 treatises, while in the last year of his life, in Campania, he completed the last nine, sending them to Porphyry before he died. As well as writing a biography of his master (*On the life of Plotinus and the order of his treatises*),

Porphyry prepared an edition of his treatises in the form of *Enneads* (54 treatises divided into six groups of nine (= 'ninth', *ennead*)) about 30 years after Plotinus' death. He arranged them thematically, although he also took pains to indicate the chronological order of composition. The first *Ennead* is on moral subjects; the second deals with physics and the sensible world; the third examines cosmological questions; the fourth, fifth and sixth are on the soul, the intellect and the one respectively, that is, the three fundamental principles – or 'hypostases' – of Plotinus' doctrine.

Plotinus' most characteristic doctrine (Gerson 1994; O'Meara 1993; Rist 1967) is that of the three 'hypostases' which articulate the whole of reality: the one, the intellect and the soul. Unlike the Platonic tradition, which had identified the cause and principle of the physical world in the intelligible world of transcendent Platonic ideas, in various ways associated with a demiurgic intelligence that makes use of them to produce the sensible cosmos, Plotinus identified the first principle of everything in a reality that is absolutely simple and one to which we can attribute the conventional denomination of 'one' or 'good'. Without exercising any voluntary, intelligent or providential act, this emanates, through its infinite power, 'super-abundant' portions of itself, thus giving rise to inferior realities. The intellect (Emilsson 2007) is placed in the second degree of reality, consists of the totality of the intelligible world of ideas, and, according to Plato's teaching, constitutes the model for the sensible world. The soul (Blumenthal 1971) is placed in the third degree of reality, and is a degradation of the intellect and the intelligible on the spatial-temporal plane of extension and division. It has the task of transposing ideal models, in the form of rational principles acting on matter, in the sensible world. Below the soul remains the sensible world, which owes its ontological substance to the form it receives from the intelligible, by virtue of the action of the soul, but possesses a material dimension that depends on the gradual exhaustion of the generating action of the one.

Plotinus introduces three main innovatory features into the Platonic tradition. (a) Previous commentary on Plato had treated the *Timaeus* as the most important dialogue, but Plotinus considered it alongside the *Parmenides*, and the second part of this dialogue in particular, which contains a series of deductions concerning the one that he reads as an anticipation of his doctrine of the three hypostases. (b) In the first series of deductions, Plotinus identifies a principle that is absolutely first, one and simple, partly drawing on the description of the idea of the good that Plato gives at the end of *Republic* bk 6, and situates it completely beyond being and reality. Being therefore unattainable by thought and discourse, it can only be expressed in negative terms, by approximations to it in terms of what it is not. (c) Plotinus elaborates an account of the real that is extremely unified and simplified, in that it derives from an absolutely single and simple principle, and he gives it a fully rational and necessary articulation, against any form of religious influence connected with theurgy, Gnostic doctrines or contemporary astrological currents of thought. In Plotinus' original synthesis, as well as the Platonic doctrinal elements, there emerges a significant Stoic philosophical influence, but also a closely argued reflection on Aristotle's work.

(**II**) *Neoplatonism after Plotinus*

Plotinus' most important disciple, Porphyry (*c.* 232–301 CE), composed an enormous body of work, which has been almost wholly lost and that partly questions Plotinus and shows the influence of his previous master, Longinus (Smith 1974). Significantly, it emphasized the importance of Aristotle's thought although its theoretical framework was essentially Platonic. As well as his biography of Plotinus and his edition of the *Enneads*, on which he also wrote a commentary (fragments of which have survived with the title *Sentences*), he also wrote commentaries on Plato's and Aristotle's works, an *Introduction to Aristotle's Categories* (*Isagogê*), a treatise in which he claimed that Plato's and Aristotle's thinking converged (*That the Schools of Plato and Aristotle are one only*), a *History of Philosophy* and a *Life of Pythagoras*, also taking an interest in theurgy and vegetarianism, practicing allegory and writing a lengthy treatise *Against the Christians*.

Iamblichus (*c.* 240–325 CE) directed a school of philosophy at Apamea in Syria, in which he introduced a vast study programme that involved the reading of the works of Aristotle, an introduction to Pythagorean philosophy and the study of Plato's dialogues, culminating in the interpretation of the *Ti.* and the *Prm.* He wrote commentaries, most of them lost, on some of Plato's dialogues (*First Alcibiades*; *Phaedo*; *Phaedrus*; *Philebus*; *Prm.*; *Sophist.*; *Ti.*) and on some of Aristotle's works (*Prior Analytics*; *De interpretatione*; *De caelo*); some fragments remain of other treatises – *On the Soul*, *On the Chaldean Oracles*, *On the Gods*; while four out of ten books have survived of a treatise *On the Pythagorean School* (with the titles *Life of Pythagoras*, *Exhortation to Philosophy*, *Common Mathematical Theory*, *On Nicomachus' Introduction to Mathematics*). Unlike Plotinus, Iamblichus saw Plato's philosophy as a theology related to Pythagoreanism, culminating in a level he

identified as superior even to Plotinus' first principle, designated as an 'Ineffable beyond the One' (Dillon 1987; Shaw 1995; Steel 1978).

This position aroused wide-ranging debate among the successive exponents of the School of Athens (Plato's Academy), who were active between the end of the fourth century and the first decades of the sixth-century CE. Plutarch of Athens (late fourth- early fifth-century CE) is regarded as its founder. Of him we know very little and none of his works have come down to us. His successor, Syrianus (d. in 437), drew up a scholastic teaching programme not unlike that of Iamblichus, and wrote commentaries on *Beta*, *Gamma*, *Mu* and *Nu* of Aristotle's *Metaphysics*, on Plato's *Phdr.*, and above all on the *Prm.*, of which, according to his pupil Proclus, he suggested a particularly detailed interpretation. Proclus (*c.* 412–85) is the best known exponent of the school, as we possess a good part of his works: comments on Plato's dialogues (on the *Alc. I*, *Ti.*, *R.*, *Cratylus* and *Prm.*), school treatises, and above all the *Platonic Theology*, in which Proclus provided a systematic exposition of the main Neoplatonic doctrines (Gersh 1973), once again establishing the one as first principle of everything, in conformity with Plotinus' doctrine and in opposition to Iamblichus. Damascius (462–>532), who led the School of Athens until it was closed by Justinian in 529 CE, took a different view: for Damascius, who wrote a commentary on the *Prm.* and a treatise *On First Principles*, the first of Plotinus' hypostases – the one – is preceded by another, absolutely ineffable, principle, while the one is divided into inferior principles that, by degeneration, lead to the production of the whole of reality.

Of the Alexandrian School (Blumenthal and Lloyd 1982; Watts 2006) little has survived beyond a few names, although it must have had a certain intellectual influence in the fourth century. Some philosophers, such as Hermias, Hierocles, Isidorus, as well as Proclus and Damascius, who were born in Alexandria, received their philosophical education in Athens; of Hypatia, the daughter of the mathematician and astronomer Theon, we know that she taught Synesius of Cyrene, who later converted to Christianity, and that her successor was Hierocles, the head of a Platonic school around 430. Those who taught at Alexandria during the fifth and sixth centuries probably included Hermias, his son Ammonius, whose lessons were published by Philoponus, a certain Eutocius and Olympiodorus, the last pagan head of the School and author of commentaries on some of the works of Plato and Aristotle.

Late Neoplatonism displayed a clear tendency to defend the substantial theoretical convergence between the doctrines of Plato and Aristotle, explaining why many of its exponents, philosophers with a Platonic background, devoted themselves to commenting on the works of Aristotle: the most famous case is Simplicius, who was educated in Alexandria and active in Athens until the Academy was closed; he was the author of commentaries on Aristotle's works and can be placed at the end of the long history of Neoplatonism.

Section B: The Influence of Plato in the Middle Ages and Renaissance

MEDIEVAL ISLAMIC PLATONISM

Taneli Kukkonen

In classical Arabic philosophy Plato features as the least familiar member in a line of godly

philosophers stretching from Socrates (q.v.) to Aristotle (q.v.): his portrait was not drawn as vividly as Socrates' in the wisdom literature, nor yet were his works studied as Aristotle's were. Still, the spectre of Plato looms large over Islamic philosophy, to the extent that one may legitimately ask whether Arabic philosophy in the classical period should be dubbed Platonizing Aristotelianism, as is now common, or whether what we have is rather a Neoplatonic (q.v.) tradition dressed in Aristotelian garb. The Arabic philosophers read almost nothing of Plato, and yet their scholarly work over and over again returns to Platonic and Neoplatonic themes, whether as an intellectual resource to be grasped (as with the immortality of the soul) or a temptation to be resisted (as was the case with the theory of ideas).

It is in the school of Alexandria's pervasive influence that an explanation is to be sought. The sixth-century Alexandrians had had to justify their dwelling on Aristotle when it was the divine Plato who held the key to true transcendent wisdom: their explanation took the form of a teleologically interpreted history of philosophy which helped to build the case for Aristotle, not Plato, as the foremost Greek thinker in the minds of Syriac and Arabic scholars. This in turn appears to have led to Plato's dialogues being largely neglected in the translation movement that took place from the eighth- to the tenth-century CE. Certainly, there was no systematic effort to render Plato into Arabic the way there was for Aristotle or even, say, Galen or Ptolemy.

At the same time, philosophizing in the Near East retained the broad soteriological and cosmological orientation it had inherited from the ancient Platonic schools. Neoplatonic texts such as the *Theology of Aristotle* and the *Book on the Highest Good* (in reality, adaptations from *Enneads* 4–6 and Proclus' *Elements of Theology*) therefore quickly found an audience, as they answered a perceived need for describing the great chain of being in broader terms than anything found in the more scientific Greek literature. The *Theology of Aristotle* also provided materials for bridging the gap between the Platonic view of the soul present in Jewish, Christian and Muslim spirituality – the tripartite division in moral psychology, the dualistic conception of the soul's true nature and its destiny – with the more mundane musings of Aristotle's *De anima*. In this way, the Peripatetic curriculum adopted by Muslim *falsafa* could be situated in the larger framework of god, cosmos and soul, and within the grand story of process and return (*al-mabda' wa al-ma'âd*).

What resulted was a general conception of philosophy that would have appeared familiar to a sixth-century Platonist, with the important difference that all references to traditional Greek religion had been carefully excised and with it the notion of *henads* and other principles beyond the intellectual. The First Principle might still be placed beyond the reach of reason, limit or quiddity, though not beyond being or existence (this is the single most important transformation of Plotinian Platonism effected by the Arabic philosophers); the other supernal principles were filled from the ranks of the Aristotelian separate intelligences, and the Agent Intellect made into a repository for the intelligibles.

As concerns doctrines commonly attributed to Plato, doxographies such as Pseudo-Plutarch's *Placita philosophorum* sufficed in introducing these. They would also serve to contrast Plato's and the Academy's teachings with those of the other schools. The disagreements between Plato and Aristotle received much play, for instance, and acted as a useful counterweight to the harmonizing tendencies exemplified by al-Fârâbî's (d. 950) *Agreement between the Opinions of the Two Sages*. On a personal level, a respectful and admiring attitude between Plato and Aristotle was consistently maintained (in some more fabulous stories Plato adopted the orphan Aristotle). Fresh gnomological and doxographical compilations were put together from older materials and reached yet wider audiences.

What is missing from the Arabic scene is any deeper engagement with the intricacies of actual Platonic dialogues. This may have been due partly to the forbidding character of fifth-/sixth-century commentaries, exceedingly complex and replete with religious allusions, or it may have had more to do with the socioeconomic facts on the ground when it came to finding translating work. The renowned translator Hunayn Ibn Ishâq lists Proclus as the most dependable guide to Plato, but this may simply repeat received wisdom. Whatever the reason, no Platonic text has come to us in Arabic translation, and there is reason to doubt that a single dialogue was ever translated in full in the first place.

Among the Peripatetics the record is particularly scant. Bibliographical sources attest to the *Republic* and *Laws* receiving some kind of comments from Hunayn, and according to the Christian Peripatetic Yahyâ Ibn 'Adî (d. 974) Hunayn's son Ishâq translated the *Sophist* along with Olympiodorus' commentary. These works seem to have had no impact: the abridgements of the *Lg.* and the *R.* produced by al-Fârâbî and Ibn Rushd (the Latin Averroes, 1126–98) are more likely to have been written on the basis of Galen's compendia. Still, lengthy citations of individual passages from the *R.* have at least been detected: certainly this work above all others interested the Peripatetics, due to the unavailability of Aristotle's *Politics*. Other citations and close paraphrases that were in circulation come from predictable sources: *Phaedo* on metempsychosis, *Crito* on Socrates' death. Finally, al-Fârâbî's *Philosophy of Plato* attests to a working knowledge of some of the main positions advanced in Plato's dialogues (all of the familiar works minus the *Minos* are listed), though the dogmatic presentation – likely derivative of some Middle Platonic compendium – distorts Plato into the shape of an Aristotelian systematic philosopher. None of this evidences a serious attempt to advance beyond the popular imagination.

Plato exercised a wider influence in the medical tradition, principally due to Galen's pronounced yet vague Platonic leanings. The noted bibliophile Ibn al-Nadîm in his *Catalogue* reports that he personally had managed to get a hold of Galenic compendia on the *Cratylus, Sph., Statesman, Parmenides, Euthydemus, R., Timaeus* and the *Lg.*: this covers the first half of Galen's *Synopsis*. It is probably because of his background in medicine that the notorious philosopher-physician al-Râzî (the Latin Rhazes, d. 925) pledged allegiance to Plato above others: al-Râzî is said to have produced a treatise on the *Ti.*, and certainly his cosmology bears a (pre-Plotinian) Platonic stamp, though again nothing we know concerning his teachings reflects an actual knowledge of Plato beyond Plutarch's or Galen's compendia, and in fact any detailed knowledge of the *R.* is explicitly ruled out. That a putative Platonic identity could be postulated on such a flimsy scholarly basis shows the ultimate thinness of Platonism under Islam. The same goes double for al-Suhrawardî (d. 1191), the Illuminationist philosopher who claimed that he was reinstituting Platonic

ideas when in fact the function served by his ideas was quite different. The notion of a later Persian Platonism should therefore be approached cautiously, as an ideological construct rather than a substantial continuation of the Platonic tradition: it is only Platonic to the extent that Avicenna (980–1037) and the Muslim Peripatetic tradition in general can be regarded as Platonic. But this is problematic.

MEDIEVAL JEWISH PLATONISM

Oliver Leaman

Jewish philosophy in the middle ages operated largely within the context of Islamic culture, and worked with the philosophical curriculum then current in that culture. Islamic philosophy grew out of Neoplatonism (q.v.), which had been the leading school of thought in the Greek world when philosophy started to be translated into Arabic, and moved subsequently into the medieval Jewish world. Neoplatonism had involved the study of both Platonic and Aristotelian texts, but this did not, in medieval times, entail the common Neoplatonist belief that Aristotle was in harmony with Plato. Rather it led to a certain blurring of the distinctions between them. The Islamic world particularly favoured Aristotle, and saw Plato as having been replaced by Aristotle on those issues where he was not in agreement with him. This view was expressed very clearly by the greatest Jewish philosopher, Moses Maimonides.

Before Maimonides three Jewish thinkers made considerable use of Plato. Saadya Gaon (882–942), Solomon Ibn Gabirol (*c.* 1021–*c.* 1057) and Bahya ben Asher (mid-thirteenth century; c. 1340) all accept Platonic philosophical psychology, where the soul and body are two substances conjoined temporarily during this life. In some ways it is reasonable to divide up the Jewish Middle Ages as before and after Maimonides. The latter's influence, plus that of Ibn Rushd (Averroes), emphasized what they took to be the rigour of Aristotelianism, and this was to dominate the philosophical curriculum of the Jewish world until the Renaissance and the uses of Plato, then to establish some form of humanism. It is as always very difficult to distinguish between Platonism and Neoplatonism in the medieval period, not so much because the classical Neoplatonic themes are difficult to distinguish from Plato, because they are not, but because there seems to have been very little reading of Plato without the accretions of interpreters and commentators, and so even where Platonic themes are evident, it is not clear that these actually come from Plato himself. Isaac Israeli, for instance, mentions what became very much a theme of Jewish thought within this period, the idea of *imitatio Dei*, through a purification of the soul. Plato was also often linked with a theory of the creation of the world out of a pre-existing matter, where the heavenly bodies are both everlasting and generated, as in the *Timaeus* 41a–b, a doctrine which Isaac Abravanel also refers to favourably (Feldman 2003).

In the Jewish world Plato was used widely in moral and political philosophy, and also aesthetics. It is often argued that this was because it was so helpful to have a doctrine available that linked politics with religion, and it was quite easy to see the *Republic* as basing authority in the state not only on the knowledge of philosophy but also on what can be taken as its source,

divine knowledge and ultimately on God and his representatives (Melamed 1997). Plato was the basis of political philosophy in the Islamic world also, largely because of the availability of the R. and, perhaps, the absence of Aristotle's *Politics*. On the other hand, availability was not the only issue, since what was translated into Hebrew was selective (Leaman 2005). Maimonides suggested that Plato is not worth reading, the idea being that whatever he had to say that was valuable was also said by Aristotle, and much better said. This attitude was not to change much until the onset of the Renaissance, when Plato was largely rediscovered in the Christian world; his thought then became very much used by Jewish thinkers like Judah Abravanel (c. 1465–c.1523), Yohanan Alemanno (c. 1435–d. after 1534) and Judah Moscato (c. 1530–c. 1593; cf. Feldman 1997). But even towards the end of the medieval period Isaac Abravanel (1437–1508) took a decidedly Platonic line on issues of significance such as the existence of an individual soul, where he found Plato's thought far more amenable to the various Aristotelian approaches that emphasize the soul's links with the body, its relationship with the active intellect and the importance of intellectual perfection for immortality. The Platonic idea of a separate soul was far more amenable to the defence of traditional religion that Isaac Abravanel had in mind, and this strategy should not be seen as a problematically eclectic approach to philosophy, since the Neoplatonic nature of most philosophy during this period makes such an orientation towards Plato easy to understand.

The disapproval that Maimonides had for Plato could be expected to have had a considerable effect on subsequent Jewish medieval thinkers, given Maimonides' high status, even among many of those firmly opposed to him. On the other hand, it has often been pointed out that much of his work is not that far from Plato (Frank 2009) and that it is quite easy to talk about a joint approach to moral and political thought followed by Plato and Aristotle (Jacobs 2010). The idea that law must have a rationale and not be based entirely on the will of god is one that Maimonides uses a great deal in his arguments about the basis of divine legislation. Maimonides sees the great leaders of the Jewish people as not just skilful politicians but also deep thinkers, whose inspiration comes from God of course, and yet who are able through their intellect to work out much of how legislation should operate. Maimonides has nothing but contempt for those who follow the law without understanding something at least of its theoretical background, and it is not difficult to see Plato's thought here being used to elucidate the links between Torah, Jewish religious law and *nomos*, rational law (Rosenthal 2010).

Much Jewish mystical work presents an account of the soul which resembles that of the *R.*, and if we are to find real evidence of Plato's thought in the medieval period it is to the kabbalah, or Jewish mysticism, that we must turn. Ideas work their way through much of the kabbalah (Leaman 2010) and resonate with a good deal of Plato's thought, especially as interpreted by the Neoplatonists (Idel 2002), including a sharp distinction between love of the body and love of God, the latter attainable by abstracting our thinking and concentrating and developing its form, and an enthusiasm for asceticism, the notion of spiritual and intellectual growth, together with a firm doctrine of the soul and its distinctiveness from the body. Socrates was seen in Islamic culture as a proto-Sufi and mystic,

and when the need was felt to challenge an overrational attitude to the world, Aristotle in other words, Plato could often be recruited as a more sympathetic intellectual source in both the Islamic and Jewish traditions.

MEDIEVAL CHRISTIAN PLATONISM

Margaret Cameron

A thoroughgoing history of medieval Christian Platonism remains to be written. The task will be difficult – not because the traces of Platonic thought are so few (although there are few *direct* points of transmission), but because there are so many (albeit *indirect*). According to a recent author, 'both Christian Greek and Latin writers were so affected by Neoplatonic thinking that one would find it hard to disentangle even the doctrine of Christianity, as understood in the Middle Ages, from it' (Marenbon 2007).

Direct access to Plato's texts was limited and, for the most part, coextensive with the history of the influence of the *Timaeus* (Hankins 1987; Steel 1990). The Latin *Ti.* (up to 53C) was translated and extensively commented on by the fourth-century Calcidius, many of whose ideas were often confused with Plato's. It was introduced into the university curriculum, only to be removed from the syllabus around 1255, presumably due to its 'replacement' by other available texts by Aristotle (Dutton 1997). The other dialogues available in Latin were: *Phaedo* and *Meno*, translated in the twelfth century by Henricus Aristippus, and the *Parmenides*, translated in the thirteenth century by William of Moerbeke. These dialogues, sometimes circulating with other 'Platonic' and 'naturalist' material did not go unnoticed, but were not the subject of serious study.

The high point of direct contact with Plato's work occurred during the twelfth century. Masters associated with the 'school' of Chartres (see most recently Jeauneau 2010) commented directly on the available version of Plato's *Ti.* (along with other Platonic materials, such as Boethius' *Consolation of Philosophy* and Macrobius' commentary on the *Dream of Scipio*, a version of Plato's Myth of Er). There was among many masters a keen interest in Platonic cosmology and eschatology, especially the origin of the world, the nature of time and eternity, providence and fate, the world soul and the human soul. These masters were characterized as *Platonici*, among whom Bernard of Chartres was singled out as 'the most perfect Platonist of our age' (John of Salisbury, *Metalogicon*). Not everything that Plato wrote, however, was easily compatible with Christian doctrine, and so these masters – commenting on every word of the Platonic texts available to them – had to devise a mechanism by which to interpret the doctrines without raising difficulties with Church authorities. Plato's true meaning was often concealed, they thought, under a veil, and the troublesome teachings were explained away as an *involucrum* or *integumentum* (Jeauneau 1957) whose proper interpretation could in the end be reconciled with Christian doctrine. For example, that women ought to be held in common (*Republic* bk 5) was given this reading: what Socrates meant was that women should be held in common *affection* (see Dutton 2005). This enabled some philosophers (Peter Abelard and William of Conches) to interpret Plato's world soul as the Holy Spirit which, as defended by Abelard, had a beginning in time (Peter Abelard, *Theologia summi boni*; Gregory 1955; Marenbon 1997).

Two primary *indirect* sources for the views of Plato and the Neoplatonists were St. Augustine and the fifth-century Roman philosopher Boethius, both of whose Platonic views were filtered through the lens of Porphyry. This filter afforded medieval thinkers insight into the ancient opinion that the doctrines of Plato and Aristotle are, ultimately, harmonious (see Ebbesen 1990; Gerson 2005; Karamanolis 2006). Augustine's writings were everywhere used by medieval thinkers, although it is more appropriate to talk about 'Augustinianism' (rather than 'Platonism'). Boethius' aim to translate and provide commentaries on every work of Aristotle and Plato, and to show how their views are in agreement (Boethius, *In peri hermeneias*), was thwarted by early imprisonment and death. Nonetheless his extant commentaries were a rich source of information on Neoplatonic interpretations of Aristotelian logic. Medieval thinkers there confronted Plato's doctrine of the pre-existence and transmigration of souls, doctrines usually either explained away or sharply rejected as contrary to Christian faith. At the same time, the commentary tradition on just one of the Neoplatonic poems of Boethius' is massive (Nauta 2009).

Other sources included Isidore of Seville's *Etymologiae*, Martianus Capella's *The Marriage of Mercury and Philology*, and the Christian fathers, including Jerome and Ambrose who provided insight into Plato's views on the origins of the world. Especially important sources of Platonic (in fact Proclean) doctrine were the *Liber de causis* and the works from the 'Dionysian' corpus (*On the celestial hierarchy*, *On the ecclesiastical hierarchy*, *On the divine names*, *On mystical theology*, along with several letters), thought to have been written by Dionysius the Areopagite and thus treated with extraordinary reverence. The understanding of Plato and Platonism changed in the late thirteenth century with the translation of Proclus' *Elementatio theologica*. Proclus' commentaries on *Ti.* and *Prm.* were also translated. This allowed philosophers to begin to distinguish Plato's thought from his systematizers', especially Proclus (q.v. Neoplatonism).

It ought to be noted that, despite the frequent tendency by scholars to characterize early medieval philosophy (i.e. before the recovery of the bulk of Aristotle's corpus and the start of the universities) as 'Platonic', there are in fact few references to Plato and his work, and fewer still that engage with his thought in a systematic way. Plato was indeed praised, such as by the ninth-century John Scottus Eriugena who considered Plato 'the greatest of all those who philosophize about the world', not least because Plato 'discovered the creator'. But 'Plato' was often simply cited as an authority for parts of the quadrivium. In these early years of the middle ages, pithy Platonic sayings are most frequent, usually learned at second hand (e.g. that cities are fortunate to have philosophers as rulers, that the place of the soul is the brain, not the heart and so on; see Marenbon 2002).

Scholars have remarked on the surprising marginality of Plato's thought, in direct transmission, in the middle ages, wondering why medieval thinkers did not seek out a complete set of Plato's texts, and why indeed those that were translated lay nearly untouched. Perhaps Aristotle's texts were simply more assimilable to a university curriculum, and his ideas more conducive to the development of natural science (Wieland 1985). Aquinas recognized that Plato and Aristotle took different philosophical approaches (*viae*):

> The diversity of these two positions stems from this, that some, in order to seek the truth about the nature of things, have

proceeded from intelligible reasons, and this was the particular characteristic of the Platonists. Some, however, have proceeded from sensible things, and this was the particular characteristic of the philosophy of Aristotle, as Simplicius says in his commentary *On the Categories* (*De spiritualibus creaturis*; tr. in Hankey 2002).

On the basis of Aristotle's criticisms of Plato in the first book of *Metaphysics*, medieval philosophers could see Aristotle as a corrector of Plato, although their views were taken to be essentially harmonious. Like the twelfth-century effort to interpret Plato's views metaphorically or in a transferred sense, Aquinas too notes that 'Plato had a bad way of teaching: for he says everything figuratively and teaches through symbols, intending something other through his words than what they themselves say' (*Sententia libri De Anima*; cited in Hankey 2002).

For further information, see Bos and Meijer (1992), Dobell (2009), Dutton (2003), Gersh (1986) and Klibansky (1939).

RENAISSANCE PLATONISM

Sarah Hutton

Renaissance Platonism is important for two reasons: for the rediscovery of Plato's dialogues and for developing a view of Platonism which values it for its moral teachings and spiritual insight. Since late antiquity, thanks to Christian churchmen like Augustine, Plato had a respectable reputation as the pagan philosopher who came closest to Christian truth. But direct knowledge of Plato's works was fragmentary in the Middle Ages (q.v. Christian Platonism, early; Medieval Christian Platonism). We owe our knowledge of the corpus of Plato's writings to the efforts of Italian Renaissance editors and translators, who acquired original manuscripts of Plato's dialogues from Byzantine Greeks who were the heirs of a tradition of interpretation unbroken since classical times. Since that legacy was soon to be truncated, with the fall of Constantinople in 1453, the preservation of Plato's philosophy was one of the greatest services rendered by Renaissance Humanism to European philosophy. The recovery of Plato's dialogues established Plato as an important philosopher in the Renaissance setting the mould for interpreting Plato for the next 300 years.

The first fruits of the humanist study of Plato were manuscript translations of individual dialogues into Latin. One of the most important early translators was Leonardo Bruni (1369–1444), who translated several dialogues, including the *Phaedo* and *Republic*. Another was George of Trebizond who translated the *Laws* and *Epinomis* in 1451, followed in 1459 by *Parmenides* dedicated to Nicholas of Cusa (1401–64). Cusanus is an example of a Renaissance philosopher who was interested in Plato's philosophy, but unable to read Greek. The most important Plato translator of the Renaissance was the Florentine, Marsilio Ficino (1433–99), who translated into Latin all 36 dialogues of the Thrasyllan canon, which were printed in 1484. Ficino's Plato translations were part of a larger project, which involved translating a substantial number of Neoplatonist texts (q.v. Neoplatonism), including the *Enneads* of Plotinus, Iamblichus' *De mysteriis Aegyptiorum* and the *Corpus Hermeticum*. His plans for a Greek edition of Plato had to be abandoned because of the death of his patron, Cosimo de'Medici. The first Greek

editions of Plato's complete works were published in the sixteenth century: the Aldine *editio princeps* (1513) and the 1578 edition by the French scholar, Henri Estienne (Stephanus), which established the referencing system still in use today. Ficino's translation is remarkable for its accuracy, and it was not superseded by later Renaissance translations of the complete dialogues by the German humanist, Janus Cornarius (Johann Hainpol 1561), and by the French scholar, Jean de Serres (published with the Stephanus edition).

The historical circumstances of the recovery of Plato in the fifteenth century account in large measure for the character of Renaissance Platonism. Plato was mediated by the Byzantines, notably Manuel Chrysoloras (1350–1414), George Gemisthius Pletho (c. 1360–1452) and Cardinal Bessarion (c. 1403–1472) who originally travelled to Italy in the hope of forming political and religious alliances with the beleaguered Byzantine empire. Plato's dialogues were read through the prism of the philosophical, religious and social conditions of Early Modern Europe, where scholastic Aristotelianism prevailed in the universities. Unlike Aristotle's philosophy which had been subject to over a century of accommodation to Christian theology within the institutions of higher learning, Platonism lacked a time-honoured tradition of interpretation in the institutions of the Christian West. Platonism never succeeded in breaking the Aristotelian monopoly on university study – notwithstanding the efforts of Francesco Patrizzi da Cherso (1529–97), who sought to replace Aristotelianism with Platonism, on the grounds that Aristotle's philosophy contradicted Christian teaching (see his *Discussionum peripateticorum libri XV*, 1571, and *Nova de universis philosophia*, 1591).

To modern readers, unacquainted with historical Platonism, Renaissance Platonism might appear to be more properly a variety of eclectic Neoplatonism. In fact, the modern habit of reading Plato separately from other philosophers of the Platonic tradition developed only recently. Through most of its history, Platonism has been read in relation to the so-called Neoplatonist philosophers. Renaissance Platonism was no exception. Ficino regarded Plotinus as the greatest interpreter and systematizer of Plato. But Ficino was more than a translator of Plato; he was a thinker who, by means of his commentaries, and his philosophical writings, provided a framework for reading and interpreting Plato's philosophy which combined faithfulness to the text with a Christian understanding of the wisdom to which Plato aspired. Although he acknowledged the diversity of the themes of the dialogues, he regarded Plato's underlying philosophical outlook as unified. Ficino's *Theologia Platonica de immortalitate animae* (1469–74) offers a systematic philosophy of the soul, set out as a Neoplatonic hierarchy of being, and defended in terms of scholastic arguments.

Adapting Plato for Renaissance consumption meant tackling the culturally unacceptable aspects of Plato's dialogues. This was done in a variety of ways. Paedophilia (q.v. Paederastia) and homoeroticism were reinvented as Platonic love. On the religious side, Platonism had been associated since early Christian times with theologically dangerous positions, especially Trinitarian heresies. Old theological controversies were reignited by the new influx of Plato's texts, fuelling the attack on Plato by George of Trebizond (*Comparatio Platonis et Aristotelis*, 1458), which provoked Bessarion's defence, *In calumniatorem Platonis* (1469). Plato's admirers emphasized religious and philosophical concordism. The most striking instance of this is the concept of a *prisca sapientia* which was developed by Ficino (adapted from Iamblichus' idea of *perennial philosophy*), which stressed the commonalities between Platonism, Christianity and the best of other philosophies (including Aristotelianism). The mytho-poetic aspects of Plato's philosophy lent themselves to allegorical interpretation, which Ficino exploited chiefly to elucidate what he regarded as the veiled religious content. His allegorism is relatively restrained by comparison with the Neoplatonists of antiquity.

In the fifteenth and sixteenth centuries Platonism was taken up outside the academies, and developed as a philosophy for laymen. The aspects of Plato's philosophy which gave it a secular and broadly cultural appeal included the Socratic conception of philosophy as the pursuit of wisdom, the dialogic, *non academic* format of Plato's philosophy, and its potential for symbolic interpretation. The most striking instance of a Renaissance development of Platonic philosophy was the adaptation of Plato's philosophy of love in the *dialoghi d'amore* (dialogues of love), such as Pietro Bembo's *Gli Asolani* (1505). These enjoyed wide currency as a genre throughout the Renaissance, the most popular of all being Baldessare Castiglione's *Il libro del cortegiano* (1528). Another secular arena for Plato's philosophy in the Renaissance was political, especially the idea of the perfect government – the most creative and enduring Renaissance engagement with Plato's *R.* being Thomas More's *Utopia* (1516).

For more information, see Allen (1984), Celenza (2007), Copenhaver (1992) and Hankins (1990).

THE CAMBRIDGE PLATONISTS

Sarah Hutton

Cambridge Platonism is a modern term used to designate a form of English Platonism which flourished in the seventeenth century. The name Cambridge Platonism derives from the fact that its chief proponents were all associated with the University of Cambridge: Benjamin Whichcote (1609–83), Peter Sterry (1613–72), John Smith (1618–52), Nathaniel Culverwell (1619–51), Henry More (1614–87) and Ralph Cudworth (1617–89). Their wider circle included George Rust (d. 1670), Anne Conway (1630–79) and John Norris (1657–1711). Their interest in Plato's philosophy may be accounted for partly by their desire to find an alternative to outdated scholastic Aristotelianism, and partly by their anti-Calvinist theological convictions, which are characterized by a firm persuasion of the compatibility of reason and faith, an optimistic view of human nature and belief in the freedom of the will. They studied Plato in relation to the full corpus of classical philosophy which had been made available by the editorial and translating endeavours of Renaissance humanists. And they studied ancient philosophy in relation to contemporary scientific and philosophical developments – principally the philosophy of Descartes, Hobbes and Spinoza as well as the ideas of Bacon, Boyle and the Royal Society (Smith, Culverwell, Cudworth and More were among the first Englishmen to read Descartes). Plato was for them first among philosophers, and they regarded Plotinus as his key interpreter. They viewed Plato's philosophy as the highest achievement of the human mind, unassisted by revelation. Plato is the philosopher who exemplifies the compatibility of reason and spirituality, and

offers profound insights into the nature and workings of the human soul. But they also regarded Platonism as compatible with atomist natural philosophy, and looked to Plato to supply the metaphysics which they regarded as wanting in Cartesianism and other contemporary philosophy.

Contrary to views purveyed by scholars like Cassirer (1963) and Koyré (1957) the Cambridge Platonists were not mystics, but apologists for religion who sought to defend religious belief by philosophical means. Platonism, with its combination of abstract reasoning and spiritual insight met that aim well. They devoted their considerable philosophical learning to religious and moral issues, to defending the existence of god and the immortality of the soul and to formulating a practical ethics for Christian conduct. Their anti-determinism led them to propose arguments for human liberty and autonomy. The broadly Platonist features of their philosophy included their holding the eternal existence of both moral principles and of truth. Their epistemology and ethics is underpinned by their view that the human mind is equipped with the principles of reason and morality. They were all dualists for whom mind is ontologically prior to matter, and for whom the truths of the mind are superior to sense-knowledge.

There are certainly aspects of their view of Plato which we no longer share. Plato was to them the 'divine Plato', the 'Attic Moses', the Greek philosopher who had achieved the greatest insight into the truth of the Bible. In his attempt to square Platonism with Christian doctrine, Cudworth, for example, went to some lengths to argue that Plato was not just a monotheist, but a Trinitarian. Readings of this kind are heavily dependent on accepting as genuine texts of controversial authenticity, notably the second letter. However, their Platonism was not an antiquarian predilection, but fully engaged with contemporary thought. Although they respected Ficino, and adopted a similar model of perennial philosophy to his, the sources of their Platonism were more recent (they used the Stephanus edition) as was the philosophical prism through which they interpreted it. They accepted post-Galilean science, and subscribed to an atomistic theory of matter. But they repudiated the mechanistic natural philosophies of Hobbes and Descartes, arguing that spirit is the fundamental causal principle in the operations of nature. Both More's hypothesis of the 'spirit of Nature' and Cudworth's concept of 'Plastic Nature' are theories of intermediate causality which owe something to Plato's *anima mundi*.

The Cambridge Platonists continued and developed a strand of thought that was already present in early modern England – in John Colet (1467–1519) and Thomas Jackson (1578–1640). Their influence endured well into the eighteenth century, notably through Lord Shaftesbury (1671–1713) and Richard Price (1723–91).

Section C: The Influence and Interpretation of Plato in Modern and Contemporary Philosophy

EARLY MODERN PHILOSOPHY: FROM DESCARTES TO BERKELEY

Stuart Brown

Early modern philosophy was the new philosophy of the seventeenth and eighteenth centuries, modelled primarily on the mathematical or the experimental sciences and invoking no authority but what was available to everyone: common reason and the evidence of the senses. 'Modern philosophy' is often presented loosely in retrospect as dividing into the rationalist tradition led by René Descartes (1596–1650), for which the mathematical sciences provided the paradigm or at least the ideal; and the empiricist tradition, begun by Francis Bacon (1561–1626) and re-shaped by John Locke (1632–1704), who took their inspiration from the burgeoning empirical sciences and sought to show how ideas all came from experience.

At the centre of the debates between philosophers of the period are the interrelated Platonic topics of innate ideas and eternal truths. Locke, consistently with his programme of showing how all ideas come from experience, denied the existence of innate ideas. Truths that seem to be necessary and so appear to be eternal truths must, according to him, be understood in some other way, as depending on definitions of terms. In opposition to Locke, Gottfried Leibniz (1646–1716) allied himself consciously with the Platonic tradition. Leibniz not only defended innate ideas but took the same side as the Cambridge Platonists in the debate as to whether or not the eternal truths were subject to god's will. He held that the standards of goodness and justice would be 'arbitrary' if they were subject to the will of god. But in such controversies original philosophers often took a different view from what might be expected. Thus Descartes, though committed to innate ideas, denied that the truths of reason were independent of the will of god. And on the other side, the Irish philosopher George Berkeley (1685–1753) though he accepted the empiricist tenet that all ideas come from experience, could still find much in common with the Platonic tradition, finding room for innate 'notions'.

One difficulty in assessing the reception and influence of Plato on the first generation of 'modern' philosophers is that they set about doing philosophy in a radically new way, and most made little mention of their predecessors. The merits of the views expressed by a philosopher were to be decided not by their pedigree but by the strength of the arguments given in support of them. Benedict de Spinoza (1632–77) presented his *Ethics* as if he were writing a treatise on geometry, which provided an ideal of rational argument he and Descartes shared, as did many other philosophers of the period.

Nicolas Malebranche (1638–1715) aimed to reconcile the Christian thought of Augustine with the secular philosophy of Descartes. Though Malebranche made no acknowledgement of any debt to Plato himself, he was sometimes referred to as 'the French Plato'. His 'Christianization' of Descartes allowed others to think of the 'father' of modern philosophy as a reviver of Plato. Thus, Leibniz credited Descartes with having restored the study of Plato by leading the mind away from the senses and by raising the doubts of the (Platonic) Academy.

Leibniz was one of the first of the modern philosophers to be willing to place himself within a philosophical tradition. When he was in Paris in the 1670s, he was part of a group keen to promote the revival of neglected philosophers of the past. He himself had written some Latin abridgements of the *Phaedo* and the *Theaetetus*, and encouraged others to produce French translations of Plato's dialogues. One of Descartes' many critics, the 'Academic' sceptic Simon Foucher (1644–96), presented himself as a modern follower of the later Platonic Academy in ancient Athens, whose principles he professed to revive.

Leibniz, though he would have disliked any (sectarian) label such as 'Platonist' being attached to him, regarded Plato as 'the greatest of the idealists' (i.e. those who opposed materialism). He told one correspondent that if Plato's philosophy were to be stated rigorously and systematically, it would 'come quite close' to his own.

There is always some prospect of finding common ground between philosophers in the rationalist epistemological tradition and Plato. In the case of those labelled 'empiricists', however, it might be expected that looking for points in common with Plato would be particularly fruitless. But one of them, George Berkeley (1685–1753), wrote a book (*Siris*) in later life in which he affirmed that the Platonists 'had a notion of the true System of the World':

> They allowed of mechanical principles, but actuated by soul or mind . . . they saw that a mind, infinite in power, unextended, invisible, immortal, governed, connected and contained all things: they saw that there was no such thing as real absolute space: that mind, soul, or spirit truly and really exists: that bodies exist only in a secondary and dependent sense. (Sec. 266)

It is a matter of controversy whether Berkeley was being true, in this later work, to his youthful *Principles of Human Knowledge*, on which his reputation as one of the leading philosophers of his age is based. Muirhead (1931), who provides a survey of the continuing tradition of Platonism in Anglo-Saxon philosophy from the time of the Cambridge Platonists, treats Berkeley as a follower of Locke's way of ideas and his later sense of a connection with Plato as not relevant to an overall interpretation of his thought. (For a more recent assessment, see Hedley and

Hutton 2008.) But even in the *Principles* there are obvious debts to Plato, as in his emphasis on spirits and his curiously 'rationalistic' argument for the immortality of the soul. Like Descartes and Leibniz, Berkeley held that souls, being indivisible, were not corruptible, and so were 'naturally immortal', allowing as piety demanded that it was within the omnipotence of god to destroy them. On this – to him – fundamental point Berkeley does not fit comfortably in the space once allotted to him, between Locke and Hume. He also belongs, as they did not, to the tradition of Christian Platonism.

For more information, see Brown (1995), Brown (1997), Mercer (2001) and Muirhead (1931).

NINETEENTH-CENTURY PLATO SCHOLARSHIP

Frederick Beiser

In fundamental respects German idealism of the nineteenth century was a revival of Platonism. The source of its idealism was Plato's theory of ideas; the inspiration for its *Naturphilosophie* was Plato's cosmology; and the basis for its epistemology was Plato's rationalism. In some idealists – Hegel and Trendelenburg – Aristotelian motifs seem to overshadow Plato's influence; but even in these cases Aristotle proves to be a mediator of Platonic themes. Kant was also a fundamental source of German idealism; but his significance too lies in his transmission of Platonic themes. German idealism of the nineteenth century was essentially Platonized transcendental idealism, that is, Kant's idealism minus the thing in itself, regulative constraints and the transcendental subject.

Idealism in nineteenth-century Germany begins with the early romantic movement or *Frühromantik* (1797–1802), which has been described as 'the greatest revival of Platonism since the Renaissance' (Walzel). Inspired by J. J. Winckelmann and the revival of Plato scholarship in the eighteenth century, Friedrich Schlegel (1772–1829), Friedrich Hölderlin (1770–1843), F. W. J. Schelling (1775–1845), F. D. Schleiermacher (1767–1834) and G. W. F. Hegel (1770–1831) all read Plato in the original Greek in their youth and received their philosophical education from him. Of special importance for them were *Phaedrus*, *Symposium* and *Timaeus*. The metaphysics of the early romantics was monistic, organic and idealist. The monism came from Spinoza's single universal substance; but the organicism and idealism came from Plato. They saw the universe as a single living organism following Plato's description of the world in the *Ti.* as 'a living being with soul and intelligence' (*Ti.* 30b). This organism was governed by intelligence, and had a unified rational structure, according to 'the idea of ideas' (Schelling). There was also a profound aesthetic dimension to early romantic metaphysics: the universal organism was a work of art; and the rational structure of things, the ideas, were grasped only through aesthetic intuition. The chief source of this aestheticism was Plato's *Phdr*. Romantic ethics lays the greatest importance on love, whose source is as much Platonic as Christian. No less than their eighteenth-century forbears, the early romantics were Diotima's children.

Of all nineteenth-century German idealists, the most influential was Hegel. Although his philosophy is usually interpreted as a modernized form of Aristotle, it is still, apart from its Aristotelian theory of universals, fundamentally Platonic. Having been nurtured in a romantic nursery, Hegel upheld the same basic romantic doctrines – monism, organicism and idealism – having the same Platonic roots. Even in his later years Hegel would pay handsome tribute to Plato, whom he always regarded as the father of idealism. After 1801 he broke with his romantic friends and contemporaries, chiefly with regard to the status of art and the powers of aesthetic intuition in providing knowledge of the absolute. But this was not a complete renunciation of the Platonic legacy; it was rather playing off one Platonic motif (the dialectic of the *Republic*) against another (the aestheticism of the *Phdr.*).

The Platonic inspiration of nineteenth-century idealism continues with Friedrich Adolf Trendelenburg (1802–72). Trendelenburg, who was professor of philosophy in Berlin for 40 years, was a seminal influence on German philosophy from the 1840s to 1870s. Though he is most famous for his critique of Hegel, he was also an important teacher for the young Kierkegaard, Dilthey, Cohen and Brentano. The chief source of his influence lay in his transmission of the classical legacy. Very much a late romantic, Trendelenburg saw himself as a spokesman for Plato and Aristotle's philosophy in the modern world. The express aim of his philosophy, as expounded in his *Logische Untersuchungen*, was to defend 'the organic worldview' of Plato's *Ti.* against modern naturalism and materialism. Trendelenburg became famous for his Aristotle scholarship, especially his critical edition of *De Anima*, and has been seen as a major champion of modern Aristotelianism; yet he always saw Aristotle's philosophy as fundamentally Platonic.

Another major idealist of the mid-nineteenth century, and transmitter of Platonism, was Hermann Lotze (1816–81). As professor in Göttingen for 35 years (1844–81), Lotze's influence on his age was immense; among his students were Frege, Brentano, Husserl, Windelband and Royce. Like Trendelenburg, Lotze's aim was to uphold the organic worldview against the growing naturalism and materialism of the modern age. In his *Mikrokosmus* (1856–64) he battled against these forces by stressing the normative dimension of the universe, which he understood in essentially Platonic terms as the realm of ideas. With Lotze, Plato becomes a warrior against modern materialism and naturalism. In his 1874 *Logik*, Lotze made an important distinction between the realm of truth or validity and that of existence and placed the Platonic ideas solely and squarely in the realm of truth or validity. The point of Plato's theory of ideas was to distinguish between these realms, so that ideas must not be understood as entities but as truths whose validity transcends the realm of existence. Lotze claimed that Aristotle had misunderstood Plato's theory of ideas and that Plato's theory, properly understood, gives a glimpse into a completely new world, that of truth or validity. Lotze's interpretation of Plato, and his distinction between truth and existence, proved fundamental for phenomenology and neo-Kantianism.

Nineteenth-century idealism reaches its culmination in the Marburg school of neo-Kantianism, whose chief members were Hermann Cohen (1842–1918), Paul Natorp (1854–1924) and Ernst Cassirer (1874–1945). Cohen was the father of the Marburg school, and in him the Platonic influence is most visible. With no exaggeration, Cassirer once described Cohen as 'one of the most resolute Platonists in the history of philosophy'. Though his philosophy grew out of his interpretation of Kant, Cohen understood Kant in Platonic terms. He regarded Plato as 'the founder of idealism', and he saw Kant as his modern interpreter and transmitter. In some early essays – 'Die Platonische Ideenlehre' (1866) and *Platos Ideenlehre und die Mathematik* (1878) – Cohen interprets the theory of ideas in methodological terms. The ideas are not things but stand for 'hypotheses', that is, the first principles of reasoning. In his later work, *Die Logik des reinen Denkens* (1902), the ideas have a more metaphysical status, because they are not only principles of thinking and reasoning but also principles of being itself. In his *Platos Ideenlehre* (published in 1902, written in 1887) Natorp applied Cohen's approach to Plato's intellectual development, interpreting the ideas in terms of laws and scientific method. It was typical of the Platonic legacy of the Marburg school that Natorp saw Plato's philosophy as the best introduction to idealism. 'In Plato, idealism is primal, as it were native . . . Plato's theory of ideas is the birth of idealism in the history of humanity.' Those lines from Natorp's preface could be taken as the fundamental conviction of all nineteenth-century German idealism.

NINETEENTH-CENTURY PLATONIC SCHOLARSHIP

Hayden W. Ausland

Modern Platonic scholarship began around the turn of the eighteenth to nineteenth centuries, when a reconceived 'critical' philology emerged in Germany that soon supplanted the older, humanistic style centred in the Netherlands. W. G. Tennemann's attempt to cull the Platonic corpus of spurious dialogues and to distil from a supposedly genuine remainder a systematic philosophy arranged in accordance with Kantian principles (1792–95) was promptly eclipsed by

a novel programme announced in the introduction to an opening volume of Friedrich Schleiermacher's translations of the dialogues into German (1804). Schleiermacher initiated a largely still regnant approach, according to which Plato is to be understood from his dialogues, which are in turn to be understood in the light of an accurate reconstruction of their original order. By the last, however, Schleiermacher understood a methodical series deliberately designed as such by Plato from first to last. His approach was shortly modified crucially by K. F. Hermann's philological thesis that the dialogues reflect the unfolding of Plato's thought according to definite principles over which he himself did not have authorial control. Hermann worked under the twin theoretical influences of Friedrich Schlegel's romanticism and the idealism of thinkers such as J. G. Fichte and G. W. F. Hegel (Ausland 2002).

During the nineteenth century, various scholars were for a variety of reasons moved to athetize critically one or more of a wide range of dialogues, culminating in the extreme of A. Krohn's conclusion that the *Republic* alone was a genuine dialogue of Plato. The general ordering assumed by Schleiermacher and Hermann alike, which viewed the other dialogues as preliminary to a 'final' exposition this dialogue would introduce, has undergone but important modification since their day. This has resulted in the significantly different view of Plato's development still often assumed, which has it that the *R.*, together with several other characteristically idealistic dialogues, is to be placed in a 'middle' period, with Plato's 'late' period now occupied instead by a number of more logically-oriented dialogues, which most nineteenth-century developmentalists, following Schleiermacher and Hermann's lead, tended to associate with an immediately post-Socratic 'Megarian' phase in Plato's thought.

The change in outlook responsible for this shift arose first in Great Britain, but later also more or less independently in Germany, in either case prompted by what may be broadly termed 'stylistic' considerations. For the first half of the nineteenth century, efforts to order the dialogues relied mostly on historical and doctrinal considerations of various kinds. (Friedrich Überweg 1855 embodies the fullest such treatment of the question. For a contemporary review of the *status quaestionis*, with extensive references to previous scholarship, cf. Franz Susemihl 1855–57, updated in Eduard Zeller 1889.) More empirically oriented scholarship in Britain was strongly sceptical of the entire approach (thus George Grote 1965), but in his 1867 edition of the *Sophist* and *Politicus*, Lewis Campbell found affinities in the diction of the presumably late *Laws* with that found in five other dialogues (*Sph., Plt., Philebus, Timaeus and Critias*). With this observation he paired a surmise that Plato had later in life reconsidered both the political and the metaphysical idealism of the *R.* in favour of a compromise with the real world in both regards. Campbell's study remained unnoticed for some time on the continent, where around the same time an interest developed in reconstructing historically Plato's competitive interactions with contemporaries like Isocrates, which led, in turn, to a series of often minute examinations of Plato's stylistic devices. By the end of the century, these could be gathered together as the putative data for a 'stylometric science' that promised to solve once and for all the question of the order of the dialogues (see Lutoslawski 1897). The sheer variety and inconsistency of the results so obtained (cf. Brandwood 1990) has called this entire approach into question (Ausland

2000; Howland 1991), but the twentieth century nevertheless inherited and retained a scholarly consensus in favour of the reordering proposed first by Campbell (1867; cf. 1889 and 1896). Moreover, despite an early attempt to read the same newly 'late' dialogues in more metaphysical a vein (Jackson 1881:85), the scholarly mainstream has tended to assume that Plato later in life moved away from thought of the kind informing the *R.* The following syncopated orderings will illustrate the difference involved (for further comparisons, see the tables in Ritter 1910 and Ross 1951):

Hermann (1839)	Ross (1951)
Under Socratic influence: *Charmides, Laches, Euthyphro, Hippias Major*	Before Sicilian visits: *Chrm., La., Euthphr., Hp. Ma.*
Under Megarian influence: *Cratylus, Theaetetus, Sph., Plt., Parmenides*	After first Sicilian visit: *Cra., Symposium, Phaedo, R., Phaedrus, Prm., Tht.*
During tenure as director of the Academy: *Phdr., Smp., Phd., Phlb., R., Ti., Criti., Lg.*	After second Sicilian visit: *Sph., Plt.* After third Sicilian visit: *Ti., Criti., Phlb., Epistle 7, Lg.*

It is noteworthy that with neither general ordering exemplified above could analogously 'scientific' criteria be found for isolating the common grouping of 'Socratic' dialogues, whose association in a hypothetically early Platonic phase rests instead largely on a particular interpretation of certain criticisms Aristotle directs against Plato, originally designed to rehabilitate Socrates as a philosopher in a sense adequate to nineteenth century demands (Ausland 2005). But the conjectural three-period ordering and explanation proposed by Campbell in 1867 still remain those most often habitually assumed by Platonic scholars today, if usually without a sufficiently critical appreciation of their historical genesis or scientific fragility.

DEVELOPMENTALISM

William Prior

Developmentalism is a theory concerning the order of composition and the interpretation of Plato's dialogues. It is a modern phenomenon; ancient interpreters of Plato were 'unitarians' (Annas 1999:3–5; unitarians believe that there is a systematic unity of Platonic doctrine or belief among all the dialogues). There are several varieties of developmentalism; what is common to them all is the idea that the philosophical views contained in the dialogues, which are taken to reflect Plato's own views, changed significantly over time.

In order for a developmentalist theory of Plato's philosophy to exist it is necessary to determine, at least in broad outlines, the order in which the dialogues were written. Until the advent of stylometry (the measurement of changes in Plato's style, some of them unconscious) in the latter part of the late nineteenth century there was no agreement on this order. The research of Campbell and other scholars led to the establishment of a late group of dialogues, including the *Timaeus, Critias, Philebus, Sophist, Statesman* and *Laws*, a penultimate group of dialogues, including the *Phaedrus, Republic, Parmenides* and *Theaetetus*, and an early group consisting the remaining dialogues (for thorough surveys of stylometric studies, see Brandwood 1992:90–120; Kahn 2002:93–112; Thesleff 2009:213–30). Stylometry was unable to establish divisions within this latter group (Kahn 1996:43–4)

The existence of three groups of dialogues does not in itself establish the truth of developmentalism, though it does provide a basis for it. It is possible to hold that the dialogues were written in a certain order and to deny that this chronology reflects any significant changes in Plato's view (Kahn 1996; Shorey 1903:4). The most influential version of developmentalism was motivated by a desire to restrict the scope of Plato's most famous theory, the theory of forms (q.v.). Unitarians since ancient times had regarded the theory of forms as a distinctive and enduring feature of Plato's philosophy. In the middle decades of the twentieth century, however, this doctrine came under scrutiny. Some scholars took the critique of the theory in the *Prm.* to be either a refutation of the theory of forms (Ryle 1939a:134) or a call for significant changes in it (Owen 1953a; cf. Kraut 1992c:14–19).

This criticism required modification of the three stylometric groups of dialogues. The strategy behind this grouping was to confine the theory of forms, or at least objectionable versions of it, to the middle group of dialogues. On this interpretation the 'middle dialogues' become precisely 'dialogues containing the theory of (paradigm) Forms'. In order to accomplish this it was necessary to move three dialogues in the first stylometric group, the *Cratylus, Phaedo* and *Symposium*, into the middle group of dialogues. The remaining dialogues in the first group labelled 'Socratic' or 'early' were held by some to represent the philosophy of the historical Socrates (Vlastos 1991a). This Socratic group was held to be purely ethical in content and not to contain any reference to the theory of forms. Two dialogues belonging to the penultimate stylometric group, the *Tht.* and *Prm.*, which were thought to be critical of the doctrines of the middle period, were placed by some scholars into a late, 'critical' group of dialogues. One scholar boldly proposed moving the *Timaeus*, which contains the paradigm version of the theory of forms, from the late group of dialogues to the middle group (Owen 1953a).

This version of developmentalism was the dominant interpretation of Plato among analytical scholars in the middle years of the twentieth century. Questions about it arose, however. Some dialogues did not fit the early-middle-late schema. The *Meno*, a dialogue of the first stylometric group of dialogues, seemed in some respects to be a Socratic dialogue, yet it contained the doctrine of recollection (q.v.), which was associated in the *Phd.* (72e–7a) with the theory of forms. Some scholars regarded it as 'transitional' between the early and middle dialogues. Some scholars (Allen 1970; Prior 2004) argued that some Socratic dialogues contain an early version of the theory of forms. The greatest impediment to acceptance of this version of the developmentalist picture, however, has been the *Ti.* Owen's (1953a) attempt to re-date the dialogue to the middle period was criticized by Cherniss (1957) and, despite vigorous and prolonged scholarly debate, has not won the support of a majority of scholars (cf., e.g. Brandwood 1992:112–14; Irwin 2008:80; Silverman 2002:12).

The presence or absence of the theory of forms is not the only criterion used to distinguish groups of Platonic dialogues. Penner (1992) has argued that the relevant distinction is between a simple and a tripartite theory of the soul, and that the breaking point between the early Socratic account of the soul and the Platonic theory comes in bk 4

of the *R.* This version of developmentalism does not involve modification of the first and second stylometric groups of dialogues, as does the version outlined above. Differing conceptions of dialectic provide the basis for yet another conception of developmentalism: the Socratic elenchus being succeeded by the Platonic method of hypothesis and finally by the method of collection and division (Robinson 1953).

As noted above, the chief opposing view to developmentalism is unitarianism, the view that Plato's view altered little or not at all over the course of his career. It is often assumed that one must be either a developmentalist or a unitarian. This, however, is not necessarily the case. Unitarianism and developmentalism are polar opposites: there is space, inhabited by many scholars, between the options of radical change and little or no change in Plato's view. It is also possible to reject the stylometric chronology on which developmentalism is based, or the idea that the dialogues represent (stages of) Plato's thought. Even if the stylometric chronology is accepted, however, the most fruitful reading of the dialogues remains a matter of interpretation.

COMPOSITIONAL CHRONOLOGY

Debra Nails

It was once hoped that determining the order in which Plato composed his dialogues would permit the mapping of his philosophical development, but that approach, dominant for some 150 years, now creaks unreliably. Two data from ancient times motivate inferences about the order of composition of Plato's dialogues: Aristotle's remark (*Politics* 1264b26) that *Republic* antedates *Laws*, and Diogenes Laertius' statement that *Lg.*, 'in the wax' at Plato's death, was transcribed by Philip of Opus (3.37). Glaring linguistic mannerisms in *Lg.* (e.g. notable synchysis, plummeting rate of hiatus, absence of certain clausulae, etc., catalogued in Thesleff 2009:63–81) are shared by *Timaeus, Critias, Politicus, Sophist, Philebus* and *Epistles 7 and 8*, marking all as *late* and edited with the same stylistic principles in view, perhaps those of Philip, whom Diogenes credits with writing the non-Platonic *Epinomis*, stylometrically indistinguishable from the bulk of the *Lg.* and the last half of *Plt.* Not unreasonably, scholars sought definitive style markers of *R.* that would permit the identification of a set of *R.*-like dialogues, leaving a third and earlier set, yet more remote from *Lg.* Although that effort has failed to distinguish the 'early' and 'middle' groups reliably, the bulk of modern scholarship has nevertheless followed Campbell's nineteenth century identification of three periods of productivity. Efforts to establish the order of composition once for all on (1) literary, (2) stylometric, (3) thematic and (4) historical foundations are yet alive.

(1) A common literary basis for compositional order takes the predominance of Socratic questioning as early, of constructive speeches as middle. Despite the general uselessness of dramatic dates for determining composition order, others have used the dramatic date of *Theaetetus* to claim that it was written just before *Sph.* and *Plt.* Diogenes (3.38) reports an ancient story that *Phaedrus*, exhibiting youthfulness (*meirakiôdês*), was Plato's first dialogue, a view defended by Tomin (1997). Another effort takes literally the suggestion that such formulaic expressions as 'I said' and 'he agreed' should give way to direct speech (*Tht.* 143b–c; cf. *R.* 3.392c–8b). By this criterion, dialogues with direct speech were to be counted as later than *Tht.* However,

the criterion founders on the exceptions: for example, *Laches* and *Ion* would be post-*Tht.*; *Ti.* and *Parmenides* would be pre-*Tht.*, defying considerations of content. To complicate matters, several dialogues mix the dramatic and narrative styles.

(2) Stylometry, measuring aspects of Plato's conscious and unconscious style (e.g. participle frequency, incidence of particles, formulae of reply) promised 'scientific' accuracy in relative dating; and hundreds of studies appeared after Campbell (1867) initiated the effort. Stylometry famously crossed swords with content when Owen (1953a) proposed a 'middle' date for *Ti.* against the stylistic evidence, though Cherniss (1957) trounced that bold suggestion. The advent of computers allowed measurement and correlation of very large numbers of stylistic features and heralded a new interest in stylometry, but the problem of how to programme the computer reiterated Campbell's original problem: the only invulnerable datum was the relationship between *R.* and *Lg.*, insufficient for generating secure results. Ledger (1989) marked an advance with new programmes that did not require prior assumptions about what to count as *early* style; but his preliminary results did not confirm scholars' preconceptions about the order of the dialogues (see Brandwood 1990; Young 1994), less concerned about what he had to assume to produce his results, delivered more palatable fare, that is, confirming expectations. Again complicating matters, both *R.* bk 1 and the first part of *Prm.* usually cluster with the Socratic dialogues considered early. Kahn (2002) mounts a robust defence of stylometry, in reply to which Griswold (2002) canvasses reasons to doubt its usefulness to our understanding of Plato.

(3) Thematic development was supposed (since Socher 1820) to demonstrate that

Plato's views evolved over time (e.g. about forms, knowledge, political theory) and that the order in which the dialogues were written could be determined by placing the least evolved first. As evidence for such thematic development Aristotle's various remarks on Socratic vs. Platonic positions are often cited, and often criticized (Kahn 1996:79–87). Two insurmountable difficulties arise: (a) the view considered most highly evolved depended entirely on the existing views of the scholars who performed the investigations; and (b) when dialogues addressing more than one subject were compared, a dialogue might be 'highly developed' on one subject and introductory on another, while another dialogue would have the reverse configuration, leaving no obvious way to determine which had been written earlier. Using criterion (3) with a dash of (1), Vlastos (1991a:46–9) proposed that the *historical* Socrates, depicted in dialogues deemed 'early', and Plato, in 'middle and late' dialogues – though usually using the *character* Socrates as his mouthpiece – addressed different subject matters and in different ways. For contrary views, see Press (2000).

(4) Less frequently than with the three approaches above, relative dates of composition have been derived from absolute dates proffered for particular dialogues, usually by linking their themes to historical events, for example, Plato's experiences (Grote 1865; Tennemann 1792); the death of Theaetetus (if in 392, Kirchner 1901; if in 369, Vogt 1909–10); Theban politics (Dušanić 1979, 1980); or to positions advocated by rivals whom Plato was said to be answering, for example, Antisthenes or Isocrates (Rick 1931; Ries 1959); or sometimes to nascent schools such as the Cynics or Cyrenaics.

Consensus about the order of composition has stayed firmly out of reach for several reasons. Despite the wondrously exact results achieved by many of these scholars, their results contradict one another within and across the methods used (Nails 1995:53–63). Moreover, a circularity problem confounds (1)–(4): each suggested order depends on first positing a pre-*R.* exemplar for which no independent confirmation has ever been credible, though the *Apology* has been an unfortunate favourite – unfortunate because court speeches are not reliably compared to dialogues.

(5) Further, there is textual evidence and testimony that Plato edited or rewrote dialogues in his lifetime, confounding any single date.

(6) Also, short dialogues may have been written during the periods when longer ones – *Grg.*, *R.*, *Lg.* – were being conceived and executed, resisting any linear chronology. Evidence for 5) and 6) undermines all purportedly discrete chronologies.

(7) Several dialogues show clear evidence of editing or rewriting: for example, *Grg.* (Tarrant 1982), *Protagoras* (Frede 1986), *Cratylus* (Sedley 2003:6–21) and *Tht.* (Tarrant 2010). Inconsistencies in *Lg.* prompted Morrow (1960) and Ryle (1966) to support the view that there was a proto-*Lg.*; and Nails and Thesleff (2003) argue that the *Lg.* exhibits the accretion of later material onto a Platonic stem, as allowed for in the actual encouragement of change in the law code. As for testimony, Dionysius of Halicarnassus (*de Compositione Verborum* 25.207–18), said Plato 'combed and curled in every direction' the first line of *R.* bk 1.

(8) *R.* presents an especially complex case; and the extent to which it was revised during Plato's lifetime casts further suspicion on single dates of composition for any of the longer dialogues while it also makes it more plausible that short dialogues were composed along the way. Although this remains

controversial, it is likely that before the *R.* as we know it was compiled, there was both (a) a freestanding version of the first book, *On Justice* or *Thrasymachus*; and (b) a proto-*R.* or *Ideal State* of two scrolls that comprised much of *R.* bk 2, most of *R.* bk 3 and the beginning of *R.* bk 5 (for exact passages, see Thesleff 2009:521).

Among the reasons cited for a discrete composition of *R.* bk 1, regardless of whether it preceded or followed the proto-*R.*, are the natural break before the remainder of the dialogue; and *R.* bk 1's featuring of several persons whose active dates in Athens cannot be reconciled with the lives of Adeimantus and Glaucon, who would then have been children (Nails 1998). In addition, Socrates' elenctic interaction with Cephalus, Polemarchus and Thrasymachus resembles that of other Socratic dialogues; in *R.* bks 2–10, Socrates takes a constructive role. Among those who have supported the view that *R.* bk 1 was composed separately, deploying arguments about content, are Vlastos (1991a:248–51) and Kraut (1992a:xii); Kahn (1993) has opposed it. Stylometric analyses (Arnim 1914; Ritter 1888:35–7, 1910:236–7) likewise supported separate composition (Brandwood's 1990:67–73 data is claimed by both sides; and Ledger (1989) did not test for variation between *R.* bk 1 and *R.* bks 2–10).

There is abundant, though not conclusive, evidence for a proto-*R.* or *Ideal State* – well known for some time before Plato composed *R.* – most of it provided by philologists (Hermann 1839; Hirmer 1897:592–8; Thesleff 2009:519–39 with further references). Aulus Gellius (*Attic Nights* 14.3.3) mentions the two scroll version that Xenophon opposed; and Diogenes (5.22, 5.43) names a two scroll epitome of Plato's *R.* from the libraries of Aristotle and Theophrastus. A proto-*R.* explains how Aristophanes' *Ecclesiazusae* of

392 or 391 BCE could have included more than a score of exact parallels to the language and proposals of *R.* bks 2–3 and 5. It explains why there is a dearth of contemporaneous references to other parts of *R.*; why the explicit summary of the ideal state at the beginning of the *Ti.–Criti.* summarizes *only* those very same parts of *R.*; why a summary of the same material appears at the beginning of *R.* bk 8; and why Aristotle summarizes the same material in *Politics* II.

Ryle (1966:216–300) offers a comprehensive, common sense discussion of the order of composition of the dialogues. In shorter compass, but nevertheless taking a number of approaches into account, Irwin (2008:77–84) makes a case for the Anglo-American 'standard view' of the order of composition, distinguishing it from simple developmentalism, as criticized effectively by Cooper (1997:xii–xviii).

ANALYTIC APPROACHES TO PLATO

J. H. Lesher

During the past half-century a number of scholars have sought to apply the techniques of modern analytic philosophy to Plato's writings. This has involved recasting portions of the dialogues as concisely stated deductive arguments, exploring questions relating to validity as well as to truth, exposing contradictions and equivocations and making explicit all essential assumptions. The rationale behind this approach, as Gregory Vlastos has explained, is that:

> By means of these techniques we may now better understand some of the problems Plato attempted to solve and we are, therefore, better equipped to assess

the merits of his solutions. The result has been a more vivid sense of the relevance of his thought to the concerns of present-day ontologists, epistemologists, and moralists. (Vlastos 1971a:vii)

The classic example of the genre is Vlastos' study of the Third Man Argument (TMA) in Plato's *Parmenides* (Vlastos 1954). Although the name derives from Aristotle's restatement of the argument, the *Prm*. version holds that positing the existence of a form such as largeness commits us to the existence of an infinite number of forms of largeness. Vlastos identified two assumptions essential to the validity of the TMA: (a) self-predication (that the form of F is itself F); and (b) nonidentity (that anything that has the character of F must be nonidentical with that in virtue of which it has that character). Vlastos maintained that while the two assumptions are inconsistent (they imply among other things that the form of F cannot be identical with itself), Plato never clearly saw the inconsistency or he would have stepped back from embracing both principles. Vlastos concluded that the TMA reflected Plato's 'honest perplexity', but others have argued that Plato introduced the TMA to call attention to inadequacies in earlier formulations of his theory of forms.

Three other studies by Vlastos focused attention on issues in Socratic philosophy. (a) A 1974 account of Socrates' attitude towards civil disobedience prompted a series of discussions of how the apparently inconsistent positions Socrates embraces in the *Apology* and *Crito* might be reconciled. (b) A 1983 exploration of the Socratic method of *elenchus* or 'cross-examination' sparked debate on the assumptions underlying Socrates' distinctive approach to philosophizing. (c) A 1985 analysis of Socrates' disavowal of knowledge as constituting 'a complex irony' exploiting two

distinct senses of 'know' prompted others to reflect on Socrates' conception of knowledge and its relation to virtue.

In his famous 1963 paper David Sachs charged that the main argument of Plato's *Republic* traded on two different conceptions of justice and was therefore fallacious. 'Platonic justice' consisted in the parts of the soul working in harmony with one another while 'vulgar justice' consisted in refraining from behaviour normally counted as unjust (acts of theft, sacrilege, etc.). Since the challenge posed to Socrates by Glaucon and Adeimantus was to show, in effect, that vulgar justice is profitable, Socrates' explanation of the benefits of Platonic justice was irrelevant. The many published 'responses to Sachs' failed to yield a consensus, but most found a greater degree of coherence in Plato's account than Sachs had claimed.

Analytic techniques have also been put to use in connection with epistemological and metaphysical aspects of the *R*. One example of this approach, with a positive objective in view, is Richard Ketchum's inquiry into the grounds for Plato's rejection of the knowability of things in the sensible world (Ketchum 1987). As Ketchum explains the situation, Plato's thesis that we can have no knowledge of things in the sensible realm assumes a distinctive view of the nature of truth. To assert the truth, as Plato sees it, is to assert of a thing that is that it is (or of things that are that they are). But of any occupant of the sensible world it can be said not only that it is (in some respect) but also that it is not (in some respect), and therefore one cannot say of it that it is *tout court*. And since knowledge (both for us and for Plato) requires truth, it follows that, strictly speaking, no occupant of the sensible world can be known. While Ketchum leaves unanswered the question of why Plato might have embraced this rather demanding view of the requirements for truth (*Prm.* B2 seems a likely candidate here), his explanation of the rationale behind Plato's denial of knowledge of things in the sensible realm has much to recommend it.

Few passages in Plato's writings have attracted greater attention than Socrates' refutation of Euthyphro's third definition of piety. When Euthyphro (unwisely) states that the gods love what is pious *because it is pious* (*Euthphr.* 10d) Socrates explains that if this were the case, and if 'pious' did mean 'beloved by all the gods', then the gods would be loving what is beloved *because it is beloved* – which contradicts the principle established at *Euthphr.* 10c that no one can love a thing *because it is beloved*. Socrates' refutation of Euthyphro's definition has been thought to pose problems for any attempt to ground moral values in acts of will or approval, divine or otherwise. A second issue posed by the *Euthphr.*, memorialized in Peter Geach's charge of 'fallacy' (Geach 1966), is whether Plato held that we can discover the essential nature from an inspection of individual instances *and* that we must first know the essential nature of a thing in order to identify genuine instances of it.

Two dialogues generally regarded as works of Plato's maturity have also been thought to anticipate issues of interest to contemporary philosophers. In his *Philosophical Investigations* (Secs. 48 ff.), Ludwig Wittgenstein identified the account of simples and complexes in 'Socrates' Dream Theory' in the *Theaetetus* as a forerunner of the philosophy of logical atomism embraced by Bertrand Russell, Wittgenstein himself and others. Similarly, Gilbert Ryle claimed that the alphabet model of language introduced in the *Tht.* and *Sophist* anticipates aspects of Frege's theory of meaning (Ryle 1960), and many consider Plato's conception

of knowledge as 'true belief plus a *logos* or rational account' a forerunner of the modern standard or tripartite analysis of knowledge.

These studies lend credence to the claim that the use of modern techniques of analysis can help us to understand and assess Plato's achievements as a philosopher. But in focusing attention on texts that lend themselves to logical analysis we run the risk of slighting other important if less logically structured aspects of Plato's thought. It would clearly be an error, for example, to develop an interpretation of a Platonic dialogue without attending to details relating to setting and characterization. Nor can the analysis of individual arguments, however expertly done, determine the larger significance of the dialogues in which those arguments appear. Thus we can profit from Vlastos' analyses of individual arguments without necessarily agreeing with his claim that the dialogues give us an 'early or *elenctic* Socrates' as well as a 'mature' one (see Beversluis 1993), or that they divide into 'early', 'middle' and 'late' works (see Nails 1993). The relevance of Platonic thought to modern philosophy has also sometimes been overstated. Plato's conception of knowledge, for example, may bear a formal resemblance to the standard analysis of knowledge as justified true belief; but at *Tht.* 206c Socrates describes the *logos* as what we add to a belief we already have, not (as required by the standard analysis) as some body of evidence or reasoning that led us to adopt the belief we already have.

VLASTOSIAN APPROACHES

M. L. McPherran

Gregory Vlastos (1907–91) was one of the most prolific, influential and well-regarded scholars of ancient Greek philosophy of the twentieth century. His work ranged from essays in pre-Socratic philosophy to Platonic epistemology/metaphysics and Socratic moral theory. He seems to have consistently assumed throughout his career that Plato's dialogues can be arranged into a tripartite order of early, middle and late dates of composition, with the early, 'aporetic' dialogues offering our best evidence – as opposed to, say, the testimony of Aristophanes (q.v. Aristophanes and 'intellectuals') or Xenophon (q.v. Other Socratics) for the views and methods of the historical Socrates (q.v.; q.v. Compositional chronology). Vlastos thus offers a paradigm case of the developmentalist approach (q.v. Developmentalism) to the dialogues – as opposed to the Unitarian or Straussian (q.v. Straussian approaches) interpretation.

According to Vlastos, Plato's dialogues can be ordered into three groups: (a) The first group listed alphabetically as follows. (i) Early Elenctic: *Apology, Charmides, Crito, Euthyphro, Gorgias, Hippias Minor, Ion, Laches, Protagoras, Republic* 1; (ii) Transitional: *Euthydemus, Hippias Major, Lysis, Menexenus, Meno*. (b) The Middle Dialogues, listed in probable order of composition: *Cratylus, Phaedo, Symposium, Republic* bks 2–10, *Phaedrus, Parmenides, Theaetetus*. (c) The Late Dialogues, listed in probable order of composition: *Timaeus, Critias, Sophist, Politicus, Philebus, Laws* (Vlastos 1991a:46–7). In Vlastos' account, Plato represents the views of his teacher in the early dialogues, but then moves on in his middle dialogues to use Socrates as his mouthpiece to introduce his original and distinctive theory of forms (q.v.) and associated doctrines. Subsequently, and with the criticisms of that theory he put forward in the *Prm.* in mind, Plato then modified his views in various ways in the late dialogues.

In his later life, Vlastos returned to his earlier work on Socrates with a view to publishing a book on the topic. After hosting a number of National Endowment for the Humanities Summer Seminars on Socrates, where this ongoing work was exposed to the criticisms of many participants, he published his results as *Socrates: Ironist and Moral Philosopher* (Vlastos 1991a). Chs 2 and 3 make a sustained effort to solve the 'Socratic Problem', namely, the problem of how to construct a Socratic philosophy that is distinct from that of Plato (or his other followers), despite the fact that we have no textual evidence by Socrates himself, and that the evidence we do have (such as Plato or Xenophon) appears not to be wholly consistent.

On Vlastos' strategy, the primarily nondialogical *Ap.* is regarded as capturing the tone and essential substance of what Socrates actually said in the courtroom, and is thus able to serve as a rough historical touchstone (Vlastos 1991a:49–50, n. 15). The rest of Plato's early works are then understood to be *imaginative recreations* – and so not necessarily *reproductions* – in dialogue form of the methods and doctrines of the historical Socrates. One then proceeds on the assumption that the early dialogues are the product of a Plato who, in the initial stages of his philosophical career, was a convinced Socratic and so philosophized after the manner of his teacher, pursuing through his writing the Socratic insights he had made his own (an assumption justified by the independent testimony of Aristotle (and Xenophon to some small extent) to the doctrines held by the historical Socrates). On this view the early dialogues *exhibit* Socratic doctrine and method without necessarily or always involving the conscious attempt to reproduce an exact copy of them. This position in no way *excludes* the influence of Plato's artistic craftsmanship and independent philosophical intentions, and so does not hold that literally all the claims and positions in a text are ones Socrates (or Plato) was himself committed to (Vlastos 1991a:50–3, explains that he makes the fundamental assumption that Plato's dialogues record the development of *Plato's* (not Socrates') mind, with a sharp change of direction in his way of thinking marked by the *Men.*'s introduction of the theory of recollection (q.v. Recollection) and followed by the middle dialogues). An early dialogue may appear to end in perplexity, but given this interpretation of their composition, that surface perplexity need not mean to a developmentalist that Plato himself had no view on the issue at hand or on what the position of the historical Socrates was. On this approach, it is thus well within reasonable historiographic procedures to bring to the interpretation of the early dialogues the hypothesis that 'authentic Socratic thought survives in Plato's recreation of it' (Vlastos 1988:108).

Vlastos uses Aristotle's testimony to nail down the distinction between the Socrates of the early dialogues (SE) and the Socrates of the middle dialogues (SM) to make plausible the working hypothesis that the ideas of the historical Socrates survive in Plato's early dialogues. Vlastos (1991a:92) is particularly taken by Aristotle's remark that:

> Socrates occupied himself with the excellences of character, and in connection with them became the first to raise the problem of universal definitions . . . But Socrates did not make the universals or the definitions exist apart; his successors [viz. Plato], however, gave them separate existence, and this was the kind of thing they called ideas. (*Metaphysics* 1078b7–32. Tr. after Jonathan Barnes)

On the basis of such evidence as this, Vlastos finds ten key trait differences between SE and SM; for example, SE is exclusively a practical moral philosopher, disavowing knowledge and possessing no theory of separated forms or a complex account of the nature of the soul or its immortality, whereas SM is a philosopher of wide-ranging theoretical interests, confident that he has found knowledge, knowledge backed by a theory of separated forms and of the tripartite structure of the immortal soul (Vlastos 1991a:47–9).

Some commentators, however, are unimpressed with Aristotle as a witness and as a historian of philosophy, holding that his testimony derives from his knowledge of Plato's dialogues and possibly other Socratic testimonia. On this view Aristotle is thus but the first reader of a long line of readers (including Vlastos) taken in by the optical illusion created by Plato's masterful fictions (Kahn 1996:3; see further Beversluis 1993; Nehamas 1992; Rowe 2006, who criticize Vlastos' approach because of its reliance on the assumption that Aristotle is an independent witness). Others focus their attack on Vlastos' attempt to impose a tripartite order on the dialogues and what they see as developmentalists' unwarranted assumption that *Ap.* can be treated as historically accurate in any useful sense (see, e.g. Morrison 2000; Nails 1993; Prior 2006; for a reply to all these criticisms on behalf of the study of Socrates based on a qualified developmentalism, see Brickhouse and Smith 2003).

CONTINENTAL APPROACHES

Francisco Gonzalez

'Continental approaches' to Plato are best understood by tracing them back to their source, arguably Friedrich Nietzsche (1844–1900), because Nietzsche (1999, 2005) first articulates the principal traits that characterize most readings of Plato in continental philosophy despite the great diversity they otherwise exhibit.

(1) Nietzsche and his successors treat Plato not as an object of philology and history, but rather as an interlocutor with whom one can pursue a philosophical dialogue today, while at the same time assigning him a definite place, and therefore a definite distance from us, in the history of philosophy. For continental philosophers starting with Nietzsche, doing philosophy today is inseparable from confronting and coming to terms with the philosophical tradition; in such a confrontation Plato becomes the privileged interlocutor.

(2) In line with this, Nietzsche and his successors are most interested not in Plato's specific conclusions or the arguments by which he arrives at them, but rather in his fundamental assumptions, which usually go unsaid and must be discovered indirectly behind the texts. In Nietzsche this takes the form of an emphasis on the 'personalities' of Plato and other Greek philosophers (1996), but in later continental philosophers the general approach survives the abandonment of this 'psychologising'.

(3) Given this emphasis on fundamental assumptions, Plato is seen not just as one philosopher among others, but rather as a spokesman for the entire philosophical tradition he initiated.

(4) Thus, the confrontation with the philosophical tradition takes the form of a radical critique of Plato. Plato is seen as representing all of those assumptions of the philosophical tradition from which continental philosophers seek to distance themselves: in particular, the opposition of a 'true' world

to the world of appearances, the rejection of becoming in favour of being, understood as eternal static presence, the degrading of the sensible in favour of the 'supersensible', the disparagement of the body, the dismissal of poetry in favour of logic, the belief in Truth as opposed to truths.

(5) Despite this critique, or rather because of it, continental philosophers starting with Nietzsche himself express a great indebtedness to, and respect for, Plato. If the Greek philosopher is an adversary, he is a most worthy one.

The next important name in the continental approach to Plato, Martin Heidegger (1889–1976), represents another turning point: Heidegger's profound ambivalence to Plato will come to characterize later continental readings and even produce a split among them. On the one hand, Heidegger is deeply influenced by Nietzsche's critique and like him sees Plato as the representative of the metaphysical tradition that must be overcome. Specifically, Heidegger (2003) sees in Plato the inauguration of a naïve conception of being as static enduring presence arrived at from the perspective of a naïve conception of time in terms of the present (with past and future understood as what is no longer or not yet present). Furthermore, Heidegger (1998, 2004) sees in Plato the transformation of truth from an event of unconcealing taking place in beings themselves to mere correctness in a speaking that corresponds to beings, a transformation he identifies with Plato's 'unsaid' teaching. Plato is thus seen as setting the West on its course towards a reduction of beings to a 'standing reserve' and a reduction of truth to 'information' in the age of modern technology. Yet, at the same time, Heidegger's reading of Plato's texts (a reading much more sustained, nuanced and faithful than Nietzsche's) uncovers fundamental tendencies and characteristics that run counter to the tradition with which he seeks to identify Plato. He repeatedly encounters in Plato's dialogues not the Platonism he seeks to overcome but rather something much more akin to his own task of thinking. A similar ambivalence can be seen in Emmanuel Levinas (1906–95), for whom Plato is both the representative of that ontological tradition that is to be surpassed and at least the first step towards surpassing it (see Benso and Schroeder 2008).

This ambivalence leads to a split among later continental philosophers in their relation to Plato. Many, following in the footsteps of Nietzsche and Heidegger, continue to see themselves as anti-Platonist and anti-Plato (failing, as Nietzsche and Heidegger *sometimes* did before them, to make a distinction here; q.v. Anti-Platonism). The best known and most influential of these is Jacques Derrida (1930–2004), who sees in Plato a representative of logocentrism and the metaphysics of presence, though his nuanced readings of Plato, like Heidegger's before him, also uncover in the texts elements at odds with this position (Derrida 1983).

On the other hand, some of Heidegger's own students, for example, Leo Strauss (2003; q.v. Straussian readings) and H. G. Gadamer (1983, 1991), were inspired by him to pursue a much more sympathetic reading and positive appropriation of Plato, seeing in Plato not a representative or father of the dominant philosophical tradition, but rather an alternative to it, a trace of something left behind by it.

This tendency within contemporary continental philosophy towards a more sympathetic reading of Plato has grown exponentially in recent years, as evidenced, for example, by the works of Stanley Rosen (1999, 2008), Drew Hyland (1995, 2004),

John Sallis (1996, 2004) and their pupils. More and more philosophers trained within the continental tradition are finding, when they turn to Plato's dialogues, not the opposition of philosophy to poetry and rhetoric but their marriage, not a contemplation of the universal but a sensitivity to the particularities and contingencies of praxis, not a final and absolute Truth but many approximate truths, not the rejection of sensible appearances but their validation as the resplendent shining forth of the supersensible (beauty), not the disparagement of the body and its desires but a recognition of their indispensability to the erotic pursuit of wisdom and virtue. One could say that for this group of continental philosophers Plato has become more of a 'contemporary' though still not 'up to date'. For, continental philosophers today believe they can critique the tradition, and therefore everything that has come to be 'up to date' on the basis of this tradition, *with* Plato rather than against him.

STRAUSSIAN READINGS OF PLATO

Catherine Zuckert

Leo Strauss (1899–1973) developed a distinctive way of reading Plato after studying the Islamic philosopher Al-farabi's account of *The Philosophy of Plato* (Mahdi 1962:53–67). He described his way of reading and the reasons for it at the beginning of his essay 'On Plato's *Republic*' in *The City and Man* (Strauss 1964:50–62).

In his dialogues, Strauss emphasized, Plato presents exclusively the speeches and deeds of others. The dialogues must, therefore, be read like dramas in which one never identifies the views of the author with any particular character. It may be tempting to take

Socrates as Plato's spokesman; but Socrates is not the only philosopher who appears in the dialogues, and Socrates is explicitly said to be ironic. Socrates did not write, moreover, but his student Plato obviously did. Plato had to be aware of the essential defect of writing that Socrates stresses at the end of the *Phaedrus* – that writings say the same thing to all people. Plato's dialogues thus show Socrates saying different things to different people.

The different teachings presented in the different dialogues do not merely reflect the different characters of the participants in the conversation, however, nor are they simply matters of rhetoric or persuasion. 'Plato's work consists of many dialogues because it imitates the manyness, the variety, the heterogeneity of being . . . There are many dialogues because the whole consists of many parts'. Unlike numerical units, however, the parts cannot simply be added up to constitute the whole. 'Each dialogue . . . reveals the truth about that part. But the truth about a part is a partial truth, a half-truth' (Strauss 1964:61–2). In order to see the way in which the truth presented in each dialogue is only partial, readers have to pay particular attention to the dramatic elements. 'The principle guiding the specific abstraction which characterizes [a] dialogue . . . is revealed primarily by the setting . . . : its time, place, characters, and action' (Strauss 1989:155). The setting is what gives rise to and limits, that is, literally defines, the conversation depicted. The task confronting the reader of a Platonic dialogue is thus to see the way in which the drama, that is, the setting, characters and action, shape or distort the argument. Plato does not tell us what he thinks; he shows us by presenting the speeches and deeds of others.

Reading the *Republic* in light of the action as well as the argument, Strauss concluded that Plato thought an individual could indeed be just; that individual would be a philosopher who seeks the truth above and beyond any other good. A city could not and never would be just, therefore, if it were not ruled by a philosopher. However, precisely because a philosopher seeks the truth rather than recognition or wealth, he will never want to rule and other people neither can nor will try to force him to do so (Strauss 1964:112–38). Without philosophers to rule on the basis of knowledge, political associations will always be based on opinion. Indeed, they need to formulate and enforce authoritative views to hold them together. The best form of such authoritative opinions is the kind of rational religion or 'political theology' put forward in Plato's *Laws* (Strauss 1989).

Applying Strauss' dramatic way of reading the dialogues, his students and their many students have emphasized a variety of different, though related themes. Allan Bloom (1968:307–436, 1993) and his students (Bruell 1999; Ludwig 2002; Pangle 1980; and Bruell's student, Stauffer 2001, 2006) show the way in which Socrates appeals to an erotic desire for justice in his young, politically ambitious interlocutors, which he then moderates with a philosophical education. Seth Benardete (2000) and his students (Burger 1984 and Davis 2006) bring out the way in which the action of a dialogue undermines its apparent surface teaching or 'argument'. In the case of the *R.*, for example, Benardete emphasizes the difference between the 'dialogic community' Socrates forms with his interlocutors and the thumotically ordered *politeia* they found in speech (Benardete 1989). Although Plato shows that the world is not completely intelligible, Joseph Cropsey (1995) and his students (Nichols 1987, 2009; Stern 1993, 2008; Zuckert 2009) argue, he nevertheless shows in Socrates how a human being can not only live a fully satisfying life but also care for friends. Writing as professional 'philosophers' rather than as political scientists or classicists, Stanley Rosen (1983, 1986) and his students (Griswold 1986, 1998; Howland 1993, 1998; Hyland 1995, 2004; Roochnik 1998) have insisted on the advantages of dramatic readings of Plato in opposition to deconstructive or purely analytical approaches. In his last book-length interpretation of *Plato's 'Republic'*, Rosen (2005) nevertheless explicitly breaks with Strauss with regard to the conclusion, although not the mode of his reading. Although Rosen agrees that the *R.* reveals the insoluble problem of politics rather than its solution, he contends that the philosopher wants to rule, but learns that he cannot.

PLATO'S 'UNWRITTEN DOCTRINES'

Hayden W. Ausland

The postulate of a body of unwritten doctrines of Plato originates in an enigmatically unique mention in Aristotle, where he says that Plato identified 'matter' with 'space' in the *Timaeus* but with 'the great and the small' in 'what are called the unwritten opinions' (*Physics* 209b11–17; for the translation of 'what are called' rather than a still usual 'so-called', cf. Szlezák 1999). 'The great and the small' is one of several designations Aristotle employs in criticizing Plato in contexts where he speaks in his own idiom of certain basic 'principles' (or 'elements') Plato espoused in some way continuous with the 'ideas'. In the wake of a later debate on the status of universals, the idealism with which Aristotle credits Plato seems easier to locate in the dialogues than the Platonic principles of which Aristotle speaks, so that the later

theory he mentions has been associated further with the idea of a Platonic 'Esotericism' (q.v.), which will then have conditioned the doctrines left unwritten. Aristoxenus reports a comment of Aristotle regarding a lecture Plato gave publically on the good (on which, see Gaiser 1980), and the Greek Aristotelian commentators, with other later writers, speak in expansive terms of Plato's unwritten associations or lectures, of which written accounts were worked up by his pupils, including Aristotle. But sceptical arguments have been vigorously urged against giving this amplified tradition any credence, or even taking what Aristotle himself says at face value (Shorey 1903:82–5, anticipating Cherniss 1944). Whence Aristotle has the materials for his account of a Platonic teaching on principles thus remains a real question. However this may stand, his technique of referring to the two basic principles with which he credits Plato falls into two main kinds: the first is regularly called 'the one', but in contexts informed by physical conceptions, he pairs this with 'the great and the small', while in those focusing on mathematical conceptions, he tends to substitute 'the indefinite dyad' (for a catalogue of these with other variants, see Ross 1924:lvii–lix). In both kinds of context, however, Aristotle speaks further of Plato's having posited mathematical things intermediate between ideas and sensibles, as well as having somehow identified the ideas themselves with numbers. (For translations of the key Aristotelian passages as supported by later writers' contributions, see Appendix 1 in Findlay 1974.)

Confronted with this evidence, modern scholars have pursued two general paths. Some – and this originally with a view to dispelling any vestiges of the older attribution of a mysterious esotericism to Plato – have undertaken to reconstruct a unified Platonic doctrine on the basis of Aristotle's statements per se (so Trendelenburg 1826; cf. Gentile 1930 and Robin 1908). Others have sought to explain a variety of tantalizing passages in the dialogues as confirming a more creditable esotericism once these are fleshed out with the doctrinal content of what is denominated its complementary, 'indirect tradition' (q.v. Tübingen Approach and Merlan 1953). Special examinations of mathematical 'intermediates' (Annas 1975; Wedberg 1955) and 'idea-numbers' (Dumoncel 1992; Scolnicov 1971) have tended to follow suit, either eking out the evidence with Aristotelianizing or modernizing mathematico-metaphysical speculation to yield a coherent theory of some kind (e.g. Cleary 2003, 2004; Taylor 1926–27), or searching for some way to integrate what Aristotle and later authors tell us with the idealism held to be present in works like the *Republic* (Miller 2007), or with a supposedly less idealistic, 'later' phase of Platonic thought reflected in the *Theaetetus-Sophist-Statesman* trilogy, the *Ti.* and the *Philebus* (see Sayre 1983 and Stenzel 1924; cf. Miller 2003). The second general approach falls subject to criticism for holding to be present in Plato's writings doctrines *ex hypothesi* left unwritten by him (see Cherniss 1945); from a less rigidly doctrinal perspective, however, it usefully explores the senses in which views conceivably held by Plato may be meaningfully held to be present in the dialogues at all (Miller 1995a).

Readings of either general kind have perhaps predictably yielded a wide variety of hypotheses regarding Plato's views or literary meaning, raising a question whether they may be anything more than occasions for supplanting the gaps in our evidence with one's own favoured mathematical and metaphysical views – whether ancient or modern. Plato may have engaged in

some intellectual experimentation late in life (Thesleff 1999:91–107). And he will doubtless have intended to spur his readers' autonomous philosophical impulses. But when an interpretive method – even with due acknowledgement for varying degrees of speculative supplement – issues in the charitable allowance that further inferences from what is actually said in the dialogues may be present in these without Plato having fully appreciated the fact (Miller 1995b), we may see exemplified the very Aristotelian method conditioning the historical-philosophical dimension of the problem in the first place (Cherniss 1945).

While scholarly agreement on the question of Aristotle's doxographical reliability will likely remain elusive (for the fundamental difference clearly depicted, cf. Shorey 1924 with Taylor 1926), his critical remarks on Plato's distinctions between radically different kinds of number (*Metaphysics* 13.6–8 passim; cf. 1.6, 987b14–18 and 14.3, 1090b32–6) suggest a fuller understanding of important limits Plato may have placed on the powers of rational expression as such (see Hopkins 2009 on Klein 1934–36 and 1964; contra Gadamer 1968).

ESOTERICISM

Hayden W. Ausland

Reference to esoteric philosophical teaching originates in antiquity, where it can suggest a deliberate limitation on one's outward discourse, like that observed by the initiates of various mystery cults or within certain cults of personality. A prominent case of the last is the reserve practised in the school of Pythagoras, whose initially exclusive mathematical speculation appears to have influenced Plato to some extent, according to Aristotle even inspiring his metaphysical idealism (*Metaphysics* 1.6). It may be doubted whether Aristotle's own references to 'exoteric discourses' in his ethical works (Bonitz, *Ind. Arist.* 104b44–5a48) are to be taken as complementary with such a practise, but at least subsequent 'neopythagorean' speculation credited Platonism with a quasimysterious appreciation of such reserve, tracing this to Plato himself. Characters in the dialogues will on occasion speak of such reserve as becoming a thinker (e.g. *Theaetetus* 152c) or of themselves for various reasons having to hold back something they might otherwise wish to say (e.g. *Republic* 506d–e), but any straightforward inferences from such literary passages invite controversy. Indeed, in key respects, the modern historical assessment of Plato's philosophy is founded on a flat rejection of the notion of a Platonic esotericism of any such kind (Hegel 1840–43; cf. Tigerstedt 1974). Yet it has from the outset retained at least a latent strain of appreciation for the delicacy of the question (Schleiermacher 1804; cf. Strauss 1986).

Pragmatic conditions of the twentieth century brought the question closer to the surface. Paul Friedländer's post World War I attentions to the existential dimensions of the dialogues (Friedländer 1921, 1928, 1930) set the stage for some European scholars working under the adverse political conditions of the 1930s to consider whether the dramatic form of Plato's writings might well be owing to prudential considerations (Strauss 1986 – written in 1939). In the wake of World War II, Friedländer's own work underwent important revisions and translation into English (Friedländer 1954, 1957, 1960), while other expatriates (Klein 1965; Strauss 1964) undertook to set out a more curiously literary reading of Plato's dialogues

for a now primarily American audience. Meanwhile, back in Germany, an alternative esoteric approach began to read the dialogues in the light of the foundational role it accorded Plato in a European metaphysical tradition (Gaiser 1963; Krämer 1959). As a result, there came to exist side-by-side two interpretations of Plato both denominated 'esoteric', but of decidedly different inspirations and orientations (Ausland 2002).

The esotericism integral to Straussian readings of Plato (q.v.) takes as its model a prudential hermeneutics acknowledging several levels of meaning, as developed in medieval Jewish and Arabic philosophy for the sake of pursuing speculation within a society governed by religious law (Strauss 1945), for which the analogue in Plato's time will have been the Athenian political conditions under which the trial and execution of Socrates proved possible. Strauss revives an earlier understanding generally forgotten since the birth of nineteenth-century Platonic scholarship (q.v.), by acknowledging the real prospect of political persecution as a permanently inescapable condition of the practise and writing, of philosophy. Where he avoided confronting metaphysical questions posed by the ideas, esotericism of the Tübingen approach (q.v.) postulates a founding role for Plato in a European tradition of 'Geistesmetaphysik' (Krämer 1964, 1990, on which see Sayre 1993) and so more broadly as a key player in an ideal 'History of Philosophy' as developed by Hegel (1840–43). Both approaches have prompted tangential efforts (e.g. Rosen 1968 and Oehler 1965, respectively) and all have encountered animated criticism, but where disparagement of Strauss and the Straussians has – in seeming confirmation of his premises – assumed a politicized form in the sphere of public intellectual discourse (e.g. Burnyeat 1985), a scholarly critique has lain bare several problems with methodical assumptions of the 'new scientific paradigm' claimed by the Tübingen approach (Brisson 1990 on Richard 1986; Brisson 1995; Fritz 1966; Fronterotta 1993; cf. Fritz 1967 contra Oehler 1965; Ilting 1965; Isnardi Parente 1984, 1993, 1995; Vlastos 1963).

Although the latter arose independently, some affinities emerged, as it at length spread beyond Tübingen (where it also evolved somewhat) resulting in two distinguishable styles. The more dogmatic of these is visible in the form adopted by an Italian school centred at Milan, which elaborated an ecclesiastically oriented interpretation, as a companion of sorts to a similarly conditioned reading of Aristotle's *Metaphysics* (Reale 1986 with Reale 1967; cf. Rizzerio 1993). Tübingen proper has meanwhile pursued a path more compatible – but thereby also more competitive – with Strauss' understanding, by employing a rather greater sensitivity to the dialogues' literary and dramatic nature (Szlezák 1985, 1993; with Krämer 1988). Especially in the terms of the mathematical side of Plato's thought, some unduly neglected writings by J. Klein (1965, 1966, 1977) have anticipated this approximation, but there remains much in this area still to be done (q.v. Unwritten Doctrines). The special approach of W. Wieland (1982, 1987) is analogously intermediate, acknowledging a literary reserve explained as conditioned by limits to communicability in propositional form.

THE TÜBINGEN APPROACH

Thomas Alexander Szlezák

The new way of understanding Plato's philosophy introduced half a century ago by H. J. Krämer (1959) and K. Gaiser (1963)

can be characterized in the following way. As to methodology, the so-called Tübingen School, which is now an international movement represented by scholars in well over a dozen countries – though largely absent from and unknown in the Anglo-Saxon world – (a) takes seriously, unlike the common practise since Schleiermacher (1804), clear indications in the dialogues that they are not meant by their author to be autarchic, self-sufficient and comprehensive accounts of his philosophy. The fact that the dialogues point beyond themselves not only casually and incidentally, but systematically and consistently (Szlezák 1985, 2004), is essential for their being understood. (b) The school does not set aside or play down the importance of Plato's criticism of writing nor does it try to convert its meaning into a recommendation of a particular form of writing, viz. the dialogue form. (c) Its adherents are not convinced that the Seventh Letter was written by somebody other than Plato, pending discovery of the long sought proof of its inauthenticity. But it is essential to note that the Tübingen position in no way depends on the assumption of the authenticity of the Letter. (d) Likewise, its adherents reject as methodologically ill-conceived and wholly unconvincing the attempt (undertaken by Cherniss 1944) to discard the testimony of Aristotle and other sources concerning Plato's *agrapha dogmata* or 'unwritten doctrines' (q.v.). There are two sources of our knowledge of Plato's philosophy: the direct tradition, that is, the dialogues, and the indirect tradition, that is, the Testimonia Platonica (as collected by Gaiser 1963 and Richard 1986). Neither of the two branches of the transmission should be ignored.

As to the contents, the picture of Plato resulting from the Tübingen School's use of the above methods can be sketched as follows. (a) In his search for the first principles

303

of reality, Plato integrated and developed the Heraclitean theory of flux, the Pythagorean (q.v.) philosophy of number, the Orphico-Pythagorean creed of the immortality of the soul, and the Eleatic dialectic of the One and the Many. (b) By giving all these approaches a new and deeper interpretation and by combining them with the Socratic care for the soul he created a synthesis of the whole of Greek philosophy before him which amounts to no less than the second foundation of philosophy (after its first foundation by the pre-Socratics). Therefore, it is inadequate to see Plato exclusively or mainly as a 'Socratic' – he was at the same time an unwavering Heraclitean, a committed Pythagorean and a daring Eleatic dialectician. (c) With Plato begins the metaphysical epoch of Western philosophy (Krämer 1982) which came to an end by the late nineteenth and the early twentieth centuries in the philosophies of Nietzsche and Heidegger (q.v. Continental approaches) on the one side, and by the analytical approach (q.v. Analytic approaches) and pragmatism on the other. (d) The structure of reality arrived at by Plato's methodologically multiple approach is reflected in the dialogues, though not in its entirety. Taking into account both branches of the transmission, we can see that Plato opted for a twofold procedure (which is reflected in the way up and the way down in the simile of the cave): the analysis of the phenomena is meant to lead to the recognition of the first principles and elements (*archai* and *stoicheia*) of reality, starting from which the dialectician will show in a second, synthetic move how things are 'derived' from the principles or 'generated' by their interaction. As highest principles Plato posited the One and the Indefinite Duality (*hen* and *aoristos dyas*). The One he equated with the Good (q.v.), while the Dyad was for him the ultimate source of evil.

The first products of the progressive limitation of the Unlimited by the One were the (ideal) numbers. The realm of the Ideas had a hierarchical order (hinted at in *Republic* 485b6; cf. 500c2). Between the Ideas and the sensible things, the objects of mathematics, *ta mathêmatika*, occupied an intermediate (*metaxy*) position. The Soul, which itself stands between the Ideas, which it receives, and the sensible things, which it orders, is akin to the realm of the *mathêmatika*. There is a structural kinship (*oikeiotês*) or communion (*koinônia*) between the mathematical disciplines among themselves and with the structure of reality as a whole, which is mentioned in the dialogues (*R.* 537c; *Laws* 967e), but not explained in detail – the exact elaboration of this theory being, like the derivation of all reality from the One and the Indefinite Dyad, a topic for the oral theory of the principles expounded in what Aristotle called Plato's *agrapha dogmata*.

Contrary to a widespread opinion, Aristotle's reports on Plato's philosophy of principles and numbers are neither inconsistent nor obscure (Richard 2005; Robin 1908). That the Testimonia Platonica are of great use for the interpretation of the dialogues has been shown by Gaiser (1963, 2004) and Reale (1984). Aristotle's own philosophy is clearly influenced by the 'unwritten' Plato in his theory of *aretê* as *mesotês* (Krämer 1959) and in his use of the concept of matter (Happ 1971). Likewise, Speusippus and Xenocrates build not only on the written dialogues of their common master, but also on the philosophy of the *agrapha dogmata*. In historical perspective, Plato's oral philosophy proves to be the highest point of Greek speculation on the ultimate principles of reality, both resuming earlier attempts and enriching later ones. Present-day meta-axiomatic theory has rediscovered the importance of

Plato's philosophy of mathematics (Surányi 1999).

It is hard for our culture of literacy to understand Plato's decision not to commit all of his philosophy to writing. Yet the dialogues show his reasons: Socrates does not tell his view on the essence of the *megiston mathêma*, nor does he give a sketch of dialectics, because the interlocutors would not be able to grasp it (*R.* 506e, 533a). In his criticism of writing, Plato recommends not addressing 'those who have no business with it (sc. philosophy)' (*Phaedrus* 275e3, 276a7). The *Epistle 7* (q.v. Letters) merely confirms this attitude. Thus the Letter is not needed as an independent witness for Plato's views on the worth of writing. Conversely, the anti-esoteric position depends on the unproved assumption of its inauthenticity, since it is very clear about the fact that Plato favoured an esotericist (q.v. Esoterism) use of his theory of principles (Szlezák 1985:386–405, 2004:54–8).

ANTI-PLATONISM, FROM ANCIENT TO MODERN

Monique Dixsaut

Opposition to Plato's thought, sometimes called anti-Platonism, has existed since antiquity; but it is a more complex phenomenon than the single name would suggest.

Quite obviously, to be an anti-Platonist is to oppose Platonism. But what is less obvious is how it is possible to oppose a philosophy which does not offer an articulated set of principles and consequences and is frequently objecting against its own theses, and why should one bother to refute a philosopher who never asserts anything in his own name? But from the absence of Platonism in

Plato there has followed a proliferation of Platonisms (q.v. Academy, Neoplatonism), that is, a multiplicity of constructions freely elaborated by opponents or supporters at a given time, answering a variety of strategies. The histories of Platonism and anti-Platonism are constantly interacting, so that the term 'Platonism' tends to become more and more devoid of content and is commonly used to point to some great 'error' – transcendental realism, idealism, elitism or totalitarianism. It refers little or not at all to what Plato wrote, but rather to the representation one has of it. Yet, if Platonism is a variable, what consistency could conceivably be found in the numerous anti-Platonisms?

(I) CRITIQUES OF PLATONSIM FROM OUTSIDE PHILOSOPHY

It might be useful to set out a first distinction. 'Platonism' did not mainly provide philosophers with theories to refute: from Antiquity to the first half of the eighteenth century, two extra-philosophical forms of anti-Platonism developed continuously, one devoted to the defence of rhetoric (and its modern form, literature), and the other periodically reasserting the subordination of philosophy to the true (Christian) faith. The counterattack of the supporters of rhetoric began with Isocrates (q.v.), proceeded with Aelius Aristides (117–81 CE) and the second sophistic, and was born again in the seventeenth century with the 'Moderns' whose spokesman in France is Charles Perrault (1688). The controversy was introduced into England by Temple's essay 'Of Ancient and Modern Learning' (1692) and Swift, in his *Battle of the Books* (1704), shows Duns Scot and his master Aristotle concerting to turn out Plato 'from his antient Station among the Divines'. But in Diderot and d'Alembert's

Encyclopaedia (Jaucourt 1736) the word 'Platonism' is endowed with a purely theological meaning and connected with the theory of the three hypostases. The twelfth and thirteenth centuries had been punctuated with quarrels between Roman and Greek Fathers, Trinitarians and anti-Trinitarians, 'philosophical' theologians and theologians of the true faith (von Ivánka 1964). 'Platonism', which had been accused of having perverted Origen, blamed for the outrageous claims of philosophy as expounded in Boethius' *De consolatione Philosophiae* (524) where no mention is made of Christ or of the Christian religion, is found to be responsible for Abelard's scandalous theses: Plato is 'the purveyor of every single heresy'. What is at stake under the name Platonism is merely symbolic, and its 'subtlety' is charged with corrupting the 'simplicity' either of fine language or of the Christian faith.

(II) CRITIQUES OF PLATONISM FROM WITHIN PHILOSOPHY.

While they do not vanish entirely – cf. Nietzsche (1888) on Plato's tedious prolixity and 'hybrid' style – these debates no longer are in the foreground and 'Platonism' is no more the word used by outside opponents to expose the *hubris* of philosophy from the moment Kant makes it a well defined theoretical object. The first philosophical objections levelled at Plato came from the Socratic Antisthenes, from some Cynics – mainly Diogenes: from the group of anecdotes attributed to him in D. L. 4 there emerges a Plato who is his antitype, a paradigmatic metaphysician and plutocrat – and from the sceptics, Timon of Phlius (*c.* 320–230 BCE) among others; but for Aristotle, on the contrary, Plato was too Socratic because of his immoderate trust in dialectical *logos*.

Aristoxenus of Tarentum (fourth century BCE) and Antigonus of Carystus (third century BCE) are also often mentioned for their anti-Platonism.

While disagreeing on a definition of philosophy which oscillated between its (Socratic) figure of an ever possible questioning, and its scientific (Aristotelian) figure of a knowledge of first principles and first causes, they were all agreed on a rejection of Plato's conception of forms as separate substances endowed with causal power over sensible particulars. The various criticisms first aimed by Aristotle (q.v.) and more radically formulated by Averroes, Aquinas and Duns Scot have made up a 'Platonism' which is but the paradigm of a realistic theory of universals, under its purest and most nonsensical form: 'Phantasticus Plato', in the words of that trueborn anti-Platonist William of Ockham. This medieval form of opposition dies out with scholasticism when Plato is at last allowed to speak again thanks to Marsilio Ficino (1433–99). Yet, this same realism of universals is to be found at the core of the mathematical anti-Platonism of those (Russell, the later Wittgenstein, Carnap or Dummet) who stress that mathematical objects are constructed, not objectively given, and are conventions ruled by logical syntaxes (Balaguer 1998).

In the Kantian 'History of pure reason' (in Kant 1787), Plato is also a prototype, not of a 'realist' but of the 'intellectualist' philosopher fought by Epicurus' sensualism, and of the 'noologist' philosopher criticized by Aristotle's empiricism. Kant's 'battlefield' recalls the Battle of Giants between the Sons of the Earth and the Friends of Ideas (*Sph.* 246aff), with this difference, that Plato, the creator of a now dead and buried speculative metaphysic, is supposed to belong to the latter. This paves the way for accusations of despising the body and the earth or discarding the pleasures of the flesh, but earlier representations went directly counter to that ascetic pre-Christian figure: according to Athenaeus, Plato keeps writing erotic speeches, while George of Trebizond (1469) judges Epicurus to be a second Plato who, like the first one, decrees *voluptas* to be the supreme good. What becomes at last patent with Kant is that, if their answers may be contradictory, the anti-Platonists share their problems and postulates with the Platonists; consequently, one must become aware that being an anti-Platonist is just another way of being a Platonist. The most evident sign of this new awareness is a semantic mutation: from then on no philosopher attacks or refutes Platonism, he 'reverses' or 'inverts', 'surpasses' or 'overcomes' it. The two different translations of the title of Carnap's paper, 'Überwindung der Metaphysik durch logische Analyse der Sprache' (1932), plainly show that what is meant by *Überwindung* is far from clear: is it 'elimination' or 'overcoming'?

(III) APPEALS TO PLATO AGAINST PLATONISM

Every attempt to go beyond Platonism seems however to find its best ally in Plato (or his Socrates). When Kant (1796; cf. Derrida 1983) makes Platonism responsible for any form of mystical exaltation in philosophy, he adds: 'Platonism, not Plato'. Though the Platonic 'non-problem' of the existence of Ideas is to Schlick (1937) the very example of a confusion between question of meaning and question of fact, Socrates is said to be 'the true father of our philosophy' (logical positivism). Heidegger calls upon Sartre to come and 'philosophize with him far beyond all Platonism', and chooses a sentence from the *Sophist* as an epigraph to *Sein und Zeit*,

that same *Sph.* to which the 'Conclusion' of *L'Etre et le Néant* acknowledges its debt. And while Levinas (1972) feels the demand for a fundamental meaning to be kept open beyond the world of established significations closed in by Plato, he finds it possible to 'return to Plato in a new way'. But it is certain that Plato is always accused of missing (or ignoring) something, and that that 'something' is in the accuser's mind reality itself. For Nietzsche, Bergson or Deleuze, it is the creative power of life; for those who are called 'existentialists' it is the movement of negativity which preserves existence from being submitted to essence (Sartre), or the horizon which enables being and truth to unveil themselves while remaining veiled (Heidegger). The charge is that Platonism not only ignores reality, it creates fictions more fictive than any of those it sought to expose. It must therefore not be philosophically criticized but discarded as an ideology, since it is, if one may say so, ideology in itself. It is then easy to understand how Marxism manages to find in the dualism of the two worlds, one of which is a world of ideas governed by unchanging relations, an 'ideological' transposition of the 'real' division between the working class and the idle one.

(IV) CRITIQUES OF PLATO EMPHASIZING POLITICS

This brings us to the point which has always excited the most brutal reaction, not against Platonism, but against Plato himself. The epithet used by Epicurus, *dionysokolax*, is aimed at the comedy under which Plato conceals his desire for power (Nietzsche 1886) – to put it more bluntly with Crossman or Popper, whoever flatters Denys may one day flatter Hitler. Perrault (1688:58) draws on the diatribe by Athenaeus (*Deipnosophists*

XI.505–8) when he writes: 'the nature brimming over with pride to be seen in Socrates [. . .] is quite insufferable to me', and Crossman (1945:190) echoes George of Trebizond, who 'always detested Plato': 'the more I read the *Republic*, the more I hate it'; as for the *idea* of the philosopher-king, it is to Popper (1945:I.137) 'a monument of human smallness', and he contrasts 'Socrates' simple humanity with the hatred Plato is filled with'. It is not a matter of pleading for the democratic interplay of opinions and interests, but of answering violently to what is felt as an act of violence: Plato's negation of any kind of equality among men, whether it be natural or social, religiously revealed or politically instituted, guaranteed by law or acquired by means of a method. Plato is surely not the only enemy of democracy among philosophers, but he is the only one to base on intelligence a hierarchical organization of State and City, a fairly attractive and dangerous proposition. The intensity of the repulsion is equal to the power of his magic – 'The Spell of Plato' – as if Plato could only be either divine or diabolical.

BIBLIOGRAPHY

Adam, James. 1902. *The Republic of Plato.* Cambridge.

Adamson, Peter. 2002. *The Arabic Plotinus.* London.

Albert, Karl. 1989. *Über Platons Begriff der Philosophie.* Sankt Augustin.

Algra, Keimpe. 1995. *Concepts of Space in Greek Thought.* Leiden.

Allen, Michael. 1984. *The Platonism of Marsilio Ficino.* Berkeley and London.

Allen, R. E. (ed.). 1965a. *Studies in Plato's Metaphysics.* London and New York.

— 1965b. 'Participation and Predication in Plato's Middle Dialogues', in R. E. Allen (ed.), 1965, pp. 43–60.

— 1970. *The Euthyphro and Plato's Earlier Theory of Forms.* London.

— 1971. 'Plato's Earlier Theory of Forms', in Gregory Vlastos (ed.), *The Philosophy of Socrates.* Plato II: A Collection of Critical Essays. Ethics, Politics and Philosophy of Art and Religion. Garden City, pp. 319–34.

Alline, Henri. 1915. *Histoire du Texte de Platon.* Paris.

Anagnostopoulos, Mariana. 2006. 'The Divided Soul and the Desire for Good in Plato's Republic', in Gerasimos Santas (ed.), *The Blackwell Guide to Plato's Republic.* Oxford, pp. 166–88.

Anderson, D. E. 1993. *The Masks of Dionysos: A Commentary on Plato's Symposium.* Albany.

Annas, Julia. 1974. 'On the "Intermediates,"' *Archiv für Geschichte der Philosophie.* 57, 146–65.

— 1976. 'Plato's Republic and Feminism', *Philosophy.* 51, 307–21.

— 1977. 'Plato and Aristotle on friendship and altruism', *Mind.* 86, 532–54.

— 1981. *An Introduction to Plato's Republic.* Oxford.

— 1985. 'Self-Knowledge in Early Plato', in D. J. O'Meara (ed.), *Platonic Investigations.* Washington, pp. 111–38.

— 1999. *Platonic Ethics: Old and New.* Ithaca.

Annas, Julia and Christopher Rowe (eds). 2002a. *New Perspectives on Plato, Modern and Ancient.* Harvard and Cambridge.

— 2002b. 'What are Plato's Middle Dialogues in the Middle of?' in Julia Annas and Christopher Rowe (eds), 2002b, pp. 1–25.

Apelt, Otto. 1919. *Platons Dialog 'Parmenides'.* Leipzig.

Ardley, Gavin. 1967. 'The Role of Play in the Philosophy of Plato', *Philosophy.* 42, 226–44.

Arieti, James. 1993. 'Plato's Philosophical Antiope: the Gorgias', in Gerald A. Press (ed.), *Plato's Dialogues: New Studies and Interpretations*. Lanham.

Armstrong, David. 1973. *Belief, Truth, and Knowledge*. Cambridge.

Arnim, Hans von. 1914. 'Thrasymachos über die Gerechtigkeit', in Hans von Arnim (ed.), *Platons Jugenddialoge und die Entstehungszeit des Phaidros*. Leipzig.

Aronadio, Francesco. 2008. *Dialoghi spuri di Plato*ne. Torino.

Atwill, Janet. 2009. *Rhetoric Reclaimed*. Ithaca.

Ausland, Hayden W. 2000. 'The Euthydemus and the Dating of Plato's Dialogues', in Thomas M. Robinson and Luc Brisson (eds), *On Plato: Euthydemus, Lysis, Charmides. Selected Papers from the Fifth Symposium Platonicum*. Sankt Augustin, pp. 20–2.

— 2002. 'Plato's Ideal Cosmopolitanism', in K. J. Boudouris (ed.), *Fourteenth Annual Conference on Greek Philosophy. 'Polis and Cosmopolis: Problems of a Global Era II'*. Athens, pp. 33–50.

— 2005. 'Socrates' Definitional Inquiries and the History of Philosophy', in Rachana Kamtekar and Sara Ahbel-Rappe (eds), *The Backwell Companion to Socrates*. Oxford, pp. 493–510.

— 2008. 'Proëmial Prolepsis in Plato's Politeia', *Symbolae Osloenses*. 83, 18–44.

Bailey, D. T. 2006. 'Plato and Aristotle on the Unhypothetical', *Oxford Studies in Ancient Philosophy*. 30, 101–26.

Bailly, Jacques. 2004. *The Socratic Theages: Introduction, English Translation, Greek Text and Commentary*. Hildesheim, Zürich and New York.

Balaguer, Mark. 1998. *Platonism and Anti-platonism in Mathematics*. Oxford.

Baltes, Matthias. 1997. 'Is the Idea of the Good in Plato's Republic Beyond Being?' in M. Yoal (ed.), *Studies in Plato and the Platonic Tradition, Essays Presented to J. Whittaker*. Hampshire, pp. 3–23.

— 1999. 'Is the Idea of the Good in Plato's Republic beyond being?' in Matthias Baltes (ed.), *Dianoémata. Kleine Schriften zu Platon und zu Platonismus*. Stuttgart and Leipzig, pp. 351–71.

Baltzly, Dirk. 1992. 'Plato and the New Rhapsody', *Ancient Philosophy*. 12, 29–52.

— 1996. 'To an Unhypothetical First Principle', *History of Philosophy Quarterly*. 13, 149–65.

— 1999. 'Aristotle and Platonic Dialectic in *Metaphysics* gamma 4', *Apeiron*. 32, 171–202.

Barker, Andrew. 1982. 'Aristides Quintilianus and Constructions in Early Music Theory', *Classical Quarterly*. 32, 184–97.

— 1989. *Greek Musical Writings*. Cambridge.

— 2000. 'Timaeus on Music and the Liver', in M. R. Wright (ed.), *Reason and Necessity: Essays on Plato's Timaeus*. London, pp. 85–99.

— 2007. *The Science of Harmonics in Ancient Greece*. Cambridge.

Barnes, Jonathan. 1979. *The Presocratic Philosophers, Vol. 1: Thales to Zeno*. London.

Barney, Rachel. 2001. *Names and Nature in Plato's Cratylus*. New York and London.

— 2010. 'Notes on Plato on the Kalon and the Good', *Classical Philology*. 105, 363–77.

Baxter, Timothy M. S. 1992. *The Cratylus: Plato's Critique of Naming*. Leiden.

Beiser, Frederick. 2002. *German Idealism*. Cambridge.

— 2003. *The Romantic Imperative*. Cambridge.

Belfiore, Elizabeth. 1983. 'Plato's Greatest Accusation against Poetry', *Canadian Journal of Philosophy*. 9, 39–62.

— Forthcoming. 'Poets at the Symposium', in Pierre Destrée and Fritz-Gregor Herrmann (eds), *Plato and the Poets*.

Bélis, Annie. 2008. 'Un Fragment de Traité Musical sur Papyrus (P. Tebt. III, 694)', in J.-L. Périllié (ed.), Platon et les Pythagoriciens, Hierarchie des Savoirs et des Pratiques: Cahiers de Philosophie Ancienne. 20, 225–36.

Benardete, Seth. 1989. *Socrates' Second Sailing: On Plato's 'Republic'*. Chicago.

— 1991. *The Rhetoric of Morality and Philosophy: Plato's 'Gorgias' and 'Phaedrus'*. Chicago and London.

— 2000. *The Argument of the Action: Essays on Greek Poetry and Philosophy*. Chicago.

Benitez, Eugenio. 2000. 'Cowardice, Moral Philosophy, and Saying What You Think', in Gerald A. Press (ed.), *Who Speaks for Plato?* Savage, pp. 83–98.

— 2009. 'Plato's Music', Special Issue of *Literature and Aesthetics*. 19.

Benoit, William L. 1991. 'Isocrates and Plato on Rhetoric and Rhetorical Education', *Rhetoric Society Quarterly*. 21, 60–71.

Benso, Silvia and Brian Schroeder (eds). 2008. *Levinas and the Ancients*. Indianapolis.

Benson, Hugh H. 2000. *Socratic Wisdom: The Model of Knowledge in Plato's Early Dialogues*. New York.

— 2003. 'The Method of Hypothesis in the Meno', *Proceedings of the Boston* Area Colloquium in Ancient Philosophy. 18, 95–126.

— 2006. *A Companion to Plato*. Oxford.

Betegh, G. 2004. *The Derveni Papyrus, Cosmology, Theology and Interpretation*. Cambridge.

Beversluis, John. 1993. 'Vlastos's Quest for the Historical Socrates', *Ancient Philosophy*. 13, 293–312.

Blank, David. 1993a. 'The Arousal of Emotions in Plato's Dialogues', *Classical Quarterly*. 43, 428–39.

— 1993b. 'Review article on: T. A. Szlezák, Platon und die Schriftlichkeit der Philosophy, and M. Erler, Der Sinn der Aporien in den Dialogen Platons', *Ancient Philosophy*. 13, 414–26.

Bloedow, Edmund F. 1975. 'Aspasia and the "Mystery" of the Menexenos', *Wiener Studien*. 88, 32–48.

Blondell, Ruby. 2002. *The Play of Character in Plato's Dialogues*. Cambridge.

Bloom, Allan (trans.). 1968. *The Republic of Plato*. New York.

— 1987. 'An Interpretation of Plato's Ion', in Thomas L. Pangle (ed.), *The Roots of Political Philosophy: Ten Forgotten Socratic Dialogues*. Ithaca, pp. 371–95.

— 1991. 'Interpretive Essay', in *The Republic of Plato*. New York, pp. 305–436.

— 1993. *Love and Friendship*. New York.

Bluck, R. S. 1956. 'Logos and Forms in Plato', *Mind*. 65, 522–9.

— 1961. *Plato's Meno*. Cambridge.

— 1963. 'Knowledge by Acquaintance in Plato's Theaetetus', *Mind*. 72, 259–63.

— 1965. *Plato's Meno*. Cambridge.

Bluestone, N. H. 1987. *Women and the Ideal Society: Plato's Republic and Modern Myths of Gender*. Amherst.

Blumenthal, H. J. 1971. *Plotinus' Psychology*. The Hague.

Blumenthal, H. J. and A. C. Lloyd (eds). 1982. *Soul and the Structure of Being in Late Neoplatonism*. Liverpool.

Bobonich, Christopher. 1994. 'Akrasia and Agency in Plato's Laws and Republic', *Archiv für Geschichte der Philosophie*. 76, 3–36.

— 2002. *Plato's Utopia Recast*. Oxford.

Bolotin, David. 1979. *Plato's Dialogue on Friendship: An Interpretation of the Lysis*. Ithaca.

Bolton, Robert. 1975. 'Plato's Distinction between Being and Becoming', *Review of Metaphysics*. 29, 66–95.

Bonazzi, Mauro. 2008. 'Towards Transcendence: Philo and the Renewal of Platonism in the Early Imperial Age', in Francesca Alesse (ed.), *Philo of Alexandria and Post Aristotelian Philosophy*. Leiden, pp. 233–52.

Bordt, Michael. 1998. *Platon: Lysis*. Göttingen.

Bos, E. P. and P. A. Meijer (eds). 1992. *On Proclus and his Influence in Medieval Philosophy*. Leiden, Köln and New York.

Brancacci, Aldo. 2005. *Antisthène: Le discours propre*. Paris.

Brandwood, Leonard. 1976. *A Word Index to Plato*. 'Index of Quotations'. Leeds, pp. 991–1003.

— 1990. *The Chronology of Plato's Dialogues*. Cambridge.

— 1992. 'Stylometry and Chronology', in Richard Kraut (ed.), *The Cambridge Companion to Plato*. Cambridge, pp. 90–120.

Brickhouse, Thomas C. and Nicholas D. Smith. 1989. *The Trial of Socrates*. Oxford and Princeton.

— 1994. *Plato's Socrates*. Oxford.

— 2007. 'Socrates on Akrasia, Knowledge, and the Power of Appearance', in Christopher Bobonich and Pierre Destrée (eds), *Akrasia in Greek Philosophy*. Leiden, pp. 1–17.

— 2009. 'The Socratic Paradoxes', in Hugh Benson (ed.), *A Companion to Plato*. Oxford, pp. 263–77.

Brink, David. 2007. 'The Autonomy of Ethics', in M. Martin (ed.), *The Cambridge Companion to Atheism*. Cambridge, pp. 149–65.

Brisson, Luc. 1987. *Platon: Lettres*. Paris.

— 1999. *Plato: The Mythmaker*. Chicago and London.

— 2004. *How Philosophers Saved Myths: Allegorical Interpretation and Classical Mythology*. Chicago.

— 2006. 'Agathon, Pausanias, and Diotima in Plato's Symposium. Paiderastia and Philosophia', in James H. Lesher, Debra Nails and Frisbee Sheffield (eds), *Plato's Symposium: Issues, interpretation and reception*. Washington DC, 229–51.

Brisson, Luc and Gerard Naddaf. 1994. *Le Même et l'Autre dans la structure ontologique du Timée de Platon*. Sankt Augustin.

Brown, Eric. 2000. 'Justice and Compulsion for Plato's Philosopher-Rulers', *Ancient Philosophy*. 20, 1–17.

— 2004. 'Minding the Gap in Plato's Republic', *Philosophical Studies*. 117, 275–302.

Brown, Lesley. 1986. 'Being in the Sophist: a syntactical enquiry', *Oxford Studies in Ancient Philosophy*. 4, 49–70.

— 2008. 'The Sophist on statements, predication, and falsehood', in Gail Fine (ed.), *The Oxford Handbook of Plato*. Oxford, pp. 437–62.

— 2010. 'Definition and Division in Plato's Sophist', in David Charles (ed.), *Definition in Greek Philosophy*. Oxford, pp. 151–71.

Brown, Stuart. 1995. 'Leibniz and the Classical Tradition', *International Journal of the Classical Tradition*. 2, 68–89.

— 1997. 'Platonic Idealism in Modern Philosophy from Malebranche to Berkeley', in G. A. J. Rogers, J. M. Vienne, and Y. C. Zarka (eds), *Cambridge Platonists in Philosophical Context*. Dordrecht, pp. 197–214.

Bruell, Christopher. 1999. *On the Socratic Education*. Lanham.

Brumbaugh, Robert S. 1961. *Plato on the One: The hypotheses in the 'Parmenides'*. New Haven.

Bruns, Ivo. 1896. *Das literarische Porträt der Griechen*. Berlin (repr. Darmstadt 1961).

Brunt, Peter A. 1993. *Studies in Greek History and Thought*. Oxford.

Buchan, Morag. 1999. *Women in Plato's Political Theory*. London and New York.

Burger, Ronna L. 1980. *Plato's 'Phaedrus': A Defense of a Philosophic Art of Writing*. Tuscaloosa.

— 1984. *The Phaedo: A Platonic Labyrinth*. New Haven.

Burgess, J. P. 2009. *Philosophical Logic*. Princeton.

Burkert, Walter. 1960. 'Platon oder Protagoras? Zum Ursprung des Wortes "Philosophie"', *Hermes*. 88, 159–77.

— 1972. *Lore and Science in Ancient Pythagoreanism*. Cambridge.

— 1985. *Greek Religion*. Cambridge.

— 1987. *Ancient Mystery Cults*. Cambridge.

Burnet, John. 1916. 'The Socratic Doctrine of the Soul', *Proceedings of the British Academy*. 7, 235 ff.

— 1920. *Early Greek Philosophy* (3rd ed.). London.

— 1924. *Plato's Euthyphro, Apology of Socrates, and Crito*. Oxford.

Burnyeat, M. F. 1970. 'The Material and Sources of Plato's Dream', *Phronesis*. 15, 101–22.

— 1978. 'The Philosophical Sense of Theaetetus' Mathematics', *ISIS*. 69, 489–513.

— 1990. *The Theaetetus of Plato*. Indianapolis.

— 1997. 'The Impiety of Socrates', *Ancient Philosophy*. 17, 1–12.

— 1999a. 'Culture and Society in Plato's Republic', *The Tanner Lectures on Human Values*. 20, 217–324.

— 1999b. 'Culture and Society in Plato's Republic', in Grethe B. Peterson (ed.), *The Tanner Lectures on Human Values*. Salt Lake City, pp. 215–324.

— 2000. 'Plato on Why Mathematics is Good for the Soul', in Timothy Smiley (ed), *Mathematics and Necessity: Essays in the History of Philosophy*. Oxford, pp. 1–81.

— 2005. 'ΕΙΚΩΣ ΜΥΘΟΣ', *Rhizai*. 2, 143–66.

Bury, R. G. (trans.). 1942. *Plato. Laws*. Harvard.

Byrd, Miriam. 2007. 'Dialectic and Plato's Method of Hypothesis', *Apeiron*. 40, 141–58.

Caizzi, Fernanda D. 1966. *Antisthenis Fragmenta*. Varese and Milano.

Campbell, Lewis. 1867. *The 'Sophistes' and 'Politicus' of Plato*. Oxford (repr. in Salem, 1988).

— 1889. 'On the Position of the Sophistes, Politicus, and Philebus in the Order of the Platonic Dialogues and on Some Characteristics of Plato's Latest Writings', *Transactions of the Oxford Philological Society*. 25–42 (repr. in Oxford, 1894).

— 1896. 'On the Place of the Parmenides in the Chronological Order of the Platonic Dialogues', *Classical Review*. 10, 129–36.

Carey, C. 2000. 'Old Comedy and the Sophists', in D. Harvey and J. Wilkins (eds), *The Rivals of Aristophanes*. London, pp. 419–38.

Carlini, Armando. 1962. 'Alcuni dialoghi pseudoplatonici e l'Accademia di Arcesilao', *Annali della Scuola Normale Superiore di Pisa*. 31, 33–63.

Carnap, Rudolf. 1932. 'Überwindung der Metaphysik durch logische Analyse der Sprache', *Erkenntnis*. 2, 219–41.

Carone, Gabriela Roxana. 1998. 'Socrates' Human Wisdom and Sophrosune in Charmides 164c ff.', *Ancient Philosophy*. 18, 267–76.

Carpenter, Rhys. 1933. 'The Antiquity of the Greek Alphabet', *American Journal of Archaeology*. 37, 8–29.

Cassirer, Ernst. 1963. *The Individual and the Cosmos in Renaissance Philosophy* (trans. M. Domandi). Oxford (first published in German, 1927).

Celenza, Christopher S. 2007. 'The Revival of Platonic Philosophy', in James Hankins (ed.), *The Cambridge Companion to Renaissance Philosophy*. Cambridge.

Chappell, Timothy. 2004. 'Alternative Interpretations of the Theaetetus as a Whole', *Reading Plato's Theaetetus*. Indianapolis, pp. 16–21.

Cherniss, Harold F. 1936. 'The Philosophical Economy of the Theory of Ideas', *American Journal of Philology*. 57, 445–56.

— 1944. *Aristotle's Criticism of Plato and the Academy. Vol. I*. Baltimore and New York.

— 1945. *The Riddle of the Early Academy*. Berkeley and Los Angeles.

— 1951. 'Plato as Mathematician', *The Review of Metaphysics*. 4, 395–425.

— 1957. 'The Relation of the Timaeus to Plato's Later Dialogues', *American Journal of Philology*. 75, 225–66 (repr. as Studies in Plato's Metaphysics, London 1965, pp. 1–12).

Chisholm, R. M. 1996. *Theory of Knowledge*. New York.

Chung-Hwa, Chen. 1978. 'On Plato's Charmides 165c4–175d', *Apeiron*. 12, 13–28.

Clavaud, Robert. 1980. *Le Ménexène de Platon et la Rhétorique de son Temps*. Paris.

Clay, Diskin. 1994. 'The Origins of the Socratic Dialogue', in P. A. Vander Waerdt (ed.), *The Socratic Movement*. Ithaca and London, pp. 23–47.

— 2005. 'The Comic Poet of Plato's Symposium', *Skepsis: A Journal for Philosophy and Interdisciplinary Research*. 16, 73–81.

Cleary, John J. (ed.). 1997. *The Perennial Tradition of Neoplatonism*. Leuven.

— 2003. 'Aristotle's Criticism of Plato's Theory of Form Numbers', in G. Damschen, R. Enskat and A. G. Vigo (eds), *Platon und Aristoteles – Sub Ratione Veritatis. Festschrift für Wolfgang Wieland zum 70 Geburtstag*. Göttingen, pp. 3–30.

— 2004. 'Aristotle's Criticism of Plato's First Principles', in J.-M. Narbonne and A. Reckermann (eds), *Pensées de L'un Dans L'histoire de la Philosophie: Études en Hommage au Professeur Werner Beierwaltes*. Paris and Québec, pp. 70–97.

Code, Alan. 1986. 'Aristotle: Essence and Accident', in Richard E. Grandy and Richard Warner (eds), *Philosophical Grounds of Rationality*. Oxford, pp. 411–39.

Cohen, Hermann. 1866. 'Die platonische Ideenlehre, psychologish entwickelt', in *Zeitschrift für Sprachwissenschaft und Völkerpsychologie IV*. 403–64.

— 1876. *Kants Theorie der Erfahrung* (2nd edn). Berlin.

— 1878. *Platonsideenlehre und die Mathematik*. Marburg.

— 1902. *Logik des reinen Denkens*. Berlin.

Cohen, Marc. 1971. 'The Logic of the Third Man', *Philosophical Review*. 80, 448–75.

Cohen, S. Marc and David Keyt. 1992. 'Analysing Plato's Arguments: Plato and Platonism', in James C. Klagge and Nicholas D. Smith (eds), *Methods of*

Interpreting Plato and His Dialogues.
Oxford, pp. 173–200.

Cole, Thomas. 1991. *The Origins of Rhetoric in Ancient Greece.* Baltimore.

Conacher, Desmond. 1998. *Euripides and the Sophists.* London.

Cooper, John M. 1970. 'Plato on Sense-Perception and Knowledge (Theaetetus 184–6)', *Phronesis.* 15, 123–46.

— 1974. *Plato on the Trial and Death of Socrates.* Ithaca.

— 1977. 'The Psychology of Justice in Plato', *American Philosophical Quarterly.* 14, 151–7.

— 1984. 'Plato's Theory of Human Motivation', *History of Philosophy Quarterly.* 1, 3–21.

— (ed.). 1997a. *Plato: Complete Works.* Indianapolis.

— 1997b. 'Introduction', in John. M. Cooper (ed.), 1997, pp. vii–xxvi.

— 1998. 'Socrates', in Edward Craig (ed.), *Routledge Encyclopedia of Philosophy.* London and New York, pp. 8–19.

— 2004. 'Two Theories of Justice', in John M. Cooper, *Knowledge, Nature, and the Good: Essays on Ancient Philosophy.* Princeton, pp. 247–69.

Copenhaver, Brian. 1992. *Renaissance Philosophy.* Cambridge.

Cornford, Francis M. 1935. *Plato's Theory of Knowledge.* London.

— 1937. *Plato's Cosmology.* London.

— 1939. *Plato and Parmenides.* London.

— 1964. *Plato's Theory of Knowledge: The Theaetetus and the Sophist of Plato.* London.

— 1971. 'The Doctrine of Eros in Plato's Symposium', in Gregory Vlastos (ed.), *Plato: A Collection of Critical Essays: Ethics, Politics, and Philosophy of Art and Religion. Vol. II.* Garden City, pp. 126–8.

Creese, David. 2010. *The Monochord in Ancient Greek Science.* Cambridge.

Cropsey, Joseph. 1995. *Plato's World: Man's Place in the Cosmos.* Chicago.

Crossman, Richard. 1945. *Plato to-day.* London.

Crotty, Kevin. 2009. *The Philosopher's Song: The Poets' Influence on Plato.* Lanham.

Csapo, Eric. 2004. 'The Politics of New Music', in Penelope Murray and Peter Wilson (eds), *Music and the Muses: The Culture of Mousike in the Classical Athenian City.* Oxford, pp. 207–48.

Cummins, Joseph W. 1981. 'Eros, Epithumia, and Philia in Plato', *Apeiron.* 15, 10–18.

Dahl, Norman O. 1991. 'Plato's Defense of Justice', *Philosophy and Phenomenological Research.* 51, 809–34.

Dancy, J. and E. Sosa. 1992. *A Companion to Epistemology.* Oxford.

Dancy, R. M. 2007. *Plato's Introduction of Forms.* Cambridge.

Darwall, S. 1992. *British Moralists and the Internal Ought.* Cambridge.

Davidson, Donald 1985. 'Plato's Philosopher', *The London Review of Books.* 7, 15–17.

Davies, J. K. 1971. *Athenian Propertied Families 600–300 BC.* Oxford.

Davis, Michael. 2006. *Wonderlust.* South Bend.

de Romilly, Jacqueline. 1975. *Magic and Rhetoric in Ancient Greece.* Cambridge.

De Stryker E. and S. R. Slings. 1994. *Plato's Apology of Socrates: A Literary and Philosophical Study with Running Commentary.* Leiden and New York.

De Vries, G. J. 1949. *Spel bij Plato.* Amsterdam.

— 1953. 'Isocrates' Reaction to the Phaedrus', *Mnemosyne*. 6, 39–45.

Denyer, Nicholas (ed.). 2001. *Plato: Alcibiades*. Cambridge.

— 2007. 'Sun and Line: The Role of the Good', in G. R. F. Ferrari (ed.), *The Cambridge Companion to Plato's Republic*. Cambridge, pp. 284–309.

— 2008. *Plato: Protagoras*. Cambridge.

Derrida, Jacques. 1972a. 'Plato's pharmacy', in *Disseminations*. (trans. Barbara Johnson). Chicago (repr. of 'La pharmacie de Platon', Quel Tel 32–3).

— 1972b. 'La pharmacie de Platon', in Jacques Derrida, *La dissemination*. Paris, pp. 71–197.

— 1983. *D'un ton Apocalyptique Adopté Naguère en Philosophie*. Paris (English trans. by P. D. Fenves in Raising the Tone of Philosophy, 1993, Baltimore).

Desjardins, Rosemary. 1988. 'Why Dialogues? Plato's Serious Play', in Charles L. Griswold, Jr (ed.), *Platonic Writings, Platonic Readings*. New York, pp. 110–25.

Destrée, Pierre and Nicholas D. Smith. 2005. 'Socrates' Divine Sign: Religion, Practice, and Value in Socratic Philosophy', *Apeiron* 38, xii–180.

Devereux, Daniel. 1995. 'Socrates' Kantian Conception of Virtue', *Journal of the History of Philosophy*. 33, 381–408.

Dillon, John M. 1987. 'Iamblichus of Chalcis', in Wolfgang Haase and Hildegard Temporini (eds), *Aufstieg und Niedergang der Römischen Welt, Teil II, Band 36.2*. Berlin and New York, pp. 862–909.

— 1989. 'Tampering with the Timaeus: Ideological Emendations in Plato, with Special Reference to the Timaeus', *American Journal of Philology*. 110, 50–72.

— 1996. *The Middle Platonists: a Study of Platonism 80 B.C. to A.D. 220* (2nd edn). London.

— 2003a. 'Philip of Opus and the Theology of Plato's Laws', in Samuel Scolnicov and Luc Brisson (eds), *Plato's Laws: From Theory into Practice*. Sankt Augustin, pp. 304–11.

— 2003b. *The Heirs of Plato. A Study of the Old Academy (247–274 BC)*. Oxford.

Dillon, John and Luc Brisson (eds). 2010. *Plato's Philebus: Selected Papers from the Eighth Symposium Platonicum*. Sankt Augustin.

Dillon, Matthew. 2000. 'Dialogues with Death: The Last Days of Socrates and the Buddha', *Philosophy East and West*. 50, 525–58.

Dimas, P. 2003. 'Recollecting Forms in the Phaedo', *Phronesis*. 48, 175–214.

Dittmar, Heinrich. 1870. *Aischines von Sphettos Studien zur Literaturgeschichte der Sokratiker*. Berlin.

Dixsaut, Monique. 1985. *Le Naturel philosophe: Essai sur les dialogues de Platon*. Paris.

— 1986. 'Isocrate contre des sophistes sans sophistique', in B. Cassin (ed.), *Le Plaisir de Parler*. Paris, pp. 63–85.

— ed. 1993. *Contre Platon 1: Le Platonisme Dévoilé*. Paris.

— ed. 1995. *Contre Platon 2: Renverser le Platonisme*. Paris.

Dodds, Eric R. 1928. 'The Parmenides of Plato and the Origin of the Neoplatonic "One"', *The Classical Quarterly*. 22, 129–42.

— 1951. The Greeks and the Irrational. Berkeley.

— (ed.). 1959. *Plato: Gorgias. A Revised Text with Introduction and Commentary*. Oxford.

— 1985. *Plato Gorgias*. Oxford.

Dönt, Eugen. 1963. 'Die Stellung der Exkurse in den pseudoplatonischen Dialogen', *Wiener Studien*. 76, 27–51.

Dorandi, T. (ed). 1991. *Philodemi Academicorum Historia, in Storia dei Filosofi, Platone e l'Academia*. Naples.

Döring, Klaus. 1972. *Die Megariker Kommentierte Sammlung der Testimonien*. Amsterdam.

— 2004. [Platon], *Theages. Übersetzung und Kommentar*. Göttingen.

Döring, Klaus, Michael Erler and Stefan Schorn (eds). 2005. *Pseudoplatonica*. Stuttgart.

Dörrie, Heinrich. 1987. *Der Platonismus in der Antike. Die geschichtlichen Wurzeln des Platonismus. Vol. 1*. Stuttgart and Bad Cannstatt.

Dorter, Kenneth. 2006. *The Transformation of Plato's Republic*. Lanham.

Douglas, Mary. 2007. *Thinking in Circles: An Essay on Ring Composition*. New Haven and London.

Dover, Kenneth J. (ed.). 1968. *Aristophanes: The Clouds*. Oxford.

— (ed.). 1980. *Plato: Symposium*. Cambridge.

— 1989. *Greek Homosexuality*. Cambridge.

— (ed.). 1993. *Aristophanes: Frogs*. Oxford.

Du Bois, Page. 1988. *Sowing the Body: Psychoanalysis and Ancient Representations of Women*. Chicago.

Duke, E. A., W. F. Hicken, W. S. M. Nicoll, D. B. Robinson and J. C. G. Strachan (eds). 1995. *Platonis Opera I*. Oxford.

Dumoncel, J. C. 1992. 'La Théorie platonicienne des Idées-Nombres', *Revue de Philosophie Ancienne*. 10, 3–34.

Düring, Ingemar. 1957. *Aristotle in the Ancient Biographical Tradition*. Göteborg.

Dušanić, Slobodan. 1979. 'L'académie de Platon et la Paix Commune de 371 av. J.-C.', *Revue des Études Grecques*. 92, 319–47.

— 1980. 'Plato's Academy and Timotheus' Policy, 365–359 B.C.', *Chiron*. 10, 111–44.

— 1990. *Историја и Политика у Платоновим "Законима."* Beograd.

Dutton, Paul. 1997. 'Material Remains of the Study of the Timaeus', in C. Lafleur and J. Carrier (eds), L'enseignement de la Philosophie au XIII Siècle: Autour du 'Guide de L'étudiant' du ms. Ripoll 109: Actes du Colloque International. Turnhout, pp. 208–19.

— 2003. 'Medieval Approaches to Calcidius', in G. Reydams-Schils (ed.), *Plato's Timaeus as Cultural Icon*. Notre Dame, pp. 183–205.

— 2005. 'Holding Women in Common. A Particular Problem in the Twelfth Century', in T. Leinkaut and C. Steel. (eds), *Plato's Timaeus and the foundations of cosmology in Late Antiquity, the Middle Ages, and Renaissance*. Louvain.

Easterling, Patricia (ed.). 1995. *Greek Literature: The Cambridge History of Classical Literature. Vol. I*. Cambridge.

Ebbesen, Sten. 1990. 'Porphyry's Legacy to Logic: A Reconstruction', in R. Sorabji (ed.), *Aristotle Transformed: the Ancient Commentators and their Influence*. London, pp. 141–71.

Ebert, Theodor. 1973. 'Plato's Theory of Recollection Reconsidered: An Interpretation of Meno 80a–86c', *Man and World*. 6, 163–80.

Edelstein, Ludwig. 1945. 'The Role of Eryximachus in Plato's Symposium', *Transactions of the American Philological Association*. 76, 85–103.

— 1962. 'Platonic Anonymity', *American Journal of Philology*. 83, 1–22.

— 1966. *Plato's Seventh Letter*. Leiden.

Edmonds, J. M. 1957. *Fragments of Attic Comedy, Vol. 1*. Leiden.

Edmonds III, R. G. 2004. *Myths of the Underworld Journey: Plato, Aristophanes, and the 'Orphic' Gold Tablets*. Cambridge.

Emilsson, Eyjólfur K. 2007. *Plotinus on Intellect*. Oxford.

Endress, Gerhard. 1973. *Proclus Arabus: Zwanzig Abschnitte aus der Institutio Theologica in Arabischer Übersetzung*. Beirut.

Erler, Michael. 1987. *Der Sinn der Aporien in den Dialogen Platons*. Berlin.

— 2007. *Ueberwegs Grundriss der Geschichte der Philosophie*. Antike 2/2. Platon. Basel.

Evans, Matthew. 2008. 'Plato on the Possibility of Hedonic Mistakes', *Oxford Studies in Ancient Philosophy*. 35, 89–124.

Feldman, Seymour. 2003. 'The End and Aftereffects of Medieval Jewish Philosophy', in D. Frank and O. Leaman (eds), *Cambridge Companion to Medieval Jewish philosophy*. Cambridge, pp. 414–45.

Ferber, Rafael. 1984. *Platos Idee des Guten*. Sankt Augustin.

— 1989. *Platos Idee des Guten*. Sankt Augustin.

— 2002. 'The Absolute Good and the Human Goods', in Giovanni Reale and Samuel Scolnicov (eds), New Images of Plato: Dialogues on the Idea of the Good. Sankt Augustin, pp. 187–96.

— 2005. 'Ist die Idee des Guten Nicht Transzendent Oder ist sie es Doch? Nochmals Platons EPEKEINA TES OUSIAS', in D. Barbaric (ed.), *Platon über das Gute und die Gerechtigkeit / Plato on Goodness and Justice / Platone sul Bene e sulla Giustizia*. Würzburg, pp. 149–74.

— 2010. 'Plato's Side Suns: Beauty, Symmetry and Truth. Comments Concerning Semantic Monism and Pluralism of the "Good" in the Philebus (65a1–5)', *Elenchos*. 41, 51–76.

Ferejohn, Michael. 1982. 'The Unity of Virtue and the Objects of Socratic Inquiry', *Journal of the History of Philosophy*. 20, 1–21.

— 1984. 'Socratic Thought Experiments and the Unity of Virtue Paradox', *Phronesis*. 39, 105–22

Ferguson, John. 1963. 'Sun, Line, and Cave Again', *Philosophical Quarterly*. 13, 188–93.

Ferrari, G. R. F. 1987. *Listening to the Cicadas: A Study of Plato's Phaedrus*. Cambridge.

— 1989. 'Plato and Poetry', in George A. Kennedy (ed.), *Cambridge History of Classical Criticism, Vol. 1*. Cambridge, pp. 92–148.

— 1992. 'Platonic love', in Richard Kraut (ed.), *The Cambridge Companion to Plato*. Cambridge, pp. 248–76.

— (trans.). 2000. *Plato: The Republic*. Cambridge.

— 2005. *City and Soul in Plato's Republic*. Chicago.

— 2007. The Cambridge Companion to Plato's Republic. Cambridge.

— 2009. 'Glaucon's Reward, Philosophy's Debt: the Myth of Er', in C. Partenie (ed), *Plato's Myths*. Cambridge, pp. 116–33.

Ficino, Marsilio (trans.). 1484. *Plato [Complete Works]*. No t.p. Florence.

Findlay, J. N. 1974. *Plato: The Written and Unwritten Doctrines*. London.

Fine, Gail. 1979. 'Knowledge and Logos in the Theaetetus', *Philosophical Review*. 88, 367–97.

— 1990. 'Knowledge and Belief in Republic V–VII', in Stephen Everson (ed.), *Epistemology*. Cambridge, pp. 65–115.

— 1992. 'Inquiry in the Meno', in Richard Kraut (ed.), *The Cambridge Companion to Plato*. Cambridge, pp. 200–26.

— 1993. *On Ideas: Aristotle's Criticism of Plato's Theory of Forms*. Oxford.

Finley, Moses I. 1985. 'Athenian Demagogues', in Moses I. Finley (ed.), *Democracy Ancient and Modern*. (2nd edn). London, pp. 38–75 (repr. of Past and Present 21, 3–24).

Flashar, Hellmut. 1958. *Der Dialog Ion als Zeugnis platonischer Philosophie*. Berlin.

Ford, Andrew. 2002. *The Origins of Criticism: Literary Culture and Poetic Theory in Classical Greece*. Princeton and Oxford.

Foucault, Michel. 1988. *Technologies of the Self: A Seminar with Michel Foucault*, Luther H. Martin, Huck Gutman, and Patrick Hutton (eds). Amherst.

Fowler, David H. 1999. *The Mathematics of Plato's Academy: A New Reconstruction* (2nd edn). Oxford.

Fowler, H. N. (trans.). 1999. *Plato: Euthyphro. Apology. Crito. Phaedo. Phaedrus*. Cambridge.

Frank, Daniel. 2009. 'Divine Law and Human Practices', in S. Nadler and T. Rudavsky (eds), *Cambridge History of Jewish Philosophy*. Cambridge, pp. 790–806.

Franklin, L. 2005. 'Recollection and Philosophical Reflection in Plato's Phaedo', *Phronesis*. 50, 289–314.

Frede, Dorothea. 1985. 'Rumpelstiltskin's Pleasures: True and False Pleasures in Plato's Philebus', *Phronesis*. 30, 151–80 (repr. as Fine, Gail (ed.). 1999. *Plato 2 Ethics, Politics, Religion, and the Soul*. Oxford. (pp. 345–72)).

— 1986. 'The Impossibility of Perfection: Socrates' Criticism of Simonides' Poem in the Protagoras', *The Review of Metaphysics*. 39, 729–53.

— 1992. 'Disintegration and Restoration: Pleasure and Pain in Plato's Philebus', in Richard Kraut (ed.), *The Cambridge Companion to Plato*. Cambridge, pp. 425–63.

— 1993. *Plato Philebus*. Indianapolis.

— 1997. *Platon Philebos: Übersetzung und Kommentar*. Göttingen.

Frede, Michael. 1967. *Praedikation und Existenzaussage*. Gottingen.

— 1987. 'The Original Notion of Cause', in Michael Frede, Essays in Ancient Philosophy. Minneapolis.

— 1988. 'Being and Becoming in Plato' *Oxford Studies in Ancient Philosophy*. Supplementary volume. 53–60.

— 1992a. 'Plato's Sophist on False Statements', in Richard Kraut (ed.), *The Cambridge Companion to Plato*. New York, pp. 397–424.

— 1992b. 'Plato's Arguments and the Dialogue Form', in James C. Klagge and Nicholas D. Smith (eds), *Methods of Interpreting Plato and His Dialogues*. Oxford, pp. 201–19.

— 1996. 'The Literary Form of the Sophist', in C. Gill and M. M. McCabe (eds), *Form and Argument in Late Plato*. Oxford, pp. 135–51.

Frege, G. 1879. *Begriffsschrift, eine der Arithmetischen Nachgebildete Formelsprache des Reinen Denkens*. Halle.

Freydberg, Bernard. 1997. *The Play of the Platonic Dialogues*. New York.

Friedländer, Paul. 1958. *Plato Vol. I, An Introduction* (trans. H. Meyerhoff). London.

— 1965. *Plato Vol. II* (trans. H. Meyerhoff). London.

Fussi, Alessandra. 2006. '"As the Wolf Loves the Lamb." Need, Desire, Envy, and

Generosity in Plato's Phaedrus', *Epoché.* 11, 51–80.

Gabbey, Alan. 1982. 'Philosophia cartesiana triumphata: Henry More and Descartes, 1646–71', in T. M. Lennon, J. M. Nicholas and J. W. Davis (eds), *Problems in Cartesianism.* Kingston, pp. 171–249.

Gadamer, H.-G. 1968. 'Plato und die Dichter', in Platos Dialektische Ethik und Andere Studien zur Platonischen Philosophie. Hamburg.

— 1980. 'Plato's Unwritten Dialectic', in P. C. Smith (trans.), *Dialogue and Dialectic: Eight Hermeneutical Studies on Plato.* New Haven, pp. 124–55.

— 1983. *Dialogue and Dialectic: Eight Hermeneutical Studies on Plato* (trans. P. C. Smith). New Haven.

— 1991. *Plato's Dialectical Ethics: Phenomenological Interpretations Relating to the Philebus* (trans. Robert M. Wallace). New Haven.

Gaiser, Konrad. 1959. *Protreptik und Paränese.* Stuttgart.

—1963. *Platons Ungeschriebene Lehre* (1st edn). Stuttgart.

— 1968. *Platons Ungeschriebene Lehre* (2nd edn). Stuttgart.

— 1980. 'Plato's Enigmatic Lecture on the Good', *Phronesis.* 25, 8–37.

— 2004. *Gesammelte Schriften.* Sankt Augustin.

Gall, Robert S. 2009. 'From Daimonion to the "Last" God: Socrates, Heidegger, and the God of the Thinker', *Philosophy Today.* 53, 265–72.

Gallop, David. 1984. *Parmenides of Elea, Fragments: A Text, with an Introduction.* Toronto.

Geach, Peter. 1966. 'Plato's Euthyphro: An Analysis and Commentary', *The Monist.* 50, 369–82.

Gentile, Marino. 1930. *La Dottrina Platonica Delle Idee Numeri e Aristotele.* Pisa.

Gersh, Stephen E. 1973. *Kinesis Akinetos: A Study of Spiritual Motion in the Philosophy of Proclus.* Leiden.

— 1986. *Middle Platonism and Neoplatonism: The Latin tradition.* Notre Dame.

Gerson, Lloyd P. 1990. *God and Greek Philosophy. Studies in the Early History of Natural Theology.* London and New York.

— 1994. *Plotinus.* London.

— 2003a. *Knowing Persons: A Study in Plato.* Oxford.

— 2003b. 'Akrasia and the Divided Soul in Plato's Laws', in Samuel Scolnicov and Luc Brisson (eds), *Plato's Laws: From Theory into Practice* (Proceedings of the VI Symposium Platonicum). Sankt Augustin, pp. 149–54.

— 2005. *Aristotle and Other Platonists.* Ithaca.

Giannantoni, Gabriele. 1983–5. *Socraticorum Reliquiae.* Naples.

Gill, Christopher. 1979. 'Plato and Politics: The Critias and the Politicus', *Phronesis.* 24, 148–67.

— 1985. 'Plato and the Education of Character', *Archiv für Geschichte der Philosophie.* 67, 1–26.

— 1996. *Personality in Greek Epic, Tragedy and Philosophy: The Self in Dialogue.* Oxford.

— 1998. 'Is Plato Proleptic?' *Polis.* 15, 113–21.

— 2002. 'Dialectic and the dialogue form', in J. Annas and C. Rowe (eds), *New Perspectives on Plato, Modern and Ancient.* Cambridge, pp. 145–71.

Gill, Mary Louise. 1996. *Plato: Parmenides.* Indianapolis.

— 2010. 'Division and Definition in Plato's Sophist and Statesman', in D. Charles (ed.), *Definition in Greek Philosophy.* Oxford, pp. 172–99.

Glaser, Konrad. 1935. 'Gang und Ergebnis des Platonischen Lysis', *Wiener Studien.* 53, 47–67.

Glucker, John. 1978. *Antiochus and the Late Academy.* Göttingen.

Goethe, Johann Wolfgang. 1796. 'Plato als Mitgenosse Einer Christlichen Offenbarung', in *Ion.* Cambridge, pp. 42–6.

Gomez-Lobo, Alfonso. 1999. *The Foundations of Socratic Ethics.* Indianapolis and Cambridge.

Gonzalez, Francisco J. 1995a. 'Plato's Lysis: An Enactment of Philosophical Kinship', *Ancient Philosophy.* 15, 69–90.

— (ed). 1995b. *The Third Way: New Directions in Platonic Studies.* Lanham.

— 1998a. *Dialectic and Dialogue: Plato's Practice of Philosophical Inquiry.* Evanston.

— 1998b. 'Nonpropositional Knowledge in Plato', *Apeiron.* 31, 235–84.

— 2000. 'Socrates on Loving One's Own: A Traditional Conception Radically Transformed', *Classical Philology.* 95, 379–98.

— 2002. 'The Socratic Elenchus as Constructive Protreptic', in Gary Alan Scott (ed.), *Does Socrates have a Method?* University Park, pp. 161–82.

— 2003. 'How to Read a Platonic Prologue: Lysis 203a–207d', in Ann N. Michelini (ed.), *Plato as Author.* Leiden, pp. 15–44.

Goody, Jack. 1977. *The Domestication of the Savage Mind.* Cambridge.

Gordon, Jill. 1999. *Turning Toward Philosophy: Literary Device and Dramatic Structure in Plato's Dialogues.* University Park.

Gorgias, 1972. 'Encomium of Helen', in Rosamond Kent Sprague (ed.), *The Older Sophists.* Columbia, pp. 50–4.

Gosling, J. C. B (trans.). 1975. *Plato Philebus.* Oxford.

Gosling, J. C. B. and C. C. W. Taylor. 1984. *The Greeks on Pleasure.* Oxford.

Gould, Thomas. 1991. *The Ancient Quarrel Between Poetry and Philosophy.* Princeton.

Goulet-Cazé, M.-O. 1999. 'L' Ordre Succession des Socratiques', in Marie-Odile Goulet-Cazé (ed.), *Diogène Laërce vie et Doctrine des Philosophes Illustres.* Paris, pp. 161–5.

Greene, W. C. 1944. *Moira. Fate, Good, and Evil in Greek Thought.* Cambridge.

Griswold, Charles L. 1986. *Self-knowledge in Plato's Phaedrus.* New Haven.

— 1988a. *Platonic Writings/Platonic Readings.* New York.

— 1988b. 'Unifying Plato', *Journal of Philosophy.* 85, 550–1.

— 1999. 'E Pluribus Unum? On the Platonic "Corpus,"' *Ancient Philosophy.* 19, 361–97.

— 2000. 'E Pluribus Unum? On the Platonic "Corpus:" the Discussion Continued', *Ancient Philosophy.* 20, 195–7.

— 2001. *Platonic Writings/Platonic Readings.* University Park (repr. of New York and London, 1988).

— 2002. 'Comments on Kahn', in Julia Annas and Christopher Rowe (eds), *New Perspectives on Plato, Modern and Ancient.* Cambridge, pp. 129–44.

— 2009. 'Plato on Rhetoric and Poetry', in Edward N. Zalta (ed.), *The Stanford Encyclopedia of Philosophy.* http://plato. stanford.edu/archives/fall2009/entries/ plato-rhetoric/ (accessed 1 March 2010).

Grote, George. 1865. *Plato and the Other Companions of Socrates.* London.

Grube, G. M. A. 1926. 'On the Authenticity of the Hippias Major', *Classical Quarterly.* 20, 134–48.

— 1929. 'The Logic and Language of the Hippias Major', *Classical Philology*. 24, 369–75.

— (trans.). 2002. *Plato: Five Dialogues*. Indianapolis.

Gulley, Norman. 1954. 'Plato's Theory of Recollection', *Classical Quarterly*. 4, 194–213.

— 1968. *The Philosophy of Socrates*. London.

Gutas, Dimitri. 2000. *Greek Philosophers in the Arabic Tradition*. Aldershot.

— 2003. 'Suhrawardî and Greek Philosophy', *Arabic Sciences and Philosophy*. 13, 303–9.

Guthrie, W. K. C. 1969. *A History of Greek Philosophy, Vol. 2: The Presocratic Tradition from Parmenides to Democritus*. Cambridge.

— 1971a. *The Sophists*. Cambridge.

— 1971b. *Socrates*. Cambridge.

— 1975. *A History of Greek Philosophy, Vol. 4: Plato, The Man and His Dialogues, Earlier Period*. Cambridge.

— 1978. *A History of Greek Philosophy, Vol. 5: The Later Plato and the Academy*. Cambridge.

Hackforth, Reginald. 1972. *Plato's Phaedrus*. Cambridge.

Haden, James. 1983. 'Friendship in Plato's Lysis', *Review of Metaphysics*. 37, 327–56.

Hager, Fritz-Peter. 1970. *Der Geist und das Eine: Untersuchungen zum Problem der Wesensbestimmung des höchsten Prinzips als Geist oder als Eines in der griechischen Philosophie*. Bern.

Halfwassen, Jens. 1993. *Der Aufstieg zum Einen. Untersuchungen zu Platon und Plotin*. Stuttgart.

— 2004. 'Platons Metaphysik des Einen', in Marcel van Ackeren (ed.), *Platon Verstehen*. Darmstadt, pp. 263–78.

Hall, Dale. 1980. 'Interpreting Plato's Cave as an Allegory of the Human Condition', *Apeiron*. 14, 74–84.

Hall, Rupert. 1990. *Henry More. Magic Religion and Experiment*. Oxford.

Halliwell, Stephen. 1990. 'Traditional Greek Conceptions of Character', in Christopher Pelling (ed.), *Characterization and Individuality in Greek Literature*. Oxford, pp. 32–59.

— 2000. 'The Subjection of Muthos to Logos: Plato's Criticism of the Poets', *Classical Quarterly*. 50, 94–112.

— 2002. *The Aesthetics of Mimesis: Ancient Texts and Modern Problems*. Princeton.

— 2007. 'The Life-and-Death Journey of the Soul: Interpreting the Myth of Er', in G. R. F. Ferrari (ed.), *The Cambridge Companion to Plato's Republic*. Cambridge, pp. 445–73.

Halperin, David M. 1990. *One Hundred Years of Homosexuality: And Other Essays on Greek Love*. New York and London.

— 1993. 'Is There a History of Sexuality?' in Henry Abelove, Michèle Aina Barale, and David M. Halperin (eds), *The Lesbian and Gay Studies Reader*. New York, pp. 416–31.

Hankey, Wayne. 2002. 'Aquinas and the Platonists', in S. Gersh and Maarten J. F. M. Hoenen (eds), *The Platonic Tradition in the Middle Ages: A Doxographic Approach*. Berlin and New York, pp. 279–324.

Hankins, James. 1987. 'Plato in the middle ages', in J. Strayer (ed.), *Dictionary of the Middle Ages. Vol. IX*. New York, pp. 694–704.

— 1990. *Plato in the Italian Renaissance*. Leiden.

Hankinson, R. J. 1998. *Cause and Explanation in Ancient Greek Thought*. Oxford.

Hansen, Mogens H. 1991. *The Athenian Democracy in the Age of Demosthenes.* Oxford.

Happ, Heinz. 1971. *Hyle: Studien zum Aristotelischen Materie-begriff.* Berlin.

Harriott, Rosemary. 1969. *Poetry and Criticism Before Plato.* London.

Harris, William. 1989. *Ancient Literacy.* Cambridge and New York.

Harte, Verity. 2002. *Plato on Parts and Wholes: The Metaphysics of Structure.* Oxford.

— 2003–4. 'The Philebus on Pleasure: The Good, the Bad and the False', *Proceedings of the Aristotelian Society.* 2, 111–28.

— 2008. 'Plato's Metaphysics', in Gail Fine (ed.), *The Oxford Handbook to Plato.* Oxford, 191–216.

Havelock, Eric. 1963. *Preface to Plato.* Cambridge.

Hawtrey R. S. W. 1981. *Commentary on Plato's Euthydemus.* Philadelphia.

Heath, Malcolm. 2002. *Interpreting Classical Texts.* London.

Heath, S. Arthur. 1921. *A History of Greek Mathematics.* Oxford.

Heath, Thomas. 1981. *A History of Greek Mathematics, Vol. I: From Thales to Euclid.* New York.

Hedley, Douglas and Sarah Hutton (eds). 2008. *Platonism at the Origins of Modernity: Studies on Platonism and Early Modern Philosophy.* Dordrecht.

Heidegger, Martin. 1998. 'Plato's Doctrine of Truth', in William McNeill (ed.), *Pathmarks.* Cambridge, pp. 155–82

— 2003. *Plato's Sophist* (trans. Richard Rojcewicz and André Schuwer). Indianapolis.

— 2004. *Essence of Truth: On Plato's Parable of the Cave and Theaetetus* (trans. Ted Sadler). London.

Henry, Madeleine Mary. 1995. *Prisoner of History: Aspasia of Miletus and her Biographical Tradition.* Oxford.

Hermann, Karl Friedrich. 1839. *Geschichte und System der Platonischen Philosophie.* Heidelberg.

Hirmer, Joseph. 1897. 'Entstehung und Komposition der Platonischen Politeia', *Jahrbücher für Classische Philologie* (Supplementband). 23, 579–678.

Hobbs, Angela. 2000. *Plato and the Hero: Courage, Manliness and the Impersonal Good.* Cambridge.

— 2006. 'Female Imagery in Plato', in J. H. Lesher, Debra Nails and Frisbee C. C. Sheffield (eds), *Plato's Symposium: Issues in Interpretation and Reception.* Cambridge and London, pp. 252–70.

Hoenen, Maarten J. F. M. and L. Nauta (eds). 1997. *Boethius in the Middle Ages: Latin and Vernacular Traditions of the Consolatio Philosophiae.* Leiden.

Hoerber, R. G. 1959. 'Plato's Lysis', *Phronesis.* 4, 15–28.

Hopkins, Burt. 2009. 'Jacob Klein on the Myth of Learning', *The St. John's Review.* 51, 5–39.

Howland, Jacob. 1991. 'Re-Reading Plato: The Problem of Platonic Chronology', *Phoenix.* 45, 189–214.

— 1993. *The Republic: The Odyssey of Philosophy.* New York.

— 1998. *The Paradox of Political Philosophy.* Lanham.

— 2007. 'Plato's Dionysian Music? A Reading of the Symposium', *Epoche.* 12, 17–47.

Howland, R. L. 1937. 'The Attack on Isocrates in the Phaedrus', *Classical Quarterly.* 31, 151–9.

Huby, Pamela M. 1957. 'The Menexenus Reconsidered', *Phronesis.* 2, 104–14.

Huffman, Carl A. 1993. *Philolaus of Croton: Pythagorean and Presocratic.* Cambridge.

— 1999. 'Limite et Illimité chez les Premiers Philosophes Grecs', in Monique Dixsaut (ed.), *La Fêlure du Plaisir.* Paris, pp. 11–31.

— 2005. *Archytas of Tarentum.* Cambridge.

— 2008. 'Two Problems in Pythagoreanism', in Patricia Curd and Daniel W. Graham (eds), *The Oxford Handbook of Presocratic Philosophy.* Oxford, pp. 284–304.

— 2009. 'The Pythagorean conception of the soul from Pythagoras to Philolaus', in Dorothea Frede and Burkhard Reis (eds), *Body and Soul in Ancient Philosophy.* Berlin, pp. 21–43.

— 2010. 'Reason and Myth in Early Pythagorean Cosmology', in Joe McCoy (ed.), *Early Greek Philosophy: Reason at the Beginning of Philosophy.* Washington, DC. Forthcoming.

Hunter, Richard. 2004. *Plato's Symposium.* Oxford.

Hutchinson, D. S. 1997. 'Alcibiades', in J. M. Cooper (ed.), *Plato: Complete Works.* Indianapolis.

Hutter, Horst. 1978. *Politics as Friendship: The Origins of Classical Notions of Politics in the Theory and Practice of Friendship.* Waterloo.

Hutton, Sarah (ed.). 1990. *Henry More (1614–1687): Tercentenary Studies.* Dordrecht.

— 1992. 'The Cambridge Platonists', in S. Nadler (ed.), *Blackwell Companion to Early Modern Philosophy.* Oxford.

— 2007. 'The Cambridge Platonists', in Edward N. Zalta (ed.), *The Stanford Encyclopedia of Philosophy.* http://plato. stanford.edu/archives/fall2008/entries/ plato/ (accessed 29 June 2010).

Hyland, Drew. 1968. 'Why Plato Wrote Dialogues', *Philosophy and Rhetoric.* 1, 38–50.

— 1981. *The Virtue of Philosophy: An Interpretation of Plato's Charmides.* Athens.

— 1995. *Finitude and Transcendence in the Platonic Dialogues.* Albany.

— 2004. *Questioning Platonism: Continental Interpretations of Plato.* Albany.

— 2008. *Plato and the Question of Beauty.* Bloomington.

Idel, Moshe. 2002. *Absorbing Perfections: Kabbalah and Interpretation.* New Haven.

Irwin, Terence H. 1977a. *Plato's Moral Theory: The Early and Middle Dialogues.* Oxford.

— 1977b. 'Plato's Heracliteanism', *The Philosophical Quarterly.* 27, 1–13.

— (trans., comm.). 1979. *Plato: Gorgias.* Oxford.

— 1995. *Plato's Ethics.* Oxford.

— 2005. 'Was Socrates Against Democracy?' in Rachana Kamtekar (ed.), *Plato's Euthyphro, Apology, and Crito: Critical Essays.* London and Boulder, pp. 127–49.

— 2006. 'Socrates and Euthyphro: The Argument and Its Revival', in L. Judson and V. Karasmanis (eds), *Remembering Socrates.* Oxford, pp. 58–71.

— 2008. 'The Platonic Corpus', in Gail Fine (ed.), *The Oxford Handbook of Plato.* Oxford, pp. 63–87.

Isnardi Parente, Margherita. 1969. 'Sugli apocrifi platonici Demodoco e Sisifo', *La Parols del Passato.* 9, 425–31.

— 1980. *Speusippo. Frammenti.* Naples.

— 1982. *Senocrate-Ermodoro. Frammenti.* Naples.

— 1997 and 1998. *Per una raccolta delle principali testimonianze sul legomena agrapha dogmata di Platone in Atti della Accademia Nazionale dei Lincei* (2 vols.). Rome.

Ivánka, Endre von. 1964. *Plato Christianus*. Einsiedeln.

Jackson, Henry. 1881–5. 'Plato's Later Theory of Ideas', *Journal of Philology*. 10, 253–98; 11, 287–331; 13, 1–40 and 242–72; and 14, 173–230.

Jacobs, Jonathan. 2010. *Law, Reason, and Morality in Medieval Jewish Philosophy*. Oxford.

Jaeger, Werner. 1939–44. *Paideia, the ideals of Greek culture*. (3 vols) (trans. Gilbert Highet). New York and Oxford.

— 1962. *Aristotle. Fundamentals of the History of his Development*. Oxford.

Janaway, Christopher. 1995. *Images of Excellence: Plato's Critique of the Arts*. Oxford.

Janko, Richard. 2009. 'Socrates the Freethinker', in S. Ahbel-Rappe and R. Kamtekar (eds), *A Companion to Socrates*. Oxford, pp. 48–62.

Jantzen, J. 1989. *Hippias minor oder Der Falsche Wahre: über den Ursprung der moralischen Bedeutung von 'gutt'*. Weinheim.

Jarratt, Susan. 1991. *Rereading the Sophists*. Carbondale.

Jaucourt, Chevalier de. 1736. *Art. 'Platonisme' in Encyclopédie raisonnée des sciences, des arts et des métiers, Vol. 12*. Paris.

Jay, Martin. 1993. *Downcast Eyes. The Denigration of Vision in Twentieth-century French Thought*. Berkeley.

Jeauneau, Édouard. 1957. 'L'usage de la notion d'integumentum à travers les gloses de Guillaume de Conches', *Archives D'histoire Doctrinaire Littéraire du Moyen Age*. 24, 35–100 (repr. in Id. Lectio philosophorum: recherches sur l'Ecole de Chartres, Amsterdam 1973, pp. 127–92).

— 2010. *Rethinking the School of Chartres* (trans. Claude Paul Desmarais). Toronto.

Jenks, Rod. 2008. *Plato on Moral Expertise*. Lanham.

Johansen, Thomas K. 2004. *Plato's Natural Philosophy: A Study of the Timaeus-Critias*. Cambridge.

— 2008. 'The Timaeus on the Principles of Cosmology', in Gail Fine (ed.), *Oxford Handbook of Plato*. Oxford, pp. 463–83.

Johnson, D. M. 1999. 'God as the True Self: Plato's Alcibiades I', *Ancient Philosophy*. 19, 1–19.

Jouanna, Jacques. 1998. 'The Birth of Western Medical Art', in Mirko D. Grmek (ed.), *Western Medical Thought from Antiquity to the Middle Ages* (trans. Antony Shugaar). Cambridge, pp. 22–71.

Jouët-Pastré, Emmanuelle. 2006. *Le jeu et le Sérieux dan les Lois de Platon*. Sankt Augustin.

Joyal, Mark. 1995. 'Tradition and Innovation in the Transformation of Socrates' Divine Sign', in L. Ayres (ed.), *The Passionate Intellect: Essays on the Transformation of Classical Traditions Presented to I.G. Kidd*. New Brunswick, pp. 39–56.

— 2000. *The Platonic Theages: An Introduction, Commentary and Critical Edition*. Stuttgart.

Justin, Gale. 2005. 'Identification and Definition in the Lysis', *Archiv für Geschichte der Philosophie*. 87, 75–104.

Kahn, Charles H. 1963. 'Plato's Funeral Oration: The Motive of the Menexenus', *Classical Philology*. 58, 220–34.

— 1966. 'The Greek Verb "To Be" and the Concept of Being', *Foundations of Language*. 2, 245–65.

— 1968. 'Review of G. Ryle, Plato's Progress', *Journal of Philosophy*. 65, 364–75.

— 1981. 'Did Plato Write Socratic Dialogues?' *Classical Quarterly*. 31, 305–20.

— 1983. 'Drama and Dialectic in Plato's Gorgias', *Oxford Studies in Ancient Philosophy*. 1, 75–121.

— 1988. 'Plato's Charmides and the Proleptic Reading of Plato's Dialogues', *Journal of Philosophy*. 69, 541–9.

— 1993. 'Proleptic Composition in the Republic, or Why Book I was Never a Separate Dialogue', *Classical Quarterly*. n.s. 43, 131–42.

— 1994. 'Aeschines on Socratic Eros', in P. A. Vander Waerdt (ed.), *The Socratic Movement*. Ithaca and London, pp. 87–106.

— 1996. *Plato and the Socratic Dialogue: The Philosophical Use of a Literary Form*. Cambridge.

— 2000. 'Response to Griswold', *Ancient Philosophy*. 20, 189–93.

— 2001. *Pythagoras and the Pythagoreans: A Brief History*. Indianapolis.

— 2002. 'On Platonic Chronology', in Julia Annas and Christopher Rowe (eds), *New Perspectives on Plato, Modern and Ancient*. Cambridge, pp. 93–127.

— 2007. 'Why Is the Sophist a Sequel to the Theaetetus?' *Phronesis* 52, 33–57.

— 2008. 'Response to Christopher Rowe', *Plato* 2. http://gramata.univer-paris1.fr/Plato/article31.html (accessed 15 June 2010).

— 2010. 'The Place of Cosmology in Plato's Later Dialogues', in Richard Mohr and Barbara Slater (eds), *One Book, The Whole Universe: Plato's Timaeus Today*. Las Vegas, pp. 69–77.

Kamtekar, Rachana. 2004. 'What's the Good of Agreeing? Homonoia in Platonic Politics', *Oxford Studies in Ancient Philosophy*. 24, 131–72.

— 2006. 'Socrates and Euthyphro: The Argument and its Revival', in L. Judson and V. Karasmanis (eds), *Remembering Socrates*. Oxford, pp. 58–71.

— 2010. 'Ethics and politics in Socrates' defense of justice', in Mark McPherran (ed.), *The Cambridge Critical Guide to Plato's Republic*. Cambridge, pp. 65–82.

Kant, Immanuel. 1787. *Kritik der reinen Vernunft*. Riga (English trans. Smith N. K. (2nd ed.) (1933). *Immanuel Kant's Critique of Pure Reason*. Edinburgh).

— 1796. *Von Einem Neuerdings Erhobenen Vornehmen Ton in der Philosophie*, (Engl. trans. Fenves, P. D. 1993. 'On a Newly Arisen Superior Tone in Philosophy', in P. D. Fenves (ed.), *Raising the Tone of Philosophy*. Baltimore).

Karamanolis, George. 2006. *Plato and Aristotle in Agreement? Platonists on Aristotle from Antiochus to Porphyry*. Oxford.

Keller, Evelyn and Christine Grontkowski. 1983. 'The Mind's Eye', in Sandra Harding and Merill Hintikka (eds), *Discovering Realities*. Dordrecht.

Kelly, Eugene (ed.). 1984. *New Essays on Socrates*. Lanham.

Kennedy, George A. 1963. *The Art of Persuasion in Ancient Greece*. Princeton.

— 1994. *A New History of Classical Rhetoric*. Princeton.

Kennedy, J. B. 2010. 'Plato's Forms, Pythagorean Mathematics, and Stichometry', *Apeiron*. 43, 1–31.

— 2011. *The Musical Structure of Plato's Dialogues*. Durham.

Kerferd, G. B. 1950. 'The First Greek Sophists', *Classical Review*. 64, 8–10.

— 1981. *The Sophistic Movement*. Cambridge.

Ketchum, Richard. 1987. 'Plato on the Unknowability of the Sensible World',

History of Philosophy Quarterly. 4, 291–305.

Kierkegaard, Søren. 1841. *On the Concept of Irony with Continual Reference to Socrates* (trans. L. M. Capel). New York.

Kimball, Bruce. 1986. *Orators and Philosophers*. New York.

Kingsley, Peter. 1995. *Ancient Philosophy, Mystery and Magic*. Oxford.

Kirchner, Johannes. 1901. *Prosopographia Attica*. Berlin.

Kirk, G. S. 1962. *Heraclitus: The Cosmic Fragments* (2nd edn). Cambridge.

Klagge, James C. and Nicholas D. Smith (eds). 1992. *Methods of Interpreting Plato and His Dialogues*. Oxford.

Klein, Jacob. 1965. *A Commentary on Plato's Meno*. Chapel Hill.

— 1966. 'A Note on Plato's Parmenides', in R. Williamson and E. Zuckerman (eds), *Lectures and Essays*. Annapolis, pp. 285–7.

— 1992. *Greek Mathematical Thought and the Origin of Algebra* (trans. Eva Brann). New York.

Klein-Franke, Felix. 1973. 'Zur Überlieferung der platonischen Schriften in Islam', *Israel Oriental Studies*. 3, 120–39.

Klibansky, Raymond. 1939. *The Continuity of the Platonic tradition during the Middle Ages: Outlines of a Corpus Platonicum Medii Aevi*. London.

Klosko, George. 1984. 'The Refutation of Polus in Plato's Gorgias', *Greece & Rome*. 31, 126–39.

— 2006. *The Development of Plato's Political Theory* (2nd edn). Oxford.

Kneale, William and Martha Kneale. 1964. *The Development of Logic*. Oxford.

Knorr, Wilbur. 1989. *Textual Studies in Ancient and Medieval Geometry*. Boston.

Knox, B. M. W. 1985. 'Books and Readers in the Greek World: From the Beginnings to Alexandria', in P. E. Easterling and B. M. W. Knox (eds), *Greek Literature: The Cambridge History of Classical Literature I*. Cambridge, pp. 1–15.

Kosman, Aryeh. 1976. 'Platonic Love', in W. H. Werkmeister (ed.), *Facets of Plato's Philosophy*. Amsterdam, pp. 53–69.

— 2007. 'Justice and Virtue: the Republic's Inquiry into Proper Difference', in G. R. F. Ferrari (ed.), *The Cambridge Companion to Plato's Republic*. Cambridge, pp. 116–37.

— 2010. 'Beauty and the Good: situating *to kalon*', *Classical Philology*. 105, 341–57.

Koyré, Alexander. 1957. *From the Closed World to the Infinite Universe*. Baltimore.

Krämer, Hans J. 1959. *Arete bei Platon und Aristoteles* (1st edn). Heidelberg.

— 1964. *Der Ursprung der Geistmetaphysik. Untersuchungen zur Geschichte des Platonismus zwischen Platon und Plotin* (1st edn). Amsterdam.

— 1982. *Platone e i fondamenti della metafisica*. Milano.

— 1990. *Plato and the Foundations of Metaphysics: A Work on the Theory of the Principles and Unwritten Doctrines of Plato with a Collection of the Fundamental Documents* (trans. J. R. Catan). New York.

Krauss, Heinrich. 1911. *Aischinis Socratici reliquiae*. Leipzig.

Kraut, Richard. 1979. 'Two Conceptions of Happiness', *Philosophical Review*. 88, 167–97.

— 1984. *Socrates and the State*. Princeton.

— (ed.). 1992a. *The Cambridge Companion to Plato*. Cambridge.

— 1992b. 'The Defense of Justice in Plato's Republic', in Kraut (ed.), 1992a, pp. 311–37.

— 1992c. 'Introduction to the Study of Plato', in Kraut (ed.), 1992a, pp. 1–50.

— 1992d. 'Chronology', in Kraut (ed.), 1992a, pp. xii–xiii.

Kretzmann, Norman. 1971. 'Plato on the Correctness of Names', *American Philosophical Quarterly*. 8, 126–38.

Krohn, August. 1876. *Der Platonische Staat*. Halle.

Lacey, A. R. 1971. 'Our Knowledge of Socrates', in Gregory Vlastos (ed.), The Philosophy of Socrates. Plato II: A Collection of Critical Essays. Ethics, Politics and Philosophy of Art and Religion. New York, pp. 22–49.

Lafrance, Yvon. 1986. *Pour Interpréter Platon: La Ligne en République VI, 509d–511e*. Montréal and Paris.

— 1987. *Pour Interpréter Platon, I, La Ligne en République VI, 509d–511e. Bilan analytique des études (1804–1984)*. Montréal and Paris.

— 1994. *Pour Interpréter Platon, II, La Ligne en République VI, 509d–511e. Le Texte et son Histoire*. Montréal and Paris.

Laín Entralgo, Pedro. 1970. *The Therapy of the Word in Classical Antiquity*. New Haven (trans. Lelland J. Rather and John M. Sharp).

Laird, Andrew. 2003. 'Death, Politics, Vision and Fiction in Plato's Cave (After Saramago)', *Arion*. 10, 1–30.

Lamberton, Robert and John Keaney (eds). 1992. *Homer's Ancient Readers: The Hermeneutics of Greek Epics Earliest Exegets*. Princeton.

Landy, Tucker. 1998. 'Limitations of Political Philosophy: An Interpretation of Plato's Charmides', *Interpretation*. 26, 183–99.

Lane, Melissa S. 1998. *Method and Politics in Plato's Statesman*. Cambridge.

Leaman, Oliver. 2005. 'Plato's Republic in Jewish philosophy', in M. Vegetti and M. P. Pissavino (eds), *I Decembrio e la Traduzione Della Repubblica di Platone tra Medioevo e Umanesimo*. Naples, pp. 13–30.

— 2010. *Judaism: An Introduction*. London.

Lear, G. R. 2007. 'Permanent Beauty and Becoming Happy in Plato's Symposium', in James Lesher, Debra Nails, and Frisbee Sheffield (eds), *Plato's 'Symposium': Issues in Interpretation and Reception*. Cambridge, pp. 96–123.

Lear, J. 1992. 'Inside and Outside the Republic', *Phronesis*. 37, 184–215.

Lebeck, Anne. 1971. *The Oresteia. A Study in Language and Structure*. Washington D. C. and Cambridge.

Ledger, Gerard R. 1989. *Re-Counting Plato: A Computer Analysis of Plato's Style*. Oxford.

Lee, Mi-Kyoung. 2005. *Epistemology after Protagoras: Responses to Relativism in Plato, Aristotle and Democritus*. Oxford.

— 2008. 'The Theaetetus', in Gail Fine (ed.), *Oxford Handbook on Plato*. Oxford, pp. 411–36.

Lesher, J. H. 1987. 'Socrates' Disavowal of Knowledge', *Journal of the History of Philosophy*. 25, 275–88.

— 1992. *Xenophanes of Colophon*. Toronto.

Lesher, J. H., Debra Nails and Frisbee C. C. Sheffield. 2006. *Plato's Symposium: Issues in Interpretation and Reception*. Cambridge, Massachusetts and London.

Lesky, Albin. 1996. *A History of Greek Literature*. London.

Levin, Donald N. 1971. 'Some Observations Concerning Plato's Lysis', in J. P. Anton and G. L. Kustas (eds), *Essays in Greek Philosophy*. Albany, pp. 236–58.

Levin, Susan B. 2000. *The Ancient Quarrel Between Philosophy and Poetry Revisited: Plato and the Greek Literary Tradition*. New York and Oxford.

— 2007. 'Is Medicine a Technê? Health and End-of-Life Care in Plato's Republic', *Philosophical Inquiry*. 29, 125–53.

— 2008. 'Platonic Metaphysics and Semantics: The Cratylus' Ties to the Sophist and Politicus', in Dagfinn Føllesdal and John Woods (eds), *Logos and Language: Essays in Honour of Julius Moravcsik*. London, pp. 73–98.

Levinas, Emmanuel. 1972. *Humanisme de L'autre Homme*. Montpellier.

Lewis, V. Bradley. 2000. 'The Seventh Letter and the Unity of Plato's Political Philosophy', *Southern Journal of Philosophy*. 38, 231–50.

Lindberg, David. 1976. *Theory of Vision from Al-Kindi to Kepler*. Chicago.

Livingstone, Niall. 2001. *A Commentary on Isocrates' Busiris*. Leiden.

Lloyd, A. C. 1990. *The Anatomy of Neoplatonism*. Oxford.

Lloyd, G. E. R. 1968. *Aristotle. The Growth and Structure of his Thought*. Cambridge.

— 1979. *Magic, Reason, and Experience*. Cambridge.

— 1992a. *Polarity and Analogy: Two Types of Argumentation in Early Greek Thought*. Bristol.

— 1992b. 'The Meno and the Mysteries of Mathematics', *Phronesis*. 37, 166–83.

Lobel, Edgar. 1919. 'Aeschines Socraticus, Alicibiades', in *Papyri Oxyrhynchus*. XII n. 1608.

Long, A. A. 1996. 'The Socratic Tradition: Diogenes, Crates and Hellenistic Ethics', in R. Bracht Branham and Marie-Odile Goulet-Cazé (eds), *The Cynics The Cynic Movement in Antiquity and its Legacy*. Berkeley, Los Angeles and London.

— (ed). 1999. *The Cambridge Companion to Early Greek Philosophy*. Cambridge.

— 2004. 'Eudaimonism, divinity, and rationality in Greek ethics', *Proceedings of the Boston Area Colloquium in Ancient Philosophy, Vol. XIX*. Leiden and Boston, pp. 123–43.

Long, Christopher P. 2003. 'Dancing Naked with Socrates: Pericles, Aspasia and Socrates at Play with Politics, Rhetoric and Philosophy', *Ancient Philosophy*. 23, 49–69.

Loraux, Nicole. 1986. *The Invention of Athens: The Funeral Oration in the Classical City* (trans. A. Sheridan). Cambridge.

Lorenz, Hendrik. 2006. 'The Analysis of the Soul in Plato's Republic', in Gerasimos Santas (ed.) *Blackwell Guide to Plato's Republic*. Oxford, pp. 125–45.

Lotze, Hermann. 1856–64. *Mikrokosmus*. Leipzig.

— 1874. System der Philosophie: Logik. Leipzig.

Lovibond, Sabina. 1990. 'True and False Pleasures', *Proceedings of the Aristotelian Society*. 90, 213–30.

Ludwig, Paul. 2002. *Eros and Polis*. Cambridge.

Lutoslawski, Wicenty. 1897. *The Origin and Growth of Plato's Logic. With an Account of Plato's Style and of the Chronology of his Writings*. London.

Luz, Menahem. 1994. 'The Transmission of Antisthenes' Hercules in Hellenistic Philosophy and Literature', in K. J. Boudouris (ed.), *Hellenistic Philosophy*. Athens, pp. 88–95.

— 1996. 'Antisthenes' Prometheus Myth', in John Glucker and André Laks (eds), *Jacob Bernays: un Philologue Juif*. Villeneuve d'Ascq, pp. 89–103.

— 2000. 'Disgracefulness is Disgraceful: Antisthenes' Logic, Ethics and Sources', in Konstantine Boudouris (ed.), *Greek Philosophy and the Fine Arts*. Athens, pp. 88–95.

Lycos, Kimon. 1987. *Plato on Justice and Power: Reading Book I of Plato's Republic*. Albany.

Mahdi, Muhsin (trans.). 1962. *Alfarabi's Philosophy of Plato and Aristotle*. Glencoe.

Mahoney, T. 1992. 'Do Plato's Philosopher-Rulers Sacrifice Self-interest to Justice?' *Phronesis*. 38, 265–82.

Maiatsky, Michail. 2005. *Platon, Penseur du Visuel*. Paris.

Malcolm, John. 1981. 'The Cave Revisited', *Classical Quarterly*. 31, 60–8.

— 1991. *Plato on the Self Predication of Forms*. Oxford.

Mannebach, Erich. 1961. *Aristippi et Cyrenaicorum Fragmenta*. Leiden.

Mansfeld, Jaap. 1994. *Prolegomena: Questions to be Settled before the Study of an Author, or a Text*. Leiden.

Manuwald, Bernd. 2005. 'The Unity of Virtue in Plato's Protagoras', *Oxford Studies in Ancient Philosophy*. 29, 115–35.

Marenbon, John. 1997. *The philosophy of Peter Abelard*. Cambridge.

— 2002. 'Platonism–a Doxographic Approach: the Early Middle Ages', in S. Gersh and Maarten J. F. M. Hoenen (eds), *The Platonic Tradition in the Middle Ages: A Doxographic Approach*. Berlin and New York, pp. 67–89.

— 2007. *Medieval Philosophy: An Historical and Philosophical Introduction*. New York.

Marrou, Henri-Irénée. 1956. *A History of Education in Antiquity* (trans. George Lamb). New York.

Matthews, Gareth. 2008. 'The epistemology and metaphysics of Socrates', in Gail Fine (ed.), *Oxford Handbook on Plato*. Oxford, pp. 114–38.

McCabe, Mary Margaret. 1994. *Plato's Individuals*. Princeton.

— 2000. *Plato and his Predecessors: the Dramatisation of Reason*. Cambridge.

— 2008. 'Plato's Ways of Writing', in Gail Fine (ed.), *The Oxford Handbook of Plato*. Oxford, pp. 88–113.

McCoy, Marina. 2007. *Plato on the Rhetoric of Philosophers and Sophists*. Cambridge.

— 2009. 'Alcidamas, Isocrates, and Plato on Speech, Writing, and Philosophical Rhetoric', *Ancient Philosophy*. 29, 45–66.

McKim, Richard. 1985. 'Socratic Self-knowledge and Knowledge of Knowledge in Plato's Charmides', *Transactions of the American Philological Association*. 115, 59–77.

McKirahan, Voula Tsouna. 1994. 'The Socratic Origins of the Cynics and Cyrenaics', in P. A. Vander Waerdt (ed.), *The Socratic Movement*. Ithaca, pp. 367–91.

McPherran, Mark L. 1996. *The Religion of Socrates*. University Park.

— 2000. 'Does Piety Pay? Socrates and Plato on Prayer and Sacrifice', in Nicholas D. Smith and Paul Woodruff (eds), *Reason and Religion in Socratic Philosophy*. Oxford, pp. 89–114; also in Thomas C. Brickhouse and Nicholas D. Smith (eds). 2002. *The Trial and Execution of Socrates: Sources and Controversies*. Oxford, pp. 162–89.

— 2002. 'Elenctic Interpretation and the Delphic Oracle', in Gary A. Scott (ed.), *Does Socrates Have a Method?* University Park, pp. 114–44.

— 2003. 'The Aporetic Interlude and Fifth Elenchos of Plato's Euthyphro', *Oxford Studies in Ancient Philosophy*. 25, 1–37.

— 2006a. 'Platonic Religion', in Hugh Benson (ed.), *A Companion to Plato*. Malden, pp. 244–60.

— 2006b. 'The Gods and Piety of Plato's Republic', in Gerasimos X. Santas (ed.), *The Blackwell Guide to Plato's Republic*. Malden, pp. 84–104.

— 2006c. 'Medicine, Magic, and Religion in Plato's Symposium', in James H. Lesher, Debra Nails, and Frisbee Sheffield (eds), *Plato's Symposium: Issues in Interpretation and Reception*. Cambridge, pp. 71–95.

— 2010. 'Love and Medicine in Plato's Symposium and Philebus', in Luc Brisson and John Dillon (eds), *Plato's Philebus: Selected Papers from the Eighth Symposium Platonicum*. Sankt Augustin, pp. 204–8.

Méasson, Anita. 1986. *Du char ailé de Zeus à l'Arche d'Alliance: Images et Mythes Platoniciens chez Philon d'Alexandrie*. Paris.

Meinwald, Constance C. 1991. *Plato's 'Parmenides'*. Oxford.

— 1998. 'Prometheus's Bounds: Peras and Apeiron in Plato's Philebus', in Jyl Gentzler (ed.), *Method in Ancient Philosophy*. Oxford, pp. 165–80.

Melamed, Abraham. 1997. 'Medieval and Renaissance Jewish Political Philosophy', in D. Frank and O. Leaman (eds). *History of Jewish Philosophy*. London, pp. 415–49.

Menn, Stephen. 2002. 'Plato and the Method of Analysis', *Phronesis*. 47, 193–223.

Mercer, Christia. 2001. *Leibniz's Metaphysics: Its Origins and Development*. Cambridge.

Merker, Anne. 2003. *La Vision chez Platon et Aristote*. Sankt Augustin.

Merlan, Philip. 1947. 'Form and Content in Plato's Philosophy', *Journal of the History of Ideas*. 8, 406–30.

— 1953. *From Platonism to Neoplatonism*. The Hague.

Michelini, A. N. 2003. *Plato as Author: The Rhetoric of Philosophy*. Leiden and Boston.

Migliori, Maurizio. 1990. *Dialettica e Verità: Commentario Filosofico al 'Parmenide' di Platone*. Milan.

Miles, Murray. 2001. 'Plato on Suicide (*Phaedo* 60c–63c)', *Phoenix*. 55, 244–58.

Miller, Fred D. 2005. 'Plato on the Rule of Reason', *Southern Journal of Philosophy*. 43, 50–83.

Miller, Mitch Jr. 1985. 'Platonic Provocations: Reflections on the Soul and the Good in the Republic', in D. J. O'Meara (ed.), *Platonic Investigations*. Washington, pp. 165–93.

— 1986. *Plato's Parmenides: The Conversation of the Soul*. Princeton.

— 1995a. 'The Choice between the Dialogues and the Unwritten Teachings: A Scylla and Charybdis for the Interpreter?' in Francisco J. Gonzales (ed.), *The Third Way: New Directions in Platonic Studies*. Lanham, pp. 25–44.

— 1995b. '"Unwritten Teachings" in the Parmenides', *Review of Metaphysics*. 48, 591–633.

— 2003. 'The Timaeus and the Longer Way', in G. Greydam-Schils (ed.), *Plato's Timaeus as Cultural Icon*. Notre Dame, pp. 17–59.

— 2004. *The Philosopher in Plato's Statesman*. Parmenides.

— 2007. 'Beginning the "Longer Way,"' in G. R. F. Ferarri (ed.), *The Cambridge Companion to Plato's Republic*. Cambridge, pp. 310–44.

— 2008. 'The Pleasures of the Comic and of Socratic Inquiry: Aporetic Reflections on Philebus 48a–50b', *Arethusa*. 41, 263–89.

Mirhady, David C. 2001. 'Dicaearchus of Messana: The Sources, Text and Translation', in William W. Fortenbaugh and Eckart Schütrumpf (eds),

Dicaearchus of Messana. New Brunswick and London, pp. 1–142.

Mirhady, David C. and Yun L. Too. 2000. *Isocrates I.* Austin.

Moes, Mark. 2000. *Plato's Dialogue Form and the Care of the Soul.* New York.

Moline, Jonathan. 1969. 'Meno's Paradox?' *Phronesis.* 14, 153–61.

Monoson, Sara S. 1992. 'Remembering Pericles: The Political and Theoretical Import of Plato's Menexenus', *Political Theory.* 26, 489–513.

Moravcsik, Julius. 1970. 'Learning as Recollection', in Gregory Vlastos (ed.), *Plato: A Collection of Critical Essays.* Vol. I. Garden City, pp. 53–69.

— 1973. 'The Anatomy of Plato's Divisions', in E. N. Lee, A. P. D. Mourelatos, and R. M. Rorty (eds), *Exegesis and Argument: Studies in Greek Philosophy Presented to Gregory Vlastos.* New York, pp. 324–48.

— 1992. *Plato and Platonism.* Oxford.

Moreau, Joseph. 1941. 'La platonisme de "L'Hippias Majeur,"' *Revue des Etudes Grecques.* 54, 19–42.

Morgan, Kathryn A. 2000. *Myth and Philosophy from the Presocratics to Plato.* Cambridge.

— 2010. 'Inspiration, Recollection, and Mimêsis in Plato's Phaedrus', in David Sedley and Andrea Nightingale (eds), *Ancient Models of Mind: Studies in Human and Divine Rationality.* Cambridge, pp. 45–63.

Morgan, Michael L. 1990. *Platonic Piety: Philosophy and Ritual in Fourth-Century Athens.* New Haven and London.

Morrison, Donald. 2000. 'On the Alleged Historical Reliability of Plato's Apology', *Archiv für Geschichte der Philosophie.* 82, 235–65.

Morrow, Glenn R. 1935. *Studies in the Platonic Epistles.* Urbana.

— 1960. 'Aristotle's Comments on Plato's Laws', in I. Düring and G. E. L. Owen (eds), *Plato and Aristotle in the Mid-fourth Century.* Göteborg, pp. 145–62.

— 1993. *Plato's Cretan City.* Princeton (repr. of Princeton 1960).

Most, G. W. 1993. 'A Cock for Asclepius', *Classical Quarterly.* N.S. 43 No. 1, 96–111.

Mourelatos, A. P. D. 1970. *The Route of Parmenides: A Study of Word, Image, and Argument in the Fragments.* New Haven.

Mueller, Ian. 1992. 'Mathematical Method and Philosophical Truth', in Richard Kraut (ed.), *The Cambridge Companion to Plato.* New York, pp. 170–99.

Mugler, Charles. 1964. *Dictionnaire Historique de la Terminologie Optique des Grecs.* Paris.

Muir, J. V. 2001. *Alcidamas: The Works and Fragments.* London.

Muirhead, John H. 1931. *The Platonic Tradition in Anglo-Saxon Philosophy.* London.

Mulhern, J. J. 1984. 'Tropos and Polytropia in Plato's Hippias minor', *Phoenix.* 22, 283–8.

Murdoch, Iris. 1977. *The Fire and the Sun: Why Plato Banished the Artists.* Oxford.

Murphy, David J. 2000. 'Doctors of Zalmoxis and Immortality in the Charmides', in Thomas M. Robinson (ed.), *Plato: Euthydemus, Lysis Charmides: Proceedings of the V'Symposium Platonicum.* Sankt Augustin, pp. 287–95.

Murray, Oswyn. (ed.). 1990. *Sympotica: A symposium on the Symposium.* Oxford.

Murray, Penelope. 1981. 'Poetic inspiration in early Greece', *Journal of Hellenic Studies.* 101, 87–100.

— 1993. 'Inspiration and mimesis in Plato', in Andrew Barker and Martin Warner (eds), *The Language of the Cave*. Edmonton, pp. 27–46 (repr. in 2004, *Apeiron* 25, 4).

Nagy, Gregory. 1989. 'Early Greek View of poets and poetry', in George Kennedy (ed.), *The Cambridge History of Classical Criticism. Vol. I*. Cambridge.

Nails, Debra. 1993. 'Problems with Vlastos's Platonic Developmentalism', *Ancient Philosophy*. 13, 273–91.

— 1994. 'Plato's Middle Cluster', *Phoenix*. 48, 62–7.

— 1995. *Agora, Academy, and the Conduct of Philosophy*. Dortrecht.

— 1998. 'The Dramatic Date of Plato's Republic', *The Classical Journal*. 93, 383–96.

— 2002. *The People of Plato: A Prosopography of Plato and Other Socratics*. Indianapolis and Cambridge.

Nails, Debra and Holger Thesleff. 2003. 'Early Academic Editing: Plato's Laws', in Samuel Scolnicov and Luc Brisson (eds), *Plato's Laws: From Theory into Practice*. Sankt Augustin, pp. 14–29.

— 2006. 'The Life of Plato of Athens', in Hugh Benson (ed.), *A Companion to Plato*. Oxford, pp. 1–12.

— 2009. 'Socrates', The Stanford Encyclopedia of Philosophy, Edward N. Zalta (ed.), http://plato.stanford.edu/entries/socrates/ (accessed 19 February 2010).

Napolitano Valditara, Linda. 1994. *Lo Sguardo nel Buio. Metafore Visive e Forme Grecoantica Della Razionalità*. Roma-Bari.

Narcy, Michel. 1984. *Le Philosophe et son Double: Un Commentaire de l'Euthydème de Platon*. Paris.

Natorp, Paul. 1903. *Platonsideenlehre*. Leipzig.

Nauta, Lodi. 1996. 'The preexistence of the soul in medieval thought', *Recherches de Théologie Ancienne et Médiévale*. 63, 93–135.

— 2009. 'The Consolation: the Latin commentary tradition 800–1700', in J. Marenbon (ed.), *The Cambridge Companion to Boethius*. Cambridge.

Navia, Luis E. 2001. *Antisthenes of Athens: Setting the World Aright*. Westport.

Nehamas, Alexander. 1975. 'Plato on the Imperfection of the Sensible World', *American Philosophical Quarterly*. 12, 105–17 (reprinted in Fine, Gail (ed.). 1999. *Plato I: Metaphysics and Epistemology*. Oxford, pp. 171–91; also in Nehamas, A. 1999. *Virtues of Authenticity*. Princeton, pp. 138–58).

— 1979. 'Self-predication and Plato's Theory of Forms', *American Philosophical Quarterly*. 16, 93–103.

— 1982a. 'Participation and Predication in Plato's Later Dialogues', *Review of Metaphysics*. 36, 343–74 (also in Nehamas, A. 1999. *Virtues of Authenticity*. Princeton, pp. 196–223).

— 1982b. 'Plato on Imitation and Poetry', in Julius Moravcsik and Philip Temko (eds), *Plato on Beauty, Wisdom, and the Arts*. Totowa: NJ, pp. 47–78.

— 1992. 'Voices of Silence: On Gregory Vlastos' Socrates', *Arion: A Journal of Humanities and the Classics*. 2, 157–86.

— 1999. *Virtues of Authenticity: Essays on Plato and Aristotle*. Princeton.

Nettleship, Richard Lewis. 1929. *Lectures on the Republic of Plato*. London.

— 1935. *The Theory of Education in Plato's Republic*. Oxford.

Nichols, Mary P. 1987. *Socrates and the Political Community*. Albany.

— 2009. *Socrates on Friendship and Community: Reflections on Plato's*

Symposium, Phaedrus, and Lysis. Cambridge.

Nietzsche, Friedrich. 1886. *Jenseits von Gut und Böse.* 1888. *Götzen-Dämmerung, oder Wie man mit dem Hammer philosophirt,* 'Was ich den Alten verdanke'§2.

— 1888. *Twilight of the Idols, What I Owe to the Ancients* §2.

— 1996. *Philosophy in the Tragic Age of the Greeks* (trans. Mariane Cowan). Washington, D.C.

— 1999. *The Birth of Tragedy and Other Writings* (trans. Raymond Geuss and Ronald Speirs). Cambridge.

— 2005. *The Anti-Christ, Ecce Homo, Twilight of the Idols and Other Writings* (trans. Judith Norman). Cambridge.

Nightingale, Andrea W. 1995. *Genres in Dialogue: Plato and the Construct of Philosophy.* Cambridge.

— 2004. *Spectacles of Truth in Classical Greek Philosophy: Theoria in its Cultural Context.* Cambridge.

North, Helen. 1966. *Sophrosyne: Self-Knowledge and Self-Restraint in Greek Literature.* Ithaca.

Notomi, Noburu. 1999. *The Unity of Plato's Sophist: Between the Sophist and the Philosopher.* Cambridge.

— 2007. 'Plato on what is not', in D. Scott (ed.), *Maieusis.* Oxford, pp. 254–75.

Nussbaum, Martha C. 1986. *The Fragility of Goodness: Luck and Ethics in Greek Tragedy and Philosophy.* Cambridge.

— 1994. *The Therapy of Desire.* Princeton.

O'Connor, David K. 2007. 'Rewriting the Poets in Plato's Characters', in G. R. F. Ferrari (ed.), *The Cambridge Companion to Plato's Republic.* Cambridge, pp. 55–89.

O'Meara, Dominic J. 1993. *Plotinus: An Introduction to the Enneads.* Oxford.

O'Sullivan, Neil. 1992. *Alcidamas, Aristophanes and the Beginnings of Greek Stylistic Theory.* Stuttgart.

Ober, Josiah. 1989. *Mass and Elite in Democratic Athens.* Princeton.

Ohly, Kurt. 1928. *Stichometrische Untersuchungen.* Leipzig.

Okin, Susan Moller. 1977. 'Philosopher-Queens and Private Wives: Plato on Women and the Family', *Philosophy and Public Affairs.* 6, 345–69.

— 1979. *Women in Western Political Thought.* Princeton.

Ong, Walter. 1982. *Orality and Literacy: The Technologizing of the Word.* London.

Osborne, Catherine. 1994. *Eros Unveiled: Plato and the God of Love.* Oxford.

— 1995. 'Perceiving Particulars and Recollecting the Forms in the *Phaedo*', *Proceedings of the Aristotelian Society.* N.S. 95, 211–33.

Oswiecimski, Stefan. 1978. 'The Enigmatic Character of some of Plato's Apocrypha', *Eos.* 66, 31–40.

— 1979. 'The Acephalous Dialogues', *Eos.* 67, 55–67.

Owen, G. E. L. 1953a. 'The Place of the Timaeus in Plato's Dialogues', *Classical Quarterly.* 3, 70–95 (repr. in R. E. Allen (ed), *Studies in Plato's Metaphysics.* London 1965, pp. 1–12 and repr. in G. E. L. Owen and Martha Nussbaum (eds), *Logic, Science, and Dialectic.* Ithaca 1986, pp. 65–84).

— 1953b. 'The Place of the Timaeus in Plato's Dialogues', *Classical Quarterly.* n.s. 3, 79–95.

— 1957. 'A Proof in the Peri Ideon', *Journal of Hellenic Studies.* 77, 103–11.

— 1965. 'The Place of the Timaeus in Plato's Dialogues', in R. E. Allen (ed.), *Studies in Plato's Metaphysics.* London, pp. 313–38.

— 1970. 'Plato on Not-Being', in Gregory Vlastos (ed.), *Plato I*. New York, pp. 223–67.

— 1971. 'Plato on Not-Being', in Gregory Vlastos (ed.), *Plato: A Collection of Critical Essays, Vol. 1*. Notre Dame, pp. 223–67 (repr. in Martha Nussbaum (ed.), 1986. *Logic, Science, and Dialectic*. Ithaca, pp. 104–37).

— 1986. 'The Platonism of Aristotle', in Martha Nussbaum (ed.), *Logic, Science and Dialectic*. London and New York, pp. 200–20.

Pakaluk, M. 2003. 'Degrees of Separation in the *Phaedo*', *Phronesis*. 48, 89–115.

Palmer, John. 1999. *Plato's Reception of Parmenides*. Oxford and New York.

Pangle, Thomas L. 1980. 'Interpretive Essay', in *The Laws of Plato*. Thomas L. Pangle (trans.), Chicago, pp. 375–510.

Pappas, Nickolas. 2003. *Routledge GuideBook to Plato and the Republic* (2nd edn). London.

Paquet, Léonce. 1973. *Platon. La Médiation du Regard*. Leiden.

Parry, Richard. 1996. *Plato's Craft of Justice*. Albany.

— 2007. 'The Unhappy Tyrant and the Craft of Inner Rule', in G. R. F. Ferrari (ed.), *The Cambridge Companion to Plato's Republic*. Cambridge, pp. 386–414.

Partenie, Catalin (ed.). 2009. *Plato's Myths*. Cambridge.

Passmore, J. A. 1951. *Ralph Cudworth, an Interpretation*. Cambridge.

Patrizzi da Cherso, Francesco. 1571. *Discussionum Peripateticorum Libri XV*. Basle.

— 1591. *Nova de Universis Philosophiae*. Ferrara.

Patterson, Richard. 1985. *Image and Reality in Plato's Metaphysics*. Indianapolis.

— 1997. 'Philosophos Agonistes: Imagery and Moral Psychology in Plato's Republic', *Journal of the History of Philosophy*. 35, 327–54.

— 2007. 'Diagrams, Dialectic, and Mathematical Foundations in Plato', *Apeiron*. 40, 1–33.

Pellegrin, Pierre. 2009. 'Ancient Medicine and its Contribution to the Philosophical Tradition', in Mary L. Gill and Pierre Pellegrin (eds), *A Companion to Ancient Philosophy*. Malden, pp. 664–85.

Pender, E. E. 1992. 'Spiritual Pregnancy in Plato's Symposium', *Classical Quarterly*. 42, 72–86.

— Forthcoming. 'The Rivers of the Underworld: Plato's Geography of Dying and Coming-back-to-Life', in C. Collobert, P. Destrée, F. J. Gonzalez (eds), *Platonic Myths: Uses and Statuses*. Leiden, ch. 11.

Penner, Terry. 1971. 'Thought and Desire in Plato', in Gregory Vlastos (ed.), *Plato II*. Garden City, pp. 96–118.

— 1973. 'The Unity of Virtue', *The Philosophical Review*. 82, 35–68.

— 1990. 'Plato and Davidson: Parts of the Soul and Weakness of Will', in David Copp (ed.), *Canadian Philosophers, Supplementary Vol. 16, Canadian Journal of Philosophy*. pp. 35–74.

— 1991. 'Desire and Power in Socrates: The Argument of Gorgias 466a–468c that Orators and Tyrants have no Power in the City', *Apeiron*. 24, 147–202.

— 1992. 'Socrates and the Early Dialogues', in Richard Kraut (ed.), *The Cambridge Companion to Plato*. Cambridge, pp. 121–69.

— 2002. 'The Historical Socrates and Plato's Early Dialogues: Some Philosophical Questions', in Julia Annas and Christopher Rowe (eds), *New*

Perspectives on Plato, Modern and Ancient. Cambridge, pp. 189–212.

— 2005. 'Socratic Ethics, Ultra-realism, Determinism, and Ethical truth', in Christopher Gill (ed.), *Virtue, Norms & Objectivity: Issues in Ancient and Modern Ethics*. Oxford, pp. 157–87.

Penner, Terry and Christopher Rowe. 2005. *Plato's Lysis*. Cambridge.

Perl, Eric. 1995. 'The Living Image: Forms and the Erotic Intellect in Plato', *American Catholic Philosophical Quarterly*. 69, 191–204.

Perrault, Charles. 1688. *Parallèle des Anciens et des Modernes en ce qui Concerne les Arts et les Sciences* (4 vol.). Paris.

Philip, J. A. 1970. 'The Platonic Corpus', *Phoenix*. 24, 296–308.

Pieper, Josef. 1964. *Enthusiasm and Divine Madness* (trans. Richard Winston and Clara Winston). New York.

Plass, Paul. 1964. 'Philosophic Anonymity and Irony in the Platonic Dialogues', *American Journal of Philology*. 85, 254–78.

— 1967. '"Play" and Philosophical Detachment in Plato', *Transactions and Proceedings of the American Philological Association*. 98, 343–64.

Polansky, Ronald. 1992. Philosophy and Knowledge: *A Commentary on Plato's Theaetetus*. Lewisburg.

Popper, Karl. 1945. *The Open Society and its Enemies, Vol. I: The Spell of Plato*. London.

— 1962. *The Open Society and Its Enemies* (4th edn, vol. 1). Princeton.

Post, L. A. 1934. *The Vatican Plato and its Relations*. Middletown.

Pottenger, John R. 1995–6. 'The sage and the sophist: a commentary on Plato's Lesser Hippias', *Interpretation*. 23, 41–60.

— 1995. *Sophistical Rhetoric in Classical Greece*. Columbia.

Pownall, Frances. 2004. *Lessons from the Past: The Moral Use of History in Fourth-Century Prose*. Ann Arbor.

Pratt, Louise. 1993. *Lying and Poetry from Homer to Pindar: Falsehood and Deception in Archaic Greek Poetics*. Ann Arbor.

Press, Gerald A. (ed.). 1993. *Plato's Dialogues: New Studies & Interpretations*. Lanham.

— 1995a. 'Knowledge as Vision in Plato's Dialogues', *Journal of Neoplatonic Studies*. 3, 61–89.

— 1995b. 'Plato's Dialogues as Enactments', in Francisco Gonzalez (ed.), *The Third Way: New Directions in Platonic Studies*. Lanham, pp. 133–52.

— 2000. (ed.) *Who Speaks for Plato? Studies in Platonic Anonymity*. Lanham.

— 2007. *Plato: A Guide for the Perplexed*. New York.

Price, Anthony W. 1989. *Love and Friendship in Plato and Aristotle*. Oxford.

— 1995. *Mental Conflict*. London.

Price, Jonathan. 2001. *Thucydides and Internal War*. Cambridge.

Prier, Raymond. 1989. *Thauma Idesthai: The Phenomenology of Sight & Appearance in Archaic Greek*. Tallahassee.

Prior, William J. 1985. *Unity and Development in Plato's Metaphysics*. Chicago and La Salle.

— 1996. *Socrates: Critical Assessments*. London and New York.

— 2001. 'The Historicity of Plato's Apology', *Polis*. 18, 41–57.

— 2004. 'Socrates Metaphysician', *Oxford Studies in Ancient Philosophy*. 27, 1–14.

— 2006. 'The Socratic Problem', in Hugh Benson (ed.), *A Blackwell Companion to Plato*. Malden, pp. 25–36.

Proclus. 1970. *A Commentary on the First Book of Euclid's Elements* (trans. Glenn Morrow). Princeton.

Quine, W. V. 1986. *Philosophy of Logic* (2nd edn). Cambridge.

Rademaker, Adriaan. 2005. *Sôphrosynê and the Rhetoric of Self-Restraint*. Leiden.

Randall, John Herman. 1970. *Plato: Dramatist of the Life of Reason*. New York.

Rankin, H. D. 1967. 'Laughter, Humour and Related Topics in Plato', *Classica et Medievalia*. 28, 186–213.

— 1986. *Antisthenes Sokratikos*. Amsterdam.

Ranta, Jerrald. 1967. 'The Drama of Plato's Ion', *Journal of Aesthetics and Art Criticism*. 26, 219–29.

Raven, J. E. 1953. 'Sun, Divided Line, and Cave', *Classical Quarterly*. 3, 22–32.

Rawls, John. 1971. *A Theory of Justice*. Cambridge.

Reale, Giovanni. 1984. *Per una Nuova Interpretazione di Platone*. Milano.

Reeve, C. D. C. 1988. *Philosopher-Kings: The Argument of Plato's Republic*. Princeton.

Reisman, David. 2004. 'Plato's Republic in a Newly Discovered Passage', *Arabic Sciences and Philosophy*. 14, 263–300.

Rexine, John E. 1985. 'Daimon in classical Greek literature', *Platon*. 37, 29–52.

Richard, Marie-Dominique. 1986. *L'enseignement Orale de Platon* (1st edn). Paris.

Richardson, Henry S. 1990. 'Measurement, Pleasure, and Practical Science in Plato's Protagoras', *Journal of the History of Philosophy*. 28, 7–32.

Richardson, Nicholas. 1975. 'Homeric Professors in the Age of the Sophists', *Proceedings of the Cambridge Philological Society*. 21, 65–81.

Rick, Hubert. 1931. *Neue Untersuchungen zu platonischen Dialogen*. Bonn.

Rickless, Samuel. 2007. *Plato's Forms in Transition: A Reading of the Parmenides*. Cambridge.

Ries, Klaus. 1959. *Isokrates und Platon im Ringen um die Philosophie* (Dissertation). Munich.

Riginos, Alice. 1976. *Platonica. The Anecdotes Concerning the Life and Writings of Plato*. Leiden.

Rist, John M. 1967. *Plotinus: The Road to Reality*. Cambridge.

Ritter, Constantin. 1888. *Untersuchungen über Platon*. Stuttgart.

— 1910a. 'Eidos, idea und verwandte Wörter in den Schriften Platons', in Ritter Constantin, *Neue Untersuchungen über Platon*. München, pp. 228–326.

— 1910b. *Platon: sein Leben, seine Schriften, seine Lehre*. Munich.

— 1933. *The Essence of Plato's Philosophy*. New York.

Robb, Kevin. 1994. *Literacy and Paideia in Ancient Greece*. Oxford.

Robin, Léon. 1908. *La Théorie Platonicienne des Idées et des Nombres D'après Aristote*. Paris.

— 1964. *La Théorie Platonicienne de L'amour* (2nd edn). Paris.

Robinson, David B. 1986. 'Plato's Lysis: The Structural Problem', *Illinois Classical Studies*. 11, 63–83.

Robinson, Richard. 1953. *Plato's Earlier Dialectic*. Oxford.

— 1966. *Plato's Earlier Dialectic* (2nd edn). Oxford.

Robinson, Thomas. 1995. *Plato's Psychology* (2nd edn). Toronto.

Rogers, G. A. J., J.-M. Vienne and Y.-C. Zarka (eds). 1997. *The Cambridge Platonists in Philosophical Context:*

Politics, Metaphysics and Religion. Dordrecht.

Roochnik, David. 1984. 'The Riddle of the Cleitophon', *Ancient Philosophy.* 4, 132–45.

— 1996. *Of Art and Wisdom: Plato's Understanding of Techne.* University Park.

— 2003. *Beautiful City: The Dialectical Character of Plato's Republic.* Ithaca and London.

Rorty, Richard. 1979. *Philosophy in the Mirror of Nature.* Princeton.

Rösel, Martin. 1994. *Übersetzung als Vollendung der Auslegung: Studien zur Genesis Septuaginta.* Berlin.

Rosen, Stanley. 1983. *Plato's Sophist: The Drama of Original and Image.* New Haven (repr. in 1999, South Bend).

— 1988. *The Quarrel between Philosophy and Poetry.* New York.

— 2005. *Plato's Republic: A Study.* New Haven.

Rosenstock, Bruce. 1994. 'Socrates as Revenant: A Reading of the Menexenus', *Phoenix.* 48, 331–47.

Rosenthal, Erwin. 2010. 'Torah and nomos in medieval Jewish philosophy', *Judaism, Philosophy, Culture, Selected Studies by E I J Rosenthal.* London, pp. 309–24.

Rosenthal, Franz. 1940. 'On the Knowledge of Plato's Philosophy in the Islamic World', *Islamic Culture.* 14, 387–422.

— 1941. 'Addenda', *Islamic Culture.* 15, 396–8.

Ross, W. D. 1924. *Aristotle's Metaphysics: A Revised Text with Introduction and Commentary.* Oxford.

— 1951. *Plato's Theory of Ideas.* Oxford.

— 1955. *Aristotelis Fragmenta Selecta.* Oxford.

Roth, Michael. 1995. 'Did Plato Nod? Some Conjectures on Egoism and Friendship in the Lysis', *Archiv für Geschichte der Philosophie.* 77, 1–20.

Rowe, Christopher. 1986. 'The argument and structure of Plato's Phaedrus', *Proceedings of the Cambridge Philological Society.* 32, 106–25.

— 1990. 'Philosophy, Love, and Madness', in Christopher Gill (ed.), *The Person and the Human Mind.* Oxford, pp. 227–46.

— 1993. *Plato Phaedo.* Cambridge.

— 1995. 'Introduction', in Christopher J. Rowe (ed.) *Plato: Statesman.* Warminster, pp. 1–20.

— 2006. 'Interpreting Plato', in Hugh Benson (ed.), *A Companion to Plato.* Malden, pp. 13–24.

Rudebusch, George. 1999. *Socrates, Pleasure, and Value.* Oxford.

— 2002. 'Dramatic Prefiguration in Plato's Republic', *Philosophy and Literature.* 26, 75–83.

— 2004. 'True Love Requited: the Argument of Lysis 221d–222a', *Ancient Philosophy.* 24, 1–14.

Runia, David T. 1986. *Philo of Alexandria and the Timaeus of Plato.* Leiden.

— 1993a. *Philo in Early Christian Literature: A Survey.* Assen- Minneapolis.

— 1993b. 'Was Philo a Middle Platonist? a Difficult Question Revisited', *The Studia Philonica Annual.* 5, 112–40.

Russell, Daniel C. 2005. *Plato on Pleasure and the Good Life.* Oxford.

Rutherford, Richard B. 1995. *The Art of Plato: Ten Essays in Platonic Interpretation.* London.

Ryle, Gilbert. 1939a. 'Plato's Parmenides', in R. E. Allen (ed.), *Studies in Plato's Metaphysics.* London, pp. 97–147.

— 1939b. 'Plato's Parmenides', *Mind.* 48, 129–51 and 302–25.

— 1949. *The Concept of Mind.* New York.

— 1960. 'Letters and Syllables in Plato', *Philosophical Review*. 69, 431–51.

— 1966. *Plato's Progress*. Cambridge.

Sachs, David. 1963. 'A Fallacy in Plato's Republic?' *Philosophical Review*. 72, 141–58.

Saffrey, H. D. 2007. 'Retour sur le Parisinus Graecus 1807: le manuscrit A de Platon', in C. d'Ancona (ed.), *The Libraries of the Neoplatonists*. Leiden, pp. 3–28.

Salkever, Stephen G. 1993. 'Socrates' Aspasian Oration: The Play of Philosophy and Politics in Plato's Menexenus', *American Political Science Review*. 87, 133–43.

Sallis, John. 1996. *Being and Logos: Reading the Platonic Dialogues*. Indianapolis.

— 2004. *Platonic Legacies*. Albany.

Santas, Gerasimos X. 1972. 'The Socratic Fallacy', *Journal of the History of Philosophy*. 10, 127–41.

— 1973. 'Socrates at Work on Virtue and Knowledge in Plato's Charmides', in Edward N. Lee, Alexander P. D. Mourelatos, and Richard M. Rorty (eds), *Exegesis and Argument*. New York, pp. 105–32.

— 1985. 'Two Theories of Good in Plato's Republic', *Archiv für Geschichte der Philosophie*, 67, 223–45.

— 1988. *Plato and Freud: Two Theories of Love*. Oxford.

Saunders, Trevor J. 1962. 'The Structure of State and Soul in Plato's Laws', *Eranos*. 9, 37–55.

— 1994. *Plato's Penal Code*. Oxford.

Saunders, Trevor J. and Luc Brisson. 2000. *Bibliography on Plato's Laws*. Sankt Augustin.

Saxonhouse, Arlene. 1976. 'The Philosopher and the Female in the Political Thought of Plato', *Political Theory*. 4, 195–212.

Sayre, Kenneth M. 1969. *Plato's Analytic Method*. Chicago.

— 1983. *Plato's Late Ontology: A Riddle Resolved*. Princeton (expanded edition Las Vegas, 2005).

— 1992. 'A Maieutic View of Five Late Dialogues', in James C. Klagge and Nicholas D. Smith (eds), *Methods of Interpreting Plato and His Dialogues*. Oxford, pp. 221–43.

— 1995a. *Plato's Literary Garden: How to Read a Platonic Dialogue*. Notre Dame.

— 1995b. 'Why Plato Never Had a Theory of Forms', in John J. Cleary and William Wians (eds), *Proceedings of the Boston Area Colloquium in Ancient Philosophy*, Vol. IX. Boston, pp. 167–99.

— 2002. 'The Multilayered Incoherence of Timaeus' Receptacle', in Gretchen Reydams–Schils (ed.), *Plato's Timaeus as Cultural Icon*. Notre Dame, pp. 60–79.

— 2005. *Plato's Late Ontology: A Riddle Resolved*. Parmenides.

— 2006. *Metaphysics and Method in Plato's Statesman*. Cambridge.

Schaper, Eva. 1968. *Prelude to Aesthetics*. London.

Schenke, Stefan. 1985. 'Der Logik des Rückstiegs', *Philosophisches Jahrbuch*. 92, 316–34.

Schiappa, Edward. 1991. *Protagoras and Logos*. Columbia.

— 1994. 'Plato and hê kaloumenê rhêtorikê: A Response to O'Sullivan', *Mnemosyne*. 47, 512–14.

— 2003. *Protagoras and Logos: A Study in Greek Philosophy and Rhetoric*. Columbia.

Schindler, D. C. 2008. *Plato's Critique of Impure Reason. On Goodness and Truth in the Republic*. Washington DC.

Schleiermacher, Friedrich. 1836. *Schleiermacher's Introductions to the Dialogues of Plato* (trans. W. Dobson). Cambridge, pp. 1–47.

Schlick, Moritz. 1937. 'L'École de Vienne et la philosophie traditionnelle', in *Travaux, du IXe congrès international de philosophie, IV*. Paris, pp. 99–107.

Schmid, Walter T. 1992. *On Manly Courage: A Study of Plato's Laches*. Carbondale.

— 1997. *Plato's Charmides and the Socratic Ideal of Rationality*. Albany.

Scolnicov, Samuel. 1971. 'On the Epistemological Significance of Plato's Theory of Ideal Numbers', *Museum Helveticum*. 28, 72–97.

— 1976. 'Three Aspects of Plato's Philosophy of Learning and Instruction', *Paideia*. 5, 50–62.

— 1988. *Plato's Metaphysics of Education*. London and New York.

— 1994. 'Derrida's drug and Plato's antidote: Socratic dialogue as moral philosophy', in L. Toker (ed.), *Reflective Commitment: Essays in Literature and Moral Philosophy*. New York, pp. 3–23.

— 2003. *Plato's Parmenides*. Berkeley.

— 2004. 'Plato's ethics of irony', in M. Migliori (ed.), *Plato Ethicus*. Sankt Augustin.

Scott, Dominic. 1990. *Recollection and Explanation: Plato's Theory of Learning and its Successors*. Cambridge.

— 2006. *Plato's Meno*. Cambridge.

Scott, Gary A. 2002. *Does Socrates have a Method?: Rethinking the Elenchus in Plato's Dialogues and Beyond*. University Park.

— (ed.). 2007. *Philosophy in Dialogue: Plato's Many Devices*. Evanston.

Sedley, David. 1989. 'Is the Lysis a Dialogue of Definition?' *Phronesis*. 34, 107–8.

— 1990. 'The Dramatis Personae of Plato's Phaedo', in T. Smiley (ed.), Philosophical Dialogues: Plato, Hume, Wittgenstein. Proceedings of the British Academy 85. Oxford, pp. 3–26.

— 1997. 'Becoming like God in the Timaeus and Aristotle', in Tomás Calvo and Luc Brisson (eds), *Interpreting the Timaeus-Critias*. Sankt Augustin.

— 1998. 'Platonic Causes', *Phronesis*. 43, 114–32.

— 1999. 'The Ideal of Godlikeness', in Gail Fine (ed.), *Plato. Vol. II: Ethics, Politics, Religion, and the Soul*. Oxford, pp. 309–28.

— 2003. *Plato's Cratylus*. Cambridge.

— 2004. *The Midwife of Platonism: Text and Subtext in Plato's Theaetetus*. Oxford.

— 2007a. *Creationism and its Critics in Antiquity*. Berkeley, Los Angeles and London.

— 2007b. 'Philosophy, the Forms, and the Art of Ruling', in G. R. F. Ferrari (ed.), *The Cambridge Companion to Plato's Republic*. Cambridge, pp. 256–83.

— 2008a. 'The Ideal of Godlikeness', in Gail Fine (ed.), Plato. *Oxford Readings in Philosophy*. Oxford, pp. 791–810.

— 2008b. *Creationism and its Critics in Antiquity*. Berkeley.

— 2009a. 'Myth, punishment, and politics in the Gorgias', in C. Partenie (ed.), *Plato's Myths*. Cambridge, pp. 51–76.

— 2009b. 'A Thrasyllan Interpretation of Theaetetus', *Papyri Oxyrhynchus*. LXXIII 4941, 65–71.

Seel, Gerhard. 2006. 'If you Know What is Best, you Do it: Socratic Intellectualism in Xenophon and Plato', in L. Judson and V. Karasmanis (eds), *Remembering Socrates*. Oxford, pp. 20–49.

— 2007. 'Is Plato's Conception of the Form of the Good Contradictory?' in Douglas Cairns, Fritz-Gregor Herrmann, and Terry Penner (eds), *Pursuing the Good, Ethics and Metaphysics in Plato's Republic*. Edinburgh, pp. 168–96.

Segal, Charles. 1962. 'Gorgias and the Psychology of Logos', *Harvard Studies in Classical Philology*. 66, 99–155.

Segvic, Heda. 2002. 'No One Errs Willingly: The Meaning of Socratic Intellectualism', *Oxford Studies in Ancient Philosophy*. 19, 1–46.

Sharma, Ravi. 2009. 'Socrates' New Aitia: Causal and Metaphysical Explanations in Plato's Phaedo', *Oxford Studies in Ancient Philosophy*. 36, 137–77.

Sharples, R. W. (trans.). 1985. *Plato: Meno*. Chicago.

Shaw, Gregory. 1995. *Theurgy and the Soul: The Neoplatonism of Iamblichus*. University Park.

Shorey, Paul. 1903. *The Unity of Plato's Thought*. Chicago.

— 1924. 'Review of Stenzel 1924', *Classical Philology*. 19, 381–3.

— (trans.). 1930. *Plato: The Republic, Books 1–5*. Cambridge.

— 1933. *What Plato Said*. Chicago.

— (trans.). 1937. *Plato: The Republic*. Cambridge.

Shortridge, Andrew. 2007. 'Law and Nature in Protagoras' Great Speech', *Polis*. 24, 12–25.

Sickinger, James P. 1999. *Public Records & Archives in Classical Athens*. Chapel Hill.

Sider, David. 1977. 'Plato's Early Aesthetics: The Hippias Major', *Journal of Aesthetics and Art Criticism*. 35, 465–70.

Silverman, Allan. 2002. *The Dialectic of Essence: A Study of Plato's Metaphysics*. Princeton.

Simon, Gérard. 1988. *Le Regard, L'être et l'Apparence dans l'Optique de l'Antiquité*. Paris.

Sinaiko, Herman L. 1965. *Love, Knowledge, and Discourse in Plato: Dialogue and Dialectic in Phaedrus, Republic, Parmenides*. Chicago.

Singpurwalla, Rachel. 2005. 'Plato's Defense of Justice', in G. Santas (ed.), *The Blackwell Guide to Plato's Republic*. Oxford, pp. 263–82.

Slings, Simon. R. 1975. 'Some Remarks on Aeschines' Miltiades', in *Zeitschrift für Papyrologie und Epigraphik 16*. pp. 301–8.

— 1981. *A Commentary on the Platonic Clitophon*. Amsterdam.

— 1999. *Plato: Clitophon*. Cambridge.

Slings, Simon R., Gerard Boter and J. M. van Ophuijsen. 2005. *Critical Notes on Plato's Politeia*. Leiden.

Smith, Andrew. 1974. *Porphyry's Place in the Neoplatonic Tradition–A Study in Post-Plotinian Neoplatonism*. The Hague.

Smith, Imogen. 2008. 'False Names, Demonstratives and the Refutation of Linguistic Naturalism in Plato's Cratylus 427d1–431c3', *Phronesis*. 53, 125–51.

Smith, Nicholas D. 1979. 'Knowledge by Acquaintance and Knowing What in Plato's Republic', *Dialogue*. 18, 281–8.

— 1996. 'Plato's Divided Line', *Ancient Philosophy*. 16, 25–46.

— 2000. 'Plato on Knowledge as a Power', *Journal of the History of Philosophy*. 38, 145–68.

— 2004. 'Did Plato Write the Alcibiades I?' *Apeiron*. 37, 93–108.

Socher, Joseph. 1820. *Über Platons Schriften*. Munich.

Solmsen, Friedrich. 1975. *Intellectual Experiments of the Greek Enlightenment.* Princeton.

— 1981. 'The Academic and the Alexandrian Editions of Plato's Works', *Illinois Classical Studies.* 6, 102–11.

Sommerstein, A. H. (ed.). 1982. *Aristophanes: Clouds.* Warminster.

— (ed.). 1987. *Aristophanes: Birds.* Warminster.

Sparshott, Francis E. 1966. 'Socrates and Thrasymachus', *Monist.* 50, 421–59.

Sprague, Rosamond Kent. 1962. *Plato's Use of Fallacy: A Study of the Euthydemus and Some Other Dialogues.* London.

— (trans.). 1965. *Plato: Euthydemus.* New York.

— (ed). 1972. *The Older Sophists.* Columbia (repr. in Indianapolis, 2001).

Stalley, R. F. 2000. 'Sôphrosynê in the Charmides', in Thomas M. Robinson (ed.), *Plato:* Euthydemus, Lysis Charmides: Proceedings of the V'Symposium Platonicum. *Sankt Augustin,* pp. 265–77.

— 2009. 'Myth and Eschatology in the *Laws*', in C. Partenie (ed.), *Plato's Myths.* Cambridge, pp. 187–205.

Stauffer, Devin. 2001. *Plato's Introduction to the Question of Justice.* Albany.

— 2006. *The Unity of Plato's Gorgias.* Cambridge.

Steel, Carlos G. 1978. *The Changing Self. A Study on the Soul in later Neoplatonism: Iamblichus, Damascius, and Priscianus.* Brussels.

— 1990. 'Plato Latinus (1939–1989)', in Rencontres de Cultures dans la Philosophie Médiévale: Traductions et Traducteurs de l'Antiquité Tardive au XIVe Siècle. Louvain-la-Neuve, pp. 301–16.

— (dir.). 2002. 'Proclus: Fifteen Years of Research (1990–2004). An Annotated Bibliography', *Lustrum.* 44, 1–367.

Stefanini, Luigi. 1932. *Platone.* Padua (2nd edn, repr. Padua, 1991).

Stenzel, Julius. 1924. *Zahl und Gestalt bei Platon und Aristoteles.* Berlin and Leipzig.

— 1928. *Platon der Ezieher.* Leipzig.

— 1973. *Plato's Method of Dialectic* (trans. D. J. Allen). New York.

Stern, Paul. 1993. *Socratic Rationalism and Political Philosophy.* Albany.

— 1999. 'Tyranny and Self-Knowledge: Critias and Socrates in Plato's Charmides', *American Political Science Review.* 93, 399–412.

— 2008. *Knowledge and Politics in Plato's Theaetetus.* Cambridge.

Stern-Gillet, Suzanne. 2004. 'On (mis) interpreting Plato's Ion', *Phronesis.* 49, 169–201.

Strauss, Leo. 1975. *The Argument and the Action of Plato's Laws.* Chicago.

— 1989. *The Rebirth of Classical Political Rationalism.* Chicago.

— 2003. *Leo Strauss on Plato's Symposium.* Seth Bernadete (ed.). Chicago.

Striker, Gisela. 1970. *Peras und Apeiron: Das Problem der Formen in Platons Philebos.* Göttingen.

Strohmaier, Gerhard. 2002. 'Platon in der arabischen Tradition', *Würzburger Jahrbücher für die Altertumswissenschaft, Neue Folge.* 26, 185–200.

Struck, Peter. 2004. *Birth of the Symbol: Ancient Readers at the Limits of their Texts.* Princeton.

Surányi, László. 1999. *Metaaxiomatische Probleme.* Frankfurt am Main.

Susemihl, Franz. 1855–7. *Die genetische Entwicklung der Platonischen Philosophie.* Leipzig.

Szlezák, Thomas A. 1985. *Platon und die Schriftlichkeit der Philosophie*. Berlin and New York.

— 1993. 'Zur üblichen Abneigung gegen die Agrapha Dogmata' *Methexis*. 6, 155–74. [English trans. 2001. 'On the Standard Aversion to the Agrapha dogmata', Graduate faculty Philosophy Journal 22, 147–63.]

— 1999. *Reading Plato*. London and New York.

— 2004. *Das Bild des Dialektikers in Platons späten Dialogen*. Berlin and New York.

Taran, Leonardo. 1981. *Speusippus of Athens*. Leiden.

Tarrant, Dorothy. 1928. *The Hippias Major, Attributed to Plato*. Cambridge.

— 1952. 'Metaphors of Death in the Phaedo', *The Classical Review*. n.s. 2, 64–6.

— 1960. 'Greek Metaphors of Light', *Classical Quarterly*. 10, 181–7.

Tarrant, Harold. 1982. 'The Composition of Plato's Gorgias', *Prudentia*. 14, 3–22.

— 1993. *Thrasyllan Platonism*. Ithaca and London.

— 2000. *Plato's First Interpreters*. London.

— 2005. 'Socratic Synousia: A Post-Platonic Myth?' *Journal of the History of Philosophy*. 43, 131–55.

— 2006. 'Socratic Method and Socratic Truth', in Sara Ahbel-Rappe and Rachana Kamtekar (eds), *A Companion to Socrates*. Malden, pp. 254–72.

— 2007a. 'Olympiodorus and Proclus on the Climax of the Alcibiades', *International Journal of the Platonic Tradition* 1, 3–29.

— 2007b. 'Moral Goal and Moral Virtues in Middle Platonism', in Robert Sharples and Richard Sorabji (eds), *Philosophy 100 BC to AD 200. Bulletin of the Institute of Classical Studies Suppl*. London, pp. 419–29.

— 2008. 'The Dramatic Setting of the Arguments with Callicles, Euripides Antiope, and the Date of an Athenian Anti-Intellectual Argument', *Antichthon* 4, 20–39.

— 2009. 'The Object of Alcibiades' Love', *Literature and Aesthetics* 19, 74–87.

— 2010. 'The Theaetetus as a Narrative Dialogue?' *Australasian Society for Cognitive Science Proceedings*. 31. http://www.classics.uwa.edu.au/ascs31.

Tate, Jonathan. 1929. 'Plato and Allegorical Interpretation', *Classical Quarterly*. 23, 142–54.

— 1939. 'On the History of Allegorism', *Classical Quarterly* 28, 105–19.

Taylor, A. E. 1926. 'Review of Stenzel 1924', *Gnomon*. 2, 396–405.

— 1926-7. 'Forms and Numbers: A Study in Platonic Metaphysics', *Mind*. 35, 419–40 and 36, 12–33.

— 1934. *The 'Parmenides' of Plato*. Oxford.

— 1960. *Plato: The Man and his Work*. London.

Taylor, C. C. W. 1969. 'Forms as Causes in the Phaedo', *Mind*. 78, 45–59.

— 1976. *Plato: Protagoras*. Oxford.

— 1982. 'The End of the Euthyphro', *Phronesis*. 27, 109–18.

— 2008. 'Plato's Epistemology', in Gail Fine (ed.), *The Oxford Handbook of Plato*. Oxford, pp. 165–90.

Tecuşan, Manuela. 1992. 'Speaking about the Unspeakable: Plato's Use of Imagery', in Andrew Barker and Martin Warner (eds), *The Language of the Cave*. Edmonton.

Tejera, Victorino. 1984. *Plato's Dialogues One by One*. New York (repr. New York, 1998).

— 1990. 'On the Form and Authenticity of the Lysis', *Ancient Philosophy*. 10, 173–91.

Temko, Philipp and Julia Moravscsik (eds). 1982. *Plato on Beauty, Wisdom and the Arts*. Totowa.

Tennemann, Wilhelm Gottlieb. 1792–5. *System der Platonischen Philosophie I*. Leipzig.

Thayer, H. S. 1975. 'Plato's Quarrel with Poetry: Simonides', *Journal of the History of Ideas*. 36, 3–26.

Thesleff, Holger. 1967. *Studies in the Styles of Plato*. Helsinki (repr. in *Platonic Patterns*. Las Vegas 2009, pp. 1–142).

— 1982. *Studies in Platonic Chronology*. Helsinki (repr. in *Platonic Patterns*. Las Vegas 2009, pp. 143–382).

— 1990. 'Theaitetos and Theodoros', *Arctos*. 24, 147–59 (repr. in *Platonic Patterns*. Las Vegas 2009, pp. 509–18).

— 1993. 'Looking for Clues: An Interpretation of Some Literary Aspects of Plato's "Two-Level Model,"' in Gerald A. Press (ed.), *Plato's Dialogues: New Studies & Interpretations*. Lanham, pp. 17–45.

— 1997. 'The Early Version of Plato's Republic', *Arctos*. 31, 149–74 (repr. in *Platonic Patterns*. Las Vegas 2009, pp. 519–39).

— 1999. *Studies in Plato's Two-Level Model*. Helsinki (repr. in *Platonic Patterns*. Las Vegas 2009, pp. 383–497).

Thomas, Rosalind. 1992. *Literacy and Orality in Ancient Greece*. Cambridge.

Thompson, E. S. 1901. *The Meno of Plato*. London.

Thompson, W. H. 1868. *The Phaedrus of Plato*. London.

Tigerstedt, E. N. 1970. 'Plato's Idea of Poetical Inspiration', *Commentationes Humanarum Litterarum*. 44, 18–20.

— 1977. *Interpreting Plato*. Uppsala.

Tomin, Julius. 1997. 'Plato's first dialogue', *Ancient Philosophy*. 17, 31–45.

Trendelenburg, Adolf. 1837. *De Platonis Philibi Consilio*. Berlin.

— 1840. *Logische Untersuchungen*. Berlin.

Trendelenburg, F. A. 1826. *Platonis de Ideis et Numeris Doctrina ex Aristotele Illustrata*. Leipzig.

Trevaskis, J. R. 1967. 'Division and its relation to dialectic and ontology in Plato', *Phronesis*. 12, 118–29.

Trivigno, Franco V. 2009. 'The Rhetoric of Parody in Plato's Menexenus', *Philosophy and Rhetoric*. 42, 29–58.

Tschemplik, Andrea. 2008. *Knowledge and Self-Knowledge in Plato's Theaetetus*. Lanham.

Tsouna, Voula. 1997. 'Socrates' attack on intellectualism in the Charmides', *Apeiron*. 30, 63–78.

Tuozzo, Thomas M. 2000. 'Greetings from Apollo: Charmides 164c–165b, Epistle III and the Structure of the Charmides', in Thomas M. Robinson (ed.), *Plato: Euthydemus, Lysis, Charmides: Proceedings of the V'Symposium Platonicum. Sankt Augustin*, pp. 296–305.

— 2001. 'What's Wrong with These Cities? The Social Dimension of Sophrosyne in Plato's Charmides', *Journal of the History of Philosophy*. 39, 321–50.

Überweg, Friedrich. 1861. *Untersuchungen über die Echtheit und Zeitfolge Platonischer Schriften und über die Hauptmomente aus Plato's Leben*. Vienna.

Untersteiner, Mario. 1954. *The Sophists* (trans. Kathleen Freeman). Oxford.

Usener, Sylvia. 1994. *Isokrates, Platon und ihr Publikum: Hörer und Leser von Literatur im 4. Jahrhundert v. Chr.* (ScriptOralia 63). Tübingen.

Van den Berg, Robbert M. 2008. *Proclus' Commentary on the Cratylus in Context: Ancient Theories of Language and Naming*. Leiden.

Van Eck, Job. 1994. '*Skopein en logois*: on Phaedo 99d–103c', *Ancient Philosophy*. 14, 21–40.

Vander Waerdt, P. A. (ed.). 1994a. *The Socratic Movement*. Ithaca.

— 1994b. 'Socrates in the Clouds', in P. A. Vander Waerdt (ed.), *The Socratic Movement*. Ithaca.

Vasiliu, Anca. 1997. *Du Diaphane. Image, Milieu, Lumière dans la Pensée Antique et Médiévale*. Paris.

Velardi, Roberto. 1989. *Enthousiasmòs: Possessione Rituale e Teoria Della Comunicazione Poetica in Platone*. Rome.

Verdenius, W. J. 1962. 'Der Begriff der Mania in Platons Phaidros', *Archiv für Geschichte der Philosophie*. 44, 132–50.

— 1983. 'The Principles of Greek Literary Criticism', *Mnemosyne*. 36, 14–59.

Vernant, J.-P. 1980. *Myth and Society in Greek Thought*. Atlantic Highlands.

Vicaire, Paul. 1960. *Platon: critique littéraire*. Paris.

Vidal-Naquet, Pierre. 1981. 'Athènes et l'Atlantide', in Pierre Vidal-Naquet, *Le Chasseur Noir: Formes de Pensée et Formes de Société dans le Monde Grec*. Paris, pp. 335–60.

Vlastos, Gregory. 1954. 'The Third Man Argument in the Parmenides', *Philosophical Review*. 63, 319–49 (repr. as Allen, R. E. (ed.). 1965. *Studies in Plato's Metaphysics*. London, pp. 231–63).

— 1965. 'Creation in the Timaeus: is it a fiction?' in Reginald E. Allen (ed.), *Studies in Plato's Metaphysics*. London and New York, pp. 401–19.

— 1967. 'Was Polus refuted?' *American Journal of Philology*. 88, 454–60.

— 1969. 'Reasons and Causes in the Phaedo', *Philosophical Review*. 78, 291–325.

— 1971a. 'Introduction', in Gregory Vlastos (ed.), *Plato II: Ethics, Politics and Philosophy of Art and Religion*. Garden City, pp. vii–xi.

— 1971b. 'Justice and Happiness in the Republic', in Gregory Vlastos (ed.), *Plato: A Collection of Critical Essays. Vol. II.* Garden City, pp. 66–95.

— 1971c. 'The Paradox of Socrates', in Gregory Vlastos (ed.), *The Philosophy of Socrates*. New York, pp. 1–21.

— 1972. 'The Unity of the Virtues in the Protagoras', *Review of Metaphysics*. 25, 415–58

— 1974. 'Socrates on Political Obedience and Disobedience', *Yale Review*. 63, 517–34.

— (ed.). 1978a. *Plato I, A Collection of Critical Essays: Metaphysics and Epistemology*. Notre Dame.

— (ed.). 1978b. *Plato II, A Collection of Critical Essays: Ethics, Politics, and Philosophy of Art and Religion*. Notre Dame.

— 1981. 'Degrees of Reality in Plato', in Gregory Vlastos, *Platonic Studies* (2nd edn). Princeton, pp. 58–75.

— 1983. 'The Socratic Elenchus', *Oxford Studies in Ancient Philosophy*. 1, 27–58 (repr. in Fine, Gail (ed.). *Plato I: Oxford Readings in Philosophy*. New York and Oxford. 1999).

— 1985. 'Socrates' Disavowal of Knowledge', *Philosophical Quarterly*. 35, 1–31.

— 1987. 'Socratic Irony', *Classical Quarterly*. 37, 79–80.

— 1988. 'Socrates', *Proceedings of the British Academy*. 74, 87–111.

— 1991a. *Socrates: Ironist and Moral Philosopher*. Ithaca.

— 1991b. 'Elenchus and Mathematics', in Vlastos, Gregory. *Socrates: Ironist and Moral Philosopher*. Cambridge, pp.107–31 (repr. of *American Journal of Philology*. 109, 362–96).

— 1997. 'Was Plato a Feminist?' in Richard Kraut (ed.), *Plato's Republic: Critical Essays*. Lanham.

— 1999. 'Happiness and virtue in Socrates' moral theory', in G. Fine (ed.), *Plato 2: Ethics, Politics, Religion and the Soul*. Oxford, pp.105–63.

Vogt, Heinrich. 1909–10. 'Die Entdeckungsgeschichte des Irrationalen nach Plato und anderen Quellen des 4. Jahrhunderts', *Bibliotheca Mathematica*. 10, 97–155.

Wagner, Ellen (ed). 2001. *Essays in Plato's Psychology*. Lanham.

Walbridge, John. 2000. *The Leaven of the Ancients: Suhrawardî and the Heritage of the Greeks*. Albany.

Walker, Paul. 1994. 'Platonisms in Islamic Philosophy', *Studia Islamica*. 79, 5–25.

Wallis, R. T. 1972. *Neoplatonism*. London.

Walzel, Oskar. 1908. *Deutsche Romantik*. Leipzig.

Watts, Edward J. 2006. *City and School in Late Antiquity: Athens and Alexandria*. Berkeley.

Waugh, Joanne. 1995. 'Neither Published nor Perished: The Dialogues as Speech, Not Text', in Francisco Gonzalez (ed.), *The Third Way: New Directions in Platonic Studies*. Lanham, pp.61–77.

Wedberg, Anders. 1955. *Plato's Philosophy of Mathematics*. Stockholm.

Weineck, Silke-Maria. 2002. *The Abyss Above: Poetic and Philosophical Madness in Plato, Hoelderlin, and Nietzsche*. Buffalo.

Weiss, Roslyn. 1981. 'Ho agathos as Ho dunatos in the Hippias Minor', *Classical Quarterly*. 21, 287–304 (reprinted of New York, Essays on the Philosophy of Socrates).

— 1998. *Socrates Dissatisfied: An Analysis of Plato's Crito*. Oxford.

— 2001. *Virtue in the Cave: Moral Inquiry in Plato's Meno*. New York.

Welliver, Warman. 1977. *Character, Plot and Thought in Plato's Timaeus-Critias*. Leiden.

Wender, Dorothea. 1973. 'Plato: Misogenist, Paedophile and Feminist', *Arethusa*. 6, 75–80.

Wersinger, A. Gabrièle. 2001. *Platon et la Dysharmonie: Recherches sur la Forme musicale*. Paris.

— 2007. 'Socrate, fais de la musique! Le destin de la musique entre paideia et philosophie', in Florence Malhomme and A. Gabrièle Wersinger (eds), *Mousikè et Aretè: La Musique et l'Ethique de l'Antiquité à l'Âge moderne*. Paris, pp.45–62.

— 2008a. 'Pourquoi dans la République de Platon, l'Harmonique est-elle la Science Propédeutique la plus haute? Perspective Nouvelle sur une Question Négligée', in Jean-Luc Périllié (ed.), 'Platon et les Pythagoriciens, Hierarchie des savoirs et des pratiques', *Cahiers de Philosophie Ancienne*. 20, 159–80 and 171–3.

— 2008b. *La Sphère et l'Intervalle: Le Schème de l'Harmonie dans la Pensée des Anciens Grecs d'Homère à Platon*. Grenoble.

— 2011. 'De 'l'Âme-Harmonie' et du "Corps-Lyre" au paradoxe du corps immortel: les aventures d'une métaphore, de Platon et Aristote à Dicéarque de Messène', in Florence Malhomme and Elisabetta Villari (eds), *Musica Corporis, Savoirs et Arts du corps, de l'Antiquité à l'âge Humaniste et Classique*. Turnhout.

West, M. L. 1992. *Ancient Greek Music*. Oxford.

White, David A. 1993. *Rhetoric and Reality in Plato's Phaedrus*. Albany.

— 2007. *Myth, Metaphysics and Dialectic in Plato's Statesman*. Farnham.

White, F. C. 1989. 'Love and Beauty in Plato's Symposium', *The Journal of Hellenic Studies*. 109, 149–57.

— 2006. 'Socrates, Philosophers and Death: Two Contrasting Arguments in Plato's Phaedo', *The Classical Quarterly*. 56, 445–58.

White, Michael. 2006. 'Plato and Mathematics', in Hugh Benson (ed.), *A Companion to Plato*. Oxford, pp. 228–43.

White, Nicholas P. 1976. *Plato on Knowledge and Reality*. Indianapolis.

— 1979. *A Companion to Plato's Republic*. Indianapolis.

— (trans.). 1993. *Plato: Sophist*. Indianapolis.

— 2002. *Individual and Conflict in Greek Ethics*. Oxford.

Whitman, John. 1986. *Allegory: The Dynamics of an Ancient and Medieval Technique*. Oxford.

Wieland, Georg. 1985. 'Plato oder Aristoteles? Überlegungen zur Aristoteles-Rezeption des lateinischen Mittelalters', in *Tijdschrift voor filosofie*. 47, pp. 605–30.

Wilcox, Joel F. 1987. 'Cross-Metamorphosis in Plato's Ion', in Donald G. Marschall (ed.), *Literature as Philosophy: Philosophy as Literature*. Iowa City, pp. 155–74.

Wildberg, Christian. 2006. 'Socrates and Euripides', in S. Ahbel-Rappe and R. Kamtekar (eds), *A Companion to Socrates*. Oxford, pp. 21–35.

Wilkes, Kathleen. 1979. 'Conclusions in the Meno', *Archiv für Geschichte der Philosophie*. 61, 143–53.

Wilson, J. R. S. 1995. 'Thrasymachus and the Thumos: A Further Case of Prolepsis in Republic 1', *Classical Quarterly*. 45, 58–67.

Winston, David. 1979. *The Wisdom of Solomon*. New York.

Wittgenstein, Ludwig. 1958. *Philosophical Investigations* (trans. G. E. M. Anscombe). New York.

Wolfsdorf, David. 2006. 'The Ridiculousness of Being Overcome by Pleasure: Protagoras 352b1–358d4', *Oxford Studies in Ancient Philosophy*. 31, 113–36.

Woodbridge, Frederick J. E. 1929. *The Son of Apollo*. New York.

Woodruff, Paul (trans.). 1982. *Plato: Hippias Major*. Indianapolis.

— 1990. 'Plato's Early Theory of Knowledge' in Stephen Everson (ed.), *Companions to Ancient Thought: 1 Epistemology*. Cambridge, pp. 60–84.

Woozley, A. D. 1971, 1980. 'Socrates on Disobeying the Law', in G. Vlastos (ed.), *The Philosophy of Socrates*. Notre Dame, pp. 299–318.

Wundt, Max. 1935. *Platons 'Parmenides'*. Berlin.

Young, Charles M. 1994. 'Plato and Computer Dating', *Oxford Studies in Ancient Philosophy*. 12, 227–50.

— 1997. 'First Principles of Socratic Ethics', *Apeiron*. 29, 13–23.

— 2006. 'Plato's Crito on the Obligation to Obey the Law', *Philosophical Inquiry*. 27, 79–90.

Zaidman, Louise B. and Pauline S. Pantel. 1992. *Religion in the Ancient Greek City* (trans. P. Cartledge). Cambridge.

BIBLIOGRAPHY

Zaslavsky, Robert. 1981. *Platonic Myth and Platonic Writing*. Washington, DC.

Zeller, Eduard. 1888. *Plato and the Older Academy* (4th edn) (trans. S. F. Alleyne and A. Goodwin). London, pp. 389–1049.

Zeyl, Donald (trans.). 2000. *Plato: Timaeus*. Indianapolis.

Zuckert, Catherine. 2000. 'Who's a Philosopher? Who's a Sophist? The Stranger v. Socrates', *The Review of Metaphysics*. 54, 65–97.

— 2009. *Plato's Philosophers: The Coherence of the Dialogues*. Chicago.

INDEX

Numbers in bold (e.g. **129–30**) indicate important discussions.